CW00656139

January 2006

For Tom
With admiration and
congratulations on
your book!

CONSTITUTIONAL
PROPERTY LAW

André

CONSTITUTIONAL PROPERTY LAW

AJ van der Walt

BIur Honns (BA) LLB LLD (Potchefstroom) LLM (Witwatersrand)
Professor of Law, Stellenbosch University

JUTA
AND COMPANY LTD

For Christa

First edition 2005

This book is the successor to the 1997 publication
*The constitutional property clause: A comparative analysis of
section 25 of the South African Constitution of 1996*

© Juta & Co, Ltd
Mercury Crescent, Wetton, Cape Town, 7780

ISBN: Hard cover   0 7021 7108 5
        Soft cover   0 7021 7318 5

Designed and set by G.J. du Toit Fine Typography
Cover design by Jacques Nel

Printed and bound in South Africa by Creda Communications

Copyright

This book is the successor to *The constitutional property clause: A comparative analysis of section 25 of the South African Constitution of 1996* (1997). Because this is the first re-working of the text in almost eight years, and since I have kept working in the field during this time, it was inevitable that I should rely in this edition on sections from journal articles that I wrote since 1996. In some cases I simply refer to the articles quite frequently, in others I summarized or paraphrased sections of the articles, and in one or two cases I followed sections of the articles quite closely. Obviously the relevant articles always had to be worked into the structure and argument of the book and new cases and material had to be worked in as well, but in some instances the articles were written with this new edition of the book already in mind and then the resemblances are quite close. Copyright in all these articles belongs to me, but I thought it advisable to record and specify the instances where I relied on previous articles quite heavily.

The publishers (in the case of *SA Public Law*, which is the only affected journal not published by Juta & Co) and editors of the relevant journals graciously gave their permission for the use of the journal article material as set out below.

- Van der Walt AJ 'Compensation for excessive or unfair regulation: A comparative overview of constitutional practice relating to regulatory takings' (1999) 14 *SA Public Law* 273–331 (in chapter 5.4)
- Van der Walt AJ 'Civil forfeiture of instrumentalities and proceeds of crime and the constitutional property clause' (2000) 16 *SAJHR* 1–45 (in chapter 5.3)
- Van der Walt AJ 'Exclusivity of ownership, security of tenure, and eviction orders: A model to evaluate South African land-reform legislation' 2002 *TSAR* 254–289 (in chapter 6.3)
- Van der Walt AJ 'Exclusivity of ownership, security of tenure, and eviction orders: A critical evaluation of recent case law' (2002) 18 *SAJHR* 371–419 (in chapters 6.3 and 7.3)
- Van der Walt AJ 'Overview of developments since the introduction of the con-stitutional property clause' (2004) 19 *SA Public Law* 46–89 (in chapters 3.1–3.6, 4.1 and 5.1, 5.8)
- Van der Walt AJ 'Striving for the better interpretation—A critical reflection on the Constitutional Court's *Harksen* and *FNB* decisions on the property clause' (2004) 121 *SALJ* 854 878 (in chapter 4.5, 4.6 and 5.2)
- Van der Walt AJ 'Retreating from the *FNB* arbitrariness test already? *Mkontwana v Nelson Mandela Metropolitan Municipality; Bissett v Buffalo City Municipality; Transfer Rights Action Campaign v MEC for Local Government and Housing, Gauteng* (CC)' (2005) 122 *SALJ* 75–89 (in chapter 4.5)

- Van der Walt AJ 'The state's duty to protect property owners vs the state's duty to provide housing: Thoughts on the *Modderklip* case' (2005) 21 *SAJHR* (forthcoming) (in chapters 6.3, 7.3 and 7.5)
- Van der Walt AJ 'Transformative constitutionalism and the development of South African property law' 2005 *TSAR*; 2006 *TSAR* (forthcoming) (in chapters 2.4 and 7.5)

Preface

Since 1997 the field of constitutional property has changed almost unrecognizably. Dozens of new property- and constitution-related laws have been promulgated; dozens of new cases have been reported on constitutional property issues; and the academic literature on this topic has also expanded and improved in quality, both in South Africa and abroad. A new edition was therefore long overdue.

Certain changes in the format and structure of the book were necessitated by developments since the first edition. For one thing, it was immediately apparent that a new edition would be more comprehensive, if only because the material was so much more extensive than before. Secondly, the changes that took place over the last seven years were so numerous and, above all, so fundamental that a slight editing of the existing text was out of the question—I had to write from scratch. In the end I could use probably less than 10% (even then heavily edited) of the existing text and the rest had to be written new. Fortunately I was able to use quite a substantial amount of material from another book and from some journal articles that I wrote during the last few years, as I indicate further down below. In view of the scope and degree of rewriting that was required I also decided that an amended title was in order, and accordingly the title of the book was simplified and shortened—instead of the cumbersome *The constitutional property clause: A comparative analysis of section 25 of the South African Constitution of 1996* of the first edition (1997), I decided to change the title to *Constitutional property law*. The name change was not inspired purely by a desire for greater brevity, but also necessitated by the realisation that this field of law, which admittedly started out from what was the norm in 1996, namely fascination with the text of the constitutional provision, the property clause, has grown and expanded over the last few years; it now has a well-documented and explored historical as well as a constitutional context, and the topics for discussion have extended beyond the text of the property clause to include a range of constitutional provisions, legislation, case law and theory. It has become constitutional property law. Accordingly, what started out as a second edition became a new book; a successor to the original.

The structure and organization of the chapters also had to change. The discussion of the structure of section 25, the purpose of the property clause and the interpretation, application and limitation issues have been removed from Chapter 1 and moved into a new Chapter 2 that brings together all the so-called operational aspects of section 25: interpretation, application, and limitation. In the process, Chapter 1 became what it should have been from the beginning: a brief introduction to the rest of the book. In this edition the brief historical overview was extended to describe new developments since 1997. Chapter 3 is still more or less the same, focusing on the scope of the property clause and the nature of property interests protected by it, but new subsections have been added on new developments, particularly in the wake of the Constitutional Court decision in the *FNB* case,[1] but also to reflect some of the specialized debates that developed around aspects of the property concept (such as dephysicalization and conceptual severance).

Chapters 4 and 5, dealing with deprivation and expropriation of property respectively, were kept in their original position but revised and expanded extensively to reflect new case law and literature. Extensive reworking of the section on arbitrary deprivation was required by the *FNB* decision, but new subsections were also added to Chapter 4 to relate developments in specialized areas such as forfeiture and planning and development law to the discussion of deprivation. A new subsection on exclusivity and eviction was also added to highlight the importance of new, sometimes controversial, laws that restrict the traditionally strong right of eviction in the context of landownership and land reform. In the chapter on expropriation a new section on constructive expropriation was added to emphasize the difficulties of dealing with the grey area in between deprivation and expropriation. A new section on forfeiture was also added to show how certain forfeiture laws and powers highlight the grey area where deprivation of property can fade into expropriation. The section on compensation was removed from its original position in a separate Chapter 6, extended with reference to new case law and included as the last part of Chapter 5 on expropriation.

The chapter on land reform, now Chapter 6, was rewritten and expanded extensively with reference to the new land reform laws and cases since 1997, and new sections were added on equitable access to land and housing and to water and mineral resources. This chapter reflects an effort to emphasize the close interrelationship between the first and second parts of section 25, which not only protects existing property rights but also mandates extensive land and other reforms. Finally, a new chapter 7 was added on the development of the common law in view of sections 8 and 39 of the Constitution, again in an effort to reflect the close relationship between the protective and the reformist aspects of section 25. This chapter simultaneously replaces the now defunct chapter 8.

In preparing this new edition I was able to draw upon some of my earlier work from a larger comparative book that was completed and published after the first edition of this one,[2] which enabled me to increase the volume of comparative examples and references from the first edition. (I was also able in certain places to rely, to a larger or smaller extent, on sections and passages from journal articles on eviction, forfeiture, expropriation and property theory that I have written over the last seven years, as indicated in the relevant footnotes in the chapters that follow.) The emphasis on comparative references made me think that it might be a good idea to make life

---

[1] *First National Bank of SA Ltd t/a Wesbank v Commissioner, South African Revenue Service; First National Bank of SA Ltd t/a Wesbank v Minister of Finance* 2002 (4) SA 768 (CC). The case is discussed in chapter 4.5.

[2] AJ van der Walt *Constitutional property clauses: A comparative analysis* (1999).

easier for the reader by including the texts of selected foreign property clauses in this book. In addition, I realized that the book relied much more on cross-references to other sections in the Constitution than was the case in the first edition, which could become quite confusing for readers who are not that familiar with the South African Constitution, and therefore I also decided to include the full text of the first two chapters of the South African Constitution in an appendix, in addition to the relevant sections that I quote at the beginning of each chapter of the book. These two new additions appear after Chapter 7 as Appendix 1 and Appendix 2.

Since 1997 the field of constitutional property law and the case law and literature have expanded to such an extent that it has become difficult to cover all areas equally thoroughly, and certain areas inevitably had to be neglected to an extent. However, my approach was to write the new edition in a way that would reflect the fact that section 25 consists of two closely intertwined parts; a first, more traditional part that protects existing property rights and a second, more innovative part that authorizes and mandates reform of property law. In my discussion I also attempted to indicate how the emerging jurisprudence of especially the Constitutional Court reflects this double-sidedness of section 25 and how the cases illustrate the necessity of inter-preting and applying section 25 within a larger historical and constitutional frame-work. Comparative foreign case law has long illustrated the fact that a constitutional property clause cannot be applied abstractly, as if it functioned separate and inde-pendent of any political, social and economic context. One significant implication of the contextual approach is demonstrated quite dramatically in South African law by the increasing recognition that section 25 functions in a close relationship with sec-tion 26. The emerging case law on sections 25 and 26 of the South African Constitu-tion perhaps goes further than most in illustrating the importance of taking account of the history of property holdings in a particular society as well. It is probably fair to say that the recent case law of the Constitutional Court on section 26 illustrates how unnecessary our initial concerns about the constitutionalization of property was, showing that the property clause—understood within its proper historical and con-stitutional context—can and should be an instrument of change as well as a guarantee of stability. The fact that property is guaranteed in the Bill of Rights does not mean that existing property holdings or the property system or property law should or can be insulated from change, provided the property clause is understood as a specific instrument within a much larger, transformation-oriented constitutional scheme that has to be interpreted and applied with proper attention for the injustices of the past, the exigencies of the present and the possibilities of the future. At the same time a contextual and reform-friendly reading of the Bill of Rights does not mean that prop-erty holdings are undervalued or left unprotected—emerging case law also demon-strates that the constitutional protection of property is strong. I hope that this new edition will do justice to my effort to show how such an understanding of constitu-tional property is emerging in South African law.

I am indebted to many institutions and persons who helped me in completing this new edition. Stellenbosch University made it possible for me to write the bulk of the new edition in one more or less uninterrupted stint by graciously allowing me to take an unprecedented long sabbatical during 2003–2004. During this period of leave I was able to travel abroad, including a couple of longer research visits to Germany and the UK, thanks to generous financial support from the National Research Foundation, the Alexander von Humboldt Stiftung, Stellenbosch University, and the Master and Fellows of Trinity College, Cambridge. I would like to record my gratitude towards these institutions, but the opinions and results expressed in this book should not be ascribed to any of them. Several large sections of the manuscript were written during extended visits to the Universities of Cologne and Freiburg in Germany and Trinity College, Cambridge, and I am extremely grateful to colleagues and friends who received me at these institutions and who made it possible for me to feel at home and work comfortably and efficiently there; in this regard I am particularly indebted to Klaus Stern, Michael Sachs, Friedrich Schoch and Kevin Gray. I also enjoyed much needed and warmly appreciated assistance and support from colleagues who helped me in finding and interpreting sources or who generously gave their time to read and comment on sections of the manuscript and to discuss it with me. In this regard I would like to single out Greg Alexander (Cornell), Tom Allen (Durham), Lourens du Plessis (Stellenbosch), Kevin Gray (Trinity College, Cambridge), Fanie Grobler (Johannesburg Bar), Irma Kroeze (Unisa), Sandra Liebenberg (Stellenbosch), Frank Michelman (Harvard), Juanita Pienaar (Stellenbosch), Theunis Roux (Witwatersrand and SAIFAC), Michael Sachs (Cologne), Friedrich Schoch (Freiburg), Joe Singer (Harvard), Klaus Stern (Cologne), Laura Underkuffler (Duke) and Gerry Whyte (Trinity College, Dublin). Gerhard du Toit and Jacques Jacobs read and commented on sections of the manuscript; and Gerhard du Toit provided excellent, tireless and enthusiastic research assistance throughout and also compiled the bibliography and indexes.

I would like to thank Ria de Kock, Patty Searle and Ute Kuhlmann of Juta & Co and Gawie du Toit for making the production and publication process as painless as possible.

Case law and legislation have been updated until 30 September 2005, and all URLs referred to in the footnotes are correct as on the same date.

STELLENBOSCH, OCTOBER 2005

Preface to
The Constitutional Property Clause[1]

This book started out as a journal article, but soon got out of hand and ended up in the present format, not least because of the inspiration and encouragement of some of my close friends and colleagues, both in South Africa and abroad.

The property clause in section 25 of the Constitution of the Republic of South Africa of 1996 is so fraught with possibilities and problems that it is almost impossible to say anything about it without getting caught up in all kinds of debates and controversies. In saying anything whatsoever about this property clause, one inevitably says both too much and too little. In most countries with an entrenched bill of rights, the property clause is regarded as one of the most difficult provisions to interpret and apply, and this is no different in South Africa. However, one consideration exacerbates the situation for South African lawyers: we have never had the opportunity to get used to a proper constitutional system in general, and the private-law tradition is extremely strong and deeply embedded in our legal system. For a property lawyer brought up in the private-law tradition, some of the possibilities and all of the problems posed by a constitutional property clause are new, frightening, and fascinating. Since the introduction of the new constitutional order in 1994, South African lawyers in general and private lawyers in particular have been confronted with the realities of our past, the demands of our present and the spectres of our future in no uncertain terms, and as private-law specialists we have to adapt very quickly or get left behind irrevocably. In the process we are constantly faced with new or unfamiliar areas of the law, strange sources and outdated methodologies, and consequently the journey is characterised by the constant need to learn new things and to experiment with uncertain possibilities. I hope that the reader will find this adventure as challenging and as satisfying as I do.

I owe a huge debt of gratitude to many people and institutions who helped me during the research on which this book is based and during the writing phase. At an early stage in the research process the Centre for Research Development at the Human Sciences Research Council (Pretoria) provided partial support for research assistance on some of the initial research on foreign law. Further research in this area was funded by the Alexander von Humboldt Stiftung (Bonn) and the Research and Bursaries Committee at the University of South Africa. I wish to express my gratitude

---

[1] This book's predecessor, published in 1997, was entitled *The constitutional property clause: A comparative analysis of section 25 of the South African Constitution of 1996.*

for the financial support from all of these institutions, but the conclusions and opinions expressed in this work should not be attributed to any of them in any way.

I am heavily indebted to my research assistants. During the first two years of the research on foreign law Denise Prévost provided excellent and tireless support in finding, collecting and exploring constitutional property clauses and case law from many different countries, and in establishing a data base with which we could make the mountain of information we collected accessible. In the last year Karen Prinsloo took over the thankless job of maintaining and expanding the data base, and of assisting me with finding sources, checking references for the manuscript and compiling of the indexes. Without them this book would have been impossible.

Over the last few years, many of my colleagues and friends in South Africa and elsewhere have helped me in the difficult enterprise of establishing myself in a new field of learning, and I am grateful to all of them for the assistance, advice, comments and encouragement they gave me. I must nevertheless take full credit for the remaining errors and shortcomings in this book. A special word of thanks to Neville Botha (Unisa), Peter Butt (Sydney), Gretchen Carpenter (Unisa), Mathew Chaskalson (Witwatersrand), Duard Kleyn (Pretoria), Jenny Nedelsky (Toronto), Clement Ng'ong'ola (Botswana), Carol Rose (Yale), Joe Singer (Harvard), Klaus Stern (Cologne), Johann van der Westhuizen (Pretoria) and Dawid van Wyk (Unisa) for numerous discussions of the property clause and the Bill of Rights, and for comments on this and earlier publications or draft publications. I am particularly indebted to Johan van der Walt (Rand Afrikaans), Henk Botha (Unisa), Wessel le Roux (Unisa) and Karen van Marle (Unisa), from whom I continue to learn during our weekly discussion meetings. They also provided valuable comments and discussions on the first draft of the manuscript. In addition to numerous earlier discussions, Frank Michelman (Harvard) took enormous trouble to provide me with extensive comments on the first draft of the manuscript, and since then we have conducted a wonderfully educational and enjoyable discussion by e-mail, for which I am extremely grateful. Laura Underkuffler-Freund (Duke) also provided some valuable insights and comments on the first draft, for which I am extremely grateful. Johan Erasmus (Unisa) read through the whole final manuscript and gave me the benefit of his comments and criticisms. Henk Botha (Unisa) read through the original manuscript as well as the final manuscript of chapter 3, and provided incisive and helpful comments and suggestions. With mentors, colleagues and friends like mine the difficulties and problems of academic research and writing fade away, and one is again reminded of the joys and excitement that could be part of our work.

Finally, I am always grateful for the support and enthusiasm of my publishers, Juta & Co, and especially for the friendship and trust of Richard Cooke, Simon Sephton and André Struwig.

PRETORIA, JULY 1997

Contents

Introduction

1.1 THE EARLY YEARS OF CONSTITUTIONALISM

Ever since the possibility of the introduction of an entrenched bill of rights (and a property clause) in the constitution of a future, democratic South Africa was mooted towards the end of the 1980s, property lawyers have been at pains to determine whether such a development would have any negative effect on existing property law and established property rights. It is trite that private law, including and perhaps above all property law, was characterized during the apartheid era by its systematic and consistent ignorance of apartheid laws and their effect on individual property rights. It was only after Cowen's landmark lecture on 'New patterns of landownership' at the University of the Witwatersrand on 26 April 1984[1] that South African property lawyers began to pay serious attention to legislation and its effects on the structure and paradigm of property law.[2] Some of the early publications following this new trend focused more or less exclusively on the 'private-law' legislation concerned with sectional titles, property timesharing, airspace development, environmental conservation and so forth,[3] specifically concerning themselves with the question how these

---

[1] Subsequently published by the Law Students' Council of the University of the Witwatersrand as DV Cowen *New patterns of landownership. The transformation of the concept of landownership as* plena in re potestas (1984). For a discussion of this lecture and its influence on the development of property theory see AJ van der Walt 'Introduction' in AJ van der Walt (ed) *Land reform and the future of landownership in South Africa* (1991) 1–7.

[2] See the contributions in 1985 *Acta Juridica*, (also published separately as TW Bennett et al (eds) *Land ownership—Changing concepts* (1985)). Of particular importance in this volume are the contributions by CH Lewis 'The modern concept of ownership of land' at 241–266; DJ van der Post 'Land law and registration in some of the black rural areas of Southern Africa' at 213–240; and TRH Davenport 'Some reflections on the history of land tenure in South Africa, seen in the light of attempts by the state to impose political and economic control' at 53–76.

[3] See DV Cowen 'From sectional to airspace title' 1985 *Acta Juridica* 333–347; DW Butler 'Time-shares conferring ownership' 1985 *Acta Juridica* 315 332; GJ Pienaar 'Ontwikkelings in die Suid-Afrikaanse eiendomsreg in perspektief' 1986 *TSAR* 295–308; GJ Pienaar 'Eiendomstydsdeling: Die aard van die reghebbende se reg' 1986 *TRW* 1–14; MA Rabie 'The impact of environmental conservation on land ownership' 1985 *Acta Juridica* 289–313; JRL Milton 'Planning and property' 1985 *Acta Juridica* 267–288; AJ van der Walt 'The effect of environmental conservation measures on the concept of landownership' (1987) 104 *SALJ* 469–479. Numerous publications since 1986 testify to the continued importance of this line of research.

'new patterns of landownership' fit into the traditional framework of real rights; but at least some authors were more interested in another area of the expanded law of property, namely the socio-political aspects of apartheid legislation and the role it played in property law.[4] Since 1990, this has given rise to a vast literature on post-apartheid property law and land law, and a sizeable portion of the new literature has concerned itself with yet another addition to the list of exciting new topics in the expanded view of property law: constitutional property.

In the discussions prior to 1993, much of the debate about constitutional property was focused on the pros and cons of including a property clause in the Constitution, and some voices (including my own)[5] were raised against the constitutionalization of property in the South African Bill of Rights.[6] However, since the promulgation of the interim Constitution of the Republic of South Africa 200 of 1993, which contained a property clause in section 28,[7] political realities rendered the constitutionalization debate more or less irrelevant and the attention shifted away from the

---

[4]Early publications include the contributions in 1985 *Acta Juridica* referred to in footnote 2 above; compare C Visser 'Rent control' 1985 *Acta Juridica* 349–368; D van der Merwe 'Land tenure in South Africa: A brief history and some reform proposals' 1989 *TSAR* 663–692; D van der Merwe 'Land tenure in South Africa: Changing the face of property law' (1990) 1 *Stell LR* 321–335; AJ van der Walt 'Developments that may change the institution of private ownership so as to meet the needs of a non-racial society in South Africa' (1990) 1 *Stell LR* 26–48; AJ van der Walt 'Towards the development of post-apartheid land law: An exploratory survey' (1990) 23 *De Jure* 1–45; and compare T Marcus 'Land reform—Considering national, class and gender issues' (1990) 6 *SAJHR* 178–194; Z Skweyiya 'Towards a solution to the land question in post-apartheid South Africa: Problems and models' (1990) 6 *SAJHR* 195–214. See further A Sachs 'Rights to the land: A fresh look at the property question' in A Sachs *Protecting human rights in a new South Africa* (1990) 104–138.

[5]See AJ van der Walt 'Towards the development of post-apartheid land law: An exploratory survey' (1990) 23 *De Jure* 1–45 at 43. I subsequently changed my mind when I realised that it was possible to use the constitutional property clause to promote land reform and the redistribution process; see AJ van der Walt 'Towards a theory of rights in property: Exploratory observations on the paradigm of post-apartheid property law' (1995) 10 *SA Public Law* 298–345 at 339ff; AJ van der Walt 'The constitutional property clause: Striking a balance between guarantee and limitation' in J MacLean (ed) *Property and the constitution* (1999) 109–146. The last-mentioned essay was a response to the most convincing arguments against constitutionalization, forwarded by J Nedelsky 'Should property be constitutionalized? A relational and comparative approach' in GE van Maanen & AJ van der Walt (eds) *Property on the threshold of the 21st century* (1996) 417–432 at 422ff. See footnote 8 below.

[6]See AJ van der Walt 'Property rights, land rights, and environmental rights' in DH van Wyk, J Dugard, B de Villiers & D Davis (eds) *Rights and constitutionalism: The new South African legal order* (1994) 455–501 at 461ff, 479ff for a discussion and references. The arguments against the inclusion of a property clause were heavily influenced by the Canadian experience and the decision to exclude the property clause from the Canadian Charter of Rights and Freedoms 1982. See further footnote 8 below and chapter 2.3.4.

[7]See the interesting discussion of the drafting process by M Chaskalson 'Stumbling towards section 28: Negotiations over the protection of property rights in the interim Constitution' (1995) 11 *SAJHR* 222–240.

desirability of a property clause to a discussion of the content and meaning of the property clause. Despite some opposition, a (different) property clause was also included in section 25 of the final Constitution of the Republic of South Africa 1996, and the debate on the desirability of a property clause is now over.[8]

Although the differences between section 28 of the 1993 Constitution and the final property clause in section 25 of the 1996 Constitution are interesting and instructive, so much has already been written about section 28 that such a comparison is not worthwhile here.[9] Some references to section 28 will be necessary for purposes of the discussion, but by and large the focus of this book is on section 25.

Until quite recently there was not much by way of South African case law that could give an indication of the way in which the property clause should be interpreted and applied. In the *First Certification Case*, the first decision which contained more than just a passing reference to section 25,[10] the Constitutional Court briefly

---

[8] A powerful argument against the constitutionalization of property was made by J Nedelsky *Private property and the limits of American constitutionalism: The Madisonian framework and its legacy* (1990) chapter 6; and again in J Nedelsky 'Should property be constitutionalized? A relational and comparative approach' in GE van Maanen & AJ van der Walt (eds) *Property on the threshold of the 21st century* (1996) 417–432 at 422ff. At 428ff Nedelsky deals with the question of the 'dialogue of democratic accountability' and the creation of property jurisprudence in the situation where property is included in the Bill of Rights. Some of the liberal arguments in favour of the constitutionalization of private property that are criticized by Nedelsky are also discussed (and rejected) by FI Michelman 'Socio-political functions of constitutional protection for private property holdings (in liberal political thought)' in GE van Maanen & AJ van der Walt (eds) *Property on the threshold of the 21st century* (1996) 433–450. See further CM Rose 'Property as the keystone right?' (1996) 71 *Notre Dame LR* 329–365; AJ van der Walt 'The constitutional property clause: Striking a balance between guarantee and limitation' in J MacLean (ed) *Property and the constitution* (1999) 109–146.

[9] For a comparative analysis of the two provisions see AJ van der Walt *Constitutional property clauses: A comparative analysis* (1999) 320–358. See further DG Kleyn 'The constitutional protection of property: A comparison between the German and the South African approach' (1996) 11 *SA Public Law* 402–445; AJ van der Walt 'Towards a theory of rights in property: Exploratory observations on the paradigm of post-apartheid property law' (1995) 10 *SA Public Law* 298–345; M Chaskalson 'The problem with property: Thoughts on the constitutional protection of property in the United States and the Commonwealth' (1993) 9 *SAJHR* 388–411; M Chaskalson 'The property clause: Section 28 of the Constitution' (1994) 10 *SAJHR* 131–139; AJ van der Walt 'Notes on the interpretation of the property clause in the new constitution' (1994) 57 *THRHR* 181–203; J Murphy 'Property rights and judicial restraint: A reply to Chaskalson' (1994) 10 *SAJHR* 386–398; J Murphy 'Property rights in the new Constitution: An analytical framework for constitutional review' (1993) (56) *THRHR* 623–644; J Murphy 'Interpreting the property clause in the Constitution Act of 1993' (1995) 10 *SA Public Law* 107–130; M Chaskalson & C Lewis 'Property' in M Chaskalson et al (eds) *Constitutional law of South Africa* (1996) chapter 31; W Du Plessis & NJJ Olivier 'The old and the new property clause' (1997) 1(5) *Human Rights & Const LJ SA* 11–16.

[10] The so-called *First Certification Case*, in which the Constitutional Court was asked (and refused, for reasons not connected with the property clause) to certify the validity of the 1996 Constitution: *Ex Parte Chairperson of the Constitutional Assembly: In re Certification of the Constitution of the Republic of South Africa, 1996* 1996 (4) SA 744 (CC). The 1996 Constitution was eventually certified in the *Second Certification Case: Ex Parte Chairperson of the Constitutional Assembly: In re Certification of the*
(continued on next page ...)

discussed certain aspects of the property clause and its content.[11] The three points discussed in this decision concerned the objections (raised against the proposed text of the final Constitution) that section 25 (a) did not make express provision for the protection of the right to acquire, hold and dispose of property; (b) contained inadequate provisions regarding expropriation and payment of compensation; and (c) did not protect intellectual property. The Constitutional Court concluded that (a) 'no universally recognised formulation of the right to property exists'[12] and that the negative formulation in section 25 appears to be widely accepted as an appropriate formulation which provides implicit protection for the holding of property; (b) it is internationally accepted that there is a wide range of criteria for the calculation of compensation for expropriation and that these criteria include but are not restricted to market value, and section 25 complies with that position; and (c) it is not true that the separate protection of intellectual property is universally accepted. This decision did not provide very much by way of guidelines for the interpretation of section 25, but it did indicate certain parameters within which at least some interpretation problems could be considered. As will appear from the case law discussed in this book, some of these problems indeed surfaced at a later stage.

1.2 NEW DEVELOPMENTS SINCE 1997

Since 1997 things have changed dramatically. A whole series of decisions with regard to section 28 of the 1993 Constitution and section 25 of the 1996 Constitution were reported, starting with the important case of *Harksen v Lane NO*,[13] which dealt with the definition of expropriation in terms of section 28 of the 1993 Constitution. Since then, the Constitutional Court set out its views about arbitrary deprivation in terms of section 25(1) of the 1996 Constitution in the authoritative decision in *First National*

(*. . . from previous page*)
Amended Text of the Constitution of the Republic of South Africa, 1996 1997 (2) SA 97 (CC). The amendments did not affect section 25. Section 28 was referred to in two other early cases: *Transkei Public Servants Association v Government of the Republic of South Africa and Others* 1995 (9) BCLR 1235 (Tk) (the possibility was mooted that 'property' in section 28 was wide enough to include state contracts, pension benefits and employment rights); *Transvaal Agricultural Union v Minister of Land Affairs and Another* 1997 (2) SA 621 (CC) (decision on the validity of certain provisions in the Restitution of Land Rights Act 22 of 1994 in terms of section 28). See the discussion of the latter case by T Roux 'Turning a deaf ear: The right to be heard by the Constitutional Court' (1997) 13 *SAJHR* 216–227.
[11] *Ex Parte Chairperson of the Constitutional Assembly: In re Certification of the Constitution of the Republic of South Africa, 1996* 1996 (4) SA 744 (CC) paras [70]–[75] at 797D–800A.
[12] Par [72] at 798E–F.
[13] 1998 (1) SA 300 (CC). For discussions of the property aspects of the decision see AJ van der Walt & H Botha 'Coming to grips with the new constitutional order: Critical comments on *Harksen v Lane NO*' (1998) 13 *SA Public Law* 17–41 at 19–26; AJ van der Walt *Constitutional property clauses: A comparative analysis* (1999) 333, 336–339; AJ van der Walt 'Striving for the better interpretation—A critical reflection on the Constitutional Court's *Harksen* and *FNB* decisions on the property clause' (2004) 121 *SALJ* 854–878 at 861.

Bank of SA Ltd t/a Wesbank v Commissioner, South African Revenue Service; First National Bank of SA Ltd t/a Wesbank v Minister of Finance or *FNB*,[14] followed by the equally important decision in *Mkontwana v Nelson Mandela Metropolitan Municipality; Bissett and Others v Buffalo City Municipality; Transfer Rights Action Campaign and Others v Member of the Executive Council for Local Government and Housing, Gauteng and Others*.[15]

Apart from these decisions section 25 featured in a number of high court and Supreme Court of Appeal decisions as well, based on issues that ranged from the constitutional validity of land reform laws[16] to the calculation of compensation for expropriation.[17] In addition, a range of Constitutional Court cases that did not necessarily deal with section 25 directly nevertheless had a direct bearing on property rights, land reform and the development of property in common law.[18] Between them, these new decisions have made it possible to start tracing and debating the outlines of a new constitutional property jurisprudence, and a large part of this book embodies an attempt to describe, analyse and critique this jurisprudence.

Since 1997 several significant new reform laws have been promulgated,[19] ranging from land reform laws and laws to increase access to natural resources such as water

---

[14]2002 (4) SA 768 (CC). See further AJ van der Walt 'Striving for the better interpretation—A critical reflection on the Constitutional Court's *Harksen* and *FNB* decisions on the property clause' (2004) 121 *SALJ* 854–878 at 864.

[15]2005 (1) SA 530 (CC). See further AJ van der Walt 'Retreating from the *FNB* arbitrariness test already? *Mkontwana v Nelson Mandela Metropolitan Municipality; Bissett v Buffalo City Municipality; Transfer Rights Action Campaign v MEC for Local Government and Housing, Gauteng* (CC)' (2005) 122 *SALJ* 75–89.

[16]See eg *Joubert and Others v Van Rensburg and Others* 2001 (1) SA 753 (W). An application to appeal directly to the Constitutional Court against the order given in this case was denied by the Constitutional Court in *Katazile Mkangeli and Others v Joubert and Others* 2001 (2) SA 1191 (CC). Eventually the decision a quo was overturned by the Supreme Court of Appeal in *Mkangeli and Others v Joubert and Others* 2002 (4) SA 36 (SCA). See the discussion in chapter 6.3.

[17]See eg *Du Toit v Minister of Transport* 2003 (1) SA 586 (C); *Modderfontein Squatters, Greater Benoni City Council v Modderklip Boerdery (Pty) Ltd; (Agri SA and Legal Resources Centre, Amici Curiae); President of the Republic of South Africa and Others v Modderklip Boerdery (Pty) Ltd (Agri SA and Legal Resources Centre, Amici Curiae)* 2004 (6) SA 40 (SCA). See the discussion in chapter 5.8 and compare AJ van der Walt 'Overview of developments since the introduction of the constitutional property clause' (2004) 19 *SA Public Law* 46–89.

[18]See eg *Government of the Republic of South Africa and Others v Grootboom and Others* 2001 (1) SA 46 (CC); *Minister of Public Works and Others v Kyalami Ridge Environmental Association and Another (Mukhwevo Intervening)* 2001 (3) SA 1151 (CC); *Jaftha v Schoeman and Others; Van Rooyen v Stoltz and Others* 2005 (2) SA 140 (CC); *Zondi v Member of the Executive Council for Traditional and Local Government Affairs and Others* 2005 (3) SA 589 (CC); and particularly *Port Elizabeth Municipality v Various Occupiers* 2005 (1) SA 217 (CC). See further *President of the Republic of South Africa and Another v Modderklip Boerdery (Pty) Ltd (Agri SA and Others, Amici Curiae)* 2005 (5) SA 3 (CC). See the discussion of these cases in chapters 6 and 7.

[19]Such as the Extension of Security of Tenure Act 62 of 1997; the Prevention of Illegal Eviction from and Unlawful Occupation of Land Act 18 of 1998; the Housing Act 107 of 1997 and the Rental Housing Act 50 of 1999; the Water Services Act 108 of 1997 and the National Water Act 36 of 1998; and the Mineral and Petroleum Resources Development Act 28 of 2002. See the discussion of these laws in chapter 6.

and minerals to housing laws and crime prevention laws. Every one of the laws discussed in this book includes provisions that in one way or another have an effect on property rights, thereby making it necessary to decide whether these laws establish deprivation or expropriation of property and to evaluate the effect and constitutional legitimacy of the relevant provisions.

Perhaps not unexpectedly, academic literature on the property clause has increased and improved quite dramatically since 1997 as well.[20] In an overview of recent developments I wrote elsewhere that academic discussion about finding the constitutionally legitimate and politically appropriate balance between the preservation of existing rights and the promotion of land reform 'has lost some of its original air of transformation anxiety and developed into a more rigorous, critical debate about the respective places and functions of land rights and land reform in South African society in the post-apartheid era.'[21] To a large degree the same applies to constitutional property in general—academic commentary and debate have become more specialized, more rigorous and more critical during the first decade of democratic rule, thereby establishing constitutional property as an independent and exciting field of academic and theoretical inquiry.

The new law of constitutional property covers a vast field of specialization, including obvious topics directly and traditionally associated with the constitutional property clause such as the legitimacy and validity of police-power regulation (deprivation of property) and expropriation (including compensation), but in the South African context it also includes a number of other, less obvious topics such as constitutional theory, constitutional and statutory interpretation, land reform (including access to land and natural resources such as water and minerals) and others. From an interesting addition to the expanded law of property, constitutional property has grown into a topic that is itself so vast that it is practically impossible to have a specialized knowledge of all areas. This development has made it possible but also much more difficult to write an expanded commentary on section 25 of the Constitution.

In the chapters that follow section 25 is analysed and discussed, in the broader context of other constitutional provisions, according to the following scheme. Chapter 2 provides a structural analysis and overview of section 25, followed by a discussion of the so-called operational aspects of the property clause: interpretation, application, and limitation. The section on interpretation places special emphasis on

---

[20] In addition to a large number of journal articles, the most substantial and up to date academic commentaries are AJ van der Walt *Constitutional property clauses: A comparative analysis* (1999) 320–358; AJ van der Walt 'Striving for the better interpretation—A critical reflection on the Constitutional Court's *Harksen* and *FNB* decisions on the property clause' (2004) 121 *SALJ* 854–878; T Roux 'Section 25' in S Woolman et al (eds) *Constitutional law of South Africa* (2nd ed 2003 original service Dec 2003) chapter 46; and T Roux 'Property' in MH Cheadle, DM Davis & NRL Haysom (eds) *South African constitutional law: The bill of rights* (2002) 429–472.

[21] AJ van der Walt 'Overview of developments since the introduction of the constitutional property clause' (2004) 19 *SA Public Law* 46–89 at 48.

the so-called purposive interpretation of section 25 and the influence of the historical and constitutional context. The section on application deals particularly with the question whether section 25 can and should find horizontal application and the beneficiaries of the property clause. The discussion of limitation concentrates particularly on the applicability of limitation analysis on the property clause.

Chapter 3 deals with the definition of property for purposes of the property clause, the scope and nature of property interests that qualify for its protection and special issues relating to the property threshold question such as dephysicalization and conceptual severance. Examples of important categories of property interests that qualify for protection under section 25 are discussed, eg commercial property, immaterial property interests, social and welfare participation interests and so forth. The chapter also raises the question whether property has a special meaning or content in the constitutional sphere and how this view of property relates to its private law meaning.

Chapter 4 relates to deprivation of property. The chapter includes a general discussion of the meaning of deprivation and its distinction from expropriation as well as analysis of the requirements for legitimate and valid deprivation in terms of the requirements in section 25(1). The purpose of the deprivation provision is discussed with reference to the police power principle. Special attention is paid to the non-arbitrariness requirement in view of the *FNB* and *Mkontwana* decisions of the Constitutional Court,[22] and the effect of these decisions on the adjudication of section 25 cases is analysed and evaluated. Finally, three special statutory applications of the police power principle and the deprivation requirements are explained: planning and development regulation; search and seizure and forfeiture powers; and the effect of anti-eviction and public accommodations laws on the exclusivity of landownership.

Expropriation is discussed in chapter 5, first in relation to the distinction between deprivation and expropriation and then with reference to the section 25 requirements for valid expropriation. The distinction between deprivation and expropriation and the grey area between the two are explained with reference to two special topics that illustrate the problems, namely forfeiture laws and powers and the doctrine of constructive expropriation. The question whether constructive expropriation can and should find application in South African law is discussed with reference to comparative examples. Thereafter the section 25 requirements for valid expropriation are set out and discussed, with special attention for the public purpose and compensation requirements.

The second part of section 25 authorizes and requires extensive land reforms to take place, and in conjunction with other provisions of the Bill of Rights further reforms that have an effect on property are also made possible. In chapter 6 the three

---

[22] *First National Bank of SA Ltd t/a Wesbank v Commissioner, South African Revenue Service; First National Bank of SA Ltd t/a Wesbank v Minister of Finance* or *FNB* 2002 (4) SA 768 (CC); *Mkontwana v Nelson Mandela Metropolitan Municipality; Bissett and Others v Buffalo City Municipality; Transfer Rights Action Campaign and Others v Member of the Executive Council for Local Government and Housing, Gauteng and Others* 2005 (1) SA 530 (CC).

categories of land reform (redistribution, security of tenure reform and redistribution to increase access to land and housing) are analysed with reference to the most important legislation and case law, followed by a similar analysis of legislation and case law relating to reforms in water law and mining and minerals law. The overall question is whether the constitutional and statutory authorization of these reforms are compatible with the property clause, given the double function of section 25 already alluded to, namely to protect property and simultaneously reform what remains of the inequalities of apartheid property relations.

Chapter 7 is dedicated to a topic that has become increasingly problematic and important since 1994, namely the development of the common law and customary law to promote the spirit, purport and objects of the Constitution. The discussion of this topic is structured around a brief overview of the historical hegemony that seems to isolate the common law against constitutional reforms, a discussion of eviction as a paradigmatic issue that illustrates the problem and the case law dealing with it to date, an analysis of other developments and a discussion of the theoretical issues involved in the development of the common and customary law.

Interpretation, Application, Limitation

2.1 INTRODUCTION

In this chapter the focus is on the background (or so-called operational) issues relating to the interpretation and application of the property clause, as well as on general limitation issues in terms of section 36 of the Constitution. One issue that also relates to the interpretation of the property clause, namely the development of the common law, is not discussed here but separately in chapter 7.

The chapter starts out with a general overview and analysis of the structure of section 25. The South African property clause is longer and more complex than most similar constitutional provisions and unique in its combination of two seemingly contradictory guarantees; first a guarantee that protects existing property interests against unconstitutional interference (section 25(1)–(3)) and then a guarantee of state action to promote land and other related reforms (section 25(4)–(9)). Given the structural and substantive complexity of the clause it is important to understand the overall structure and appreciate the potential conflicts and tensions built into section 25. The overview of section 25 in 2.2 below sets out the structure and explains the complexities of the clause.

A second issue that enjoys attention in this chapter is the interpretation of the property clause. Apart from general interpretation issues this chapter pays special attention to purposive interpretation and to the use of foreign and international law in interpreting section 25. Given the seemingly contradictory structure and content of section 25 it is obviously important to decide what the purpose of the provision is and to determine how that affects its interpretation and application. The courts have indicated that constitutional provisions will be interpreted purposively, making it even more important to consider the purpose of the property clause. A purposive interpretation of section 25 requires a teleological framework within which the courts can interpret and apply the section in such a way that both the protective and the reformative purposes of section 25 are respected, protected, promoted and fulfilled[1] harmoniously. Various facets of the interpretation of section 25 are discussed in chapter 2.3 below.

---

[1] See section 7(2): 'The State must respect, protect, promote, and fulfil the rights in the Bill of Rights.' This formulation of the state's duty towards the rights in the Bill of Rights has recently enjoyed some attention in literature on international human rights; see S Liebenberg 'The interpretation of socio-economic rights' in S Woolman et al (eds) *Constitutional law of South Africa* (2nd ed original service 2003) 33-6–33-7 and references there. The relevant literature and its implications for constitutional rights (especially social and economic rights, but also the rights of unlawful occupiers in an eviction dispute) have been referred to in recent South African case law; see especially *Modderklip Boerdery (Edms) Bpk v President van die Republiek van Suid-Afrika* 2003 (6) BCLR 638 (T) 680I par [44]; *Modderfontein Squatters, Greater Benoni City Council v Modderklip Boerdery (Pty) Ltd; (Agri SA and Legal Resources Centre, Amici Curiae); President of the Republic of South Africa and Others v Modderklip Boerdery (Pty) Ltd (Agri SA and Legal Resources Centre, Amici Curiae)* 2004 (6) SA 40 (SCA) at 55 footnote 17. This question is discussed in chapter 7 under 'Theoretical and conceptual issues' on page 431.

The third issue discussed in this chapter is the application of section 25. One of the application questions that initially concerned South African commentators and courts most is the problem of horizontal application. In more recent literature there seems to be less concern about this issue, but the application problem, stated more generally, involves the effect and impact of the Constitution (and the property clause) on and in private law and therefore application remains important. The general relationship between the constitutional property clause and private law and the development of the common law are discussed in chapter 7, but the horizontal application of section 25 is initially discussed in chapter 2.4 below. Apart from horizontal application the application issue includes the question of beneficiaries. The state is usually not considered a beneficiary of the property clause, because the Bill of Rights is aimed at the protection of private or citizens' rights and not state interests. For much the same reason it is not self-evident that juristic persons (as opposed to natural persons) should benefit from the protection of the property clause, although some constitutions either provide explicitly or are interpreted to the effect that juristic persons are protected by the property clause and other provisions in the Bill of Rights. The beneficiaries of section 25 are considered in chapter 2.4.4 below.

The fourth aspect discussed in this chapter is the limitation of property rights. The limitation issue attracted much more attention in early literature on section 25 than it does now, but it remains important to reflect upon the implications of the general limitation clause in section 36 of the Constitution for section 25. The South African courts follow a two-stage approach to constitutional disputes. The first stage requires proof of the existence of a constitutional right and an infringement of that right, while the second stage allows justification of an infringement according to the requirements of the general limitation clause in section 36(1). The structure of a constitutional property dispute is considered in view of the general limitation provision and with reference to the *FNB* decision,[2] and the question is raised whether limitation analysis under section 36 has any application in property disputes. The implications of the general limitation provision for constitutional property disputes are discussed in chapter 2.5 below.

2.2 STRUCTURE OF SECTION 25

25. Property

(1) No one may be deprived of property except in terms of law of general application, and no law may permit arbitrary deprivation of property.
(2) Property may be expropriated only in terms of law of general application—
   (*a*) for a public purpose or in the public interest; and
   (*b*) subject to compensation, the amount of which and the time and manner of payment of which have either been agreed to by those affected or decided or approved by a court.

---

[2] *First National Bank of SA Ltd t/a Wesbank v Commissioner, South African Revenue Service; First National Bank of SA Ltd t/a Wesbank v Minister of Finance* 2002 (4) SA 768 (CC).

(3) The amount of the compensation and the time and manner of payment must be just and equitable, reflecting an equitable balance between the public interest and the interests of those affected, having regard to all relevant circumstances, including—
  (a) the current use of the property;
  (b) the history of the acquisition and use of the property;
  (c) the market value of the property;
  (d) the extent of direct state investment and subsidy in the acquisition and beneficial capital improvement of the property; and
  (e) the purpose of the expropriation.
(4) For the purposes of this section—
  (a) the public interest includes the nation's commitment to land reform, and to reforms to bring about equitable access to all South Africa's natural resources; and
  (b) property is not limited to land.
(5) The state must take reasonable legislative and other measures, within its available resources, to foster conditions which enable citizens to gain access to land on an equitable basis.
(6) A person or community whose tenure of land is legally insecure as a result of past racially discriminatory laws or practices is entitled, to the extent provided by an Act of Parliament, either to tenure which is legally secure or to comparable redress.
(7) A person or community dispossessed of property after 19 June 1913 as a result of past racially discriminatory laws or practices is entitled, to the extent provided by an Act of Parliament, either to restitution of that property or to equitable redress.
(8) No provision of this section may impede the state from taking legislative and other measures to achieve land, water and related reform, in order to redress the results of past racial discrimination, provided that any departure from the provisions of this section is in accordance with the provisions of section 36(1).
(9) Parliament must enact the legislation referred to in subsection (6).

2.2.1 Overview

In this part of the chapter the structure of the property clause is set out by way of an overview of the provisions in section 25. The purpose of this overview is to highlight the general structure and coherence of the section and to point out the subdivisions within the section. Important provisions and some specific issues and problems deriving from them (such as the property concept, deprivation and expropriation) are discussed separately in later chapters of the book.

Broadly speaking section 25 contains four clusters of provisions:
• Deprivation (section 25(1)).
• Expropriation (section 25(2) and 25(3)).
• Interpretation (section 25(4)).
• Land and other reforms (section 25(5) to 25(9)).

These four clusters can be divided into two main parts that respectively embody the protective and reform purposes of the property clause. The interpretation provision in section 25(4) affects both parts and falls somewhere in the middle between these two parts of the section:

- Protective purpose: to guarantee or protect existing property rights and interests, mainly (but not exclusively) against unconstitutional state interference (deprivation provision in section 25(1) and expropriation provisions in section 25(2) and 25(3), read with interpretation provision in section 25(4)).
- Reform purpose: to legitimate and promote land and related reforms in property holdings and property law (land reform provisions in section 25(5) to 25(9), read with interpretation provision in section 25(4)).

The four clusters of provisions and the two main parts into which they are divided above dictate the framework within which the property clause has to be interpreted and applied, because it embodies and explains the tension between individual provisions in section 25; between section 25 and other constitutional or statutory provisions; and between section 25 and the common law. A single provision in section 25 should not be interpreted or applied abstractly without reference to this structure.

2.2.2 Section 25(1): Deprivation

Section 25(1), which corresponds roughly with section 28(2) of the 1993 Constitution,[3] contains the deprivation provision of the property clause. The deprivation provision is phrased negatively, and unlike section 28(1) of the interim Constitution, it does not include a positive guarantee of property. The function of the deprivation provision is twofold:

- To confirm that the property clause does not render property absolute or inviolate by establishing the constitutional police power principle that state interferences with and limitations of the use, enjoyment and exploitation of property are legitimate, provided they are in the public interest and comply with the requirements set out in section 25(1).
- To ensure that necessary and legitimate regulatory limitations of property are not imposed arbitrarily and unfairly by requiring that they should comply with the constitutional requirements.

In other words, the deprivation provision confirms that property may be limited legitimately through regulatory deprivation of property, and lays down the require-

---

[3] The two subsections are not identical. Perhaps the most crucial difference is that section 28(2) requires that a deprivation of property should be 'in accordance with a law', whereas section 25(1) requires it to be 'in terms of law of general application'. The provision in section 25(1) that 'no law may permit arbitrary deprivation of property' did not appear in section 28(2) at all. The deprivation provision is discussed in chapter 4.

ments for regulatory limitation of property to be valid.[4] Like the rest of section 25, section 25(1) must be interpreted and applied in terms of a balance which has to be struck between the protection of individual rights and the promotion and protection of social or public responsibilities and duties.[5] The deprivation provision in section 25(1) is dealt with in chapter 4. The relationship between the deprivation requirements and the general limitation provision is discussed in chapter 2.5 below.

2.2.3 Section 25(2) and 25(3): Expropriation

Subsections 25(2) and 25(3), which correspond roughly with section 28(3) of the 1993 Constitution, lay down the general provisions for the validity of expropriation. The expropriation provision consists of two parts:

- Section 25(2) establishes the general principle that expropriation is legitimate provided that it complies with certain specified requirements: it must be imposed by law of general application; it must serve a public purpose or be in the public interest, and it must be accompanied by compensation.[6]

- Section 25(3) specifies that compensation for expropriation must be just and equitable and it sets out the general principle according to which compensation should be determined, namely that it should reflect an equitable balance between the interests of those affected and the public interest, having regard to all the relevant factors.[7]

Building on the assumption that property may be limited subject to certain requirements, the expropriation provision enumerates the requirements with which expropriation has to comply (above and beyond the general requirements of section 25(1)) to be valid. Section 25(3) indicates that compensation must establish a just and equitable balance between the individual interest affected and the public interest, which creates the impression that all the expropriation requirements, like the deprivation requirements, should be interpreted in terms of a balance that should be struck between individual rights and the public interest.

---

[4]The requirements in section 25(1) are discussed in chapter 4. With regard to the general limitation clause in section 36 see the discussion in chapter 2.5 below and compare DG Kleyn 'The constitutional protection of property: A comparison between the German and the South African approach' (1996) 11 *SA Public Law* 402–445 at 424ff; AJ van der Walt 'Towards a theory of rights in property: Exploratory observations on the paradigm of post-apartheid property law' (1995) 10 *SA Public Law* 298–345 at 303ff. Compare G Carpenter 'Internal modifiers and other qualifications in bills of rights—Some problems of interpretation' (1995) 10 *SA Public Law* 260–282; S Woolman 'Limitations' in M Chaskalson et al (eds) *Constitutional law of South Africa* (1996 Revision Service 2, 1998) chapter 12 at 13ff; IM Rautenbach *General provisions of the South African bill of rights* (1995) 105ff.

[5]See chapter 2.3.6 below and compare DG Kleyn 'The constitutional protection of property rights: A comparison between the German and the South African approach' (1996) 11 *SA Public Law* 402–445 at 408ff.

[6]As is explained in chapter 5.2 below, expropriation is a special subcategory of deprivation and therefore also subject to section 25(1).

[7]Compensation is discussed in chapter 5.8.

A particularly vexing question is the distinction between deprivation (section 25(1)) and expropriation (section 25(2)). It is clear from the *FNB* decision that the former category is the wider one, so that all expropriations are deprivations while only some deprivations are expropriations.[8] However, it is widely recognized that there is a grey area in between where actions not intended as expropriations may have an expropriatory effect, and in some jurisdictions these actions are treated as expropriations of a kind. In this area the problem, as far as South African law is concerned, is to identify deprivations that have the same effect as expropriation and to decide whether they could and should be treated as constructive expropriation by South African courts. It seems inevitable that South African courts will have to deal with this question sooner or later. This problem is discussed in chapter 5.4.

The characteristic that most clearly distinguishes expropriation from non-expropriatory deprivation is compensation, because compensation is required only for expropriation and not for deprivation. Section 25(2) establishes the duty to compensate for expropriation and section 25(3) sets out some general principles for the calculation of just and equitable compensation. Compensation is discussed in chapter 5.8.

2.2.4 Section 25(4): Interpretation

Section 25(4) is an interpretation provision that applies to section 25 only.[9] It is aimed at excluding certain interpretations of section 25:

*   The term 'public interest' (which appears in section 25(2)(a) and 25(3) with regard to expropriation) is not restricted to public use of property but includes 'the nation's commitment to land reform, and to reforms to bring about equitable access to all South Africa's natural resources'. This makes it possible to justify expropriation aimed at land redistribution, where the ultimate beneficiary (owner or user) of the land is a private person and not the state or the public.[10]
*   Property is not limited to land. This makes it possible to argue that movable corporeal property as well as intangibles such as commercial interests and intellectual property is included under the protection in section 25 as a matter of course.[11]

The first definitional provision ensures that certain land reforms, and especially those which have the eventual redistribution of land as their aim, are not attacked on the basis of the public-interest requirement, and also that the public interest is considered

---

[8] *First National Bank of SA Ltd t/a Wesbank v Commissioner, South African Revenue Service; First National Bank of SA Ltd t/a Wesbank v Minister of Finance* 2002 (4) SA 768 (CC) paras [57]–[58] at 796E–797A; see chapter 5.2.

[9] The interpretation provision affects the land reform provisions in section 25(5) to 25(9) because it makes clear that, although land reform is central to these provisions, property is not limited to land and by giving legitimacy to land reform goals; but it also applies to the public interest provision in section 25(2)(a) by specifying that property is not limited to land and that the public interest includes land reform aspirations and goals.

[10] See the discussion in chapter 5.7.

[11] See the discussion in chapter 3.

duly when determining just and equitable compensation for expropriation. From the whole of section 25 it is obvious that the constitutional assembly was particularly anxious to ensure that the legitimacy and efficacy of land reform would not be detrimentally affected by the property clause. The public purpose or public interest requirement for expropriation is discussed in chapter 5.7 and the relationship between land reform and the protection of existing property rights in terms of the property clause in chapters 6 and 7.

Section 25 is so heavily involved with land rights and land reform that it is easy to think that the clause deals with land only. The second definitional provision ensures that the term 'property' in section 25 is not read so restrictively. This provision applies especially to section 25(1), 25(2), 25(3) and 25(7) since the other sections deal specifically with land in any event. The effect of this provision, the special status of land as an important category of 'property', and the interpretation problems caused by section 25(4)(*b*) and by the status of land in section 25 are discussed in chapter 3.

2.2.5 Section 25(5) to 25(9): Land reform

Subsections 25(5) to 25(9) deal with various aspects of land and other reforms. In the redrafting of the property clause the constitutional assembly was obviously very concerned about the continued efficacy and legitimacy of land reform, and these provisions are therefore quite important to the overall structure and effect of section 25. The scope of these provisions can be summarized as follows:

• Section 25(5) places a general duty upon the state to take reasonable legislative and other steps, within its available resources, to foster conditions which promote equitable access to land.[12]
• Section 25(6) places a specific duty upon the state to ensure security of tenure for persons or communities whose tenure of land is legally insecure as a result of past discriminatory laws or practices, by providing for such security or comparable redress in legislation.[13]

---

[12] The Land Reform (Labour Tenants) Act 3 of 1996 and the Communal Property Associations Act 28 of 1996 are examples of land reform laws aimed at this goal. See chapter 6.4 for a discussion of land reform laws concerned with access to land and housing.

[13] The Land Reform (Labour Tenants) Act 3 of 1996, the Extension of Security of Tenure Act 62 of 1997, the Prevention of Illegal Eviction from and Unlawful Occupation of Land Act 18 of 1998 and the Interim Protection of Informal Land Rights Act 31 of 1996 fall into this category. See chapter 6.3 for a discussion of land reform laws concerned with security of tenure.

- Section 25(7) entitles a person or community dispossessed of property after 19 June 1913 as a result of past racially discriminatory laws or practices to restitution or equitable redress, as provided for in a law.[14]
- Section 25(8) ensures that no provision of section 25 may impede the state from taking legislative and other measures to achieve land, water and related reforms in order to redress the results of past racially discriminatory laws and practices, provided that such measures (in so far as they limit property rights that are guaranteed in section 25) are in accordance with the limitation requirements in section 36.[15]
- Section 25(9) states that parliament must enact the legislation referred to in section 25(6). Various laws have been promulgated to give effect to this duty.[16]

These land-reform provisions (and especially section 25(8), which creates some interesting interpretation problems) reflect the constitutional assembly's anxiety about land reform and the importance of reform and transformation as inherent part of the property clause. The effect of the land-reform provisions and the relationship between the protection of existing property rights and the promotion of land reform in terms of the property clause are discussed in chapter 6.

2.2.6 Evaluation

The structure of section 25 is complex and the first part (section 25(1)–(3): protection of existing property interests) may seem to be in conflict with the last part (section 25(5)–(9): land reform). However, it is both necessary[17] and possible to read the provision as a coherent whole that embodies a creative tension within itself without being self-conflicting or contradictory. Such a coherent, non-conflicting approach to section 25 presupposes a purposive interpretation of the property clause.[18] This book is based on the assumption that section 25 should and can be interpreted as a coherent whole, within the historical and constitutional context. The book is accordingly inspired by the idea that the double function of section 25 embodies a creative tension rather than a fatal conflict, and it is argued here that the emerging case law of the

---

[14]The Restitution of Land Rights Act 22 of 1994 is the law this section refers to, and in that sense this section replaces section 121(1) of the interim 1993 Constitution. In a sense the Land Reform (Labour Tenants) Act 3 of 1996 also functions as a restitution law and not simply as a redistribution law. See chapter 6.2 on land reform laws concerned with restitution. See further *Transvaal Agricultural Union v Minister of Land Affairs and Another* 1997 (2) SA 621 (CC) (sections 11(7) and 11(8) of the Restitution of Land Rights Act 22 of 1994 are not in conflict with section 28 of the 1993 Constitution, or if they are, the infringements so caused are justified by section 33). Compare W du Plessis & NJJ Olivier 'The old and the new property clause' (1997) 1(5) *Human Rights & Const LJ SA* 11–16.

[15]See chapter 6.6 for a discussion of this provision.

[16]See footnote 13 above; and compare chapter 6.3.

[17]In terms of the presumption that legislation is valid and purposeful; see further JR de Ville *Constitutional and statutory interpretation* (2000) 167–169; L du Plessis *Re-interpretation of statutes* (2002) 187–191.

[18]See 2.3 below on the purposive interpretation of the property clause.

Constitutional Court demonstrates the possibility of such a reading of the section. The possibility of a purposive interpretation of section 25 and emerging case law on it are discussed in 2.3 below. Various aspects of these and related assumptions are worked out in the chapters that follow, especially in chapter 6 (land and other reforms) and chapter 7 (influence of the Constitution on the common law).

2.3 INTERPRETATION

39. Interpretation of Bill of Rights

(1) When interpreting the Bill of Rights, a court, tribunal or forum—
   (a) must promote the values that underlie an open and democratic society based on human dignity, equality and freedom;
   (b) must consider international law; and
   (c) may consider foreign law.
(2) When interpreting any legislation, and when developing the common law or customary law, every court, tribunal or forum must promote the spirit, purport and objects of the Bill of Rights.
(3) The Bill of Rights does not deny the existence of any other rights or freedoms that are recognized or conferred by common law, customary law or legislation, to the extent that the are consistent with the Bill.

25. Property

(4) For the purposes of this section—
   (a) the public interest includes the nation's commitment to land reform, and to reforms to bring about equitable access to all South Africa's natural resources; and
   (b) property is not limited to land.

2.3.1 Introduction

A number of recent publications[19] have made it unnecessary to write much here about constitutional interpretation in general, but it remains necessary to consider certain interpretation issues as they apply to the property clause. The main issues that are considered here are the use of international and foreign law, the purposive approach to interpretation and the effect of the interpretation provision in section 25(4).

---

[19]See particularly JR de Ville *Constitutional and statutory interpretation* (2000); L du Plessis *Reinterpretation of statutes* (2002). For a discussion of interpretation issues (with reference to these books) and their implications for constitutional property adjudication compare AJ van der Walt 'Striving for the better interpretation—A critical reflection on the Constitutional Court's *Harksen* and *FNB* decisions on the property clause' (2004) 121 *SALJ* 854–878 at 854–860.

2.3.2 International and foreign law

Section 39(1)(b) of the Constitution provides that a court, tribunal or forum must consider international law when interpreting the Bill of Rights, and section 39(1)(c) adds that such a court, tribunal or forum may consider foreign law.[20] The use of comparative reference to foreign and international law in interpreting and applying the property clause is a complex and contentious issue. In the early days, when the 1993 Constitution was still in its drafting stages and shortly after its acceptance, South African lawyers (and especially property lawyers, who were mostly private law specialists with little or no knowledge of or experience in constitutional law) almost automatically (and somewhat frantically) fell back upon comparative analysis in interpreting the property clause. Every private property lawyer with an interest in constitutional issues suddenly became a comparatist in order to find out what constitutional property was all about. However, at that stage South African lawyers had limited knowledge of the comparative constitutional property sources and issues and consequently comparative analysis was often haphazard and unsystematic.[21]

Since then South African lawyers and courts have improved their knowledge and understanding of constitutional comparison, both in general and as far as constitutional property is concerned. The growth of literature and case law on constitutional property has reduced the broad, general or introductory need for reliance upon comparative sources and has refined the use of comparative materials. Above all it is now understood that comparative analysis for the sake of comparison alone is senseless; comparative analysis should bring some benefit in the form of new solutions and alternatives or greater clarity (even when it is of no more assistance than avoiding errors made in other jurisdictions), in specific areas and on specific points of law or interpretation.[22]

Although reference to international law in the interpretation of the Bill of Rights is obligatory,[23] case law on section 25 contains few references to international law—

---

[20]The comparable section 35(1) of the interim Constitution provided that a court of law which interprets the Bill of Rights 'shall, where applicable, have regard to public international law' and 'may have regard to comparable foreign case law'.

[21]See AJ van der Walt *Constitutional property clauses: A comparative analysis* (1999) 27–37 on the methodological problems.

[22]See the criticism of T Roux 'Section 25' in S Woolman et al (eds) *Constitutional law of South Africa* (2nd ed 2003 original service Dec 2003) 46–23 against the extensive comparative analysis in *First National Bank of SA Ltd t/a Wesbank v Commissioner, South African Revenue Service; First National Bank of SA Ltd t/a Wesbank v Minister of Finance* 2002 (4) SA 768 (CC) paras [71]–[99] at 801D–810G; and compare the criticism of AJ van der Walt & H Botha 'Coming to grips with the new constitutional order: Critical comments on *Harksen v Lane NO*' (1998) 13 *SA Public Law* 17–41 at 20–23 on the much less ambitious comparative analysis of the Court in *Harksen v Lane NO and Others* 1998 (1) SA 300 (CC) paras [29]–[40] at 314G–318I. See further in general the comments on comparative sources in AJ van der Walt 'Moving towards recognition of constructive expropriation?' (2002) 65 *THRHR* 459–473 at 464–468. See further footnote 24 below.

[23]Compare sections 231, 232 and 233 of the Constitution, which concern the general applicability of international law.

by and large there are more references in the literature and in the cases to foreign law than to international law as far as property is concerned, and references to international law are almost exclusively restricted to case law on the European Convention on Human Rights.[24] This is probably a result of the fact that constitutional property has enjoyed relatively little attention in international law, except for the extensive case law on the property provision in article 1 of the First Protocol to the European Convention. In areas where property did enjoy attention in international law the benefits for comparative constitutional law were often limited.[25]

In this book, reference is made to a variety of constitutional property clauses and case law dealing with them, from a number of often widely divergent foreign jurisdictions.[26] As will appear in the course of the analysis, it is my contention that differ-

---

[24]The most significant Constitutional Court decision to date, *First National Bank of SA Ltd t/a Wesbank v Commissioner, South African Revenue Service; First National Bank of SA Ltd t/a Wesbank v Minister of Finance* 2002 (4) SA 768 (CC) paras [71]–[99] at 801D–810G, refers to the following jurisdictions: the US, Australia, the Council of Europe (European Convention), Germany, and the UK. However, T Roux 'Section 25' in S Woolman et al (eds) *Constitutional law of South Africa* (2nd ed 2003 original service Dec 2003) 46-23 criticized this comparative analysis because none of its results was actually applied in the case. In the first extensive judicial analysis of the property clause (section 28 of the 1993 interim Constitution), *Harksen v Lane NO and Others* 1998 (1) SA 300 (CC) paras [29]–[40] at 314G–318I, the Constitutional Court referred to Zimbabwean and Indian law. See AJ van der Walt & H Botha 'Coming to grips with the new constitutional order: Critical comments on *Harksen v Lane NO*' (1998) 13 *SA Public Law* 17–41 at 20–23 for critical comments on the suitability and usefulness of the Court's comparative analysis.

[25]See AJ van der Walt *Constitutional property clauses: A comparative analysis* (1999) 96–120 on this source of comparative materials. At the time of writing Tom Allen was preparing a book on the European Convention law and its meaning for UK law, entitled *Property and the Human Rights Act 1998* (forthcoming, Hart Publishing, 2005). JD van der Vyver 'Property in international human rights law' in GE van Maanen & AJ van der Walt (eds) *Property law on the threshold of the 21st century* (1996) 451–486 provides an overview of some of the more general international law principles that are relevant. See further J Murphy 'Compensation for nationalization in international law' (1993) 110 *SALJ* 79–99.

[26]I rely extensively on the analysis of comparative materials in AJ van der Walt *Constitutional property clauses: A comparative analysis* (1999), but also on T Allen *The right to property in Commonwealth constitutions* (2000). At the time of writing Gregory Alexander was preparing a comparative analysis of constitutional property in German, South African and US law entitled *The global debate over constitutional property* (forthcoming, University of Chicago Press, 2006). T Roux 'Section 25' in S Woolman et al (eds) *Constitutional law of South Africa* (2nd ed 2003 original service Dec 2003) 46-23 considers the contextual similarities between Commonwealth jurisdictions and South Africa regarding their history of colonialism, similar stage of economic development and—particularly— the fact that Commonwealth courts have tended not to treat different sticks in the bundle of property rights as independent property interests as an important reason for these jurisdictions to play a meaningful role in South Africa. Roux is certainly right that Commonwealth jurisprudence is an important source of comparative information on section 25, and he does qualify its significance with reference to textual differences and the dangers of poor decisions. However, apart from Roux's considered arguments the more general preference amongst lawyers and judges for comparison with Commonwealth countries may also be inspired either by the relative inaccessibility of

(continued on next page ...)

ences in the phraseology and structure of a property clause, and even larger structural differences such as between the common-law and civil-law traditions, are often less influential in the interpretation of any given property clause than one might expect, especially judging from a private law background.[27] Very often the problems which arise and some of the possible solutions are not so much the result of the phraseology or structure of the property clause, but rather a function of the role assigned to property and to the constitutional property clause in the historical, social, political and legal context of the specific society. To a large extent this role always concerns the tensions and conflicts which emanate from a society's efforts to mediate between existing, private interests (the socio-economic *status quo*) on the one hand and the public interest (socio-economic development or transformation) on the other.[28] For purposes of interpreting and applying the South African property clause I therefore argue that one may (and should) make extensive use of examples from a wide range of foreign law, provided these differences and the social and political contexts are kept in mind.

The purpose of reference to foreign law should be, firstly, to note the problems of interpretation and application that have already been uncovered there, and secondly to observe and analyse different approaches, arguments, tendencies and trends in the solution of those problems, while remaining careful to ensure that the eventual interpretation and application of section 25 is suited to current, local needs and demands, within the historical, social and political context of South African legal development. It is obviously necessary to always consider and apply foreign law with proper sensitivity for systemic, structural, historical and contextual differences between contexts and for the unique characteristics of the South African Constitution and the South African socio-economic setting. In some cases the whole point of comparative analysis could be to establish that a certain jurisdiction is not suitable

---

(... from previous page)
German, French and similar examples or by the impression that specifically German constitutional property law, with its emphasis on the institutional guarantee, would steer South African law in the wrong direction. In response to this impression it should be mentioned that many Commonwealth examples are not only poorly decided or out of date, but that some of the more interesting recent examples come from jurisdictions such as Australia and Ireland that do not share with South Africa the characteristics mentioned above, and that pose particularly daunting comparative problems. At the same time, despite its own problems, it should be acknowledged that the German property clause shares some textual characteristics with section 25 and that German case law developed (at least initially) in a context where social responsibilities and social democratic sensibilities were emphasized, which means that German case law often demonstrates exactly the kind of reform-awareness that South African courts have to take note of, rather than the opposite.

[27]See AJ van der Walt *Constitutional property clauses: A comparative analysis* (1999) 10–38 for analysis and examples.

[28]See AJ van der Walt *Constitutional property clauses: A comparative analysis* (1999) 10–38; compare further LS Underkuffler-Freund 'Takings and the nature of property' (1996) 9 *Can J Law & Jur* 161–205, especially at 169ff. Compare the *First Certification Case: Ex Parte Chairperson of the Constitutional Assembly: In re Certification of the Constitution of the Republic of South Africa, 1996* 1996 (4) SA 744 (CC) par [34] at 786D.

or useful as a comparative source on a specific point, even though it may well be useful and instructive on other points.[29] However, this does not mean that one should be unnecessarily skeptical about or suspicious of foreign law.[30] To consider foreign law does not commit the courts to following foreign law—on the contrary, reference to foreign law can often be useful in avoiding mistakes made elsewhere. Moreover, it seems logical that a decision not to follow foreign law should result from rather than preclude consideration of foreign law, which means that the general warning against 'unnecessary importation' of foreign law should not be used as an excuse not to investigate, analyse and consider the applicability and usefulness of foreign law, but should in fact follow from and be justified by such analysis. Across-the-board skepsis about foreign law will deprive the courts of much useful and stimulating input, and will often demand of them to reinvent the wheel or induce them to make the same mistakes that have already been made (and perhaps rectified) elsewhere. Fear of making the same mistakes that were made in other countries (the Indian example and the American experience with *Lochnerism* are often cited)[31] should be an argument in favour of, and not against, extensive but careful and reflective consultation of foreign law.

2.3.3 Purposive interpretation I: Introduction

Perhaps the most important issue concerning the interpretation of section 25 is the fact that it, like the rest of the Constitution, is supposed to be interpreted purposively, according to the general trend in constitutional and statutory interpretation adopted by the courts since 1994.[32] Section 25 is particularly difficult to interpret because of the tension between protection of existing rights and reform of the property regime that is built into the clause. In this case, purposive interpretation can solve the

---

[29] The best example in this book is the conclusions about comparative sources with regard to the public purposes requirement for expropriation; see chapter 5.7.3 and especially footnotes 254–268 and accompanying text there.

[30] See *Qozeleni v Minister of Law and Order and Another* 1994 (3) SA 625 (E) at 633F–G; *Park-Ross and Another v Director: Office for Serious Economic Offences* 1995 (2) SA 148 (C) at 160G–H for examples of judgments that are careful about the 'unnecessary importation' of foreign law, albeit not in the area of constitutional property.

[31] See especially M Chaskalson 'The problem with property: Thoughts on the constitutional protection of property in the United States and in the Commonwealth' (1993) 9 *SAJHR* 388–411; compare J Murphy 'Insulating land reform from constitutional impugnment: An Indian case study' (1992) 8 *SAJHR* 362–388.

[32] See *Brink v Kitshoff NO* 1996 (4) SA 197 (CC) for an example of a decision where the Constitutional Court indicated that it will follow a purposive interpretation. Compare *Park-Ross and Another v Director: Office for Serious Economic Offences* 1995 (2) SA 148 (C) at 160Cff; see further footnote 89 below. In *Minister of Home Affairs v National Institute for Crime Prevention and the Reintegration of Offenders (NICRO) and Others* 2005 (3) SA 280 (CC) par [21] at 290B it was confirmed that, although the Constitution was interpreted according to the values enshrined in section 1 of the Constitution, these values did not 'give rise to discrete and enforceable rights in themselves.'

problem by making it possible to read section 25 as a coherent whole. Such an approach to the interpretation of section 25 depends on the following premises:

- All constitutional property clauses contain an inherent tension between the protection of existing rights and the state's power to infringe upon existing rights in the public interest; in this regard the South African clause is not unique, despite its heavy emphasis on land reform. The land reform provisions in section 25 are not conflicting foreign bodies that render the property clause uniquely problematic or unworkable, but rather the result of a context-specific emphasis on a particular category of constitutionally legitimate public-interest state limitations imposed on private property. In other contexts, other categories of limitation may be more important.[33]

- The legitimacy of land reform as a special category of constitutionally sanctioned state limitations imposed on private property derives from the historical context within which the South African Constitution functions; it is a result of the historical injustice that is being repaired by constitutionally sanctioned transformation and reform efforts. Neither the Constitution nor the property clause can be abstracted from or interpreted and applied without consideration for that historical context. The Constitution sanctions and promotes legitimate efforts to overcome and repair the injustices of the past as part of its central transformative function, and therefore land and related reforms feature as a special category of legitimate public purpose limitations of private property.

- The transformative focus of the Constitution and the property clause does not mean that the Constitution does not value or protect private property; the property clause still serves this classic protective purpose alongside its transformative purpose. However, the purpose of the constitutional protection of private property must be seen in the broader context of the Constitution and the Bill of Rights and the central values of human dignity, equality and justice.

This book is based on the assumptions that section 25 should and can be interpreted purposively and that such an interpretation should depend on the creative tension between the two seemingly conflicting purposes in the clause. This approach explains and finds support in the history and contextual background of the clause and in other debates about its nature and purpose. It also finds support in the emerging case law of the Constitutional Court.[34]

---

[33] In Switzerland special emphasis is placed on land use and development regulation; a search of the website of the Swiss Federal Supreme Court reveals that a large percentage of cases had their origin in land use planning and control measures. See AJ van der Walt 'The property clause in the new Federal Constitution of the Swiss Confederation 1999' (2004) 15 *Stell LR* 326–332 at 329.

[34] See especially *Port Elizabeth Municipality v Various Occupiers* 2005 (1) SA 217 (CC) paras [8]–[23] at 222A–229G, setting out the historical context of discriminatory land law and the new constitutional context within which conflicting land rights are adjudicated.

2.3.4 Purposive interpretation II: The constitutionalization debate[35]

A constitutional property clause is by no means a logical or self-evident part of a bill of rights or of a constitutional order. Although many constitutional states have enshrined the right to private property in an entrenched bill of rights,[36] others have not.[37] It is therefore useful to reflect on the purpose of a constitutional property guarantee as it emerges from the constitutionalization debate before embarking upon analysis of section 25.

Much has been written about the pro's and cons of constitutionally entrenching property in a bill of rights and it is unnecessary to repeat the whole debate about constitutionalization here,[38] but it is useful to refer to a central issue that has a direct

---

[35]The constitutionalization issue relates directly to the question whether section 25 can be described as a guarantee of property (see 2.3.5 below) and the notion of property as a truncated right (see chapter 3.2).

[36]Examples of constitutions often referred to in the literature are the United States, the Federal Republic of Germany, Malaysia, Zimbabwe and Namibia. Less well-known but equally interesting examples are Austria, Ireland, Jamaica, Botswana and Gambia. An even less obvious example is Australia, where a property guarantee is read into what is not a classic bill of rights at all. For more detail see the relevant chapters in AJ van der Walt *Constitutional property clauses: A comparative analysis* (1999).

[37]The United Kingdom has no written constitution (and hence no property clause), but still some interesting and important case law on the interpretation of a property clause: see *Attorney-General v De Keyser's Royal Hotel, Ltd* [1920] AC 508 HL; and compare GR Rubin *Private property, government requisition and the constitution, 1914–1927* (1994); SE Finer, V Bogdanor & B Rudden *Comparing constitutions* (1996). As from 2 October 2000 the Human Rights Act 1998 incorporated provisions of the European Convention on Human Rights into UK law; see D Rook *Property law and human rights* (2001) 11–15; T Allen *Property and the Human Rights Act 1998* (forthcoming, Hart Publishing, 2005). The unentrenched Canadian Bill of Rights 1960 contains a property clause (section 1(*a*)), but in the Canadian Charter of Rights and Freedoms 1982 there is no property clause. The property clause (sections 19, 31) was removed from the Bill of Rights in the Indian Constitution in 1978, and what remains is just a prohibition against arbitrary deprivation of property (section 300A). See the chapters on Canada and India in AJ van der Walt *Constitutional property clauses: A comparative analysis* (1999).

[38]J Nedelsky 'Should property be constitutionalized? A relational and comparative approach' in GE van Maanen & AJ van der Walt (eds) *Property on the threshold of the 21st century* (1996) 417–432 at 419 sets out and defends arguments against a constitutional property clause, including the argument of CH Lewis 'The right to private property in a new political dispensation in South Africa' (1992) 8 *SAJHR* 389–430. One argument that is not considered by Nedelsky (and that is discussed in AJ van der Walt 'The constitutional property clause: Striking a balance between guarantee and limitation' in J McLean (ed) *Property and the constitution* (1999) 109–146) is the possibility that the constitutional property clause itself can be interpreted as the basis and authority for land reform and the redistribution of property. See further FI Michelman 'Socio-political functions of constitutional protection for private property holdings (in liberal political thought)' in GE van Maanen & AJ van der Walt (eds) *Property on the threshold of the 21st century* (1996) 433–450; CM Rose 'Property as the keystone right?' (1996) 71 *Notre Dame LR* 329–365; AJ van der Walt 'Property rights, land rights, and environmental rights' in DH van Wyk, J Dugard, B de Villiers & D Davis (eds) *Rights and constitutionalism: The new South African legal order* (1994) 455–501 at 455–462; and generally
(continued on next page ...)

bearing on the purpose (and therefore the interpretation) of a constitutional property clause.

Most of the arguments against constitutionalization of property relate to concerns that the property clause would either entrench existing property rights too strongly (frustrating land reform) or that it would undermine existing property rights for the sake of land reform.[39] In this book I argue that it is possible (and in fact obligatory) to interpret and apply section 25 in such a way that both these results are avoided by striving for a just and equitable balance between existing, private property interests and the public interest in the transformation of the current property regime. According to this approach the entrenchment of existing private property holdings cannot be the only or even the main purpose of the property clause; both the protection and the regulatory limitation of property rights have to be seen in the light of the fundamental constitutional purpose of establishing a just and equitable balance

---

(… from previous page)
AJ van der Walt 'Unity and pluralism in property theory: A review of property theories and debates in recent literature: Part I' 1995 *TSAR* 15–42; 'Subject and society in property theory: A review of property theories and debates in recent literature: Part II' 1995 *TSAR* 322–345; 'Rights and reforms in property theory: A review of property theories and debates in recent literature: Part III' 1995 *TSAR* 493–526.

[39] Constitutionalization was opposed by M Chaskalson 'The problem with property: Thoughts on the constitutional protection of property in the United States and in the Commonwealth' (1993) 9 *SAJHR* 388–411 at 402; J de Waal, G Erasmus & I Currie *Bill of rights handbook* (4th ed 2001) 422, 426–428; M Chaskalson & C Lewis 'Property' in M Chaskalson et al (eds) *Constitutional law of South Africa* (1st ed 1998) par 31.5(*b*)(ii)(bb); G Budlender 'The constitutional protection of property rights: Overview and commentary' in G Budlender, J Latsky & T Roux (eds) *Juta's new land law* (1998) chapter 1 at 25–26, 34–36. See 2.3.4 below and chapter 4.5.1 for a discussion of the issues in the constitutionalization debate. The (admittedly strong) arguments forwarded by both J Nedelsky 'Should property be constitutionalized? A relational and comparative approach' (at 417) and FI Michelman 'Socio-political functions of constitutional protection for private property holdings (in liberal political thought)' (at 433) in GE van Maanen & AJ van der Walt (eds) *Property law on the threshold of the 21st century* (1996) do not allow for a constitutional property theory and practice that does not follow the predictable route of political liberalism. My first reaction was against constitutionalization; see AJ van der Walt 'Towards the development of post-apartheid land law: An exploratory survey' (1990) 23 *De Jure* 1–45. Later on I subscribed to the more nuanced view proposed by J Murphy 'Property rights in the new Constitution: An analytical framework for constitutional review' (1993) 26 *CILSA* 211–233 at 217; see AJ van der Walt 'Property rights, land rights, and environmental rights' in D van Wyk, J Dugard, B de Villiers & D Davis (eds) *Rights and constitutionalism: The new South African legal order* (1994) 455–501 at 480. Eventually I became convinced that the constitutionalization of property need not frustrate land reform and that it can in fact, if interpreted in a transformation-sensitive way, become an instrument of transformation; see AJ van der Walt 'The constitutional property clause: Striking a balance between guarantee and limitation' in J MacLean (ed) *Property and the constitution* (1999) 109–146. T Roux 'Property' in MH Cheadle, DM Davis & NRL Haysom *South African constitutional law: The bill of rights* (2002) 429–472 at 432 footnote 8 provides an interesting insight into the differences between strong initial anti-constitutionalization sentiments and the later, less skeptical approach in terms of which the constitutionalization of property is regarded as a political compromise.

between existing rights and the public interest in the process of transforming and reforming the property regime. The property clause recognizes reform of the property regime as a legitimate reason for regulatory limitation of existing property holdings; consequently, reform-oriented deprivation and expropriation of property is just as much part of the purpose of the property clause as is the protection of existing property interests and rights. The only sensible and legitimate interpretation of section 25 is therefore one that allows (and actually obliges) the courts to strike an equitable balance between the protection of existing rights and the public interest (which includes land reform goals).

This approach to section 25 takes the sting out of anti-constitutionalization arguments, but it also implies that section 25 should be interpreted and applied purposively, with due regard for its double-sided protective and reform purpose and function.

2.3.5 Purposive interpretation III: Property clause or property guarantee?[40]

An interesting theoretical question with implications for the interpretation of section 25 is whether the property clause could be described as a property guarantee. In the *First Certification Case*[41] there were objections to the fact that the phraseology of section 25 deviated from section 28 of the 1993 Constitution in that it does not make explicit provision for the protection of the right to acquire, hold and dispose of property.[42] This raises the question whether a purely negative property clause like section 25[43] is fundamentally different from a positive property clause,[44] which guarantees the right to acquire, hold and dispose of property, in one form or another, explicitly and in positive terms.[45] In the *First Certification Case* the Constitutional Court accepted that positive or negative formulation of the property clause makes no fundamental

---

[40]This issue relates directly to the constitutionalization debate; see 2.3.4 above. See further chapter 3.2, where the notion of property as a truncated right is discussed. The two issues are related.

[41]*Ex Parte Chairperson of the Constitutional Assembly: In re Certification of the Constitution of the Republic of South Africa, 1996* 1996 (4) SA 744 (CC) par [70] at 798A.

[42]Section 28(1) of the Constitution of 1993 provided that '[e]very person shall have the right to acquire and hold rights in property and, to the extent that the nature of the right permits, to dispose of such rights.'

[43]Like the Fifth and Fourteenth Amendments to the US Constitution; section 51(xxxi) of the Commonwealth of Australia Constitution Act 1900 (UK); section 13 of the Federal Constitution of Malaysia 1957 and many others.

[44]Or, more accurately, a combination between a negative and a positive clause. The German article 14 GG combines a positive guarantee of property with a negative guarantee against state interference. See footnote 45 below.

[45]Examples are article 14(1) of the German *Grundgesetz (GG)* (1949); section 5 of the Basic Law of 21 December 1867 which is incorporated by article 149(1) into the Austrian Federal Constitution (revised 1929); the first rule in article 1 of the First Protocol to the European Convention on Human Rights (1950); section 40.3.2 and section 43.1.1 and 43.1.2 of the Constitution of Ireland (1937); section 16(1) of the Constitution of the Republic of Namibia Act 1990.

difference, in the sense that neither can be described as a 'universally recognised for-mulation' and that even a negative property clause is an 'appropriate' formulation for the constitutional protection of property.[46] This attitude, which is confirmed by case law in most jurisdictions, implies that a negative property clause does provide adequate protection for property and that it is not necessary for a property clause to be phrased in positive terms to be regarded as a property guarantee.[47]

The issue involves several related but discrete problems. The first problem is most easily disposed of: the idea that a property clause should include a positive as well as the usual negative formulation to ensure that it guarantees a positive claim right is simply misguided. It is generally accepted that a property clause (even when it includes a positive formulation to the effect that the clause protects the right to acquire, hold and dispose of property) does not create a positive claim right that entitles anybody to claim or receive property from the state. This is simply not the function of a constitutional property clause; it is unknown in constitutional property law and it can have no effect on the debate about whether section 25 can be described as a property guarantee.

However, the question whether section 25 can be said to guarantee property is not without meaning.[48] Subsection 36(1) of the Constitution provides that '[t]he *rights in the Bill of Rights* may be limited only in terms of ... [the requirements laid down in that subsection]', and subsection 36(2) states that '[e]xcept as provided in subsection (1) or in any other provision of the Constitution, no law may limit any *right entrenched in the Bill of Rights*' (my emphasis). One could argue that section 25 does not guar-antee the right to property in the Bill of Rights because of its negative phraseology; insisting that it in fact protects nothing more than the right not to be deprived or expropriated of property other than in terms of the provisions of section 25 itself, which would then imply that what is protected by section 25 is neither 'a right in the Bill of Rights' nor 'a right entrenched in the Bill of Rights', which would in turn mean that section 25 is effectively excluded from limitation scrutiny in terms of sec-tion 36, with the substantive proportionality analysis that it entails. Consequently, any deprivation or expropriation of property would be subjected to the thinnest possible scrutiny in terms of the formal requirements in section 25(1)–(3) and nothing more— once a deprivation was imposed by law of general application that did not allow arbitrary deprivation it would be constitutionally beyond impugnment; expropriation authorized by law of general application would be beyond substantive scrutiny as long as it served a public purpose and was accompanied by just compensation. Moreover, the formal requirements could presumably be applied in the form of relatively thin

---

[46] *Ex Parte Chairperson of the Constitutional Assembly: In re Certification of the Constitution of the Republic of South Africa, 1996* 1996 (4) SA 744 (CC) par [72] at 798F–G.

[47] The same assumption is evident from the argument of DP Currie 'Positive and negative consti-tutional rights' (1986) 53 *Univ Chicago LR* 864–890, who goes even further in construing a positive claim-right (that places a positive obligation on the state to provide or guarantee certain rights and freedoms) from negative clauses in the Bill of Rights.

[48] I am indebted to Frank Michelman for bringing this aspect to my attention.

rationality control, which means that state limitation of property would, effectively, never be subjected to substantive constitutional review as long as it was not obviously and patently irrational. In short, the argument that section 25 does not protect property was intended to ensure that state limitation of property would not be subjected to substantive, *Lochner*-like judicial review.

The avoidance of section 36 limitation analysis, with its substantive proportionality test, was in turn inspired by fear that substantive scrutiny of limitations of property rights could frustrate legitimate regulatory and land reform goals of the state in *Lochner*-style judicial resistance against state-sponsored reform initiatives. However, in response to this argument it is worth mentioning that the traditional and very common negative formulation of property clauses is a result of the basically liberal, *laissez-faire* context within which bills of rights (and especially property clauses in bills of rights) were originally conceived as purely defensive barriers against state interference in the private sphere. In the post-liberal, reformist context within which the South African Constitution originated and functions, this attitude is patently outdated and unsuitable. In this perspective the skeptical approach towards negatively framed property clauses is, at best, an unnecessary and a-contextual effort to combat admittedly real but not very threatening enemies while better, more suitable weapons are available in the interpretation and adjudication theories that accept section 25 as a constitutional property guarantee but concentrate on finding the interpretation that would best suit and explain its constitutional function. The better strategy, as far as avoidance of *Lochner*-like judicial resistance against legitimate government policy is concerned, is not to exclude substantive review but to develop a suitable interpretation and adjudication theory that suits the post-liberal nature and content of the South African Constitution. In a purposive approach the South African Constitution should be interpreted with reference to a set of norms and values that embody the principles of constitutionalism and democracy[49] and that preclude exactly the reform-resistant approach that the sceptics want to avoid.

Moreover, technically ingenious as the no-property-guarantee argument may appear, it seems counter-intuitive in view of the way in which negatively formulated property clauses are usually interpreted and applied in foreign law.[50] Firstly, although the majority of constitutional property clauses around the world are phrased negatively, both foreign case law and academic commentary suggest that a purely negative view of constitutional rights is outdated, and that a purposive or functional interpretation of a constitutional bill of rights requires a different view of even those rights that are framed negatively. In line with the judgment in the *First Certification Case*, it

---

[49] See in this regard *Public Servants' Association of South Africa v Minister of Justice and Others* 1997 (3) SA 925 (T) at 632J; *Fedsure Life Assurance Ltd and Others v Greater Johannesburg Transitional Metropolitan Council and Others* 1997 (5) BCLR 657 (W) at 665C–E.

[50] Apart from section 25 (property), the following sections in chapter 2 are also framed negatively: section 13 (slavery, servitude and forced labour); 20 (citizenship); 31 (cultural, religious and linguistic communities).

is accepted generally that a negative property clause protects property in much the same manner that a positive clause does, except that it does not even raise the question whether the property clause creates positive claim rights. In fact, the discussion of the concept of property in chapter 3.2 suggests that the exact phraseology of the property clause is not as influential in its interpretation as one would expect and that divergent formulations ('ownership', 'property', 'peaceful enjoyment of possessions') from different jurisdictions with very different socio-economic, legal and constitutional backgrounds are all interpreted within the same broad constitutional framework, as if they refer to the protection of basically the same right and provide basically the same kind of guarantee.

This impression is supported by the fact that the courts in some of the major jurisdictions with a positive property clause (or, rather, a property clause consisting of a combination of a positive and a negative part) have accepted that the negative part of the property clause already protects and guarantees property in the 'normal' or 'classic' way, and therefore sought to attach a separate meaning to the positive part of the guarantee.[51] The German courts (followed by the Swiss and Austrian courts) accepted that the negative part of article 14 GG contains the individual property guarantee, and therefore attached a separate, different meaning to the positive part of the guarantee, saying that it contains an institutional guarantee of property.[52] Since the scrapping of section 28(1) of the South African interim Constitution the concept of an institutional guarantee is no longer relevant for the South African property clause[53] and it is not really worthwhile to discuss the technical detail of an institutional

---

[51] Positively phrased guarantees also appear in the Irish Constitution and in the European Convention on Human Rights.

[52] AJ van der Walt 'Property rights, land rights, and environmental rights' in DH van Wyk, J Dugard, B de Villiers & D Davis (eds) *Rights and constitutionalism: The new South African legal order* (1994) 455–501 at 469; AJ van der Walt 'Towards a theory of rights in property: Exploratory observations on the paradigm of post-apartheid property law' (1995) 10 *SA Public Law* 298–345 at 308–310; DG Kleyn 'The constitutional protection of property: A comparison between the German and the South African approach' (1996) 11 *SA Public Law* 402–445 at 414–418 for a discussion of the institutional guarantee. FI Michelman 'Socio-political functions of constitutional protection for private property holdings (in liberal political thought)' in GE van Maanen & AJ van der Walt (eds) *Property on the threshold of the 21st century* (1996) 433–450 at 444 does point out that there are sound reasons why American lawyers tend to assume that the 'constitutional protection of property' means the negative protection of private property against state interference and nothing more.

[53] DG Kleyn 'The constitutional protection of property: A comparison between the German and the South African approach' (1996) 11 *SA Public Law* 402–445 at 418 argues that an institutional guarantee can still be construed on the basis of the negative guarantee in section 25. While (as argued above) it is no doubt true that the negative formulation does not exclude the implicit guarantee of property rights in the positive sense, this does not amount to an institutional guarantee as meant in German, Swiss or Austrian law, and Kleyn's argument in this regard is unconvincing. An institutional guarantee is always concerned with the institution of private property in general, whereas the standard individual guarantee (whether it is the negatively framed wording of the clause or the implicit positive guarantee associated with it) is concerned with concrete, individual property rights.

guarantee here, but it is important to note that the German-language concept of an institutional guarantee lends credence to the view that the use of a negative structure and language does not mean that the property clause in question does not 'guarantee property'. In fact, it seems clear that constitutional practice and theory in foreign law support the notion that the negative part of a constitutional property clause (whether it is combined with a positive provision or not) constitutes a guarantee of individual property rights (without thereby already determining exactly what is guaranteed).

It seems that the positive element of the South African property clause in section 28(1) of the 1993 Constitution was left out of the final property clause in section 25 in order to avoid the debate about an institutional guarantee, which is more suitable in a legal system with a complete private-law code than in the uncodified South African law of property; which again means that one should perhaps not attach too much meaning to the absence of a positive guarantee in section 25. Instead, it seems justifiable to assume that the more or less classic negative formulation of subsections 25(1) and 25(2) should be interpreted in the same way as the classic examples of such a negative guarantee such as the American or Malaysian property clauses. Judging from case law and academic analysis there does not seem to be a convincing reason to state that either of these classic property clauses should not be or is not regarded as a property guarantee, or that they do not guarantee property, or that property (as opposed to just the right not to be deprived of property except as provided for) is not protected in the respective bills of rights. In so far as the statement that section 25 does not protect property means that it does not provide a positive claim right, or that it does not guarantee existing property holdings absolutely in the sense of insulating them against legitimate limitation, the argument is not so much unconvincing as unnecessary.

The phraseology and context of the South African Bill of Rights cannot support a strong argument to the effect that section 25 is just a guarantee of the right not to be deprived of property except as provided for either.[54] It is true that the majority of provisions in the South African Bill of Rights are framed positively, or that they start off with a kind of founding or essential statement of the right, followed by exclusions, qualifications and limitation provisions, while section 25 launches into the limitation provisions and qualifications without any introduction. However, as was pointed out earlier, this is not unusual for property clauses, and avoidance of any positive formulation or statement is understandable in view of the wish to avoid the complexities of a theory of institutional guarantees, which is possible in the case of property clauses with a positive element. If the property clause is unique within the South African Bill of Rights in this regard that should not cause too much concern, because of the history of property clauses and experience elsewhere. However, that does not justify the conclusion that the property clause only protects the right not to be deprived of property except as provided, as opposed to property as such. And, as is argued in chapter 3.2, even if such a truncated meaning is attached to section 25 it does not

---

[54]This notion of property as a so-called truncated right is discussed in chapter 3.2.

make much difference in practice once it is accepted that section 25 does not merely insulate existing property holdings against reforms.

Finally, the Constitutional Court practically deprived the no-property-guarantee argument of all meaning by attaching a thick, substantive but flexible interpretation to the non-arbitrariness requirement in section 25(1) in the *FNB* case.[55] By introducing a (variable) element of substantive proportionality analysis into the first stage of a constitutional property dispute the Court rendered all efforts to exclude proportionality analysis from constitutional property adjudication meaningless, and the no-property-guarantee should perhaps be forgotten as a consequence.

In view of these arguments it is assumed, for purposes of this book, that it is justifiable (within the parameters set out below) to refer to section 25 as a property guarantee; and it is also assumed that property is both a right in the Bill of Rights as meant in section 36(1) and a right entrenched in the Bill of Rights as meant in section 36(2). However, to say that section 25 protects property does not mean that the protection of private property is the main or only purpose of the property clause, or that it entrenches existing property rights in the sense of insulating them from any state interference, or in the sense of 'freezing' the status quo as far as existing property holdings are concerned, or that it enables the courts to frustrate legitimate state limitation of property through unjustified substantive second-guessing of government policy. The spirit and values of the Bill of Rights indicate that this cannot be the case and that the aim of section 25 is to establish a just and equitable balance between the protection of private property and the promotion of the public interest. In other words, it is argued here that section 25 can be seen as a property guarantee without necessarily falling foul of the typically libertarian view that the main function of the Bill of Rights is to insulate private property from state interferences and transformation programmes, and also without making the error of opening the door on unjustified and purely obstructive judicial activism. The assumption in this book is that section 25 does protect and indeed guarantee property, but then in a way that is characteristic of the new constitutional order in general and of the Bill of Rights in particular. It is argued in 3.6 that property, for purposes of section 25 of the Constitution, is a characteristically constitutional right, which means that it is neither the same as nor protected in the same manner as private-law property. In the terminology of Michelman[56] this means that the property clause, far from insulating and entrenching existing property holdings, protects existing rights in the form of derivative rights, that is, by way of a guarantee that 'attaches only to such instances of entitlement as do happen to arise, under such standing laws as do happen to provide for them, protecting these contingent but actual entitlement relations against certain

---

[55] *First National Bank of SA Ltd t/a Wesbank v Commissioner, South African Revenue Service; First National Bank of SA Ltd t/a Wesbank v Minister of Finance* 2002 (4) SA 768 (CC). The case is discussed in chapter 4.5 and 4.6.

[56] FI Michelman 'Property as a constitutional right' (1981) 38 *Wash & Lee LR* 1097–1114, especially at 1099.

kinds of governmental impairment'.[57] This view corresponds essentially with the German notion of property rights that are subject to immanent restrictions as embodied in the laws,[58] and is quite compatible with describing the property clause as a constitutional guarantee of property, given the context of the double function that the property clause assumes in the South African context.

2.3.6 Purposive interpretation IV: Striking a balance between private and public interests

In the previous section it was argued that section 25 has to be interpreted purposively, with reference to a balancing function that has proper regard for the protection of existing property rights and for the public interest, including the public interest in reforms that are foreseen and authorized by the Constitution. Comparative sources show that this is not a unique interpretation of a constitutional property clause. It is often said that the function of the property clause in article 14 of the German Basic Law of 1949 (*Grundgesetz*) is to establish a balance between the protection of private, individual property rights and the promotion of the public weal, or between private interests and the public interest.[59] The German Federal Constitutional Court describes this balance as a tension between personal freedom and the social function of property, and interprets and applies the property clause explicitly in such a manner that it contributes to the establishment and maintenance of a balance between private and social interests in property. In the German context, this purposive interpretation is explained with reference to the *Leitmotiv* for the interpretation of article 14: creating and protecting a sphere of personal freedom, where the individual is enabled to (and expected to take responsibility for the effort to) realize and promote the development of her own life and personality, within the social context.[60] According to this purposive guideline, the constitutional protection of property serves the freedom of the individual person, but it does so while simultaneously protecting the public interest in property, and with due regard for the social context within which property rights are established, acquired, exercised, recognized and protected.[61]

---

[57] FI Michelman 'Property as a constitutional right' (1981) 38 *Wash & Lee LR* 1097–1114 at 1099.
[58] In terms of article 14(1) and 14(2) GG. See chapter 4.5.1.
[59] AJ van der Walt *Constitutional property clauses: A comparative analysis* (1999) 124; DG Kleyn 'The constitutional protection of property: A comparison between the German and the South African approach' (1996) 11 *SA Public Law* 402–445, especially at 408–419.
[60] Compare chapter 3.7. See AJ van der Walt *Constitutional property clauses: A comparative analysis* (1999) 124; DG Kleyn 'The constitutional protection of property: A comparison between the German and the South African approach' (1996) 11 *SA Public Law* 402–445 at 410, with references to relevant decisions of the German Federal Constitutional Court and literature in footnote 42.
[61] Purposive interpretation of the property clause finds support in other jurisdictions besides Germany; see D Davis, M Chaskalson & J De Waal 'Democracy and constitutionalism: The role of constitutional interpretation' in DH van Wyk, J Dugard, B de Villiers & D Davis (eds) *Rights and constitutionalism: The new South African legal order* (1994) 1–130 at 77, with references in footnote

(continued on next page ...)

An interesting example of the German approach is the *Deichordnung* case, which involved legislation that transformed certain private land into public land and restricted the use of other private land in a dyke area in Hamburg. The legislation was promulgated subsequent to a major flood and aimed at preventing future flooding by restricting and controlling development on dyke land. In terms of this decision, the public interest in preventing further floods justified a shift in the existing balance between private property rights and public control over the use of property, even up to the point where a certain category of property (dyke land) was practically removed from private ownership altogether.[62] In a later case[63] the German Federal Constitutional Court went so far as to justify a law which practically nationalised a private settlement fund for delictual damages, with reference to the need to establish the correct balance between individual interests and the public interest in the proper management and distribution of the fund. The fund was created by a settlement agreement between victims of serious side-effects caused by a pregnancy drug and the producers of the drug, and the law in question transformed the fund into a public fund against which all victims (and not only the ones involved in the settlement agreement) could claim, thereby reducing the value of the claims of original claimants but allowing other claimants to submit their claims as well. This fundamental transformation (and concomitant reduction) of existing private rights was not seen as an unconstitutional interference with property, but rather as a constitutionally justified exercise of state regulatory control to protect the public interest.

This interpretation of the property clause in terms of a central, normative guideline focused on achieving an equitable balance between individual interests in property and the public interest in property is carried through consistently by the German courts, whether the question is the content of property, the justification of a particular limitation of property or the amount of compensation for an expropriation. An important implication of this approach, which has interesting comparative possibilities for the South African situation, is that both natural and legal persons in the private sphere are allowed to benefit from the property guarantee, but not legal persons in

---

(... from previous page)

446; and at 99ff. For a purposive analysis of Austrian case law, see M Holoubek 'Die Interpretation der Grundrechte in der jüngeren Judikatur des VfGH' in R Machacek, WP Pahr & G Stadler (eds) *70 Jahre Republik: Grund- und Menschenrechte in Österreich. Grundlagen, Entwicklung und Internationale Verbindungen* (1991) 43–83 at 48ff. In Holoubek's analysis, the most important decision is *VfSlg 12227/1989*, which involved a law that imposed a compulsory reserve contract on oil importers. One can also see the analysis of W Peukert 'Protection of ownership under article 1 of the First Protocol to the European Convention on Human Rights' (1981) 2 *Human Rights LJ* 37–78 as a purposive reading of case law on the European Convention on Human Rights 1950. In this case, the most important decision is *Sporrong and Lönnroth v Sweden* [1982] 5 EHRR 35.

[62] See *BVerfGE* 24, 367 [1968] (*Deichordnung*). See AJ van der Walt *Constitutional property clauses: A comparative analysis* (1999) 130–131.

[63] *BVerfGE* 42, 263 [1976] (*Contergan*). See AJ van der Walt *Constitutional property clauses: A comparative analysis* (1999) 131.

the public sphere like state organs, state departments and local authorities.[64] If the purpose of the property clause is to establish an equitable balance between private interests in property and the public interest and the protection of private interests is associated with the protection of private autonomy within the social context, there is no reason why state organs should enjoy this protection.

Perhaps the most well-known contemporary constitutional argument for an interpretation of the Bill of Rights in terms of a balancing of interests is the Canadian decision in *R v Oakes*.[65] In this decision, a proportionality test was worked out in terms of which it could be determined whether a limitation of a constitutional right was reasonable and justified. This test involves the question whether the cost involved in upholding a limitation is justified by the purpose it serves, and it closely resembles the proportionality test also applied in German law and in the jurisprudence of the European Court of Human Rights. This question is of particular importance in the context of the limitation of fundamental rights; for the moment it suffices to note that the notion of a purposive or functional approach to the interpretation of the Bill of Rights in general is closely linked to the idea of proportionality and a balancing of interests in general. (The proportionality question is again discussed in chapters 4 and 5.) This suggests that a purposive, context-sensitive and reform-friendly interpretation and adjudication theory would be easier to develop and apply in the South African context when substantive proportionality analysis is embraced; not when it is avoided at all cost. As will be argued in later chapters, this conclusion is borne out by recent case law of the Constitutional Court.

The US courts have not been able to formulate a single, definitive, purposive principle, deriving from the American Constitution, in terms of which the Bill of Rights can be interpreted, but there is a trend towards functionalism in US constitutional law as well. US constitutional property law since about 1987 was not exactly aimed at social transformation, but academic commentary shows that a purposive interpretation of the US property clause is possible and that it has arguably formed part of the post-realist movement in American legal thinking since the early decades of the previous century.[66] An important indication of such an approach is that the Bill

---

[64]See *BVerfGE* 4, 7 [1954]; *BVerfGE* 61, 82 [1982]; *BVerfGE* 68, 139 [1984]; *BVerfGE* 75, 192 [1987]; *BVerfGE* 78, 101 [1988]. See AJ van der Walt *Constitutional property clauses: A comparative analysis* (1999) 126; compare further 2.4.4 below.

[65](1986) 26 DLR 4th 200. For a discussion see PW Hogg *Constitutional law of Canada* (3rd ed 1992) 866ff; D Gibson *The law of the Charter: General principles* (1986) 133ff.

[66]In this regard WN Hohfeld 'Some fundamental legal conceptions as applied in judicial reasoning' (1913) 23 *Yale LJ* 16–59; WN Hohfeld 'Fundamental legal conceptions as applied in judicial reasoning' (1917) 26 *Yale LJ* 710–770 was of particular importance, since it transformed the conventional private-law concept of property into a system of legal relationships, which is much more amenable to a functional interpretation of the Constitution than was conventional conceptualism. Recent examples of American thinking that fit in with this balancing-of-interests approach (although not necessarily with relation to the property clause) are J Nedelsky *Private property and the limits of American constitutionalism: The Madisonian framework and its legacy* (1990) at

(continued on next page ...)

of Rights is not regarded as a simple negative defence of existing rights against state interference. As Davis, Chaskalson & De Waal point out,[67] the implications of a functional or purposive approach in the development of positive rights have been worked out more aggressively by the German and Indian courts, but a tendency towards a purposive or functional approach that requires a balance to be struck between private and public interests can also be observed in American law.[68]

In a journal article generally acknowledged as a watershed event in American jurisprudence,[69] Frank Michelman[70] argued in favour of a purposive, outcomes-based or pragmatist rather than a random case-by-case approach to the takings problem.[71] The outcomes-based approach is different from the traditional or conventional analysis of constitutional property conflicts in that it is said to be more scientific, system-

---

(... from previous page)

204; JW Singer & JM Beermann 'The social origins of property' (1993) 6 *Can J Law & Jur* 217–248 at 218ff; LS Underkuffler 'On property: An essay' (1990) 100 *Yale LJ* 127–148 at 142; FI Michelman 'Property as a constitutional right' (1981) *Wash & Lee LR* 1097–1114 passim; GS Alexander *Commodity and propriety: Competing visions of property in American legal thought, 1776–1970* (1997); JW Singer *Entitlement: The paradoxes of property* (2000); LS Underkuffler *The idea of property: Its meaning and power* (2003). Compare further JW Singer 'Property and social relations: From title to entitlement' in GE van Maanen & AJ van der Walt (eds) *Property on the threshold of the 21st century* (1996) 69–90.

[67] See D Davis, M Chaskalson & J De Waal 'Democracy and constitutionalism: The role of constitutional interpretation' in DH van Wyk, J Dugard, B de Villiers & D Davis (eds) *Rights and constitutionalism: The new South African legal order* (1994) 1–130 at 126.

[68] See AJ van der Walt *Constitutional property clauses: A comparative analysis* (1999) 398–409; compare D Davis, M Chaskalson & J De Waal 'Democracy and constitutionalism: The role of constitutional interpretation' in DH van Wyk, J Dugard, B de Villiers & D Davis (eds) *Rights and constitutionalism: The new South African legal order* (1994) 1–130 at 122ff, with references to literature. Compare LH Tribe & MC Dorf *On reading the Constitution* (1991) 65ff.

[69] See GS Alexander 'The concept of property in private and constitutional law: The ideology of the scientific turn in legal analysis' (1982) 82 *Col LR* 1545–1599; WW Fisher 'The development of modern American legal theory and the judicial interpretation of the bill of rights' in MJ Lacey & K Haakonssen (eds) *A culture of rights. The bill of rights in philosophy, politics, and law—1791 and 1991* (1991) 266–365 at 335–348.

[70] FI Michelman 'Property, utility and fairness: Comments on the ethical foundations of "just compensation" law' (1967) 80 *Harv LR* 1165–1258. Compare FI Michelman 'Property as a constitutional right' (1981) 38 *Wash & Lee LR* 1097–1114; FI Michelman 'Possession vs distribution in the constitutional idea of property' (1987) 72 *Iowa LR* 1319–1350; and FI Michelman 'Socio-political functions of constitutional protection for private property holdings (in liberal political thought)' in GE van Maanen & AJ van der Walt (eds) *Property on the threshold of the 21st century* (1996) 433–450.

[71] See also JL Sax 'Takings and the police power' (1964) 74 *Yale LJ* 36–76; JL Sax 'Takings, private property and public rights' (1971) 81 *Yale LJ* 149–186; B Ackerman *Private property and the Constitution* (1977); and generally GS Alexander 'The concept of property in private and constitutional law: The ideology of the scientific turn in legal analysis' (1982) 82 *Col LR* 1545–1599 on the 'scientific turn' represented by these publications.

atic, and teleological or, to use the currently fashionable term, purposive.[72] In his 1967 essay, Michelman departs from 'the assumption that case-by-case adjudication should or must be the prime method for refining society's compensation practices',[73] and 'return[s] as far as may be necessary to first principles in order to form a clear understanding of just *what purposes society might be pursuing* when it decrees that compensation payments shall sometimes be made'.[74] In the course of this inquiry, Michelman argues that the only test which is 'responsive to society's purpose in engaging in a compensation practice is the test of fairness', which is a test that can indicate when it is fair, in terms of public policy, to promote a specific social measure without granting a specific claim for compensation for private loss caused by the action in question.[75] The effect of Michelman's approach is comparable to the German effort at finding an equitable balance between private interests and the public interest (which balance is regarded as the purpose of the German *Grundgesetz*), in the sense that both these approaches to constitutional interpretation are attempts to escape from a simple conceptual or intentional interpretation[76] and to move towards a purposive interpretation that acknowledges the social context and political function of property.

Obviously there are differences between German and American law,[77] but for present purposes the important aspect is that there is support in both systems for a move away from a static, typically private-law conceptualist view of the constitution as a guarantee of the *status quo* to a dynamic, typically public-law view of the constitution as an instrument for social change and transformation under the auspices of entrenched constitutional values.

---

[72] See D Davis, M Chaskalson & J De Waal 'Democracy and constitutionalism: The role of constitutional interpretation' in DH van Wyk, J Dugard, B de Villiers & D Davis (eds) *Rights and constitutionalism: The new South African legal order* (1994) 1–130 especially at 122ff for a discussion of the origin and characteristics of this approach to constitutional interpretation. Compare GS Alexander 'The concept of property in private and constitutional law: The ideology of the scientific turn in legal analysis' (1982) 82 *Col LR* 1545–1599 at 1549ff.

[73] FI Michelman 'Property, utility, and fairness: Comments on the ethical foundations of "just compensation" law' (1976) 80 *Harv LR* 1165–1258 at 1171.

[74] FI Michelman 'Property, utility, and fairness: Comments on the ethical foundations of "just compensation" law' (1976) 80 *Harv LR* 1165–1258 at 1171. My emphasis; italics not in the original.

[75] FI Michelman 'Property, utility, and fairness: Comments on the ethical foundations of "just compensation" law' (1976) 80 *Harv LR* 1165–1258 at 1171–1172, compare 1258.

[76] FI Michelman 'Property, utility, and fairness: Comments on the ethical foundations of "just compensation" law' (1976) 80 *Harv LR* 1165–1258 at 1166 expresses doubt about the question whether his inquiry amounts to an essay in constitutional law at all, but for present purposes it can be assumed that if it were it could be regarded as a functional or purposive rather than an intentionalist or a purely ad hoc approach to constitutional interpretation. In his own terminology Michelman's essay should probably be described as pragmatist.

[77] For a comparative analysis of German and US law see GS Alexander 'Constitutionalising property: Two experiences, two dilemmas' in J McLean (ed) *Property and the constitution* (1999) 88–108.

2.3.7 Purposive interpretation V: Balancing and purposive interpretation

The casting of the property clause within a normative, purposive, interpretive framework is extremely important for the interpretation of section 25 of the South African Constitution. Its main advantage compared to a conceptualist or intentionalist interpretation is that it ensures that the property clause is not simply regarded as a 'thin' two-dimensional instrument for the protection of individual rights, interests and privileges against state interference. Instead, it presents the property guarantee as a 'thick' multi-dimensional instrument of constitutionalism,[78] which has to be interpreted and applied with due regard for the tensions between the individual and society, between the privileged and the underprivileged, between the haves and the have-nots, between the powerful and the powerless.[79] The potential importance of such an approach in the South African context is obvious—above all, it enables a transformative or reform-oriented interpretation of the property clause that will support and promote rather than frustrate land and related reforms.

A second advantage is that a purposive approach provides an explicitly constitutional framework for the interpretation and application of the Bill of Rights, thereby reducing the possibility that this process will be influenced unwittingly by hidden or subconscious, and perhaps unsuitable, private-law presuppositions.[80] One major

---

[78] See further chapter 4.5.1.

[79] See in a similar vein AJ van der Walt 'Towards a theory of rights in property: Exploratory observations on the paradigm of post-apartheid property law' (1995) 10 *SA Public Law* 298–345, especially at 334–345; and compare DP Currie *The Constitution of the Federal Republic of Germany* (1994) 290; AJ van der Walt 'Notes on the interpretation of the property clause in the new constitution' (1994) 57 *THRHR* 181–203 at 185ff; J Murphy 'Property rights and judicial restraint: A reply to Chaskalson' (1994) 10 *SAJHR* 386–398; D Davis, M Chaskalson & J De Waal 'Democracy and constitutionalism: The role of constitutional interpretation' in DH van Wyk, J Dugard, B de Villiers & D Davis (eds) *Rights and constitutionalism: The new South African legal order* (1994) 1–130 at 122ff; J Murphy 'Property rights in the new Constitution: An analytical framework for constitutional review'(1993) 26 *CILSA* 211–233. An interesting historical and philosophical perspective on this argument is offered by Hannah Arendt *The human condition* (1958, paperback ed 1989), who argues (at 23ff, 28ff, 52ff, especially 58ff) that the balance at stake here is a social rather than a political one, meaning that the kind of balance in question is not a political process of simultaneously relating and separating people around the common world (at 52, 55, 63), but a social process of transforming everything into an object of wealth and consumption, whereby both the private and the public realms are ultimately threatened (at 69).

[80] These subconscious presuppositions are what Gary Peller refers to as the 'metaphysics' of American law: G Peller 'The metaphysics of American law' (1985) 73 *Cal LR* 1151–1290. Compare AJ van der Walt 'Marginal notes on powerful(*l*) legends: Critical perspectives on property theory' (1995) 58 *THRHR* 396–420; AJ van der Walt 'Tradition on trial: A critical analysis of the civil-law tradition in South African property law' (1995) 11 *SAJHR* 169–206. As is pointed out in the course of the argument later on (chapter 4.5), this also means that the spectre of *Lochnerism* is reduced substantially, even when the courts assume the job of testing the proportionality or suitability of laws that interfere with private property.

advantage of an overtly constitutional interpretive framework is, as Kleyn[81] points out, that some of the problems which characterize the interpretation and application of a constitutional property clause are removed from the purely private sphere and recast in the mould of the greater, overarching tension between individual rights and social responsibilities or interests. By doing so the courts are enabled to adjudicate property disputes with greater social realism, and to judge a variety of different problems and disputes with a sense of social responsibility, continuity and consistency. Of course, this does not suddenly solve these problems, but it does provide a vantage point from which they can be approached with a greater emphasis on historical and social context.

Another advantage is that this approach recognizes the Constitution as the driving force which inspires the transformation (or development, in terms of section 39(2) of the 1996 Constitution) of common law and customary law as part of the total transformation of the legal system.[82] Interestingly enough, this approach has the potential to overcome the misgivings of those who are against the constitutionalization of property or the 'thicker' reading of the property clause because they think that it might revive the spectre of substantive due process and *Lochnerism*. It is pointed out in chapter 4.5 that this fear is misplaced because the proportionality test concerns the constitutional justifiability of a limitation of constitutional rights and not the wisdom or suitability of laws or government policies that impose such limitations. In other words, it does not rely on subjective judgment but on an objective constitutional evaluation of the balance between the purpose and the cost of legislative interferences with constitutional rights.[83]

These remarks should not create the impression that the (or a) purposive or balancing of interests approach is without problems or that it will necessarily have superior results compared to any other approach to constitutional interpretation. On the contrary—there are arguments to the effect that it may not be all that different from earlier, conceptualist or intentionalist approaches in the final analysis.[84] The merits or possible shortcomings of balancing as a constitutional approach will to a large extent depend on the way in which the courts apply it,[85] but a purposive approach explains many of the otherwise perhaps bewildering elements of current constitutional juris-

---

[81]DG Kleyn 'The constitutional protection of property: A comparison between the German and the South African approach' (1996) 11 *SA Public Law* 402–445 at 415. See K Govender 'The virtues of balancing' (1997) 1(6) *Human Rights & Const LJ SA* 2–3.

[82]See chapter 7 on the development of the common law and the effect of the Constitution in private law.

[83]See *S v Makwanyane and Another* 1995 (3) SA 391 (CC) par [104] at 449–450; *Public Servants' Association of South Africa and Another v Minister of Justice and Others* 1997 (3) SA 925 (T) at 983H, where a similar distinction is made with reference to Canadian law.

[84]See GS Alexander 'The concept of property in private and constitutional law: The ideology of the scientific turn in legal analysis' (1982) 82 *Col LR* 1545–1599; G Peller 'The metaphysics of American law' (1985) 73 *Cal LR* 1151–1290.

[85]For an analysis of balancing see H Botha 'Metaphoric reasoning and transformative constitutionalism (part 2)' 2003 *TSAR* 1–36 at 25–31.

prudence, it has some advantages compared to old-style formalism, and judging from case law it will be followed by South African courts more likely than not.[86]

For purposes of this book, it is taken for granted that a purposive approach of sorts will form the basis of analysis and interpretation of section 25 of the South African Constitution; whether in the form of an explicit balance-of-interests approach (as followed by the German courts) or of a more general constitutional functionalism.[87] It is assumed that the analysis of section 25 cannot be undertaken as if there were a simple, flat layer of meaning which simply has to be 'opened up'. Instead, the meaning of section 25 has to be determined, in each specific case, within an interpretive framework that takes due cognisance of the inevitable tensions which characterize the operation of the property clause. This tension between individual rights and social responsibilities has to be the guiding principle in terms of which the section is analysed, interpreted and applied in every individual case. This is particularly important in understanding and dealing with the tension between the two goals that are arguably both embodied in section 25: the protection of existing, private property rights and the protection of the public interest (referred to mainly in terms of land reform, although the public interest extends far beyond that). From the structure and the phraseology of section 25 it is clear that the property clause has to be seen in relation to both these functions, and that a balance has to be struck between the protection of existing, private land rights and the promotion of land reform initiatives. This does not mean that there is some kind of essential or fundamental equilibrium between the protection of individual rights and the promotion of the public interest and that the courts simply have to find the magic formula to establish or maintain the balance. It does mean that there will always be an inherent tension between these two aspects of the constitutional protection of property, and that the courts may never consider the property clause without overtly recognizing and dealing with that tension.

A purposive approach requires a central guideline or principle, similar to the *Leitmotiv* of the German Basic Law mentioned earlier, in terms of which the balance between individual and public interest could be construed. In the South African Constitution, several phrases repeat a sentiment which could be identified as the heart of the Bill of Rights: 'a society based on democratic values, social justice and fundamental human rights' in the Preamble; 'human dignity, the achievement of equality and the advancement of human rights and freedoms' in section 1(*a*); 'the democratic values of human dignity, equality and freedom' in section 7(1); '[a] limitation [which] is reasonable and justifiable in an open and democratic society based on human dig-

---

[86]See *Brink v Kitshoff NO* 1996 (4) SA 197 (CC) for an example of a decision where the Constitutional Court indicated that it might follow a purposive interpretation. Compare *Park-Ross and Another v Director: Office for Serious Economic Offences* 1995 (2) SA 148 (C) at 160Cff; and see further footnote 89 below.

[87]See further T Roux 'Section 25' in S Woolman et al (eds) *Constitutional law of South Africa* (2nd ed 2003 original service Dec 2003) 46–2.

nity, equality and freedom' in section 36(1); and 'the values that underlie an open and democratic society based on human dignity, equality and freedom' in section 39(1). The strong emphasis placed on these phrases and the central role of the constitutional values of human dignity, equality and freedom in an open and democratic society indicate, in the context in which these phrases are used in the Preamble and in section 36, that these values embody an aspiration towards a human-rights practice that is characterized by a just and equitable balance between existing, private interests and the public interest. In the first edition of this book it was suggested that these values could describe the purpose that should guide interpretation of section 25. In its subsequent case law the Constitutional Court came closer to sketching the outlines of such an interpretive framework.

2.3.8 Purposive interpretation VI: The *FNB* decision

Several provisions of the 1996 Constitution support a balance-of-interests approach to the interpretation of the Bill of Rights.[88] Section 39(1) and (2) explicitly provide that the Bill of Rights and other legislation must be interpreted so as to promote the 'values that underlie and open and democratic society based on human dignity, equality and freedom' and the 'spirit, purport and objects' of the Constitution respectively. Accordingly, the Constitutional Court has repeatedly indicated that a purposive approach is suitable in interpreting the Bill of Rights.[89] Since the first edition of this book appeared in 1997 the Constitutional Court has indicated in the *FNB* deci-

---

[88]See the Preamble (' ... adopt this Constitution as the supreme law of the Republic so as to ... [h]eal the divisions of the past and establish a society based on democratic values, social justice and fundamental human rights ... '); section 1(a) (the Republic is one, sovereign, democratic state founded on the values of, *inter alia* '... [h]uman dignity, the achievement of equality and the advancement of human rights and freedoms'); section 7(1) (the Bill of Rights is the cornerstone of democracy; it enshrines the rights of all people in the country and affirms the democratic values of human dignity, equality and freedom; but is subject to the limitations in section 36 or elsewhere in the Bill); section 36 (limitations clause: limitations of the rights are only permitted in terms of law of general application and to the extent that the limitation is reasonable and justifiable in an open and democratic society based on human dignity, equality and freedom, taking into account all relevant factors, including some specified factors which basically protect the interests of those affected and the public interest); section 39 (interpretation clause: when interpreting the Bill a court, tribunal or forum must promote the values that underlie an open and democratic society based on human dignity, equality and freedom; and every court, tribunal and forum has to promote the spirit, purport and objects of the Constitution when interpreting any law or when developing the common law or customary law). See footnote 89 below for case law where it was indicated that the courts might follow a purposive approach.

[89]See JR de Ville *Constitutional and statutory interpretation* (2000) 250–254; L du Plessis *Re-interpretation of statutes* (2002) 118–119 and references there. De Ville (at 250) indicates that the South African courts adopted the purposive approach from the Canadian decision in *R v Big M Drug Mart Ltd* (1985) 18 DLR (4th) 321 at 359–360. The Constitutional Court has indicated repeatedly that a purposive approach, which gives expression to the underlying values and principles of the Constitution, should be followed when interpreting the Constitution and especially the Bill of Rights:
(continued on next page ...)

sion that it will indeed approach the property clause from a purposive perspective and that the clause has to be interpreted with due regard for its historical context and constitutional purpose:[90] section 25(1) must be construed in its context 'as part of a comprehensive and coherent Bill of Rights in a comprehensive and coherent constitution.'[91]

In *FNB* the Court confirmed its purposive approach by attaching a 'thick', context-sensitive, balancing interpretation to the non-arbitrariness provision in section 25(1).[92] By defining arbitrariness on a sliding scale that reflects the soundness of the reason for a deprivation in terms of the nature of the property, the nature and scope of the deprivation, the relationship between the owner and the property and the relationship between the property and the purpose of the deprivation,[93] the Court effectively characterized the arbitrariness test as a balancing test, with the implication that the legitimacy of deprivation depends upon the question whether the deprivation reflects a fair balance between the public interest in the regulatory purpose and the private property interest that is affected by it.

Although the *FNB* decision has been criticized,[94] its advantage is that it clearly characterizes the arbitrariness test in section 25(1) as a relatively[95] substantive balancing test that should reflect a fair balance between the individual property interests affected by regulatory action and the public interest in regulating property in the

---

(*... from previous page*)

S v Zuma and Others 1995 (2) SA 642 (CC) par [15] at 651E–I; *S v Makwanyane and Another* 1995 (3) SA 391 (CC) par [9] at 403C–G; *Ferreira v Levin NO and Others; Vryenhoek and Others v Powell NO and Others* 1996 (1) SA 984 (CC) paras [46] at 1012G–1013D, [172] at 1086B–D, [213] at 1098G–I; *Bernstein and Others v Bester and Others NNO* 1996 (2) SA 751 (CC) paras [148] at 816B–E, [151] at 817B–F; *Pretoria City Council v Walker* 1998 (2) SA 363 (CC) par [43] at 383D–384A; *De Lange v Smuts NO and Others* 1998 (3) SA 785 (CC) par [25] at 797G–I.

[90]See *First National Bank of SA Ltd t/a Wesbank v Commissioner, South African Revenue Service; First National Bank of SA Ltd t/a Wesbank v Minister of Finance* 2002 (4) SA 768 (CC) paras [47]–[50] at 792D–794D.

[91]*First National Bank of SA Ltd t/a Wesbank v Commissioner, South African Revenue Service; First National Bank of SA Ltd t/a Wesbank v Minister of Finance* 2002 (4) SA 768 (CC) par [63] at 798B.

[92]See further chapter 4.5 and 4.6 below.

[93]The test is discussed in more detail in chapter 4.5.

[94]See particularly T Roux 'Section 25' in S Woolman et al (eds) *Constitutional law of South Africa* (2nd ed 2003 original service Dec 2003) 46-2–46-5, 46-22–46-25.

[95]T Roux 'Section 25' in S Woolman et al (eds) *Constitutional law of South Africa* (2nd ed 2003 original service Dec 2003) 46–24 points out that the Court reserved a large measure of discretion for itself in determining the level of scrutiny, an observation that is apparently borne out by the decision in *Mkontwana v Nelson Mandela Metropolitan Municipality; Bissett and Others v Buffalo City Municipality; Transfer Rights Action Campaign and Others v Member of the Executive Council for Local Government and Housing, Gauteng and Others* 2005 (1) SA 530 (CC). However, see 4.6 below.

particular context. In the *Port Elizabeth Municipality* case[96] the Constitutional Court elaborated on the position in *FNB* by explaining extensively how conflicting individual rights (of landowners and unlawful occupiers) should be reconciled with proper consideration for the historical background of land rights in South Africa, the social and economic context, and the current constitutional process of transformation. This case now probably embodies the interpretive approach that is most suited to property conflicts in terms of section 25 and section 26, but it could also find application in property cases generally.

2.3.9 Section 39

It has already been pointed out above that subsections 39(1) and (2) require a purposive interpretation of section 25 in that they instruct courts, tribunals and forums to interpret the Bill of Rights so as to promote the values that underlie an open and democratic society based on human dignity, equality and freedom; and to interpret legislation so as to promote the spirit, purport and objects of the Bill of Rights.

Section 39 also requires special attention for interpretation in that it clearly presupposes a particular relationship between the Constitution, the Bill of Rights, other legislation, and the common law and customary law. Of particular importance in this regard is the superiority of the Constitution (other rights and legislation are recognized as far as they are consistent with the Constitution) and the obligation to develop the common law and customary law to bring them in line with the Constitution.[97] The development of the common law is discussed in chapter 7.

2.3.10 Section 25(4)

The interpretation of section 25 is also influenced by the interpretation provision in section 25(4), which provides that (for purposes of section 25) the public interest includes the nation's commitment to land and other, similar reforms aimed at creating fair access to natural resources; and that (for purposes of section 25) property is not restricted to land. These provisions and their effect on the interpretation of section 25 are discussed in 2.2.4 above.

---

[96] *Port Elizabeth Municipality v Various Occupiers* 2005 (1) SA 217 (CC) paras [8]–[23] at 222A–229G. See the discussion of this decision in chapters 6 and 7. Another example, although not ultimately decided on property grounds, is the SCA and Constitutional Court decisions in *Modderfontein Squatters, Greater Benoni City Council v Modderklip Boerdery (Pty) Ltd; (Agri SA and Legal Resources Centre,* Amici Curiae*); President of the Republic of South Africa and Others v Modderklip Boerdery (Pty) Ltd (Agri SA and Legal Resources Centre,* Amici Curiae*)* 2004 (6) SA 40 (SCA); *President of the Republic of South Africa and Another v Modderklip Boerdery (Pty) Ltd (Agri SA and Others,* Amici Curiae*)* 2005 (5) SA 3 (CC).

[97] See further in this regard section 8(3).

2.4 APPLICATION[98]

2.4.1 Horizontal application I: Introduction

During the early phases of the new constitutional era commentators differed sharply on the question whether the provisions in the Bill of Rights could or should apply horizontally. Proponents of the view that the fundamental rights should apply horizontally as well as vertically argued that the new constitutional order should not countenance the privatization of inequality and discrimination:[99] if the fundamental

---

[98] This section is partially based upon and resembles portions of two forthcoming journal articles: AJ van der Walt 'Transformative constitutionalism and the development of South African property law' 2005 *TSAR*, 2006 *TSAR* (forthcoming); AJ van der Walt 'The state's duty to protect property owners vs the state's duty to provide housing: Thoughts on the *Modderklip* case' (2005) 21 *SAJHR* 144–161. See further chapter chapter 7.5.

[99] This was the crux of many early pleas for horizontal application; see eg A Sachs 'Towards a Bill of Rights in a democratic South Africa' (1990) 6 *SAJHR* 1–24 at 3–4; H Botha 'Privatism, authoritarianism and the Constitution: The case of Neethling and Potgieter' (1995) 58 *THRHR* 496–499; LM du Plessis 'Enkele gedagtes oor historiese interpretasie van Hoofstuk 3 van die Oorgangsgrondwet— *Du Plessis v De Klerk* 1994 (6) BCLR 124 (T)' (1995) 58 *THRHR* 504–513; JD van der Vyver 'Constitutional free speech and the law of defamation' (1995) 112 *SALJ* 572–602; G Carpenter & C Botha 'Constitutional attack on private law: Are the fears well founded?' (1996) 59 *THRHR* 126–135; MLM Mbao 'The province of the South African Bill of Rights determined and redetermined—A comment on the case of *Baloro & Others v University of Bophuthatswana & Others*' (1996) 113 *SALJ* 33–45; S Woolman 'Defamation, application, and the interim Constitution: An unqualified and direct analysis of *Holomisa v Argus Newspapers Ltd*' (1996) 113 *SALJ* 428–454; JWG van der Walt 'Justice Kriegler's disconcerting judgment in *Du Plessis v De Klerk*: Much ado about direct horizontal application (read nothing)' 1996 *TSAR* 732–741; JWG van der Walt 'Perspectives on horizontal application: *Du Plessis v De Klerk* revisited' (1997) 12 *SA Public Law* 1–31; S Woolman & D Davis 'The last laugh: *Du Plessis v De Klerk*, classical liberalism, creole liberalism, and the application of fundamental rights under the Interim and Final Constitutions' (1996) 12 *SAJHR* 361–404; H Cheadle & D Davis 'The application of the 1996 Constitution in the private sphere' (1997) 13 *SAJHR* 44–66; IM Rautenbach 'The Bill of Rights applies to private law and binds private persons' 2000 *TSAR* 296–316; JWG van der Walt 'Die toekoms van die onderskeid tussen die publiekreg en die privaatreg in die lig van die horisontale werking van die Grondwet' 2000 *TSAR* 416–427, 605–618; and S Woolman 'Application' in M Chaskalson et al (eds) *Constitutional law of South Africa* (Revision Service 3 1998).

rights in the new Constitution were only enforced vertically against the state, private individuals and institutions would be able to continue the very same discriminatory practices that were supposed to be proscribed by the Constitution. In order to outlaw and uproot private discrimination and inequality, it was said, the fundamental rights should be enforceable not only against the state but also between private persons and against private institutions. In terms of these arguments the Constitution has to apply on the horizontal level as well as the purely state-oriented vertical level, which means that the fundamental rights provisions in the Bill of Rights could when necessary be enforced—in some way or another—in what otherwise was a private law dispute.[100] The horizontality debate is no longer as active or relevant as it was, because the 1996 Constitution is much clearer in favour of at least indirect horizontality, although it could also support arguments against horizontality.[101]

2.4.2 Horizontal application II: Direct vs indirect horizontal application

Pro-horizontality authors initially favoured a strong version of horizontal application referred to as direct horizontal application.[102] When saying that the Constitution applies directly horizontally the horizontalists meant that private persons could rely

---

[100]S Woolman 'Application' in M Chaskalson et al (eds) *Constitutional law of South Africa* (Revision Service 3 1998) at 10–1 points out that the dichotomy between vertical and horizontal application of the Bill of Rights 'represented a vast oversimplification of the existing range of possibilities', by which he apparently means to suggest that the two should rather be seen as points on a continuum, with many nuances in between. According to Woolman 10–1, verticalists and horizontalists agree that (*a*) statutes, when relied upon by the state, are subject to constitutional review; (*b*) the common law, when relied upon by the state, is subject to constitutional review; and (*c*) statutes, when relied upon by a private party, is subject to constitutional review; so that the remaining issue is whether the common law, when relied upon by a private party in a private dispute, is subject to constitutional review.

[101]In the 1996 Constitution, the strongest textual support for a horizontal reading is located in section 8(1) (the Bill of Rights applies to all law and binds the legislature, the executive and the judiciary). Section 8(2) provides that the Bill of Rights binds all natural and juristic persons if (and to the extent that) it is applicable, taking into account the nature of the right and any duty imposed by the right. Section 8(3) provides that a court, in applying the Bill of Rights to a natural or juristic person in terms of section 8(2), must apply (or where necessary develop) the common law to the extent that legislation does not give effect to the right (and may develop the common law to limit the right in accordance with section 36). According to S Woolman 'Application' in M Chaskalson et al (eds) *Constitutional law of South Africa* (Revision Service 3 1998) at 10–61, section 39(2) (when developing the common law a court must promote the spirit, purport and objects of the Bill of Rights) has the same function as the old section 35(3), namely to ensure indirect horizontal seepage, but now the courts are obliged to ensure such seepage ('must promote' instead of just 'having due regard'). C Sprigman & M Osborne 'Du Plessis is *not* dead: South Africa's 1996 Constitution and the application of the Bill of Rights to private disputes' (1999) 15 *SAJHR* 25–51 deny that the 1996 Constitution applies horizontally—in their view, the 1996 Constitution allows indirect horizontal application as foreseen in *Du Plessis v De Klerk,* but does not mandate it.

[102]JWG van der Walt 'Justice Kriegler's disconcerting judgment in *Du Plessis v De* Klerk: Much ado about direct horizontal application (read nothing)' 1996 *TSAR* 732–741 at 736.

directly on a provision in the Constitution to found a cause of action for a constitutional attack on another private party in a private dispute. At a later stage most commentators abandoned the idea of direct horizontal application and accepted that 'the
distinction between direct and indirect horizontality is indeed of no real significance
for the administration of justice under the Final Constitution.'[103] The only real application issue is, therefore, whether the Constitution applies horizontally, either
directly[104] or indirectly,[105] to a private dispute between two private parties, in such a
way that the (statutory or common law) private law rules that govern the dispute are
open to amendment or influence from the Constitution, even though a state threat
against either party is not directly in issue. Most pro-horizontality authors now accept
that direct horizontal application cases—instances where a private person relies
directly on a constitutional provision to found a cause of action against another private person in a private dispute—would constitute a small minority of cases, and that
the effect of the Constitution on private law would in fact largely take place indirectly
via the so-called radiating (or, in a probably weaker version, indirect seepage) effect
of constitutional principles and values.[106] However, most commentators leave open
the possibility that application of the Constitution could vary according to the context of a specific case (particularly the nature of the specific right involved and any
duty imposed by it), and accordingly it is still possible that a specific constitutional
provision could require or prescribe direct rather than indirect horizontal application.[107] Because it is accepted that horizontal application takes place through horizontal radiation or seepage that affects the development of the common law, the
distinction between direct and indirect horizontal application seems to have lost most
if not all of its meaning and urgency in the literature.

---

[103] JWG van der Walt 'Perspectives on horizontal application: *Du Plessis v De Klerk* revisited' (1997)
12 *SA Public Law* 1–31 at 3.

[104] Terminology on this point varies to some extent, but I follow the argument as developed by
JWG van der Walt and use the term 'direct horizontal application' to refer to instances where a
private party can rely directly on a provision in the Constitution to found a cause of action in a
private dispute against another private party, without involving or relying upon any other statutory
or common law rule

[105] See the previous footnote. By extension, this would refer to instances where the cause of action
is founded upon a statutory or common law rule, but the interpretation or application of that rule
is affected by the Constitution in some way in order to give effect to a specific constitutional
provision or to the 'spirit, purport or object' of the Constitution, as it is stated in section 39(2) of
the Constitution.

[106] The effect of the Constitution on private law is discussed in chapter 7. See JWG van der Walt
'Perspectives on horizontal application: *Du Plessis v De Klerk* revisited' (1997) 12 *SA Public Law* 1–
31 at 16–17; JWG van der Walt '*Progressive* indirect horizontal application of the Bill of Rights:
Towards a co-operative relation between common-law and constitutional jurisprudence' (2001) 17
SAJHR 343–361; S Woolman 'Application' in M Chaskalson et al (eds) *Constitutional law of South
Africa* (Revision Service 3 1998) at 10-46–10-49.

[107] See eg JWG van der Walt 'Perspectives on horizontal application: *Du Plessis v De Klerk* revisited'
(1997) 12 *SA Public Law* 1–31 at 11; H Cheadle & D Davis 'The application of the 1996 Constitution in the private sphere' (1997) 13 *SAJHR* 44–66 at 59.

In the case law horizontal application was taken for granted from the outset as most courts accepted that the Constitution intended to transform South African society, that the inequities and injustices of the past were not restricted to exercises of state power, and that the fundamental rights provisions in the Constitution therefore had to apply horizontally in one way or another to ensure that private law (and the private relations governed by it) was also included in the transformation process. One high court decision that rejected horizontal application of the fundamental rights provisions because it would cause 'the whole body of our private law to become unsettled'[108] was subsequently overturned by the Constitutional Court. The draft of the 1996 Constitution was already in an advanced state of completion when this case went on appeal and it was reasonably clear that the Final Constitution would make provision for horizontal application in any event, but the decision of the Constitutional Court in *Du Plessis v De Klerk*[109] nevertheless settled the matter as far as the 1993 Constitution was concerned: the majority of the Court held that the resolution of the horizontality issue must ultimately depend upon the specific provisions of the Constitution; that general (direct) horizontal application in the sense of direct invocation of constitutional rights in private litigation was not intended;[110] that a party in private litigation may nonetheless contend that a statute or executive act relied on by the other party was inconsistent with the Constitution; and that the fundamental rights provisions do apply to private law, so that government actions or omissions in reliance upon private law may be attacked by a private litigant in a dispute against the state for being inconsistent with the Constitution.[111]

Following upon the decision in favour of indirect horizontal application in *Du Plessis v De Klerk*, it could not be argued that there would be no form of horizontal application under the 1996 Constitution, especially since section 8 of the Constitution made provision for some form of horizontal application. Since the 1996 Constitution came into power it has therefore been accepted widely that the fundamental rights provisions apply horizontally. By and large it is accepted that horizontal application will for practical purposes mostly be restricted to indirect horizontal application, although direct horizontal effect is not excluded altogether—in a small minority of suitable instances it is still possible. The question is: does section 25 allow for direct horizontal application, in other words for a situation where one private party can rely directly on section 25 in a constitutional attack against another private person, in what would otherwise have been a private dispute?

---

[108] *De Klerk v Du Plessis* 1995 (2) SA 40 (T).

[109] *Du Plessis v De Klerk* 1996 (3) SA 850 (CC).

[110] In *Du Plessis v De Klerk* 1996 (3) SA 850 (CC) Ackermann J dedicated the entire 5 pages of his analysis of German law (paras [92]–[106] at 704F–709E) to a detailed consideration of the reasons why German courts and scholars rejected (and why South African courts should also reject) direct horizontal application and instead work with indirect horizontal application only.

[111] *Du Plessis v De Klerk* 1996 (3) SA 850 (CC) per Kentridge J par [49].

2.4.3 Horizontal application of section 25

In the so-called enforcement decision that preceded the Supreme Court of Appeal's decision in the *Modderklip* case[112] the High Court made a statement that amounts to an explicit—but unsubstantiated—acknowledgement of direct horizontal application of section 25(1): 'It is declared that: 1.1 the applicant's rights as set out in section 25(1) of the Constitution are infringed upon by the refusal of the 8th respondent [the unlawful occupiers] to vacate the relevant land in terms of the eviction order ... '[113] The impression created by this statement is that the unlawful occupiers were infringing upon the landowner's property right by depriving him of his property in conflict with section 25(1) of the Constitution, rather than that the state deprived him of his property by failing to put into place the housing strategy that would prevent or remove the obstacle in the way of his full enjoyment of his property. Despite the impression created by this seemingly clear wording, the enforcement order was granted against the state, which negates the idea that the case concerned a direct horizontal application issue.

In the subsequent SCA judgment the reference to direct horizontal application was accepted as being correct in one place,[114] but the problem of deciding whether section 25 in fact applies horizontally was avoided by rephrasing the enforcement order to emphasize the fact that the state was infringing upon the landowner's section 25(1) right by failing to implement housing policies that would prevent or remove the current obstacles in the way of the landowner's enjoyment of his property.[115] Too much should not be read into the unsubstantiated and probably largely unconsidered statement in either the High Court or the SCA judgment to the effect that section 25(1) operates horizontally. On appeal the Constitutional Court declined the oppor-

---

[112] *Modderfontein Squatters, Greater Benoni City Council v Modderklip Boerdery (Pty) Ltd; (Agri SA and Legal Resources Centre*, Amici Curiae*); President of the Republic of South Africa and Others v Modderklip Boerdery (Pty) Ltd (Agri SA and Legal Resources Centre*, Amici Curiae*)* 2004 (6) SA 40 (SCA). In this case, the SCA simultaneously dealt with two related matters; an application for leave to appeal against the judgment in *Modderklip Boerdery (Pty) Ltd v Modder East Squatters* 2001 (4) SA 385 (W) (the 'eviction case') and an appeal against the decision in *Modderklip Boerdery (Edms) Bpk v President van die Republiek van Suid-Afrika* 2003 (6) BCLR 638 (T) (the 'enforcement' case).

[113] My translation from the Afrikaans. See par 1.1 of the enforcement order in *Modderklip Boerdery (Edms) Bpk v President van die Republiek van Suid-Afrika* 2003 (6) BCLR 638 (T) at 693–694. The words in brackets were inserted in the SCA judgment.

[114] *Modderfontein Squatters, Greater Benoni City Council v Modderklip Boerdery (Pty) Ltd; (Agri SA and Legal Resources Centre*, Amici Curiae*); President of the Republic of South Africa and Others v Modderklip Boerdery (Pty) Ltd (Agri SA and Legal Resources Centre*, Amici Curiae*)* 2004 (6) SA 40 (SCA) par [21] at 831B–C.

[115] *Modderfontein Squatters, Greater Benoni City Council v Modderklip Boerdery (Pty) Ltd; (Agri SA and Legal Resources Centre*, Amici Curiae*); President of the Republic of South Africa and Others v Modderklip Boerdery (Pty) Ltd (Agri SA and Legal Resources Centre*, Amici Curiae*)* 2004 (6) SA 40 (SCA) par [52](*b*)(i) at 841H.

tunity to decide whether section 25 applied horizontally, preferring to decide the matter on another basis altogether.[116]

The possibility that section 25 may operate horizontally has been mooted but mostly denied in the literature.[117] The strongest indication that section 25 does not apply to 'private conduct that is not authorized by law'[118] derives from the Constitutional Court decision in *Phoebus Apollo Aviation CC v Minister of Safety and Security*,[119] where it was said explicitly (but arguably *obiter*) that section 25 does not apply horizontally. The strongest analytical or logical argument against direct horizontal application is that the notions of 'deprivation' and 'expropriation' of property have acquired a more or less technical (even if unclear and contested) meaning that relates to actions carried out in the exercise of state powers (the regulatory or police power and the power of expropriation or eminent domain respectively).[120] Of course these powers can be exercised by private persons, but then their actions will be ascribed to the state as explained by Roux. However, when a private person is exercising private rights in a way neither directly nor indirectly authorized by law *that regulates the exercise of state powers* (to extend Roux's formulation somewhat further), the chances that such action could amount to or should be treated as a deprivation or expropriation in terms of section 25 are slim. In this regard, section 25(1)–(3) relates to the negative defensive aspect of fundamental rights and should not find any direct horizontal application (although the rest of section 25, dealing with land reform, could support different arguments). By and large, however, it does not at this stage look as if there is any realistic possibility that section 25(1)–(3) could find any direct horizontal application.

2.4.4 Beneficiaries

Natural persons qualify for the protection of most of rights in the Bill of Rights in principle, although some rights are specifically reserved for citizens.[121] In terms of

---

[116] *President of the Republic of South Africa and Another v Modderklip Boerdery (Pty) Ltd (Agri SA and Others,* Amici Curiae) 2005 (5) SA 3 (CC) par [26] at 17H.

[117] See T Roux 'Property' in S Woolman et al (eds) *Constitutional law of South Africa* (2nd ed original service 2003) 46-6–46-8 and sources referred to there.

[118] T Roux 'Property' in S Woolman et al (eds) *Constitutional law of South Africa* (2nd ed original service 2003) 46–6.

[119] 2003 (2) SA 34 (CC) par [4] at 35D. T Roux 'Property' in S Woolman et al (eds) *Constitutional law of South Africa* (2nd ed original service 2003) 46–7 footnote 1 refers to the enforcement order in *Modderklip* 2003 (6) BCLR 638 (T) at 693–694 as an example of direct horizontal application and suggests that it was overruled (days later) by the decision in *Phoebus Apollo Aviation*. It is perhaps more accurate to say that, if and in so far as the statement in *Modderklip* was indeed intended or is read as saying that section 25 applies horizontally outside of private conduct not authorized by law, this statement was indeed overruled by *Phoebus Apollo Aviation*.

[120] See T Roux 'Property' in S Woolman et al (eds) *Constitutional law of South Africa* (2nd ed original service 2003) 46-6–46-7.

[121] Such as the political rights in section 19 and the right to citizenship in section 20. T Roux 'Property' in S Woolman et al (eds) *Constitutional law of South Africa* (2nd ed original service 2003) 46–9 mentions that other jurisdictions limit the constitutional protection of property to citizens.

section 8(4) of the 1996 Constitution a juristic person is also entitled to the rights in the Bill of Rights 'to the extent required by the nature of the rights and the nature of that juristic person', which means that juristic persons are entitled to the protection of section 25 in principle.[122]

There is nothing in section 25 to indicate that juristic persons should not qualify for the protection of the property clause, although section 8(4) provides that the nature of the property right in question and the requirements of the juristic person in question have to be taken into account in every individual case before this question can be answered. In principle, however, there is no reason why juristic persons such as companies and clubs should not enjoy the protection of the property clause. In the *FNB* case the Constitutional Court held that juristic persons should enjoy the benefit of section 25 for two reasons: firstly because the property rights of individual persons can only be realized fully and properly when the protection is also extended to companies; and secondly because denying companies the protection of section 25 would lead to grave disruptions and undermine the fabric of the democratic state.[123] From the *FNB* decision it is therefore clear that the constitutional property clause protects natural as well as juristic persons.[124]

---

[122]See T Roux 'Property' in S Woolman et al (eds) *Constitutional law of South Africa* (2nd ed original service 2003) 46–9. Roux is probably correct when saying that companies and other juristic persons should enjoy this protection regardless of whether their headquarters are situated in South Africa or elsewhere.

[123] *First National Bank of SA Ltd t/a Wesbank v Commissioner, South African Revenue Service; First National Bank of SA Ltd t/a Wesbank v Minister of Finance* 2002 (4) SA 768 (CC) paras [41]- [45] at 790D–791I, referring to the Court's earlier decisions in *Ex Parte Chairperson of the Constitutional Assembly: In re Certification of the Constitution of the Republic of South Africa, 1996* 1996 (4) SA 744 (CC) par [57] at 792G–793B (regarding the general objection that juristic persons should not be protected); *Investigating Directorate: Serious Economic Offences and Others v Hyundai Motor Distributors (Pty) Ltd and Others: In re Hyundai Motor Distributors (Pty) Ltd and Others v Smit NO and Others* 2001 (1) SA 545 (CC) par [18] at 557F–I (with regard to privacy).

[124]A Kok 'Why the finding that juristic persons are entitled to the property rights protected by section 25 of the Constitution?' (2004) 67 *THRHR* 683–686 argues that the finding in paras [41]–[45] of *FNB* was unnecessary because the Court had already decided in *Ferreira v Levin NO and Others; Vryenhoek v Powel NO and Others* 1996 (1) SA 984 (CC) that a litigant would have standing to bring a case if he or she could show that he or she has a sufficient interest in the matter. Kok argues that FNB clearly had an interest in the matter and should therefore have standing regardless of whether section 25 protects juristic persons; and that the only reason why the Court made the finding on juristic persons was to 'put foreign investors at ease that their investments in Africa would be safe and that this court would look after their interests in interpreting the property right' (at 686). Kok therefore argues that the finding in *FNB* was unnecessary because the decision in '*Ferreira* still stands: the court will follow a broad approach to standing (para 165), a litigant need only show a sufficient interest in the remedy it seeks from the court (para 168) and would only need to illustrate (*sic*) an objective inconsistency between the Bill of Rights and the impugned Act (par 163)' (at 686). However, the argument against the beneficiaries finding in *FNB* is spurious, because Kok underplays the significance of section 8(4): juristic persons are entitled to the rights in the Bill of Rights to the extent required by the nature of the rights and of the juristic persons, and not

(continued on next page ...)

In German law it is said that the purpose of the Bill of Rights is to protect the individual liberty and personal freedom of people, and that state organs, state departments and local authorities are therefore excluded from the protection of the Bill of Rights, including the property guarantee.[125] Special exceptions are allowed in German law for state bodies that need and deserve the same protection of their property as other juristic persons,[126] and also for exceptional situations, such as cases where private legal persons perform certain state functions. A similar principle could well apply in South Africa, and consequently (except in some cases, particularly with regard to semi-state and semi-autonomous state bodies) state organs and state departments should not enjoy the protection of the property clause. This could apply particularly with regard to former state or trust land that has been transferred to provincial and local authorities subsequent to the abolition of apartheid laws. Second- and third-tier government structures such as local authorities could therefore, in the absence of exceptional circumstances,[127] be excluded from attacking the validity of laws and actions that 'deprive' them of land or other property.

(... from previous page)
simply because they can show a real interest in the right or an objective inconsistency between the right and the impugned act. In view of the fact that the protection of the constitutional property clause does not necessarily extend to juristic persons with property interests and that it has been denied non-citizens and juristic persons in other jurisdictions it seems justified and indeed necessary to make clear what the South African Constitutional Court's position on the scope of section 25 is; *FNB* was the first suitable occasion to do so.

[125]See AJ van der Walt *Constitutional property clauses: A comparative analysis* (1999) 126. Compare further *BVerfGE* 4, 7 [1954]; *BVerfGE* 61, 82 [1982]; *BVerfGE* 68, 139 [1984]; *BVerfGE* 75, 192 [1987]; *BVerfGE* 78, 101 [1988].

[126]See *BVerfGE* 61, 82 [1982]; *BVerfGE* 68, 193 [1984].

[127]An example would be where a local authority bought land for a specific purpose and the land is then needed by a central department for land reform. In such a case some kind of compensation or redress might be acceptable, although it could well be argued that even in such a case the aggrieved state organ should make use of the provisions in Chapter 3 of the Constitution (co-operative government) rather than Chapter 2 (Bill of Rights).

2.5 LIMITATION

7. Rights

(1) This Bill of Rights is a cornerstone of democracy in South Africa. It enshrines the rights of all people in our country and affirms the democratic values of human dignity, equality and freedom.

(2) ...

(3) The rights in the Bill of Rights are subject to the limitations contained in or referred to in section 36, or elsewhere in the Bill.

8. Application

(1) ...

(2) ...

(3) In applying the provisions of the Bill of Rights to natural and juristic persons in terms of subsection (2), a court—

   (*a*) in order to give effect to a right in the Bill, must apply, or where necessary, develop, the common law to the extent that legislation does not give effect to that right; and

   (*b*) may develop rules of the common law to limit the right, provided the limitation is in accordance with section 36(1).

36. Limitation of rights

(1) The rights in the Bill of Rights may be limited only in terms of law of general application to the extent that the limitation is reasonable and justifiable in an open and democratic society based on human dignity, equality and freedom, taking into account all relevant factors including—

   (*a*) the nature of the right;

   (*b*) the importance of the purpose of the limitation;

   (*c*) the nature and extent of the limitation;

   (*d*) the relation between the limitation and its purpose; and

   (*e*) less restrictive means to achieve the purpose.

(2) Except as provided in subsection (1) or in any other provision of the Constitution, no law may limit any right entrenched in the Bill of Rights.

2.5.1 Limitation of rights: Introduction

In the first edition of this book a substantial part of the discussion about limitation was dedicated to the relationship between so-called internal modifiers in section 25 and the general limitation provision in section 36.[128] In this edition that discussion is left

---

[128] The internal modifiers are distinguished from the general limitation provision in that internal modifiers define or restrict the scope of the right abstractly and initially without limiting any specific individual rights. Section 16(2) excludes war propaganda, incitement to violence and race hate speech from the right to freedom of speech; a law that subsequently regulates hate speech will not amount to a limitation of free speech when preventing someone from publishing hate speech based on race, because such speech was excluded when the right was modified or restricted internally and not by way of the subsequent general limitation. See in this regard AJ van der Walt 'The limits of constitutional property' (1997) 12 *SA Public Law* 275–330 and references there.

out because it now appears less relevant for the property clause than was initially anticipated. In the first place comprehensive discussions of the general limitation issue have been published, making an extensive discussion of limitation issues unnecessary here.[129] Secondly, the *FNB* decision has cleared up the issues about the level of scrutiny that should apply during the first stage of a property dispute,[130] making it unnecessary to continue the debate about the relationship between internal modifiers and the general limitation clause in so far as that debate was inspired by preferences for a thinner or thicker review of limitation during the first stage of a constitutional property challenge. Thirdly, it is becoming increasingly clear that second-stage limitation analysis will only rarely apply in constitutional property disputes,[131] which again makes it unnecessary to pay too much attention to limitation issues here. The discussion of limitation issues is therefore restricted to a small number of points. Apart from the few general remarks about limitation that follow directly below, the two stage approach is explained in 2.5.2 below. The possibility that general limitation analysis could apply to a constitutional property dispute under section 25 is discussed in 2.5.3 below.

Section 36 provides that the rights in the Bill of Rights may only be limited in accordance with the provisions of that section. Limitations must therefore either comply with the requirements in section 36(1) or with limitation provisions elsewhere in the Constitution. Of these two possibilities the former is clearly the general norm that applies to the vast majority of cases. In terms of section 36(1), rights in the Bill of Rights may only be limited by law of general application, and only to the extent that such limitation is reasonable and justifiable in an open and democratic society based on human dignity, equality and freedom, taking into account all relevant factors, including the nature of the right, the importance of the purpose of the limitation, the nature and extent of the limitation, the relation between the limitation and its purpose, and less restrictive means to achieve the purpose. Section 36(1) is based on the Canadian general limitation provision[132] and amounts to a general proportionality test that ensures that the rights in the Bill of Rights are limited only by general law and in a reasonable and justifiable manner. The requirement that rights may only be limited in terms of law of general application appears twice in section 25 and is therefore not foreign to the property clause; the meaning of the requirement is discussed in the appropriate chapters.[133]

---

[129]See S Woolman 'Limitations' in M Chaskalson et al (eds) *Constitutional law of South Africa* (1996 Revision Service 2, 1998) and literature referred to there.

[130]The *FNB* decision and its implications for the level of scrutiny issue are discussed in chapter 4.5 and 4.6; the two stages of a property dispute are discussed in 2.5.2 below.

[131]See 2.5.3 below.

[132]See S Woolman 'Limitations' in M Chaskalson et al (eds) *Constitutional law of South Africa* (1996 Revision Service 2, 1998) 12-4–12-17 on the history and the comparative debts of this provision.

[133]The same requirement appears in section 25(1) (deprivation may only take place in terms of law of general application) and section 25(2) (expropriation may only take place in terms of law of general application); see the discussion in chapters 4.4 and 5.6 respectively.

The requirement that limitations should be reasonable and justifiable as described in section 36(1) amounts to a proportionality test that is probably similar in spirit but stronger in force than the (variable) non-arbitrariness test laid down in the *FNB* decision.[134] Given the similarities between the section 36(1) proportionality test and the *FNB* non-arbitrariness test, the wealth of literature on the general limitation test and the improbability of section 36(1) proportionality analysis in fact applying to constitutional property disputes, it is unnecessary to discuss the proportionality test any further here.[135]

2.5.2 The structure of a constitutional property challenge

The Constitutional Court has indicated in its first few decisions[136] that it will follow the Canadian 'two stage' approach when inquiring into the constitutional validity of a statute that limits a fundamental right. The first stage, in which the applicant bears the onus of proof, involves the question whether there has been an infringement of a right protected in the Bill of Rights. The case proceeds to the second stage only if the first stage results in an affirmative answer. In the second stage, where the state or the party relying on the validity of the statute bears the onus of proof, the question is whether the infringement can be justified under the limitation provision (section 36 of the Constitution).

If it is assumed that the same approach will be followed in a constitutional property dispute, the applicant will have to prove during the first stage that there was an infringement of a property right which is protected by section 25. Of course this involves two separate questions, namely whether there is proof of property that qualifies for the protection of section 25, and whether there is an infringement of that property. If the applicant succeeds in proving the existence of a protected property right and of an infringement, the case proceeds to the second stage. In the second stage the state, or the party relying on the validity of the relevant act, has to prove that the infringement can be justified, either in terms of section 25 or in terms of section 36 or both.

---

[134]It was said in *FNB* that the arbitrariness test operates on a sliding scale that varies from mere rationality to something almost (but apparently not quite) as substantive as the proportionality test in section 36(1): *First National Bank of SA Ltd t/a Wesbank v Commissioner, South African Revenue Service; First National Bank of SA Ltd t/a Wesbank v Minister of Finance* 2002 (4) SA 768 (CC) par [100](G) at 811D–E; see further T Roux 'Property' in S Woolman et al (eds) *Constitutional law of South Africa* (2nd ed original service 2003) 46–24.

[135]See S Woolman 'Limitations' in M Chaskalson et al (eds) *Constitutional law of South Africa* (1996 Revision Service 2, 1998) and compare further 4.5 on page 145, 5.2 on page 181, and 2.5.3 on page 56 below.

[136]See *S v Makwanyane and Another* 1995 (3) SA 391 (CC) paras [100]–[102] at 435C–436A; *Ferreira v Levin and Others; Vryenhoek and Others v Powell NO and Others* 1996 (1) SA 984 (CC) par [44] at 1012B.

In the *FNB* decision[137] the Constitutional Court amended (or at least particularized) the two stage approach's application to constitutional property disputes in terms of section 25. According to the methodology proposed in that decision a constitutional property dispute would generally proceed as follows:

- The starting point for all constitutional property disputes is section 25(1). The first question is therefore whether there was a deprivation that infringes property in conflict with section 25(1), in other words arbitrarily.[138] The threshold questions (whether the applicant is a beneficiary who qualifies for the protection of section 25, whether the affected interest is property and whether the property interest was indeed infringed) are apparently 'sucked into' the arbitrariness test.
- If there is a deprivation in conflict with section 25(1), the second question would be whether such deprivation is justifiable under section 36(1). If not, the limitation is unconstitutional and the matter ends there.
- If the deprivation passes scrutiny under section 25(1) (does not conflict with it) or under section 36(1) (does conflict with section 25(1) but is reasonable and justifiable under section 36(1)) the next question is whether the deprivation amounts to expropriation. If it amounts to expropriation it must again pass scrutiny under section 25(2) and 25(3).
- If the deprivation amounts to expropriation and passes scrutiny under section 25(2) and 25(3) it is constitutionally legitimate and valid and the matter ends there.
- If the deprivation amounts to expropriation but does not pass scrutiny under section 25(2) or 25(3) it could again be justified under section 36(1). If it cannot be justified the expropriation is unconstitutional and the matter ends there.
- If the deprivation amounts to expropriation and conflicts with section 25(2) or 25(3) but can be justified under section 36(1) it is constitutional and the matter ends there.

In the procedure as set out above the matter can move from first-stage analysis under section 25 to second-stage limitation analysis under section 36(1) at two points: first when it appears that there is a deprivation in conflict with section 25(1) and second when a deprivation that is either not in conflict with section 25(1) or is in conflict with section 25(1) but was justified under section 36(1) then proves to be in conflict with section 25(2) or 25(3).

However, the apparently pleasing symmetry of this procedure is misleading. Theunis Roux has argued convincingly that it is unlikely, if the procedure as set out in *FNB* is followed, that a constitutional property dispute would actually proceed

---

[137] *First National Bank of SA Ltd t/a Wesbank v Commissioner, South African Revenue Service; First National Bank of SA Ltd t/a Wesbank v Minister of Finance* 2002 (4) SA 768 (CC) paras [58]–[60] at 797H–798D. See chapter 4.5 and 4.6 for further discussion. Compare T Roux 'Property' in S Woolman et al (eds) *Constitutional law of South Africa* (2nd ed original service 2003) 46-2–46-5 for a graphic illustration of the procedure.

[138] Of course a deprivation could also conflict with section 25(1) for not being authorized by a law of general application, but this is unlikely—the majority of cases would turn on arbitrariness.

through all the stages set out above.[139] There are two main reasons why the *FNB* approach makes it unlikely that a constitutional property challenge would proceed through all the stages as set out:

- Firstly, if the *FNB* procedure is followed it is highly likely that a challenge based on non-compliance with the section 25(2) or 25(3) requirements for expropriation will already surface during the section 25(1) arbitrariness test. Comparison of the requirements for valid deprivation in section 25(1) and valid expropriation in section 25(2) and 25(3) shows that both deprivation and expropriation are subject to law of general application and public purpose or public interest requirements, while non-arbitrariness is required for deprivation only and compensation for expropriation only.[140] However, in terms of the *FNB* approach expropriation is a subcategory of deprivation and it must also (first) comply with the non-arbitrariness requirement, which is unlikely if a specific expropriation is attacked for not complying with the one requirement that applies to expropriation only, namely compensation. In short, an expropriation that does not provide for compensation as required in section 25(2) and 25(3) will fail the non-arbitrariness test before it can even be considered as an expropriation, and therefore it is unlikely to ever reach the expropriation stage of the analysis.

- Secondly, it is unlikely as a matter of logic that any deprivation (whether it also amounts to expropriation or not) that fails the non-arbitrariness test can ever be justified in terms of section 36(1).[141] The logic of this observation can be tested by isolating every reason why a deprivation could fail the non-arbitrariness test and then asking whether the deprivation could still be reasonable and justifiable as meant in section 36(1), given that reason. Obviously a deprivation that failed the section 25(1) test because it was not imposed by law of general application must also fail the section 36(1) test, because section 36(1) also requires law of general application. Similarly, it would be unlikely if not impossible to hold that a deprivation is reasonable as meant in section 36(1) once it has been described as arbitrary for one of the reasons set out in *FNB*. Accordingly, it is argued in 2.5.3 below that section 36(1) limitation analysis is unlikely to apply to constitutional property disputes in all but the most singular and abnormal cases.

If one accepts that it is unlikely that section 25(1) constitutional property disputes would ever proceed to either the section 36(1) limitation analysis or the section 25(2)

---

[139]See T Roux 'Property' in S Woolman et al (eds) *Constitutional law of South Africa* (2nd ed original service 2003) 46-2–46-5, 46-21–46-25; and compare the discussion in chapter 4.6 and chapter 5.4.5.

[140]Compare chapters 4.3 (deprivation: public purpose), 4.4 (deprivation: law of general application) and 4.5 (deprivation: non-arbitrariness) with chapter 5.5 (expropriation: general requirements), 5.6 (expropriation: law of general application), 5.7 (expropriation: public purpose) and 5.8 (expropriation: compensation).

[141]See AJ van der Walt 'The limits of constitutional property' (1997) 12 *SA Public Law* 275–330 at 325–327; T Roux 'Property' in S Woolman et al (eds) *Constitutional law of South Africa* (2nd ed original service 2003) 46–36.

and 25(3) expropriation analysis foreseen in *FNB* one must conclude, as Theunis Roux did, that all constitutional property disputes that follow the *FNB* procedure are likely to get stuck in the section 25(1) arbitrariness analysis and end there.[142]

2.5.3 Section 25 and limitation analysis

Finally it remains to conclude that it is highly unlikely that a constitutional property dispute in terms of section 25 will ever reach the section 36(1) limitation analysis—the second stage in a two stage process—if the courts follow the procedure as set out in *FNB*.[143] Put very simply and briefly one could summarize the argument as follows:

- Deprivation or expropriation that fails the section 25(1) or 25(2) law of general application requirement will necessarily also fail the section 36(1) law of general application argument.
- It is highly unlikely that deprivation or expropriation that fails the public purpose or public interest requirement (implicit in section 25(1) but explicit in section 25(2)) can pass muster under section 36(1) limitation analysis, because such deprivation or expropriation would arguably not be reasonable and justifiable as meant in section 36(1). Section 36(1) attempts to find an equitable balance between the individual interest and the public interest, which is impossible if the action in question does not serve the public interest in the first place.
- It is highly unlikely that deprivation that is arbitrary and therefore in conflict with section 25(1) can be reasonable in terms of section 36(1). One of the central meanings usually attached to 'arbitrary' is 'not reasonable'.
- It is highly unlikely that expropriation that fails to satisfy the compensation requirement, within the already very context-sensitive ambit of section 25(3), could ever be reasonable and justifiable under section 36(1). In view of the nuances built into section 25(3) expropriation can be legitimate and valid even in the absence of or against unusually low compensation; accordingly, expropriation that offends even the contextual and flexible standard of compensation in section 25(3) will probably always be unreasonable and unjustifiable.[144]

The inevitable conclusion therefore seems to be that, although section 25 is not explicitly excluded from limitation analysis in terms of section 36(1), it is highly improbable that any deprivation or expropriation that is in conflict with section 25

---

[142]T Roux 'Property' in S Woolman et al (eds) *Constitutional law of South Africa* (2nd ed original service 2003) 46-2–46-5, 46-21–46-25; and compare the discussion in chapter 4.6 and chapter 5.4.5.
[143]See AJ van der Walt 'The limits of constitutional property' (1997) 12 *SA Public Law* 275–330 at 325–327; T Roux 'Property' in S Woolman et al (eds) *Constitutional law of South Africa* (2nd ed original service 2003) 46–36.
[144]In *Nhlabati and Others v Fick* 2003 (7) BCLR 806 (LCC) par [35] at 818A–819E the Land Claims Court accepted that section 36 limitation analysis could apply in certain cases when expropriation without compensation was mandated by law, and that the limitation could be reasonable and justifiable. The effect of the *FNB* decision was not considered. See chapter 5.8.5 text surrounding footnote 217 for a discussion.

could be saved in terms of section 36(1). Consequently section 36(1) is not really significant for purposes of section 25: limitation of property that does not comply with the specific internal requirements in section 25 will probably always be unconstitutional.[145]

---

[145]See the somewhat similar argument regarding section 27 rights and the justification of limitations in terms of section 36 in *Khosa and Others v Minister of Social Development and Others; Mahlaule and Others v Minister of Social Development and Others* 2004 (6) SA 505 (CC) paras [83], [105], [106] at 540B–D, 549C–F.

CHAPTER 3

Property

3.1 INTRODUCTION

25. Property

(1) No one may be deprived of property except in terms of law of general application, and no law may permit arbitrary deprivation of property.
(2) Property may be expropriated only in terms of law of general application—
    (*a*) ...
    (*b*) ...
(3) ...
(4) For the purposes of this section—
    (*a*) ...
    (*b*) property is not limited to land.

When the possibility of a constitutional property clause was first raised in the late 1980s the meaning of the term 'property' in such a clause was initially regarded as the most important interpretation problem created by the constitutionalization of property.[1] The central question was whether 'property', for purposes of the constitutional property clause, should be construed generously or restrictively. Those who opposed the inclusion of property in the Bill of Rights because they feared that the constitutionalization of property might impede land reform by immunizing existing property holdings against transformation and reform initiatives favoured a restrictive, less than generous interpretation.[2] Others countered that the property concept should rather be interpreted generously, because it would be ironic if the property rights that have been denied the majority of the population for decades were finally guaranteed by the Constitution, only to be restricted through judicial interpretation.[3]

Discussions about the property clause were therefore initially dominated by arguments based on the possibly reform-inhibiting effects of a constitutional property guarantee. A political compromise ensured the inclusion of a property clause in the Constitution, rendering the effect of this debate negligible, but anti-constitutionaliz-

---

[1] See M Chaskalson 'The property clause: Section 28 of the Constitution' (1994) 10 *SAJHR* 131–139 at 132; AJ van der Walt 'Notes on the interpretation of the property clause in the new constitution' (1994) 57 *THRHR* 181–203 at 191ff; AJ van der Walt 'Towards a theory of rights in property: Exploratory observations on the paradigm of post-apartheid property law' (1995) 10 *SA Public Law* 298345 at 307ff; DG Kleyn 'The constitutional protection of property: A comparison between the German and the South African approach' (1996) 11 *SA Public Law* 402–445 at 419ff for examples. Compare the *First Certification Case* judgment of the Constitutional Court: *Ex Parte Chairperson of the Constitutional Assembly: In re Certification of the Constitution of the Republic of South Africa, 1996* 1996 (4) SA 744 (CC) par [72] at 798E–F, where it was confirmed that 'no universally recognised formulation of the right to property exists'. In the guiding *FNB* decision the Constitutional Court acknowledged the *First Certification* dictum and the fact that property is not restricted to land for purposes of section 25 (section 25(4)), but found it practically impossible, judicially unwise and unnecessary to give a comprehensive definition of property, although it accepted that ownership of corporeal movables (and land) must 'lie at the heart of our constitutional concept of property, both as regards the nature of the right involved as well as the object of the right': *First National Bank of SA Ltd t/a Wesbank v Commissioner, South African Revenue Service; First National Bank of SA Ltd t/a Wesbank v Minister of Finance* 2002 (4) SA 768 (CC) par [51] at 794E–F.

[2] T Roux 'Property' in MH Cheadle, DM Davis & NRL Haysom *South African constitutional law: The bill of rights* (2002) 429–472 at 432 footnote 8 provides an interesting insight into the differences between strong initial anti-constitutionalization sentiments and the later, less skeptical approach in terms of which the constitutionalization of property is regarded as a political compromise. See further M Chaskalson 'Stumbling towards section 28: Negotiations over the protection of property rights in the interim constitution' (1995) 11 *SAJHR* 222–240.

[3] My first reaction was against constitutionalization; see AJ van der Walt 'Towards the development of post-apartheid land law: An exploratory survey' 1990 *De Jure* 1–45. Later on I subscribed to the more nuanced view proposed by J Murphy 'Property rights in the new Constitution: An analytical framework for constitutional review' (1993) 26 *CILSA* 211–233 at 217, see AJ van der Walt 'Property rights, land rights, and environmental rights' in D van Wyk, J Dugard, B de Villiers & D Davis (eds) *Rights and constitutionalism: The new South African legal order* (1994) 455–501 at 480. Eventually I was convinced that the constitutionalization of property need not frustrate land reform and that it can in fact, if interpreted in a transformation-sensitive way, become an instrument of transformation; see AJ van der Walt 'The constitutional property clause: Striking a balance between guarantee and limitation' in J MacLean (ed) *Property and the constitution* (1999) 109–146. See further chapter 2.3.4.

ation arguments cannot simply be dismissed[4]—what is required is a nuanced analysis that distinguishes separate aspects of the problem and considers them independently —conflation of the issues merely causes confusion. Aspects of the debate about property that relate to the constitutionalization debate and that are discussed in this chapter include the notion of property as a truncated right (3.2 below), dephysicalization (3.3 below) and conceptual severance (3.4 below).

Judging from recent publications, some commentators now think that the exact meaning of the property concept as such might not be all that important. This attitude finds some support in foreign case law, where differently phrased property clauses are often interpreted roughly the same;[5] the trend seems to be to focus on the constitutional justifiability of a specific limitation of property rather than on the question whether a specific right or interest can or cannot be defined as property or whether a specific limitation should be classified as one rather than another category of state action. Accordingly, the property question is usually either ignored completely or subjected to a lower level of scrutiny than justification issues. It appears as if South African jurisprudence might follow the international trend to interpret the property concept generously, because one of the side-effects of the Constitutional Court decision in the *FNB* case[6] might be that the meaning of 'property' in section 25 will play a smaller role in constitutional litigation than was originally anticipated. The effect of the *FNB* case on the property concept is discussed in 3.5 below.

Of course, this does not mean that the property concept is irrelevant. The purpose of this chapter is to emphasize the aspects of this issue that are still relevant and to discuss them in view of South African case law to date and foreign law. Experience in other jurisdictions shows that the manner in which the constitutional property concept relates to the existing private law property tradition is important. In Anglo-American

---

[4]For a comprehensive analysis of anti-constitutionalization arguments see J Nedelsky 'Should property be constitutionalized? A relational and comparative approach' in GE van Maanen & AJ van der Walt (eds) *Property law on the threshold of the 21st century* (1996) 417–432; compare for a critical view of these arguments AJ van der Walt 'The constitutional property clause: Striking a balance between guarantee and limitation' in J MacLean (ed) *Property and the constitution* (1999) 109–146, and see chapter 2.3.4.

[5]The following two examples illustrate the point. Firstly, property clauses from German-language jurisdictions and from Commonwealth jurisdictions are interpreted roughly similarly even though the German-language constitutions refer to *Eigentum* or 'ownership', which is a more restricted concept than 'property' in German-language systems of private law; the later usually refers to full dominium of corporeals only. Secondly, the European Convention on Human Rights refers to 'peaceful enjoyment of possessions' and not to property, but the provision is interpreted much like other provisions that refer to property. See AJ van der Walt *Constitutional property clauses: A comparative analysis* (1999) 21–22 and compare the discussion below for details.

[6]*First National Bank of SA Ltd t/a Wesbank v Commissioner, South African Revenue Service; First National Bank of SA Ltd t/a Wesbank v Minister of Finance* 2002 (4) SA 768 (CC) par [57] at 796F–H. See further T Roux 'Section 25' in S Woolman et al (eds) *Constitutional law of South Africa* (2nd ed 2003 original service Dec 2003) 46-2–46-5, 46-9–46-11, 46-23–46-25; AJ van der Walt 'Striving for the better interpretation—A critical reflection on the Constitutional Court's *Harksen* and *FNB* decisions on the property clause' (2005) 123 *SALJ* 854–878 at 872–874.

law this aspect does not create much of a problem, but in the Roman-Germanic private law systems property traditionally tends to be defined restrictively (as far as its objects are concerned) and absolutely (as far as its nature and scope are concerned). Should the constitutional property concept be interpreted similarly? Property acquired a special (wider) constitutional meaning in jurisdictions where it has a restricted meaning in private law, with the result that the constitutional and private law meanings of property are different. However, the private law meaning of property cannot be isolated from its constitutional meaning completely—the two affect and influence each other, and in a very fundamental sense property embodies a link between private and constitutional law. When a property clause is introduced into an established legal system the implication is that constitutional law must have due regard for the meaning of property in private law and, on the other hand, private law might have to adjust to constitutional law. This is particularly important in a reform-oriented context like the South African post-1994 situation. The implications of this perspective for the constitutional transformation of private law are worked out in more detail in chapter 7, but some of the issues relating to the property concept are discussed in 3.6 below.

Once it is accepted that property, for purposes of section 25, should be seen specifically as a constitutional right it becomes necessary to consider the scope of the property clause. Even in jurisdictions where the substantive issues concerning the justifiability of a limitation on property attract more attention than conceptual analysis of the term 'property' there is still some concern with the meaning and scope of the property concept. In German law one can distinguish between an initial phase during which a suitable principle for the definition of property was developed and a subsequent phase during which the principle was merely applied and more emphasis was placed on substantive justification issues; one could perhaps expect a similar shift of focus in South African case law once the initial work of sketching out a paradigm for constitutional property has been completed.

The constitutional meaning of property involves two aspects,[7] namely the objects of property rights[8] and the content and scope of property rights.[9] The first aspect involves the question whether a wider or narrower category of objects should be recognized as objects of property rights for purposes of the constitutional property guarantee. Different aspects of this problem are discussed in 3.7 below. The second aspect involves the question whether the entitlements that accompany property as a right should be treated restrictively or generously in constitutional law. This question

---

[7] As far as property as a right is concerned, private law property in the Roman-Germanic systems is traditionally associated with full ownership as opposed to other, lesser real and personal rights in property.

[8] As far as the object of the right is concerned, private law property is traditionally restricted to corporeal things in the Roman-Germanic systems. See 3.7 below for references and examples.

[9] In the Roman-Germanic systems private law ownership is traditionally regarded as the most complete real right, characterized by its absoluteness and exclusivity. The absoluteness principle presents a potential problem for constitutional interpretation because of its inhibiting implications for regulatory exercises of the state's police power. See 3.8 below for references and examples.

has significant implications for the state, since a too generous approach to the scope of property rights, combined with an overly strict review of the state's powers of regulation, could result in the impossible situation that the state must compensate property owners and holders for every little regulatory limitation of their rights. The implications of different approaches to the scope of property as a right are discussed in 3.8 below.

In terms of the 'two stage' approach followed by the courts in adjudicating disputes about the limitation of constitutional rights the first stage requires the complainant to provide proof of a constitutional right that was subjected to a limitation.[10] For purposes of section 25 this means that the first stage of the case will require proof of a property right that is protected in terms of section 25, as well as proof that the right was affected by a limitation imposed on it. Proof of a property interest will often (in the 'easy' cases distinguished below) not be difficult, but it still has to be considered in every case as a threshold question, even if such an inquiry is conducted on a very low level of scrutiny. This makes it necessary to consider the question whether certain interests will qualify as property for purposes of section 25, and in 3.9 below some guidelines for this process are distilled from South African case law to date and foreign law.[11]

3.2 PROPERTY AS A TRUNCATED RIGHT[12]

It was said in the introduction above that, once a property clause was included in the 1996 Constitution,[13] those who initially opposed the constitutionalization of property favoured a restrictive, less than generous interpretation of the clause because they were concerned that constitutional protection could immunize existing property

------

[10]See chapter 2.5.2 for a discussion of the two stage approach and references.

[11]Since this aspect of section 28 of the 1993 interim Constitution was analysed exhaustively elsewhere it is not necessary to discuss all the possibilities in detail here. Accordingly, this chapter highlights a few problems but does not attempt to discuss all forms of property for purposes of section 25. See AJ van der Walt 'Towards a theory of rights in property: Exploratory observations on the paradigm of post-apartheid property law' (1995) 10 *SA Public Law* 298–345 at 311ff. Compare DG Kleyn 'The constitutional protection of property: A comparison between the German and the South African approach' (1996) 11 *SA Public Law* 402–445 at 419ff; W Du Plessis & NJJ Olivier 'The old and the new property clause' (1997) 1(5) *Human Rights & Const LJ SA* 11–16 at 12; T Roux 'Section 25' in S Woolman et al (eds) *Constitutional law of South Africa* (2nd ed 2003 original service Dec 2003) at 46-15–46-17.

[12]This section is based upon and resembles parts of AJ van der Walt 'Overview of developments since the introduction of the constitutional property clause' (2004) 19 *SA Public Law* 46–89. See further chapter 2.3.5, where the question is whether section 25 can be said to embody a property guarantee. The two issues are related.

[13]It is more difficult to make the same argument with regard to section 28 of the 1993 Constitution because of the 'positive' guarantee in section 28(1), which is perhaps one of the reasons why the positive formulation was dropped in the 1996 text. See M Chaskalson 'Stumbling towards section 28: Negotiations over the protection of property rights in the interim constitution' (1995) 11 *SAJHR* 222–240 at 234–236 for reasons raised during negotiations.

holdings against reform initiatives.[14] Accordingly, these commentators favoured a restrictive interpretation of what was considered property for purposes of section 25. One argument forwarded in favour of such a restricted interpretation was that the property clause guaranteed what has been described as a 'truncated right'.[15] This truncated right is not property as such, but the right that property would not be infringed upon other than in accordance with the Constitution. In Roux's words, the truncated right argument emphasizes that section 25 protects not property in general but 'two distinct rights',[16] namely the right not to be deprived of property except in terms of law of general application that does not permit the arbitrary deprivation of property, and the right that property would not be expropriated except in terms of law of general application, for a public purpose or in the public interest, and on payment of compensation, the amount of which and the time and manner of payment of which, if not agreed, is just and equitable. In other words, according to this truncated right argument, section 25 protects the right not to be deprived of property or expropriated other than in accordance with the provisions of section 25, as opposed to the view that section 25 simply protects property generally.

Leaving structural and contextual differences aside for a moment, this argument could be transplanted onto most negative property clauses, for example by saying that the property clause in the US Constitution[17] does not protect a general right to property, but rather the right not to be deprived of property without due process of law, and for property not to be taken for public use without just compensation. Seen like that, the truncated right argument merely emphasizes the fact that the South African and the American property clauses—unlike their German counterpart[18]—are negatively framed and therefore do not support an institutional guarantee of property as an economic system. However, when transplanted onto negative property clauses in established systems the argument also shows—in view of experience in those systems

---

[14]See footnotes 2–4 above and accompanying text and chapter 2.3.4.

[15]This is Frank Michelman's term (in informal discussions) for the argument, which is explained most clearly by T Roux 'Property' in MH Cheadle, DM Davis & NRL Haysom *South African constitutional law: The bill of rights* (2002) 429–472 at 440.

[16]T Roux 'Property' in MH Cheadle, DM Davis & NRL Haysom *South African constitutional law: The bill of rights* (2002) 429–472 at 440, with reference to J de Waal, I Currie & MG Erasmus *The bill of rights handbook* (2000) at 393–394.

[17]Fifth and Fourteenth Amendments to the US Constitution; see AJ van der Walt *Constitutional property clauses: A comparative analysis* (1999) 398 ff.

[18]Article 14.1 of the German *Grundgesetz* provides explicitly (or positively) that property is guaranteed, and a special (so-called institutional) interpretation is attached to this positive guarantee: see AJ van der Walt *Constitutional property clauses: A comparative analysis* (1999) 128. A similar institutional guarantee, which guarantees the preservation of the institution of private property, is not read into the American property clause, and should arguably not be read into the South African clause either, because neither of these clauses includes such a positive guarantee of property: AJ van der Walt *Constitutional property clauses: A comparative analysis* (1999) at 326–327; but see D Kleyn 'The constitutional protection of property: A comparison between the German and the South African approach' (1996) 11 *SA Public Law* 402–445 at 418.

—that a negatively framed property guarantee does not immunize existing property holdings against normal regulatory action. Once it is accepted that the property clause does not restrict or prevent normal regulatory action it is reasonably easy to argue that it does not prevent constitutionally sanctioned reform initiatives either, and at that point it becomes clear that the truncated right argument does not make much difference to the interpretation of section 25. As Roux points out, it can at most have an effect on the onus of proof and the question whether and how limitation analysis should apply to section 25, and even then it will not affect the outcome in many cases.[19] The possibly reform-inhibiting effects that generous interpretation of section 25 might have was perhaps a legitimate concern during the constitution-drafting process, but experience since 1994 suggests that the courts are treating the provision with the necessary contextual sensitivity and that existing rights will not be insulated from reforms. Consequently, if the courts' interpretation of the property clause does not in fact threaten or frustrate reform initiatives, the motivation for the truncated right argument falls away. In effect this truncated rights argument was nothing more than the result of initial anxiety about the possible reform-inhibiting results of constitutionalization of property; once this anxiety was laid to rest the argument lost much of its force.

It could in fact be argued that concern about the reform-inhibiting effects of section 25 was always unnecessary in view of the historical and constitutional context. Judging from experience in foreign law, constitutional property is not protected in the sense that existing property holdings are guaranteed absolutely against any interference or invasion not authorized or consented to by the owner. Constitutional protection of property is different from private-law protection of property in that the purpose is not to guarantee and insulate the existing position of the property holder against any interference, but to establish and maintain a balance between the individual's vested rights and the public interest, which often means that the individual's interest has to be subjected to controls, regulations, restrictions, levies, deprivations and changes that promote or protect a legitimate public interest, sometimes with relatively serious negative effects for the property owner but nevertheless without compensation. In this constitutional context it should be clear that legitimate reforms of the property regime should be possible despite constitutionalization and that existing property holdings cannot be immunized against them; a result that is strengthened by the explicit reform-oriented aims and obligations set out and legitimized in the South African Constitution.[20]

This history- and context-sensitive explanation of the legitimacy of 'normal' business-as-usual regulation of property and of politically inspired property reforms is

---

[19]T Roux 'Property' in MH Cheadle, DM Davis & NRL Haysom *South African constitutional law: The bill of rights* (2002) 429–472 at 440.

[20]Section 25(4)–(8) makes it clear that certain reform initiatives are not only legitimate, but that the state is obliged to establish and implement them. See further sections 26 (housing) and 39(3) (development of the common law), and compare chapters 6 and 7.

backed up by theoretical argument and by recent Constitutional Court judgments.[21] Apartheid systematically eroded black land rights by depriving owners and occupiers of security and denying them the normal protection of the laws of the land. The Constitution imposes legislative and other duties upon the legislature and the executive to change this situation by providing those people who were disadvantaged by apartheid with the security and the protection that was taken away from or denied them. If this is the purpose of the constitutional property clause it is unnecessary to worry too much about its reactionary potential and it makes more sense to focus on its transformational possibilities. Accordingly, the truncated rights argument appears to be a somewhat forced and not very convincing effort to solve what is turning out to be a non-problem. It was argued in chapter 2.3 that, in as far as it is a problem to ensure that section 25 is interpreted and applied with due regard for its historical and constitutional context, the best strategy is not to restrict the scope of the property clause but to focus on developing the best possible interpretation and adjudication theory for it. Recent case law of the Constitutional Court suggests that the Court is indeed moving in that direction by focusing on a contextualized and reform-sensitive interpretation framework within which property issues are considered and judged substantively rather on strategies that would limit the application of the property clause (or reduce its adjudication to thin rationality review).

3.3 DEPHYSICALIZATION[22]

In the *FNB* case,[23] the Constitutional Court indicated that it was impossible to define property comprehensively for purposes of section 25 and restricted itself to the statement that ownership of corporeal movables and of land is at the heart of the constitutional property concept. However, that does not mean that constitutional property is limited to these categories, and most South African commentators agree that a relatively wide or accommodating notion of property is appropriate when interpreting section 25, to ensure that economically significant intangible property interests that might not be considered property in private law are nevertheless included in

---

[21] See particularly *Port Elizabeth Municipality v Various Occupiers* 2005 (1) SA 217 (CC) paras [8]–[23] at 222A–229G, setting out the historical context of discriminatory land law and the new constitutional context within which conflicting land rights are adjudicated. Compare the discussion of the case in chapters 6 and 7.

[22] Parts of this section are based upon sections of AJ van der Walt 'Overview of developments since the introduction of the constitutional property clause' (2004) 19 *SA Public Law* 46–89.

[23] *First National Bank of SA Ltd t/a Wesbank v Commissioner, South African Revenue Service; First National Bank of SA Ltd t/a Wesbank v Minister of Finance* 2002 (4) SA 768 (CC) par [51] at 794E.

its protection.[24] Roux has pointed out that the approach adopted by the Constitutional Court in *FNB* might mean that the Court will in future place very little
emphasis on the threshold property question and prefer to postpone the essential
balancing of interests to a later stage of the proceedings by focusing on the question
whether there was proof of an arbitrary deprivation of property.[25] Such a generous
attitude towards the property question would be in line with and reflect the theoretical notion of the 'dephysicalization of property', which has become more or less
commonplace in constitutional property cases in most foreign jurisdictions.[26]

   The notion of dephysicalization refers to the complex social, economic and legal
processes by which incorporeal or intangible property are becoming increasingly
important for personal wealth and security and for social welfare, while the importance of traditional tangible property such as land declines.[27] This development takes
place in private and in constitutional law. It may even be said that recognition of the
process of dephysicalization precipitated (or at least is linked to) the general trend,
in Roman-Germanic legal systems, for the constitutional property concept to be
interpreted more generously than is the case in private law.[28] In any event this
process involves recognition, at least in constitutional law but often in private law as
well, of the fact that certain intangibles (mostly in the form of rights) have become
so important and valuable in modern society that they have to be treated and protected as property, even when it was or is not regarded as property in that specific
private law tradition. The most obvious intangible interests and assets that became
classified as property in this sense are intellectual property (copyright, patents and
trade marks) and commercial interests such as debts, shares, and the goodwill of a

---

[24]See in general AJ van der Walt *Constitutional property clauses: A comparative analysis* (1999) at 351–
353; T Roux 'Property' in MH Cheadle, DM Davis & NRL Haysom *South African constitutional
law: The bill of rights* (2002) 429–472 at 449–452. For an early analysis see AJ van der Walt 'Toward
a theory of rights in property: Exploratory observations on the paradigm of post-apartheid property
law' (1995) 10 *SA Public Law* 298–345. See the discussion in 3.7 below.
[25]T Roux 'Section 25' in S Woolman et al (eds) *Constitutional law of South Africa* (2nd ed 2003
original service Dec 2003) at 46-2–46-5, 46-21–46-25. See the discussion in chapter 4.5 and 4.6.
[26]The dephysicalization issue is linked to but extends beyond the constitutional protection of
property interests. In general see KJ Vandevelde 'Developing property concepts' (1980) 29 *Buffalo
LR* 333–340; AJ van der Walt 'Unity and pluralism in property theory—A review of property
theories and debates in recent literature: Part I' 1995 *TSAR* 15–29 at 28–29.
[27]See the previous footnote, and compare TC Grey 'The disintegration of property' in JR
Pennock & JW Chapman (eds) *Property (Nomos XXII)* (1980) 69–85; C Reich 'The new property'
(1964) 73 *Yale LJ* 733–787 for discussions of similar or related processes.
[28]The best example is German law. German private law restricts property to corporeals, but in
constitutional law a wider concept of property is recognized: see the discussion in 3.7.5 below.
Reich had a similar process in mind with his plea for the recognition of the 'new property'; see C
Reich 'The new property' (1964) 73 *Yale LJ* 733–787, and compare AJ van der Walt 'Protecting
social participation rights within the property paradigm: A critical reappraisal' in E Cooke (ed)
Modern studies in property law (2002) 27–41. However, not all the categories of 'new property' that
Reich enumerated have been accepted in either private or constitutional law as property; see 3.7.5
below.

company. The rights deriving from the acquisition and exploitation of commercial licenses, permits and quotas are also sometimes regarded as property, but recognition of so-called 'new property' or public participation claims as constitutional property is more controversial.[29]

The dephysicalization process has several implications for constitutional property. On the one hand the mere fact that this process is given effect in private law has had an impact in constitutional law, because it is difficult to deny constitutional protection to interests and assets that are recognized and protected as such in private law. On the other hand constitutional law sometimes tends to be more generous in recognizing and protecting even interests that are not treated as property in private law. This creates a potential dilemma in that giving effect to the economic realities of dephysicalization could result in an unrestricted proliferation of constitutionally recognized intangible property interests. Accordingly, there is concern that 'an overly expansive definition of constitutional property, one that recognized virtually every interest capable of being assessed in money terms, would run counter to the courts' developing jurisprudence on the fundamental values underlying the final Constitution'.[30] This concern is particularly relevant with regard to interests that are not recognized or protected as property in private law or in statutory law.

It was argued in the previous section above that constitutionalization concerns (and their subsequent embodiment in concerns about the scope of section 25) based on the argument that the constitutional protection of property should not impede or frustrate land reform or economic and social transformation have little or no force in view of the constitutional context and early indications in case law. At the same time, a restrictive approach to the interpretation of property in section 25 is not necessarily the best way of promoting the efficacy of land reform—it could be argued that the battlefield where these concerns have to be addressed is not the scope of property that enjoys the protection of section 25, but the interpretation and application of the regulation and expropriation provisions that apply to all property. Theunis Roux's analysis of the *FNB* decision[31] suggests that the Constitutional Court might in future leave the substantive balancing of interests for decision on the arbitrary deprivation issues, while applying the property threshold in a relatively accommodating manner. This would be in accordance with the approach adopted in German constitutional law, where a fairly generous approach is adopted with regard to what qualifies as

---

[29]See 3.7.5 below for a discussion and references.

[30]T Roux 'Property' in MH Cheadle, DM Davis & NRL Haysom *South African constitutional law: The bill of rights* (2002) 429–472 at 446.

[31]T Roux 'Section 25' in S Woolman et al (eds) *Constitutional law of South Africa* (2nd ed 2003 original service Dec 2003) at 46-2–46-5, 46-21–46-25. See the discussion in chapter 4.5 and 4.6.

property for purposes of protection in terms of Article 14 of the Basic Law.[32] As far as the protection of intangible property interests is concerned, the scope of property for purposes of section 25 should therefore not be restricted simply for the sake of transformation.

The dephysicalization of property is an economic reality that is already acknowledged even in South African private law, and therefore it cannot be ignored in constitutional law. Intangible assets and interests that are regarded and protected as property in private law or in independent legislation should be recognized as constitutional property and protected in constitutional law as well. Other intangible interests should be regarded as constitutional property and protected on the same basis as any corporeal property interest—probably by determining whether the interest has constitutionally relevant value for the claimant and whether it has vested or has been acquired in accordance with the applicable principles of law.[33]

3.4 CONCEPTUAL SEVERANCE[34]

The greatest concern caused by the dephysicalization of property is not that intangible rights would be treated as objects of property, but that little chunks would be separated from these or other, more traditional property rights and treated as independent property rights. The classic example is the situation where a landowner is prevented from building a commercially viable development on her land and then claims that her property, in the form of the right to develop her land, has been taken away or expropriated. One chunk of entitlements that follow from or accompany ownership of the land, namely the right to develop the land, is severed from the whole and presented as an independent and separate property right, with the result that regulatory denial of that entitlement can be described as expropriation of property—it cannot be said that the landowner loses the land, but it is argued that she loses the right to develop the land. When the property is regarded as a whole that entitlement is just one strand or one stick in the bundle that makes up property; denial of the one stick could perhaps more readily be justified as a legitimate regulatory deprivation, whereas an expropriation of a whole independent right might be more difficult to justify. Separating individual strands or entitlements off from the bigger bundle is therefore a rhetorical strategy that makes it more difficult to justify specific regulatory limitations placed on the exercise or exploitation of property rights, particularly in land.

---

[32]The threshold does still apply, though, and not just any interest is included as property. It is generally accepted in German constitutional law that two principles restrict the liberal approach: only concrete rights and interests are protected and not general wealth; and only vested or acquired rights are protected and not expectancies. The latter requirement finds application, in some form or another, in most if not all foreign jurisdictions. See AJ van der Walt *Constitutional property clauses: A comparative analysis* (1999) at 153.

[33]For detail and examples see 3.7.2 below.

[34]This section is based upon and resembles sections of AJ van der Walt 'Overview of developments since the introduction of the constitutional property clause' (2004) 19 *SA Public Law* 46–89.

Margaret Jane Radin described the construction that underlies the expropriation argument in the example above as 'conceptual severance', a rhetorical practice by which claimants construct constitutional compensation claims for state interferences that destroy or take one aspect of their property holdings, while leaving the rest intact.[35] By relying on the Realist notion of property as a bundle of sticks and 'severing' the affected stick or aspect of the property holding (such as the right to develop the property into a holiday resort, or the right to enjoy the use of the property free from traffic noise) conceptually from the undisturbed rest, it becomes possible to argue that the affected stick was expropriated, thereby founding a compensation claim for what otherwise would be considered nothing more than a regulatory deprivation that would not easily support a compensation claim unless the affected part amounts to a substantial or essential chunk of the whole. Treating state action that interferes with just one aspect of property as expropriation of that aspect as a separate property interest subjects state action to potentially crippling compensation claims and accordingly the intellectual and rhetorical strategy of conceptual severance is regarded with well-founded skepticism by all but the most hardened libertarians.

During the drafting of the South African Constitution the restrictive potential of conceptual severance arguments caused concern in pro-reform circles, as it could be abused to frustrate almost any reform effort by the government by subjecting it to impossible compensation duties.[36] Although concerns in this regard have to be taken seriously, they have perhaps been overstated, since there are several reasons why the practice of conceptual severance should not feature large or at all in South African law. Firstly, this practice developed out of the context of American takings jurisprudence, which is not easily transplanted to South Africa because of the unique American understanding of takings. Secondly, even in the US (where the notion was developed) courts and commentators have so far mostly rejected conceptual severance arguments and it has found very limited application in fact.[37] Thirdly, the

---

[35] Margaret Jane Radin 'The liberal conception of property: Crosscurrents in the jurisprudence of takings' (1988) 88 *Col LR* 1667–1696. See further on Radin's work in this regard AJ van der Walt 'Subject and society in property theory—A review of property theories and debates in recent literature: Part II' 1995 *TSAR* 322–345.

[36] See M Chaskalson 'Stumbling towards section 28: Negotiations over the protection of property rights in the interim constitution' (1995) 11 *SAJHR* 222–240 at 234–236.

[37] See LS Underkuffler *The idea of property: Its meaning and power* (2003) at 22–24. The Supreme Court particularly rejected conceptual severance in its earlier decisions; compare *Andrus v Allard* 444 US 51 (1979); *Penn Central Transportation Co v City of New York* 438 US 104 (1978). In *Tahoe-Sierra Preservation Council, Inc v Tahoe Regional Planning Agency* 535 US 302 (2002) the US Supreme Court again showed its resistance against conceptual severance arguments, in this case by refusing to recognize a temporal ban on development as a taking. There are earlier decisions in which conceptual severance was perhaps accepted, although these decisions could be explained differently as well; compare *Hodel v Irving* 481 US 704 (1987); *First English Evangelical Lutheran Church v County of Los Angeles* 482 US 304 (1987), and see Frank I Michelman 'Takings, 1987' (1988) 88 *Col LR* 1600–1629 at 1617–1618. See further in this regard *Lucas v South Carolina Coastal Council* 505 US 1003 (1992) (deprivation of all economic use is a taking).

viability of conceptual severance arguments depends on acceptance of two theoretical concepts or constructions that do not fit easily and therefore might not be accepted in South African law, namely the notion of property as a bundle of rights[38] and the notion of regulatory taking or constructive expropriation.[39] In a nutshell, concern about the importation of conceptual severance arguments is justified and has to be taken seriously, but the greatest danger is that analysts or courts would not realize that they are arguing on the basis of conceptual severance logic. Once alerted to that possibility, the construction should be rejected more often than not.

Unfortunately the Constitutional Court has perhaps made it more difficult to avoid conceptual severance arguments. Theunis Roux pointed out that the *FNB* decision and methodology could support conceptual severance arguments:[40] in order to arrive at the stage where the court can apply its arbitrariness test, it first has to accept that the affected interest is indeed property for purposes of section 25. However, in the arbitrariness test the court is allowed to take cognizance of the fact that just one or a few incidents of ownership have been affected by the deprivation, which means that single-entitlement deprivations are considered as deprivations of property —which amounts to a version of conceptual severance. Stated differently, the property test is effectively 'telescoped' into the arbitrariness test; with the result that the court's taking cognizance of the effect of deprivations on separate incidents of ownership would reinforce rather than inhibit conceptual severance claims. This is a strong argument, and it means that conceptual severance logic can only be avoided in South African law to the extent that the court recognizes single-entitlement deprivations for what they are and refuse to treat them as deprivations of property. However, doing so would involve a slight but significant deviation from the methodology set out and followed in *FNB*.

---

[38] Acceptance of which is unlikely in Roman-Dutch law, which regards ownership as an abstract right that is more than the sum of its constituent entitlements: CG van der Merwe *Sakereg* (2nd ed 1989) at 175–176.

[39] Which means that courts could treat extraordinarily harsh or unfair regulatory limitation of property as constructive expropriation that requires compensation. Acceptance of this doctrine is possible but unlikely in South African law as matters stand now—see chapter 5.4, where it is explained that recognition of constructive expropriation is doubtful in view of the *FNB* decision. Conceptual severance relies on regulatory takings doctrine or (in South African terminology) recognition of constructive expropriation because it involves treating excessive regulatory action as expropriation.

[40] See T Roux 'Section 25' in S Woolman et al (eds) *Constitutional law of South Africa* (2nd ed 2003 original service Dec 2003) at 46–13 with reference to *First National Bank of SA Ltd t/a Wesbank v Commissioner, South African Revenue Service; First National Bank of SA Ltd t/a Wesbank v Minister of Finance* 2002 (4) SA 768 (CC) par [100](*f*) at 811C.

3.5 EFFECT OF THE *FNB* DECISION

As a result of the Constitutional Court decision in the *FNB* case[41] the meaning of
'property' in section 25 could play a smaller role in constitutional litigation than was
originally anticipated. The Court accepted that ownership of corporeal movables
(and land) must 'lie at the heart of our constitutional concept of property, both as
regards the nature of the right involved as well as the object of the right', but found
it 'practically impossible and judicially unwise' to attempt a comprehensive definition
of property.[42] However, the greatest effect of the decision on the meaning of the
property concept could be a result of the methodology followed by the Court and
the 'vortex' effect of that methodology as it was described by Theunis Roux.[43]

The methodology followed by the Court means that practically all attention in a
constitutional property challenge is focused on the arbitrariness test in the sense that
the balancing at the heart of all such challenges takes place with regard to arbitrariness
rather than any other issue, including the property issue.[44] Accordingly, the question
whether the affected interest is property is glossed over or even ignored altogether,
except in so far as it is relevant to the arbitrariness test.[45] However, as Roux correctly
points out,[46] by the time that the arbitrariness test is applied the court must already
have assumed that the affected interest was property, and consideration of the nature
of the property interest is not part of a property analysis as such. This could mean that

---

[41] *First National Bank of SA Ltd t/a Wesbank v Commissioner, South African Revenue Service; First
National Bank of SA Ltd t/a Wesbank v Minister of Finance* 2002 (4) SA 768 (CC) par [57] at 796F–
H. See further T Roux 'Section 25' in S Woolman et al (eds) *Constitutional law of South Africa* (2nd
ed 2003 original service Dec 2003) 46-2–46-5, 46-9–46-11, 46-23–46-25; AJ van der Walt 'Striving
for the better interpretation—A critical reflection on the Constitutional Court's *Harksen* and *FNB*
decisions on the property clause' (2005) 123 *SALJ* 854–878 at 872–874.

[42] *First National Bank of SA Ltd t/a Wesbank v Commissioner, South African Revenue Service; First
National Bank of SA Ltd t/a Wesbank v Minister of Finance* 2002 (4) SA 768 (CC) par [51] at 794E–F.

[43] See T Roux 'Section 25' in S Woolman et al (eds) *Constitutional law of South Africa* (2nd ed 2003
original service Dec 2003) 46-2–46-5, 46-9–46-11, 46-23–46-25.

[44] T Roux 'Section 25' in S Woolman et al (eds) *Constitutional law of South Africa* (2nd ed 2003
original service Dec 2003) 46 3 explains that balancing could also take place with regard to several
other issues: (*a*) Does that which is taken away from the complainant amount to property? (*b*) Has
there been a deprivation of that property by the state? (*c*) Is that deprivation consistent with the
requirements in section 25(1)? (*d*) If not, is the deprivation justified under section 36(1)? (*e*) If it
is, does it amount to expropriation? (*f*) If it does, does the expropriation comply with section 25(2)
and 25(3)? (*g*) If not, is the expropriation justified by section 36(1)? The arbitrariness test in *FNB*
results in all focus being placed on just one requirement in issue (*c*). Compare the discussion of the
arbitrariness test in chapter 4.5.

[45] According to the *FNB* test it is relevant to determine whether corporeal property or a right is
affected, whether ownership or a lesser right is affected, and whether just one or all entitlements
of ownership are affected. See *First National Bank of SA Ltd t/a Wesbank v Commissioner, South
African Revenue Service; First National Bank of SA Ltd t/a Wesbank v Minister of Finance* 2002 (4) SA
768 (CC) par [100](*d*), (*e*) and (*f*) at 811A–D.

[46] T Roux 'Section 25' in S Woolman et al (eds) *Constitutional law of South Africa* (2nd ed 2003
original service Dec 2003) 46–13.

the question whether the affected property is property will receive less attention than it deserves as a threshold consideration, or even that it will receive no attention at all.

Despite the force of Roux's analysis of the 'vortex' effect of the *FNB* arbitrariness test it remains possible that the Constitutional Court (or another court) will in future depart from the seemingly strict logic of the *FNB* methodology and apply some sort of threshold property test. In the significant constitutional challenges to date[47] the claimant was always clearly owner of property, and therefore it was not necessary for the courts to indulge in threshold property analysis to date; perhaps they will focus on property analysis as and when the need arises. The exception that might prove the rule of glossing over the property issue for pragmatic reasons is *Lebowa Mineral Trust Beneficiaries Forum v President of the Republic of South Africa*.[48] In this case the Transvaal High Court argued that mineral rights are not fundamental rights or property that is protected by section 25, because 'if the drafters of the Constitution intended to protect mineral rights, they would have done so expressly as in other jurisdictions'.[49] Although the decision was arguably wrong in making that assumption, the decision does indicate that the courts will perhaps consider the property issue more carefully when it is not clear that the interest in question is property for purposes of the Constitution. This could be the case either because the object of the right is problematic —in *Lebowa Mineral Trust* the object was mineral rights—but probably especially when the right in question is not ownership of tangible property.

3.6 PROPERTY AS A CONSTITUTIONAL RIGHT

Many of the problems posed by the property concept in the constitutional context result from obvious inconsistencies between the characteristics of property in private law on the one hand and the nature and function of the Constitution and the Bill of Rights on the other. In the South African context the Constitution and the Bill of Rights commit the state to a process of transformation that is difficult to reconcile with a libertarian entrenchment of existing property holdings, but even in the normal cause of events constitutional property involves recognition of restrictive state powers

---

[47] Particularly *First National Bank of SA Ltd t/a Wesbank v Commissioner, South African Revenue Service; First National Bank of SA Ltd t/a Wesbank v Minister of Finance* 2002 (4) SA 768 (CC), but also *Harksen v Lane NO* 1998 (1) SA 300 (CC); *Phoebus Apollo Aviation CC v Minister of Safety and Security* 2003 (2) SA 34 (CC); *Mkontwana v Nelson Mandela Metropolitan Municipality; Bissett and Others v Buffalo City Municipality; Transfer Rights Action Campaign and Others v Member of the Executive Council for Local Government and Housing, Gauteng and Others* 2005 (1) SA 530 (CC); see further the Supreme Court of Appeal and High Court decisions in *Du Toit v Minister of Transport* 2003 (1) SA 586 (C); *Minister of Transport v Du Toit* 2005 (1) SA 16 (SCA); *Nyangane v Stadsraad van Potchefstroom* 1998 (2) BCLR 148 (T); *Steinberg v South Peninsula Municipality* 2001 (4) SA 1243 (SCA).

[48] 2002 (1) BCLR 23 (T). The decision is discussed more fully in 3.7.2 below.

[49] *Lebowa Mineral Trust Beneficiaries Forum v President of the Republic of South Africa* 2002 (1) BCLR 23 (T) at 29G–H. See in this regard AJ van der Walt 'Resisting orthodoxy—again: Thoughts on the development of post-apartheid South African law' (2002) 17 *SA Public Law* 258–279. Compare the discussion in 3.7.2 below.

that conflict with absolute protection of private property. To overcome this difficulty commentators and courts have pointed out that constitutional property is related to but not identical with property in private law—in the constitutional sphere, property is specifically a constitutional right.

Emphasizing that property is a constitutional right places a specific spin on the constitutional protection of property: for purposes of the constitutional property clause property is not a pre-social, natural right but a social construct that is subject to public interest amendment and regulation. This indicates that both the protection of property interests and the legitimacy of state interferences with property must be understood—and weighed against each other—with reference to constitutional principles, goals and values. According to the German approach a property right can be restricted according to its proximity to the individual and the social interests involved: the closer the right is to the individual personality and liberty of the person, the smaller the range of acceptable limitations; the further the right is removed from the individual and the closer it comes to the social interest, the greater the range of possibly legitimate limitations.[50] Both the typically private-law characteristics of property, namely absoluteness (being unlimited in principle) and exclusivity, are undermined in the constitutional perspective by subjecting property interests to balancing and therefore constitutional property is never absolute; it is just as unlimited and just as exclusive as the law allows it to be, depending on the proper balance between individual and public interests in that property.

The German Federal Constitutional Court established a typically constitutional interpretation of the term *Eigentum* which is different from the traditional private-law meaning of this term, both in its meaning of the objects of property rights (*property* as opposed to *things*) and in its meaning of property rights (*property* as opposed to *ownership*). The constitutional meaning of the term *Eigentum* as property was developed by interpreting it according to the constitutional question whether the inclusion of a specific object or right of property under the protection of article 14 GG would serve the constitutional purpose of creating and protecting a sphere of personal freedom where the individual is enabled to (and expected to take responsibility for the effort to) realize and promote the development of her own life and personality, within the social context. This interpretation moved away from the typically private-law view that property rights are basically absolute and exclusive, and subjected the freedom of a property holder to typically constitutional restrictions.

---

[50]See DG Kleyn 'The constitutional protection of property: A comparison between the German and the South African approach' (1996) 11 *SA Public Law* 402–445 at 425–426, and compare the German examples in *BVerfGE* 21, 73 [1967] (*Grundstücksverkehrsgesetz*) (limitation on ownership of forest land); *BVerfGE* 24, 367 [1968] (*Deichordnung*) (limitation on use and expropriation of dyke land in flood area); *BVerfGE* 42, 263 [1976] (*Contergan*) (state transforms private-law settlement claims into public-law claims to protect public interest); *BVerfGE* 52, 1 [1979] (*Kleingarten*) and *BVerfGE* 87, 114 [1992] (*Kleingarten*) (limitations on rent levels and sale of allotment gardens, with good examples of how perceptions of acceptable limitations change according to economic and social context). Compare the rent-control cases referred to in footnote 114 below for similar examples.

In Anglo-American law it is also recognized that constitutional property is not absolute.[51] Although American case law places heavy emphasis on the physical integrity and exclusivity of property,[52] post-realist American law (which is largely reflected in constitutional property case law) has expanded the property concept in such a way that it focuses on property relations rather than on the objects of property, thereby inevitably making the tension between individual property interests and the public interest part of the property concept.[53] The result is that constitutional property cannot really be regarded as a fundamentally unlimited or absolute right. Frank Michelman provides the theoretical framework within which property is explained as a constitutional right,[54] arguing that some of the property rights vindicated or

---

[51] See *Government of Malaysia and Another v Selangor Pilot Association* (1977) 1 MLJ 133 (Malaysia); *Manitoba Fisheries Ltd v The Queen* (1978) 88 DLR 3d 462; *R v Oakes* (1986) 26 DLR 4th 200 (Canada); *Trade Practices Commission and Another v Tooth & Co Ltd and Another* (1979) 142 CLR 397; *The Commonwealth of Australia and Another v The State of Tasmania and Others* (1983) 158 CLR 1 (Australia); *Central Dublin Association and Others v Attorney General* [1975] 109 ILTR 69; *Dreher v Irish Land Commission and Others* [1984] ILRM 94; *Electricity Supply Board v Gormley* [1985] IR 129 (Ireland); *State of Madras v VG Row* 1952 SCJ 253 (India); *Davies and Others v Minister of Land, Agriculture and Water Development* 1997 (1) SA 228 (ZSC) (Zimbabwe); *Village of Euclid v Amber Realty Co* 272 US 365 (1926); *Penn Central Transportation Co v New York City* 438 US 104 (1978); *Keystone Bituminous Coal Association v DeBenedictis* 480 US 470 (1978) (US).
[52] See *Kaiser Aetna v United States* 444 US 164 (1979); *Loretto v Teleprompter Manhattan CATV Corp* 458 US 419 (1982); *Nollan v California Coastal Commission* 483 US 825 (1987).
[53] LS Underkuffler-Freund 'Takings and the nature of property' (1996) 9 *Can J Law & Jur* 161–205, especially 167–168 suggested an explanation in terms of her comparison between the 'Apparent' and 'Operative' models of property. The 'Apparent' model holds that property as individual rights, seen in the 'normal' or 'common-sense' perspective of the person in the street, are protected against state power. This model is static and focuses on the protection of the *status quo*. The 'Operative' model holds that property describes or embodies the tension between the individual and the collective. This model is dynamic and focuses on necessary social change. According to Underkuffler-Freund's perspective, none of these models can provide sufficient answers to the takings problem on its own. Important differences between the 'Apparent' and 'Operative' models (including the fact that all property is not protected with equal stringency in the 'Operative' model, while it is in the 'Apparent' model; and that the content and protection of property can be subject to changes in the 'Operative' model, while it is not in the 'Apparent' model) can be explained by Underkuffler-Freund's theory in terms of the fact that questions relating to the tension between the individual and the collective are external to the 'Apparent' property concept, but inherent to the 'Operative' property concept (at 187, 191ff). The 'Apparent' model, which corresponds roughly to the statist, private-law perspective on property, does not take any notice of the public interest or questions of social necessity; the 'Operative' model, which corresponds roughly with the dynamic, constitutional perspective of property encountered in German case law, reflects these issues as a matter of course. For a further development of this model see LS Underkuffler *The idea of property: Its meaning and power* (2003) 37ff.
[54] See FI Michelman 'Property as a constitutional right' (1981) 38 *Wash & Lee LR* 1097–1114, especially at 1099, 1104–1105, 1110, 1114; compare FI Michelman 'Possession vs. distribution in the constitutional idea of property' (1987) 72 *Iowa LR* 1319–1350. I am indebted to Frank Michelman for extensive debates and exchange of ideas on this topic.

protected by the US Supreme Court[55] were not derived from 'the standing law', but were 'directly rooted in the Constitution' itself—these are direct (as opposed to derivative) or constitutional property rights.

Whereas the German courts were forced by their Basic Law and by socio-economic realities to formulate and work with an explicitly constitutional guideline in answering these questions,[56] Anglo-American courts often worked on the assumption that the property concept is clear and unambiguous, and that differences between the private-law and public-law content of this concept are irrelevant or non-existent.[57] In most cases the result is comparable to the position in German law, but in some instances this has resulted in a situation where the implicit and often unspoken historical, philosophical and political baggage of the property concept, which even in the Anglo-American common-law tradition is often of a purely private-law character, was imported into constitutional law uncritically.[58] This is clear in constitutional cases where a typically private-law view, in terms of which either the physical integrity or the exclusivity of property rights was described as the most important or central aspect of property rights, was accepted in constitutional analysis without criticism or reflection, either generally[59] or specifically in public-accommo-

---

[55] He refers specifically to *Kaiser Aetna v United States* 444 US 164 (1979) and *Pennsylvania Coal Co v Mahon* 260 US 393 (1922).

[56] The reason is that German courts realized that, given the social reality of post-World War II housing shortages and the strong social responsibility focus in the Basic Law, they cannot simply apply the restricted property concept of private law in the constitutional context, so that they were forced to create an overtly constitutional property concept.

[57] Here, the need to develop a specifically constitutional property concept is much weaker, because of the strong perception that the private-law concept of property is so wide and flexible anyway. As is pointed out in the course of the analysis, this perception is not always accurate, and typically private-law elements of the property concept have crept into constitutional discourse as a result.

[58] See K Gray 'Property in thin air' (1991) 50 *Cambridge LJ* 252–307, and compare G Peller 'The metaphysics of American law' (1985) 73 *Cal LR* 1151–1290 at 1160ff, 1175ff, 1193ff. Compare G Minda *Postmodern legal movements: Law and jurisprudence at century's end* (1995) 13ff, 24ff; GS Alexander 'The concept of property in private and constitutional law: The ideology of the scientific turn in legal analysis' (1982) 82 *Col LR* 1545–1599, especially at 1560ff. See further GS Alexander *Commodity and propriety—Competing visions of property in American legal thought 1776–1970* (1997) 72ff, 277ff, 311ff; JW Singer *Entitlement: The paradoxes of property* (2000) 95ff.

[59] Such as *Loretto v Teleprompter Manhattan CATV Corp* 458 US 419 (1982) at 435 per Marshall J for the Court (physical invasion); *Kaiser Aetna v United States* 444 US 164 (1979) at 180 per Rehnquist J for the Court; *Nollan v California Coastal Commission* 483 US 825 (1987) (right to exclude). Compare K Gray 'Property in thin air' (1991) 50 *Cambridge LJ* 252–307 with reference to different aspects of exclusivity. The US Supreme Court used to rely on the so-called positivist approach in property cases, accepting that the existence of a property interest relied on an outside (non-constitutional) source such as (inter alia) state (private) law: *Board of Regents v Roth* 408 US 564 at 577 (1972); *Phillips v Washington Legal Foundation* 524 US 156 (1999). However, in *Phillips v Washington Legal Foundation* 524 US 156 (1999) and *Palazzolo v Rhode Island* 533 US 606 (2001) there are signs that the US Supreme Court could be moving away from the positivist approach and that constitutional law might have a bigger influence on what is regarded as property than was thought before. See footnote 66 below.

dations cases.[60] The result is that the private interests of property holders can easily be overemphasized vis-à-vis the public interest, resulting in some questionable or puzzling decisions.

However, despite these aberrations and confusing exceptions, the general effect of the developments set out above is that the content and scope of property in civil-law jurisdictions came closer to the property concept of Anglo-American jurisdictions, so that this concept is rendered relatively independent of the exact terminology used to describe it. In effect, whether the term used is *property, ownership* or *possession*, the outcome is roughly the same: the objects included in the constitutional guarantee are not restricted to corporeal things; the rights included in the constitutional guarantee are not restricted to or dominated by ownership; and it is assumed that property rights can be limited by or in accordance with the provisions of the property clause or the bill of rights. Instances where the limitation of property rights (and particularly limitations of the absolute right of disposal, physical integrity and exclusivity of ownership) still creates problems are often the result of the unwitting importation of the private-law tradition of absoluteness and exclusivity into the constitutional sphere.

Describing property as a constitutional right implies at least two vital differences from the protection of property in private law (or property as a private-law right). Firstly, as a constitutional right property is not protected in the sense that every entitlement that is recognised or protected by private law is guaranteed against or insulated from state interference, even if that entitlement has been exercised lawfully before. Existing entitlements can be changed, restricted, and subjected to new or stricter controls, limitations and levies without compensation, if the change is justified by the public interest (the police power). The best formulation of the principle is that, when faced with the inevitable social need to regulate the use of property by legislation, the legislature is not restricted to two alternatives (leaving existing rights intact or expropriating them against compensation)—the state can subject existing uses to the controls and regulations required by the police power.

Secondly, as a constitutional right property interests that are not recognised or protected by private law can be acknowledged and protected under the property clause if that protection is justified by the constitutional function of the property clause and the public interest. This principle is illustrated by several foreign cases that are mentioned in this chapter below, and it opens up the possibility to argue that the property clause itself forms the basis of land reform.

In accordance with these two principles property, for purposes of section 25, can be described as a constitutional right, which is fundamentally different from property as a private-law right. The differences are not restricted to the concept of property or to the range of property interests that can be included under the property clause in the

---

[60]See JW Singer 'No right to exclude: Public accommodations and private property' (1996) 90 *Northwestern Univ LR* 1283–1497; especially 1352ff and references to case law there; see further *PruneYard Shopping Center v Robins* 447 US 74 (1980). See K Gray 'Property in thin air' (1991) 50 *Cambridge LJ* 252–307.

Constitution, but extend to the kind of protection that each right can get and, most importantly, the reasons why and the considerations in terms of which the protection is afforded in any individual case. Constitutional protection can only be obtained and should only be given on the basis of the Constitution itself, taking into account the fundamental purpose of the Constitution and of the Bill of Rights in general and of the property clause in particular. This means that the protection of the property clause must always function in the broader framework of establishing and maintaining a just and equitable balance between the protection of existing property rights and the protection of the public interest in regulating the use of property (including land reform as a tool of transformation of the property system). Rights can only be protected in so far and in such a way as is indicated by this balance, and by the values of an open and democratic society based on human dignity, the promotion of equality and freedom. Property as a constitutional right can never be protected or limited unless the protection or limitation in question is justifiable and reasonable in view of these values. In this perspective, the protection of property as a fundamental right can neither threaten existing rights nor entrench them unreasonably and unfairly, and consequently it should not impede but rather promote and encourage land reform.

The implications of this analysis for South African law can be summarized as follows:

*   Insofar as South African private law forms part of the Roman-Germanic tradition, and therefore subscribes to the traditional, private-law interpretation of property, the constitutional meaning of property in section 25 will differ from the private-law meaning.[61]
*   The difference between the traditional private-law meaning and the constitutional meaning of property implies that the objects of property rights in section 25 are not restricted to corporeal things; that the property rights in section 25 are not restricted to ownership; and that the property rights in section 25 are not absolute or exclusive, because they can be and are inherently limited by or in accordance with the property clause and the Bill of Rights.
*   For purposes of section 25 'property' can therefore relate to a wide range of objects both corporeal and incorporeal, a wide range of traditional property rights and interests both real and personal, and a wide range of other rights and interests which (in the civil-law tradition) have never been considered in terms of property before.

---

[61] This is particularly relevant for the Afrikaans text of section 25, which refers to 'eiendom' for 'property'. The Afrikaans 'eiendom' is typically Germanic in the sense that it can refer to either the object of property rights or to the right itself in the sense of ownership. The fact that the English 'property' is a foreign term as far as property law is concerned makes it much easier to accept and understand 'property' in section 25 as a wider, constitutional concept that is distinguished from the narrower, private-law 'ownership' or 'things'. For this purpose the Afrikaans 'eiendom' in section 25 is much more confusing, and actually the phrase 'regte in eiendom' (rights in property) in section 28 of the interim Constitution of 1993 was much clearer. See in this regard AJ van der Walt 'Towards a theory of rights in property: Exploratory observations on the paradigm of post-apartheid property law' (1995) 10 *SA Public Law* 298–345.

- This implies that the change from 'rights in property' in section 28 of the interim Constitution to 'property' in the 1996 Constitution should make no difference to the meaning and scope of the property guarantee in principle.

- The exact range of objects and rights that can or should be included under the property clause might be determined, in every individual case, with reference to a general principle or guideline for the interpretation of the whole Bill of Rights, such as the promotion of the values that underlie an open and democratic society based on human dignity, the achievement of equality and freedom or the just and equitable balance that has to be struck between the protection of private interests and the promotion of the public interest.

3.7 OBJECTS OF PROPERTY RIGHTS

3.7.1 Corporeal objects

South African private law shares in the Roman-Germanic tradition, in which the objects of property rights are generally limited to corporeal things.[62] German law, which also shares in this private law tradition, has developed extensive case law and academic writing on constitutional property and is therefore the obvious comparative example to consider.[63] The German civil code (*Bürgerliches Gesetzbuch—BGB*) explicitly restricts property (referred to as 'ownership' or *Eigentum*) to corporeal

---

[62] For this reason Property Law as a field of study is often referred to in the Roman-Germanic (and South African) private law tradition as the Law of Things. Two significant examples from private law textbooks are HJ Erasmus, CG van der Merwe & AH van Wyk *Lee and Honore: Family, things and succession* (2nd ed 1983); CG van der Merwe *The law of things* in WA Joubert *The law of South Africa* vol 27 (published separately as *The law of things* in 1987). CG van der Merwe *Sakereg* (2nd ed 1989)—the most authoritative Afrikaans-language textbook on private law property—has never been translated, but if it were it would probably have been published as *The law of things*. The equally authoritative English-language H Silberberg *The law of property* (1975; now in its 4th ed 2003 by PJ Badenhorst, JM Pienaar & H Mostert) exemplifies a different approach. See footnote 64 below.

[63] Although Dutch private law is also closely related to South African private law for historical reasons, Dutch law is less interesting for constitutional purposes than German law because the property provision in the Dutch Constitution is not entrenched. With reference to private law it is interesting that the Dutch civil code recently moved away from its earlier narrow focus on the law of things (*zakenrecht*) to the wider law of property (*goederenrecht*). However, the shift is more apparent than real; Book 5 of the new civil code is still focused on rights in corporeal things, and this is merely complemented by the wider patrimonial focus in Book 3. (Although Book 3 deals with legal relationships involving wider patrimonial rights, in other words involving both corporeal and incorporeal objects, the definition of things is included in Book 3 with other definitions.) This brings the Dutch private law in line with the German situation. See HJ Snijders & EB Rank-Berenschot *Goederenrecht* (1994) 8–12, 136–137. Compare footnote 64 below.

things.[64] The German Basic Law (*Grundgesetz*—*GG*) also refers to 'ownership' or *Eigentum*,[65] but unlike the civil code it does not define the objects of property. The German Federal Constitutional Court decided that it would be unacceptable to restrict the objects of constitutional property in terms of article 14 GG to corporeals. A wider constitutional property concept was therefore developed by the Court, based on but distinct from the narrower, private-law concept. Although the private-law concept of property as things is the starting point, for purposes of article 14 the meaning and content of the term have been determined with reference to the Basic Law and not purely according to private law.[66] Consequently, a wider interpretation is attached to the objects of property rights in constitutional law than in private law and in effect the term *Eigentum* (as referring to the objects of property rights) is interpreted as 'things' for purposes of private law and as 'property' for purposes of constitutional law. Apart from corporeal things, a range of incorporeal objects, rights and interests are regarded as property for purposes of the property clause. A similar result

---

[64]In German private law the objects of property interests are defined in terms of 'things', which are restricted to corporeals by § 90 of the civil code *(BGB)* of 1900: 'Sachen im Sinne des Gesetzes sind nur körperliche Gegenstände' (things in terms of the law are restricted to corporeal objects). The same applies to the definition of 'things' in Book 3 article 2 of the new Dutch civil code (*Nieuw Burgerlijk Wetboek*—*NBW*) of 1992: 'Zaken zijn de voor menselijke beheersing vatbare stoffelijke objecten' (things are corporeal objects that are susceptible to human control). The South African law of property was also traditionally restrictively interpreted as the law of things, but recently this approach has been criticized and some authors work with a wider concept of property: see DG Kleyn & A Boraine *Silberberg & Schoeman: The law of property* (3rd ed 1992) 9ff; PJ Badenhorst, JM Pienaar & H Mostert *Silberberg & Schoeman's The law of property* (4th ed 2003) 2, 4ff; AJ van der Walt & GJ Pienaar *Introduction to the law of property* (4th ed 2002) chapter 2. Compare *Cooper v Boyes NO and Another* 1994 (4) SA 521 (C) (shares are incorporeal movable property over which a usufruct can be established), where Van Zyl J undermines the historical argument for a restricted concept in common law. It is uncertain whether these recent developments discredit the traditional view that property was in principle restricted to corporeals in common law. Compare footnotes 62 and 63 above.

[65]Both § 903 of the German civil code (*Bürgerliches Gesetzbuch*—*BGB*) and article 14 of the German Constitution or *Basic Law* (*Grundgesetz*—*GG*) refer to *Eigentum*, the correct technical translation of which is 'ownership' rather than 'property'. However, as is pointed out below, this term is interpreted as 'property' for purposes of the constitutional text.

[66]See *BVerfGE* 58, 300 [1981] (*Naßauskiesung*) at 335. Compare AJ van der Walt *Constitutional property clauses: A comparative analysis* (1999) 151–153; DG Kleyn 'The constitutional protection of property: A comparison between the German and the South African approach' (1996) 11 *SA Public Law* 402–445 at 419ff. Although the so-called positivist approach of the US Supreme Court meant that it used to defer to sources outside the Constitution on the identification of property interests, there are signs that the Court may be moving away from this approach and recognizing that the Constitution plays a role in identifying property interests; see footnote 59 above.

was reached, at least partly under the influence of German law, with regard to the term *Eigentum* in the Austrian[67] and Swiss[68] constitutions.

These developments in the Roman-Germanic legal tradition are also echoed by the interpretation of the property concept in the European Convention on Human Rights 1950.[69] Article 1 of the First Protocol to the Convention does not refer to either property or ownership—it provides that every natural or legal person is entitled to the 'peaceful enjoyment of their possessions', and that they shall not be deprived of the peaceful enjoyment of their possessions except as provided for in article 1.[70] Despite the differences in phraseology and terminology,[71] the phrase 'peaceful enjoyment of their possessions' in article 1 has been interpreted by the European Commission of Human Rights and the European Court of Human Rights as if

[67] The property clause appears in article 5 of the Austrian Bill of Rights, which is the Constitution of 21 December 1867, incorporated in terms of section 149(1) of the Federal Constitution of Austria 1929. See *VfSlg 8212/1977*; *VfSlg 9911/1983*; *VfSlg 9913/1984*; *VfSlg 12227/1989*; and compare AJ van der Walt *Constitutional property clauses: A comparative analysis* (1999) 82.

[68] Article 22*ter*, which contains the property clause, was inserted in the Swiss Constitution by an amendment of 1969, and was replaced by article 26 of the new Constitution of the Swiss Confederacy on 1 January 2000. See *BGE* 106 Ia 163 [1980] (*Graf*) on the old clause and compare AJ van der Walt *Constitutional property clauses: A comparative analysis* (1999) 373–375. See AJ van der Walt 'The property clause in the new federal Constitution of the Swiss Confederation 1999' (2004) 15 *Stell LR* 326–332; KA Valender 'Art. 26' in B Ehrenzeller, P Mastronardi, RJ Schweizer, & KA Vallender (eds) *Die Schweizerische Bundesverfassung—Kommentar* (St Gallen Kommentar) (2002) 328–352 at 333–336 on the new clause.

[69] European jurisdictions (like Germany, the UK, Ireland and Austria) that are interesting for comparative purposes are signatories to and therefore bound by this part of international law, and therefore it makes sense to see their domestic case law against the background of the Convention. Very often the case law on the Convention itself is indicative of general trends in European law. See AJ van der Walt *Constitutional property clauses: A comparative analysis* (1999) 96–97.

[70] See AJ van der Walt *Constitutional property clauses: A comparative analysis* (1999) 116–118; W Peukert 'Protection of ownership under article 1 of the First Protocol to the European Convention on Human Rights' (1981) 2 *Human Rights LJ* 37–78 for a discussion of article 1 and the case law dealing with it. Compare JA Frowein & W Peukert *Europäische MenschenRechtsKonvention—EMRK Kommentar* (1985) sv article 1; DJ Harris, M O'Boyle & C Warbrick *Law of the European Convention on Human Rights* (2nd ed 1995) 517ff; E Schwelb 'The protection of the right of property of nationals under the First Protocol to the European Convention on Human Rights' (1964) 13 *Am J Comp L* 518–541.

[71] The differences between ownership, possession and property are of the utmost importance in the Roman-Germanic private-law tradition, including South African law. In his influential medieval definition of *dominium*, which is still at the heart of the modern civil-law definition of ownership, Bartolus de Saxoferrato relied on the difference between *dominium* and *possessio* to define ownership in contrast with possession. See Bartolus' commentary on D 41.2.17.1 n 4, and compare AJ van der Walt 'Bartolus se omskrywing van *dominium* en die interpretasies daarvan sedert die vyftiende eeu' (1986) 49 *THRHR* 305–321; AJ van der Walt 'Marginal notes on powerful(*l*) legends: Critical perspectives on property theory' (1995) 58 *THRHR* 396–420; AJ van der Walt 'Der Eigentumsbegriff' in R Feenstra & R Zimmermann (eds) *Das römisch-holländische Recht: Fortschritte des Zivilrechts im 17. und 18. Jahrhundert* (1992) 485–520.

it were exactly the same as 'property'.[72] As far as it refers to the object of property, this property concept is interpreted widely to include corporeal things as well as a range of incorporeals and vested rights.[73]

The South African Constitutional Court confirmed that land and movable corporeals must be property for purposes of the property clause, but has not yet found it necessary to decide whether 'property' in section 25 of the Constitution is restricted to corporeals. In the *First Certification Case* judgment it confirmed that 'no universally recognised formulation of the right to property exists' and that it was unnecessary to decide whether section 28 of the 1993 Constitution was invalid for not explicitly including intellectual property.[74] In the *FNB* decision the Constitutional Court accepted that ownership of corporeal movables (and land) must 'lie at the heart of our constitutional concept of property, both as regards the nature of the right involved as well as the object of the right',[75] but besides referring to the *First Certification Case* dictum and the fact that property is not restricted to land for purposes of section 25[76] the Court found it 'practically impossible and judicially unwise' to attempt a comprehensive definition of property. However, most commentators assume that the property concept will be interpreted widely for constitutional purposes and that it will include but extend well beyond corporeal objects.[77]

---

[72] See the *Handyside* case [1976] ECHR Series A volume 24; the *Marckx* case [1979] ECHR Series A vol 31; compare AJ van der Walt *Constitutional property clauses: A comparative analysis* (1999) 116–118; W Peukert 'Protection of ownership under article 1 of the First Protocol to the European Convention on Human Rights' (1981) 2 *Human Rights LJ* 37–78 at 42; DJ Harris, M O'Boyle & C Warbrick *Law of the European Convention on Human Rights* (2nd ed 1995) 517 (the latter explains the role of the French text of article 1). For decisions in which incorporeals or vested rights were acknowledged see *Pine Valley Developments Limited and Others v Ireland* [1991] 14 EHRR 319; the *Tre Traktörer AB* case [1989] ECHR Series A vol 159.

[73] See *X v Sweden* [1974] 2 DR 123 (not an academic's possible earnings from future research); the *Marckx* case [1979] ECHR Series A vol 31 (not an unborn child's possible right to a legacy); *De Napoles Pacheco v Belgium* [1977] 15 DR 143 (not a conditional claim if the condition has not been realized yet); *A & B Company v Federal Republic of Germany* [1978] 14 DR 146 (a debt is property if the applicant can prove the claim); *Pine Valley Developments Limited and Others v Ireland* [1991] 14 EHHR 319 (an established development right is property); the *Tre Traktörer AB* case [1989] ECHR Series A vol 159 (an economic interest in a restaurant business, including a liquor licence, is property). Compare AJ van der Walt *Constitutional property clauses: A comparative analysis* (1999) 116–118.

[74] *Ex Parte Chairperson of the Constitutional Assembly: In re Certification of the Constitution of the Republic of South Africa, 1996* 1996 (4) SA 744 (CC) par [72] at 798 E–F.

[75] *First National Bank of SA Ltd t/a Wesbank v Commissioner, South African Revenue Service; First National Bank of SA Ltd t/a Wesbank v Minister of Finance* 2002 (4) SA 768 (CC) par [51] at 794E–F.

[76] As stated in section 25(4).

[77] See AJ van der Walt *Constitutional property clauses: A comparative analysis* (1999) 351–353; T Roux 'Section 25' in S Woolman et al (eds) *Constitutional law of South Africa* (2nd ed 2003 original service Dec 2003) 46-15–46-17. Roux offers three reasons for his view: (*a*) a blanket exclusion of incorporeal property from the protection of section 25 would be a very crude way of balancing competing private and public property interests; (*b*) the overwhelming preponderance of foreign law favours a wider interpretation; and (*c*) the second reason given in *FNB* for extending the protection of section 25 to juristic persons, namely the role they play in economic growth and the consolidation of democracy, applies equally well to the protection of incorporeal property.

3.7.2 Incorporeal property: General

In legal systems based on the Roman-Germanic private law tradition the central question is whether constitutional property includes rights and interests in incorporeal or intangible assets. Private and public law are not distinguished so strictly and the property concept has always been wider in Anglo-American jurisdictions than in Roman-Germanic law, with the result that the inclusion of incorporeal objects is basically a typically Roman-Germanic issue. Besides, post-realist American takings jurisprudence is not focused strongly on conceptual analysis of the property concept, although the meaning of 'property' did enjoy some attention in 20th century US constitutional jurisprudence, which confirms that certain intangibles are property for purposes of the constitutional property clause.[78] The general tendency since the early decades of the 20th century has been, in keeping with post-realist jurisprudence, to see all property in terms of rights as relationships and not in terms of objects, even if the right in fact relates to some property object. Property is, therefore, described in terms of a number of theories which all attempt to grasp the definitive concept of rights as relationships,[79] and not in terms of a classification of objects of property. It is perhaps possible to argue that the emphasis that is sometimes placed on exclusivity as the core or essential stick in the bundle of property rights[80] indicates that even the post-realist US property concept is still haunted by the ghost of an older, more thing-oriented view of property, but in case law and literature the objects of property play a distinctly minor role. It is therefore unsurprising that a wide range of objects are regarded as property in American and Commonwealth constitutional law, including some

---

[78]See *Hadacheck v Sebastian* 239 US 394 (1915), and compare *Bell v Burson* 402 US 535 (1970); *Perry v Sindermann* 408 US 593 (1971); *Board of Regents v Roth* 408 US 564 (1971). However, not any interest is recognised as property. The US Supreme Court has held that the following interests are not constitutional property: general financial interests rather than identifiable assets: *Eastern Enterprises v Apfel* 524 US 498 (1998); contingent future interests such as prospective clients for a business: *College Savings Bank v Florida Prepaid Secondary Educational Expense Board* 527 US 666 at 672 (1999); benefits that derive directly from the government, such as future social security payments described as 'mere expectancies': *Flemming v Nestor* 363 US 603 at 608 (1960). For an analysis and more examples compare LS Underkuffler-Freund 'Takings and the nature of property' (1996) 9 *Can J Law & Jur* 161–205 at 169ff; Underkuffler *The idea of property: Its meaning and power* (2003) 11–15. See further AJ van der Walt *Constitutional property clauses: A comparative analysis* (1999) 441. See further footnotes 90–92 below and accompanying text.

[79]Examples are theories that focus on the concept of property as a bundle of rights, on the ordinary meaning of property, or on the content of property in terms of reasonable, investment-backed or historical expectations; see LS Underkuffler-Freund 'Takings and the nature of property' (1996) 9 *Can J Law & Jur* 161–205 at 169ff for a summary and references to case law and literature, and see further L Underkuffler *The idea of property: Its meaning and power* (2003) 11–15.

[80]See cases like *Loretto v Teleprompter Manhattan CATV Corp* 458 US 419 (1982); *Kaiser Aetna v United States* 444 US 164 (1970).

personal or creditor's rights, intellectual property interests, other commercial interests[81] and certain social or welfare interests.[82]

As was pointed out in 3.7.1 above, the tendency in German-language jurisdictions
is similar—for constitutional purposes, *Eigentum* is interpreted widely as property
rather than narrowly as corporeal things. Consequently, a range of incorporeal interests are recognized as objects of property for purposes of the property clause: copy-

---

[81]See T Allen *The right to property in Commonwealth constitutions* (2000) 119–161; T Allen
'Commonwealth constitutions and the right not to be deprived of property' (1993) 42 *Int & Comp
LQ* 523–552 at 534ff; M Chaskalson 'The problem with property: Thoughts on the constitutional
protection of property in the United States and in the Commonwealth' (1993) 9 *SAJHR* 388–411
at 389ff in general; for examples compare *Clunies-Ross v Commonwealth of Australia* (1984) 155 CLR
193 at 201 (right of access to an island); *Smith-Kline & French Laboratories (Australia) Ltd v Secretary,
Department of Community Services and Health* (1990) 95 ALR 87 (FC) at 134–135 (confidential industrial information); *Peverill v Health Insurance Commission* (1991) 104 ALR 449 (FC) at 454 (state
debt) (all Australia); *Shah v Attorney-General (No. 2)* [1970] EA 523 (UHC) (state debt) (Uganda);
Attorney-General for The Gambia v Momodou Jobe [1985] LRC (Const) 556 (PC) (claim to bank
account) (The Gambia); *Revere Jamaica Alumina v Attorney General* (1977) 15 JLR 114 (state
contract) (Jamaica); *Deokinandan Prasad v The State of Bihar and Others* AIR 1971 SC 1409 (state
pension); *State of Madhya Pradesh v Ranorijao Shinde* 1968 (3) SCR 489 (state pension); *Madhav Rao
Scindia and Others v Union of India* AIR 1971 SC 530 (state debt); *Madan Mohan Pathak and Another
v Union of India and Others* AIR 1978 SC 803 (wages, cash bonus for state employment); *State of
Rajasthan v Union of India* AIR 1977 SC 1361 (salary of members of government); *Tilkayat Shri
Govindlalalj Maharaj v State of Rajasthan and Others* AIR 1963 SC 1638; *Kakinada Annadana Samajam
v Commissioner of Hindu Religious and Charitable Endowments, Hyderabad and Others* AIR 1971 SC
891 (hereditary trust of religious office is not property) (all India); *Nobrega v Attorney-General of
Guyana* (1967) 10 WIR 187 (CAG); *Attorney-General v Alli and Others* [1989] LRC (Const) 474
(CAG) (salary and wages) (Guyana); *Attorney-General v Lawrence* [1985] LRC (Const) 921 (CAStK)
(right to manage a business) (St Christopher & Nevis); *State (Pheasantry Ltd) v Donelly* [1982] ILRM
512 (right to earn a livelihood); *Hand v Dublin Corporation* [1991] 1 IR 409 (certain licences are
privileges and not rights); *Hempenstall and Others v Minister for the Environment* [1994] 2 IR 20
(licence or quota with financial value might be property) (all Ireland). In Irish law, it is also accepted
that the right to bring an action in tort, and perhaps even an action for breach of statutory duty,
might be property: *Byrne v Ireland* [1972] IR 241; *O'Brien v Keogh* [1972] IR 144; but compare
Moynihan v Greensmyth [1977] IR 71; *O'Brien v Manufacturing Engineering Limited* [1973] IR 334;
see B Doolan *Constitutional law and constitutional rights in Ireland* (3rd ed 1994) 278–281; G Hogan
& G Whyte (eds) *JM Kelly: The Irish Constitution* (4th ed 2003) 1978–1993. In the case of *In the
Matter of Article 26 of The Constitution & In the Matter of the Health (Amendment) (No. 2) Bill 2004*
[2005] IESC 7 (Supreme Court of Ireland, decision of 16 Feb 2005) the Irish Supreme Court
confirmed that the right of patients to reclaim from the state charges unlawfully imposed upon
them for certain medical services was a constitutionally protected property right known as a chose
in action, and the Court held that a law purporting to prevent those patients from reclaiming the
money by extinguishing the debt retroactively was an unconstitutional 'unjust attack' on property
rights.
[82]See 3.7.5 below on welfare rights, and see GS Alexander *Commodity and propriety: Competing
visions of property in American legal thought, 1776–1970* (1997) 311–378.

right,[83] trade marks,[84] workers' rights,[85] contractual claims,[86] and certain participatory 'new property' or so-called public-law participation rights.[87] In German law these 'extensions' of the traditional private law property concept is justified in terms of the general *Leitmotiv* for the interpretation of the Bill of Rights, namely whether the inclusion of a specific form of property under the protection of article 14 would serve the central constitutional purpose of creating and protecting a sphere of personal freedom where the individual is enabled to (and expected to take responsibility for the effort to) realise and promote the development of her own life and personality, within the social context.[88] A purposive or functional approach, which relies on the constitutional purpose of the property clause, therefore ensured that a generous interpretation of the objects of property rights is followed even in German-language jurisdictions, where such an approach is counterintuitive in view of the much narrower definition of ownership and property in the private law tradition.

The general principle laid down by the German courts in view of this guideline is that all valuable rights (*vermögenswerte Rechtspositionen*) which a person can use for her own benefit in the social context (as explained by the purpose of the property clause) will qualify as property for purposes of article 14 GG.[89] However, extensions of the property concept in terms of this principle are restricted by two conditions: only vested (and not contingent) rights are recognized as property,[90] and article 14 protects concrete, specific property rights and not a person's estate or wealth as such.[91]

---

[83]See *BVerfGE* 31, 229 [1971] (*Urheberrecht*); compare AJ van der Walt *Constitutional property clauses: A comparative analysis* (1999) 152.

[84]See *BVerfGE* 51, 193 [1979] (*Warenzeichen*); compare AJ van der Walt *Constitutional property clauses: A comparative analysis* (1999) 152.

[85]See *BVerfGE* 50, 290 [1979] (*Mitbestimmung*); compare AJ van der Walt *Constitutional property clauses: A comparative analysis* (1999) 152.

[86]See *BVerfGE* 42, 263 [1976] (*Contergan*); *BVerfGE* 83, 201 [1991] (*Vorkaufsrecht*); compare AJ van der Walt *Constitutional property clauses: A comparative analysis* (1999) 131, 152.

[87]See *BVerfGE* 69, 272 [1985] (*Eigenleistung*); compare AJ van der Walt *Constitutional property clauses: A comparative analysis* (1999) 152, 156–157. See the discussion in 3.7.5 below.

[88]See AJ van der Walt *Constitutional property clauses: A comparative analysis* (1999) 152; DG Kleyn 'The constitutional protection of property: A comparison between the German and the South Africa approach' (1996) 11 *SA Public Law* 402–445 at 410, and references there in footnote 42.

[89]See *BVerfGE* 89, 1 [1993] (*Besitzrecht des Mieters*); compare AJ van der Walt *Constitutional property clauses: A comparative analysis* (1999) 151; DG Kleyn 'The constitutional protection of property: A comparison between the German and the South African approach' (1996) 11 *SA Public Law* 402–445 at 420.

[90]See *BVerfGE* 28, 119 [1970]; *BVerfGE* 45, 142 [1977]. The same principle applies in Swiss law, as demonstrated by the *Graf* case: *BGE 106 Ia 163* (1980); compare AJ van der Walt *Constitutional property clauses: A comparative analysis* (1999) 153, 373. The US Supreme Court also refused to recognize contingent future interests such as prospective clients for a business: *College Savings Bank v Florida Prepaid Secondary Educational Expense Board* 527 US 666 at 672 (1999); see footnote 78 above.

[91]See *BVerfGE* 4, 7 [1954]; compare AJ van der Walt *Constitutional property clauses: A comparative analysis* (1999) 153. The US Supreme Court also protects identifiable assets and not general financial interests: *Eastern Enterprises v Apfel* 524 US 498 (1998); see footnote 78 above.

The last-mentioned restriction is particularly important in the area of taxation and economic regulation, because it means that laws and regulations that affect an individual's wealth in a general way cannot be attacked unless they can be shown to interfere with a specific, concrete property right as well.[92]

The functional or purposive approach to the definition of property fits in well with South African constitutional law,[93] and therefore a similar approach can be followed when the courts are forced to decide whether incorporeal property qualifies for the protection of section 25. To date the courts have mostly dealt with cases where corporeal movables or land was involved, and therefore the scope of the property clause has not been raised in many court cases. Two objections were raised against the draft section 25 in the *First Certification Case*,[94] but both were rejected rather summarily by the Constitutional Court. The first objection, that the provision does not include a positive formulation of property and an explicit guarantee of the right to acquire and dispose of property, was rejected on the ground that there is no universally recognized formulation of the constitutional guarantee of property.[95] The

---

[92] Compare the decision in *Diepsloot Residents' and Landowners' Association and Another v Administrator, Transvaal* 1994 (3) SA 336 (A) at 349I (the fact that the administrator was empowered to establish less formal townships implies that he was also empowered to cause the possible decline in property values in the vicinity, and that means that nearby property owners cannot claim that the establishment of such a township is invalid just because their property values were indeed affected). In *Du Toit v Minister of Transport* 2003 1 SA 586 (C) the Cape High Court decided that a landowner could claim compensation for gravel removed from his land for the building of a road, although the state averred that it should only pay compensation for the temporary use of the land from which the gravel was removed. The Supreme Court of Appeal reversed the decision and awarded compensation for temporary use of the land only, which suggests that, contrary to the approach followed in foreign law, it ignored the loss of actual property (the gravel) and focused on the overall loss of value for the owner: see *Minister of Transport v Du Toit* 2005 (1) SA 16 (SCA) par [16] at 25G–I. The majority of the Constitutional Court confirmed the SCA decision, but the minority placed the focus on the gravel. See *Du Toit v Minister of Transport* CCT 22/04 8 September 2005 paras [39], [76], and compare chapter 5.8.5. See further footnotes 78 and 90–91 above.

[93] The Constitutional Court has accepted the suitability of a purposive approach to interpretation of the Constitution and other legislation; see LM du Plessis *Re-interpretation of statutes* (2002) 115–117 for explanation and references, and compare chapter 2.3.3, especially footnote 89 there.

[94] *Ex parte Chairperson of the Constitutional Assembly: In re Certification of the Constitution of the Republic of South Africa, 1996* 1996 (4) SA 744 (CC) paras [70]–[75] at 797D–800A.

[95] *Ex parte Chairperson of the Constitutional Assembly: In re Certification of the Constitution of the Republic of South Africa, 1996* 1996 (4) SA 744 (CC) par [72] at 798D. The one case that does refer to the positive guarantee of the right to acquire and dispose of property in section 28(1) of the 1993 Constitution, *Prior v Battle* 1999 (2) SA 850 (Tk), merely suggested in passing that retention of the marital power in civil marriages in terms of Transkei legislation might be contrary to section 28(1) in that it 'impacts negatively' on women's right to acquire and dispose of their separately held property. It is uncertain whether such a claim and this decision would still be possible in terms of section 25 of the 1996 Constitution. If the legislative retention of the marital power is seen as a negation of a German-type institutional guarantee of property, this argument becomes less likely in the absence of a positive formulation such as section 28(1); if it is treated as a state-aided arbitrary deprivation of property the same decision would be possible under section 25(1).

second objection, that the draft failed to recognize a right to intellectual property or mineral rights explicitly, was rejected on the same ground.[96] On both counts the decision seems to be correct, as it was the Constitutional Court's duty in the certification process to ensure that the proposed provisions comply with established and universally recognized norms, and there simply is no universally recognized norm for the formulation of a constitutional property clause, particularly not as far as the description of property is concerned. At the same time, it is fairly obvious from comparative case law that failure to mention a particular class or kind of property (such as intellectual property) specifically in the property clause does not necessarily mean that that class of property is excluded, because it is unusual to list or specify all or indeed any class or type of property that is generally accepted to be included in the generic term 'property'.[97] To state the obvious, section 25 does not specify that movable corporeal property is property for purposes of the clause, but everyone (including the Constitutional Court) accepts that it is.[98] Failure to specify that a particular category of objects is property for purposes of section 25 is therefore neither a fatal shortcoming in the provision nor an indication that such an object is not property.

Surprisingly, in the one case where a court concerned itself with the property issue the Transvaal High Court decided that mineral rights are not included in the property that is protected by section 25, because 'if the drafters of the Constitution intended to protect mineral rights, they would have done so expressly as in other jurisdictions'.[99] Although the Constitutional Court stated in the *First Certification Case* that mineral rights were not a discrete set of fundamental human rights and therefore do not need to be specified in the Bill of Rights,[100] this statement has to be read in the context of the judgment and the constitutional function of the Court in that case, and it certainly is not authority for the general proposition that mineral rights are not property for purposes of section 25. In the context of the certification process, the Court held that it was extremely rare for a property clause to make explicit mention of mineral rights, and that mineral rights as such can therefore not be said to constitute (separate or independent) fundamental human rights that, based on universally recognized practice, deserve or need to be mentioned and protected explicitly in such a clause. It cannot be inferred from that statement that mineral rights are not included

---

[96] *Ex parte Chairperson of the Constitutional Assembly: In re Certification of the Constitution of the Republic of South Africa, 1996* 1996 (4) SA 744 (CC) paras [75] and [74] at 799E and 799D respectively.

[97] See AJ van der Walt *Constitutional property clauses: A comparative analysis* (1999) at 352–353; T Roux 'Property' in MH Cheadle, DM Davis & NRL Haysom *South African constitutional law: The bill of rights* (2002) 429–472 at 451.

[98] See *First National Bank of SA Ltd t/a Wesbank v Commissioner, South African Revenue Service; First National Bank of SA Ltd t/a Wesbank v Minister of Finance* 2002 (4) SA 768 (CC) par [51] at 794E–F.

[99] *Lebowa Mineral Trust Beneficiaries Forum v President of the Republic of South Africa* 2002 (1) BCLR 23 (T) at 29G–H. See in this regard AJ van der Walt 'Resisting orthodoxy—again: Thoughts on the development of post-apartheid South African law' (2002) 17 *SA Public Law* 258–279.

[100] *Ex parte Chairperson of the Constitutional Assembly: In re Certification of the Constitution of the Republic of South Africa, 1996* 1996 (4) SA 744 (CC) par [74] at 799D.

in the general protection afforded to property of all kinds and categories. In fact, in view of the general formulation of the property clause and the general absence of explicit references to any kind or category of property interests, the converse conclusion seems much more obvious—if property is protected in general, and no mention is made of any specific kind of property, it has to be inferred that any kind of property interest that is not excluded explicitly or by necessary implication is included, probably as long as it is recognized as property by law. This is particularly the case when the relevant category of interests is recognized as property in private law, as mineral rights are.[101] The Transvaal High Court missed this point and arrived at what has to be the wrong conclusion, possibly inspired by old-fashioned privatist orthodoxy about the restricted scope of property in Roman-Dutch law.[102] Decisions in which property is closely associated with land—despite the explicit provision in section 25(4) of the Constitution[103]—may be inspired by the courts' inability to depart from pre-constitutional tradition, according to which expropriation (which is associated most directly with property in the constitutional sphere) pertained mostly to land.[104] However, it is doubtful whether this decision is explained even by such private law conservatism, because in fact mineral rights are regarded as property in South African private law, which renders the *Lebowa Mineral Trust* decision even more puzzling.[105]

It is reasonably clear that at least some incorporeals will be treated as property in South African constitutional law. At the very least the assets that are protected under section 25 should include incorporeal objects or interests that are accepted as objects of property rights in private law.[106] In view of foreign examples one would also expect constitutional property to include intellectual property (copyright, trade marks and patents), certain 'rights in rights' (mineral rights, leases, security interests, other commercial property based on contract) and other commercial property interests (shares, licences). As a general rule, the inclusion of these interests under the protection of section 25 should probably depend on questions regarding their independent existence

---

[101]See PJ Badenhorst, JM Pienaar & H Mostert (assisted by M van Rooyen) *Silberberg and Schoeman's The law of property* (4th ed 2002) at 335.

[102]See AJ van der Walt 'Resisting orthodoxy —again: Thoughts on the development of post-apartheid South African law' (2002) 17 *SA Public Law* 258–279.

[103]Stating that, for purposes of section 25, property is not limited to land.

[104]See eg *Harksen v Lane NO* 1998 (1) SA 300 (CC) par [32] at 315E–G; compare AJ van der Walt & H Botha 'Coming to grips with the new constitutional order: Critical comments on *Harksen v Lane NO*' (1998) 13 *SA Public Law* 17–41 at 19–26.

[105]CG van der Merwe *Sakereg* (2nd ed 1993) 559, PJ Badenhorst, JM Pienaar & H Mostert (assisted by M van Rooyen) *Silberberg and Schoeman's The law of property* (4th ed 2002) 335–336; *Ex parte Pierce* 1950 (3) SA 628 (O) 634; *Erasmus v Afrikander Proprietary Mines* 1976 (1) SA 950 (W) 956E; *Apex Mines Ltd v Administrator, Tvl* 1988 (3) SA 1 (A); *Du Preez v Beyers* 1989 (1) SA 320 (T).

[106]Compare *Cooper v Boyes NO and Another* 1994 (4) SA 521 (C) (shares are incorporeal movable property over which a usufruct can be established), where Van Zyl J undermines the historical argument for a restricted concept of property in common law. It is uncertain whether these developments discredit the traditional view that property was in principle restricted to corporeals in common law. See the previous footnote and compare footnotes 62–64 above.

and the vesting in or acquisition of these rights by the claimant, according to normal law (common law or statute). Workers' rights have been included in other jurisdictions but may be both controversial and unnecessary in South African law because these rights are protected separately and explicitly in the Constitution.[107] The participatory 'new property' or so-called public-law rights have also been included to a limited extent elsewhere, but their recognition is controversial and complicated, and since certain socio-economic rights are protected explicitly in the South African Constitution it might also not be necessary to protect them as property.[108] Commercial property and 'new property' interests are discussed in 3.7.4 and 3.7.5 below respectively.

3.7.3 Non-proprietary rights

The German Basic Law refers to *Eigentum* in article 14, and the South African Constitution to *eiendom* in the Afrikaans version of section 25 of the Constitution.[109] In its traditional, Roman-Germanic private-law sense, this term is translated with 'ownership' rather than 'property', and it is traditionally associated with full ownership, so that ownership (in this restricted sense) is contrasted with other, lesser property interests such as a lease or a bond.[110] Consequently, significant and commercially valuable property interests such as leases are not regarded as property in the narrow private-law sense (ownership). Of course, this peculiarity of private law is remedied in Roman-Germanic legal systems by legislation or other private law rules that strengthen the value and protection of the non-proprietary rights for private-law purposes. However, in a modern economy such a narrow private-law perception of property as ownership

---

[107]Sections 17 (assembly, demonstration, picket and petition), 22 (trade, occupation and profession), 23 (labour relations).

[108]Sections 24 (environment), 26 (housing), 27 (health care, food, water, and social security), 28 (rights of children), 29 (education), 30 (language and culture), 31 (cultural, religious and linguistic communities). Section 27(5)–(8) (providing for land reform) can also be seen as protecting social and welfare rights, particularly in so far as they support the right to housing in section 26. See in this regard *Port Elizabeth Municipality v Various Occupiers* 2005 (1) SA 217 (CC), where the relationship between section 25 and section 26 is explained with reference to the historical background and the socio-economic and political context. This case and its implications are discussed in chapter 6.3.8 an chapter 7.3.4.

[109]'Eiendom' can of course refer to either the objects of property rights as discussed in 3.7.1 above or to property as rights, although it is more likely that 'ownership' would be translated into Afrikaans as 'eiendomsreg'. It is therefore possible that the intention with the use of this term in section 25 was to refer to a wide range of objects rather than to a restricted category of rights. However, that would be a curious approach, because it is unusual in the post-realist world to focus so strongly on the objects of property rights. My approach is to analyse the term in both possible meanings, in other words both as referring to objects of property rights (3.7.1 above) and as referring to property as rights (3.7.2 above).

[110]See AJ van der Walt 'Marginal notes on powerful(l) legends: Critical perspectives on property theory' (1995) 58 *THRHR* 396–420; AJ van der Walt 'Tradition on trial: A critical analysis of the civil-law tradition in South African property law' (1995) 11 *SAJHR* 169–206; AJ van der Walt 'Der Eigentumsbegriff' in R Feenstra & R Zimmermann *Das römisch-holländische Recht: Fortschritte des Zivilrechts im 17. und 18. Jahrhundert* (1992) 485–520.

restricts the scope of the property clause and of the Constitution unduly: once the objects of property rights are understood for constitutional purposes to include incorporeal rights and interests, it makes no sense to restrict property as a right to only one kind of property interest. Accordingly, even the Roman-Germanic systems tend to interpret property as a right generously in the constitutional context so that it includes non-proprietary rights and interests that are not regarded as property in the narrow private-law sense (ownership).

The best example of the fact that the term 'property' is interpreted generously in constitutional law to include non-proprietary rights and interests is a recent German decision in the Federal Constitutional Court confirmed that the possessory right of a lessee of immovable property is also protected by article 14 GG, which underlines the fact that not only ownership but other property rights (as opposed to other property objects) are included in the Federal Constitutional Court's understanding of the term *Eigentum*,[111] even in a situation where this right is protected against the property owner herself. This decision of the German Constitutional Court means that various rights of different persons with regard to the same object can all qualify as property for purposes of the constitutional guarantee; a conclusion that is easily justified in the constitutional sphere (and perhaps even in private law) as long as 'property' is not equated with 'ownership'—to recognize more than one kind of ownership or simultaneous ownership rights for more than one person is problematic in Roman-Germanic private law.[112] Moreover, in constitutional law such a conclusion is

---

[111]See *BVerfGE* 89, 1 [1993] (*Besitzrecht des Mieters*). This decision is controversial in German law and particularly private law specialists reject it as being bad in law and logic; see AJ van der Walt 'Ownership and eviction: Constitutional rights in private law' (2005) 9 *Edinburgh LR* 32–64 at 32–40 and compare the next footnote below. Similar but less controversial examples are *BVerfGE* 42, 263 [1976] (*Contergan*) (public-law claims against a compensation fund); *BVerfGE* 50, 290 [1979] (*Mitbestimmung*) (worker's rights to participate in management of a company); *BVerfGE* 52, 1 [1979] (*Kleingarten*) and *BVerfGE* 87, 114 [1992] (*Kleingarten*) (lease rights of allotment gardens); *BVerfGE* 83, 201 [1991] (*Vorkaufsrecht*) (statutory right of pre-emption); as well as the rent-control cases in footnote 114 below. See further AJ van der Walt *Constitutional property clauses: A comparative analysis* (1999) 152.

[112]This is the reason why critics of the German Landlord-Tenant decision regard the constitutional development as a move back towards feudalism; see AJ van der Walt 'Ownership and eviction: Constitutional rights in private law' (2005) 9 *Edinburgh LR* 32–64 at 32–40. The main critics are O Depenheuer 'Entwicklungslinien des Verfassungsrechtlichen Eigentumsschutzes in Deutschland 1949–2001' in T von Danwitz, O Depenheuer & C Engel *Bericht zur Lage des Eigentums* (2002) 109–213 at 124–126, 129–131, 186–187; O Depenheuer 'Der Mieter als Eigentümer' (1993) 46 *NJW* 2561–2564; M Ruffert *Vorrang der Verfassung und Eigenständigkeit des Privatrechts* (2001) 366–392. The main criticisms were that this decision brought about a functional splitting of ownership between the landlord and the tenant, that the functional splitting of ownership threatened the modern institution of private ownership (and with it the free market economy) and pushed it back towards feudalism; and that the decision was simply bad in law because it is not correct to say, as the Court did, that the lessee acquires an (even partial) right of disposal—in fact he acquires nothing more than a limited right of use and occupation as described in the lease agreement, while

(continued on next page ...)

unnecessary: it is clear that more than one person can have different property rights (eg ownership, tenancy, a bond and a servitude) with respect to the same property object at the same time, and as long as all of them are recognized as property for constitutional purposes it serves no purpose to even discuss the question whether they are all forms of ownership in the narrow (private-law) sense as well.

In accepting that non-proprietary rights also qualify as property for purposes of the constitutional guarantee, the German courts rely on the fundamental constitutional guideline mentioned earlier: a right will be in- or excluded from the property concept (and protected) according to the question whether in- or exclusion will serve the creation of a sphere of personal freedom which will allow the individual person to take responsibility for the development and management of her own affairs within the social context.[113] On the basis of this test, certain non-proprietary rights (and particularly the socially important land-use rights of residential lessees[114] and lessees of garden allotments,[115] as well as the participatory rights of employees in a large firm[116] and the claim rights of beneficiaries of a socially important compensation fund for victims of a pregnancy drug[117]) have been included in the property guarantee, while

---

(... from previous page)
the right of disposal remains with the landlord exclusively. It should be noted that the South African Constitutional Court was faced by a similar situation recently in the Port Elizabeth Municipality and Modderklip cases, where the 'rights' of unlawful occupiers were also in effect upheld against the landowner in the sense that they were not to be evicted before alternative accommodation could be provided, but in these cases the Court avoided the pitfalls of the German decision by deciding the cases on the basis of establishing a balance between the rights of the landowner and the occupiers in terms of the applicable constitutional provision (section 26(3)) and land reform laws (Port Elizabeth Municipality v Various Occupiers 2005 (1) SA 217 (CC)) or on the basis of section 34 (access to courts) (President of the Republic of South Africa and Another v Modderklip Boerdery (Pty) Ltd (Agri SA and Others, Amici Curiae) 2005 (5) SA 3 (CC)).

[113]See BVerfGE 89, 1 [1993] (Besitzrecht des Mieters). See further AJ van der Walt Constitutional property clauses: A comparative analysis (1999) 138–139; AJ van der Walt 'Ownership and eviction: Constitutional rights in private law' (2005) 9 Edinburgh LR 32–64 at 32–40.

[114]See BVerfGE 37, 132 [1974] (Wohnraumkündigungsschutzgesetz); BVerfGE 38, 248 [1975] (Zweckentfremdung von Wohnraum); BVerfGE 68, 361 [1985] (Wohnungskündigungsgesetz); BVerfGE 79, 292 [1989] (Eigenbedarfskündigung); BVerfGE 89, 1 [1993] (Besitzrecht des Mieters); BVerfGE 89, 237 [1993] (Eigenbedarfskündigung); BVerfGE 91, 294 [1994] (Fortgeltung der Mietpreisbindung). See further AJ van der Walt Constitutional property clauses: A comparative analysis (1999) 136–137; AJ van der Walt 'Ownership and eviction: Constitutional rights in private law' (2005) 9 Edinburgh LR 32–64 at 32–40.

[115]See BVerfGE 52, 1 [1979] (Kleingarten); BVerfGE 87, 114 [1992] (Kleingarten).

[116]See BVerfGE 50, 290 [1979] (Mitbestimmung). See further AJ van der Walt Constitutional property clauses: A comparative analysis (1999) 140.

[117]See BVerfGE 42, 263 [1976] (Contergan). This case is an interesting example. The rights in question derived from a private-law settlement agreement concerning delictual damages, but the whole situation was judged to be of so much social importance that the Court deemed it suitable for a law to transform the claims into public-law claims against a public fund and to allow potential claimants who were not parties to the settlement agreement to also submit claims. See further AJ van der Walt Constitutional property clauses: A comparative analysis (1999) 131.

others (especially some social participatory rights[118] and some claim rights[119]) have been excluded. As is pointed out in 3.7.2 above, the requirement for the inclusion of rights under the property clause is usually that the right must have vested before it will be protected. Case law indicates that the law which applies to the source of the right in question (contract, statute, court order) will also indicate whether the right has vested or not—in other words, if the right is based on contract, the normal rules of contract law will determine whether the right has vested or not; when it is based on legislation, the legislation will indicate whether it has vested or not.[120]

Despite the difficult cases and remaining uncertain areas, there are examples in foreign law of the way in which the protection of rights as property can be combined with a functional or purposive approach to reach a sensible and context-sensitive result, at least in the majority of cases. In German law, the protection of the rights of lessees of garden allotments is a good example. The allotment gardens were established before World War I, and they proved their worth during both World Wars by providing urban people the opportunity to survive by growing their own fruit and vegetables on allotments within the city. After World War II the land on which these allotment gardens were situated became extremely valuable, and there were efforts to use the land for building and development. The land was often owned by the local government or the churches, and the courts withstood pressure from these land-owners to evict the lessees so that the land could be used for development, arguing that the use of the allotment gardens was of vital importance for the lessees, many of whom relied on food grown on their allotments for their survival. Consequently, the extremely low rentals and anti-eviction measures that applied during the War were upheld, even in cases where contractual lease periods have run out, as long as the lessees desired to retain the use of the gardens and were willing to pay the nominal rent. When it was argued later that the initial reasons for the protection of lessees of allotment gardens were no longer applicable, and after it was demonstrated that only a few lessees still used the gardens to grow food, the Court acknowledged the change

---

[118] Especially those rights that have not vested yet, or that did not meet the requirements laid down by the courts—see footnote 90 above. Examples are certain state subsidies and family allowances —see *BVerfGE* 53, 257 [1980]; *BVerfGE* 69, 272 [1985] (*Eigenleistung*); *BSG* 1987 *NJW* 463; *BVerfGE* 78, 232 [1988]. See AJ van der Walt *Constitutional property clauses: A comparative analysis* (1999) 153–155. See the previous footnote above.

[119] Especially those claims that have not vested yet; see *BVerfGE* 28, 119 [1970]; *BVerfGE* 45, 142 [1977]; *BGHZ* 83, 1 [1982]. See AJ van der Walt *Constitutional property clauses: A comparative analysis* (1999) 153–155.

[120] This does not always solve the problem, as is illustrated by the Zimbabwean case of *Chairman, Public Service Commission, and Others v Zimbabwe Teachers' Association and Others* 1997 (1) SA 209 (ZSC), which concerned the annual bonus of state employees. The majority of the Zimbabwe Supreme Court decided that the bonus was not a normal part of the employees' salary and therefore not vested before a specific work year was completed, while the minority decided that the bonus was contractually part of the salary and therefore vested. See AJ van der Walt *Constitutional property clauses: A comparative analysis* (1999) 488–489. Recent US case law also suggests that the source of a private property right might be contested or unclear in some cases: see footnote 59 above.

in circumstances by somewhat relaxing the controls on eviction and by making it possible to charge a reasonable rent, but it nevertheless upheld the protection of the lessees because of the socio-economic importance of these gardens in the urban context.[121] The fact that the land in question was mostly owned by large corporate owners, local authorities and churches played a role in this decision, since it was not so important to uphold the property of these landowners, seeing that it could not possibly affect their personal freedom; whereas the protection of the lessees was directly relevant to the protection of their individual freedom. The second *Kleingarten* decision of 1992 can be described as an effort to apply the protection of article 14 GG in such a way that it established a just and equitable balance between the rights and freedom of individual landowners, lessees of allotment gardens in the cities and the public interest in the use of urban land in general. In the process the use and occupation rights of lessees were recognized and treated as property for purposes of the constitutional property clause.

In Anglo-American law,[122] the property concept is not traditionally associated so strongly with ownership as is the case in Roman-Germanic law, and the principle is that many rights are regarded as property for purposes of the constitutional property clause.[123] Moreover, the methodological turn in post-realist jurisprudence (away from

---

[121] Compare the first *Kleingarten* decision: *BVerfGE* 52, 1 [1979] with the second *Kleingarten* decision: *BVerfGE* 87, 114 [1992]. See AJ van der Walt *Constitutional property clauses: A comparative analysis* (1999) 137.

[122] The private-law perspective on this view is interesting; see K Gray 'Property in thin air' (1991) 50 *Cambridge LJ* 252–307. On the one hand, Gray emphasizes the extreme 'openness' and flexibility of the property concept, which can include a wide range of incorporeals, interests and rights. On the other hand, the ultimate test which is suggested for in- or excluding rights and interests from the property concept is 'excludability', which is a more static, private-law yardstick (although it admittedly can accommodate changes, as Gray indicates). For case law on the range of rights protected as property in the constitutional sphere, see 3.7.2 above. The question whether a property right is infringed when a state debt is cancelled by statute or when a private business is closed down by law and replaced by a state monopoly has not been answered very consistently, thereby creating some uncertainty about the scope of this wider concept of rights; see 3.7.4 below, text accompanying footnotes 142–144. See further *Chairman, Public Service Commission, and Others v Zimbabwe Teachers' Association and Others* 1997 (1) SA 209 (ZSC) (unlike salaries, annual bonuses are contingent rights that do not vest until they become payable, and therefore they can be reduced or cancelled by law, so that salaries can qualify as property, while bonuses cannot; a special provision in section 16(3) of the Constitution of Zimbabwe includes both vested and contingent rights in pensions.) Either the normal rules of contract law or the statute in question could be used as an indicator of whether the right has vested.

[123] However, as has been pointed out earlier, not any or every property interest is recognized as property for purposes of the property clause. The US Supreme Court has held that the following interests are not constitutional property: general financial interests rather than identifiable assets: *Eastern Enterprises v Apfel* 524 US 498 (1998); contingent future interests such as prospective clients for a business: *College Savings Bank v Florida Prepaid Secondary Educational Expense Board* 527 US 666 at 672 (1999); benefits that derive directly from the government, such as future social security payments described as 'mere expectancies': *Flemming v Nestor* 363 US 603 at 608 (1960). In each of these respects US law resembles German law; see footnotes 90–92 and accompanying text above.

identifying property with the objects of property towards seeing property as property relations) ensured that legal analysis would acknowledge a wide range of rights as property. There are, however, some indications that some remnants of an earlier, stronger emphasis on ownership as an important form of property still remain at the heart of property analysis. This appears most strongly in decisions in which attempts have been made to identify the most important or essential sticks in the bundle which makes up property.[124] The point of this tendency to characterize property in terms of the most essential stick in the ownership bundle is that, for purposes of constitutional law, some sticks in the bundle are protected more stringently than others:[125] the right to exclude[126] or the right to pass on property to one's heirs[127] are important examples. The well-known *Loretto* case[128] is a good illustration of this point: although the actual physical invasion of the property (and any conceivable damage or loss) was really negligible, the fact that an invasion was physical and permanent was sufficient to constitute a taking of property. This illustrates the strong emphasis on the right to exclude others from the property as an essential stick in the bundle that makes up property. Interestingly enough, the physical invasion rule is relaxed when the property has already been opened up to the public by the owner, for example if the property is a shopping mall,[129] where it may be assumed that the property owner has waived or weakened the right to exclude others. The fact that strong emphasis on the physical integrity of the property and the concomitant right of the property owner to exclude is so clearly linked to the will of the property owner is an indication that this approach still reflects the old-fashioned perception of property in terms of ownership as a sphere of personal autonomy.[130] The implication is that the will of the property owner is at the centre of the protection of property, and therefore the protection may only be relaxed if it can be assumed that the owner has waived the right to exclude (either by contract or through the ballot).

---

[124]See *Penn Transportation Co v New York City* 438 US 104 (1978); *Agins v City of Tiburon* 447 US 255 (1980).

[125]See the analysis of LS Underkuffler-Freund 'Takings and the nature of property' (1996) 9 *Can J Law & Jur* 161–205 at 185ff, to whom I am indebted for this insight.

[126]See particularly *Kaiser Aetna v United States* 444 US 164 (1979); *Loretto v Teleprompter Manhattan CATV Corp* 458 US 419 (1982); *Nollan v California Coastal Commission* 483 US 825 (1987).

[127]*Hodel v Irving* 481 US 704 (1978).

[128]*Loretto v Teleprompter Manhattan CATV Corp* 458 US 419 (1982). In *Nollan v California Coastal Commission* 483 US 825 (1987) and *Dolan v City of Tigard* 512 US 374 (1994) the Supreme Court indicated that it may expand the physical-occupation category of regulatory takings in the sphere of exactions (free transfer of private land in exchange for development permission), thereby emphasizing the importance of physical integrity or the right to exclude as a core strand of landownership.

[129]See *Pruneyard Shopping Center v Robins* 447 US 74 (1980), and compare further the exhaustive analysis of JW Singer 'No right to exclude: Public accommodations and private property' (1996) 90 *Northwestern Univ LR* 1283–1497. For an interesting South African comparison see *Victoria & Alfred Waterfront (Pty) Ltd and Another v Police Commissioner, Western Cape, and Others (Legal Resources Centre as* Amicus Curiae*)* 2004 (4) SA 444 (C) and compare chapter 4.7.3.

[130]See in this regard G Peller 'The metaphysics of American law' (1985) 73 *Cal LR* 1151–1290.

The analysis above indicates that jurisprudence in Roman-Germanic jurisdictions, where property as a right is traditionally associated with ownership in private law, has developed a wider interpretation of the property concept for purposes of constitutional law, thereby including non-proprietary rights even in competition with ownership itself. In German law, this process of extension was guided by the fundamental constitutional question whether the in- or exclusion of certain rights would serve the establishment and maintenance of an equitable balance between individual and social interests. In some cases this served to extend the property guarantee to non-proprietary interests that are extremely sensitive and important socially. In Anglo-American law, where the division between private and public law is not so clear, a wide range of property rights is taken for granted, although analysis suggests that the characteristics of the narrower private-law property concept can in some cases still be identified in the constitutional property concept.

In conclusion it can be said that most objections against the extension of the constitutional property concept to include non-proprietary rights arise from remnants of (often unarticulated) unsuitable and largely discarded private-law assumptions about the nature of property as individual ownership. Despite the continued influence of these remnants of private-law thinking in constitutional law, both the Roman-Germanic and Anglo-American systems of constitutional law have extended constitutional property to at least some instances of non-proprietary rights and interests. The decision whether or not to include a specific non-proprietary right often depends, as in the case of other constitutional property rights, on issues regarding the separate or independent existence of the right and its vesting in or acquisition by the property holder according to normal law. Courts tend to treat non-proprietary interests as constitutional property whenever the particular interest is generally accepted or recognised as an independent right in private or commercial law, or when it is socio-economically or constitutionally justified to recognise and protect the right or interest as such although it is not necessarily recognised in private law, and provided that the claimant acquired the right according to the legal rules that control the existence of the right.

3.7.4 Commercial property

Among the incorporeal objects and interests that are recognized as property for constitutional purposes, the commercial interests are particularly important. As has been mentioned above, a variety of commercial interests have been recognized and protected as constitutional property in Anglo-American and in Roman-Germanic jurisdictions: contract-based rights, intellectual property interests, business goodwill and others.[131] A few of them deserve special attention.

Arguably the least controversial category of commercial property, as far as constitutional recognition is concerned, is intellectual property: patents, copyright, and

---

[131] See footnotes 81–87 above.

trade marks are generally regarded as property for purposes of the constitutional property clause.[132] Since these rights are creatures of statute and established in accordance
with a special statutory regime, the requirement is usually that the right should be
established and vested according to the applicable statutory prescriptions before it will
be recognized and protected under the constitutional property clause.[133] For the same
reason recognition and the scope of these rights are subject to statutory amendments
and to the usual provisos with regard to police power regulation, but generally a right
that was properly vested and exercised according to the existing statutory controls will
be recognized and protected.

In the South African *First Certification Case*[134] the Constitutional Court held that
it was not universal custom to protect intellectual property explicitly and separately
in bills of rights. Although this point was not made by the Court, the reason for this
omission in bills of rights is the generally accepted view that intellectual property is
regarded as property and that it does not have to be mentioned separately. The same
applies to other commercial interests that are widely accepted and protected as property, such as mineral and mining rights.[135] The High Court decision in which the
court decided that mineral rights are not constitutional property because 'if the
drafters of the Constitution intended to protect mineral rights, they would have done
so expressly as in other jurisdictions' interpreted the *First Certification Case* wrongly.[136]
The fact that mineral rights (or intellectual property or other commercial rights) are

---

[132]See T Allen *The right to property in Commonwealth constitutions* (2000) 122 with regard to
Commonwealth law; *BVerfGE* 31, 229 [1971] (*Urheberrecht*) (copyright); *BVerfGE* 36, 281 [1974]
(patents); *BVerfGE* 51, 193 [1979] (*Warenzeichen*) (trade marks) for German law; *Smith-Kline &
French Laboratories (Australia) Ltd and Others v Secretary, Department of Community Services and Health;
Alphapharm Pty Ltd v Secretary, Department of Community Services and Health and Others* (1990) 95
ALR 87 (FC) (Australia); *Harper & Row, Publishers, Inc v Nation Enterprises* 471 US 539 (1985); *San
Francisco Arts & Athletics, Inc v US Olympic Committee* 107 S Ct 2971 (1987) (US). See further AJ van
der Walt 'Police-power regulation of intangible property and the constitutional property clause: A
comparative analysis of case law' in P Jackson & DC Wilde (eds) *Property law: Current issues and
debates* (1999) 208–280 at 253–257; LH Tribe *American constitutional law* (2nd ed 1988) 888.
[133]AJ van der Walt 'Police-power regulation of intangible property and the constitutional property
clause: A comparative analysis of case law' in P Jackson & DC Wilde (eds) *Property law: Current
issues and debates* (1999) 208–280 at 256.
[134]*Ex Parte Chairperson of the Constitutional Assembly: In re Certification of the Constitution of the
Republic of South Africa, 1996* 1996 (4) SA 744 (CC) par [75] at 799E–800A.
[135]Mineral and mining rights are traditionally recognized and protected as *sui generis* property in
South African private law and should therefore also be recognized and protected for constitutional
purposes; see Expropriation Act 63 of 1975 section 12(1)(a); A Gildenhuys *Onteieningsreg* (2nd ed
2001) 155, 299. The new Mineral and Petroleum Resources Development Act 28 of 2002 changed
the statutory framework and the nature of mineral and mining rights completely, but recognition
of these rights for constitutional property purposes will probably be unaffected; see chapter 6.5.3
for a discussion and references.
[136]*Lebowa Mineral Trust Beneficiaries Forum v President of the Republic of South Africa* 2002 (1) BCLR
23 (T) at 29G–H. See in this regard AJ van der Walt 'Resisting orthodoxy—again: Thoughts on
the development of post-apartheid South African law' (2002) 17 *SA Public Law* 258–279; footnotes
99–105 and accompanying text above.

not usually specifically and explicitly mentioned and protected in constitutional property clauses (as was correctly held in the *First Certification Case*) means that it was not necessary for the South African 1996 Constitution to mention and protect them explicitly, but it does not mean that these rights are therefore not protected. They are not mentioned explicitly exactly because they are generally understood to be included in the usual generic reference to property.[137]

Debts and claims that sound in money have been recognized as constitutional property in most jurisdictions.[138] Two different kinds of debt should be distinguished in this regard. On the one hand, private debts and similar claims (usually based on contract and sounding in money)[139] are recognized as constitutional property. The most common problem with this category is whether regulatory action that destroys debts of this nature could or should be regarded as deprivation or rather as expropriation of property and whether compensation is payable. In this regard the German *Contergan* decision[140] and an Australian decision[141] established the principle that legit-

---

[137]See footnotes 99–105 and accompanying text above.

[138]See *Madan Mohan Pathak v Union of India* AIR 1978 SC 803; *Deokinandan Prasad v Bihar* AIR 1971 SC 1409 (India); *Georgiadis v Australian and Overseas Telecommunications Corporation* (1994) 179 CLR 297; *Mutual Pools & Staff Pty Limited v The Commonwealth of Australia* (1994) 179 CLR 155 (Australia); *BVerfGE* 42, 263 [1976] (*Contergan*); *BVerfGE* 83, 201 [1991] (*Vorkaufsrecht*) (Germany); *Phillips v Washington Legal Foundation* 524 US 156 (1999); *Webb's Fabulous Pharmacies v Beckwith* 449 US 155 (1980) (US). See AJ van der Walt *Constitutional property clauses: A comparative analysis* (1999) 131, 152. See further AJ van der Walt 'Police-power regulation of intangible property and the constitutional property clause: A comparative analysis of case law' in P Jackson & DC Wilde (eds) *Property law: Current issues and debates* (1999) 208–280 at 216–228; T Allen *The right to property in Commonwealth constitutions* (2000) 122.

[139]Apart from other contractual and commercial interests the German courts also recognized a right of pre-emption and a lessee's right to the lease object as constitutional property; see *BVerfGE* 83, 201 [1991] (*Vorkaufsrecht*); *BVerfGE* 89, 1 [1993] (*Besitzrecht des Mieters*); compare AJ van der Walt *Constitutional property clauses: A comparative analysis* (1999) 152.

[140]*BVerfGE* 42, 263 [1976] (*Contergan*); see AJ van der Walt *Constitutional property clauses: A comparative analysis* (1999) 131, 152. The case concerned money claims for damages against the insolvent estate of the company that produced the drugs that caused the Thalidomide scandal in the 1970s. Victims who had proven their claims against the company were affected when the government nationalized the private fund from which the claims were to be paid in order to ensure that other victims not involved in the original court actions could also claim. The private law claims for damages were thereby transformed into public law claims, and their value was probably decreased, for the sake of public justice and equal treatment of all victims.

[141]*Mutual Pools & Staff Pty Limited v The Commonwealth of Australia* (1994) 179 CLR 155. See further AJ van der Walt *Constitutional property clauses: A comparative analysis* (1999) 44–45; T Allen *The right to property in Commonwealth constitutions* (2000) 122, 176–177. The case concerned repayment of a tax to certain private companies. The companies had previously charged their customers with the tax, and the government took steps to ensure that the repaid taxes would be paid to the customers who actually paid the tax and not to the companies. The regulatory action therefore deprived one private person of a debt formally owed to it and redirected payment to another person, in order to ensure that the relief payment reached the persons who originally paid the debt. See footnote 144 below.

imate and justifiable regulatory action that destroys or changes the nature or value of a debt or a money claim or that awards the claim to someone else is valid like any other normal, legitimate regulatory deprivation of property. In both the German and Australian cases the purpose of the regulatory action was to adjust or regulate conflicting private claims and therefore the regulatory deprivation was upheld as a legitimate regulation of private conflicts rather than a state acquisition of private rights.

The second kind of debt that has been controversial in constitutional property cases is debts against the state, particularly in situations where the debts are cancelled or destroyed by state action, without compensation.[142] In a sense this issue is concerned with the definition of expropriation and not the definition of property, since it was acknowledged in the relevant cases that the debt constituted property, but in one of them (the Zimbabwean *Hewlett* case) the court decided that cancellation of the debt did not constitute state acquisition of the debt because the state did not acquire any property, which casts doubt over the seriousness of the court's recognition of the debt as property in the first place (as is argued in 3.7.5 below). However, the court's reasoning in the *Hewlett* is questionable[143] and, most importantly, it does not in principle contradict or detract from the general agreement that debts against the state are recognized as constitutional property. The most convincing argument regarding state action that affects debts against the state was developed in Australian constitutional case law, where it was held that the state acquires property compulsorily not only when it takes the property as such from the owner, but also when it derives any benefit of any kind, however slight or insubstantial, from its own action.[144] In this perspective the fact that the cancellation of a state debt benefits the state would be sufficient to qualify the action as a compulsory acquisition of property even though that which the property owner lost (the debt) is not identical to what the state acquires (release from the debt),

---

[142]See *Peverill v Health Insurance Commission* (1991) 104 ALR 449 (FC) at 454 (Australia); *Shah v Attorney-General (No. 2)* [1970] EA 523 (UHC) (Uganda); *Attorney-General v Lawrence* [1985] LRC (Const) 921 (CA) (St Christopher & Nevis); *Hewlett v Minister of Finance and Another* 1982 (1) SA 490 (ZSC) (Zimbabwe). Compare the discussion in 3.7.5 below. It should be noted that the cases concerning a debt against the state shade into the cases concerning salaries and benefits of state employees, which is a different matter although the two categories share some features; compare 3.7.5 below. See further on these cases AJ van der Walt 'Police-power regulation of intangible property and the constitutional property clause: A comparative analysis of case law' in P Jackson & DC Wilde (eds) *Property law: Current issues and debates* (1999) 208–280 at 216–228.

[143]For criticism of the decision see T Roux 'Property' in MH Cheadle, DM Davis & NRL Haysom *South African constitutional law: The bill of rights* (2002) 429–472 at 454–456; AJ van der Walt *Constitutional property clauses: A comparative analysis* (1999) 485–489.

[144]*Georgiadis v Australian and Overseas Telecommunications Corporation* (1994) 179 CLR 297 at 305; compare chapter 5.4. Note the connection between this Australian decision and the case of *Mutual Pools & Staff Pty Limited v The Commonwealth of Australia* (1994) 179 CLR 155 mentioned in footnote 141 above; the link is that cancellation of a state debt is a valid and legitimate regulatory action when the purpose is to settle a private dispute about the debt, and not purely to benefit the state by relieving it from the duty to pay. In this regard these Australian cases should be distinguished carefully from other cases such as *Hewlett v Minister of Finance and Another* 1982 (1) SA 490 (ZSC) (Zimbabwe).

provided that the debt is recognized as property in the first place. A point that bears mentioning here is that cancellation of a state debt, once regarded as a state acquisition of property, can only result in the action being declared unconstitutional and void— it makes no sense to 'compensate' someone for loss of a property interest that sounds in money. If the action is declared void the debt is again payable.

Shares in companies constitute a special category of contract-based personal rights and are generally regarded as constitutional property, even in jurisdictions where shares are not necessarily regarded as property in private law.[145] Apart from the shares themselves special privileges connected with ownership of shares, such as special voting rights,[146] are apparently not generally regarded as constitutional property.[147]

It is generally assumed that an established and operating business concern is recognized as constitutional property in German law, although the German Federal Constitutional Court has repeatedly left this issue open.[148] Significantly, the business property is regarded as something more than the sum of the business' individual property holdings. Business goodwill, a special part of business property, is in itself also sometimes regarded as constitutional property, although such recognition has been controversial in foreign constitutional case law. Recognition of goodwill as constitutional property creates problems in instances where an existing business is prohibited, destroyed or taken over by the state as a result of regulatory action.[149] It has been decided in several major cases[150] that regulatory closing down and takeover of a pri-

---

[145]See *Bank of New South Wales v The Commonwealth* (1948) 76 CLR 1 (Australia); *BVerfGE* 50, 290 [1979] (*Mitbestimmung*) (Germany); *Charanjit Lal Chowdhury v The Union of India and Others* AIR (38) 1951 SC 41 (India); *Government of Mauritius v Union Flacq Sugar Estates Co Ltd and Others* [1993] 1 LRC 616 (PC) (Mauritius); *May, Thomas Family, Cairns Family Trust & Frogmore Tobacco Estates (Pvt) Ltd v Reserve Bank of Zimbabwe* 1986 (3) SA 107 (ZSC) (Zimbabwe). In *Cooper v Boyes NO and Another* 1994 (4) SA 521 (C) the South African Cape High Court recognized shares as incorporeal movable property over which a usufruct can be established, thereby making it much easier to recognize shares as constitutional property in South African law.

[146]See *Government of Mauritius v Union Flacq Sugar Estates Co Ltd and Others* [1993] 1 LRC 616 (PC) at 622c-624b (Mauritius); see AJ van der Walt *Constitutional property clauses: A comparative analysis* (1999) 306.

[147]See *Charanjit Lal Chowdhury v The Union of India and Others* AIR (38) 1951 SC 41 par [53] at 55 (India); see further AJ van der Walt *Constitutional property clauses: A comparative analysis* (1999) 222–223. Arguing that the special privileges associated with shareholding are separate and independent property rights probably amounts to conceptual severance, see 3.4 above. If conceptual severance is not accepted in constitutional property adjudication the refusal to recognize the special voting rights as property makes sense.

[148]See AJ van der Walt *Constitutional property clauses: A comparative analysis* (1999) 152–153.

[149]See AJ van der Walt 'Police-power regulation of intangible property and the constitutional property clause: A comparative analysis of case law' in P Jackson & DC Wilde (eds) *Property law: Current issues and debates* (1999) 208–280 at 228–235.

[150]See *Government of Malaysia and Another v Selangor Pilot Association* (1977) 1 MLR 133 (Malaysia); *Manitoba Fisheries v The Queen* (1978) 88 DLR 3d 462 (Canada); *Société United Docks and Another v Government of Mauritius* (1985) LRC (Const) 801 (PC) (Mauritius); *Saghir Ahmad v The State of Uttar Pradesh and Others* [1955] 1 SCR 707 (India). Compare *La Compagnie Sucriere de Bel Ombre Ltee v The Government of Mauritius* [1995] 3 LRC 494 (PC).

vate business does not amount to an acquisition of property, which could suggest that the courts in question applied a restricted property concept that excludes business goodwill or, alternatively, that they applied a restricted notion of expropriation. These decisions should not necessarily be regarded as authority for the general proposition that goodwill is not recognized as constitutional property or that state closure and takeover of private businesses does not involve a takeover of goodwill—the decisions vary too much and are too contradictory for such a general conclusion. A more nuanced and justifiable conclusion is that some regulatory closures of private businesses could be justified, even when the business was taken over by the state without compensation, but that compensation could nevertheless be required for a state takeover or expropriation of goodwill in suitable cases.[151]

Although the view that goodwill is constitutional property could resemble a conceptual severance argument,[152] one could also say that goodwill is raised in these cases because it is a clear indication of the benefit that the state derives from closing down and taking over private business. The purpose of the goodwill argument is therefore not to sever goodwill from the business property but to prove that closure and taking over of the business does benefit the state, and that compensation is therefore required. In that sense the property that is acquired when the state closes down and takes over a private business is not the goodwill but the business as a going concern —the goodwill is just the visible aspect of the value that the state acquires from taking over the business, as opposed to instances where the state closes a business down for regulatory purposes without itself benefiting from its acquisition (and trading on its goodwill).

Apart from goodwill, business interests can also clash with regulatory attempts to impose control over the management of private business concerns.[153] In the sense that these state actions are regarded as state interferences with property it could perhaps be argued that the right to manage private business concerns independently is constitutional property, but on the other hand foreign case law also illustrates the fact that not every state interference with the management of a business is regarded as an acquisition of property that requires compensation—attempting to construe state regulation of businesses as expropriation of management is a typical conceptual severance

[151] See AJ van der Walt *Constitutional property clauses: A comparative analysis* (1999) 89–90, 270–272, 293–300; AJ van der Walt 'Police-power regulation of intangible property and the constitutional property clause: A comparative analysis of case law' in P Jackson & DC Wilde (eds) *Property law: Current issues and debates* (1999) 208–280 at 228–235.

[152] See 3.4 above.

[153] See AJ van der Walt 'Police-power regulation of intangible property and the constitutional property clause: A comparative analysis of case law' in P Jackson & DC Wilde (eds) *Property law: Current issues and debates* (1999) 208–280 at 235–248; compare *Charanjit Lal Chowdhury v The Union of India and Others* AIR (38) 1951 SC 41; *Dwarkadas Shrinivas v The Sholapur Spinning and Weaving Co Ltd and Others* AIR (41) 1954 SC 119 (India); *Attorney-General v Lawrence* [1985] LRC (Const) 921 (CA) (St Christopher & Nevis); *Bank of New South Wales v The Commonwealth* (1948) 76 CLR 1 (Australia); *BVerfGE* 50, 290 [1979] (*Mitbestimmung*) (Germany); *PruneYard Shopping Center v Robins* 447 US 74 (1980) (US).

argument. Consequently it remains unclear to what extent the right to manage a private business concern is regarded as an independent property right for purposes of constitutional law. Generally speaking the right to manage a private business independently could be said to be part of the business as a going concern and not a separate property right—failure to award compensation for a taking of the right to independent management of a business can therefore be explained as a rejection of conceptual severance.[154]

The commercial property interests discussed so far are uncontroversial in the sense that they are widely regarded as constitutional property, but the same cannot be said for commercial interests in state-granted and controlled licences, permits and quotas.[155] Licences, permits and quotas are usually created by state grants and awards and therefore subject to state powers of cancellation, amendment and regulation, and they are often not regarded as property. However, in the world of commerce these interests can acquire great value, especially when they give access to valuable services, trading or manufacturing opportunities and when they can be sold and transferred. Because of their origin in administrative awards, there is some resistance to the notion that commercial interests in licences, permits and quotas could be protected as property, but some of these interests have enjoyed limited constitutional protection in foreign case law. The tendency is to regard licences, permits and quotas as constitutional property only if they have commercial value and once they have been vested and acquired according to the relevant (statutory or regulatory) requirements.[156]

Recognition of the property value of these interests does not change the fact that property interests created by administrative grants are subject to administrative regulation, amendment and cancellation. The general police power principle, according to which all property interests are subject to uncompensated deprivation caused by legitimate, justifiable and proportionally fair regulatory action, applies even more

---

[154]See 3.4 above.

[155]See AJ van der Walt 'Police-power regulation of intangible property and the constitutional property clause: A comparative analysis of case law' in P Jackson & DC Wilde (eds) *Property law: Current issues and debates* (1999) 208–280 at 248–253. See the decisions in *Tre Traktörer AB v Sweden* [1989] ECHR Series A vol 159; *Hand v Dublin Corporation* [1991] (1) IR 409; *Bahadur v Attorney General* [1989] LRC (Const) 632 (CAT&T); *Lawlor v Minister of Agriculture* [1988] ILRM 400 (= [1990] 1 IR 356); *Hempenstall v Minister for the Environment* [1994] 2 IR 20.

[156]Prior to vesting and acquisition it is highly unlikely that the right to property could be invoked, and therefore constitutional review of a decision not to award (or not to renew) a licence, permit or quota would take place on the basis of the right to just administrative action rather than the property clause; see section 33 of the South African Constitution and the Promotion of Administrative Justice Act 3 of 2000. In some instances previous awards may give a renewal applicant a legitimate expectation, which is a right to enjoy certain procedural benefits (such as a hearing) but not a substantive right to the award. On the overlap between constitutional property and administrative justice issues see AJ van der Walt 'Sosiale geregtigheid, prosedurele billikheid, en eiendom: Alternatiewe perspektiewe op grondwetlike waarborge' (2002) 13 *Stell LR* 59–82, 206–229; T Roux 'Section 25' in S Woolman et al (eds) *Constitutional law of South Africa* (2nd ed 2003 original service Dec 2003) 46-2–46-5 at 46-25.

strongly in the case of property interests created by administrative grant and award, but it does not necessarily mean that these interests cannot or should not be regarded as property for purposes of the property clause. Consequently, severe substantive reduction (through regulatory amendment) or even complete destruction (through regulatory cancellation) of recognized property interests of this nature could be legitimate and justifiable without compensation, despite the fact that they are recognized and protected as constitutional property.[157]

3.7.5 'New property'

Protection of participatory claims against state welfare and social benefits—the so-called 'new property' interests—is controversial and constitutional practice in this regard varies, although the essential features are fairly common. In general one could say that state welfare payments and subsidies are not usually regarded as property, although certain pension interests and similar interests could, in carefully circumscribed circumstances, qualify as property. The main reason why protection of this kind of interest is resisted in the context of the property clause is similar to the reaction to protection of other state grants such as licences, permits and quotas: these interests originate in state grants and awards and are usually subject to unilateral administrative withdrawal, reduction or cancellation, and therefore it is often argued that they cannot or should not be regarded as property.[158] However, even within the limits of these objections limited constitutional protection within the property paradigm is possible for certain interests and protection has been granted to some of them in foreign jurisdictions.

In terms of the guidelines according to which German courts interpret the property concept widely for constitutional purposes certain so-called public-law entitlements (*subjektive öffentliche Rechte*) are included under the protection of the property guarantee (eg certain state pensions), while others are excluded (eg child subsidies). Three requirements have been formulated by the German courts for the acknowledgement of a public-law participatory right as constitutional property: the public-law entitlement must (*a*) accrue to a beneficiary exclusively, like a private-law right; (*b*) be based substantially on the personal or own efforts (*Eigenleistung*) of the beneficiary

---

[157]See generally AJ van der Walt 'Police-power regulation of intangible property and the constitutional property clause: A comparative analysis of case law' in P Jackson & DC Wilde (eds) *Property law: Current issues and debates* (1999) 208–280 at 248–253.

[158]For a general discussion of the theoretical problems associated with protection of welfare and social awards as constitutional property see AJ van der Walt 'Sosiale geregtigheid, prosedurele billikheid, en eiendom: Alternatiewe perspektiewe op grondwetlike waarborge' (2002) 13 *Stell LR* 59–82, 206–229; AJ van der Walt 'Protecting social participation rights within the property paradigm: A critical reappraisal' in E Cook (ed) *Modern studies in property law* (2003) 27–41. For a general discussion of welfare rights in US law see GS Alexander *Commodity and propriety: Competing visions of property in American legal thought 1776–1970* (1997) 311–378; GS Alexander 'The concept of property in private and constitutional law: The ideology of the scientific turn in legal analysis' (1982) 82 *Col LR* 1545–1599.

(although the mere fact of own contributions or personal effort in itself is not sufficient to guarantee that the interest will be recognized as property); and (c) serve to secure or ensure the beneficiary's personal survival.[159] These requirements are based on the fundamental guideline which ensures that an equitable balance can be struck between the interests of the individual and the public interest. On the one hand, recognition of a public-law participatory right as property means that it is protected just like any other property, although the usual principles of constitutional property apply: only concrete rights are protected and not wealth in general; and only vested or acquired rights are recognized. Accordingly, regulatory actions that affect the monetary value or actual calculation of a public-law right cannot be attacked unless it can be shown that they do not affect just the general wealth of the individual concerned, but the substance of a concrete right itself; and the particular interest must have been acquired through substantial own effort (*Eigenleistung*) of the beneficiary and not purely by way of state grant. On the other hand the public interest is also taken into account: the German Federal Constitutional Court has decided that the public-law rights, funded as they are from public money, are not absolute entitlements but relative to the state of the economy in the sense that their monetary value can be amended to suit the state's financial situation, without the amendment amounting to an unlawful deprivation or expropriation.[160]

Although participatory 'new property' rights are not recognized as property in Austrian law, they are protected in Swiss law if the rights have become vested.[161] The phrase 'peaceful enjoyment of their possessions' in article 1 of the European Convention has also been interpreted by the European Commission of Human Rights and the European Court of Human Rights, as far as it refers to the object of property, to

---

[159]See *BVerfGE* 69, 272 [1985] (*Eigenleistung*); compare AJ van der Walt *Constitutional property clauses: A comparative analysis* (1999) 156–157; DG Kleyn 'The constitutional protection of property: A comparison between the German and the South African approach' (1996) 11 *SA Public Law* 402–445 at 421. A similar restrictive test is applied with reference to the European Convention on Human Rights 1950: see *X v The Netherlands* [1971] YB 12 224.

[160]See AJ van der Walt *Constitutional property clauses: A comparative analysis* (1999) 156–157; DG Kleyn 'The constitutional protection of property: A comparison between the German and the South African approach' (1996) 11 *SA Public Law* 402–445 at 421; and compare *BVerfGE* 69, 272 [1985] (*Eigenleistung*); *BVerfGE* 53, 257 [1980]. This regulatory amendment principle, which is important in view of the recent economic drain on public resources caused by the reunification of Germany, is founded on the assumption that the benefit in question is recognized as property and must therefore be distinguished from the principle that only vested (and not contingent) rights are protected. For a similar decision on the European Convention on Human Rights 1950 see *Müller v Austria* [1976] 3 DR 25; and compare the Swiss decision in *BGE* 196 Ia 163 [1980] (*Graf*) (concerning a change in the calculation of pensions).

[161]Compare *VfSlg 13804/1994* (Austria) with *BGE* 106 Ia 163 [1980] (*Graf*) (Switzerland). See AJ van der Walt *Constitutional property clauses: A comparative analysis* (1999) 373–375; KA Valender 'Art. 26' in B Ehrenzeller, P Mastronardi, RJ Schweizer, & KA Vallender (eds) *Die Schweizerische Bundesverfassung—Kommentar (St Gallen Kommentar)* (2002) 328–352 at 334–336.

include certain vested participatory claims like social security rights.[162] In all these jurisdictions it is required that the public participation-entitlement must have vested in the claimant as an independent right that is not subject to arbitrary and unilateral state withdrawal or cancellation.

In US law recognition of social and welfare rights was influenced by Charles Reich's argument[163] that a number of distinctly intangible interests should be recognized as property for purposes of the constitutional guarantee. In 1960, the US Supreme Court decided that an interest in social security benefits was not an 'accrued property right' which qualified for the protection of the Bill of Rights.[164] In reaction, Reich wrote his now famous and influential article on the 'new property', in which he argued that the constitutional property concept should be extended to include what he called interests in 'government largesse', which are participatory claims with regard to state and social wealth (welfare rights like state pensions, medical aid schemes, state jobs and state contracts). In the contemporary world, Reich argued, these rights have the same value for an individual that thing-property had in earlier societies, and the 'new property' should be protected accordingly. This argument was accepted by the courts as far as the due process clause of the property guarantee is concerned,[165] but never as far as the takings clause is concerned.[166]

The interesting point of Reich's 'new property' theory is, as Alexander points out,[167] that although it never really transformed the property concept as Reich intended, it nevertheless provided the theoretical justification for the post-realist

---

[162]See *X v United Kingdom* [1970] YB 13 892; *X v The Netherlands* [1971] YB 14 224; *Müller v Austria* [1976] 3 DR 25; *X v Italy* [1977] 11 DR 114 (all concerning state pensions). Compare AJ van der Walt *Constitutional property clauses: A comparative analysis* (1999) 16–18.

[163]CA Reich 'The new property' (1964) 73 *Yale LJ* 733–787. For a discussion and further references see AJ van der Walt 'Protecting social participation rights within the property paradigm: A critical reappraisal' in E Cook (ed) *Modern studies in property law* Vol II (2003) 27–41.

[164]*Flemming v Nestor* 363 US 603 (1960). Compare GS Alexander 'The concept of property in private and constitutional law: The ideology of the scientific turn in legal analysis' (1982) 82 *Col LR* 1545–1599; GS Alexander *Commodity and propriety: Competing visions of property in American legal thought 1776–1970* (1997) 311–378.

[165]See *Goldberg v Kelly* 397 US 254 (1970); compare further GS Alexander *Commodity and propriety: Competing visions of property in American legal thought 1776–1970* (1997) 311–378.

[166]For an explanation, see GS Alexander *Commodity and propriety: Competing visions of property in American legal thought 1776–1970* (1997) 311–378; J Nedelsky *Private property and the limits of American constitutionalism: The Madisonian framework and its legacy* (1990) 242–243 and footnote 123 there; compare WH Simon 'The invention and reinvention of welfare rights' (1985) 44 *Maryland LR* 1–37; WH Simon 'Rights and redistribution in the welfare system' (1986) 38 *Stanford LR* 1431–1516; GS Alexander 'The concept of property in private and constitutional law: The ideology of the scientific turn in legal analysis' (1982) 82 *Col LR* 1545–1599.

[167]GS Alexander 'The concept of property in private and constitutional law: The ideology of the scientific turn in legal analysis' (1982) 82 *Col LR* 1545–1599 at 1551; GS Alexander *Commodity and propriety: Competing visions of property in American legal thought 1776–1970* (1997) 311–378. Compare LS Underkuffler-Freund 'Takings and the nature of property' (1996) 9 *Can J Law & Jur* 161–205 at 165.

'scientific' trend of takings jurisprudence. This approach involves that the courts often either gloss over or altogether ignore the 'threshold question' of takings conflicts, namely whether the contested interest is property, and simply focus directly on the substantive issues like due process or compensation. By widening the constitutional property concept, Reich enabled the courts to simply gloss over the threshold property question and focus on substantive issues about the justification of infringements —in Underkuffler-Freund's terminology, the limitation issues were moved from 'outside' to 'inside' the property concept.[168] This tendency also appears in other Anglo-American and in Roman-Germanic jurisdictions, where the threshold question is investigated only in 'difficult' or problem cases, where the property concept is in effect stretched to new lengths, because it is judged legitimate or equitable to consider the substantive issues raised by each case rather than rule these questions out of order on a formalistic or conceptualist approach to the property question.[169] However, it is significant that the US Supreme Court never recognized new property interests as property for purposes of the takings clause, which means that its recognition as constitutional property has been very limited.

In South African constitutional law the courts have only been confronted with the new property question twice. In one case[170] the Transkei High Court noted that the meaning of 'property' in section 28 of the 1993 Constitution was probably wide enough to include a state housing subsidy. However, this observation was made in passing only and has no more than persuasive authority. In the second case the Constitutional Court held that certain conditions of service relating to payment were not contrary to section 28 of the 1993 interim Constitution, but without directly asking or answering the question whether the relevant payments were indeed property for purposes of section 28.[171] Quite understandably this is one of the aspects of the

---

[168] I am indebted to Laura Underkuffler for this notion; see LS Underkuffler-Freund 'Takings and the nature of property' (1996) 9 *Can J Law & Jur* 161–205 at 189.

[169] In this regard the effect of the *FNB* decision would bring South African law in line with foreign tendencies: Roux predicted that the effect of the case would be that other potential balancing issues, including the question whether a particular interest should be regarded and protected as property in terms of section 25, would be sucked into the 'arbitrariness vortex' in terms of the decision. See 3.5 above and 3.7.6 below for a discussion and references.

[170] *Transkei Public Servants Association v Government of The Republic of South Africa and Others* 1995 (9) BCLR 1235 (Tk) at 1246–1247. See T Roux 'Section 25' in S Woolman et al (eds) *Constitutional law of South Africa* (2nd ed 2003 original service Dec 2003) 46-2–46-5 and particularly at 46–17; T Roux 'Property' in MH Cheadle, DM Davis & NRL Haysom *South African constitutional law: The bill of rights* (2002) 429–472 at 451–452.

[171] *Ex parte Speaker of the KwaZulu-Natal Provincial Legislature: In re KwaZulu-Natal Amakhosi and Iziphakanyiswa Amendment Bill of 1995; Ex parte Speaker of the KwaZulu-Natal Provincial Legislature: In re Payment of Salaries, Allowances and other Privileges to the Ingonyama Bill of 1995* 1996 (4) SA 653 (CC) paras [41]–[44] at 668I–669E.

constitutional property issue that attracts most attention from commentators,[172] and incidentally it is also one of the issues that might raise the spectre of a too wide notion of property that could frustrate transformation initiatives by insulating existing social and economic benefits from necessary or even inevitable regulatory amendment or placing impossible financial burdens upon the state. After all, social and economic interests derived from state welfare grants are good examples of individual rights where state regulation is simultaneously the most threatening to the wellbeing of the recipient and the most easily justifiable in terms of legitimate principles of state policy and governance. Consequently, an overzealous and poverty-sympathetic court could perhaps frustrate legitimate reform and transformation initiatives if it were to insulate vested interests in social and economic grants too easily and too strictly against further regulation and amendment.

Treating socio-economic or 'new property' interests as protected property for purposes of the property clause is therefore fraught with dangers and complications. However, it is unlikely that new property issues will feature prominently in South African constitutional law. In the significant decisions on social and economic rights[173] the protection of these social and economic rights in terms of the property clause was never raised or investigated, and since the South African Constitution explicitly makes provision for the protection of certain socio-economic rights[174] it looks unlikely that they would be protected or adjudicated in terms of the property clause in future.

One last observation is necessary. Although the notion of 'new property' is generally associated most strongly with socio-economic or welfare benefits, Reich's category of 'new property' extends well beyond these benefits and includes what have been described as commercial interests such as licences, permits and quotas in 3.7.4 above. Given the different nature of these two categories and the likelihood that

[172] For discussions see T Roux 'Property' in MH Cheadle, DM Davis & NRL Haysom *South African constitutional law: The bill of rights* (2002) 429–472 at 451–452; T Roux 'Section 25' in S Woolman et al (eds) *Constitutional law of South Africa* (2nd ed 2003 original service Dec 2003) at 46–17; AJ van der Walt *Constitutional property clauses: A comparative analysis* (1999) 350–351; AJ van der Walt 'Towards a theory of rights in property: Exploratory observations on the paradigm of post-apartheid property law' (1995) 10 *SA Public Law* 298–345 at 321, 331.

[173] *Soobramoney v Minister of Health, KwaZulu-Natal* 1998 (1) SA 765 (CC) (health care); *Government of the Republic of South Africa v Grootboom* 2001 (1) SA 46 (CC) (housing); *Minister of Health and Others v Treatment Action Campaign and Others* 2002 (5) SA 721 (CC) (health care); *Khosa and Others v Minister of Social Development and Others; Mahlaule and Others v Minister of Social Development and Others* 2004 (6) SA 505 (CC) (social security).

[174] Sections 24 (environment), 26 (housing), 27 (health care, food, water, and social security), 28 (rights of children), 29 (education), 30 (language and culture), 31 (cultural, religious and linguistic communities). Section 27(5)–(8) (providing for land reform) can also be seen as protecting social and welfare rights, particularly in so far as they support the right to housing in section 26. See in this regard *Port Elizabeth Municipality v Various Occupiers* 2005 (1) SA 217 (CC), where the relationship between section 25 and section 26 is explained. The case is discussed in chapters 6.3.8 and 7.3.4.

welfare-type participatory grants would not be litigated under section 25 while commercial-type interests might, it is probably advisable to avoid use of the term 'new property' in South African constitutional law.

3.7.6 Linking the property issue and deprivation issues

Theunis Roux correctly stated that the decision to protect a particular property interest against a particular state limitation can be taken at any of a number of stages during the review process, but that doing so at the property stage by blanket-excluding certain categories of property interests is a crude way of doing the balancing.[175] It is therefore to be expected that the decision to include a certain property interest under the protective umbrella of the property clause will not guarantee actual protection, because a substantive weighing up of private property interests and the public interest could indicate that a particular deprivation or expropriation of property is justified.

The fact that a purposive approach to constitutional interpretation results in the protection of non-traditional, incorporeal property interests does therefore not imply that private rights in general are privileged as against the public interest or insulated from legitimate state limitation. The German *Contergan* decision[176] illustrates the fact that incorporeal interests can be protected as property while the courts strike an equitable balance between private and public interests: the right (a contractual claim right) was recognized for protection in terms of article 14 of the German Basic Law, but at the same time a law which transformed the private-law claims into public-law claims to protect the public interest was approved as a legitimate regulatory interference in that the regulatory action admittedly deprived certain property holders of their vested property interests in order to harmonise conflicting private interests (as opposed to acquiring property for the state). The effect of the decision was that pre-existing private claims in terms of the settlement agreement were reduced in value so as to protect other claimants who were not part of the settlement. On the whole, private money claims were protected as property even though some claims were reduced in value—this is perhaps a paradigmatic example of what is meant with the statement that an equitable balance must be struck between private interests and the public interest.

However, in some foreign decisions a seemingly generous attitude towards recognition of a certain incorporeal property interest is not so much followed by a substantive decision against the property owner as it is counteracted by a surprisingly narrow

[175] T Roux 'Section 25' in S Woolman et al (eds) *Constitutional law of South Africa* (2nd ed 2003) original service Dec 2003) 46-2–46-5 at 46-2–46-5; see further at 46-21–46-25.
[176] BVerfGE 42, 263 [1976] (*Contergan*). See AJ van der Walt *Constitutional property clauses: A comparative analysis* (1999) 131 for a discussion. The same can be said with regard to the Australian decision in *Mutual Pools & Staff Pty Limited v The Commonwealth of Australia* (1994) 179 CLR 155, which also concerned regulatory control over monetary claims. The effect and import of the two cases are very similar. See AJ van der Walt *Constitutional property clauses: A comparative analysis* (1999) 47.

approach to the (conceptual rather than substantive) question whether the affected person was deprived of the property in fact. Case law, especially in some Commonwealth jurisdictions, provides examples of this equally crude approach. One should not be misled by the fact that the property interest is recognized in these cases because the decision often indicates that such recognition was more apparent than real. Two examples illustrate this point.

Debts have been recognized as objects of property in most Commonwealth jurisdictions,[177] but a Zimbabwean decision creates the impression that, while intangibles are regarded as property for purposes of the constitutional property clause, only tangible or corporeal property could be compulsorily acquired. A cancellation of a state debt was therefore seen as a deprivation rather than an acquisition of property, and compensation was not required, even though the state was clearly benefited by not having to pay the debt.[178] The decision did not exclude debts from the objects of property but restricted the term 'acquire' to an action by which the state actually 'gets' something, thereby excluding incorporeals and rights that are not 'acquired' through statutory cancellation.[179] This approach may appear progressive as far as the recognition of intangibles as property is concerned, but the reversal to narrow conceptualism on the acquisition issue shows that it is just as crude as other decisions in which it is simply denied that intangible interests are property. Decisions to the effect that only corporeals can be dispossessed physically,[180] as opposed to being compulsory acquired or expropriated, are less troublesome but still reflect a narrow approach in terms of which property is primarily associated with corporeal or tangible things.

A second problem is created by the question whether it amounts to expropriation of property if a private business is closed down by law and replaced by a state monopoly. The goodwill of a private company is considered property in some Commonwealth jurisdictions,[181] but in certain decisions the approach was nevertheless

---

[177] See T Allen *The right to property in Commonwealth constitutions* (2000) 122 for references.

[178] See *Hewlett v Minister of Finance and Another* 1982 (1) SA 490 (ZSC) at 501H, 503B, 506D–507A; and more recently *Chairman, Public Service Commission, and Others v Zimbabwe Teachers' Association and Others* 1997 (1) SA 209 (ZSC); *Davies and Others v Minister of Land, Agriculture and Water Development* 1997 (1) SA 228 (ZSC).

[179] In *Hewlett v Minister of Finance and Another* 1982 (1) SA 490 (ZSC), this argument was combined with the distinction between compulsory acquisitions and deprivations to argue that, when the state 'gets' nothing new, the limitation is a deprivation and not an acquisition. Even in private law this argument is spurious. The *Hewlett* decision was cited and relied on by the South African Constitutional Court in *Harksen v Lane NO* 1998 (1) SA 300 (CC) par [34] at 316D. For criticism of the *Hewlett* case see T Roux 'Property' in MH Cheadle, DM Davis & NRL Haysom *South African constitutional law: The bill of rights* (2002) 429–472 at 454–456; AJ van der Walt *Constitutional property clauses: A comparative analysis* (1999) 485–489.

[180] For this line of argument compare *Attorney-General for The Gambia v Momodou Jobe* [1985] LRC (Const) 556 (PC) at 565h (The Gambia). This argument applies only to forcible dispossessions, and can go hand-in-hand with acceptance of a wider property concept for purposes of compulsory acquisition. The central issue is that dispossession is a physical action which applies to tangibles only.

[181] See T Allen *The right to property in Commonwealth constitutions* (2000) 123 for references.

that the creation of a state monopoly and the subsequent effective prohibition or closing down of a private business did not amount to a taking of property.[182] These cases must be distinguished from instances where an existing business was prohibited or closed down in terms of the 'police power exception' as it is described with reference to the US takings clause, which means that (existing and) previously legitimate uses of property can be terminated by law without compensation if they later prove to be inimical to public wealth, safety or welfare.[183] In the first set of cases the state not only closed down the business for public health or safety reasons, but created a state monopoly and took over the business, probably with its goodwill, for the benefit of the state. To argue that such an action does not involve a taking of property suggests that the court works with an artificially narrow concept of property that excludes goodwill or with an equally artificially narrow concept of acquisition,[184] and in fact it amounts to sophistry. In the second set of cases the finding that the regulatory action does not amount to expropriation is potentially easier to justify in view of the connection between the action and the narrow police power purpose of protecting public health and safety.

In both these instances the fact that intangible interests are recognized as property in terms of a wide concept of property is counteracted by not acknowledging certain limitations of these intangible property interests as compulsory acquisitions of property. To a large extent this tendency is caused by what looks like the remnants of a

---

[182]See *Manitoba Fisheries v The Queen* (1978) 88 DLR 3d 462 (Canada); *Government of Malaysia and Another v Selangor Pilot Association* (1977) 1 MLJ 133 (Malaysia); *Societé United Docks and Others v Government of Mauritius* (1985) LRC (Const) 801 (PC) (Mauritius); *Saghir Ahmad v The State of Uttar Pradesh and Others* [1955] 1 SCR 707 (India); *Trinidad Island-Wide Cane Farmers' Association Inc and Attorney-General v Prakash Seereeram* (1975) 27 WIR 329 (CA) (Trinidad & Tobago). In German law, the general principle regarding the scope of the constitutional property concept has been applied in such a way that an established business concern (*eingerichteter Gewerbebetrieb*) is protected as property; see 3.7.4 above.

[183]See in this regard LS Underkuffler-Freund 'Takings and the nature of property' (1996) 9 *Can J Law & Jur* 161–205 at 183 and examples in footnotes 99–110 there. The major US cases in this regard are *Penn Central Transportation Co v New York City* 438 US 104 (1978); *Keystone Bituminous Coal Association v DeBenedictis* 480 US 470 (1987). A similar principle is enforced in German law; compare *BVerfGE* 25, 112 [1969]; *BVerwGE* 38, 209 [1971]; *BVerwGE* 49, 365 [1975]; and particularly *BVerfGE* 42, 263 [1976] (*Contergan*); *BVerfGE* 58, 300 [1981] (*Naßauskiesung*). See generally chapter 4.2.3 and compare chapter 5.4.

[184]Even in cases where the state does transform the property into public property the action need not amount to expropriation, and a nuanced judgment may be necessary, as is indicated by the German decision in *BVerfGE* 42, 263 [1976] (*Contergan*) (the state transformed a private-law claim fund resulting from a delictual settlement into a public fund to protect the public interest in ensuring that all possible claimants are protected and not only those who concluded the settlement agreement). The more relevant consideration was formulated by Australian courts that held that the question is whether the state acted to harmonize conflicting private interests or to acquire some benefit for itself, no matter how small or insignificant; see *Mutual Pools & Staff Pty Limited v The Commonwealth of Australia* (1994) 179 CLR 155; AJ van der Walt *Constitutional property clauses: A comparative analysis* (1999) 47. In the German *Contergan* case the state clearly obtained no benefit whatsoever.

narrow, private-law view of tangible property and not by a substantive weighing of private and public interests.

3.7.7 Conclusions

The analysis in the preceding paragraphs indicates that the constitutional courts in Roman-Germanic jurisdictions, where the object of property rights in private law is traditionally restricted to corporeal things, have developed a wider constitutional property concept, which differs from the traditional private-law concept in that it includes a range of incorporeal objects and rights, thereby bringing the constitutional property concept in these jurisdictions closer to the traditionally wider property concept in Anglo-American jurisdictions. The comparative perspective indicates that the range of objects of constitutional property is reasonably wide, regardless of the question whether the constitutional property clause itself refers to 'property', 'possessions' or 'ownership'. The main implication is that the decision to include a particular right in the protection of the property clause fairly easily does not mean that private property is privileged in relation to the public interest or some public benefit, or that private rights are insulated from legitimate state limitation. Instead, the courts often deem it necessary to gloss over the property issue more lightly and proceed to the substantive issues raised in the second stage of the constitutional dispute rather than rule cases out of order in the first stage on the basis of a conceptualist approach to the meaning of the term 'property'.

3.8 CONTENT AND SCOPE OF PROPERTY RIGHTS

In 3.7 above it was said that the property clause is generally interpreted generously as far as the objects of property rights are concerned, despite the fact that the objects of property rights are traditionally restricted to corporeal things in Roman-Germanic systems. One aspect of this generous interpretation involves the recognition of rights (rather than corporeal things) as objects of property rights for constitutional purposes, for example when a lessee's right of use and occupation or a bank's pledge over a company's book debts is treated as property. In some cases this generous approach is followed (sometimes in part) in private law as well, but in some jurisdictions it represents a constitutional departure from private law tradition.

Apart from the fact that rights and other incorporeal interests are treated as property for purposes of the constitutional property clause, property is also different in the constitutional context as far as its nature and scope are concerned. Traditionally, property is regarded as an absolute right in private law as far as the scope or range of the property holder's entitlements are concerned; it is often said that property is absolute or unlimited unless restrictions are imposed by legitimate and valid regulatory action. The question in this case is whether the same approach can be followed in constitutional law. The nature and scope of constitutional property and the differences from private law are discussed in this section.

In private law, property (especially ownership) is traditionally described as an absolute right to indicate that it is unrestricted in principle; restrictions have to be imposed
specifically and clearly by legitimate legislative or regulatory action.[185] In the Roman-
Germanic tradition, property in the sense of ownership is described as the most complete, absolute and exclusive right over property.[186] As such, it is not only distinguished from the lesser real and personal rights, but it is also regarded as a basically
absolute or unrestricted and exclusive right.[187] The German Federal Constitutional
Court considered it necessary to distinguish the constitutional property concept from
this aspect of the private-law concept, since the latter view is in conflict with the

---

[185]For a historical analysis see AJ van der Walt 'Property and personal freedom: Subjectivism in
Bernhard Windscheid's theory of ownership' (1993) 56 *THRHR* 569–589.

[186]In § 903 of the German *BGB* ownership is described with reference to the complete right of
disposal of the owner: 'Der Eigentümer einer Sache kann, soweit nicht das Gesetz oder Rechte
Dritter entgegenstehen, mit der Sache nach Belieben verfahren und andere von jeder Einwirkung
ausschliessen' (the owner of a thing can dispose of it at will and exclude everybody else from any
action with regard to it, insofar as is not prohibited by law or by the rights of others). Book 5 article
1.2 of the new Dutch civil code (*NBW*) describes ownership in almost identical terms, except that
article 1.1 adds explicitly that 'Eigendom is het meest omvattend recht dat een persoon op een zaak
kan hebben' (ownership is the most complete right which a person can have with regard to a
thing). The second part of the article, which corresponds with the German § 903, derives from the
medieval definition of *dominium* provided by Bartolus de Saxoferrato D 41.2.17.1 n 4 ('dominium
est ius de re corporali perfecte disponendi, nisi lege prohibeatur'—ownership is the right of
complete disposal over a corporeal thing, insofar as is not prohibited by law), and is also accepted
as the authoritative definition of ownership in South African property law: see CG van der Merwe
Sakereg (2nd ed 1989) chapter 5; P Badenhorst, J Pienaar & H Mostert (assisted by M van Rooyen)
Silberberg & Schoeman's The law of property (4th ed 2003) chapter 6; AJ van der Walt & GJ Pienaar
Introduction to the law of property (4th ed 2002) chapter 4. With regard to Bartolus de Saxoferrato, see
AJ van der Walt 'Bartolus se omskrywing van *dominium* en die interpretasies daarvan sedert die
vyftiende eeu' (1986) 49 *THRHR* 305–321; AJ van der Walt 'Marginal notes on powerful(*l*)
legends: Critical perspectives on property theory' (1995) 58 *THRHR* 396–420; AJ van der Walt
'Der Eigentumsbegriff' in R Feenstra & R Zimmermann (eds) *Das römisch-holländische Recht: Fortschritte des Zivilrechts im 17. und 18. Jahrhundert* (1992) 485–520.

[187]The supposed absoluteness and exclusivity of ownership in the private-law tradition does not
mean that it cannot be limited and that others cannot gain access to the property; it means that the
right of the owner is absolute and exclusive in principle, so that limitations and access of others are
exceptional, unnatural and temporary, and their legitimacy depends upon the owner's consent
(through contract or the ballot). See AJ van der Walt 'Ownership and personal freedom: Subjectivism in Bernhard Windscheid's theory of ownership' (1993) 56 *THRHR* 569–589; AJ van der
Walt 'Tradition on trial: A critical analysis of the civil-law tradition in South African property law'
(1995) 11 *SAJHR* 169–206 at 175ff for a discussion. The main debate here is about the question
whether limitations of ownership (and the right to use and exploit property) are inherent or
external. Compare in this respect LS Underkuffler-Freund 'Takings and the nature of property'
(1996) 9 *Can J Law & Jur* 161–205 at 191ff.

constitutional provisions regarding the limitation of fundamental rights.[188] In constitutional law, property is mostly regarded as an inherently limited right, even when it is regarded as a fundamentally absolute right in private law. The articulation between these two apparently conflicting views of property is of great importance for constitutional property law because it determines the legitimacy and effects of police power regulation of property.

Although the absoluteness thesis is nowadays either rejected out of hand or played down as a rhetorical overstatement even in private law, the idea that a property owner can pretty much do with her property what she likes unless she is explicitly and clearly prohibited from doing something by law has important implications for constitutional property. The main implication of the absoluteness thesis is that a property owner can exploit the property in any conceivable way in the absence of explicit and clear regulatory restrictions. Accordingly, when such regulatory restrictions are imposed and the owner is prevented from exploiting or using the property in a certain way it seems almost natural to complain that they deprive the owner of an entitlement that she would otherwise — 'normally' — have enjoyed or that she in fact enjoyed prior to the imposition of the restriction. From there it is a short step to the next question, namely whether compensation is due for the deprivation.[189]

The problem with the argument above is that the underlying 'everything goes' baseline is a false assumption. The idea behind this liberal perception of rights is that property rights are natural rights that predate social or state organization and that they are therefore absolute or inclusive of all conceivable entitlements in their 'normal' form; restriction comes later through state intervention that follows the social contract. Accordingly, restriction that limits the pre-existing right requires authorization and compensation ever, the classic liberal notion of property rights is outdated; most theorists now accept that property, like any other economic right, is a social construct that depends on social, political and legal rules for its existence, its nature and its scope.[190] This Realist or relational approach is widely accepted in US property theory, and it is also illustrated by the German Federal Constitutional Court's interpretation of article 14 GG. Article 14.1.2 provides that the content and limits of property are

---

[188] See DG Kleyn 'The constitutional protection of property: A comparison between the German and the South African approach' (1996) 11 *SA Public Law* 402–445 at 424ff for a discussion and references. The German Federal Constitutional Court accepts, for purposes of article 14 GG, that property is restricted inherently by law, as provided for in the internal limitation provisions in article 14.1 and 14.2 GG. Article 14.2 provides that property also involves obligations and that it has to be enjoyed in accordance with the general welfare; article 14.1.2 provides that the limits and content of property are determined by the laws.

[189] This is the conceptual severance argument that is discussed in 3.4 above.

[190] For a brief overview and further references see AJ van der Walt 'Subject and society in property theory: A review of property theories and debates in recent literature Part II' 1995 *TSAR* 322–345; compare further JW Singer & JM Beerman 'The social origins of property' (1993) 6 *Can J of Law & Jur* 217–248.

determined by the laws.[191] The currently accepted view in German law is that constitutional property rights are inherently restricted. This departure from traditional private-law learning is based on the provisions of article 14.1[192] and 14.2[193] GG, which
are understood as inherent restrictions of property rights for purposes of the constitutional property clause.[194] Since the content and limits of property are determined by
the laws, property is restricted to what is allowed by legislation at a specific point in
time, taking into account the fact that the legislator does not have a free hand in
determining these limits.[195] The effect of this view is that for constitutional purposes
property, in its subjective meaning of a right, is constituted by the entitlements that
are awarded and allowed to a person in terms of the legislation which exists at a
specific time. It is a moot point whether these restrictions of property should be
described as inherent, which would mean that they form part of the definition of
property (internal modifiers), or as internal, which would mean that they function as
internal or specific limitations of the property rights that are protected by article 14.
The German Federal Constitutional Court interprets this provision in such a way that
property is understood as a social construct, the content and limits of which are determined by laws and, accordingly, protected by the constitutional guarantee. However,

---

[191]'Inhalt und Schranken werden durch die Gesetze bestimmt.' In view of the fact that German
private law is codified the term 'laws' refers to statutory laws.
[192]Which provides that the substance and limits of property shall be (or are) determined by law.
('Inhalt und Schranken werden durch die Gesetze bestimmt'.) The English translation of this provision is problematic. The official English translation (March 1995, Press and Information Office of
the Federal Government, similar to the 1994 edition used by DG Kleyn 'The constitutional protection of property: A comparison between the German and the South African approach' (1996) 11
SA Public Law 402–445 at 408 footnote 34) translates 'werden bestimmt' with 'shall be determined';
it can just as well (or perhaps better) be 'are determined'. 'Substance' for 'Inhalt' can also be
'content'. See AJ van der Walt Constitutional property clauses: A comparative analysis (1999) 121 footnote 1.
[193]Which provides that property entails obligations, and that its use should also serve the public
interest. ('Eigentum verpflichtet. Sein Gebrauch soll zugleich dem Wohle der Allgemeinheit
dienen'.) Once again the translation is problematic; see the previous footnote, and see AJ van der
Walt Constitutional property clauses: A comparative analysis (1999) 121 footnote 1; DG Kleyn 'The
constitutional protection of property: A comparison between the German and the South African
approach' (1996) 11 SA Public Law 402–445 at 409 footnote 36. I agree with Kleyn that 'duties' is
better than 'obligations' for 'verpflichtet', and furthermore the exact translation of 'Wohle der
Allgemeinheit' is much more complex than the official translation suggests.
[194]See the discussion of AJ van der Walt Constitutional property clauses: A comparative analysis (1999)
132–145; DG Kleyn 'The constitutional protection of property: A comparison between the
German and the South African approach' (1996) 11 SA Public Law 402–445 at 419, where the most
important authorities are referred to.
[195]This point concerns the institutional guarantee of property. See AJ van der Walt Constitutional
property clauses: A comparative analysis (1999) 129–130; DG Kleyn 'The constitutional protection of
property: A comparison between the German and the South African approach' (1996) 11 SA Public
Law 402–445 at 413, 419 for a discussion. Compare AJ van der Walt 'Towards a theory of rights in
property: Exploratory observations on the paradigm of post-apartheid property law' (1995) 10 SA
Public Law 298–345 at 302–304.

this does not mean that the legislator has a free hand and that it can change and restrict property rights as it pleases; the constitutional property guarantee means that the legislature is limited in determining the content and the limits of property because it has to respect established property institutions (such as ownership) and vested individual property interests. In determining the content of property rights the legislature may not undermine or erode established property institutions without good reason,[196] and in determining the limits of property it may not impose unfair, excessive or disproportionate regulatory burdens upon individual property holdings.[197]

3.9 PROPERTY IN SECTION 25

It is unnecessary to speculate in detail about what might be included or excluded from the protection of the South African property clause. Some of the possibilities have been canvassed extensively elsewhere already.[198] The implication of the analysis above is that the constitutional property concept will probably differ from the traditional private-law concept, and that its exact meaning and scope has to be determined for every individual case, preferably with reference to a general, fundamental guide-

---

[196]This is known as the institutional guarantee, which means that legislative ordering may not erode established property institutions such as ownership. When legislative ordering imposes new or extraordinary limits on property institutions it must be justifiable. Examples of extraordinary but justifiable interferences with the institution of ownership are the *Deichordnung* case (*BVerfGE* 24, 367 [1968]), which removed dyke land from private ownership to improve public protection against flooding; and the *Mitbestimmung* case (*BVerfGE* 50, 290 [1979]), which imposed extraordinary burdens on private ownership of companies to improve labour relations. See AJ van der Walt *Constitutional property clauses: A comparative analysis* (1999) 132–134.

[197]This is known as the individual guarantee, based on the prohibition against excessive regulation or the proportionality principle, which provides that regulatory burdens imposed on private property holdings by way of determining the limits of property rights should establish a fair balance between the affected private interest and the public interest served by the regulation. See AJ van der Walt *Constitutional property clauses: A comparative analysis* (1999) 133–136, as well as the examples from case law at 136–141.

[198]See particularly AJ van der Walt 'Towards a theory of rights in property: Exploratory observations on the paradigm of post-apartheid property law' (1995) 10 *SA Public Law* 298–345 at 311–334, where the following possible 'rights in property' are discussed with reference to section 28 of the interim Constitution of 1993: real rights in property (ownership, limited real rights, lawful holdership rights, unlawful possession, non-entitlement 'rights', forgotten or neglected common-law land-use rights, Cowen's 'new patterns of landownership', housing and residential rights, building and development rights, environmental and land-use planning rights); creditor's rights in property (creditor's rights with regard to corporeal property, other creditor's rights, commercial rights); customary-law rights in property (customary-law property rights, historical land-restitution claims); others rights in property (existing rights like 'new property', new rights like cultural or religious property). Many more can be added to this list. Compare D Kleyn 'The constitutional protection of property: A comparison between the German and the South African approach' (1996) 11 *SA Public Law* 402–445 at 419–423; W Du Plessis & NJJ Olivier 'The old and the new property clause' (1997) 1(5) *Human Rights & Const LJ SA* 11–16 at 12; T Roux 'Section 25' in S Woolman et al (eds) *Constitutional law of South Africa* (2nd ed 2003 original service Dec 2003) at 46-15–46-17.

line deriving from the Constitution. Possible guidelines have been identified in chapter 2.3.3 above, for example in the phrase[199] 'to promote the values that underlie an open and democratic society based on human dignity, equality and freedom'; or in the notion that the Bill of Rights should be interpreted to establish an equitable balance between individual rights and the public interest in property. The suggestion is that each individual question regarding the in- or exclusion of an alleged property right or interest from the protection of section 25 may be decided, much as in the German examples mentioned earlier,[200] with reference to what would be just and equitable in terms of such a guideline; whether the in- or exclusion of a specific property right or interest would serve or frustrate the constitutional goal embodied in that guideline; and whether the result of a decision in a specific case would be justifiable in terms of the general constitutional principle stated in that guideline.

In line with experience elsewhere, one would expect the courts to be lenient in answering this particular question, and to include a right or interest rather than exclude it, so that the constitutional legitimacy and justifiability of an alleged infringe-ment of that right may be investigated in a substantive inquiry in terms of the relevant provisions of the Constitution. This would mean that, once again in line with expe-rience elsewhere, the range of objects and rights that are included under the property clause would be inclusive rather than the opposite, and that the courts should, in answering questions of this nature, neither allow themselves to be inhibited by pri-vate-law tradition when confronted with seemingly novel or strange problems, nor shy away from being inventive and creative when the situation demands it. Recent developments in the fields of public-law or 'new property',[201] information and tech-nological property,[202] medical interests and 'body rights' property,[203] cultural prop-erty[204] and so forth indicate that the meaning of the term 'property', even in the

---

[199] In the Preamble, section 1, section 7(1), section 36(1) and section 39(1).

[200] See 3.7.1 and 3.7.2 above.

[201] See CA Reich 'The new property' (1964) 73 *Yale LJ* 733–787. Compare *Transkei Public Servants Association v Government of The Republic of South Africa and Others* 1995 (9) BCLR 1235 (Tk); W Du Plessis & NJJ Olivier 'The old and the new property clause' (1997) 1(5) *Human Rights & Const LJ SA* 11–16 at 13. See 3.7.5 above.

[202] See especially J Boyle *Shamans, software and spleens* (1996) at 35ff; AR Miller 'Copyright protec-tion for computer programs, databases, and computer-generated works: Is anything new since CONTU?' (1993) 106 *Harvard LR* 977–1073; CH Kennedy 'Is the Internet a new legal frontier?' (1996) 39 *Howard LJ* 581–586; HS Reeves 'Property in cyberspace' (1996) 63 *Univ Chicago LR* 761–799; FH Cate 'Law in cyberspace' (1996) 39 *Howard LJ* 565–579; BF Marchant 'On-line on the Internet: First Amendment and intellectual property uncertainties in the on-line world' (1996) 39 *Howard LJ* 477–503. See 3.7.2 above.

[203] See SR Munzer *A theory of property* (1990) at 37ff; J Boyle *Shamans, software and spleens* (1996) at 97ff; MJ Radin *Contested commodities* (1996) at 131ff, as well as the literature referred to there.

[204] See RJ Coombe 'The properties of culture and the politics of possessing identity: Native claims in the cultural appropriation controversy' (1993) 6 *Can J Law & Jur* 249–285; B Ziff & Pratima V Rao (eds) *Borrowed power: Essays on cultural appropriation* (1997), as well as the literature referred to there. For the South African context, see André P Brink 'Speaking in voices' in *Reinventing a continent: Writing and politics in South Africa 1982–1995* (1996) 12–19.

constitutional sphere, is far from being stable or uncontested, and therefore the courts should not hesitate to allow the circumstances and requirements of each case to influence the development of the constitutional notion of property, regardless of what the situation in private law may be. Of course, courts should do well to make intelligent and sensitive use of foreign law in the interpretation of new and difficult cases. The suggestion that all 'economic rights flowing from employment relationships (eg health benefits and study or training opportunities)' and 'so-called fringe benefits (eg car and expense allowances)' might be included in the property concept for purposes of section 25 might look like a frighteningly novel departure for South African courts,[205] but it becomes much less forbidding with the assistance of established foreign examples. In German law,[206] these rights would only be protected if they were vested rights, acquired through substantial own efforts of their holders, and suitable to secure the livelihood or existence of their holders. On the other hand, German law[207] also emphasizes the social importance of property interests which secure a minimum standard of living for those who would otherwise have been destitute or dependent on the state, and although the relevant German decisions on this issue mostly deal with residential rights rather than with state subsidies, it is possible that the South African situation might justify an extension of the German example when a particular state subsidy is essential in establishing or maintaining an important welfare function.[208] In the final analysis, it seems preferable to follow the example of foreign law and restrict the constitutional protection of social participation and welfare rights to those rights that require such protection in view of the values of the Constitution, provided those rights have been acquired through substantial own effort.

Judging on the basis of foreign case law it seems that the threshold question in a constitutional dispute about property, namely whether there is proof of a property right that qualifies for the protection of the property clause (and that has been infringed), can arise with regard to easier or more difficult property interests. In the easier cases, which concern obvious examples of property such as land and movable corporeals, the courts tend to gloss over or skip the threshold question altogether and assume that the property question was answered satisfactorily. Some well-established commercial interests and rights (intellectual property, shares in a company) are treated in much the same way, although the plaintiff might have to do more to answer the threshold question by providing proof of the actual presence of property in these

[205] See W Du Plessis & NJJ Olivier 'The old and the new property clause' (1997) 1(5) *Human Rights & Const LJ SA* 11–16 at 13, with reference to *Transkei Public Servants Association v Government of the Republic of South Africa and Others* 1995 (9) BCLR 1235 (Tk).
[206] See the discussion in 3.7.2 above.
[207] See the discussion in 3.8 above.
[208] See the *Sunday Times* 18 May 1997 at 25 ('Sunday Essay'), where Charles van Onselen argues that university admission and study bursaries, grants and stipendiums provide an important social welfare safety net for disadvantaged students and for their extended families, to compensate for the absence or shortcomings of a proper state welfare system.

cases.[209] The more difficult cases require at least an initial decision or series of decisions to lay down the general principles in terms of which the property question can be investigated and answered. If the property interest at stake is a right deriving from contract, the attitude seems to be to look at the rules of contract law to determine whether the right has vested, in which case it may be protected as property. Similar considerations apply when the right derives from legislation or from a court order. If the property interest is a right against the state, different or extra requirements are laid down, such as the German rule that the right must have been earned through substantial own effort and not purely as a unilateral state grant. The most recent categories of difficult cases, which concern cultural property, body rights and so forth, require more creative effort to lay down suitable rules, but in general the tendency seems to be to accept the proof of property fairly generously (within certain boundaries and subject to certain provisos) and proceed to a substantive investigation of the averred infringement or limitation of property.[210]

An interesting case, as far as South African law is concerned, is the possible proliferation of land-use related rights that might (and should) be included under the property clause. Obviously even the Roman-Dutch common-law tradition leaves us with an almost bewildering range of rights that qualify as property in terms of section 25: ownership, limited real rights like servitude or mortgage bonds, creditor's rights like short-term leases, traditional use-rights like special leases, new developments like share block and timesharing interests or even airspace interests and many more. Customary law adds quite a few interesting rights, including residential and commonage-use rights, rights of inheritance and so forth. To that one can add interesting new statutory rights deriving from land reform legislation.[211] It is possible to say, in fact, that land and various rights and interests in land may well be the source of some of the most interesting questions regarding the meaning of 'property' in section 25, especially if one considers the great importance that land reform assumes in the section. The fact that a balance must be struck between individual rights and the public interest primarily means that conflict between the protection of existing individual rights and the promotion of land reform must be solved with reference to the constitutionally sanctioned land reforms goals, but the same goals can be used to promote the creation or recognition of new property rights for the sake of land reform.

---

[209] Examples of case law where rights and interests of this nature have been accepted are mentioned in 3.7.4 above.

[210] Examples of cases where rights and interests of this nature have already been accepted are mentioned in 3.7.4 and 3.7.5 above.

[211] Here one can think of land claims in terms of the Restitution of Land Rights Act 22 of 1994; so-called informal land rights in terms of the Interim Protection of Informal Land Rights Act 31 of 1996; rights in property associations in terms of the Communal Property Associations Act 28 of 1996; and so-called initial ownership in terms of the Development Facilitation Act 67 of 1995. See chapter 6.3 and 6.4.

Consider the following argument, which relates to the question whether section 25 of the 1996 Constitution protects or entrenches property.[212] One of the major characteristics of apartheid land law was that the 'rights' and interests of black people to use land were systematically eroded and disregarded. In the wake of the new constitutional order it now becomes possible to argue that one of the effects of the 1993 Constitution was to overturn that position and create a situation where those rights could again be recognised, not only by way of new land reform legislation, but also by simply giving those land rights the constitutional nod. This means that the land rights of a labour tenant or a long-term farm labourer are not re-created by new land reform laws: they were resurrected by the Constitution, and the new laws do no more than formalise the scope and content of those rights. This argument provides the background for construing a number of constitutional property rights on the basis of section 25. While none of these rights could be classified as straightforward claim-rights, and although most of them (consider section 25(6) and 25(7)) are 'processed' through legislation, section 25 can nevertheless be seen as the source of these rights of access to land. If this argument is sound, it means that section 25 cannot and should not be seen simply as a threat or impediment to land reform; it can also be regarded as the very basis and source of land reform itself. According to this view, and given the history of land and property law in South Africa, it seems likely that a fairly expansive and generous attitude towards the definition of property in the constitutional sphere can promote rather than hamper the cause of land reform, but perhaps this is a question that is better answered in each individual case, with reference to the guidelines derived from the Bill of Rights, than abstractly.

It remains to summarize some of the findings above regarding the possible scope of the property concept that is involved in section 25. While there are no clear answers to the property question in individual cases because each case has to be judged in its own context, there are some general guidelines in foreign case law that can assist the courts in arriving at answers in the first phase of the property dispute. It was said earlier that the first phase of a constitutional property dispute, where the existence (and limitation of) a protected property interest must be proven, can involve easier or more difficult cases. It is important to note that, although some of the categories below might be easier that does not mean that each case will always automatically qualify for protection. In some cases the property entitlement relied on may be restricted or even taken away by law, such as the entitlement to build on land. The purpose of the distinctions below is not to argue that each of these categories will automatically be protected, but that there is sufficient authority in foreign law for the argument that rights of that kind may be protected as property, depending upon the context and the specific circumstances of each case. The references below to the difficulty or ease with which the property question may be answered refer to the abstract issue as it affects each category in general, but the property question has to be argued and proven separately and concretely in each individual case.

---

[212] See the discussion in chapter 2.3.5 and in 3.2 above.

The first group of examples, where the property question hardly needs to be asked or discussed at all, and where it is indeed often passed over in foreign case law, are the easiest cases, where it will probably not even be necessary to argue the presence of property, as long as the existence of the right itself is proven. Proof will possibly take the same form as in a vindicatory or similar private-law action:

- Real rights in land and permanent attachments to land (immovable tangible property). Personal use-rights (as opposed to ownership and other real rights) with regard to immovable property usually derive from contract or legislation, and therefore fall in the second group of examples below, but generally they are protected if the right has vested and if the protection is socially justified. Judging from European case law and recent South African case law the courts might bend over backwards to protect socially or economically insecure land-use rights, and particularly residential rights that affect the human dignity and personal security of people. If a particular interest is protected by legislation it could potentially enjoy the protection of section 25, even when it is not recognized as property in private law.
- Real rights in movable tangible property.

A second group of examples concern intangible property, mostly in the form of rights. These cases are slightly more difficult, and the party who relies on the protection of section 25 will probably have to prove the existence of the right and argue the reasons why the right in question should be protected in terms of the property clause. However, in view of authority from foreign law it should not be too hard to prove that these rights can be protected as property in general:

- Personal rights in land.
- Personal rights in movable tangible property.
- Rights in immaterial property (copyright, patents, trademarks, confidential commercial information).[213] Proof of the right is usually sufficient to justify its protection as property, since these rights are recognized as property anyway, either in private or in commercial law.
- Established and well-known commercial rights based on contract (debts, claims, goodwill, shares in a company).[214] Proof of the right (that the right has vested) is usually accepted as justification for its protection, since these rights are widely

---

[213]There is ample authority for each of these examples. The most important German cases are *BVerfGE* 31, 229 [1971] (*Urheberrecht*) (copyright); *BVerfGE* 36, 281 [1974] (patents); *BVerfGE* 51, 193 [1979] (*Warenzeichen*) (trademarks). With regard to confidential information see *BVerfGE* 36, 281 [1974]; and compare *Smith-Kline & French Laboratories (Australia) Ltd and Others v Secretary, Department of Community Services and Health* (1990) 95 ALR 87 (FC) (Australia); *Harper & Row, Publishers, Inc v Nation Enterprises* 471 US 539 (1985); *San Francisco Arts & Athletics, Inc v US Olympic Committee* 107 S Ct 2971 (1987).

[214]See with regard to contractual debts: *BVerfGE* 42, 263 [1976] (*Contergan*) (delictual settlement claims); *BVerfGE* 83, 201 [1991] (*Vorkaufsrecht*) (right of pre-emption); *BVerfGE* 53, 257 [1980] (matrimonial property rights) (Germany); *Peverill v Health Insurance Commission* (1991) 104 ALR 449 (FC) (Australia); *Nobrega v Attorney-General of Guyana* (1967) 10 WIR 187 (CAG) (Guyana);

(continued on next page ...)

recognized as property. An important subdivision of this category consists of land-use rights based on contract, court order or legislation. As was pointed out earlier, some of these rights are protected even against a private landowner when such protection is justified by the social interest.

A third group of examples involve slightly more difficult cases, which involve debts and claims not based on contract. These rights are often referred to as 'new property' in terms of Reich's famous article,[215] but in fact they include different categories that should be distinguished, although all of them are based on claims against the state. Even in the abstract sense the protection of these rights is mostly problematic, although there are some general rules and guidelines in foreign law:

- Welfare claim rights against the state and not based on contract (pensions, medical benefits, subsidies).[216] Only some of these rights are regarded as property and protected. In German law, three requirements are used to distinguish between protected and unprotected welfare rights, the most important requirements being that the right in question must have been earned substantially through own effort and that it must have vested in the beneficiary. Gratuitous payments are not protected.[217]
- Licences, permits and quotas issued by the state.[218] Some of these rights are regarded as property and protected if they have vested in the claimant and if they are regarded as valuable assets.
- Other rights against the state, based on legislation (especially land- and water-use rights in terms of land reform and similar initiatives undertaken in terms of sections 24, 25, 26 and 27).[219]

(... from previous page)

but compare *Chairman, Public Service Commission, and Others v Zimbabwe Teachers' Association and Others* 1997 (1) SA 209 (ZSC) (Zimbabwe); *Phillips v Washington Legal Foundation* 524 US 156 (1999); *Webb's Fabulous Pharmacies v Beckwith* 449 US 155 (1980) (US). The general rule is that the right is protected if the debt has vested; the rules of contract law indicate whether and when a right has vested. In *BGE* 196 Ia 163 [1980] (*Graf*) (Switzerland) the right vested by way of legislation; in *Hewlett v Minister of Finance and Another* 1982 (1) SA 490 (ZSC) (Zimbabwe) the debt vested by way of an award similar to a court order. Proof that goodwill is property is problematical.

[215]CA Reich 'The new property' (1964) 73 *Yale LJ* 733–787; compare the discussion in 3.7.5 above.
[216]See the examples in 3.7.5 above. The most important German case is *BVerfGE* 69, 272 [1985] (*Eigenleistung*), where the three requirements listed in 3.7.5 above are set out and applied. The most important US case is *Flemming v Nestor* 363 US 603 (1960) at 608 .
[217]See *Tilkayat Shri Govindalalj Maharaj v State of Rajasthan and Others* AIR 1963 SC 1638 (India) (hereditary religious trust is not property); compare *Chairman, Public Service Commission, and Others v Zimbabwe Teachers' Association and Others* 1997 1 SA 209 (ZSC) (Zimbabwe) (teachers' annual bonus is not property); *Flemming v Nestor* 363 US 603 (1960) at 608.
[218]See 3.7.4 above for examples. The best examples are *Hand v Dublin Corporation* [1991] 1 IR 409; *Hempenstall and Others v Minister for the Environment* [1994] 2 IR 20 (Ireland); the *Tre Traktörer AB Case* [1989] ECHR Series A vol 159 (European Court of Human Rights).
[219]See chapter 6.3 and 6.4 for examples of land reform laws that may establish such rights. Claims in terms of land reform laws that were promulgated in accordance with subsections 25(5), 25(6), 25(7) could qualify, as well as water use rights and mineral and mining rights in terms of the new water and minerals and mining legislation discussed in chapter 6.5.

The guidelines in the summary above give an indication of the way in which the inclusion of rights and intangible assets in the property concept of the constitutional property clause inevitably involve questions about the purpose and social function of the constitutional protection of these rights. It is therefore justified to emphasize the fact that what is protected by the property clause is not property in the traditional, private-law sense; and that the protection as such is also not the traditional, private-law protection in the sense of an unconditional and absolute insulation of property against all interferences and invasions not consented to by the owner (in as far as that ever was and still is the nature of private-law protection of property). In this sense it is of the utmost importance that the property clause be seen in the context of its constitutional function: for purposes of section 25, property is a characteristically constitutional right, and its protection is also of a typically constitutional nature. Constitutional protection does not amount to protection of private rights at all cost, nor does it recognize property as a pre-social right that requires compensation for any amendment or limitation. If anything, it means that existing and new property interests are recognized and protected when and in so far as it is necessary to establish and uphold an equitable balance between individual property interests and the public interest, with due regard for the historical context within which property holdings were established and the constitutional context within which they are now protected.

Deprivation

---

25. Property

(1) No one may be deprived of property except in terms of law of general application, and no law may permit arbitrary deprivation of property.

4.1 INTRODUCTION

Section 25(1) of the 1996 Constitution deals with a special category of limitation of property, namely deprivation. The section provides that deprivation of property may only be imposed by law of general application, and that no law may provide for arbitrary deprivation.

In one sense, the term 'deprivation' is confusing in this context because it can create the mistaken impression that the term refers to the taking away of property.[1]

---

[1] See *Mkontwana v Nelson Mandela Metropolitan Municipality; Bissett and Others v Buffalo City Municipality; Transfer Rights Action Campaign and Others v Member of the Executive Council for Local Government and Housing, Gauteng and Others* 2005 (1) SA 530 (CC) par [32] at 546A–C, where the Constitutional Court confirmed that the taking away of property is not required for deprivation, citing *First National Bank of SA Ltd t/a Wesbank v Commissioner, South African Revenue Service; First National Bank of SA Ltd t/a Wesbank v Minister of Finance* 2002 (4) SA 768 (CC) par [57] at 796F–H.

The potential for confusion is increased by the fact that the relevant constitutional text in at least two foreign jurisdictions (France[2] and the European Union[3]) indeed uses the term 'deprivation' when it refers to expropriation of property. However, despite the terminological inconsistencies, 'deprivation' is distinguished relatively clearly from 'expropriation' in most jurisdictions, as is explained in 4.2 below,[4] and consequently the terminology should not create insurmountable confusion, at least not initially.[5] There is grey area between the two categories where deprivation seems to blur into expropriation, but the existence of this grey area is a function of excessive regulation and should not detract from the relative clarity of the initial distinction.

The purpose of this chapter is to provide an introduction to deprivation, to indicate how it is understood by the courts and in the literature and what it involves, and to discuss the requirements for deprivation of property in terms of section 25. The central part of the chapter is dedicated to the authoritative interpretation of the deprivation provision in section 25(1) in the Constitutional Court decision in *First National Bank of SA Ltd t/a Wesbank v Commissioner, South African Revenue Service; First National Bank of SA Ltd t/a Wesbank v Minister of Finance.*[6] This decision is important because it developed an interpretation of deprivation and a methodology for applying the requirements in section 25(1) (particularly the arbitrariness test) that have significant implications for the interpretation and application of section 25 as a whole.[7] It also

---

[2] Article 17 of the Declaration of the Rights of Man and the Citizen 1789 provides as follows: 'Property being an inviolable and sacred right, no one may be deprived of it save where public necessity, legally ascertained, clearly requires it; and then on condition of a just and previously determined compensation.' In this provision, 'deprivation' means expropriation; see AJ van der Walt *Constitutional property clauses: A comparative analysis* (1999) 522–525.

[3] The second sentence of the first paragraph (the so-called 'second rule'; see *Sporrong & Lönnroth v Sweden* [1982] 5 EHRR 35) of article 1 of the First Protocol to the European Convention on Human Rights 1950 provides that '[n]o one shall be deprived of his possessions except in the public interest and subject to the conditions provided for by law and the general principles of international law.' In this rule, 'deprive' means expropriate; see AJ van der Walt *Constitutional property clauses: A comparative analysis* (1999) 110.

[4] The distinction between deprivation and expropriation is again discussed in chapter 5.2 and 5.4.

[5] The possibility of confusion was raised and the matter was settled definitively in *First National Bank of SA Ltd t/a Wesbank v Commissioner, South African Revenue Service; First National Bank of SA Ltd t/a Wesbank v Minister of Finance* 2002 (4) SA 768 (CC) par [57] at 796E–H; see footnotes 1–3 above and surrounding text.

[6] 2002 (4) SA 768 (CC). See the discussion of the case in 4.5 and 4.6 below and compare chapter 5.2. See further on the *FNB* decision T Roux 'Section 25' in S Woolman et al (eds) *Constitutional law of South Africa* (2nd ed 2003 original service Dec 2003) 46-2–46-5 at 46-2–46-5, 46-21–46-25.

[7] The decision and its interpretive approach was already followed in a subsequent decision of the Constitutional Court: *Mkontwana v Nelson Mandela Metropolitan Municipality; Bissett and Others v Buffalo City Municipality; Transfer Rights Action Campaign and Others v Member of the Executive Council for Local Government and Housing, Gauteng and Others* 2005 (1) SA 530 (CC). This decision is discussed in 4.5.4 below, where it is argued that the *Mkontwana* decision purports to follow and apply the *FNB* test but in fact deviates from it.

represents the Court's authoritative view of the meaning and interpretation of section 25(1), at least for the moment.

Subsequent to the discussion of the definition of and requirements for valid deprivation three special categories of deprivation that have already enjoyed some attention in case law are discussed briefly in the last section of the chapter: firstly land-use planning and development and environment conservation; secondly search, seizure and forfeiture provisions; and thirdly restrictions on eviction, especially in the sphere of so-called 'public accommodations'. These three categories of regulatory deprivation explain and demonstrate the nature and purpose of and requirements for deprivation of property in more or less 'normal', business-as-usual circumstances and offer examples of how deprivation powers are applied in most foreign jurisdictions.

4.2 DEFINITION OF DEPRIVATION

4.2.1 Introduction

Deprivation is usually defined with reference to the ways in which it differs from expropriation. The distinction between deprivation and expropriation of property has become deeply embedded in constitutional property jurisprudence worldwide.[8] In countries such as Malaysia[9] and South Africa[10] there is a strong textual basis for this distinction, but it is accepted even in jurisdictions (such as Zimbabwe)[11] where there is no textual indication for making the distinction.

---

[8]The distinction is not always made explicitly, but it is totally absent in only a few cases. When the constitutional text does not make the distinction explicit it is often assumed. For South African law the Malaysian property clause (article 13 of the Federal Constitution of Malaysia 1957; see AJ van der Walt *Constitutional property clauses: A comparative analysis* (1999) 266, 271–272) is the closest match, in that section 13(1) refers to deprivation and section 13(2) to expropriation against compensation in much the same terms as subsections 25(1) and (2)–(3) respectively. In another sense, the South African provision in section 25 relates structurally (if not conceptually) to the German property provision (article 14 of the German Basic Law 1949; see AJ van der Walt *Constitutional property clauses: A comparative analysis* (1999) 121, 123), which distinguishes between expropriation (article 14.3) and the (regulatory) determination of the content and limits of property (article 14.1.2).

[9]Section 13(1) and 13(2) of the Malaysian Constitution refers to deprivation and expropriation respectively; see chapter 5.2 below and compare AJ van der Walt *Constitutional property clauses: A comparative analysis* (1999) 266, 271–272. Compare *Government of Malaysia v Selangor Pilot Association* (1977) 1 MLJ 133, where the application of the distinction is by no means simple or uncontroversial.

[10]Subsections 25(1) and 25(2) envisage and authorize the distinction by establishing two discrete categories of limitation, each with its own requirements and results. The distinction was first raised by the Constitutional Court in *Harksen v Lane NO* 1998 (1) SA 300 (CC) paras [33]–[40] at 315E–318I; see the discussion below.

[11]In *Davies and Others v Minister of Land, Agriculture and Water Development* 1997 (1) SA 228 (ZSC) at 232D the Zimbabwe Supreme Court decided that this distinction forms part of Zimbabwean law and that only expropriation requires compensation, while no compensation is payable for deprivation of property; see AJ van der Walt *Constitutional property clauses: A comparative analysis* (1999) 473–489. See further *Hewlett v Minister of Finance and Another* 1982 (1) SA 490 (ZSC). For further discussions of this distinction, see M Chaskalson 'The problem with property: Thoughts on

(continued on next page ...)

As was mentioned in the introduction above, terminology with regard to deprivation in constitutional property clauses is neither clear nor consistent.[12] Generally, deprivation is defined by contrasting it with expropriation, and it is often said that both categories involve some state interference with private property and possibly some loss or deterioration of value for the property holder, but that the state acquires property against compensation through expropriation while it merely regulates the use of property through deprivation. The obvious effect of this approach to the definition is that deprivation is usually not compensated, while expropriation is. The most common examples of deprivation referred to in this context are public health and safety laws related to property, land-use planning and development controls, building regulations and environmental conservation laws.[13] These regulatory controls restrict the owner's free use, enjoyment, exploitation and disposal of the property and so diminish its value or profitability, but none of them takes the property away—they merely impose controls on the use of the property. The loss or diminution of value caused by regulatory control varies and it can be quite substantial in some instances; in extreme cases regulation may result in total destruction of the property, but even then—so the standard argument goes—the state does not acquire the property and therefore it is not expropriation.[14] The significant elements that appear from this explanation are that regulatory deprivation is not intended to take property away but to

---

(... from previous page)
the constitutional protection of property in the United States and the Commonwealth' (1993) 9 SAJHR 388–411; M Chaskalson 'The property clause: Section 28 of the constitution' (1994) 10 SAJHR 131–139 at 134ff; AJ van der Walt 'Towards a theory of rights in property: Exploratory observations on the paradigm of post-apartheid property law' (1995) 10 SA Public Law 298–345 at 310ff; DG Kleyn 'The constitutional protection of property: A comparison between the German and the South African approach' (1996) 11 SA Public Law 402–445 at 437; AJ van der Walt 'Compensation for excessive or unfair regulation: A comparative overview of constitutional practice relating to regulatory takings' (1999) 14 SA Public Law 273–331.

[12]See footnotes 2 and 3 above and surrounding text.

[13]See the classic explanation and discussion in JL Sax 'Takings and the police power' (1964) 74 Yale LJ 36–76; see on Sax's argument T Allen The right to property in Commonwealth constitutions (2000) 173–175. Compare AJ van der Walt Constitutional property clauses: A comparative analysis (1999) 410–423 (US, the classic approach and distinction), 132–147 (Germany, with a slightly unusual approach to deprivation), 332–335 (South Africa).

[14]See eg Mugler v Kansas 123 US 623 (1887) (prohibition on sale and manufacture of liquor); Miller v Schoene 276 US 272 (1928) (one landowner's trees were destroyed to save others' from a virulent pest). T Allen The right to property in Commonwealth constitutions (2000) 180 points out that the holding in Mugler survived the challenge from Pennsylvania Coal Co v Mahon 260 US 393 (1922), which means that not every deprivation that imposes a very heavy burden (up to and including loss of the property) will necessarily be transformed into an expropriation that requires compensation. The distinction between regulatory action that destroys property without compensation and instances that mutate into expropriation and require compensation (inverse condemnation) is one of the most contentious issues in US takings law; see further on that topic chapter 5.4. See T Roux 'Property' in MH Cheadle, DM Davis & NRL Haysom South African constitutional law: The bill of rights (2002) 429–472 at 454.

regulate its use; that it always causes some diminution of value and can sometimes cause significant loss; and that it is nevertheless usually not compensated.

Although this initial, basic definition makes it relatively easy to distinguish 'normal' regulatory deprivation (such as the regulation of building standards) from 'normal' expropriation (involving compulsory acquisition of property) the distinction is not as simple as it appears. In fact the 'normal' distinction is little more than a useful starting point and the differences become blurry and contested as soon as the examples become more complex. There are many reasons why the initial distinction fails in concrete cases. One reason is that it is accepted in some jurisdictions that expropriation can occur without the state acquiring the affected property, for instance when the property is destroyed by regulatory control (inverse condemnation).[15] Similarly, it is sometimes accepted that regulatory deprivation of property can be treated as expropriation that requires compensation when the effects of the deprivation become excessive or overly burdensome, especially when they are placed on just one or a small group of owners for the benefit of society at large (regulatory taking or material or constructive expropriation).[16] A third problem is that this distinction does not explain the situation when the property is not acquired by the state but taken from the affected owner and transferred to another private person or group for a legitimate government purpose such as land reform—the narrow definition would characterize such an action as deprivation but not expropriation and therefore exclude compensation, probably unfairly.[17]

The first two of these problematic cases, where the initial distinction between deprivation and expropriation is blurred because the case is treated as expropriation although the state does not acquire the property, constitute a grey area in between deprivation and expropriation. It is widely recognized that regulatory exercise of the police power almost always involves some restriction or limitation on the use and enjoyment of property, and that it can sometimes result in quite serious loss for the property holder,[18] but the problem is that these excessive effects of deprivation cannot

---

[15]See in this regard chapter 5, especially 5.4. When the regulation serves the core goal of protecting public health and safety it is less likely that compensation will be required even when the burden is very heavy; see the previous footnote above.

[16]See in this regard chapter 5, especially 5.4. The classic US example is *Lucas v South Carolina Coastal Council* 505 US 1003 (1992), where the US Supreme Court held that regulatory action that deprived an owner of all economic use of the property has the same effect and is regarded as a taking that requires compensation.

[17]See T Roux 'Property' in MH Cheadle, DM Davis & NRL Haysom *South African constitutional law: The bill of rights* (2002) 429–472 at 453–455, and compare chapter 5.4.

[18]Consider the regulatory restriction that prevents the owner of a motor car from driving faster than the speed limit, and compare that with the restriction that prevents all building or development on a piece of land situated in a sensitive nature area. With regard to regulatory deprivation that destroys the property or all its value see *Miller v Schoene* 276 US 272 (1928) and *Lucas v South Carolina Coastal Council* 505 US 1003 (1992). In *Miller* it was considered acceptable that the affected landowner's trees were destroyed without compensation to prevent the disease from spreading; in

(continued on next page …)

always be justified with reference to the purpose served by the regulation, especially when regulation leaves the core area of public health and safety and moves into marginal areas of public interest regulation.[19] Similarly, the effects of regulatory loss become more difficult to justify when the state derives some material benefit from the regulatory action. It is in these instances, where the effect of regulatory action can result in the two categories blurring into each other, that the injustice is sometimes rectified by treating regulatory deprivation as expropriation. As a consequence it is an oversimplification to explain the distinction between deprivation and expropriation purely in terms of the question whether the state acquires the property or not.

Apart from acquisition by the state, the initial distinction often relies on the fact that expropriation is permanent and deprivation temporary,[20] but this is also an over-simplification, because deprivation is often permanent in its limiting effect on the use of property,[21] while expropriation can in certain cases be temporary.[22] Two defining characteristics of expropriation—state acquisition and permanence—are therefore unreliable in distinguishing deprivation from expropriation.

In *Mkontwana*[23] the South African Constitutional Court stated that the question whether there has been a deprivation 'depends on the extent of the interference with or limitation of use, enjoyment or exploitation' and that 'at the very least, substantial interference or limitation that goes beyond the normal restrictions on property use or

---

(... from previous page)
Lucas it was said that regulatory action that deprived an owner of all economic use of the property has the same effect as a permanent physical invasion and is regarded as a *per se* taking that requires compensation. The difference between the two cases is difficult to explain, except with reference to their respective distance to the regulatory core of protecting public health and safety, and even then *Lucas* is not easily distinguished from *Miller*. Compare the *Lucas* situation to another US decision, namely *Tahoe-Sierra Preservation Council Inc v Tahoe Regional Planning Agency* 535 US 302 (2002), where the building restrictions that prevented development for the sake of conservation were temporary. This aspect is discussed below.

[19] The most obvious example is aesthetic neighbourhood protection, which does not protect public safety or health in a direct or obvious way, although it may serve more marginal social interests.

[20] This view is sometimes deduced from the Constitutional Court decision in *Harksen v Lane NO* 1998 (1) SA 300 (CC) paras [33]–[40] at 315E–318I, where Goldstone J emphasized the permanent acquisition element in distinguishing expropriation from deprivation.

[21] This applies to most regulatory restrictions on the use of property, especially if they are imposed to serve the narrow purposes of protecting public health and safety; compare the examples in footnote 14 above.

[22] The classic examples are *Attorney General v De Keyser's Royal Hotel, Ltd* [1920] AC 508 (HL) (United Kingdom, temporary wartime requisitioning of the use of a building); *First English Evangelical Lutheran Church of Glendale v County of Los Angeles* 482 US 304 (1987) (United States, temporary taking of all use of a certain piece of land). However, in *Tahoe-Sierra Preservation Council Inc v Tahoe Regional Planning Agency* 535 US 302 (2002) the US Supreme Court refused to treat a temporary development moratorium as a taking of development rights.

[23] *Mkontwana v Nelson Mandela Metropolitan Municipality; Bissett and Others v Buffalo City Municipality; Transfer Rights Action Campaign and Others v Member of the Executive Council for Local Government and Housing, Gauteng and Others* 2005 (1) SA 530 (CC).

enjoyment found in an open and democratic society would amount to deprivation.'[24] This definition was made subject to a disclaimer[25] and should be read with care because it is problematic in several respects. Firstly, it seems odd that deprivation should be limited to that which exceeds restrictions that are 'normal in an open and democratic society', because all legitimate regulatory restrictions on the use and enjoyment of property are normal in such a society. Furthermore, regulatory control over the use of firearms, motor vehicles and explosives or regulation that ensures building standards and environmental conservation are not unique to open democracies—they are common to most or all regulated societies. Democratic values ensure open public debate about the purposes of and the means selected for regulatory control over the use of property, but they are not uniquely linked with the existence of such controls.

Secondly, it serves no useful purpose to restrict the concept of deprivation to substantial or abnormal—in other words excessive—regulatory deprivation; the purpose of section 25(1) is to legitimize the imposition of regulatory control and the deprivation of property that goes with it generally, not only in excessive cases. Generally speaking it is true that deprivation usually causes problems only in cases of excessive regulation and not when the deprivation is slight, but that does not make it necessary or even advisable to exclude slight deprivations from the definition or from constitutional scrutiny. In the constitutional framework of section 25(1) any regulatory restriction on the use and enjoyment of property, however small or insignificant, can be classified as deprivation without placing an additional burden on the state because deprivation does not in general require compensation and regulatory state action is subject to constitutional review in terms of the general legality requirement in any event.[26] However, if slight or 'normal' restrictions are excluded from the definition of deprivation—as the Court's dictum in *Mkontwana* seems to suggest—that would exclude them from the constitutional control imposed by the requirements in section 25(1), which would in its turn unleash an unnecessary interpretive struggle to determine when a particular restriction on property is substantial enough to qualify as deprivation and when not. Given the modest language of the relevant passage in *Mkontwana* the suggestion that deprivation could be defined with reference to the significance of the limitation should probably just be ignored. The simplest solution is to assume that

---

[24] Par [32] at 545J–546C.

[25] 'It is not necessary in this case to determine precisely what constitutes deprivation': par [32] at 546A–C. Of course it is possible that the Court only expressed itself unclearly in *Mkontwana* and that it really intended to say, as it did in *FNB*, that the extent of deprivation will have an effect on the level of scrutiny that applies when a specific deprivation is tested for constitutionality: see *First National Bank of SA Ltd t/a Wesbank v Commissioner, South African Revenue Service; First National Bank of SA Ltd t/a Wesbank v Minister of Finance* 2002 (4) SA 768 (CC) par [100](*g*) at 81D–E. Compare the discussion of the case in this chapter below.

[26] See *Pharmaceutical Manufacturers Association of SA and Another: In re ex parte President of the Republic of South Africa and Others* 2000 (2) SA 674 (CC) paras [17], [20] at 687B–F, 687H–688B.

every restriction on property, no matter how small or insubstantial, constitutes deprivation in terms of section 25(1) and is therefore subject to its requirements.[27]

The examples referred to above show that the distinction between deprivation
and expropriation may be relatively clear and established on a basic level, but outside
of the easy cases it soon becomes complex and context-specific. Accordingly, it is
impossible to define deprivation with the focus exclusively on the questions whether
the state acquires the property, whether the acquisition is permanent or temporary,
and whether the extent of the deprivation is slight or serious. To develop a more
context-sensitive definition requires attention for a more complex set of defining
factors. Comparative analysis reveals that such factors indeed exist and that a useful
definition of deprivation can be construed with their help.

4.2.2 Defining factors

The traditional distinction between deprivation and expropriation owes much of its
content to US law, albeit that the US Constitution, case law and literature employ
different terminology from most other jurisdictions.[28] In its simplest form, the distinction is explained by saying that expropriation refers to exercises of the state's power
of eminent domain and deprivation to exercises of the police power. This distinction
rests on the different sources of power by which each of the two limitations is authorized and suggests a reason for the fact that compensation is usually not required for
deprivation—exercises of the police power may cause (even extensive) loss or damage
but are as a rule not compensated because their purpose is to protect public health and
safety for everyone's benefit.[29] The underlying assumption is, therefore, that one

[27] Of course the *de minimis* principle will ensure that insignificant deprivations are not litigated.
However, that is not to say that a distinction between slight and substantial deprivation is useless.
In Swiss law a lower level of scrutiny applies when slight regulatory interferences are reviewed; see
AJ van der Walt *Constitutional property clauses: A comparative analysis* (1999) 367. This differentiated
approach is sensible in Swiss law because substantial deprivation could prove to be material expropriation, for which compensation is required, but the idea may also be useful in other jurisdictions.
See further AJ van der Walt 'The property clause in the new Federal Constitution of the Swiss
Confederation 1999' (2004) 15 *Stell LR* 326–332.
[28] Although the term 'expropriation' is known in US law, it is reserved for formal expropriation,
and the term used more generally is 'taking'. Deprivation is often referred to in terms of 'regulation'. See AJ van der Walt *Constitutional property clauses: A comparative analysis* (1999) 410–423. T
Allen *The right to property in Commonwealth constitutions* (2000) at 179 indicates that most Commonwealth courts took over some version of the US police power doctrine.
[29] It is true that this difference is sometimes blurred because this rule is not applied absolutely or
consistently. Compare footnote 14 above on US law. Article 26(2) of the Federal Constitution of the
Swiss Confederation 1999 explicitly guarantees compensation for material expropriation or, as the
article describes it, 'restrictions of ownership equivalent to expropriation'; see AJ van der Walt 'The
property clause in the new Federal Constitution of the Swiss Confederation 1999' (2004) 15 *Stell LR*
326–332 and compare chapter 5.4. Other jurisdictions do not necessarily guarantee compensation
for constructive expropriation but nevertheless recognize the category in case law; see chapter 5.4.
See further T Allen *The right to property in Commonwealth constitutions* (2000) at 162–163.

person gives up property in the public interest through expropriation, whereas everyone suffers more or less equal limitations and enjoys more or less equal benefits through regulatory deprivation; hence the former requires compensation but the latter does not.

Although the grey area between deprivation and expropriation—mostly consisting of what is called regulatory taking in US law—is fraught with confusing overlaps,[30] it can generally be said on the basis of US jurisprudence that the eminent domain / police power distinction is useful in the majority of cases. The confusion that makes the distinction so difficult in the grey area of regulatory taking is caused by the excessive effects of some regulatory deprivations and does not really detract from the validity of distinguishing between the two categories with reference to the power by which either category is authorized.[31] Accordingly it appears as if the source of authority for the limitation of property in US law, namely either the power of eminent domain or the police power, is a useful indicator that makes the definition of deprivation somewhat easier, at least initially. Australian law[32] emphasizes the source of the authority for state limitation of property in deciding whether the action requires compensation, with the effect that even very harsh limitations that were imposed on the authority of non-expropriatory constitutional powers are not treated as expropriation, although it is perhaps not quite clear that they are necessarily therefore classified as deprivation either.[33] In German law, the emphasis on the source of power is even stronger in that it is said that excessive or unfair regulatory deprivation could be unconstitutional and invalid for being unjustifiably unfair, but it cannot thereby be transformed into expropriation because the two kinds of action derive from different sources of authority and should each be judged according to its own source of authority.[34]

---

[30] See chapter 5.4 for a fuller discussion.

[31] This is illustrated by the famous words of Holmes J in *Pennsylvania Coal Co v Mahon* 260 US 393 (1922)—generally recognized as the origin of the notion of regulatory taking—that the state cannot be expected to compensate every loss caused by regulatory action, but when a regulation 'goes too far' it will be treated as a taking and deemed invalid unless compensation was paid (*Mahon* at 413). See LH Tribe *American constitutional law* (2nd ed 1988) 591.

[32] The Australian situation is uniquely complex in that the property clause refers only to 'compulsory acquisition' and only guarantees compensation ('just terms') for compulsory acquisitions that are authorized specifically by section 51(xxxi) of the Commonwealth Constitution and not for others; see AJ van der Walt *Constitutional property clauses: A comparative analysis* (1999) 46–48, 56; T Allen *The right to property in Commonwealth constitutions* (2000) 175–178; and compare chapter 5.3, 5.4 and 5.7 for further details.

[33] Compare the Australian decisions in *Re Director of Public Prosecutions; Ex Parte Lawler and Another* (1994) 179 CLR 270 (HC) (forfeiture); *Mutual Pools & Staff Pty Limited v The Commonwealth of Australia* (1994) 179 CLR 155 (taxes); *Health Insurance Commission v Peverill* (1994) 179 CLR 226 236 (adjustment of civil claims) discussed in chapter 5.3 and 5.4. See further T Allen *The right to property in Commonwealth constitutions* (2000) 175–179; AJ van der Walt *Constitutional property clauses: A comparative analysis* (1999) 46–48, 56.

[34] See the discussion in chapter 5.4.3 and especially the Federal Constitutional Court decision in the *Naßauskiesung* case *BVerfGE* 58, 300 [1981]; confirmed in *BVerfGE* 100, 226 [1999]. See further AJ van der Walt *Constitutional property clauses: A comparative analysis* (1999) 141–145.

On the basis of these comparative examples deprivation could be defined—and contrasted with expropriation—by referring to a cluster of context-sensitive considerations:

- The source of the power: deprivation results from exercises of the regulatory police power; expropriation from exercises of the expropriatory power of eminent domain. Compensation is usually required for exercises of the power of eminent domain but not for exercises of the police power. A particular limitation of property that is authorized by the police power could end up being recognized and treated as expropriation as a result of one of the other considerations below, but at least initially the source of power gives a useful indication of the distinction between deprivation and expropriation.[35]

- The purpose or intention behind the limitation: because the source of the power that authorizes expropriation and deprivation is so significant it is important to establish the purpose or intention behind the limitation. If the intention is to acquire property compulsorily but the source of authority is the police power the limitation may well be invalid, especially in jurisdictions such as Germany where the source of authority is extremely important in determining the validity of the limitation. This factor should be relatively easy to apply since the public purpose requirement for expropriation necessitates identification of the specific public need or duty to be fulfilled by the expropriation.[36] The real intention behind a limitation should be relevant and not the declared purpose.

- The effect of the limitation on the property holder: the effect of a limitation on the property owner or holder is relevant in the difficult cases that make up the grey area between deprivation and expropriation. As a general rule, the effect of expropriation should be that the state acquires (or destroys) property for a public purpose; the effect of deprivation should be that the burden of protecting public health and safety is spread widely and fairly throughout society by way of general or reciprocal use restrictions. In some jurisdictions excessive deprivation (that 'goes too far') is treated as expropriation and requires compensation, even though the authorizing power and the intention or purpose may have been regulatory rather than acquisitive;[37] in others excessive deprivation is simply invalid for exceeding its constitutional or statutory authority or purpose.[38]

---

[35]See T Allen *The right to property in Commonwealth constitutions* (2000) 185.

[36]See chapter 5.7 regarding the public purpose requirement for expropriation, and compare the discussion in 4.3 below with regard to the requirements for deprivation. See further T Allen *The right to property in Commonwealth constitutions* (2000) 163, 177.

[37]This is constructive expropriation; see chapter 5.4 for a discussion. The classic cases are mostly American; see especially *Pennsylvania Coal Co v Mahon* 260 US 393 (1922) at 413. See T Allen *The right to property in Commonwealth constitutions* (2000) 168.

[38]The paradigm example is Germany; see chapter 5.4.3 for a discussion. The classic case is *BVerfGE* 58, 300 [1981] (*Naßauskiesung*); confirmed in *BVerfGE* 100, 226 [1999]. See AJ van der Walt *Constitutional property clauses: A comparative analysis* (1999) 141–145.

- State acquisition of the property: the fact that the state does not acquire the property should not in itself be considered decisive—even when the state does not acquire the property other factors could indicate that the action should nevertheless be treated as expropriation rather than deprivation. However, if the state does acquire the property that should be a very strong indication that the action is expropriatory rather than regulatory in nature, regardless of the declared intention or form of the action. In Australian law (where the property clause refers to 'compulsory acquisition') it is said that state action could amount to expropriation that requires compensation if the state acquires any property or any benefit, however slight, from it—it is not necessary that the state should acquire the affected property as such.[39] The fact that the state acquires the property or some benefit merely indicates that its effects are acquisitive, but not that it should be treated as expropriation—in German law the result would be that the action is invalid because of the mismatch between authority, purpose and effect.

- Permanence: the fact that a limitation on the property is temporary should not be considered decisive proof that it is deprivation rather than expropriation, but if the limitation involves permanent loss of the property or a permanent physical invasion by the state that could in some jurisdictions indicate, depending on other factors, that the action is expropriatory rather than regulatory in nature.[40]

Apart from the factors usually referred to by the courts (state acquisition, permanence and the extent of the deprivation) deprivation could therefore be defined with reference to the power that authorizes it, its purpose and its effects. Generally speaking the purpose of the police power is to regulate and control the use, enjoyment, exploitation and disposal of property for the sake of public health and safety. In US law this is regarded as the core or narrow definition of the police power, to be distinguished from more remote or fringe regulatory functions that do not serve public health and safety directly but are nevertheless useful and in the public interest. A higher level of scrutiny should apply to limitations outside the core police power functions of promoting public health and safety.[41]

In conclusion, deprivation could be defined as properly authorized and fairly imposed limitation on the use, enjoyment, exploitation or disposal of property for the sake of protecting and promoting public health and safety, normally without compensation. When this complex set of factors is taken into account in defining deprivation other factors such as state acquisition of the property and the permanence and extent

---

[39] *Georgiadis v Australian and Overseas Telecommunications Corporation* (1994) 179 CLR 297 at 305; see AJ van der Walt *Constitutional property clauses: A comparative analysis* (1999) 54.

[40] In US law it is said that a permanent physical invasion is regarded as a *per se* taking: *Loretto v Teleprompter Manhattan CATV Corp* 458 US 419 (1982); see AJ van der Walt *Constitutional property clauses: A comparative analysis* (1999) 429.

[41] Examples would be land use planning regulation that has no direct bearing on public health and safety, such as aesthetic and neighbourhood character controls; perhaps also foreign exchange and customs controls. See chapter 5.4.2 and compare footnote 119 there for further references.

of the deprivation become more valuable and less confusing than when they are considered on their own.

One way of relating this definition of deprivation to the distinction with expropriation is to set the two categories up as opposing and exclusive parts of a dichotomy; another approach is to see deprivation and expropriation as different points on a continuum rather than exclusive domains; yet another approach is to see deprivation as a broader, encompassing category that includes expropriation, so that all expropriations are deprivations and just some deprivations are expropriations. The first approach was adopted by the South African Constitutional Court in *Harksen*;[42] the second is perhaps most characteristic of the *Mahon* view of regulatory taking in US law; the third was developed in *FNB*.[43] The advantage of the second and third approaches is that they facilitate a more flexible view in terms of which a range of regulatory deprivations can be evaluated with proper attention for their effects and context; the first approach is based on a strict conceptual dichotomy and therefore inflexible.

4.2.3 The police-power principle

Police-power regulatory deprivation restricts the use of property and can therefore cause considerable loss for the property owner or holder, but this negative effect is usually accepted because it protects public health and safety. Moreover, the burdens and losses caused by police power regulation usually affect all citizens alike, and therefore it is accepted that affected owners have to bear these burdens and losses without compensation.[44] Generally speaking, the effect of regulatory deprivation should not be excessive for any individual owner, and the burden should be reciprocal and spread more or less equally among all owners or holders of affected property (motor car owners, restaurateurs, farmers). As far as regulatory deprivation is concerned, compensation (or invalidity) only becomes an issue when the burden is not imposed fairly or not spread equally, so that one owner (or a small group of owners) is singled out and expected to bear an excessive burden for the sake of the public at large.[45]

---

[42] *Harksen v Lane NO* 1998 (1) SA 300 (CC) paras [33]–[40] at 315E–318I; compare the criticism of AJ van der Walt & H Botha 'Coming to grips with the new constitutional order: Critical comments on *Harksen v Lane NO*' (1998) 13 *SA Public Law* 17–41 at 19–21.

[43] *First National Bank of SA Ltd t/a Wesbank v Commissioner, South African Revenue Service; First National Bank of SA Ltd t/a Wesbank v Minister of Finance* 2002 (4) SA 768 (CC) paras [57]–[58] at 796E–797A. See the discussion of the cases in 4.5 and 4.6 below and compare chapter 5.2.

[44] In *Pennsylvania Coal Co v Mahon* 260 US 393 (1922) Holmes J explained that the state cannot be expected to compensate every loss caused by regulatory action because that would make government impossible—it is only when regulation 'goes too far' that it will be treated as a taking and deemed invalid unless compensation was paid (at 413). See footnote 31 above. See further T Allen *The right to property in Commonwealth constitutions* (2000) 179.

[45] This emphasizes the usefulness of looking at (among other factors) the effects of the limitation to determine its nature: if the burden is placed on one owner only for the benefit of society as a whole, the limitation should preferably be clothed as expropriation. In German-language jurisdictions this is known as the *Sonderopfertheorie*, but a version of it is followed in US law as well, albeit

(continued on next page ...)

The police-power principle, which is at the heart of uncompensated regulatory deprivation of property, is that the state is not obliged to either leave all existing property interests unaffected by state action or pay compensation for any detrimental effect that its action may have on private property. Instead, the state is authorized to regulate the use, enjoyment and exploitation of private property—even when such regulation involves limitation of the property owner's entitlements and causes financial loss— provided the regulatory deprivation is imposed generally, for a legitimate public purpose and fairly (not arbitrarily, in the South African terminology of section 25(1)). This principle was famously expounded by Holmes J in the US case of *Pennsylvania Coal Co v Mahon*:[46] government would be impossible if values incident to property could not be diminished to a certain extent through regulation without paying for every change in the law. The same constitutional principle is explicitly stated in the German property clause and confirmed in case law: property is not absolute, its use should also serve the public interest, and therefore it can be regulated to a certain extent, provided the regulation is imposed upon general legislative authority, establishes a fair balance between the public interest and the private interest and is not disproportionate.[47] In the *Contergan* case[48] the Federal Constitutional Court confirmed that the legislature, in making laws to establish the necessary balance between the public interest and private

---

(... from previous page)
on a different theoretical basis and with different results; see AJ van der Walt *Constitutional property clauses: A comparative analysis* (1999) 79, 141, 371; compare chapter 5.4 for details and references. In principle, a regulatory deprivation that imposes an unequal and unfair burden on one property owner should qualify the regulation as disproportionate and therefore should be invalid in German law, although invalidity can be avoided through so-called equalization payments in some cases. In US and in Swiss law, disproportionality will probably qualify the deprivation as a regulatory taking or material expropriation that requires compensation.

[46] 260 US 393 (1922) at 413, 415. See further *Hadacheck v Sebastian* 239 US 394 (1915), which established the principle that a legitimate exercise of the police power that protects public health and safety against a nuisance is not compensated, regardless of its effects on the landowner. See AJ van der Walt *Constitutional property clauses: A comparative analysis* (1999) 410–411. In *Lucas v South Carolina Coastal Council* 505 US 1003 (1992) the Supreme Court decided that regulatory action that deprives a landowner of all economic value constitutes a *per se* taking of property, but in *Tahoe-Sierra Preservation Council, Inc v Tahoe Regional Planning Agency* 535 US 302 (2002) the Court held that temporary development moratoria do not constitute *per se* takings under the *Lucas* doctrine. See further chapter 5.4.

[47] The property clause provides in article 14.1.2 and 14.2 that property entails obligations and that its use should also serve the public interest. See AJ van der Walt *Constitutional property clauses: A comparative analysis* (1999) 132–133. Illustrative cases are discussed by Van der Walt at 136ff.

[48] *BVerfGE* 42, 263 [1976]. The police-power principle is established very well in German case law; see AJ van der Walt *Constitutional property clauses: A comparative analysis* (1999) 131. The clearest cases are the series of decisions between 1974 and 1993 concerned with landlord-tenant law and the power of the state to limit landowner-landlords' rights for the sake of social housing interests; see *BVerfGE* 37, 132 [1974] *(Wohnraumkündigungsschutzgesetz)*; *BVerfGE* 68, 361 [1985] *(Wohnungskündigungsgesetz)*; *BVerfGE* 79, 292 [1989] *(Eigenbedarfskündigung)*; *BVerfGE* 89, 237 [1993] *(1993 Eigenbedarfskündigung)*; *BVerfGE* 89, 1 [1993].

interests, is acting within clear limits but is nevertheless not precluded from affecting and even changing private property rights detrimentally.

This principle was refined further in German cases where it was said that the extent to which a regulatory deprivation may affect private property negatively is partly determined by the nature of the property and its relation to the autonomy and privacy of the person or persons affected—the stronger the social relation and function of the property, the stronger and the wider are the regulatory powers of the legislature in determining the content and limits of that property, but the stronger the personal and individual character and function of the property, the weaker and smaller are the state's powers to limit it through regulation.[49] This principle is based on the fact that the use of property with a strong social relation and function affects not only the property holder but also other people's lives and interests and is therefore more open to regulation, while more personal property such as the family home is less susceptible to intrusive regulation than economic or commercial property. The application of this principle functions through the level of scrutiny with which the prohibition of regulatory excess is applied: high scrutiny for regulation that affects intimately individual and private property; lower scrutiny for regulation that affects commercial property.

The police-power principle therefore means that the state is not obliged to either leave private property untouched or pay compensation for every state action that has a negative effect on its value or its use and enjoyment. The alternative, to regulate the use, enjoyment and exploitation of private property for the protection of public health and safety, is a viable option, even when it affects the property or the property owner quite seriously and even when it causes financial loss, provided the regulatory action is properly authorized by a law of general application, aimed at protecting a legitimate public purpose such as protection of public health and safety, and not disproportionate in its effects.

The authority or power in terms of which regulatory limitation is imposed on property owners and holders is important because regulation usually brings about a restriction or loss—a deprivation—that diminishes the owner's use and enjoyment of or profit from the property, without compensation. Property owners can only be expected to bear such a burden without complaint and in the absence of compensation when the limitation is duly authorized and properly imposed for a purpose that fairly serves the common good, such as protecting public health and safety. Finally,

---

[49]See eg *BVerfGE* 89, 1 [1993] (*Besitzrecht des Mieters*) (subjective right of a lessee vis-à-vis investment right of the lessor) and *BVerfGE* 50, 290 [1979] (*Mitbestimmung*) (right of employees to participate in the management of a large business concern vis-à-vis investment rights of shareholders); and see the cases on the rights of lessors and lessees of garden allotments (*Kleingarten*): *BVerfGE* 52, 1 [1979]; *BVerfGE* 87, 114 [1992]. When the social interest in the regulation of a certain kind of property is particularly great, it can be subjected to especially strict and far-reaching regulation. Land, being an indispensable and limited resource of great social import, is routinely subjected to social regulation: *BVerfGE* 21, 73 [1967] (*Grundstücksverkehrsgesetz*); see AJ van der Walt *Constitutional property clauses: A comparative analysis* (1999) 140. Compare chapter 5.4.3.

regulatory deprivation that exceeds its purpose or authority in one way or another (procedural unfairness, unequal treatment, excessive effects that are unevenly distributed) will be open to attack and review, either to have it invalidated or to have it treated as expropriation for which compensation is required. As a rule, lack of authority or procedural unfairness should result in invalidity and only disproportional effects should be remedied by treating the deprivation as expropriation. The result of unfair distribution of the burden or excessive regulation depends on the jurisdiction: when the notion of constructive expropriation is recognized unfair or excessive regulatory deprivation could be salvaged by treating it as expropriation that requires compensation; in other jurisdictions the result of unfair or excessive regulation is invalidity.

Although compensation is usually not required for regulatory deprivation[50] some jurisdictions provide for or allow the damage or loss caused by excessive regulation to be compensated or 'softened' by way of so-called equalization or administrative compensation payments.[51] In French law, property owners can claim compensation for loss caused by regulatory action in administrative law on the basis of the equality principle, even when the action is not expropriation for which the Constitution requires compensation. The underlying idea is that the burden of administrative (regulatory) controls should be spread equally and if they are not, the affected person should be compensated. In German law, it is accepted that a money award for certain kinds of excessive regulation is possible, but then not as compensation for expropriation (or for regulation that comes close to expropriation), but as an equalization payment that 'softens' the impact of the burden which a regulatory measure or action places upon an individual property holder, thereby ensuring that the burden is not rendered invalid for being excessive in terms of the proportionality principle. In both cases the award is not compensation for state acquisition of the property but compensation for loss or damage caused by excessive regulation; the compensation award should not create the impression that the deprivation was transformed into or treated as expropriation. The compensation award should therefore be calculated with reference to the loss or damage and not the value of the property. The French notion that compensation of this kind is paid on the basis of the principle that the burden of regulatory action should be spread equally is especially helpful in justifying a claim for such an award. In German law the most useful explanation of equalization is the road noise example: when building of a new road causes undue hardship in the form of road noise for a few people living near the road, the state should help them mitigate the noise by either building or installing noise reduction installations or paying them money to install their own (eg double glazing).

---

[50] The exception is Switzerland; see footnote 29 above.

[51] The obvious examples are France and Germany. On French law see chapter 5.4.2 footnotes 150–151 and accompanying text; on German law see chapter 5.4.3 footnote 161 and accompanying text.

In the *Modderklip* decision[52] the South African Constitutional Court ordered the state to pay compensation to the landowner for the loss that he suffered as a result of the unlawful invasion and occupation of his land and the lack of state provision for efficient enforcement procedures. In other words, when a landowner is prevented from obtaining and executing an eviction order against unlawful occupiers because of the sheer number and the personal circumstances of the occupiers, it is unacceptable for the state to just stand by and leave it to the owner to solve the problem. If the landowner is then expected to bear the continued unlawful occupation of his land until the state can provide an effective remedy (*inter alia* by providing alternative accommodation for the occupiers), the owner might have a claim for compensation against the state. It is argued in chapter 5.4.5 that the compensation claim in *Modderklip* could be compared to the equalization payments in French and German law—the idea is not to compensate the owner for loss of a right, but to compensate her for individual and unfair or disproportionate suffering brought about by legitimate regulatory action. In the absence of such compensation the burden on one landowner would be so unfair and disproportionate that the regulatory action might be arbitrary and unconstitutional.

In view of the discussion above the difference between anti-eviction regulation that would attract *Modderklip*-style compensation and regulation that would not could perhaps be described with reference to the usual test for disproportionate regulatory action: anti-eviction regulation that affects all landowners more or less equally (such as the fact that all landowners have to go through the often costly and time-consuming procedures prescribed by land reform laws to obtain an eviction order) is a 'normal' regulatory limitation on ownership, but when anti-eviction regulation practically deprives one individual landowner or a small group of landowners completely of the possibility of obtaining an eviction under circumstances where they would otherwise have been able to do so and forces them to bear the burden of the regulation alone for a considerable time, a compensation claim may be required. This would probably be the case when, as in the *Modderklip* situation, the landowner is precluded from enforcing an eviction order because of the sheer number of people involved and their personal circumstances, combined with lack of the efficient enforcement institutions or procedures that the owner is normally entitled to in terms of section 34. Such a situation would obviously only arise when the owner is entitled to an eviction order in terms of the relevant legislation and the requirements and procedures it prescribes.

---

[52] The Constitutional Court decision was handed down on 13 May 2005 and is reported as *President of the Republic of South Africa and Another v Modderklip Boerdery (Pty) Ltd (Agri SA and Others, Amici Curiae)* 2005 (5) SA 3 (CC). The SCA decision is reported as *Modderfontein Squatters, Greater Benoni City Council v Modderklip Boerdery (Pty) Ltd; (Agri SA and Legal Resources Centre, Amici Curiae); President of the Republic of South Africa and Others v Modderklip Boerdery (Pty) Ltd (Agri SA and Legal Resources Centre, Amici Curiae)* 2004 (6) SA 40 (SCA). See AJ van der Walt 'The state's duty to protect property owners vs the state's duty to provide housing: Thoughts on the *Modderklip* case' (2005) 21 *SAJHR* 144–161. See the discussion in chapter 5.4.3 and 5.4.4 and in chapter 6.3.6 and 6.3.8.

Furthermore, the compensation option could probably only work when the delay in evicting the unlawful occupiers is temporary, as it was in *Modderklip*—if eviction proves to be completely and permanently impossible when the owner is entitled to eviction the situation changes and the deprivation of the landowner's right would be either an arbitrary deprivation or, possibly, a constructive expropriation.

4.3 FORMAL REQUIREMENTS: INTRODUCTION

Section 25(1) sets out only two requirements: deprivation must (*a*) take place in terms of law of general application; and (*b*) no law may permit arbitrary deprivation. Each of these requirements is discussed separately below.[53] In addition to the two explicit requirements, it may be argued that deprivation should serve a legitimate public purpose or the public interest. The question whether deprivation is subject to an implicit public purpose requirement is discussed below.

The two explicit requirements in section 25(1) ensure that deprivation of property is in accordance with the due process of law. They are threshold requirements in the sense that non-compliance with them will render a limitation invalid regardless of the merits of the purpose served or of the right affected. In terms of section 25(8) it is possible in principle to justify a limitation that does not satisfy the requirements in section 25(1), as long as it complies with the requirements in section 36(1), but as was pointed out in chapter 2.5 this is unlikely in practice because deprivation in conflict with the formal requirements in section 25(1) will probably also be in conflict with the justification requirements in section 36(1).

The requirements for deprivation also apply to expropriation of property; firstly because the law of general application requirement and the public purpose require-ment (if it is recognized) are both required for expropriation as well, and secondly (as far as the non-arbitrariness requirement is concerned) because of the Constitutional Court's attitude towards the relationship between deprivation and expropriation: in the Court's view, '[t]he starting point for constitutional analysis, when considering any challenge under s 25 for infringement of property rights, must be s 25(1).'[54] According to the methodology set out in the *FNB* decision,[55] expropriation is treated as a special subset of deprivation and therefore expropriation must comply with the general requirements for deprivation (and particularly the arbitrariness test) as well as the special requirements for expropriation (particularly the compensation require-

---

[53] The law of general application requirement is similar to the first requirement for expropriation, which is discussed in chapter 5.6. Accordingly, this aspect is discussed just briefly in 4.4 below. The arbitrariness test is discussed in 4.5 and 4.6 below.

[54] *First National Bank of SA Ltd t/a Wesbank v Commissioner, South African Revenue Service; First National Bank of SA Ltd t/a Wesbank v Minister of Finance* 2002 (4) SA 768 (CC) par [60] at 797C.

[55] *First National Bank of SA Ltd t/a Wesbank v Commissioner, South African Revenue Service; First National Bank of SA Ltd t/a Wesbank v Minister of Finance* 2002 (4) SA 768 (CC) paras [60] at 797C, [100] at 810G–811F. See the discussion in 4.5.3 below.

ment, the only one that does not apply to deprivation as well). The arbitrariness test and its effects are discussed in 4.5 and 4.6 below.

Although section 25(1) does not state explicitly that deprivation must be for a public purpose or in the public interest, such a requirement is arguably implicit in the provision. Foreign courts tend to be strict in requiring that deprivation of property should be for a public purpose, both in jurisdictions where there is an explicit public purpose requirement in a due-process clause[56] and in some where there is no due-process clause.[57] In German law, deprivation that limits the content or scope of property has to be imposed by a valid law and satisfy the proportionality principle (*Übermaßverbot*), which means that it must serve the public interest and the burden it imposes must not exceed what the public interest requires.[58] In addition, deprivation has to be constitutional, which means that it must be in accordance with general constitutional principles such as equality and trust.[59] The Irish courts require that a limitation should be authorized by law, in accordance with the principles of social justice, and imposed with a view to reconciling the exercise of the right with the exigencies of the common good.[60] In US law it is also accepted that police-power

---

[56]See *BVerfGE* 50, 290 [1979] (*Mitbestimmung*); *BVerfGE* 89, 1 [1993] (*Besitzrecht des Mieters*); *BVerfGE* 52, 1 [1979] (*Kleingarten*); *BVerfGE* 87, 114 [1992] (*Kleingarten*) (Germany); *BGE* 105 Ia 330 [1979] (*Meier*) (Switzerland). See AJ van der Walt *Constitutional property clauses: A comparative analysis* (1999) 132, 365.

[57]Section 51(xxxi) of the Australian Commonwealth Constitution 1900 provides only for compulsory acquisition, but the courts distinguish between compulsory acquisition and deprivation, and they also apply a general public purpose requirement: *Trade Practices Commission and Another v Tooth & Co Ltd and Another* (1979) 142 CLR 397. See AJ van der Walt *Constitutional property clauses: A comparative analysis* (1999) 48.

[58]It is usually said that the deprivation must be strictly necessary (*erforderlich*), suitable for the public purpose it serves (*geeignet*) and not disproportionate to the burden it imposes (*verhältnismäßig*, also *zumutbar*). See AJ van der Walt *Constitutional property clauses: A comparative analysis* (1999) 135; compare 4.5 below. The Swiss courts also require a valid law, public interest and proportionality, and the proportionality test is also applied with reference to necessity, suitability and an equitable balance between benefit and effect; see *BGE* 105 Ia 330 [1979] (*Meier*); AJ van der Walt *Constitutional property clauses: A comparative analysis* (1999) 368. When balancing individual and public interests, room is left for considerations of local context in each case—*örtliche Verhältnisse*. See AJ van der Walt *Constitutional property clauses: A comparative analysis* (1999) 367. In Austrian law the initial tendency was to focus on formal validity, but the courts have started looking at proportionality as well and now require that the limitation should serve the public interest; see *VfSlg 9198/1981*; *VfSlg 8981/1980*; *VfSlg 9913/1984*; *VfSlg 12227/1989*; *VfSlg 12100/1989*; AJ van der Walt *Constitutional property clauses: A comparative analysis* (1999) 78.

[59]See DG Kleyn 'The constitutional protection of property: A comparison between the German and the South African approach' (1996) 11 *SA Public Law* 402–445 at 424–425; AJ van der Walt *Constitutional property clauses: A comparative analysis* (1999) 135.

[60]As prescribed by section 43.2.1 of the Irish Constitution. For a good example see *Electricity Supply Board v Gormley* [1985] IR 129, where it was decided that the burden was so heavy as to require compensation. See *Dreher v Irish Land Commission and Others* [1984] ILRM 94 for an explanation of the basic test. See further AJ van der Walt *Constitutional property clauses: A comparative analysis* (1999) 236–237.

regulation of property must serve the public welfare or a public purpose, although such a requirement is not stated explicitly in the property clause. According to the traditional narrow construction of the police power principle the public purpose is usually associated with the core function of ensuring and promoting public health and safety, although wider regulatory purposes have been recognized and upheld.[61] The public purpose requirement is formulated similarly for regulatory exercises of the police power and for expropriatory exercises of the power of eminent domain, and in both instances the courts defer to the decisions of the legislature; the courts will only scrutinize the public purpose of a regulatory action to ensure that it is not 'palpably without reasonable foundation'.[62] In jurisprudence on the property clause in the European Convention, the right to regulate the use of property is associated with the so-called third rule of the property clause (article 1 paragraph 2 of the First Protocol), and although a 'margin of appreciation' or local discretion is left for individual states to decide what is in the public interest it is consistently required that regulatory limitation of the use of property should be in accordance with municipal law, imposed in the public interest, and establish a fair balance of proportionality between the public interest served and the private interest affected.[63]

The tendency in foreign law therefore seems to be to require that regulatory deprivation of property should be properly authorized (in accordance with law), proportional (not arbitrary), and imposed for a public purpose or in the public interest. This last requirement is not always stated explicitly and it is sometimes subjected to nothing more than rationality review, but it is widely accepted that regulatory deprivation is subject to it. At the very least, therefore, regulatory exercises of the police power will be subject to public purpose scrutiny to ensure that it is not without any foundation, arbitrary or capricious. Acceptance of this requirement is not surprising in view of the traditional function of regulatory control over the use and enjoyment of property, namely to protect and promote public health and safety— action that promotes public health and safety will usually also serve a public purpose

---

[61] See *Village of Euclid v Ambler Realty Co* 272 US 365 (1926); *Nectow v City of Cambridge* 277 US 183 (1928); *Penn Central Transportation Co v City of New York* 438 US 104 (1978); *Agins v City of Tiburon* 447 US 255 at 260 (1980) (a zoning scheme must substantially advance legitimate state interests); *Nollan v California Coastal Commission* 483 US 825 (1987); *Dolan v City of Tigard* 512 US 374 (1994) (there must be a close nexus and rough proportionality between the public purpose served by the deprivation and the sacrifice it entails for the landowner); *Tahoe-Sierra Preservation Council, Inc v Tahoe Regional Planning Agency* 535 US 302 (2002). See AJ van der Walt *Constitutional property clauses: A comparative analysis* (1999) 412–423. For a South African example see *Nyangane v Stadsraad van Potchefstroom* 1998 (2) BCLR 148 (T); compare 4.7.1 below.

[62] *Berman v Parker* 348 US 26 (1954); *Hawaii Housing Authority v Midkiff* 467 US 229 at 241 (1984). See AJ van der Walt *Constitutional property clauses: A comparative analysis* (1999) 412–413, and compare the extensive discussion of the public purpose requirement in chapter 5.7.5.

[63] See the good example in the *Tre Traktörer AB Case* [1989] ECHR Series A vol 159; compare *Sporrong and Lönnroth v Sweden* [1983] 5 EHRR 35; *James v United Kingdom* [1986] 8 EHRR 123; *Mellacher and Others v Austria* [1989] ECHR Series A vol 169. See further AJ van der Walt *Constitutional property clauses: A comparative analysis* (1999) 106.

or the public interest. It can therefore be accepted as a matter of logical necessity that regulatory deprivation in terms of the police power is subject to an implicit public purpose requirement. In the case of section 25(1) an implicit public purpose requirement can be inferred from either the legality requirement (law of general application) or the non-arbitrariness requirement; the former would possibly imply thinner rationality review and the latter more substantive proportionality review.

Recognition of an implicit public purpose requirement fits in with section 25(1) of the South African Constitution, especially in view of the fact that the Constitutional Court has now confirmed that the proscription of arbitrary deprivation is intended to ensure that deprivation of property is imposed with due regard for proportionality between the public interest served by regulation and the private interests affected by it.[64] Section 25(1) clearly recognizes the power to impose regulatory limitation on the use and enjoyment of property, even when that causes deprivation of property, because such regulatory action protects and promotes public health and safety interests, and therefore it can be accepted that section 25(1) includes an implicit requirement that deprivation of property should indeed serve a public purpose or the public interest. The test for this requirement should relate directly to the core function of the police power, namely that regulatory deprivation of property protects or promotes public health and safety.

According to comparative examples, review of the public purpose requirement for deprivation should be based on a higher level of scrutiny when regulation moves into borderline areas such as aesthetic building regulation, while a lower level of scrutiny could apply in the core areas where regulation obviously serves the protection of public health and safety. Accordingly, closer scrutiny is required when the purpose of deprivation is not to protect public health and safety as such but simply to serve other fringe purposes that are vaguely in the public interest (such as aesthetic building regulation) or to make it easier for the state to carry out its day-to-day business, for example in collection of taxes or debts. Deprivation aimed at fiscal efficiency should therefore arguably be subjected to closer scrutiny as a matter of principle. However, on the whole it seems that the public purpose issue, like many others, might continue to receive less attention than it deserves in South African law because of being sucked

---

[64] Which is the approach to the non-arbitrariness requirement followed by the Constitutional Court in *First National Bank of SA Ltd t/a Wesbank v Commissioner, South African Revenue Service; First National Bank of SA Ltd t/a Wesbank v Minister of Finance* 2002 (4) SA 768 (CC) par [100] at 810H–811F. See 4.5 below. In *National Director of Public Prosecutions v Prophet* 2003 (6) SA 154 (C) the Cape High Court decided that the public purpose for which forfeiture laws were promulgated and enforced, namely to combat organized crime more effectively, was sufficient to justify the infringements of property that resulted from it although it was still important to assess the fairness of each infringement individually. On appeal (*Prophet v National Director of Public Prosecutions* case 502/04 29 September 2005 (SCA)) the SCA confirmed its decision in *National Director of Public Prosecutions v RO Cook Properties (Pty) Ltd* 2004 (8) BCLR 844 (SCA), where it was said that proportionality analysis applies only to the second stage of the instrumentalities of crime inquiry, where the issue is whether certain property should be excluded from the forfeiture order. It does not apply during the first stage, when it is determined whether a functional relation between crime and property exists.

into the 'arbitrariness vortex' described so evocatively by Theunis Roux.[65] This observation is substantiated by the fact that the South African Constitutional Court has so far paid more attention to the effect of deprivation than to its purpose—a higher level of scrutiny is required when the deprivation in question is substantial and a lower level when it is slight, with little regard for the question how the purpose of the deprivation is related to the core function of protecting public health and safety.[66] The purpose of the deprivation is therefore subjected to judicial scrutiny, but only in relation to the nexus between the purpose and the property affected and its owner; the purpose as such is not treated as an indication of the level of scrutiny.

In the *FNB* case, which was also concerned with fiscal efficiency regulation and where the arbitrariness test was formulated and first applied, the result was that a relatively high level of scrutiny was indeed applied in the sense that the Court could not establish a sufficient reason for the deprivation in the absence of a nexus between the purpose of the deprivation (enforcement of a tax debt) and the property involved or its owner.[67] The Court accepted that exacting payment of a customs debt is 'a legitimate and important legislative purpose, essential for the financial well-being of the country and in the interest of all its inhabitants' but decided that the legislation cast the net too wide.[68] The Court stated that the level of scrutiny in arbitrariness cases should be determined with reference to the 'interplay between variable means and

---

[65] T Roux 'Section 25' in S Woolman et al (eds) *Constitutional law of South Africa* (2nd ed 2003 original service Dec 2003) 46-2–46-5 argued that the 'telescoping' effect of the *FNB* approach means that all property cases will be treated as deprivations first, which means that the law of general application issue will be decided during the deprivation analysis, and that most if not all irregularities that might disqualify an expropriation under section 25(2) or (3) would probably already taint it as an arbitrary deprivation in terms of section 25(1). See the discussion in chapter 5.4.5, 5.5 and in 4.5 below.

[66] *First National Bank of SA Ltd t/a Wesbank v Commissioner, South African Revenue Service; First National Bank of SA Ltd t/a Wesbank v Minister of Finance* 2002 (4) SA 768 (CC) par [100](g) at 81D–E; compare *Mkontwana v Nelson Mandela Metropolitan Municipality; Bissett and Others v Buffalo City Municipality; Transfer Rights Action Campaign and Others v Member of the Executive Council for Local Government and Housing, Gauteng and Others* 2005 (1) SA 530 (CC) par [32] at 545J–546C. The statement in *Mkontwana* is not exactly in line with *FNB*, as it makes the existence of deprivation rather than the level of scrutiny for evaluating the deprivation depend on the scope of the deprivation. See further AJ van der Walt 'Retreating from the *FNB* arbitrariness test already? *Mkontwana v Nelson Mandela Metropolitan Municipality; Bissett v Buffalo City Municipality; Transfer Rights Action Campaign v MEC for Local Government and Housing, Gauteng* (CC)' (2005) 122 *SALJ* 75–89.

[67] In *First National Bank of SA Ltd t/a Wesbank v Commissioner, South African Revenue Service; First National Bank of SA Ltd t/a Wesbank v Minister of Finance* 2002 (4) SA 768 (CC) the Court accepted that exacting payment of a customs debt is 'a legitimate and important legislative purpose, essential for the financial well-being of the country and in the interest of all its inhabitants', and decided that the only problem was that the legislation cast the net too wide: par [108] at 814H.

[68] *First National Bank of SA Ltd t/a Wesbank v Commissioner, South African Revenue Service; First National Bank of SA Ltd t/a Wesbank v Minister of Finance* (2002 (4) SA 768 (CC) par [108] at 814H.

ends, the nature of the property in question and the extent of its deprivation',[69] which makes it possible to engage in a public purpose inquiry, provided that the analysis of the different relationships (property and owner) to the purpose is taken seriously (which was indeed the case in *FNB*). In other words, the high level of scrutiny was determined by the interplay between the purpose of the deprivation, its effect on the owner and the lack of a nexus between purpose, owner and property. This does not guarantee that a high level of scrutiny will apply in other cases where the purpose of the deprivation is in itself a non-core purpose such as fiscal efficiency or state governance considerations. Because of the 'vortex' effect, the level of scrutiny that applies to the purpose for the deprivation will depend on the Court's view of the effect of the deprivation on the owner—if that is slight, scrutiny will be light. This approach, which takes note of the effect rather than the purpose of the deprivation when determining how strictly the action should be reviewed, is perhaps not as sophisticated as could be expected and it might require reconsideration in future.

In *Mkontwana*,[70] which again involved deprivation for fiscal efficiency purposes, the Court was indeed satisfied with a fairly low level of rationality review, merely ensuring that the regulatory measure in question was rationally related to a legitimate government function, without concerning itself with the question whether regulation should be subjected to strong or weak review in the relevant area. Moreover, the *Mkontwana* Court engaged in a less rigorous analysis of the relationships between

[69] *First National Bank of SA Ltd t/a Wesbank v Commissioner, South African Revenue Service; First National Bank of SA Ltd t/a Wesbank v Minister of Finance* 2002 (4) SA 768 (CC) par [100](g) at 811D. It is possible that the purpose of the deprivation is supposed to be considered properly in terms of the admittedly flexible and context-sensitive *FNB* test, but in fact this aspect as such received relatively little attention—beyond its rational legitimacy—in *FNB* and especially in *Mkontwana*. In the case of *FNB* one can still argue that the purpose was taken account of in the final decision that there was insufficient reason for the deprivation, but that cannot be said for *Mkontwana*, where the deprivation was upheld. See the discussion of the *Mkontwana* decision in 4.5.4 below. Despite the focus on expropriation it is arguable that *Harksen v Lane NO* 1998 (1) SA 300 (CC) should also have been treated as a deprivation case, and in that decision the Court raised the public purpose issue explicitly because it was alleged that the limitation amounted to unconstitutional expropriation. In the end the Court held that the true purpose of the provision was to ensure that insolvent estates are not deprived of property to which they are entitled (par [36] at 317G) and (in the analysis of the equality issue) that this purpose was not unconstitutional (par [65] at 329B). In that sense the closest and arguably most instructive foreign case to compare with *Harksen* is the Australian decision in *Mutual Pools & Staff Pty Limited v The Commonwealth of Australia* (1994) 179 CLR 155; see the discussion in 4.2 and chapter 5.2; compare Van der Walt AJ *Constitutional property clauses: A comparative analysis* (1999) 64.

[70] In *Mkontwana v Nelson Mandela Metropolitan Municipality; Bissett and Others v Buffalo City Municipality; Transfer Rights Action Campaign and Others v Member of the Executive Council for Local Government and Housing, Gauteng and Others* 2005 (1) SA 530 (CC) the Constitutional Court accepted that placing the risk of unpaid service charges on the property owner was 'important, laudable and has the potential to encourage regular payments of consumption charges and thereby contribute to the effective discharge by municipalities of their constitutionally mandated functions': par [38] at 548C–549C.

purpose, property and owner than was the case in *FNB*, with the result that the fairly harsh outcome of the case for property owners has the appearance of having been sanctioned by low-level rationality scrutiny. This aspect is discussed in more detail in 4.5.4 below.

4.4 LAW OF GENERAL APPLICATION

Deprivation of property in terms of section 25(1) has to be imposed by law of general application. The 'law of general application' requirement in section 25(2) is discussed in chapter 5.6, and since most of what is said there also applies to section 25(1) everything need not be repeated here. The law of general application requirement embodies the general rule of law and legitimacy principles of the Constitution, ensuring that deprivation of property shall only be lawful when it is imposed in terms of and authorized by properly promulgated and valid law.

In *Park-Ross and Another v The Director, Office for Serious Economic Offences*[71] the Cape High Court decided that section 6 of the Investigation of Serious Offences Act 117 of 1991 (which authorizes certain search and seizure procedures) was 'a law' as meant in section 28(2) of the 1993 Constitution. Roux[72] argues that this decision will be followed in cases decided under section 25 of the 1996 Constitution, and that all original and delegated legislation will accordingly qualify as 'law of general application' for this purpose, while internal administrative policy documents will probably not qualify.[73] Apart from its general applicability, laws must also be specific and accessible to satisfy this requirement.[74]

---

[71] 1995 (2) BCLR 198 (C) at 216G. See further T Roux 'Property' in MH Cheadle, DM Davis & NRL Haysom *South African constitutional law: The bill of rights* (2002) 429–472 at 458–460; and compare with regard to the law of general application requirement in section 25(1) *Deutschmann NO and Others v Commissioner for the South African Revenue Service; Shelton v Commissioner for the South African Revenue Service* 2000 (2) SA 106 (E) at 124A (regarding the Income Tax Act 58 of 1962 and the Value-Added Tax Act 89 of 1991).

[72] T Roux 'Property' in MH Cheadle, DM Davis & NRL Haysom *South African constitutional law: The bill of rights* (2002) 429–472 at 458–459; T Roux 'Section 25' in S Woolman et al (eds) *Constitutional law of South Africa* (2nd ed 2003 original service Dec 2003) 46–21. See further G Budlender 'The constitutional protection of property rights: Overview and commentary' in G Budlender, J Latsky & T Roux (eds) *Juta's new land law* (1998) chapter 1 at 34.

[73] A Gildenhuys *Onteieningsreg* (2nd ed 2001) 93. The general analysis of the law of general application requirement in section 36(1) by S Woolman 'Limitation' in M Chaskalson et al (eds) *Constitutional law of South Africa* (1st ed 5th rev service 1999) 12-28−12-32 is useful in this regard as well; see further chapter 2.5. At 12-29 footnote 3 Woolman points out that Canadian case law is divided on the question whether government policy directives or guidelines are to be regarded as laws of general application. In *De Lille and Another v Speaker of the National Assembly* 1998 (3) SA 430 (C) the Cape High Court decided that the rule of parliamentary privilege does not qualify as a law of general application, particularly because it was neither published or accessible nor precise or certain.

[74] See the discussion in chapter 5.6 for details.

The fact that section 25(1) refers to 'law of general application' as opposed to 'a law'[75] ensures that regulatory deprivation of property can also be authorized by the rules of common and customary law, and at the same time it subjects common-law and customary-law authorized deprivation of property to the requirement that they should not be arbitrary. However, in view of the fact that police power regulation is nowadays usually exercised by way of legislation it is difficult to imagine that deprivation authorized by rules of common law or customary law would raise arbitrariness problems of the kind that would bring section 25(1) into the picture—no obvious example springs to mind.[76]

However, the requirement demands more than just a valid law—law of general application means that the law that authorizes deprivation of property must be generally applicable, non-arbitrary, specific and accessible. Although most laws affect some people but not others, a law providing for deprivation that singles out and burdens just one individual or a small group of individuals (so-called bills of attainder) may fall foul of this provision.[77] Regulatory legislation that authorizes deprivation poses no special problem, because regulatory laws are usually of a general nature, and it is unlikely that statutory deprivation of property will fail the law of general application test, unless a specific law was promulgated (or is argued to have been promulgated) with the intention of targeting an individual person or a small group of persons in an unfair manner.

---

[75] As it read in the 1993 Constitution. The Afrikaans text of the 1996 Constitution reads 'algemeen geldende regsvoorskrif' as opposed to the other possible translation of 'law', namely 'wet' in the sense of 'statute'.

[76] If regulatory deprivation indeed does take place by way of common or customary law, this could be a place for horizontal application of section 25. The rest of the section deals with either expropriation or land reform, both of which are based on legislation and direct state involvement, and regulatory control over the use and exploitation of property is also normally embodied in legislation. It is therefore unlikely that this will happen. See the general discussion of the application problem in chapter 2.4; and compare H Cheadle & D Davis 'The application of the 1996 Constitution in the private sphere' (1997) 13 *SAJHR* 44–66; T Roux 'Property' in MH Cheadle, DM Davis & NRL Haysom *South African constitutional law: The bill of rights* (2002) 429–472 at 442. Roux is probably correct that the example of original acquisition of ownership mentioned in the first edition of this work (1997 p 106) does not really fit in with the technical meaning that attaches to expropriation as a specific kind of state action. The common law principles of neighbour law used to serve the same purpose now mostly promoted in land use and development and environment conservation control, and may provide a more promising area for finding an example of a common law rule that deprives a landowner of property for a regulatory purpose, but it is difficult to imagine a case where such a rule might be unconstitutional for being arbitrary. One area where this problem may possibly arise is the neighbour law rules in terms of which one landowner loses ownership of part of her land when it is transferred (or even 'transferred') to the neighbour whose buildings encroach on her land under circumstances where the court refuses to order demolition of the building and instead grants compensation; see e g *Rand Waterraad v Bothma* 1997 (3) SA 120 (O); *Trustees of the Brian Lackey Trust v Annandale* [2003] 4 All SA 528 (C); *Lombard v Fischer* [2003] 1 All SA 698 (O).

[77] See the discussion of *Lebowa Mineral Trust Beneficiaries Forum v President of the Republic of South Africa* 2002 (1) BCLR 23 (T) at 29H in chapter 5.6.

4.5 ARBITRARINESS: THE *FNB* TEST[78]

4.5.1 Introduction: 'Thin' or 'thick' review?

The term 'arbitrary' in section 25(1) causes interpretation problems. The law of general application requirement in the first part of section 25(1) already establishes that deprivation cannot be arbitrary in the sense of being aimed at a specific person or group. The law of general application requirement also ensures that deprivation cannot take place without proper authority and that the state cannot delegate the power to effect arbitrary deprivation to some state body or official. The question is, therefore: what does the second part of section 25(1) add to this requirement? One view is that the provision ensures formal procedural justice, read as a 'thin', low level of scrutiny rationality test that merely ensures that regulatory deprivation is rationally connected to some legitimate government purpose. According to this view, the non-arbitrariness requirement is a rationality requirement, and it would be satisfied when there is a legitimate government reason for the deprivation, without any substantive inquiry into the proportionality between means and ends.

According to a 'thicker' interpretation of section 25(1) the non-arbitrariness requirement means that deprivation should not impose an unacceptably heavy burden upon or demand an exceptional sacrifice from one individual or a small group of individuals for the sake of the public at large. This interpretation, which finds some support in foreign case law,[79] means that any law that authorizes deprivation of property must establish sufficient reason for the deprivation in the sense that it is not only rationally linked to a legitimate government purpose but also justified in the sense of establishing a proper balance between ends and means. Consequently, a law that authorizes an excessive burden being placed unfairly on one individual or a small group of individuals could be invalid for being arbitrary. According to this interpretation a non-expropriatory, regulatory deprivation of property would be arbitrary unless it establishes a proportionate balance between the public benefit it serves and the private harm it causes.[80]

---

[78]The discussion of the *FNB* decision in this section is based on and similar in part to AJ van der Walt 'Striving for the better interpretation. A critical reflection on the Constitutional Court's *Harksen* and *FNB* decisions on the property clause' (2004) 121 *SALJ* 854–878.

[79]Although foreign law is not at all unanimous on this point. In US law, substantive review of policy decisions is generally problematic because of the *Lochner* history (see footnote 82 below), and particularly in case of economic regulation review tends to be thin rather than thick. German-language jurisdictions tend to apply thicker, proportionality-type review (see footnotes 84–85 and surrounding text below). T Allen *The right to property in Commonwealth constitutions* (2000) 162–200 shows that Commonwealth countries differ, some (like Malaysia) preferring thin rationality review of regulatory action, while others (like Australia and Mauritius) apply thicker review. My argument is not that there is a clear preference for thicker review in foreign law, but that there is some authority for it. See further footnotes 56–61 above.

[80]See A Gildenhuys *Onteieningsreg* (2nd ed 2001) 94, who refers to the thin interpretation and adds that the provision against arbitrary deprivation was probably meant to prevent deprivation placing an unacceptably heavy burden on one person for the benefit of the public in general.

Prior to the Constitutional Court decision in *FNB*[81] it was unclear whether the 'thinner' mere rationality or the 'thicker' proportionality interpretation of the non-arbitrariness requirement would be followed. Proponents of the thin rationality approach were concerned that a proportionality approach—applied during the first stage of constitutional enquiry—would cause the same problems in South African law that the so-called substantive due process cases caused in the US during the *Lochner* era, and that the result would frustrate reformist government action in the same way that the *Lochner* court frustrated social reform efforts in the US.[82] In the American *Lochner*-era cases, the courts interpreted the due process requirement in such a way that a regulating law should not only be properly promulgated but also be reasonable in its aims and in the way in which it promotes those aims.[83] The problem with Lochnerism was that an activist (and not democratically elected) court was perceived to be second-guessing the legislature and executive about contentious policy decisions with which the court was not satisfied substantively. In other words, the courts were perceived to be substituting their own policy (and political) choices for those of the democratically elected government not because these choices were made improperly, but because the courts disagreed with their substance. The prospect that activist, politically reactionary courts would block and frustrate legitimate reform initiatives of the newly elected democratic government if they were allowed to review executive action on substantive grounds loomed large in the early days of the new democratic and constitutional order in South Africa, and therefore the notion of

---

[81] *First National Bank of SA Ltd t/a Wesbank v Commissioner, South African Revenue Service; First National Bank of SA Ltd t/a Wesbank v Minister of Finance* 2002 (4) SA 768 (CC).

[82] Proportionality review was opposed in the early South African literature by M Chaskalson 'The problem with property: Thoughts on the constitutional protection of property in the United States and in the Commonwealth' (1993) 9 *SAJHR* 388–411 at 402, referring to decisions like *PruneYard Shopping Centre v Robins* 447 US 74 (1980); *Nollan v California Coastal Commission* 483 US 825 (1987); and by J de Waal, G Erasmus & I Currie *Bill of rights handbook* (4th ed 2001) 422, 426–428; M Chaskalson & C Lewis 'Property' in M Chaskalson et al (eds) *Constitutional law of South Africa* (1st ed 1998) par 31.5(*b*)(ii)(bb); G Budlender 'The constitutional protection of property rights: Overview and commentary' in G Budlender, J Latsky & T Roux (eds) *Juta's new land law* (1998) chapter 1 at 25–26, 34–36. For criticism of Chaskalson's view see J Murphy 'Property rights and judicial constraint: A reply to Chaskalson' (1994) 10 *SAJHR* 385–398; AJ van der Walt 'The limits of constitutional property' (1997) 12 *SA Public Law* 275–330. The Lochnerism debate refers to *Lochner v New York* 198 US 45 (1905). Substantive due process review started with *Allgeyer v Louisiana* 165 US 578 (1897), where the Supreme Court applied a reasonableness test to review the purpose of regulatory laws and the relationship between the legislative purpose and the means selected to promote it, and the Supreme Court abandoned the idea of substantive due process in *West Coast Hotel Co v Parrish* 300 US 379 (1937) and switched to its current policy of judicial deference to legislative intent on matters of economic policy, according to which it will review the legislature's judgment as to what constitutes a public use only to ensure that the public use is not palpably without reasonable foundation.

[83] See M Chaskalson 'The problem with property: Thoughts on the constitutional protection of property in the United States and in the Commonwealth' (1993) 9 *SAJHR* 388–411 at 401–402 for a brief introduction and some references.

substantive or proportionality review in the first stage of a constitutional case met with considerable opposition.

However, the way in which proportionality review is applied in jurisdictions like Germany,[84] Austria[85] and the European Court of Human Rights[86] shows that there are vital differences between Lochnerism and substantive proportionality review in general, even when proportionality review takes place in the first stage of a constitutional case. Proportionality is an overtly constitutional principle, applied in terms of specific constitutional provisions, principles and values, and therefore it does not have to result in subjective or improper judicial interference with policy considerations or second-guessing of policy decisions properly taken by democratically elected legislatures and governments.[87] If the courts apply the proportionality test to evaluate the constitutional justifiability (and not the political wisdom) of a limitation the chances of a reversal towards Lochnerism are reduced. Accordingly, the thicker, proportionality-type approach was supported in the first edition of this book.[88] In the *FNB* case the Constitutional Court responded to the debate by opting for a thick, proportionality-type approach, albeit on different grounds than were previously forwarded in

---

[84]See *BVerfGE* 78, 232 [1988] 245–247; compare further L Blaauw-Wolf & J Wolf 'A comparison between German and South African limitation provisions' (1996) 113 *SALJ* 267–296; and compare DG Kleyn 'The constitutional protection of property: A comparison between the German and the South African approach' (1996) 11 *SA Public Law* 402–445 at 425ff. Compare AJ van der Walt *Constitutional property clauses: A comparative analysis* (1999) 135–141.

[85]See *VfSlg 8981/1980; VfSlg 12227/1989;* compare further M Holoubek 'Die Interpretation der Grundrechte in der jüngeren Judikatur des VfSlg' in R Machacek, WP Pahr & G Stadler (eds) *70 Jahr Republik: Grund- und Menschenrechte in Österreich. Grundlagen, Entwicklung und Internationale Verbindungen* (1991) 43–83 at 46. Compare AJ van der Walt *Constitutional property clauses: A comparative analysis* (1999) 77–79, 83–84.

[86]See *Sporrong & Lönnroth v* Sweden [1982] 5 EHRR 35; but compare MR Antinori 'Does Lochner live in Luxembourg? An analysis of the property rights jurisprudence of the European Court of Justice' (1995) 18 *Fordham Int LJ* 1778–1851. Compare AJ van der Walt *Constitutional property clauses: A comparative analysis* (1999) 119–120. Probably under the influence of the European Union, a similar tendency is developing in Irish law; see AJ van der Walt *Constitutional property clauses: A comparative analysis* (1999) 243–244.

[87]See *S v Makwanyane and Another* 1995 (3) SA 391 (CC) at 436G. The considerations mentioned in section 36(1)(a)–(e) relate to the proportionality test. See chapter 2.5, and compare S Woolman 'Out of order? Out of balance? The limitation clause of the final Constitution' (1997) 13 *SAJHR* 102–134 at 108ff.

[88](1997) at 107–108, but also more extensively (and in terminology that attracted some justified criticism) in chapter 3. See the current chapter 2.3 and 2.5 for a revised discussion, and see further AJ van der Walt 'The limits of constitutional property' (1997) 12 *SA Public Law* 275–330; compare H Mostert 'Liberty, social duty and fairness in the context of constitutional property protection and regulation' in H Botha, A van der Walt & J van der Walt (eds) *Rights and democracy in a transformative constitution* (2003) 131–161 at 140–158. See J de Waal, G Erasmus & I Currie *Bill of rights handbook* (4th ed 2001) 422, 426–428; M Chaskalson & C Lewis 'Property' in M Chaskalson et al (eds) *Constitutional law of South Africa* (1st ed 1998) par 31.5(b)(ii)(bb); G Budlender 'The constitutional protection of property rights: Overview and commentary' in G Budlender, J Latsky & T Roux (eds) *Juta's new land law* (1998) chapter 1 at 34–36 for the opposite view.

support of proportionality review.[89] This aspect of the decision is discussed in 4.5.3 below, together with the arbitrariness test, but first it is necessary to consider the new methodology introduced in the decision.

4.5.2 The *FNB* case: A new methodology

The issue in *FNB* was whether detention and sale in execution of movable property in terms of a statutory lien[90] constituted unconstitutional interference with the owner's property in circumstances where the owner had no knowledge of and neither the attached property nor its owner had any relation to the principal debt.[91] The owner, a commercial bank, held ownership of the attached property as security for a loan granted to the debtor for purchase of the property. The state established its security interest over the property to enforce payment of a separate customs debt that had no relation to either the attached property or the bank. The question was whether the statutory creation and imposition of a preferent security interest in favour of the state amounted to an unconstitutional deprivation of the 'innocent' bank's property.[92]

The Cape High Court[93] held that section 114 of the Customs and Excise Act 91 of 1964 was not unconstitutional because it established a lien or a tax that does not

---

[89] *First National Bank of SA Ltd t/a Wesbank v Commissioner, South African Revenue Service; First National Bank of SA Ltd t/a Wesbank v Minister of Finance* 2002 (4) SA 768 (CC). The same approach was again followed in the subsequent decision in *Mkontwana v Nelson Mandela Metropolitan Municipality; Bissett and Others v Buffalo City Municipality; Transfer Rights Action Campaign and Others v Member of the Executive Council for Local Government and Housing, Gauteng and Others* 2005 (1) SA 530 (CC), although AJ van der Walt 'Retreating from the *FNB* arbitrariness test already? *Mkontwana v Nelson Mandela Metropolitan Municipality; Bissett v Buffalo City Municipality; Transfer Rights Action Campaign v MEC for Local Government and Housing, Gauteng* (CC)' (2005) 122 *SALJ* 75–89 argues that the Court in fact deviated from *FNB* in the *Mkontwana* case.

[90] Created by section 114 of the Customs and Excise Act 91 of 1964.

[91] The provision that creates the statutory lien applies to all property present on the business premises of the customs debtor, including property unrelated to the customs debt. In his discussion of the decision, JC Sonnekus 'Borgstelling, verjaring en verwarring' 2003 *TSAR* 350–376 at 373 raises doubts over the question whether this was indeed the correct interpretation of section 114. If Sonnekus is correct the provision does not apply and the state would not have been able to prove a security right at all, and that would have disposed of the matter. For the sake of the argument I assume that the provision does apply and that there was a serious issue to be decided in this case.

[92] Similar issues are raised whenever statutory enforcement of state interests affects the property of third party owners, eg in the case of civil forfeiture of property belonging to innocent third parties; see chapter 5.3 (and 4.7.2 below) and compare AJ van der Walt 'Civil forfeiture of instrumentalities and proceeds of crime and the constitutional property clause' (2000) 16 *SAJHR* 1–45 for examples and a discussion.

[93] *First National Bank t/a Wesbank v Commissioner, South African Revenue Service* 2001 (3) SA 310 (C). For a critical discussion of the decision of the Cape High Court see AJ van der Walt 'Negating Grotius—The constitutional validity of statutory security rights in favour of the state' (2002) 18 *SAJHR* 86–113. The criticisms that I raised against the High Court decision are not repeated here. The Constitutional Court was also critical of some of the views expressed by the lower court; see *First National Bank of SA Ltd t/a Wesbank v Commissioner, South African Revenue Service; First National Bank of SA Ltd t/a Wesbank v Minister of Finance* 2002 (4) SA 768 (CC) paras [31]–[40] at 787C–790D.

amount to expropriation.[94] Central to this finding was the High Court's conclusion that the effect of section 114 was to turn third party owners of affected property into co-principal debtors who are liable, together with the customs debtor, for payment of the principal customs debt.[95] State enforcement of a debt against the property of the debtor is more or less uncontroversial,[96] even if the security and its priority and the enforcement mechanism are established by statute, and therefore the High Court seemed to argue that the provisions in question would be saved from constitutional impugnment if it were demonstrated that the affected parties were co-principal debtors. However, Ackermann J correctly indicated in his reasons for the Constitutional Court decision[97] that there is no authority for the proposition that the state's security right could extend so far as to transform an unrelated third party owner of the secured property into a co-principal debtor—arguing that it does and that the provision is saved thereby begs the question of constitutional validity. The issue is not how statutory authority is structured to subject third party property rights to the state's security right, but whether a statutory lien would establish unconstitutional deprivation of property if it did affect third party property. The Constitutional Court rejected the High Court's point of departure on this point and set out to investigate the constitutional legitimacy of section 114 in view of the deprivation requirements in section 25(1).

In doing so, the Court proposed that certain steps should be followed when considering the constitutional validity of any limitation of property rights, based on the Court's distinction between deprivation and expropriation as a wider, inclusive and a narrower category respectively (rather than two mutually exclusive categories). The Court argued that expropriation constitutes a subspecies of deprivation and that the subsection 25(1) requirements for valid deprivation therefore apply to what may be described as non-expropriatory deprivation as well as to expropriation (in addition to the specific subsection 25(2) requirements that apply to expropriation only). On that

---

[94] *First National Bank t/a Wesbank v Commissioner, South African Revenue Service* 2001 (3) SA 310 (C) at 330A.

[95] *First National Bank t/a Wesbank v Commissioner, South African Revenue Service* 2001 (3) SA 310 (C) at 328F. This conclusion is set out, analysed and rejected by the Constitutional Court in *First National Bank of SA Ltd t/a Wesbank v Commissioner, South African Revenue Service; First National Bank of SA Ltd t/a Wesbank v Minister of Finance* 2002 (4) SA 768 (CC) par [32] at 787F–G.

[96] Just as criminal forfeiture of property used or acquired by convicted criminals is more or less uncontroversial; it is the effect of enforcement on 'innocent' third party owners that creates controversy in the context of constitutional property protection. See chapter 5.3 and AJ van der Walt 'Civil forfeiture of instrumentalities and proceeds of crime and the constitutional property clause' (2000) 16 *SAJHR* 1–45 for examples and discussion.

[97] *First National Bank of SA Ltd t/a Wesbank v Commissioner, South African Revenue Service; First National Bank of SA Ltd t/a Wesbank v Minister of Finance* 2002 (4) SA 768 (CC) par [32] at 787F–G. See T Roux 'Section 25' in S Woolman et al (eds) *Constitutional law of South Africa* (2nd ed 2003 original service Dec 2003) 46–18.

basis an investigation regarding the constitutional validity of any limitation of property should always start with the general, all-embracing requirements in subsection 25(1):

> '[58] Viewed from this perspective s 25(1) deals with all "property" and all deprivations (including expropriations). If the deprivation infringes (limits) s 25 and cannot be justified under s 36, that is the end of the matter. The provision is unconstitutional.
>
> [59] If, however, the deprivation passes scrutiny under s 25(1) (ie it does not infringe s 25(1) or, if it does, is a justified limitation) then the question arises as to whether it is an expropriation. If the deprivation amounts to an expropriation it must pass scrutiny under s 25(2)(a) and make provision for compensation under s 25(2)(b) ...
>
> [60] The starting point for constitutional analysis, when considering any challenge under s 25 for the infringement of property rights, must be s 25(1).'

In this passage, the Court sets out a guideline for the consideration of property challenges: the Court will always start out by asking whether the interference satisfies the general requirements for valid deprivation of property in terms of subsection 25(1), regardless of whether the applicant challenges the infringement as deprivation or expropriation. In this regard, *FNB* represents a major departure from *Harksen*.[98] To begin with, the distinction between deprivation and expropriation is relegated to a later stage of the process: only once it has been established that the interference either satisfies the requirements in subsection 25(1) or is a justified limitation in terms of section 36 can the question be asked whether the interference also qualifies as expropriation, in which case it also has to satisfy the more specific requirements of subsection 25(2). In *FNB*, the latter issue simply never came up, because—in the words of Ackermann J for the Court—when a deprivation proves to be an unconstitutional deprivation in conflict with section 25(1) that cannot be justified in terms of section 36, 'that is the end of the matter'.[99] When this approach is followed, the result will probably be the same in the vast majority of cases, as it seems unlikely (as will be indicated in more detail below)[100] that many infringements will pass muster in the deprivation inquiry and then fail in the expropriation inquiry; similarly, expropriations that would fail the subsection 25(2) inquiry will probably also fail the earlier subsection 25(1) inquiry.

---

[98] In *Harksen v Lane NO* 1998 (1) SA 300 (CC) paras [31]–[40] at 315B–318I the Court assumed that deprivation and expropriation constitute discrete and mutually exclusive categories, and apparently also that the plaintiff who wanted to attack the constitutional validity of any limitation of property had to select the category under which the limitation had to be reviewed. In *Harksen* the applicant alleged that the limitation constituted an unconstitutional expropriation without compensation and the Court dismissed this allegation without considering the possibility that it might have constituted an invalid deprivation; see AJ van der Walt & H Botha 'Coming to grips with the new constitutional order: Critical comments on *Harksen v Lane NO*' (1998) 13 *SA Public Law* 17–41 at 19–21.

[99] *First National Bank of SA Ltd t/a Wesbank v Commissioner, South African Revenue Service; First National Bank of SA Ltd t/a Wesbank v Minister of Finance* 2002 (4) SA 768 (CC) par [58] at 797A.

[100] See further chapter 2.5, where the issue is discussed.

The approach in *FNB* effectively overturned the assumption in *Harksen* that a litigant is forced to argue either that there was unconstitutional expropriation or that there was unconstitutional deprivation of property and that the Court will not consider the other option of its own accord. In *Harksen* the Court decided the expropriation question raised by the applicant without considering deprivation as an alternative, but the logic of *FNB* means that the Court will always investigate the deprivation issue first, regardless of whether it was raised by the applicant at all. If this procedure were followed in *Harksen* it might have resulted in a different outcome, since it is conceivable that the Court could have regarded the effects of section 21 as unjustifiably harsh for the purpose it serves.[101]

The *FNB* decision introduced a significant methodological shift that will probably be followed in all property challenges in future. The shift boils down to the fact that limitation of property will always be regarded as deprivation and tested against the requirements of subsection 25(1) first, before the question is raised whether it also constitutes expropriation, for which further requirements are set out in subsection 25(2). The approach set out in *FNB* was already followed in the subsequent decision of the Constitutional Court in *Mkontwana*.[102]

4.5.3 The *FNB* case: The arbitrariness test

Having established its new methodology, the Constitutional Court in *FNB* focused on the provision in subsection 25(1) that no law shall authorise arbitrary deprivation of property. In its analysis of this provision the Court unexpectedly terminated the debate about the question whether first-stage limitation analysis should involve a 'thin' or a 'thick' approach.[103] As was pointed out in 4.5.1 above, a thin interpretation of the requirements in section 25(1) would mean that any deprivation of property that was authorised by a properly promulgated law of general application and that was not palpably capricious or in bad faith would pass constitutional muster. The result would be that deprivation would never be subjected to substantive scrutiny or justification analysis under section 36: deprivation imposed in terms of properly promulgated, general law will be validated relatively easily under thin rationality review and, since there is no limitation of property as long as the requirements of subsection 25(1) have

---

[101] As is indicated by the remarks of O'Regan J in connection with the equality issue; see AJ van der Walt & H Botha 'Coming to grips with the new constitutional order: Critical comments on *Harksen v Lane NO*' (1998) 13 *SA Public Law* 17–41 at 23–26, 32. It has to be remembered in this context that *Harksen* was decided on the basis of section 28 of the 1993 Constitution, and that the absence of the 'arbitrary' requirement in subsection 28(2) would have made it more difficult to arrive at the same conclusion that Ackermann J reached in *FNB* with reference to subsection 25(1), but a similar kind of argument may have been possible nevertheless.

[102] *Mkontwana v Nelson Mandela Metropolitan Municipality; Bissett and Others v Buffalo City Municipality; Transfer Rights Action Campaign and Others v Member of the Executive Council for Local Government and Housing, Gauteng and Others* 2005 (1) SA 530 (CC). In *Du Toit v Minister of Transport* CCT 22/04 8 September 2005 (CC) the Constitutional Court simply ignored the *FNB* methodology.

[103] See the preliminary discussion in 4.5.1 above and especially footnote 82 above.

been satisfied, section 36(1) would never be activated.[104] In order to establish substantive control over deprivation of property during first stage analysis I have previously argued in favour of a 'holistic' approach that would bring the justificatory aspects of limitation analysis into the first-stage deprivation analysis.[105] The logic of my proposal was problematic in view of the two-stage approach adopted by the Constitutional Court[106] and it was therefore criticised by other authors[107] and rejected by the Constitutional Court in *FNB*.[108] However, the *FNB* Court's interpretation of the 'arbitrary' requirement had roughly the effect I was looking for, albeit that my proposal was theoretically less elegant and terminologically more problematic.[109]

Ackermann J introduced a substantive element into the first-stage analysis by way of a surprisingly 'thick' interpretation of the requirement that laws may not permit arbitrary deprivation. In the literature on section 25[110] it was assumed that the non-arbitrariness requirement would be interpreted like the reasonableness requirement in administrative law, based on the countermajoritarian-inspired view that courts

---

[104]This is the interpretation favoured by J de Waal, G Erasmus & I Currie *Bill of rights handbook* (4th ed 2001) 422, 426–428; M Chaskalson & C Lewis 'Property' in M Chaskalson et al (eds) *Constitutional law of South Africa* (1st ed 1998) par 31.5(*b*)(ii)(bb); G Budlender 'The constitutional protection of property rights: Overview and commentary' in G Budlender, J Latsky & T Roux (eds) *Juta's new land law* (1998) chapter 1 at 34–36.

[105]AJ van der Walt 'The limits of constitutional property' (1997) 12 *SA Public Law* 275–330.

[106]*Coetzee v Government of the Republic of South Africa* 1995 (4) SA 631 (CC); *S v Makwanyane and Another* 1995 (3) SA 391 (CC); *S v Zuma and Others* 1995 (2) SA 642 (CC); *Bernstein and Others v Bester and Others NNO* 1996 (2) SA 751 (CC); *National Director of Public Prosecutions and Another v Mohamed NO and Others* 2003 (1) SA 561 (CC). However, see *Nhlabati and Others v Fick* 2003 (7) BCLR 806 (LCC) par [34] at 818E–F, where the Land Claims Court accepted the 'cumulative' view, without reference to the problems it created.

[107]See J de Waal, G Erasmus & I Currie *Bill of rights handbook* (4th ed 2001) 427 footnote 60; T Roux 'Property' in MH Cheadle, DM Davis & NRL Haysom (eds) *South African constitutional law: The bill of rights* (2002) at 440–442; H Mostert 'Liberty, social duty and fairness in the context of constitutional property protection and regulation' in H Botha, A van der Walt & J van der Walt (eds) *Rights and democracy in a transformative constitution* (2003) 131–161 at 140–159.

[108]*First National Bank of SA Ltd t/a Wesbank v Commissioner, South African Revenue Service; First National Bank of SA Ltd t/a Wesbank v Minister of Finance* 2002 (4) SA 768 (CC) par [70] at 801C.

[109]My proposal was inspired by the fact that the German Federal Constitutional Court established a jurisprudence in which substantive issues of suitability and justification are raised in two distinctly different ways, during two separate stages of the inquiry that are at least comparable to what we would call first- and second-stage analysis. See AJ van der Walt *Constitutional property clauses: A comparative analysis* (1999) 135–145. See footnote 106 above.

[110]The thin interpretation was supported by J de Waal, G Erasmus & I Currie (eds) *The bill of rights handbook* (4th ed 2001) 422; M Chaskalson & C Lewis 'Property' in M Chaskalson et al (eds) *Constitutional law of South Africa* (1st ed 1998) par 31.5(*b*)(ii)(bb); G Budlender 'The constitutional protection of property rights: Overview and commentary' in G Budlender, J Latsky & T Roux (eds) *Juta's new land law* (1998) chapter 1 at 34–36. The *FNB* Court refers to the thin interpretation of the non-arbitrary requirement, but adds that 'context is all-important', and that this requirement in the context of subsection 25(1) goes beyond thin rationality review: *First National Bank of SA Ltd t/a Wesbank v Commissioner, South African Revenue Service; First National Bank of SA Ltd t/a Wesbank v Minister of Finance* 2002 (4) SA 768 (CC) paras [62] at 797F, [65] at 798G–H, [70] at 801B–C.

should interfere as little as possible with policy decisions made by democratically elected legislatures and properly authorised administrative bodies.[111] In administrative law it was once assumed that administrative action would only be subject to review for arbitrariness when it was grossly unreasonable[112] or patently invalid.[113] Such a restrictive interpretation would have established a thin rationality review approach to the section 25(1) requirements, but in *FNB* the Court surprised everybody by adopting a substantive interpretation of the non-arbitrariness requirement.

The Court's substantive arbitrariness test adopts as its point of departure the view that deprivation is arbitrary when there is insufficient reason for it.[114] To decide whether there is sufficient reason for the deprivation, 'a complexity of relations' has to be considered, including the relationship between the means employed and the ends sought to be achieved; the relationship between the purpose for the deprivation and the person whose property is affected; and the relationship between the purpose of the deprivation and the nature of the property and the extent of the deprivation. Generally speaking, the purpose of the deprivation has to be more compelling when ownership is affected rather than a lesser property right, and when all rather than just some of the incidents of ownership are embraced by the deprivation.[115] The application of this arbitrariness test during the first stage of the constitutional inquiry is contextual—even the thickness of the test varies with the context:[116]

'[100] Having regard to what has gone before, it is concluded that a deprivation of property is "arbitrary" as meant by s 25 when the "law" referred to in s 25(1) does not provide

---

[111] *Roman v Williams NO* 1998 (1) SA 270 (C); *Standard Bank of Bophuthatswana Ltd v Reynolds NO* 1995 (3) SA 74 (B); *Carephone (Pty) Ltd v Marcus NO* 1999 (3) SA 304 (LAC); *Government of the Republic of South Africa v Grootboom* 2001 (1) SA 46 (CC). See the Promotion of Administrative Justice Act 3 of 2000 subsections 6(2)(f)(ii), 6(2)(h) and 6(2)(i); and compare C Hoexter (with R Lyster) *The new constitutional and administrative law Vol 2: Administrative law* (2002) 182–184; I Currie & J Klaaren *The Promotion of Administrative Justice Act benchbook* (2001) 169–173.
[112] In the sense that no other administrator in the same position would have taken the same decision, or that the action was so unreasonable as to indicate lack of authority or procedural unfairness.
[113] In the sense of being carried out in bad faith or capriciously, which would be symptomatic of its lack of authority, since it would thereby automatically exceed the authority to act.
[114] *First National Bank of SA Ltd t/a Wesbank v Commissioner, South African Revenue Service; First National Bank of SA Ltd t/a Wesbank v Minister of Finance* 2002 (4) SA 768 (CC); the Court sets out the test in par [100] at 810G–811F. The conclusion that 'arbitrary' can have this wider meaning is reached in par [98] at 810C–F.
[115] Factors not considered directly by the Court but that could enrich the analysis further are personal autonomy and the sanctity of the home. In accordance with the principle that the justifiability of regulatory limitation of property depends upon the balance between the individual property interest and the public interest, limitation could perhaps be accepted more readily the further the property interest is removed from the personal sphere and home of the individual, and less easily the closer it is to it. A similar approach is followed in German law; see AJ van der Walt *Constitutional property clauses: A comparative analysis* (1999) 135–141.
[116] *First National Bank of SA Ltd t/a Wesbank v Commissioner, South African Revenue Service; First National Bank of SA Ltd t/a Wesbank v Minister of Finance* 2002 (4) SA 768 (CC) par [100] at 810H, 811D–F.

sufficient reason for the particular deprivation or is procedurally unfair. Sufficient reason
is to be established as follows:

(a) ...

...

(g) Depending on such interplay between variable means and ends, the nature of the
property in question and the extent of its deprivation, there may be circumstances,
when sufficient reason is established by, in effect, no more than a mere rational relationship between means and ends; in others this might only be established by a proportionality evaluation closer to that required by s 36(1) of the Constitution.

(h) Whether there is sufficient reason to warrant the deprivation is a matter to be decided
on all the relevant facts of each particular case, always bearing in mind that the enquiry
is concerned with "arbitrary" in relation to the deprivation of property under s 25.'

In other words, the sufficiency of the reasons for deprivation is tested with reference
to a 'thick' complexity of contextual factors and, depending on the context, the test
can vary from mere rationality to something closer to section 36-type proportionality.
In the context of the *FNB* case, the test as set out by the Court in paragraph [100]
was thicker than mere rationality because it was clear that a strong reason for the
deprivation was required in the circumstances: the affected right was ownership, all
the incidents of ownership were affected, and there was no *nexus* or relationship
between either the affected owner or the affected property and the purpose of the
deprivation:[117]

'[108] Here the end sought to be achieved by the deprivation is to exact payment of a
customs debt. This is a legitimate and important legislative purpose, essential for the financial well-being of the country and in the interest of all its inhabitants. Section 114,
however, casts the net far too wide. The means it uses sanctions the total deprivation of a
person's property under circumstances where (*a*) such a *person* has no connection with the
transaction giving rise to the customs debt; (*b*) where such *property* also has no connection
with the *customs debt*; and (*c*) where such person has not transacted with or placed the
customs debtor in possession of the property under circumstances that have induced the
Commissioner to act to his detriment in relation to the incurring of the customs debt.

[109] In the absence of any such relevant *nexus*, no sufficient reason exists for s 114 to
deprive persons other than the customs debtor of their goods. Such deprivation is accordingly arbitrary for purpose of s 25(1) and consequently a limitation (infringement) of such
person's rights.'

The Court found it unnecessary to decide whether infringements of section 25 are
subject to section 36 justification analysis and simply assumed that they are.[118] In the

---

[117] *First National Bank of SA Ltd t/a Wesbank v Commissioner, South African Revenue Service; First
National Bank of SA Ltd t/a Wesbank v Minister of Finance* 2002 (4) SA 768 (CC) par [108] at 815A–C.
[118] Some authors have contended that section 36 finds no application to infringements of section
25, and it is certainly difficult to conceive of instances where an infringement that falls foul of
section 25 will pass the justification test under section 36; see in this regard J de Waal, G Erasmus
& I Currie *Bill of rights handbook* (4th ed 2001) 422, 426–428; AJ van der Walt 'The limits of
constitutional property' (1997) 12 *SA Public Law* 275–330. See further T Roux 'Section 25' in
(continued on next page ...)

circumstances the deprivation could not be justified under section 36 in any event, and consequently it was decided that section 114 was constitutionally invalid to the extent that it provided that the goods of persons other than the customs debtor are subject to a lien, detention or sale as foreseen in the provision.[119]

Theunis Roux[120] identified two 'keys to the unlocking' of *FNB*: first that the arbitrariness test will apply to all property challenges and that it will probably suck all aspects of the property challenge into the arbitrariness test; and second that the test leaves wide scope for judicial discretion. In his view, the test will not be applied formulaically by merely applying the factors set out in paragraph [100]; instead, 'the level of scrutiny will vacillate between two fixed poles: rationality review at the lower end of the scale, and something just short of a review for proportionality at the other.'[121] As is indicated in the next section below, it did not take long before Roux's evaluation of the *FNB* arbitrariness test and his predictions about its application were tested.

4.5.4 The *Mkontwana* case: Retreating from *FNB*?

The arbitrariness test in *FNB* was followed and applied in the *Mkontwana* decision.[122] Section 118(1) of the Local Government: Municipal Systems Act 32 of 2000[123] has the effect that a landowner is unable to transfer her land to a purchaser until unpaid consumption charges run up by a tenant—or even an unlawful occupier—during the previous two years have been settled in full. The South Eastern Cape Local Division of the High Court decided that this provision permitted arbitrary deprivation of the

---

(*... from previous page*)

S Woolman et al (eds) *Constitutional law of South Africa* (2nd ed 2003 original service Dec 2003) 46–27. The most that could now be said on this issue is that it is perhaps as well to keep the issue open, even if it is difficult to see how section 36 can save an infringement that fails the section 25 rationality test or other section 25(1) requirements. See further chapter 2.5.

[119] *First National Bank of SA Ltd t/a Wesbank v Commissioner, South African Revenue Service; First National Bank of SA Ltd t/a Wesbank v Minister of Finance* 2002 (4) SA 768 (CC) paras [113] at 816E–F, [114] at 816H.

[120] T Roux 'Section 25' in S Woolman et al (eds) *Constitutional law of South Africa* (2nd ed 2003 original service Dec 2003) at 46-23–46-25.

[121] T Roux 'Section 25' in S Woolman et al (eds) *Constitutional law of South Africa* (2nd ed 2003 original service Dec 2003) at 46–24.

[122] *Mkontwana v Nelson Mandela Metropolitan Municipality; Bissett and Others v Buffalo City Municipality; Transfer Rights Action Campaign and Others v Member of the Executive Council for Local Government and Housing, Gauteng and Others* 2005 (1) SA 530 (CC). This section is based on and similar in part to AJ van der Walt 'Retreating from the *FNB* arbitrariness test already? *Mkontwana v Nelson Mandela Metropolitan Municipality; Bissett v Buffalo City Municipality; Transfer Rights Action Campaign v MEC for Local Government and Housing, Gauteng (CC)*' (2005) 122 *SALJ* 75–89.

[123] The section limits landowners' power to transfer their immovable property by providing that transfer of the land may not be effected without a certificate issued by the municipality to the effect that consumption charges for services during the two years before the date of issue have been paid.

landowner's property and was therefore in conflict with section 25(1). The High Court's finding of unconstitutionality was referred to the Constitutional Court.[124]

The Court confirmed that the restriction imposed by section 18(1) amounts to deprivation[125] and applied the *FNB* test for arbitrariness by asking whether there was sufficient reason for the deprivation, taking into account the relationship between the purpose of the limitation and the deprivation effected by it. After having applied the *FNB* test, the Court held that the deprivation permitted by section 118(1) was not arbitrary because there was sufficient reason for it in that there was a close enough connection between the deprivation and the consumption charges and between the owner and the consumption charges, even when the land was unlawfully occupied and the charges were levied for services enjoyed by the unlawful occupiers.[126]

On the surface it looks as if the Court merely applied the test as set out in *FNB*, but in fact the Court's subtle rephrasing of the test points towards a significant shift. Firstly, the Court deviated from *FNB* by emphasizing the extent of the deprivation and downplaying the contextual factors: a mere rational connection between means and end could suffice for a minimal deprivation, while a more compelling reason and a closer relationship between means and ends would be required when the extent of the deprivation was greater.[127] Secondly, the test itself was stated in a different, streamlined format: 'there would be sufficient reason for the deprivation if the government purpose was both legitimate and compelling and if it would, in the circumstances, not be unreasonable to expect the owner to take the risk of non-payment.'[128] In other

---

[124] In *Geyser and Another v Msunduzi Municipality and Others* 2003 (5) SA 18 (N) the KwaZulu-Natal High Court decided that section 118(1) and 118(3) of the Act did not give rise to arbitrary deprivation and were not inconsistent with section 25(1) of the Constitution, but the South Eastern Cape Local Division of the High Court decided in two cases *(Mkontwana v Nelson Mandela Municipality and Others* case no 1238/02 (SECLD); *Bissett and Others v Buffalo City Municipality and Others* case no 903/02 (SECLD), 13 September 2003) that subsection 18(1) permitted arbitrary deprivation and was in conflict with section 25(1). The findings of unconstitutionality in the latter two cases were referred to the Constitutional Court for confirmation in terms of section 172(2) of the Constitution. The municipalities cited in those two cases and the minister responsible for local government in the province opposed confirmation and appealed against the High Court orders.

[125] Par [33] at 546G.

[126] Paras [39]–[40] at 549F–J; [53] at 554C–E; [54] at 554F–H. In *BOE Bank v City of Tshwane Metropolitan Municipality* 2005 (4) SA 336 (SCA) the Supreme Court of Appeal held that a charge upon immovable property in favour of the municipality that was imposed by section 18(3) of the Act was not restricted to the two year limit that applies to section 18(1) and that this charge provides the municipality with preference over a bank holding a mortgage bond. This decision therefore extends the application of *Mkontwana* to debts that are in principle unlimited in time and to rights holders who are even more remote from the debt than the landowners; less capable of preventing the incurrence of the debt and less capable of evicting unlawful occupiers or non-paying ex-tenants who are holding over from the premises.

[127] Par [35] at 547D–E. Of course, this departure was already signposted in the *FNB* decision in the sense that the *FNB* test requires stricter scrutiny when all or most (rather than just one) of the incidents of ownership were affected by the deprivation.

[128] Par [51] at 553E–H.

words, the complex test of the interplay between various factors as set out in *FNB* was adjusted to two questions: whether the purpose of the deprivation is legitimate and compelling, and whether it would be unreasonable in the circumstances to place the burden where the relevant provision does.

On the basis of this streamlined test the Court held that there was a close enough relationship between the property and consumption charges in that the services were delivered and consumed on the premises and affected the property's worth.[129] Secondly it was held that there was a close enough relationship between the owner and the consumption charge because ownership entails rights and duties, especially with regard to ensuring that the property is not occupied unlawfully and that service charges are paid regularly.[130] As far as the relationship between means and ends is concerned the Court decided that the restriction did affect an important incident of ownership, but that the deprivation was slight in that it was limited to one incident of ownership only and temporary.

In considering the reason for the deprivation, *Mkontwana* seems to require that the purpose be 'both legitimate and compelling',[131] but in fact it never goes beyond establishing that the purpose of the deprivation—enforcing payment of service charges— is 'laudable' and 'has the potential to encourage regular payments of consumption charges, contributes to the effective discharge by municipalities of their obligations and encourages owners of property to fulfill their civic responsibility'.[132] These considerations might prove that the purpose of the deprivation was legitimate, but certainly not that it was compelling. Other aspects of the stated purpose and their relationship to the deprivation were not considered; above all the possibility that the deprivation serves as a safety net or even as a replacement for inefficient municipal debt management and collection practices, which is not a legitimate public purpose at all.[133] The Court justified its judgment with the observation that section 118 could encourage landowners to ensure payment of service charges for their properties, but it did not consider the possibility that judicial support for the section 118 procedure might encourage local authorities to worry even less about proper debt collection practices, safe in the knowledge that they can recoup at least two years' worth of unpaid debts at some stage from the landowner.

The Court's analysis of this aspect underlines the necessity of developing a more sophisticated view of the public purpose requirement for deprivation. The *FNB* arbitrariness test makes it possible to consider the relationship between the purpose for the deprivation and the affected property and its owner, but apart from that it is also

---

[129] Par [40] at 549H–J.

[130] Paras [41]–[43] at 550A–I.

[131] Par [51] at 553E–H.

[132] Par [52] at 553I–554A.

[133] See the interesting report by Sabelo Ndlangisa 'Big guns of business lend a hand to councils: Captains of industry roped in to sort out local government' *The Sunday Times* 31 October 2004 at 4, where it is suggested that local government structures are incapable of responding adequately to their governance challenges, including debt management and debt collection problems.

necessary to pay more attention to the purpose in itself by asking whether the deprivation is really necessary and how high its purpose ranks amongst the purposes legitimately served by regulatory action. Overall it looks as if the purpose for the section 118 deprivation, namely efficient debt collection in public utilities, was accepted too easily and given too much weight in *Mkontwana*. By contrast, a more sophisticated approach would take into account the fact that the deprivation was imposed purely to facilitate day-to-day management of state finances, as opposed to a real financial crisis. In a recent case the Supreme Court of Ireland held that a law that abrogates private property interests (in the form of money claims against the state) purely to save the state money was unconstitutional, adding that a law that seeks to abrogate private property purely for state financial purposes could only be justified with an appeal to the public purposes requirement when it was intended, objectively speaking, to avoid an extreme financial crisis or a fundamental disequilibrium in public finances.[134] *Mkontwana* would probably not have passed that test.

The second step in the streamlined version of the arbitrariness test confirms the impression that the Court in *Mkontwana* moved away from the substantive test set out in *FNB* and back towards a thinner rationality test. The Court decided that it is not unreasonable to expect the landowner to bear the risk of non-payment, even with regard to unlawful occupiers of the land, considering the owner's relationship to the property, her duties and responsibilities with regard to it, and the relative position of the owner and the municipality with regard to ensuring payment.[135] On face value the test relied upon by the Court in reaching this decision, namely that 'there would be sufficient reason for the deprivation if the government purpose was both legitimate and compelling and if it would, in the circumstances, not be unreasonable to expect the owner to take the risk of non-payment',[136] looks like the proportionality-type test mentioned in *FNB* for cases that require more than mere rationality. In fact, however, it is much closer to a thin, mere rationality test: the second part of the test is applied by merely looking for a more or less reasonable connection between the purpose of the provision (efficient debt collection in public utilities) and the means (placing the risk of non-payment on the landowner) that serve the purpose. The

---

[134] *In the Matter of Article 26 of The Constitution & In the Matter of the Health (Amendment) (No. 2) Bill 2004* [2005] IESC 7 (Supreme Court of Ireland, 16 Feb 2005). See the discussion towards the end of 4.3 above, and especially footnotes 58, 60 and 61. In German law it is usually said that, to meet the proportionality requirement, deprivation must be strictly necessary (*erforderlich*), suitable for the public purpose it serves (*geeignet*) and not disproportionate to the burden it imposes (*verhältnismäßig*, also *zumutbar*). This tripartite test places special focus on the suitability of the deprivation in promoting the purpose for which it was authorized. That means that it must first be determined whether the deprivation is really necessary at all. In doing so varying levels of scrutiny could apply, depending on how closely the purpose is related to protection of public health and safety. On this level the extent of the deprivation can also be relevant; in Swiss law a lower level of scrutiny applies when slight regulatory interferences are reviewed and a higher level of scrutiny for substantial deprivation; see AJ van der Walt *Constitutional property clauses: A comparative analysis* (1999) 367.
[135] Paras [53]–[64] at 554B–558A.
[136] Par [51] at 553F–H.

Court found a sufficient relationship between the purpose and the property in the fact
that the services were delivered and consumed on the property; and between the
owner and the purpose in the fact that the owner benefits from the increase in value
resulting from the delivery of services. It assumed that the owner has the responsibility to ensure that the land is not occupied unlawfully or that unlawful occupiers
are evicted, and that service charges are paid regularly. It also assumed that the owner
is in a better position to enforce payment than the municipality, apparently because
the (very strong) enforcement instrument in the hands of the municipality, namely
termination of services, is a deeply unpopular action that is possibly in conflict with
the municipality's constitutional duty to deliver services.

This argument and its underlying assumptions are flawed in several ways. Firstly,
there is no conflict between the municipality's constitutional duty to deliver services
and its contractual right to terminate services for reasons of outstanding payment—
the former does not extend to delivery of unlimited free services and therefore does
not exclude the latter. Secondly, the termination of services is surely a much stronger
enforcement mechanism than anything the owner can muster. Thirdly, insufficient
attention was paid to the question whether non-payment might have been the result
of inefficient administration and poor debt enforcement strategies on the side of the
municipality; contingencies for which the owner should not be expected to stand in
and that could be rectified with other, more efficient and less intrusive measures.
Fourthly, all other arguments are overshadowed by the (largely ignored) fact that the
only enforcement instrument in the hands of the owner, namely eviction (preceded
by cancellation in suitable cases), is quite rightly subjected to severe restrictions by the
Constitution, legislation and case law, including the Constitutional Court's own
recent case law.[137]

Imposing a rather thin rationality test would have been understandable in *Mkontwana* if the deprivation was so slight that nothing more would be necessary, as was
explained in *FNB*. However, the Court accepted that the deprivation placed on the
applicants was 'not insubstantial', although it was at pains to point out that it affected

[137]A decision handed down by the Constitutional Court in the same period as *Mkontwana* sheds
interesting light on the issue. In *Port Elizabeth Municipality v Various Occupiers* 2005 (1) SA 217 (CC)
the Court decided, with reference to section 26(3) of the Constitution and the Prevention of Illegal
Eviction from and Unlawful Occupation of Land Act 18 of 1998, that the courts should be reluctant to grant an eviction order against unlawful occupiers unless it is convinced that it is just and
equitable in view of all the circumstances. Although it is not impossible to evict people from
informal settlements, this may only be done in a process that seeks concrete and case-specific solutions for the problems at hand (paras [21]–[22] at 229B–D). The overall effect is—quite
justifiably—that it becomes more difficult to evict even unlawful occupiers. If these occupiers are
also not paying their service charges the effect on the landowner can be disastrous, especially considering the difficulty of just getting a hearing date. In this context the owner is forced to pay the
outstanding service charges of a lessee or even an unlawful occupier while not being allowed to use
the one effective enforcement mechanism at her disposal, namely eviction.

only one incident of ownership and was temporary.[138] It is true that the deprivation should mostly affect just the one incident of ownership, namely disposal, and then only for service charges run up during the previous two years, but in view of the overall picture it could in fact have a devastating effect on the owner's rights, especially if unlawful occupiers are concerned and the owner cannot get them evicted.[139]

It might be concluded, in line with Theunis Roux's analysis of the effects of the *FNB* test, that the Constitutional Court in *Mkontwana* used the wide judicial discretion reserved for itself in *FNB* and located the level of scrutiny on the rationality side of the continuum rather than the proportionality side;[140] in other words, one could explain the thinness of the arbitrariness test in *Mkontwana* as a result of the discretion that the Court reserved for itself in *FNB* to judge how strict scrutiny should be, depending on the facts and circumstances. However, although the *FNB* Court reserved the discretion to decide how strict scrutiny in deprivation cases should be, that discretion has to be exercised with due regard for the factors enumerated in *FNB*, specifically the nexus between the purpose of the regulatory measure, the property and its owner. This is not how the test was applied in *Mkontwana*: the purpose of the regulatory measure, fiscal efficiency, may be legitimate and even important, but it remains a borderline public purpose for exercises of the police power and therefore it requires stricter scrutiny—it simply does not protect public health and safety in any obvious way. The nexus established between this purpose, the property and its owners in the case was tenuous at best, and the Court's scrutiny of that nexus was far from substantive. Accordingly it cannot be said that the choice for a low level of scrutiny, rationality review, was inspired by the Court's considered judgment that the case justified such a low level of scrutiny. The alternative explanation is that the Court did not choose the lower level of scrutiny on the basis of the *FNB* arbitrariness test, but retreated from its own test in *FNB* to a position that is closer to a mere rationality approach in principle.

4.5.5 Other post-*FNB* deprivation cases

Apart from *Mkontwana*, several other post-*FNB* decisions of the Constitutional Court have a bearing on deprivation of property, although some of them were not decided explicitly or even indirectly in terms of or with reference to section 25(1). These

---

[138] Par [45] at 551D–G. It bears repeating that this statement is misleading—although the owner can terminate the deprivation by paying the outstanding charges she may be unable to do so, not least because the outstanding debt can easily be higher than the value or the purchase price of the house. In that sense the deprivation can in effect be permanent. Compare in this regard the remarks made in *Harksen v Lane NO* 1998 (1) SA 300 (CC) par [37] at 318B–E, and compare the comments of AJ van der Walt & H Botha 'Coming to grips with the new constitutional order: Critical comments on *Harksen v Lane NO*' (1998) 13 *SA Public Law* 17–41 at 19–21.

[139] See Anna Cox 'Law lets down property owner in tenant row' *The Star* 22 October 2004 p 7; published on the Web by IOL at http://www.iol.co.za/.

[140] T Roux 'Section 25' in S Woolman et al (eds) *Constitutional law of South Africa* (2nd ed 2003 original service Dec 2003) at 46–24. In *Du Toit v Minister of Transport* CCT 22/04 8 September 2005 (CC) the Constitutional Court simply ignored the *FNB* methodology.

decisions are interesting in the current context because of their implications for judicial evaluation of state and private actions that might constitute arbitrary deprivation of property. The first two decisions that deserve mention in this regard will only be raised briefly here because they have been mentioned before and are discussed extensively in chapters 6 and 7.[141] Both cases deal with eviction of unlawful occupiers in terms of the anti-eviction measures in section 26(3) of the Constitution and in the Prevention of Illegal Eviction from and Unlawful Occupation of Land Act 18 of 1998 (PIE). These anti-eviction measures place limitations upon landownership in the sense that a landowner is only allowed to evict unlawful occupiers under procedural and substantive restrictions that depend, at least in part, upon the personal circumstances of the occupiers, whereas a landowner would normally—in the absence of these anti-eviction provisions—be able to evict unlawful occupiers regardless of their personal circumstances.

The remarkable characteristic of both decisions is that the Court, in giving effect to section 26(3) and the relevant legislation, explicitly subjected the landowner's right to the limiting effect of eviction proceedings that are designed to accommodate the personal, social and economic circumstances of the unlawful occupiers. By taking the occupiers' personal and social circumstances into consideration the Court gives effect to the limitation imposed by the relevant constitutional and statutory provisions, because landowners' 'normal' right to evict unlawful occupiers is thereby limited by factors that are neither relevant to the landowners' right nor under the landowners' control. Moreover, the Court considered this limitation of the rights of landowners a necessary and legitimate result of the relevant constitutional and statutory framework of land reform, seen against the background of the broad historical context within which land rights developed and are being reformed.[142] Although neither of these two cases was decided explicitly with reference to section 25(1), the decisions are congruent with the view that the anti-eviction measures impose a limitation upon landownership rights and that this limitation is a legitimate and valid deprivation of property because it serves a legitimate regulatory purpose and is not arbitrary. In other words, the anti-eviction decisions are capable of explanation and justification in terms of section 25(1).

In giving effect to these reform-oriented constitutional and statutory limitations of landownership the Court emphasized that the apparent conflict between the rights of

---

[141] *Port Elizabeth Municipality v Various Occupiers* 2005 (1) SA 217 (CC); *President of the Republic of South Africa and Another v Modderklip Boerdery (Pty) Ltd (Agri SA and Others,* Amici Curiae*)* 2005 (5) SA 3 (CC). See the discussion of these cases in chapter 6.3 and chapter 7.2.

[142] *Port Elizabeth Municipality v Various Occupiers* 2005 (1) SA 217 (CC) paras [8]–[23] at 222A–229G, [33]–[38] at 236C–239A; *President of the Republic of South Africa and Another v Modderklip Boerdery (Pty) Ltd (Agri SA and Others,* Amici Curiae*)* 2005 (5) SA 3 (CC) par [36] at 20D–F. The Constitutional Court did refer to section 25 in *Port Elizabeth Municipality v Various Occupiers* 2005 (1) SA 217 (CC) paras [15]–[16] at 225C–227B and stated that an appropriate constitutional relationship had to be established between section 25 rights and section 26 rights: par [19] at 228B–D. No specific reference was made to section 25(1), though.

landowners and the interests of unlawful occupiers had to be solved by way of an individualized, context-sensitive balancing process that takes both sets of rights and interests into account. The importance of this balancing process is particularly clear from the *Modderklip* case, where the right of the landowner to evict unlawful occupiers was limited by the anti-eviction measure in section 26(3) and the landowner therefore had to wait until the occupiers could be removed to alternative accommodation, but at the same time the state was ordered to pay compensation to the landowner for the loss suffered during the period of unlawful occupation. The landowner's right is therefore not simply ignored or diminished; it was properly recognized and protected in terms of section 25. In this instance, the Constitutional Court argued that the state was obliged, in terms of section 34 of the Constitution, to ensure that the landowner had access to court—including access to suitable and effective enforcement procedures and institutions—to enforce protection of his right. It was therefore not acceptable for the state to stand by and allow the owner to deal with the problem and therefore, because no effective enforcement measure was made available to him, the state had to pay compensation for the loss that the owner suffered as a result of the unlawful invasion and the protracted unlawful occupation of his land.

The equalization payments mentioned in 4.2.3 above have a bearing on the deprivation issue in the *Modderklip* case, especially with reference to the SCA and Constitutional Court decisions.[143] It could be argued that the compensation that had to be paid to the landowner in *Modderklip* who was unable to enforce his eviction order because of the lack of a suitable and effective enforcement procedure resembles the equalization payments that are sometimes possible in French and German law to compensate a property owner who is affected by unfairly harsh regulatory deprivation of property. As in French and German law, this payment should not be confused with compensation for expropriation of property (or even expropriation of a single incident of property)—it is much better explained as compensation that enables the property owner to mitigate or bear the unfair effects of the regulatory action. In view of this explanation it could also be possible in future cases to use equalization compensation in cases where it is legitimate and important to uphold a particular regulatory action for the public interest, but at the same time the effects on a single or small group of owners are so harsh and unfair that it would be unacceptable for the state not to come to their assistance in some way. In some cases it could be possible for the state to mitigate the effects of the regulation, and then the state arguably has a duty to do so, but in other cases payment of money might be equally good or better if it allows the property owner to undertake mitigating strategies herself.

---

[143] *Modderfontein Squatters, Greater Benoni City Council v Modderklip Boerdery (Pty) Ltd; (Agri SA and Legal Resources Centre,* Amici Curiae*); President of the Republic of South Africa and Others v Modderklip Boerdery (Pty) Ltd (Agri SA and Legal Resources Centre,* Amici Curiae*) 2004 (6) SA 40 (SCA); President of the Republic of South Africa and Another v Modderklip Boerdery (Pty) Ltd (Agri SA and Others,* Amici Curiae*)* 2005 (5) SA 3 (CC); see footnote 52 above. See further with regard to equalization payments footnote 51 above and accompanying text, as well as chapter 5.4.2 footnotes 150–151 and accompanying text (France); chapter 5.4.3 footnote 161 and accompanying text (Germany).

The *Jaftha* case[144] was decided with reference to section 26 of the Constitution and not with reference to section 25(1), but it can also be explained in terms of the constitutional proscription of arbitrary deprivation of property. Section 66(1)(*a*) of the Magistrates' Courts Act 32 of 1944 allows for attachment and sale in execution of private property, including immovable property, to satisfy a debt. In the *Jaftha* case this procedure was used to satisfy relatively small debts by attaching and selling in execution the debtors' houses, which were acquired with state subsidies as part of the government's housing programme. In evaluating the effect of the execution procedure in terms of section 66(1)(*a*) the Constitutional Court took notice of the backdrop of legislation that made it possible in the apartheid era to summarily evict people from their houses and contrasted it with the intention of section 26(3) of the Constitution, 'which speaks directly to the practice of forced removals and summary eviction from land' and guarantees that this practice will cease, replacing it by a system of strict judicial control over evictions.[145] Against this background, the Court decided, a summary execution procedure that results in eviction of people from their homes without any judicial control is untenable. Accordingly, the Court decided that the words 'a court, after consideration of all relevant circumstances, may order execution' should be read into section 66(1)(*a*) to bring it in line with constitutional requirements and prevent it from being in conflict with section 26(1).[146] The Court decided the case with reference to the effect that the execution procedure had in limiting the right to access to housing in section 26(1), but again it is also capable of being explained and justified in terms of section 25(1). It can be said that attachment and sale in execution of property to satisfy unpaid debts limits the homeowners' property rights, that this limitation amounts to a deprivation and that it is therefore subject to scrutiny in terms of section 25(1). In this particular case, the deprivation effect of the execution procedure provided for in the Act was amended by reading in a phrase to ensure that the execution procedure is subject to judicial control, because it would amount to arbitrary deprivation in the absence of such control. Although the case was not decided with reference to section 25(1) or in these terms, the decision indirectly confirms that a summary execution procedure that would result in people being evicted from their homes for insignificant debts without judicial control would amount to an arbitrary deprivation of their property rights. The reading in strategy is justified by the Court in terms of section 26(1), but it also makes sense in terms of section 25(1), read with section 26(1).

In the *Zondi* case[147] the Constitutional Court reached a similar result with regard to the Pound Ordinance 32 of 1947 (Natal), once again indirectly. The Ordinance allowed landowners and pound-keepers to seize and impound (mostly black) livestock found trespassing on (mostly white) land and to sell impounded animals to recover the

[144] *Jaftha v Schoeman and Others; Van Rooyen v Stoltz and Others* 2005 (2) SA 140 (CC). See chapter 7.4.
[145] Par [28] at 154C–155B.
[146] Par [67] at 165E.
[147] *Zondi v Member of the Executive Council for Traditional and Local Government Affairs and Others* 2005 (3) SA 589 (CC). See chapter 7.4.

pound fees, without a court order. The Constitutional Court decided the case against the background of the social, economic and political role that the Ordinance played in the scheme of apartheid land law, particularly in establishing and reinforcing the unequal positions of white landowners and black landless people,[148] and held that these provisions violated the constitutional guarantees of equality and access to justice. Since reading in could not work in this instance the Court declared the relevant sections of the Ordinance unconstitutional.[149] Once again the case was decided with reference to sections 8 and 34 and not section 25(1), but indirectly the result can also be explained by saying that the deprivation of property that was allowed by the Ordinance was arbitrary in the absence of judicial control and therefore unconstitutional.

4.6 EFFECT OF THE *FNB* TEST [150]

In 4.5.4 above it was argued that the Constitutional Court might have retreated from the *FNB* arbitrariness test in the subsequent *Mkontwana* decision, but even if it did this was a retreat in fact rather than in principle, and accordingly one can probably assume that the *FNB* arbitrariness test still stands. As was pointed out in 4.5.3 above, the *FNB* arbitrariness test ensured that first-stage property analysis need not necessarily be reduced to thin, superficial and mechanistic rationality review—in suitable cases, determined by the context, first-stage analysis can amount to no more than rationality review, but in other cases it can approach (but apparently never quite reach) thicker, proportionality-inspired methodology similar to the second-stage justification analysis prescribed by subsection 36(1). In opting for this nuanced and context-sensitive test, the decision seems to accommodate both those who oppose too much judicial inter-ference with policy decisions involving deprivation of property and those (like myself) who argue in favour of some form of substantive review during the first stage of section 25 analysis: in some cases, the guideline set out in *FNB* will justifiably require nothing more than thin rationality review, in other cases much more substantive justi-fication of deprivations will be required, even during the first stage, and the choice between the two will be determined by variable contextual factors.

This result of the *FNB* arbitrariness test must be applauded, even though it leaves some old and some new questions unanswered. Theunis Roux[151] emphasized one of the new questions raised by *FNB* with the incisive observation that this decision has the effect of 'telescoping' or 'sucking' all property issues into the 'vortex' of the

---

[148] Paras [38]–[42] at 605A–606E.

[149] The declaration of invalidity was suspended for twelve months to give the provincial legislature an opportunity to amend the ordinance in a suitable way, and various rulings were made to provide for interim justice: paras [126]–[131] at 629C–630F.

[150] Like the previous section, this section is partly based on and in some respects similar to AJ van der Walt 'Striving for the better interpretation: A critical reflection on the Constitutional Court's *Harksen* and *FNB* decisions on the property clause' (2004) 121 *SALJ* 854–878.

[151] T Roux 'Section 25' in S Woolman et al (eds) *Constitutional law of South Africa* (2nd ed 2003 original service Dec 2003) 46-1–46-37. The effect of *FNB* is discussed by Roux at 46-18–46-20.

arbitrariness test. Instead of the Court deciding separately whether the interest in question was property, whether there was deprivation of property, whether the deprivation satisfied the requirements in section 25(1), whether the deprivation amounted to expropriation and, if it did, whether it satisfied the requirements in section 25(2), whether any deprivation or expropriation in conflict with section 25 could be justified in terms of section 36 and so on, all these issues are now telescoped or sucked into just one inquiry, namely whether there was sufficient reason for the deprivation involved, as set out in paragraph [100] of *FNB*. Roux points out that this 'vortex' effect means that other issues relating to the property clause are no longer decided in a property challenge. Or, it may perhaps be added, if they are decided one can expect them to be subjected to rather superficial scrutiny.

In one sense, this vortex effect of the *FNB* decision merely conforms to what is done in other jurisdictions and by the South African courts in other contexts, namely to focus on one issue that provides the easiest or most obvious or least controversial solution to what may otherwise be a complicated or contested decision. It seems logical not to spend too much time and judicial effort on the property question, and in other jurisdictions it is (for example) often fairly easily accepted that the interest at stake is indeed protected property, while more attention is paid to the deprivation or limitation issues.[152] To telescope the property question into the arbitrariness question may therefore not be such a bad thing, provided that the property issue retains some kind of threshold function in suitable cases. After *FNB* it will probably not be necessary to concern oneself too much with instances where ownership of land or tangible movables is at stake, but other kinds of property interest could still require further attention, especially if the courts were to be confronted by potentially difficult 'conceptual severance' cases.[153] In any event, proper consideration of the extent of the deprivation will probably require the court to pay at least some attention to the property issue as a threshold matter to ensure that the interest in question deserves protection.[154]

The vortex effect of *FNB* can also have a positive effect because it could ensure that first-stage analysis would be substantive rather than mechanistic, telescoping some of the substance of second-stage justification proportionality analysis into the first stage. This does not solve the problem of deciding what the correct relationship between

---

[152] For example Germany; see AJ van der Walt *Constitutional property clauses: A comparative analysis* (1999) 132–141. See *BVerfGE* 37, 132 [1974] (*Wohnraumkündigungsschutsgesetz*); *BVerfGE* 89, 1 [1993] (*Besitzrecht des Mieters*).

[153] See the discussion in chapter 3.4.

[154] Because of the indication in *First National Bank of SA Ltd t/a Wesbank v Commissioner, South African Revenue Service; First National Bank of SA Ltd t/a Wesbank v Minister of Finance* 2002 (4) SA 768 (CC) par [100] at 810H–811F that deprivation that affects ownership rather than a lesser right and that affects all rather than just some incidents of ownership will require stronger justification. To determine the level of review it will therefore be necessary to consider the nature of the right and the extent of the deprivation rather carefully. As T Roux 'Section 25' in S Woolman et al (eds) *Constitutional law of South Africa* (2nd ed 2003 original service Dec 2003) 46–29 correctly points out, this is an example of how the property issue, which otherwise might have been investigated first as a threshold matter, is now considered only as part of the deprivation question.

thick first-stage analysis and proper second-stage analysis is, and many questions remain in this regard, but in a sense the telescoping effect that Roux refers to is what made the *FNB* approach more palatable than the thin rationality review foreseen in some early publications. The relationship between section 25 and section 36 remains problematic, and it could perhaps be argued that *FNB* exacerbated the problem by seemingly collapsing first- and second-stage issues into the arbitrariness test. However, this is perhaps less problematic than it seems. The alternative, in terms of which all substantive issues are kept out of the first stage, does not really help to clarify the relationship between section 25 and section 36 either—most authors who argue for a thin first-stage rationality interpretation of section 25(1) also hold that section 36 finds no application to the property clause. At the same time, their approach means that first-stage review of deprivations is restricted to a rather mechanistic or bloodless adjudication process, which could mean that deprivation will never be subjected to substantive review in which proportionality is considered. This alternative is too restrictive because it leaves all cards in the hands of the executive and (to a lesser extent) the legislature, leaving no room for the kind of interaction and critical debate that could give meaning to the Constitution (and the property clause) in a contextual, dynamic and transformative process. If uncertainty about the relationship between sections 25 and 36 is the price to pay for the more robust and substantive approach followed in *FNB* it seems worthwhile at least in part, especially since it is still possible to develop a meaningful distinction between substantive, proportionality-based first-stage arbitrariness review and full-blown, proportionality-based second-stage justification review. It seems better to leave the door open and work on greater clarity than close the door on any possibility of further development, just for the sake of (arguably) greater certainty.[155]

The vortex effect of *FNB*, combined with the rather prescriptive analytic guidelines set out by the Court, may have less acceptable effects in other areas. The most obvious of these is the fact that deprivation issues have been placed so strongly in the forefront that policy questions about expropriation effectively may be excluded from future decision. Even in cases where the problem obviously centres on compliance with the expropriation requirements in section 25(2)—for example whether an expropriation was for a public purpose or whether the compensation is fair—the *FNB* guideline means that the limitation first has to be judged as a deprivation, and it seems reasonable to assume that an expropriation that is not for a public purpose or which does not provide for adequate compensation would fail the non-arbitrariness test as set out in *FNB*, thus never reaching the stage where it can be judged as an expropriation. This seems like an unnecessary and unhelpful side-effect of *FNB*, and one can only hope that the Court would be willing to forego or amend the *FNB* guideline in suitable cases and go straight to the obvious heart of the matter when expropriation issues like public purpose or compensation are at stake.[156]

---

[155] See 4.5.2 above.

[156] In *Du Toit v Minister of Transport* CCT 22/04 8 September 2005 (CC) the Constitutional Court indeed simply ignored the *FNB* methodology and decided the case purely with reference to the compensation issue. See chapter 5.8.

Less obvious and more troubling is the effect of *FNB* on the possibility of recognising constructive expropriation under section 25(2).[157] The property clause does not provide for such a category explicitly, but it is possible to argue in favour of recognising it through interpretation, and it seems a pity to close the door on this possibility by default. It may be beneficial to leave this possibility open rather than close it down out of fear for burdensome compensation claims. The most convincing reason for doing so remains the possibility that an excessive or unfairly burdensome deprivation—which could be arbitrary and therefore unconstitutional in the absence of compensation—but which serves an otherwise legitimate and important land or other reform purpose, could be saved from constitutional impugnment by recognising it as a constructive expropriation for which compensation is required.[158] Again it seems useful to leave the possibility open of developing this argument if and when required later, but the problem is that *FNB* seems to have closed the door on it.

The following hypothetical example explains the point: consider a state project involving land-use regulation that freezes the current use of large areas of privately owned land, with the result that the land can no longer be used or developed for private farming. Instead, the land-use regulation imposes restrictions that ensure a return to the traditional use of the land in an effort to attract environmental or eco-tourism. According to the scheme the state does not want to buy or expropriate private land affected by the scheme. Landowners are therefore effectively precluded from using the land for commercial farming, and if they are unable or unwilling to use the land in accordance with the traditional use guidelines, they are effectively left with a worthless asset. It is possible (although by no means self-evident or necessary) that a court could decide in a specific case that such a regulatory programme was arbitrary and unconstitutional because it deprives the affected individual landowner of all economic use and benefit of the property, without compensation. If the guideline proposed in *FNB* is followed strictly, the scheme could be struck down as an arbitrary deprivation before the merits of the regulation could even be investigated. However, in a less restrictive approach, such a scheme could arguably be saved by treating it as a constructive expropriation that requires just compensation but is otherwise in accordance with section 25, especially if the social and economic benefits of the scheme could be justified. However, according to the strict analytic logic of *FNB* such a case will never reach the stage where that possibility could be considered, because such a deprivation would possibly fail the arbitrariness test, and it seems unlikely that it would subsequently be justifiable in terms of section 36.

---

[157]See chapter 5.4 on constructive expropriation. See AJ van der Walt 'Moving towards recognition of constructive expropriation?' (2002) 65 *THRHR* 459–473; AJ van der Walt 'Overview of developments since the introduction of the constitutional property clause' (2004) 19 *SA Public Law* 46–89.

[158]I refer to the example and argue the case in AJ van der Walt 'Striving for the better interpretation—A critical reflection on the Constitutional Court's *Harksen* and *FNB* decisions on the property clause' (2004) 121 *SALJ* 854–878 at 874–875.

In a procedure where the requirements for and validity of an expropriation can only be considered when deprivation either satisfies the subsection 25(1) requirements or is justified in terms of section 36, the possibility of recognizing constructive expropriation and using it to promote or facilitate land reform goals seems to be closed down. Hopefully the Court will be willing to deviate from its self-imposed guideline in this case, because there are good reasons why we should not close the door on the notion of constructive expropriation too quickly. These reasons are canvassed in chapter 5.4.

4.7 SPECIAL APPLICATIONS

4.7.1 Planning, development, environment[159]

Regulation in the areas of land use planning, development and environmental conservation is a rich source of potential constitutional challenges under the property clause, but comparative analysis shows that this kind of regulation is generally regarded as a legitimate and largely unproblematic exercise of state power, provided that the rules of procedural fairness are adhered to and that the effects of the regulation are not excessive or disproportionate or unfair.[160] It is therefore useful to set out the application of section 25(1) analysis in this area briefly.

South African law has already seen its small share of cases relating to land use regulation.[161] It was for instance decided in *Nyangane v Stadsraad van Potchefstroom*[162] that restrictive building conditions imposed on erven in a new development to ensure that the houses built there would be of a certain minimum size and character were legitimate and lawful limitations of ownership. In the relevant case, a prospective purchaser complained that the restrictive conditions discriminated against poor and disadvantaged purchasers, who could not afford to build the size house that was required, and that the conditions therefore imposed an unconstitutional limitation on ownership. The court found that other erven in the same development were available free of the restrictions, and that the restrictions served a legitimate town planning

---

[159]This section is based on and similar to one part of AJ van der Walt 'Overview of developments since the introduction of the constitutional property clause' (2004) 19 *SA Public Law* 46–89.

[160]See AJ van der Walt *Constitutional property clauses: A comparative overview* (1999) 143 (Germany), 366–368 (Switzerland), 414–416 (US). In Switzerland land use planning and building regulation is a far more contentious issue—a search of the website of the Swiss Federal Supreme Court reveals that a large percentage of cases had their origin in land use planning and control. See AJ van der Walt 'The property clause in the new Federal Constitution of the Swiss Confederation 1999' (2004) 15 *Stell LR* 326–332 at 329.

[161]The cases are also discussed by T Roux 'Property' in MH Cheadle, DM Davis & NRL Haysom *South African constitutional law: The bill of rights* (2002) 429–472 at 457; AJ van der Walt 'Overview of developments since the introduction of the constitutional property clause' (2004) 19 *SA Public Law* 46–89 at 68–70.

[162]1998 (2) BCLR 148 (T) at 160E–G. T Roux 'Property' in MH Cheadle, DM Davis & NRL Haysom *South African constitutional law: The bill of rights* (2002) 429–472 at 457 describes this as a 'routine form of regulation'.

purpose in the areas where they were imposed, namely to promote the conservation of the character of that area by placing reciprocal obligations and rights relating to the size and character of the houses on all neighbours. This decision is generally in line with developments in other jurisdictions,[163] although it deserves mention that the kind of regulation involved, namely social and aesthetic building and development controls, serves a legitimate but not necessarily central or essential public purpose. It is usually accepted that planning and building regulations that serve the primary or core public purpose function of protecting public health and safety are legitimate and require no more than low level rationality scrutiny, while fringe public purposes such as social and aesthetic building regulation may require stricter control and a higher level of scrutiny. In the South African historical context this distinction should be obvious because of the role that racially inspired land-use planning and development regulation played during the apartheid era, even when it was masquerading as aesthetic land-use planning. It is, therefore, necessary to foreground the general proviso that development, land-use planning and building regulation that does not directly serve the core function of protecting public health and safety should be subjected to closer scrutiny.

A second interesting topic relating to building and development regulation is exactions, a practice whereby local authorities require developers to provide land free of charge in return for development or building permission. Generally speaking the state is not allowed to impose exactions freely; it is usually considered reasonable to expect the developer to donate land that is required to accommodate the impact of the development, but not to expect donations of wholly unrelated land. In *Nollan v California Coastal Commission*[164] and *Dolan v City of Tigard*[165] the US Supreme Court held that exactions would only be legitimate if there was an 'essential nexus' and 'rough proportionality' between the exaction sacrifice and the expected impact of the proposed development or the purpose for which the permission is required. In line with comparative case law it was decided in *South Peninsula Municipality v Malherbe*[166] that the imposition of town planning conditions that exacted the surrender of land (free of charge) to the local authority in exchange for carrying out its normal administrative duties was *ultra vires* the town planning ordinance. In the South African case, the local authority used its power to approve a rezoning and development application to convince the applicant to transfer land, free of charge, to the local authority for purposes not connected to the development, and therefore outside of its normal powers as authorized by the provincial ordinance. In a sense this decision also confirms that the regulatory police power must be exercised in the public interest

---

[163] See AJ van der Walt *Constitutional property clauses: A comparative overview* (1999) 143 (Germany), 366–368 (Switzerland), 414–416 (US).

[164] 483 US 825 (1987).

[165] 512 US 374 (1994). See further *Kulasingam & Another v Commissioner of Lands, Federal Territory & Others* [1982] 1 MLJ 204 (Malaysia).

[166] 1999 (2) SA 966 (C) at 984G–I.

even though there is no explicit public purpose requirement in section 25(1): the attempt to exact land from the applicant in this case was not for a public purpose because it fell outside the authorized purpose of the power.[167] This general assessment of planning regulation that is used to extract free donations of land should, however, again be qualified by a proviso regarding the historical background: given the history of land use and land rights in South Africa it is at least possible that such use of planning permissions may in some cases be legitimate, especially when the context and the purpose relate to land reform. In any event the authorizing legislation should then make the power to exact donations of land clear and outline its limits.

In *Oudekraal Estates (Pty) Ltd v City of Cape Town*[168] it was argued that a regulatory deprivation of development rights was unconstitutional. The applicant wanted to develop its land in terms of development rights registered and endorsed on the title deeds of the property more than 30 years previously but, as appeared from the decision, originally granted *ultra vires* the powers of the then administrator in terms of the provincial ordinance. The local authority opposed the development. Registered rights in land are usually regarded as real rights, and the applicant argued that refusal of an application to exercise registered development rights would amount to an indirect expropriation of those rights. However, the Cape High Court decided that it had the jurisdiction to decide that the rights were granted *ultra vires* and therefore registered by mistake,[169] and that it would allow a belated collateral challenge against the validity of those rights resulting in a refusal of the current development application.[170]

In *African Billboard Advertising (Pty) Ltd v North and South Central Local Councils, Durban*[171] the Natal High Court decided that building by-laws that authorized the removal of illegally erected billboards and signs had to be interpreted in line with constitutional provisions such as sections 25(1), 34 and 39(1), promoting the rule of law. The by-law in question authorized the city engineer to direct any person who erected signs illegally to remove them within 14 days and, in the event of non-compliance, to remove the sign. The court decided that the provision which gave the city engineers the power to remove the sign due to non-compliance had to be read in such a way that a court order was required before the city engineers could move in and remove the signs themselves. Both the common law practice of the courts and the relevant constitutional provisions—including section 25(1)—were against self-help and in favour of the rule of law, and a power that was granted by the by-laws had to be exercised in accordance with the rule of law. The relevant provision could easily

---

[167] See 4.3 above.

[168] 2002 (6) SA 573 (C).

[169] In a negative registration system there is no guarantee that the register is an accurate reflection of the real state of affairs, and rights cannot be enforced merely on the strength of their being registered: *Oudekraal Estates (Pty) Ltd v City of Cape Town* 2002 (6) SA 573 (C) at 589D–G.

[170] *Oudekraal Estates (Pty) Ltd v City of Cape Town* 2002 (6) SA 573 (C) at 593–596. This decision was confirmed in *Oudekraal Estates v City of Cape Town and Others* 2004 (6) SA 222 (SCA), although on slightly differing arguments.

[171] 2004 (3) SA 223 (N) at 228A–229D.

have stated that no court order was required, and as it stands it is capable of the construction that favours the rule of law.

Generally, the South African cases on regulatory deprivation of property in the area of land-use control appear to be in line with comparative case law and the cases decided so far are unremarkable. The cases confirm that procedurally fair and proportionate deprivation of property in this context is legitimate in terms of the property guarantee, and also that the power to control land use may not be used by the state to exact unjustified and unconnected sacrifices of property by landowners who apply for normal land use permissions. However, it is always necessary to consider and apply these 'normal' principles of planning and development regulation with due consideration for the historical context and the constitutional aims relating to the origin and the transformation of land holdings.

4.7.2 Search and seizure, criminal and civil forfeiture[172]

Another area in which regulatory deprivations of property has already enjoyed a certain amount of attention in South African courts is deprivations that result from statutory powers of search and seizure and relating to criminal and civil forfeiture of property.[173] It is argued in chapter 5.3 that excessively unfair or burdensome civil forfeiture could, in specific individual cases, be treated as constructive expropriation that requires compensation. However, as a rule the 'normal' exercises of state of search and seizure and of criminal and civil forfeiture should be treated simply as deprivation of property that has to conform with the requirements in section 25(1). Private property is often confiscated temporarily to secure evidence in a criminal trial or to estab-

---

[172]See the discussion of forfeiture in chapter 5.3. This section is based on and similar to parts of AJ van der Walt 'Overview of developments since the introduction of the constitutional property clause' (2004) 19 *SA Public Law* 46–89, and compare further AJ van der Walt 'Civil forfeiture of instrumentalities and proceeds of crime and the constitutional property clause' (2000) 16 *SAJHR* 1–45.

[173]The cases are discussed by T Roux 'Property' in MH Cheadle, DM Davis & NRL Haysom *South African constitutional law: The bill of rights* (2002) 429–472 at 456–457. See further AJ van der Walt 'Civil forfeiture of instrumentalities and proceeds of crime and the constitutional property clause' (2000) 16 *SAJHR* 1–45. Somewhat surprisingly, the property clause is often not invoked in search and seizure and forfeiture challenges; see eg *National Director of Public Prosecutions v Phillips* 2002 (4) SA 60 (W); *National Director of Public Prosecutions v Rebuzzi* 2002 (2) SA 1 (SCA); *National Director of Public Prosecutions v Patterson* [2001] 4 All SA 525 (C). The one case that could have produced an interesting decision on the constitutional validity of forfeiture orders in view of the property clause is *Mohamed NO v National Director of Public Prosecutions* 2002 (4) SA 366 (W); *National Director of Public Prosecutions v Mohamed* 2002 (4) SA 843 (CC); *National Director of Public Prosecutions v Mohamed* 2003 (4) SA 1 (CC), but this case was decided on the access to court provision (section 34) and not property. In *National Director of Public Prosecutions v Prophet* 2003 (6) SA 154 (C) the Cape High Court decided that the public purpose for which forfeiture laws were promulgated, namely to combat organized crime more effectively, was sufficient to justify the infringements of property that resulted from it although it was still important to assess the fairness of each infringement individually.

lish jurisdiction or security and contraband is sometimes not only seized but forfeited (and destroyed) because its possession is illegal or dangerous. These limitations clearly amount to exercises of the state's police power in its core function of protecting public health and safety and their legitimacy must be analysed with that purpose in mind. As a rule, therefore, criminal forfeiture laws have a regulatory purpose and effect and they should be evaluated on that basis, namely as deprivation of property.[174]

In addition to previously existing laws, a number of new laws adopted since 1994 have introduced new powers or increased existing powers of search and seizure and powers of criminal and civil forfeiture. Most of these laws were promulgated as part of the government's struggle against white-collar crime, corruption, money laundering and organized crime.[175] Not unexpectedly, the exercise of these powers has already resulted in a number of interesting decisions.[176]

In a constitutional challenge against search and seizure powers granted by the Income Tax Act 58 of 1962 and the Value-Added Tax Act 89 of 1991, it was held that the applicants' property rights were not infringed by the provisions in question or by the search and seizure warrants (authorized by a judge upon application by the respondent).[177] Interestingly, the Eastern Cape High Court in this case explained its finding by pointing out (quite correctly) that the authorizing statutes are laws of general application and (more puzzlingly) that property rights were not affected by the warrant, as any person could establish his or her property entitlement in and claim delivery of the seized property.[178] A more satisfactory view is that the property rights in question were in fact affected by the warrant, but that the deprivation involved would be lawful in terms of section 25(1) if it was authorized by a law of general application (which it was) and as long as the law did not allow arbitrary deprivation, which could be decided with reference to the fact that the deprivation was subject to obtaining a warrant upon application to court, and subject to the affected person's right to reclaim his or her property as provided in the statute.

---

[174]Compare T Roux 'Property' in MH Cheadle, DM Davis & NRL Haysom *South African constitutional law: The bill of rights* (2002) 429–472 at 457 to the same effect.

[175]See AJ van der Walt 'Civil forfeiture of instrumentalities and proceeds of crime and the constitutional property clause' (2000) 16 *SAJHR* 1–45 and authorities referred to there for a general overview, as well as chapter 5.3 for a more extensive discussion of forfeiture laws.

[176]In an early case dealing with search and seizure provisions in the Investigation of Serious Economic Offences Act 117 of 1991, *Park-Ross v The Director, Office for Serious Economic Offences* 1995 (1) SA 148 (C), no challenge was raised on the property clause in section 28 of the 1993 Constitution, and the decision is interesting mostly because of its discussion of limitation issues.

[177]*Deutschmann NO and Others v Commissioner for the South African Revenue Service; Shelton v Commissioner for the South African Revenue Service* 2000 (2) SA 106 (E).

[178]*Deutschmann NO and Others v Commissioner for the South African Revenue Service; Shelton v Commissioner for the South African Revenue Service* 2000 (2) SA 106 (E) at 124C. This statement is reminiscent of the arguments in *Harksen v Lane NO* 1998 (1) SA 300 (CC) par [37] at 318B–E and *Mkontwana v Nelson Mandela Metropolitan Municipality; Bissett and Others v Buffalo City Municipality; Transfer Rights Action Campaign and Others v Member of the Executive Council for Local Government and Housing, Gauteng and Others* 2005 (1) SA 530 (CC).

In *Director of Public Prosecutions: Cape of Good Hope v Bathgate*[179] the Cape High Court decided that restraint orders and confiscation of property in terms of the Proceeds of Crime Act 76 of 1996 and the Prevention of Organized Crime Act 121 of 1998 'may ... constitute arbitrary deprivation of property in terms of section 25(1) of the Constitution',[180] but that such deprivation would be a justified limitation in terms of section 36 in view of the state's efforts to combat crime.[181] Curiously, the court did not investigate the question whether the restraint and confiscation orders in question indeed constituted arbitrary deprivation but assumed that they did and went on to deal with the limitation analysis. In a more recent decision the Cape High Court adopted a similar attitude, holding that, although it was a controversial measure, forfeiture was justified under the statutory provisions, without determining whether the deprivation was indeed arbitrary or otherwise in conflict with section 25.[182] In both cases it would have been useful if the court had analysed the provisions and actions taken in terms of them with a view to decide whether they actually constituted arbitrary deprivation. In this regard it is worth considering that the subsequent *FNB* decision also dealt with the effect of regulatory laws on the property of innocent or unconnected third parties. Arguably this would also be the most interesting scenario for review of forfeiture cases under section 25(1), but to date the matter has not enjoyed the focused attention of the courts in that specific form yet.

The Supreme Court of Appeal decided that chapter 6 of the Prevention of Organised Crime Act 121 of 1998 places a heavy burden on property owners and that the provisions that authorize forfeiture of instrumentalities of criminal activity therefore had to be interpreted restrictively, especially when the property belongs to a person not involved with the criminal activity.[183] The Court held that it was reasonable to expect that property owners should be vigilant in exercising control over the use of their property, but the Act nevertheless restricted the common law of property to a significant extent and therefore could not be applied generously, since a too wide application of the instrumentalities provision or an interpretation that expects the impossible of property owners could well result in arbitrary—and therefore unconstitutional—deprivation of property.[184] By adopting this line of argument the Court brought judicial inquiry into the legitimacy and constitutional validity of statutory forfeiture powers, at least as far as instrumentalities of crime are concerned, in

---

[179] 2000 (2) SA 535 (C).

[180] *Director of Public Prosecutions: Cape of Good Hope v Bathgate* 2000 (2) SA 535 (C) par [82] at 559A–D.

[181] *Director of Public Prosecutions: Cape of Good Hope v Bathgate* 2000 (2) SA 535 (C) paras [84]–[113] at 559G–566C.

[182] *National Director of Public Prosecutions v Prophet* 2003 (8) BCLR 906 (C) paras [29]–[32] at 917A–G.

[183] *National Director of Public Prosecutions v (1) RO Cook Properties (Pty) Ltd; (2) 37 Gillespie Street Durban (Pty) Ltd and Another; (3) Seevnarayan* 2004 (8) BCLR 844 (SCA).

[184] *National Director of Public Prosecutions v (1) RO Cook Properties (Pty) Ltd; (2) 37 Gillespie Street Durban (Pty) Ltd and Another; (3) Seevnarayan* 2004 (8) BCLR 844 (SCA) paras [24]–[26] at 855A–G; paras [23], [26]–[29] at 854F–G, 855E–856F. This test was referred to and applied in the Cape High Court decision in *National Director of Public Prosecutions v Engels* 2005 (3) SA 109 (C).

line with the framework that the Constitutional Court established in the *FNB* decision for arbitrariness analysis in general. The Supreme Court of Appeal confirmed this
line of thinking in *National Director of Public Prosecutions v Rautenbach and Others*[185] by
arguing that a court, when exercising its discretion as to granting a restraint order
under the Prevention of Organised Crime Act 121 of 1998, must limit the scope of
the restraint if there is clear evidence that the value of the property affected by the
order materially exceeds the amount of the anticipated confiscation order, so as to
avoid a lack of appropriate nexus between means and ends.

4.7.3 The right to exclude and 'public accommodations'

One of the areas in which regulatory deprivations are most visible in the post-1994
South African property law is the new tendency to restrict property owners'—and
especially landowners'—right to exclude others from their property. Traditionally the
right to exclude is regarded as one of the strongest entitlements that a landowner
has,[186] but because of the apartheid history this entitlement and the concomitant right
to evict are now treated with some care. Based on the anti-eviction provisions in
section 26(3) of the Constitution and in several land reform laws the right to obtain
an eviction order is subjected to substantive restrictions. As far as evictions from land
are concerned this topic and its role in the constitutional protection of property are
discussed in 4.5.5 above and in chapters 6.3 and 7.3. The focus in this section is on
two related but slightly different aspects of the right to exclude and the effect of regulatory deprivation on it.

The first aspect involves land reforms that make inroads upon the exclusivity of
landownership without involving restrictions on eviction. In some foreign jurisdictions it is said that state action that results in a permanent physical invasion on
private land would amount to a regulatory taking that requires compensation,
regardless of the actual effect of the invasion on the landowner or the significance of
the public purpose served by the action.[187] However, this strict rule does not seem
to apply in South African law, where regulatory deprivation that involves a
permanent physical invasion of private land seems to be possible without
compensation. The most striking case is *Nhlabati and Others v Fick*.[188] In two earlier

---

[185] 2005 (4) SA 603 (SCA) par [56] at 621B–H, referring to *FNB*. See 4.5 above.

[186] Not only in South African law; see eg K Gray 'Property in thin air' (1991) 50 *Cambridge LJ* 252–307.

[187] See particularly *Loretto v Teleprompter Manhattan CATV Corp* 458 US 419 (1982); compare AJ van der Walt *Constitutional property clauses: A comparative overview* (1999) 429.

[188] 2003 (7) BCLR 806 (LCC); see W du Plessis, N Olivier & J Pienaar 'Expropriation, restitution and land redistribution: An answer to land problems in South Africa?' (2003) 18 *SA Public Law* 491–514 at 501–504; compare chapter 6.3.8.

decisions[189] it was held that the legislature did not intend with section 6(2) of the Extension of Security of Tenure Act 62 of 1997 to grant farm labourers the right to bury occupiers or their family members on the farm without consent and against the will of the landowner. Subsequently the Act was amended and the new section 6(2)(dA) now includes the right to bury a deceased occupier or family member (who, at the time of that person's death, was residing on the land) in accordance with their religion or cultural belief, if an established practice in respect of the land exists. The occupier enjoys this burial right in balance with the rights of the owner or person in charge of the land and subject to reasonable conditions that may be imposed by the owner or person in charge. In the *Nhlabati* case the landowner argued that section 6(2)(dA) was unconstitutional because it was in conflict with section 25 of the Constitution.[190]

The Land Claims Court considered this argument against the background of the test for arbitrary deprivation as developed in *FNB* and decided that section 6(2)(dA) does not authorise arbitrary appropriation (deprivation) of a grave, because the right to appropriate a grave must be balanced with the right of the owner, which means that the right of the owner could in certain circumstances conceivably outweigh the right to a grave;[191] an occupier would only have the right to establish a grave if there is an established practice of giving permission for similar burials in the past, which presupposes some kind of consensus between the landowner and the occupiers about burials; the establishment of the grave would in most cases constitute a relatively minor intrusion into the landowner's property rights; and the right to bury an occupier or a family member according to section 6(2)(dA) was enacted to fulfil the state's constitutional mandate to provide occupiers legally secure tenure which, considering the importance of the religious or cultural beliefs of many occupiers regarding burial of family members close to their residence, would in most cases mean that the deprivation of some incidents of ownership would be justified by the constitutional

---

[189] *Serole and Another v Pienaar* 2000 (1) SA 328 (LCC); *Nkosi and Another v Bührmann* 2002 (1) SA 372 (SCA). The amendment and its history are discussed by the court in *Nhlabati and Others v Fick* 2003 (7) BCLR 806 (LCC) paras [16]–[19] at 811G–812I. On the SCA judgment see AJ van der Walt 'Property rights v religious rights: *Bührmann v Nkosi*' (2002) 13 *Stell LR* 394–414; W du Plessis, N Olivier & J Pienaar 'Progress in land reform, illegal occupation of land and judicial interpretation' (2002) 17 *SA Public Law* 178–209 at 186–187.

[190] A similar argument was raised and considered but not clearly decided in one of the earlier decisions on burial rights, where it was said that it would amount to an appropriation if an occupier were allowed to take a grave site without permission and against the will of the landowner: *Nkosi and Another v Bührmann* 2002 (1) SA 372 (SCA) par [38] at 384I–J. In *Serole and Another v Pienaar* 2000 (1) SA 328 (LCC) par [16] at 335D it was said that the granting of such a right would amount to granting of a servitude. See the references in *Nhlabati and Others v Fick* 2003 (7) BCLR 806 (LCC) par [27] at 815B–C, par [32] at 817E–F. A second argument, that section 6(2)(dA) was unconstitutional because it intruded upon a functional area of exclusive provincial legislative competence, is not discussed here. This argument was also dismissed: *Nhlabati and Others v Fick* 2003 (7) BCLR 806 (LCC) paras [21]–[26] at 813D–815B.

[191] *Nhlabati and Others v Fick* 2003 (7) BCLR 806 (LCC) par [31] at 816I.

mandate.[192] In the final result the constitutional challenge against section 6(2)(dA) was dismissed. The effect is that a regulatory deprivation that serves a particular constitutionally mandated land reform purpose would not automatically be unconstitutional even when it authorizes a permanent physical invasion of private land under prescribed circumstances. In other words, a regulatory limitation of the exclusivity of landownership can be constitutionally valid even when it involves a permanent physical invasion of private land, provided the reform-related circumstances are present to justify the limitation and as long as the requirements are satisfied. Another interpretation of the *Nhlabati* decision and the right to appropriate a burial site, namely that it allows an uncompensated expropriation of a grave, is discussed in chapter 5.8.[193]

The second aspect of the right to exclude that can be limited by public purpose regulation is known in the US as 'public accommodations' law. The notion of public accommodations refers to the fact that the right to exclude might be restricted in a particular case because the owner invited the public onto the property or because the property is generally used for a purpose that is open to the public. The most well-known US case in this regard is *PruneYard Shopping Center v Robins*,[194] where the question was whether the states could make legislation (such as a state constitution) which requires a private shopping centre owner to allow access to people who want to exercise their right of free speech and petition in the shopping centre. The majority confirmed that the right to exclude others from property is regarded as one of the essential sticks in the bundle making up property, and concluded that this right would be destroyed by allowing freedom of expression rights to the public on the premises of a privately owned shopping centre. However, in previous decisions the Supreme Court established that not every destruction of or injury to property by governmental action amounts to a taking in the constitutional sense; the question is whether the restriction on private property 'forces some people to bear alone public burdens which, in all fairness and justice, should be borne by the public as a whole.'[195] This entails consideration of factors such as the nature and economic impact of the regulation and its interference with reasonable investment-backed expectations. In the circumstances of the case the requirement to allow the petitioners to exercise their state-protected rights of free speech and petition in the shopping centre did not

---

[192] Par [31] at 817A–D.

[193] The court decided that even if section 6(2)(dA) authorised expropriation of grave sites without compensation, in conflict with section 25 of the Constitution, this result would be reasonable and justifiable under section 36 of the Constitution. The court made no finding on this point, merely accepting the possibility for argument's sake: par [32] at 817F.

[194] 447 US 74 (1980). See AJ van der Walt *Constitutional property clauses: A comparative overview* (1999) 432–43. The most extensive discussion of public accommodations law in the US is JW Singer 'No right to exclude: Public accommodations and private property' (1996) 90 *Northwestern Univ LR* 1283–1497; see also JW Singer 'Property and equality: Public accommodations and the constitution in South Africa and the United States' (1997) 12 *SA Public Law* 53–86.

[195] *PruneYard Shopping Center v Robins* 447 US 74 (1980) at 83, quoting from *Armstrong v United States* 364 US 40 at 49, 80 (1960).

amount to an unconstitutional infringement of the owner's property rights under the takings clause, because the property owner was free to adopt and enforce regulations with regard to the time, place and manner in which these activities would be permissible, so as to minimize interference with the regular activities of a shopping centre. In this perspective, the Court decided, the actions of the petitioners could not be described as a physical invasion of the property. In fact, the point is that the property owner failed in this case[196] to demonstrate that the right to exclude others from the premises was so essential to the use or economic value of the property that the state-allowed limitation amounted to a taking of the property. Accordingly, the claim based on the takings clause failed.

A recent South African case on public accommodations followed the direction of the US Supreme Court in *PruneYard* by refusing to recognize that the private owner of premises that is generally open to the public has an absolute right to exclude certain persons, even when those persons have been making a nuisance of themselves on the premises.[197]

The Cape High Court refused to grant the final interdict, arguing that such a radical and final prohibition against the affected persons ever again entering the area would be unreasonable as long as alternative, less intrusive remedies were available. In the event, the court granted an order that prohibited the affected persons from behaving in certain specified ways or doing certain specified things on the premises.[198] The owners of the premises did not have an absolute right of exclusion, particularly in what has practically become a suburb of Cape Town,[199] and therefore a blanket prohibition against entry and free movement should not be granted unless there is no other way of achieving a lawful and justifiable goal, which in fact was to prevent certain behaviour on the premises.[200] The court recognized that the owners of the

---

[196] At 84 Rehnquist J contrasted this aspect of the case with the position in *Kaiser Aetna v United States* 444 US 164 (1979). See JW Singer 'Property and equality: Public accommodations and the constitution in South Africa and the United States' (1997) 12 *SA Public Law* 53–86 at 66ff.

[197] *Victoria & Alfred Waterfront (Pty) Ltd and Another v Police Commissioner, Western Cape, and Others (Legal Resources Centre as* Amicus Curiae) 2004 (4) SA 444 (C) The owners of the Victoria & Alfred Waterfront in Cape Town applied for a permanent interdict to prohibit certain persons from ever again entering the premises, based on proven as well as uncontested evidence and unsubstantiated hearsay to the effect that these persons had been misbehaving on the premises over a period of time; threatening, harassing and attacking staff and customers of various establishments on the popular tourist site. In applying for the interdict the owners of the development relied on their allegedly absolute right of exclusion, exclusivity supposedly being one of the core entitlements of private ownership.

[198] *Victoria & Alfred Waterfront (Pty) Ltd and Another v Police Commissioner, Western Cape, and Others (Legal Resources Centre as* Amicus Curiae) 2004 (4) SA 444 (C) at 452Gff.

[199] At 449A, 451E.

[200] At 451I. Section 11 of the Constitution protects the right to life, which arguably includes the right to make a living, if needs be from begging—to prohibit the affected persons from begging raises large questions that the court did not want to decide on the evidence before it. Section 21 protects freedom of movement, which could also be compromised by a blanket prohibition.

Waterfront have a right to protect their custom and business interests and an interest in the physical integrity and security of their customers and employees, but in the court's view that did not justify a blanket prohibition of the affected persons.[201] In the result, the tension between the property owners' property rights under section 25 and the affected persons' right to free movement had to be resolved in a way that would optimize or vindicate both rights to the greatest extent possible, and in the court's view that could best be done by a prohibition of certain unlawful behaviour rather than a blanket entry prohibition.[202]

The public accommodations restrictions upon a landowner's right to exclude can be understood as deprivation of property—the relevant principles of common law or statute that place these limitations on the right to exclude limit the rights of a land-owner. The effect of the public accommodations principle is that these limitations are legitimate because they are imposed on landownership for a public purpose that is directly related to the purpose for and way in which the land is used by the land-owner. By inviting the public onto the land for commercial purposes the right to exclude is qualified, and as long as the owner retains an effective way of exercising reasonable control over unlawful behaviour on the premises this limitation of her right should not be arbitrary, even if it prevents the owner from freely excluding persons who cause a disturbance or a measure of discomfort by their presence and behaviour on the premises.

---

[201] At 452E–G.
[202] At 452B–G.

Expropriation

25. Property

(1) ...

(2) Property may be expropriated only in terms of law of general application—

    (a) for a public purpose or in the public interest; and

    (b) subject to compensation, the amount of which and the time and manner of payment of which have either been agreed to by those affected or decided or approved by a court.

(3) The amount of the compensation and the time and manner of payment must be just and equitable, reflecting an equitable balance between the public interest and the interests of those affected, having regard to all relevant circumstances, including—

    (a) the current use of the property;

    (b) the history of the acquisition and use of the property;

    (c) the market value of the property;

    (d) the extent of direct state investment and subsidy in the acquisition and beneficial capital improvement of the property; and

    (e) the purpose of the expropriation.

(4) For the purpose of this section—

    (a) the public interest includes the nation's commitment to land reform, and to reforms to bring about equitable access to all South Africa's natural resources; and

    (b) property is not limited to land.

5.1 INTRODUCTION

The purpose of this chapter is twofold. The definition and characteristics of expropriation are discussed in the first part of the chapter. Expropriation is usually defined in contrast with deprivation, which is seen as a less intrusive limitation of property. It is often said that expropriation consists of compulsory state acquisition of private property, while deprivation occurs when the state regulates the use and enjoyment of private property in the public interest.[1] However, this distinction is neither entirely clear nor consistent; there is a grey area where state actions limit private property in a way that cannot easily be described as either deprivation or expropriation. For example, forfeiture involves a legal process by which private property is lost to the state, usually but not necessarily as a result of it being involved in criminal activity, without compensation. This is clearly not expropriation, and yet it does not properly fit the mould of deprivation either, because it targets individual property and results in total loss rather than mere regulation of use. It is therefore necessary to explain the relation of forfeiture to the property clause. Constructive expropriation, sometimes also known as inverse condemnation or regulatory taking, raises some of the same concerns and questions as forfeiture because it also involves limitation of property that was not intended but might in certain instances be treated as expropriation (and compensated) because of its expropriation-like effects. It is unclear whether construc-

---

[1] See *Harksen v Lane NO* 1998 (1) SA 300 (CC) paras [32]–[33] at 315E–316C. See further A Gildenhuys *Onteieningsreg* (2nd ed 2001) 8.

tive expropriation can be recognized in South African law; the arguments for and against doing so are reviewed below with reference to comparative examples.

The second part of the chapter deals with the requirements for valid expropriation as set out in subsections 25(2) and 25(3):[2] expropriation must be undertaken in terms of law of general application; must serve a public purpose or the public interest; and may only take place against compensation. These requirements are analyse and discussed with reference to case law and, where necessary and possible, comparative law.

5.2 DEFINITION OF EXPROPRIATION

5.2.1 Background

Section 25 refers to two categories of limitation on property: deprivation and expropriation. Since the Constitutional Court's *FNB* decision[3] expropriation is regarded as a special subset of deprivation: some deprivations amount to expropriation, others do not, but expropriation is always a deprivation. Non-expropriatory deprivation is discussed in chapter 4 and expropriation in this chapter. However, despite the apparent simplicity and clarity of this distinction, it remains difficult to define expropriation accurately and to distinguish it from deprivation consistently.

Foreign constitutions employ different notions of expropriation, and the terminology is not consistent.[4] Some constitutions refer to 'expropriation';[5] some to

---

[2] As is pointed out in chapter 4.6, the implication of the *FNB* decision (*First National Bank of SA Ltd t/a Wesbank v Commissioner, South African Revenue Service; First National Bank of SA Ltd t/a Wesbank v Minister of Finance* 2002 (4) SA 768 (CC); see footnote 3 below) is that expropriation is regarded as a subset of deprivation and therefore also has to comply with the more general requirements for deprivation in subsection 25(1).

[3] *First National Bank of SA Ltd t/a Wesbank v Commissioner, South African Revenue Service; First National Bank of SA Ltd t/a Wesbank v Minister of Finance* 2002 (4) SA 768 (CC) par [57] at 796F–H. See further T Roux 'Section 25' in S Woolman et al (eds) *Constitutional law of South Africa* (2nd ed 2003 original service Dec 2003) 46–29; AJ van der Walt 'Striving for the better interpretation—A critical reflection on the Constitutional Court's *Harksen* and *FNB* decisions on the property clause' (2004) 121 *SALJ* 854–878 at 864ff.

[4] Apart from the concepts discussed below the following distinctions are important even though they are not referred to in section 25. (*a*) *Statutory* vs *administrative* expropriation: the former is not merely authorized but immediately effected by law; in the latter case expropriation is authorized by statute, but the expropriation is effected by an administrative process usually prescribed by the authorizing statute. Some constitutions allow for both, but statutory expropriations are unusual. As long as the South African Expropriation Act 63 of 1975 is valid it is improbable that statutory expropriation would be possible. A Gildenhuys *Onteieningsreg* (2nd ed 2001) 13–15 does not mention statutory expropriation but he does distinguish *judicial* expropriation, where a court effects the expropriation and vests the property in someone else in terms of legislation; Gildenhuys cites the Land Reform (Labour Tenants) Act 3 of 1996 as an example of judicial expropriation, with reference to *Khumalo and Others v Potgieter and Others* [2000] 2 All SA 456 (LCC). (*b*) *Permanent* vs *temporary* expropriation: temporary expropriation is unusual but not unknown, especially in the form of temporary requisitioning, for example in wartime. Section 37 of the South African Constitution of 1996 makes explicit provision for the limitation of rights during a state of emergency. The

(continued on next page ...)

'compulsory acquisition'[6] or 'taking' of property;[7] others simply refer to 'deprivation' as a generic term without explicitly distinguishing it from expropriation.[8] At least two property clauses use the term 'deprivation' to refer to what is otherwise known as expropriation, thereby complicating comparative analysis considerably.[9] A few constitutions use 'requisitioning'[10] and 'compulsory dispossession', the latter often in conjunction with 'compulsory acquisition'.[11] It is often assumed that these terms and

---

(... from previous page)

section does not make any specific provision with reference to property, but it is clear from section 37(4) that special limitations (styled 'derogations') from property rights are possible in the circumstances foreseen in this section. In view of these considerations the decision in *Harksen v Lane NO* 1998 (1) SA 300 (CC) to the effect that expropriation involves permanent acquisition of property by the state is problematic. (*c*) Expropriation of *title or a right* and of *possession:* expropriation of possession or 'compulsory dispossession' is also more at home in the area of emergency situations, and not in the normal course of affairs. In terms of the Expropriation Act 63 of 1975 either title or another right can be expropriated separately, and nothing in section 25 affects that position.

[5]See section 25(2) of the South African Constitution of 1996; article 5 of the Austrian Basic Law of 1867; article 14.3 of the German Basic Law of 1949; article 16(2) of the Constitution of the Republic of Namibia Act 1990; article 26(1) of the Constitution of the Swiss Confederation 1999.

[6]See section 51(xxxi) of the Australian Commonwealth Constitution 1900; article 31(2) of the Indian Constitution as amended by the Fourth Amendment in 1955; article 13(2) of the Federal Constitution of Malaysia 1957; section 16(1) of the Constitution of the Republic of Zimbabwe 1980.

[7]See the Fifth Amendment to the US Constitution; article 29 of the Constitution of Japan 1946; section 5 of the Government of Ireland Act 1920.

[8]See article 1(*a*) of the Constitution of Trinidad and Tobago 1962; section 1(*a*) of the unentrenched Canadian Bill of Rights 1960; article 1 of the First Protocol to the European Convention on Human Rights 1950. Of this group, one constitution uses the phrase 'unjust attack on property' without distinguishing between deprivation and expropriation: article 40.3.2 of the Constitution of Ireland 1937.

[9]The property clause in article 1 of the First Protocol to the European Convention on Human Rights 1950 refers to 'deprivation' in the sense of expropriation, and to 'control over the use of property' in the sense of regulatory deprivation. The property clause in article 17 of the French Declaration of the Rights of Man and the Citizen 1789 simply refers to deprivation of property against compensation, in other words in the sense of expropriation, without distinguishing it from regulatory deprivation. AJ van der Walt 'Compensation for excessive or unfair regulation: A comparative overview of constitutional practice relating to regulatory takings' (1999) 14 *SA Public Law* 273–331 explains the terminology and includes the text of various property clauses in an appendix. For further texts of constitutional property clauses see AJ van der Walt *Constitutional property clauses: A comparative analysis* (1999) passim.

[10]See article 31(2) of the Indian Constitution after the Fourth Amendment in 1955.

[11]See section 18(1)–(2) of the Constitution of the Republic of The Gambia 1970; section 8(1) of the Constitution of the Republic of Guyana 1966 and section 142(1) of the Constitution of the Co-operative Republic of Guyana Act 1980; section 18(1) of the Constitution of Jamaica 1962; section 8(1) of the Constitution of Mauritius 1968; section 8(1) of the Constitution of the Republic of Botswana 1966; section 8(1) of the Constitution of St Christopher & Nevis 1983; section 13(1) of the Constitution of the Republic of Uganda 1967 and section 26(2)(*b*) of the Constitution of the Republic of Uganda 1995. Because expropriation results in original acquisition of the property the term 'compulsory acquisition' is preferable to 'compulsory purchase'; see footnote 33 and accompanying text below and compare A Gildenhuys *Onteieningsreg* (2nd ed 2001) 8.

concepts share an element that defines expropriation and distinguishes it from non-acquisitive deprivation of property in that the state acquires property through expropriation but not through deprivation. However, as is explained in more detail below, there are situations where the loss of the affected property by its former holder rather than acquisition by the state is the functional element of expropriation, and it is often difficult to tell whether the state acquired the affected property or any property at all. Accordingly, state acquisition cannot be regarded as the defining characteristic of expropriation.

Another element that is often relied on to distinguish expropriation from deprivation is generality: non-expropriatory, regulatory deprivation is said to affect all property of a certain category,[12] whereas expropriation affects only a specific property or owner.[13] This rule of thumb does not really make it easier to define expropriation either, because some (admittedly exceptional) non-expropriatory deprivations may have a limited, specific focus on one individual or a small class of properties,[14] whereas some expropriatory state actions may affect a large class of property or owners in exactly the same way.[15] It is true, though, that deprivation that affects just one or a small group of owners and places an unfair burden on them for the sake of society at large will mostly be either invalid or treated as constructive expropriation.[16]

Because it is difficult to define expropriation accurately and distinguish it from deprivation consistently, theorists in many jurisdictions recognize a grey area between acquisitive expropriation and non-acquisitive regulatory deprivation, where every decision about the effects of a specific limitation is contested. As was pointed out in the introduction above this grey area includes forfeiture and similar loss of property without compensation—a consideration that should indicate that the action is regulatory and therefore deprivation, but in view of the extreme results of forfeiture this conclusion is sometimes difficult to justify.[17] The grey area between deprivation and

---

[12]See section 18(1)–(2) of the Constitution of the Republic of The Gambia 1970; section 8(1) of the Constitution of the Republic of Guyana 1966 and section 142(1) of the Constitution of the Co-operative Republic of Guyana Act 1980; section 18(1) of the Constitution of Jamaica 1962; section 8(1) of the Constitution of Mauritius 1968; section 8(1) of the Constitution of the Republic of Botswana 1966; section 8(1) of the Constitution of St Christopher & Nevis 1983; section 13(1) of the Constitution of the Republic of Uganda 1967 and section 26(2)(b) of the Constitution of the Republic of Uganda 1995.

[13]Eg all land along the route of a new road, or the agricultural land affected by a specific redistribution programme. There are exceptions to this rule, for instance when all agricultural land or all commercial banks are expropriated. This will usually take the form of nationalisation rather than expropriation, with the result that compensation is probably excluded.

[14]Eg Miller v Schoene 276 US 272 (1928) (one landowner's property (trees) were destroyed to save others' from a virulent disease); BVerfGE 42, 263 [1976] (Contergan) (Germany, transfer of specific class of civil claims into public fund for more equitable distribution).

[15]Eg James v United Kingdom [1986] 8 EHRR 123 (expropriation of a whole class of land rights for redistribution).

[16]See the discussion in 5.4 below.

[17]This aspect is discussed in 5.4 below and in chapter 4.7.2.

expropriation also includes state actions that simply do not make it clear whether the intention is to regulate the use and enjoyment of property or to expropriate. In some instances the intention is clear enough but unrealistic, for example when the stated intention is to regulate the use and enjoyment of property but the effect is to expropriate without compensation; in some jurisdictions the real effect rather than the intention of the state will be considered in deciding whether compensation is due. If it is possible for the courts to treat property infringements in this grey area as expropriation even when they were not intended as such, the relevant system is said to recognize constructive expropriation; a notion that is discussed in 5.4 below. For the moment being the question remains whether expropriation can be defined or described with reference to its characteristics or effects.

5.2.2 Expropriation in section 25

In the first major decision of the Constitutional Court to deal with the property clause, *Harksen v Lane NO*,[18] Goldstone J stated that expropriation is characterized by the 'acquisition of rights in property by a public authority for a public purpose', while deprivation falls short of such acquisition.[19] In reaching this decision, the Constitutional Court relied on three assumptions.[20] Firstly, the Court assumed that the distinction between expropriation and deprivation is categorical[21] in the sense that

---

[18] 1998 (1) SA 300 (CC), dealing with the property clause in section 28 of the 1993 Constitution. For discussions of the property aspects of the decision see AJ van der Walt & H Botha 'Coming to grips with the new constitutional order: Critical comments on *Harksen v Lane NO*' (1998) 13 *SA Public Law* 17–41 at 19–26; AJ van der Walt *Constitutional property clauses: A comparative analysis* (1999) 333, 336–339; AJ van der Walt 'Striving for the better interpretation—A critical reflection on the Constitutional Court's *Harksen* and *FNB* decisions on the property clause' (2004) 121 *SALJ* 854–878 at 861ff. The case involved section 21 of the Insolvency Act 24 of 1936, which determines that upon the sequestration of the estate of an insolvent spouse, the property of the solvent spouse shall vest in the master of the Supreme Court and (once one has been appointed) in the trustee of the insolvent estate. Goldstone J decided that the effect of section 21, even if it does amount to a transfer of ownership in the solvent spouse's property to the master or trustee of the insolvent estate, is of a temporary nature and not permanent, with the purpose not to acquire the property but to ensure that the insolvent estate is not deprived of property that actually belongs to it. Consequently it was decided that section 21 did not constitute expropriation and was not inconsistent with section 28(3) of the Constitution (explained paras [35]–[37] at 317C–318E, decided paras [38], [40] at 318F, G–I).
[19] Par [32] at 315E–G. The Court relied on one decision of the High Court (*Beckenstrater v Sand River Irrigation Board* 1964 (4) SA 510 (T) at 515A–C) and two Zimbabwean decisions (*Hewlett v Minister of Finance and Another* 1982 (1) SA 490 (ZSC) and *Davies and Others v Minister of Lands, Agriculture and Water Development* 1997 (1) SA 228 (ZSC)) for the conclusion that expropriation requires the state to acquire the property.
[20] See further AJ van der Walt 'Striving for the better interpretation—A critical reflection on the Constitutional Court's *Harksen* and *FNB* decisions on the property clause' (2004) 121 *SALJ* 854–878 at 862.
[21] AJ van der Walt & H Botha 'Coming to grips with the new constitutional order: Critical comments on *Harksen v Lane NO*' (1998) 13 *SA Public Law* 17–41 at 35 describe this approach as
(continued on next page ...)

they are distinct entities with different characteristics that distinguish them from each other clearly and exhaustively.[22] The conceptual dichotomy means that any state interference with property has to be either expropriation or deprivation, with no room for overlaps or grey areas in between. Secondly, the Court assumed that the distinction is associated with permanent acquisition of the property: if the property is not acquired by the state or if the acquisition is not permanent, there is no expropriation.[23] Finally, the Court assumed that a prospective litigant who wants to attack the constitutional validity of any state interference with property has to choose between the two and argue either that there was an unconstitutional expropriation or that there was an unconstitutional deprivation. By implication, the Court does not have to investigate or consider the other option of its own accord.

In its most important decision on the property clause to date, *First National Bank of SA Ltd t/a Wesbank v Commissioner, South African Revenue Service; First National Bank of SA Ltd t/a Wesbank v Minister of Finance* or *FNB*,[24] the Constitutional Court

---

(... from previous page)

conceptualism in the sense that expropriation and deprivation are treated as concepts with discrete and distinguishable contents, on the basis of which the signified entities can be distinguished clearly and confidently. See further AJ van der Walt 'Striving for the better interpretation—A critical reflection on the Constitutional Court's *Harksen* and *FNB* decisions on the property clause' (2004) 121 *SALJ* 854–878 at 862.

[22] The main characteristics that distinguish expropriation from deprivation are, in the Court's view as set out in paras [32]–[35] at 315E–317C, that the effect of (and intention with) expropriation is to (*a*) divest the former owner of the property and to vest it in the expropriating authority (*b*) permanently. If these characteristics are present, the action is expropriation, if not it is deprivation. In the *Harksen* case, the fact that the effect of section 21 was regarded as vesting of temporary control over the property rather than permanent divesting and acquisition resulted in it being classified as deprivation rather than expropriation. Despite the categorical distinction adopted by the Court it was possible to argue that section 21 brought about unconstitutional deprivation rather than unconstitutional expropriation, but this was not done, and the Court's failure to consider the other alternative of its own accord is significant as an indication of how it regarded the dichotomy.

[23] Despite the strong position adopted in *Harksen* this chapter is based on the assumption that temporary expropriation is possible, especially when the object of the expropriation is a right rather than corporeal property. This aspect is discussed again later in the chapter; see footnote 34 and accompanying text below. R Wendt 'Eigentum, Erbrecht und Enteignung' in M Sachs (ed) *Grundgesetz Kommentar* (3rd ed 2002) 651 Rdn 151 makes an interesting point that has some bearing on the decision in *Harksen*: it may be disputable whether *permanence* is a characteristic of expropriation, but it is beyond dispute that expropriation must be *final*—it could therefore be said that *provisional* 'expropriation' is not really expropriation, but that does not mean that temporary expropriation is impossible because temporary expropriations are final. This may be what the Court had in mind when deciding *Harksen*, the other possibility being that the Court thought that the deprivation was not in the nature of a state acquisition; see 5.4 below for a further discussion of this point.

[24] 2002 (4) SA 768 (CC), decided with regard to section 25 of the 1996 Constitution. FNB, a commercial bank, reserved ownership in motor vehicles to secure a loan granted to finance their purchase. The state (in the form of SARS) established a statutory lien (section 114 of the Customs and Excise Act 91 of 1964) over all movable property found on the premises of an importer to secure

(continued on next page ...)

adopted a different style of reasoning and effectively undermined the assumptions on which the decision in *Harksen* was based. The Court changed the nature of the inquiry by proposing that a certain procedure should be followed when considering the constitutional validity of an infringement of property rights. The procedure centres on the fact that expropriation is regarded as a subset of deprivation.[25]

If expropriation constitutes a subspecies of deprivation, the subsection 25(1) requirements for deprivation also apply to expropriation, in addition to the more specific subsection 25(2) and 25(3) requirements. On that basis an investigation into the constitutional validity of any limitation of property should always start with the general, all-embracing requirements in subsection 25(1),[26] which is a major departure from *Harksen*. The main difference is that a decision on the distinction between deprivation and expropriation is relegated to a later stage of the process. When a depri-

---

(*... from previous page*)
payment of outstanding customs duties owed by him. The tax debt had no relation to the vehicles or their purchase, but the vehicles were bought and used by the tax debtor and were present on its business premises, and therefore it fell within the definition of the statutory provision. In essence, the case concerned a conflict between the state's statutory interest in securing and enforcing payment of tax debts and the bank's reservation of ownership to secure repayment of its loan. The issue was whether detention and sale in execution of the movable property in terms of the statutory lien constituted an unconstitutional limitation of the bank's property. The significant fact is that the bank held its security right over the property in order to enforce payment of a principal debt established by a loan granted for the purchase of the property by the debtor, whereas the state established its security interest over property belonging not to the principal debtor but to an unrelated third party, to enforce payment of a principal debt that had no relation to either the property or its third party owner. The Court decided that this was arbitrary deprivation of the property.

[25] *First National Bank of SA Ltd t/a Wesbank v Commissioner, South African Revenue Service; First National Bank of SA Ltd t/a Wesbank v Minister of Finance* 2002 (4) SA 768 (CC) paras [57]–[58] at 796E–797A. The *FNB* decision was followed and applied, as far as the arbitrary deprivation test is concerned, in *Mkontwana v Nelson Mandela Metropolitan Municipality; Bissett and Others v Buffalo City Municipality; Transfer Rights Action Campaign and Others v Member of the Executive Council for Local Government and Housing, Gauteng and Others* 2005 (1) SA 530 (CC), but see chapter 4.5.4 and AJ van der Walt 'Retreating from the *FNB* arbitrariness test already? *Mkontwana v Nelson Mandela Metropolitan Municipality; Bissett v Buffalo City Municipality; Transfer Rights Action Campaign v MEC for Local Government and Housing, Gauteng* (CC)' (2005) 122 *SALJ* 75–89.

[26] In *First National Bank of SA Ltd t/a Wesbank v Commissioner, South African Revenue Service; First National Bank of SA Ltd t/a Wesbank v Minister of Finance* 2002 (4) SA 768 (CC) this approach was explained in paras [58]–[60] at 796I–797D:

'[58] Viewed from this perspective s 25(1) deals with all "property" and all deprivations (including expropriations). If the deprivation infringes (limits) s 25 and cannot be justified under s 36, that is the end of the matter. The provision is unconstitutional.

[59] If, however, the deprivation passes scrutiny under s 25(1) (ie it does not infringe s 25(1) or, if it does, is a justified limitation) then the question arises as to whether it is an expropriation. If the deprivation amounts to an expropriation it must pass scrutiny under s 25(2)(*a*) and make provision for compensation under s 25(2)(*b*) ...

[60] The starting point for constitutional analysis, when considering any challenge under s 25 for the infringement of property rights, must be s 25(1).'

vation proves to be in conflict with section 25(1) and it cannot be justified in terms of section 36, 'that is the end of the matter'[27]—the question whether a deprivation also constitutes expropriation can only be asked once it has been established that it either satisfies the requirements in subsection 25(1) or is justified in terms of section 36, in which case it also has to satisfy the more specific requirements of subsection 25(2). Before that, the question whether it also constitutes expropriation is simply not relevant. In *FNB*, the latter issue never came up, and the result will probably be the same in the vast majority of cases, as it seems likely that expropriations that would fail the subsection 25(2) inquiry would probably already fail the subsection 25(1) arbitrary deprivation inquiry and therefore never get to the expropriation analysis stage.[28]

The assumption that expropriation and deprivation are mutually exclusive categories that can be distinguished clearly from each other in terms of their characteristics, without overlaps or grey areas in between, can obviously still be upheld when expropriation is seen as a subset of deprivation, but in view of the *FNB* methodology it loses some of its force because the expropriation is in effect not seen next to and separate from deprivation, but as it were through it. This weakening of the dichotomy also appears from the *FNB* Court's abandoning of the third assumption in *Harksen*, that a litigant is forced to argue either that there was an unconstitutional expropriation or that there was an unconstitutional deprivation of property, and that the Court will not investigate the other option. The logic of *FNB* means that the Court will always investigate the deprivation issue first, regardless of whether it was raised by the applicant.[29] Similarly, the court will get to the expropriation question whether it was raised by the applicant or not, provided the limitation passes the section 25(1) enquiry.

If we assume, as the Constitutional Court in *FNB* apparently encourages us to do,[30] that expropriation in terms of section 25 of the South African Constitution is a

---

[27] *First National Bank of SA Ltd t/a Wesbank v Commissioner, South African Revenue Service; First National Bank of SA Ltd t/a Wesbank v Minister of Finance* 2002 (4) SA 768 (CC) par [58] at 797A.

[28] T Roux 'Section 25' in S Woolman et al (eds) *Constitutional law of South Africa* (2nd ed 2003 original service Dec 2003) at 46–29.

[29] The *FNB* Court did not pronounce upon the second assumption in *Harksen*, namely that the distinction turns on the permanent acquisition of the property by the state, but it also weakened the force of this assumption by the logic of the arbitrary deprivation test; see chapter 4.5 and compare *First National Bank of SA Ltd t/a Wesbank v Commissioner, South African Revenue Service; First National Bank of SA Ltd t/a Wesbank v Minister of Finance* 2002 (4) SA 768 (CC) par [100] at 810G–811F. In the test as set out in *FNB* the scope and impact of the deprivation on the affected property holder play a much larger role than the effect it has for the state, and because all expropriations are treated as deprivation initially this could mean that they are also evaluated in terms of proportionality rather than acquisition by the state. The only place where the permanent acquisition test could conceivably play a role would be where a deprivation passes the initial arbitrary deprivation test and the court then asks itself whether it is an expropriation, in which case it would also have to pass the section 25(2) and 25(3) tests: *FNB* par [59] at 797B. To determine whether the deprivation is an expropriation the court could at that point conceivably revert to the permanent acquisition test.

[30] *First National Bank of SA Ltd t/a Wesbank v Commissioner, South African Revenue Service; First National Bank of SA Ltd t/a Wesbank v Minister of Finance* 2002 (4) SA 768 (CC) par [57] at 796F–H. See footnotes 2 and 21 above.

subset of deprivation, the implication is that the distinguishing characteristic of expropriation, as opposed to deprivation of property, is not necessarily that expropriation involves acquisition of property, but perhaps rather that compensation is required for expropriation and not for deprivation—reading the section 25 requirements for deprivation and expropriation in the way that the Constitutional Court did in *FNB*, the only requirement that does not apply to deprivation (and therefore distinguishes it from expropriation) is compensation.[31] The fact that compensation is required for some deprivations but not for others makes it important to distinguish between deprivation and expropriation, since property holders might prefer to receive compensation for restrictive but inevitable and justifiable limitations on their property rather than attack the limitation's validity. It is therefore to be expected that limitations will often be attacked on the basis that they are invalid in the absence of compensation, rather than just invalid per se.

However, if the *FNB* methodology raised the stakes and made it more important to decide whether a particular state limitation is deprivation or expropriation, it also made this distinction more difficult by introducing a circular element into the definition: one has to distinguish between deprivation and compensation because only the latter requires compensation, but the only apparent distinguishing characteristic (requirement) in section 25 is that only the latter requires compensation. It is therefore necessary to distinguish between these two categories without relying exclusively on the provisions of section 25. The best possibility is to accept a partial and provisional definition with reference to the characteristics of expropriation and to recognize that this definition is incomplete and that it will produce inconsistent results in some instances.[32] On this basis, the following characteristics of expropriation are useful markers:

- Expropriation takes place by operation of law and is brought about unilaterally, without the cooperation (often against the will) of the affected owner. If the state or someone else does acquire the property as a result of expropriation, it does so by way of original acquisition and not transfer.[33]

---

[31]Both subsection 25(1) and subsection 25(2) require that deprivation and expropriation respectively should take place in accordance with law of general application. In addition, subsection 25(1) requires that deprivations should not be arbitrary, but according to the *FNB* reading this also applies to expropriation (as a subset of deprivation). Furthermore, subsection 25(2) requires that expropriation should be for a public purpose or in the public interest; a requirement that is not explicitly stated for non-expropriatory deprivation, although one could assume an implicit public purpose requirement in that deprivation that does not serve a public purpose or the public interest would probably be arbitrary—see chapter 4.3. Effectively, therefore, the only requirement that distinguishes deprivation from expropriation is compensation, which is required for the latter but not for the former.

[32]R Wendt 'Eigentum, Erbrecht und Enteignung' in M Sachs (ed) *Grundgesetz Kommentar* (3rd ed 2002) 650 Rdn 148: the German Federal Constitutional Court's standard description of expropriation as the complete or partial withdrawal of concrete property holdings for a specific public purpose (*BVerfGE* 70, 191 [1985] at 199; *BVerfGE* 72, 66 [1986] at 76; *BVerfGE* 101, 239 [1999] at 259) is also not intended as a complete definition but as a description of essential characteristics of expropriation.

[33]A Gildenhuys *Onteieningsreg* (2nd ed 2001) 8–9. Compare footnote 11 above.

- Expropriation always involves a loss of property, usually total and permanent, but in at least some jurisdictions partial and temporary loss of property can constitute expropriation.[34]
- The property is usually acquired by or on behalf of the state, but in some cases destruction of the property or acquisition by another private person can amount to expropriation.[35]
- The compulsory loss and the concomitant destruction or acquisition of the property is brought about for a public purpose or in the public interest.[36]
- The compulsory loss of property for a public purpose is usually accompanied by compensation.[37]
- Expropriation is a lawful exercise of a legitimate state power (usually but not necessarily granted in the constitution), and therefore compensation for expropriation must be distinguished from compensation for damages in delict.[38]

It is immediately apparent that this partial and provisional definition does not distinguish expropriation and deprivation into watertight compartments, and that it in fact leaves room for overlaps and grey areas in between. It is therefore necessary to discuss the boundaries of expropriation with reference to some of the limitations that occur in these grey areas.

5.2.3 Grey areas between deprivation and expropriation

The view that the distinction between deprivation and expropriation is exhaustive and that there is no room for grey areas and overlaps is unhelpful, because it is clear from comparative case law that this distinction is contested. It is therefore interesting

---

[34]See the discussion of the decision in *Harksen v Lane NO* 1998 (1) SA 300 (CC) in this section above. In *Harksen* the Constitutional Court argued that expropriation involves permanent acquisition of property by the state, but there is comparative authority for the proposition that certain temporary deprivations of property (especially in the form of rights) constitute expropriation. Compare especially *Attorney-General v De Keyser's Royal Hotel, Ltd* [1920] AC 508 (HL) (wartime requisitioning of a hotel for military use); *First English Evangelical Lutheran Church of Glendale v County of Los Angeles* 482 US 304 (1987) at 318. In both instances, the landowner was allowed to claim compensation for the temporary but total loss of the use of the property. The notion of partial or temporary expropriation raises the problem of conceptual severance, which is discussed in chapter 3.4. It is possible that the Court in *Harksen* intended to indicate that the deprivation in that case was provisional and not final, which would have been a more convincing argument; see footnote 23 above. See further AJ van der Walt *Constitutional property clauses: A comparative analysis* (1999) 579, 440.

[35]A Gildenhuys *Onteieningsreg* (2nd ed 2001) 8 denies that destruction of property will constitute expropriation, relying on the authority of M Chaskalson & C Lewis 'Property' in M Chaskalson et al (eds) *Constitutional law of South Africa* (1st ed 1996) at 31–12. This also reflects the position taken by the Constitutional Court in *Harksen v Lane NO* 1998 (1) SA 300 (CC), where it was said that the state has to acquire the property. However, as is argued in 5.4 below, this position is too inflexible and needs to be qualified.

[36]See 5.7 below.

[37]See 5.8 below.

[38]See A Gildenhuys *Onteieningsreg* (2nd ed 2001) 3.

that the South African Constitutional Court adopted the oversimplified view in *Harksen*—which described the distinction between deprivation and expropriation as categorical and exhaustive—only to come up in *FNB* with a methodology that attempts to ignore the distinction as far as possible.[39] A more satisfactory response is to recognize the fact that the distinction is contentious and contested, and to deal with the cases that inevitably come up in the grey areas between deprivation and expropriation as best as possible. The approach in this chapter is to suggest ways in which this response could be developed, although the *FNB* methodology admittedly makes it unlikely that the courts will in fact do so.

The classic illustration of the fact that the deprivation-expropriation dichotomy does not exhaust the limitations on property is taxation. The imposition of a tax looks like deprivation in that it is general (affecting everyone in the same way) and aimed at facilitating the regulatory exercise of the state's police power, but it also resembles expropriation in that it involves loss of property by the affected property owner and acquisition of property by the state. However, it is senseless to think of taxation as a limitation that could be rectified by way of compensation, which again militates against it being seen as expropriation.[40] Accordingly, taxation is not as a rule seen or treated as expropriation, even when it is unfair or excessive.[41] In the most important South African decision on constitutional property, *First National Bank of SA Ltd t/a Wesbank v Commissioner, South African Revenue Service; First National Bank of SA Ltd t/a Wesbank v Minister of Finance*,[42] the Constitutional Court held that a statutory

---

[39]See footnotes 26, 29 and accompanying text above.

[40]This does not mean that property lawyers do not consider the relationship between taxation and expropriation very carefully, or that the imposition of a tax can never be expropriatory. In some property clauses (eg article 1 of the First Protocol to the European Convention on Human Rights) the provision that governs regulatory control over the use and enjoyment of property (the so-called 'third rule' in the second paragraph of article 1) includes authorization for the imposition and enforcement of taxes, penalties and contributions. Equally, it is possible that the imposition of a tax or penalty could be considered unfair or unduly harsh, in which case it could probably be declared invalid, because the payment of money to compensate for a tax does not make sense. Usually it is accepted that the test for a fair tax, from a constitutional property viewpoint, is whether the contributions imposed are proportionate to the income upon which the tax is levied. See further in this regard the examples in *Gudmunder Gudmundsson v Iceland* [1960] YB 3 394; *X & Y v United Kingdom* [1973] 44 CD 29; *X v The Netherlands* [1971] YB 14 224; *X v Austria* [1979] 13 DR 27; *Nyambirai v National Social Security Authority and Another* 1996 (1) SA 6363 (SCZ); *Müller v Austria* [1976] 3 DR 25. These cases are discussed by AJ van der Walt *Constitutional property clauses: A comparative analysis* (1999) 109.

[41]An exception is *Attorney-General of Trinidad & Tobago v Ramesh Dipraj Kumar Mootoo* (1976) 28 WIR 304 (CAT&T), where it was said that the public purpose served by the tax had to be considered when deciding the validity of its imposition, which means that a consideration that usually applies only to expropriation was used to evaluate a tax. See AJ van der Walt *Constitutional property clauses: A comparative analysis* (1999) 386.

[42]2002 (4) SA 768 (CC). For similar cases in Irish law see *Orange v The Revenue Commissioners* [1995] 1 IR 517 (a law that provides for attachment of a debt in the hands of a third party is not inherently unconstitutional); *Daly v The Revenue Commissioners* [1995] 3 IR 1 (the attack on property brought about by attachment of a debt was unfair in the circumstances because it failed the proportionality test). See further on these decisions G Hogan & G Whyte (eds) *JM Kelly: The Irish Constitution* (4th ed 2003) paras [7.7.61]–[7.7.62].

provision that created a lien to support the enforcement of a tax debt amounted to an arbitrary deprivation and was therefore unconstitutional and invalid. A law that imposes or enforces a tax will therefore probably also be unconstitutional when the deprivation it creates is arbitrary or procedurally unfair or excessive, but it is highly unlikely that imposition of a tax could result in a successful compensation claim based on the expropriation provision.[43] The same result was reached in Australian case law with a helpful structural explanation: the state power to impose taxes is based upon a different 'head of power' or source of authority than the power of eminent domain, and in the Australian Commonwealth Constitution the guarantee of just terms for compulsory acquisition (compensation for expropriation) is limited to the provision that specifically deals with the latter power.[44] The structural division of powers that enabled this explanation in Australian law is not gratuitous—it embodies logic about the fundamental difference between taxation and expropriation that holds in other jurisdictions as well, and it therefore makes sense to distinguish between expropriation and taxation on the basis that they originate in different sources of state power.

A second grey area where the distinction between deprivation and expropriation is problematic is the settlement of civil disputes. It is widely acknowledged that the state may not use its expropriation power to settle private disputes by taking property from one and giving it to the other party,[45] but it is sometimes necessary and legitimate for the state to deprive private persons of their property in the course of regulating civil disputes.[46] Once again the Australian explanation, according to which this kind of deprivation takes place in terms of another 'head or power' or state authority and therefore does not fall into the same category as expropriation for which compensation has to be paid, makes it much easier to solve the attendant

---

[43] In Swiss law, excessive taxes have been struck down under the prohibition against limitations that undermine the institutional guarantee. It was said in the case of *Hausbeseitzer-Verein Basel BGE* 105 Ia 134 [1979] that the legislature must preserve the substance of existing property holdings and the possibility of building new property holdings when it imposes a tax; if a tax undermines or destroys existing wealth or the possibility of creating new wealth it is unconstitutional for being in conflict with the institutional guarantee. See also *BGE* 106 Ia 342 [1980], and compare AJ van der Walt *Constitutional property clauses: A comparative analysis* (1999) 361–362. A similar decision was reached by the German Federal Constitutional Court in *BVerfGE* 87, 153 [1992].

[44] See AJ van der Walt *Constitutional property clauses: A comparative analysis* (1999) 43. A similar argument can probably be made with reference to the statement that the US federal government exercises the police power in terms of its explicitly granted powers to regulate interstate commerce, make war, impose and collect taxes, and promote the general welfare; see AJ van der Walt *Constitutional property clauses: A comparative analysis* (1999) 410.

[45] Hence the general wariness towards expropriation for the benefit of another private person; see the full discussion of this issue in 5.7 below on the public purpose requirement.

[46] From many examples, see the Australian decision in *Mutual Pools & Staff Pty Limited v The Commonwealth of Australia* (1994) 179 CLR 155 (law to deprive certain merchants from a tax rebate to ensure that it reaches the intended beneficiaries); and the German decision in *BVerfGE* 42, 263 [1976] (*Contergan*) (law to nationalize a private compensation fund for Thalidomide victims to ensure more equal distribution among claimants is constitutional); see further AJ van der Walt *Constitutional property clauses: A comparative analysis* (1999) 47, 131 respectively.

problems. Cases involving this kind of deprivation should therefore probably be
solved with reference to the requirements for regulatory deprivation, which in South
African law means that they should be tested against the arbitrary deprivation test set
out in *FNB*.[47] In any event these cases should not be solved with reference to the
requirements for expropriation. In fact, the first major South African Constitutional
Court decision on property, *Harksen v Lane NO*,[48] was concerned with the regulation
of debts in cases of insolvency and should therefore perhaps have been decided on
this basis and not in terms of the question whether the statutory limitation in question
amounted to unconstitutional expropriation.[49]

In some instances limitations of property in these grey areas are solved in the same
way as other problematic limitations, namely by treating them as constructive expropriation. These instances are discussed in 5.4 below, after an overview of the constitutional status of forfeiture in view of the constitutional expropriation provisions.
Forfeiture is discussed in the next section because it is one of the clearest examples of
the problems emerging from the grey area between deprivation and expropriation.

5.3 FORFEITURE

5.3.1 Introduction

One of the most difficult examples of limitation of property in a grey area between
deprivation and expropriation is forfeiture.[50] Forfeiture involves a state action by
which private property is lost to the state, without the consent or cooperation of the
owner, usually but not necessarily because it was involved in crime. Not all forms of
seizure, confiscation and forfeiture are relevant for a discussion of expropriation—
various forms of these state actions against private property clearly qualify as regulatory deprivation of property, although they could involve even permanent loss or
destruction of the property. As regulatory actions that involve deprivation of property
these limitations are usually reasonably easy to justify in terms of the police power

---

[47] *First National Bank of SA Ltd t/a Wesbank v Commissioner, South African Revenue Service; First
National Bank of SA Ltd t/a Wesbank v Minister of Finance* 2002 (4) SA 768 (CC).

[48] 1998 (1) SA 300 (CC), dealing with the property clause in section 28 of the 1993 interim
Consitution. See footnote 18 above and footnote 49 below.

[49] See footnote 18 above. The Court was quite correct in pointing out that the intention with
section 21 is not to acquire property for the state, the point being to ensure that the property in
the insolvent estate is used to pay the estate's creditors. In ensuring this distribution of funds the
state is fulfilling a power that has no relation to expropriation, and accordingly the question should
have been whether the section established a valid deprivation of property. In that sense the closest
foreign cases to compare with *Harksen* are probably *Mutual Pools & Staff Pty Limited v The Commonwealth of Australia* (1994) 179 CLR 155 (Australia, see footnote 174 below) and BVerfGE 42, 263
[1976] (*Contergan*) (Germany, see footnote 114 below).

[50] See in more detail AJ van der Walt 'Civil forfeiture of instrumentalities and proceeds of crime
and the constitutional property clause' (2000) 16 *SAJHR* 1–45. This section relies on and in some
respects bears a resemblance to that article. See further JL Pretorius & HA Strydom 'The constitutionality of civil forfeiture' (1998) 13 *SA Public Law* 385–422 at 389.

principle, because they are aimed at and necessary for the protection of public health and safety. For instance, private property is often confiscated temporarily to secure evidence in a criminal trial or to establish jurisdiction or security and contraband is sometimes forfeited (and destroyed) because its possession is illegal or dangerous.[51] As is argued in chapter 4.7.2, these 'normal' seizures, confiscations and forfeitures of property clearly amount to exercises of the state's regulatory police power and their legitimacy must be analysed with that purpose in mind—they establish deprivation of property that must comply with the requirements in section 25(1).

The matter is complicated somewhat by the distinction between criminal and civil forfeiture. Criminal forfeiture is said to operate *in personam* or against a specific person,[52] which means that it depends on a conviction having been obtained against that person, and the forfeiture order is generally restricted to property that forms part of that person's assets or possessions or that was used by that person in committing a crime. Although criminal forfeiture can raise criminal-justice concerns such as excessive punishment,[53] it does not create major theoretical problems for property law because deprivation of property caused by criminal confiscation and forfeiture can normally be justified in terms of the regulatory purpose for which property is forfeited as a consequence of a criminal conviction, such as crime fighting or the prevention of a public danger. In these cases the forfeiture usually serves the narrow purpose of protecting public health and safety, and therefore the legitimacy of the forfeiture can be tested against the normal police power requirements. For purposes of expropriation the most interesting form of forfeiture is civil forfeiture, which can (in certain circumstances) raise the question whether a particular exercise of the power to declare property forfeit amounts to expropriation rather than deprivation.

---

[51] Temporary 'freezing', 'restraint' and 'preservation of property' orders are used to prevent the dissipation of property prior to or during applications for final forfeiture orders. The South African Prevention of Organised Crime Act 121 of 1998 provides for restraint orders (Part 3, sections 25–29); see further section 20(b) of the Prevention of Organised Crime Amendment Act 24 of 1999. It was pointed out correctly in *National Director of Public Prosecutions v Rautenbach and Others* 2005 (4) SA 603 (SCA) par [56] at 621B–H that the court granting a restraint order in a criminal forfeiture case should satisfy itself that there is a sufficiently close connection between the interference and the purpose to be achieved, as set out in the *FNB* case, to avoid the interference being an arbitrary and therefore invalid deprivation in terms of section 25(1). See chapter 4.5, 4.6 on the *FNB* decision and its implications and chapter 4.7.2 on the application of the *FNB* test to deprivations caused by seizure, confiscation and forfeiture.

[52] As opposed to *in rem* or against the property itself; the so-called personification or guilty-property fiction forms the basis of civil forfeiture.

[53] The major concern is that the forfeiture could constitute a separate, additional punishment that might push the aggregate beyond the limit of what is considered fair and normal punishment for the particular crime; compare LF Bittle 'Punitive damages and the Eighth Amendment: An analytical framework for determining excessiveness' (1987) 75 *Cal LR* 1433–1471; WW Taylor 'The problem of proportionality in RICO forfeitures' (1990) 65 *Notre Dame LR* 885–895. Another constitutional criminal-justice issue raised by civil forfeiture is protection of the right against self-incrimination; see JA Rosenberg 'Constitutional rights and civil forfeiture actions' (1988) 88 *Col LR* 390–406 for a discussion in the context of the US Fifth Amendment.

The most striking feature of civil forfeiture is that its purpose is not regulatory but acquisitive, namely to vest state ownership in the property and to use it for a public purpose or for a state benefit—crime-fighting bodies are often partly funded by moneys obtained from civil forfeiture and they sometimes rely on the use of forfeited property such as motor cars, boats or computer equipment. In recent years the scope of forfeiture orders was extended in most jurisdictions to include property regarded as instrumentalities[54] or proceeds[55] of crime, increasing the potential conflict between protection of private property and the public interest in effective crime-fighting.

Civil (*in rem*) forfeiture is distinguished from criminal (*in personam*) forfeiture by three considerations: (*a*) criminal forfeiture requires prior criminal conviction of the property owner, whereas civil forfeiture merely requires the state to allege that the property probably constitutes illegal contraband or that it was probably used for an illegal purpose; (*b*) the state bears a lower burden of proof in a civil forfeiture action than in a criminal action;[56] and (*c*) criminal forfeiture covers only property held by the criminal at the time of conviction, but civil forfeiture relates back to the date of illegal use of property, regardless of whether it is still owned or possessed by the criminal. The relation-back doctrine means that civil forfeiture could involve property belonging to innocent third parties who had no knowledge of and who were not involved in the criminal activity, which has interesting implications for constitutional property law.

The obvious concerns raised by these differences between criminal and civil forfeiture are countered by saying that the civil procedure is aimed at the property itself and not at any person, with the result that civil forfeiture does not depend on a criminal prosecution ever being instituted or a criminal conviction being obtained against any person. Consequently, civil forfeiture is enforced against whoever holds

[54]Defined as property used or involved in the commission of a (particular kind of) crime; see *Calero-Toledo v Pearson Yacht Leasing Company* 416 US 663 (1974). In *National Director of Public Prosecutions v (1) RO Cook Properties (Pty) Ltd; (2) 37 Gillespie Street Durban (Pty) Ltd and Another; (3) Seevnarayan* 2004 (8) BCLR 844 (SCA) paras [27]–[32] at 855H–857F the SCA held that instrumentalities of crime had to be interpreted narrowly for several reasons, one of which was that the provisions had to be interpreted in view of the constitutional requirements in section 25(1): a wide interpretation could well result in arbitrary deprivation that would be unconstitutional (par [15] at 851G–852A). In 2004 and 2005 South African authorities started using their forfeiture powers to combat drunken driving by attaching the vehicles of repeat offenders. On 25 May 2005 the Eastern Cape High Court declared these attachments unlawful on the basis that there was insufficient evidence that the cars were instrumentalities of the crime; see F Esbend 'Surprise ruling on seizure of drunk driving vehicles' *The Herald* 25 May 2005 at http://www.epherald.co.za/herald/2005/05/25/news/no2_25052005.htm. The legislation in question is aimed at fighting organized crime and not individual road crime (see 5.3.2 below) and the innocent owner problem arose in some of the drunken driving cases because the cars were in fact owned by someone else, eg the banks that financed their purchase.

[55]Defined as property obtained from or as a result of illegal activity; proceeds can range from cash received in a drug deal to property received as a gift from a suspected criminal.

[56]The onus of proof in civil forfeiture cases is preponderance of probabilities and not the criminal requirement of proof beyond reasonable doubt.

or owns the affected property, regardless of his or her involvement in or knowledge of any crime. Obviously this means that the property rights of those who were actually involved in crime may be lost through forfeiture, but by and large this is not necessarily unjust or unreasonable, as such loss would mostly be justifiable in the normal way by describing the forfeiture as an exercise of the police power that merely has to satisfy the requirements in section 25(1) in establishing a proper balance between the public purpose of the deprivation and the interests of the affected person. Normally it would not be difficult to convince a court that the public interest in crime fighting should outweigh the property interests of a proven criminal with regard to the products of the crime. More controversial is the fact that the rights of innocent third parties, such as lenders, co-owners, mortgagees and creditors can also be affected by civil forfeiture, without any guarantee of protection beyond, possibly, the constitutional property clause.

Civil forfeiture does not require a criminal investigation, prosecution or conviction ever to be completed (or even initiated), which means that the alleged crime never has to be investigated or proven. As far as innocent owners are concerned, this leaves room for abuse, especially given the incentive created by using the proceeds of forfeiture to fund crime-fighting agencies. Moreover, given the *in rem* nature of a civil forfeiture an innocent owner could find that her property is seized and forfeited or perhaps just held indefinitely by the authorities even after the criminal case against the suspected offender has been abandoned or dismissed. Civil forfeiture therefore features in a grey area between deprivation and expropriation: it is clearly not intended as 'normal' expropriation for which the affected owner is compensated, and its primary purpose is regulatory in the sense that it is employed to regulate the use of property, for a public purpose (namely to fight crime). However, its effects may sometimes appear expropriatory in that property owners who are not involved in or even aware of the crime lose their property to the state,[57] which acquires the property in a very real sense and often benefits from it in a purely financial way. When innocent owners are unable to reclaim their forfeited property the question is whether the matter should be dealt with as deprivation or expropriation and, if the latter, whether it could satisfy the requirements for expropriation.

---

[57] It is relatively easy to justify the loss of property in contraband or of property used in or acquired through criminal activity when the loss accrues to a convicted criminal, but the justifications do not apply with equal force when the affected owner is unrelated to the crime (the innocent owner). See AJ van der Walt 'Civil forfeiture of instrumentalities and proceeds of crime and the constitutional property clause' (2000) 16 *SAJHR* 1–45. In *National Director of Public Prosecutions v (1) RO Cook Properties (Pty) Ltd; (2) 37 Gillespie Street Durban (Pty) Ltd and Another; (3) Seevnarayan* 2004 (8) BCLR 844 (SCA) paras [24]–[26] at 855A–G the SCA sketched out the very limited way in which the South African Prevention of Organised Crime Act 121 of 1998 can be said to allow an innocent owner defence; see the discussion below. The fact that the property owner was acquitted of criminal charges on a technicality cut no ice with the SCA in *Prophet v National Director of Public Prosecutions* case 502/04 29 September 2005 (SCA) par [32].

5.3.2 Civil forfeiture in South African law

A number of anti-crime laws have been promulgated in South Africa,[58] the most relevant of which is the Prevention of Organised Crime Act 121 of 1998.[59] The Act provides for both criminal and civil forfeiture[60] and affects not only contraband but also instrumentalities and proceeds of crime. Chapter 5 provides for (criminal) *in personam* confiscation orders[61] and for restraint orders as an interim measure to secure the avail-

---

[58]See AJ van der Walt 'Civil forfeiture of instrumentalities and proceeds of crime and the constitutional property clause' (2000) 16 *SAJHR* 1–45 at 32–35; JL Pretorius & HA Strydom 'The constitutionality of civil forfeiture' (1998) 13 *SA Public Law* 385–422 at 387–390; L de Koker & JL Pretorius 'Conflicting orders in terms of the Proceeds of Crime Act: Some constitutional perspectives' 1998 *TSAR* 39–52, 277–283, 467–483; A Itzikowitz 'The prevention and control of money laundering in South Africa' (1999) 62 *THRHR* 88–107; A Hofmeyr 'The role of civil forfeiture in the forthcoming prevention of organised crime legislation: A closer look' 1998 *Responsa Meridiana* 41–61 for a discussion. The most important laws are the Drugs and Drug Trafficking Act 140 of 1992; The International Co-operation in Criminal Matters Act 75 of 1996; the Proceeds of Crime Act 76 of 1996; and the Prevention of Organised Crime Act 121 of 1998. See further chapter 3 of the Prevention and Combating of Corrupt Activities Act 12 of 2004, which allows for investigations in respect of possession of property disproportionate to a person's present or past known sources of income (section 23).

[59]The 1998 Act repealed the Proceeds of Crime Act 76 of 1996 and was subsequently amended several times.

[60]Although the distinction is blurred: the Act provides that the effect of a confiscation order is that of a civil judgment (section 23), but this does not mean that a confiscation in terms of Chapter 5 is a (civil) *in rem* forfeiture: section 18 provides explicitly that a confiscation can only be obtained once the person involved has been convicted. In fact, section 13 further provides that proceedings on application for a confiscation order are civil proceedings and not criminal, and that the civil rather than the criminal rules of evidence and construction and the civil onus of proof apply to them (balance of probabilities), thereby reinforcing the impression that the intention of section 23 is to ensure that the procedural and evidentiary aspects of the confiscation and of litigation connected with it are of the civil rather than the stricter criminal species. The intention could also be to isolate these proceedings against the protection that applies to criminal proceedings in terms of the Constitution (section 35), although experience elsewhere suggests that this effort could be futile and that the labelling of the confiscation proceedings as civil rather than criminal will not necessarily isolate it from the constitutional protection of accused, arrested and detained persons. In *National Director of Public Prosecutions v Phillips and Others* 2002 (4) SA 60 (W) par [45] at 111I–J it was decided that the application for a confiscation order in terms of section 35 was properly characterised as civil proceedings. In *National Director of Public Prosecutions v (1) RO Cook Properties (Pty) Ltd; (2) 37 Gillespie Street Durban (Pty) Ltd and Another; (3) Seevnarayan* 2004 (8) BCLR 844 (SCA) paras [17]–[18] at 852E–853B the SCA held that the explicitly declared civil nature and remedial purpose of the provisions does not alter the fact that it also has a palpably penal aspect.

[61]Once a defendant has been convicted of an offence the court may inquire into any benefit derived from that offence and, if the court finds that the defendant acquired a benefit from the offence or from related criminal activities it may, in addition to any punishment it may impose, make an order for payment to the state of any amount it considers appropriate. The amount which a court may order the defendant to pay shall be equal to the value of the proceeds of the offence or other related criminal activities, or the amount that may be realized at the time of making the order, whichever amount is the lowest. See AJ van der Walt 'Civil forfeiture of instrumentalities and

(continued on next page ...)

ability of property for confiscation.[62] Chapter 6 gives a court the power to grant temporary preservation of property orders[63] as well as civil (*in rem*) forfeiture orders with regard to property subject to a preservation order, if it is satisfied that the property

---

(... from previous page)
proceeds of crime and the constitutional property clause' (2000) 16 *SAJHR* 1–45 at 32–33 for more detail. In *National Director of Public Prosecutions v Rebuzzi* 2002 (2) SA 1 (SCA) it was held that the order to pay the amount of money does not deprive the victim of the crime of his or her claim for recovery of the property, and the existence of such a claim is not relevant to the exercise of the court's discretion in giving the order: par [20] at 7H, read with par [14] at 6D–F and paras [12]–[13] at 5I–6I.

[62]Sections 25–29. The National Director of Public Prosecutions may apply to a High Court for a restraint order prohibiting any person from dealing with property when a prosecution has been instituted against the defendant and a confiscation order has been made or it seems that there are reasonable grounds to believe that such an order will be made, or when the court is satisfied that the person involved will be charged with a crime and there are reasonable grounds to believe that a confiscation order will be made against that person. The court will rescind the restraint order if the person is not charged within a reasonable period. The court is compelled to make an order for the seizure of the property if it grants an application for a restraint order. The restraint order can be issued in the form of a rule *nisi*, calling upon the respondent to show cause why the order should not be made final. The restraint order shall make provision for notice to be given to persons affected and any affected person may apply for the order to be rescinded or amended, and the High Court may rescind or amend the order if it deems fit in the interests of justice. The restraint order shall remain in force when the proceedings against the defendant are concluded, pending the outcome of any appeal against the confiscation application, unless the court is convinced that the restraint order has to be rescinded or amended to prevent it from depriving the defendant of reasonable living expenses and so cause undue hardship that outweighs the risk that the property may be destroyed, lost, damaged, concealed or transferred. Once the proceedings against the defendant (including appeals) have been concluded, the court must rescind the restraint order. If there is no reasonable prospect of a confiscation being granted the court will not grant or confirm a restraint order either; see *National Director of Public Prosecutions v Tam and Others* 2004 (2) SA 500 (W) at 503H–504E. A court considering a restraint order is excercising a descretion even though it is not deciding the actual veracity of the evidence that might reasonably support a conviction and subsequent confiscation order: *National Director of Public Prosecution v Rautenbach and Others* 2005 (4) SA 603 (SCA) par [27] at 614C–G. In exercising this discretion the court should ascertain that the value of the property to be placed under restraint does not materially exceed the amount of the anticipated confiscation order; if it does, that could indicate absence of an appropriate connection between the interference with property and its purpose, which could render the restraint arbitrary and unconstitutional in view of the *FNB* decision: par [56] at 621B–H.

[63]The preservation order may be granted upon *ex parte* application by a High Court to prohibit any person from dealing with the specified property in any manner, if there are reasonable grounds to believe that the property is an instrumentality of an offence in Schedule 1 or is the proceeds of unlawful activities. Property is regarded as an instrumentality of an offence if the property is concerned in the commission or suspected commission of a listed offence in the Republic of South Africa or elsewhere. A court is compelled to make an order for the seizure of the property when it issues a preservation order. After the preservation order has been made, notice must be given to all persons known to have an interest in the property and a notice must be published in the Government Gazette, and interested persons then have 14 days to give notice of intention to oppose the application for a forfeiture order or to apply for the exclusion of his or her property from that order (section 39).

is an instrumentality of crime or the proceeds of unlawful activities.[64] The effect of the forfeiture order is that the property is forfeited to the state.[65] Affected persons who want to oppose the application or apply for the exclusion of their property must show that they acquired the property legally and neither knew nor had reason to know that the property was an instrumentality or the proceeds of criminal activities.[66]

The constitutional status of forfeiture powers in relation to the property clause has not been decided authoritatively by South African courts yet. Several cases with regard to statutory powers of search and seizure, confiscation and forfeiture dealt with temporary and provisional restraint and preservation orders and not with forfeiture.[67] In a constitutional challenge against search and seizure powers granted by the Income Tax Act 58 of 1962 and the Value-Added Tax Act 89 of 1991, it was held that the applicants' property rights were not infringed by search and seizure warrants authorized by a judge upon application, because the owners could still establish their entitlement to and claim delivery of the seized property.[68] In *Director of Public Prosecutions: Cape of Good Hope v*

---

[64] Section 50. As in the case of *in personam* confiscation of property in terms of Chapter 5, the *in rem* proceedings in Chapter 6 are also labelled civil and not criminal, and the rules of evidence and construction are specified to be the civil and not the criminal standard (section 37). The absence of a person who has an interest in the property or the outcome of any criminal investigation or prosecution does not affect the granting of the forfeiture order (section 50(3)–(4)), but a person who was entitled to receive notice of the application and did not may apply for exclusion of his/her property from the forfeiture order even after the order has been granted: section 54. The forfeiture order shall not take effect before any appeal has been disposed of or within 45 days from the date on which the making of the order was published in the *Government Gazette*: section 50(5). In *National Director of Public Prosecutions v Patterson and Another* [2001] 4 All SA 525 (C) the High Court decided that the question whether property had been instrumental in the commission of a crime had to be decided on the basis of the facts presented to the court.

[65] Section 56.

[66] Section 52. In *National Director of Public Prosecutions v (1) RO Cook Properties (Pty) Ltd; (2) 37 Gillespie Street Durban (Pty) Ltd and Another; (3) Seevnarayan* 2004 (8) BCLR 844 (SCA) paras [24]–[26] at 855A–G the SCA sketched out the very limited way in which the South African Prevention of Organised Crime Act 121 of 1998 can be said to allow an innocent owner defence. Without expressing a final view on the interpretation of section 52 of the Act, the SCA nevertheless indicated that a too wide interpretation of the notion of instrumentality or an interpretation that expects too much of a property owner in terms of vigilance with regard to use of her property could be unconstitutional. The link between the purpose of the forfeiture and the property has to be close and reasonably direct in the sense that the property must play a reasonably direct rather than an incidental role in the commission of the offence: paras [30]–[31] at 856F–857C.

[67] In an early case dealing with search and seizure provisions in the Investigation of Serious Economic Offences Act 117 of 1991, *Park-Ross v The Director, Office for Serious Economic Offences* 1995 (1) SA 148 (C), no challenge was raised on the property clause in section 28 of the 1993 Constitution.

[68] *Deutschmann NO and Others v Commissioner for the South African Revenue Service; Shelton v Commissioner for the South African Revenue Service* 2000 (2) SA 106 (E) at 584C–E. In view of the subsequent *FNB* decision (*First National Bank of SA Ltd t/a Wesbank v Commissioner, South African Revenue Service; First National Bank of SA Ltd t/a Wesbank v Minister of Finance* 2002 (4) SA 768 (CC)) a more satisfactory view would have been that the property rights in question were affected by the

(continued on next page ...)

Bathgate[69] the Cape High Court decided that restraint orders and confiscation of property in terms of the Proceeds of Crime Act 76 of 1996 and the Prevention of Organized Crime Act 121 of 1998 'may ... constitute arbitrary deprivation of property in terms of section 25(1) of the Constitution', but that such deprivation would be a justified limitation in view of the state's effort to combat crime.[70] In *National Director of Public Prosecution v Rautenbach and Others* the Supreme Court of Appeal reiterated that a material disproportionality between the value of the affected property and the anticipated confiscation order could render a restraint order arbitrary and unconstitutional in view of the *FNB* decision, but did not comment on the justifiability of such a limitation.[71] In *National Director of Public Prosecutions and Another v Mohamed NO and Others*[72] the Constitutional Court had an opportunity to pronounce upon the constitutional validity of the preservation procedure in chapter 6 of the Prevention of Organised Crime Act 121 of 1998, but it chose on a technical point to refer the matter back to the High Court that originally declared section 38 of the Act unconstitutional.[73]

In another decision the Cape High Court decided that forfeiture, although controversial, was justified by the public interest in crime fighting and legitimated by the statutory provisions that authorize it. The Court treated forfeiture as deprivation of property in terms of section 25(1) of the Constitution and not as expropriation, emphasizing that deprivation in terms of the forfeiture powers should not be implemented in a predetermined, mechanistic way and that a balance should be struck between the public interest in effective crime fighting and the interests of affected property owners.[74] In a later case the Supreme Court of Appeal refrained from expressing a final view on the interpretation of section 52 of the Act, but nevertheless

---

(... from previous page)
warrant, but that the deprivation involved would be lawful in terms of section 25(1) if it was authorized by a law of general application (which it was) and as long as the law did not allow arbitrary deprivation, which should be decided with reference to the fact that the deprivation was subject to obtaining a warrant upon application to court, and subject to the affected person's right to reclaim his or her property as provided in the statute. See further D Gupta 'Republic of South Africa's Prevention of Organised Crime Act: A comparative bill of rights analysis' (2002) 37 *Harv Civ Rights–Civ Lib LR* 159–183 at 165.

[69] 2000 (2) SA 535 (C).

[70] *Director of Public Prosecutions: Cape of Good Hope v Bathgate* 2000 (2) SA 535 (C) par [82] at 559C–D; paras [84]–[113] at 173I–180D.

[71] 2005 (4) SA 603 (SCA) par [56] at 621B–H. See further chapter 4.7.2 and compare *Prophet v National Director of Public Prosecutions* case 502/04 29 September 2005 (SCA) paras [11], [30]–[41].

[72] 2002 (4) SA 843 (CC).

[73] *Mohamed NO and Others v National Director of Public Prosecutions and Another* 2002 (4) SA 366 (W). The High Court declared section 38 unconstitutional but did not consider the matter raised in the application before it, namely that the whole of chapter 6 was unconstitutional.

[74] *National Director of Public Prosecutions v Prophet* 2003 (6) SA 154 (C) paras [29]–[32] at 167G– 168F; paras [28]–[29] at 167D–H, referring to AJ van der Walt 'Civil forfeiture of instrumentalities and proceeds of crime and the constitutional property clause' (2000) 16 *SAJHR* 1–45 at 45. The forfeiture·order was upheld by the SCA: *Prophet v National Director of Public Prosecutions* case 502/04 29 September 2005 (SCA).

indicated that a too generous interpretation of 'instrumentality of crime' or an application of the Act that would expect too much of a property owner in terms of vigilance regarding the unlawful use of her property could result in arbitrary
deprivation.[75] The Court therefore decided that, although 'instrumentalities of crime'
had to be interpreted without reference to the state of mind of the owner during the
first stage of the inquiry, this phrase nevertheless had to be interpreted narrowly: the
link between the purpose of the forfeiture and the property has to be close and reasonably direct in the sense that the property must have played a reasonably direct rather
than an incidental role in the commission of the offence. In the process the Court
placed judicial scrutiny of the constitutional validity of civil forfeiture powers, at least
as far as instrumentalities of crime are concerned, within the analytic framework of
arbitrariness established by the Constitutional Court in the *FNB* case.

It therefore seems as if civil forfeiture in terms of the South African crime fighting
legislation will be treated as deprivation and not as expropriation. This trend is in line
with other jurisdictions, although there are variations in the degree of deference with
which the courts approach civil forfeiture as a crime-fighting mechanism. The next
few sections outline the approach to forfeiture in foreign case law. The trend, as will
appear below, is either to simply exclude forfeiture from the compensation guarantee
in some way or to treat it as deprivation for which compensation does not apply. As
a rule foreign courts apply a fairly low level of scrutiny to the exercise of forfeiture
powers, although some systems are stricter with civil forfeiture than others.

5.3.3 Civil forfeiture not possible without criminal conviction

In the UK confiscation of property depends upon a criminal conviction—in other
words, only criminal (*in personam*) forfeiture is possible.[76] The justification for forfei-

---

[75] *National Director of Public Prosecutions v (1) RO Cook Properties (Pty) Ltd; (2) 37 Gillespie Street
Durban (Pty) Ltd and Another; (3) Seevnarayan* 2004 (8) BCLR 844 (SCA) paras [24]–[26] at 855A–G.
The SCA mentioned specifically that the Act placed a heavy burden on the owner of property and
so restricted the common law of property and, although property owners can be expected to
exercise reasonable care and vigilance regarding the use of their property, the Act cannot impose a
burden that expects the impossible: paras [23], [26]–[29] at 854F–G, 855E–856F. This test was
referred to and applied in the Cape High Court decision in *National Director of Public Prosecutions v
Engels* 2005 (3) SA 109 (C). See further *Prophet v National Director of Public Prosecutions* case 502/04
29 September 2005 (SCA) paras [30]–[41].
[76] The term is 'confiscation' in the UK. There is one exception where *in rem* confiscation is
possible in the absence of a criminal conviction: the Drug Trafficking Act 1994 allows seizure and
forfeiture of amounts of cash in excess of £10,000 where there are reasonable grounds for
suspecting that the money directly or indirectly represents proceeds of drug trafficking or that it is
intended for use in drug trafficking; and when the defendant has died or absconded before a conviction or a confiscation order could be obtained. In this instance, the purpose is to prevent the
commission of further crimes involving the property. See AJ van der Walt 'Civil forfeiture of
instrumentalities and proceeds of crime and the constitutional property clause' (2000) 16 *SAJHR*
1–45 at 18–19 for more detail. For a detailed analysis of the relevant legislation see AR Mitchell,

(continued on next page ...)

ture of private property is that criminals should not be permitted to benefit from their crimes, and consequently the whole process is based on the court's determination of the amount of benefit and the property that is available to satisfy the forfeiture order. Such a criminal forfeiture order relates to any property, and is not restricted to the actual proceeds of the crime, and since the Proceeds of Crime Act was introduced in 1995, proceeds of all crimes can be subjected to forfeiture orders. Moreover, the UK courts have much wider powers than their US counterparts in enforcing a compensation order to reimburse or compensate the victims of the crime first, before any property is forfeited to the state.

In the final analysis the forfeiture power authorized by UK legislation[77] resembles civil rather than criminal forfeiture in that it allows for confiscation (forfeiture) of property used in the commission of a crime regardless of the fact that the property may belong to an innocent third party, but since confiscation is premised upon prior criminal conviction the problem of innocent third parties being affected by civil forfeiture orders in the absence of any criminal conviction should not arise.[78] The result is that the possibility of disproportionate deprivation of innocent third parties' property is reduced.

5.3.4 Civil forfeiture excluded from compensation guarantee

The Australian High Court had to decide on the constitutional validity of forfeiture of property belonging to an innocent owner who was unaware of the criminal activity in *Re Director of Public Prosecutions; Ex Parte Lawler and Another*.[79] The case

---

(... from previous page)

MG Hinton, & SME Taylor *Confiscation* (published as part of the *Criminal Law Library*) (1992). See further on UK law M Hinton 'Are drug trafficking confiscation orders punitive?' 1992 *Solicitors J* 1264–1265; C Sallon & D Bedingfield 'Drugs, money and the law' [1993] *Crim LR* 165–173; DA Thomas 'The Criminal Justice Act 1993: (1) Confiscation orders and drug trafficking' [1994] *Crim LR* 93–100; A Mitchell & M Hinton 'Confiscation inquiries—What the Dickens?' (1994) 58 *J Crim L* 201–208; LJ Candler 'Tracing and recovering proceeds of crime in fraud cases: A compar-
[77]Such as the Customs and Excise Management Act 1979; see *Air Canada v United Kingdom* [1995] 20 EHRR 150 at 157–158 for particulars of the Act.
[78]See the previous footnote, and further LJ Candler 'Tracing and recovering proceeds of crime in fraud cases: A comparison of US and UK legislation' (1997) 31 *Int Lawyer* 3–40; and compare further RE Bell 'Confiscation orders under the proceeds of crime legislation' (1998) 49 *N Ir LQ* 38–59 (comparing legislation in the UK and Northern Ireland); C Sallon & D Bedingfield 'Drugs, money and the law' [1993] *Crim LR* 165–173; DA Thomas 'The Criminal Justice Act 1993: (1) Confiscation orders and drug trafficking' [1994] *Crim LR* 93–100.
[79](1994) 179 CLR 270 (HC). Lawler and Penrose owned a New Zealand registered fishing vessel and entered into a lease and sale agreement relating to the vessel with Bario Enterprises. The vessel was boarded by Australian officials while fishing illegally in Australian waters, and members of Bario Enterprises were charged under the Fisheries Management Act 1991. During the trial it was established that Lawler and Penrose, while still having a substantial interest in the vessel, had no knowledge of and no interest in the illegal fishing expedition. The vessel was nevertheless declared forfeit in terms of section 106 of the Act. Lawler and Penrose applied for writs of prohibition and

(continued on next page ...)

concerned the Fisheries Management Act 1991, which (in the interpretation given it by the courts) permits the forfeiture of property belonging to a person other than the convicted offender. The majority emphasized that the Commonwealth's power to regulate fishing was broad enough (and the public interest served by fishing regulation clear enough) to allow fishing vessels used in illegal fishing to be declared forfeit, even if they belonged to innocent third parties. This power of forfeiture is authorized by section 51(x) of the Constitution, and forfeiture is therefore structurally distinguished from compulsory acquisition in terms of section 51(xxxi) of the Constitution. Consequently, forfeiture is one of the exclusions for which the just terms guarantee in section 51(xxxi)[80] does not apply at all—in South African terminology it would be an example of regulatory deprivation and not expropriation.

Even when forfeiture serves a legitimate regulatory purpose and is distinguished from compulsory acquisition of property, the question remains whether certain forfeitures could be treated as compulsory acquisition despite their statutory designation, because (in terms of some kind of proportionality test) they exceed the limits of fairness and reasonableness. The Australian courts have struggled with the question whether regulatory deprivation can be treated as compulsory acquisition when it has disproportionately burdensome effects on a property owner, even though the intention of the state was not acquisitive. The Court did not deal with the question in *Lawler* but generally seems to lean towards a conceptual approach to expropriation, avoiding substantive review of the effects of forfeiture and reducing the likelihood that regulatory forfeiture would be treated as compulsory acquisition on the basis of a proportionality test.

5.3.5 Civil forfeiture treated as deprivation, with judicial deference

The US Supreme Court has generally treated civil forfeiture as an exercise of the police power and applied a low level of scrutiny when reviewing it. The Court

---

(... from previous page)
certiorari on the ground that, in so far as section 106 of the Act authorized the forfeiture of property belonging to innocent third parties, it was invalid in that it contravened the property guarantee in section 51(xxxi) of the Australian Commonwealth Constitution. For a discussion of the Australian property clause and the case, see AJ van der Walt *Constitutional property clauses: A comparative analysis* (1999) 39–73, especially at 42–45; and see AJ van der Walt 'Civil forfeiture of instrumentalities and proceeds of crime and the constitutional property clause' (2000) 16 *SAJHR* 1–45 at 22–24 for more detail.

[80]The notion that property can be regulated and compulsorily acquired under different 'heads of power' in the Australian Constitution is important in understanding the case law; see further 5.7.3 below, and compare AJ van der Walt *Constitutional property clauses: A comparative analysis* (1999) 48–58. The Constitution does not contain a classic bill of rights or property clause; although section 51(xxxi) guarantees 'just terms' or compensation and is treated as a property clause, several other subsections in section 51 also allow compulsory acquisition and other limitations of property, but then without a compensation guarantee. See AJ van der Walt *Constitutional property clauses: A comparative analysis* (1999) 39–46.

confirmed the constitutionality of civil forfeiture in *Calero-Toledo v Pearson Yacht Leasing Company*,[81] holding that the forfeiture of an innocent owner's property was justified by the public interest in preventing further illicit use of the property.[82] A limited exception was left open for innocent owners, but US courts have generally been reluctant to accept the innocent-owner defence.[83] Some courts developed their own methods to mitigate the effects of the relation-back doctrine,[84] such as distinguishing strictly between mandatory and permissive forfeiture statutes and giving a broad interpretation to the innocent-owner defence when it is available.[85] In *United States v Halper*[86] the Supreme Court signalled its willingness to look at the effect of a

---

[81] 416 US 663 (1974). The case concerned the constitutional validity of a Puerto Rico civil forfeiture statute, in terms of which the authorities seized and forfeited a yacht after finding a single marijuana cigarette on the vessel. The yacht was leased to two Puerto Rican citizens by Pearson Yacht Leasing Co, who only became aware of the forfeiture when it tried to recover possession after the lessees defaulted on the rental contract. See further with regard to US law on civil forfeiture LW Levy *A license to steal: The forfeiture of property* (1996); AD Ronner 'Prometheus unbound: Accepting a mythless concept of civil in rem forfeiture with double jeopardy protection' (1996) 44 *Buffalo LR* 655–776; MP Harrington 'Rethinking *in rem*: The Supreme Court's new (and misguided) approach to civil forfeiture' (1994) 12 *Yale Law & Pol Rev* 281–353; JR Maxeiner 'Bane of American forfeiture law—Banished at last?' (1977) 62 *Cornell LR* 768–902; GR Strafer 'Civil forfeitures: Protecting the innocent owner' (1985) 37 *Univ Florida LR* 841–861; M Goldsmith & MJ Lindeman 'Asset forfeiture and third party rights: The need for further law reform' (1989) 39 *Duke LJ* 1254–1301; MA Jankowski 'Tempering the relation-back doctrine: A more reasonable approach to civil forfeiture in drug cases' (1990) 76 *Vir LR* 165–195; LA Kasten 'Extending constitutional protection to civil forfeitures that exceed rough remedial compensation' (1991) 60 *George Wash LR* 194–244; DG Saltzburg 'Real property forfeitures as a weapon in the government's war on drugs: A failure to protect innocent ownership rights' (1992) 72 *Boston Univ LR* 217–242; L Smith '*In rem* forfeiture proceedings and extraterritorial jurisdiction' (1996) 45 *Int & Comp LQ* 902–909; MM Jochner 'The Supreme Court turns back the clock on civil forfeiture in *Bennis*' (1997) 85 *Ill Bar J* 314–332.

[82] *Calero-Toledo v Pearson Yacht Leasing Company* 416 US 663 (1974) at 684; see further *United States v United States Coin & Currency* 401 US 715 (1971) at 719–720.

[83] Public outcry prompted the Justice Department to introduce an innocent-owner defence in the Anti-Drug Abuse Act of 1988, but even this defence does not provide much protection for innocent third parties with an interest in property tainted by illegal use. See AJ van der Walt 'Civil forfeiture of instrumentalities and proceeds of crime and the constitutional property clause' (2000) 16 *SAJHR* 1–45 at 14–15 for more detail.

[84] Which entails that property is tainted back to the moment when the crime was committed, whereas criminal forfeiture usually affects only the property still in the hands of the convicted criminal.

[85] See AJ van der Walt 'Civil forfeiture of instrumentalities and proceeds of crime and the constitutional property clause' (2000) 16 *SAJHR* 1–45 at 14–15 for more detail.

[86] 490 US 435 (1989). The manager of a medical service company was convicted on a number of counts of filing false Medicare reimbursement claims amounting to an overpayment of $585 and was sentenced to two years imprisonment and a $5,000 fine. In addition, the government brought civil action against him in terms of the Civil False Claims Act, claiming $130,000. The Supreme Court held that the question whether a civil sanction amounts to (additional) punishment depends on the effect of the civil remedy, and not merely on the interpretation of the terminology used in the relevant statute or on the civil classification of the action. The conclusion was that a fine of more than $130,000 was so far removed from the actual damage caused by the defendant that the sanction indeed intended to punish, despite the ostensible compensatory nature of the action.

civil remedy when deciding on its validity; and in *Austin v United States*[87] the Court indicated that there were limits to the government's powers to sanction civil forfeiture through legislation, even in the struggle against organized crime, by holding that the prohibition against excessive fines in the Eighth Amendment applied to disproportionate civil forfeiture proceedings. In this case, the Court significantly abandoned all reliance on the outdated personification or guilty-property fiction and held that civil forfeiture powers rested on the notion that the owner was negligent in allowing his property to be misused and that he is properly punished for his negligence.[88] The Court insisted that civil forfeiture was at least in part punishment and that a proportionality test is therefore a suitable instrument to help decide whether a civil forfeiture is justified and reasonable under the circumstances of the case.[89] In US constitutional property law this means that excessive or disproportionate forfeiture could in principle be treated as regulatory taking or expropriation.[90]

However, in later cases the Supreme Court confirmed the constitutional justification of civil forfeiture, regardless of its effect on an innocent person. In *United States v Ursery*[91] the Supreme Court held that civil forfeiture is neither punishment nor criminal for purposes of the Double Jeopardy Clause, thereby re-opening the door for civil forfeitures being used parallel with criminal prosecutions and criminal punishment. In *Bennis v Michigan*[92] the Court reaffirmed its government-friendly attitude and reversed the earlier tendency to subject civil forfeiture to substantive, proportionality-type scrutiny of purposes, means and effects. The focus of forfeiture jurisprudence in the US was always firmly on due process considerations, and the Court's attitude in the *Ursery* and *Bennis* cases seemed to be that forfeiture that satisfies the due process requirement of the Fourteenth Amendment and therefore involves a lawful exercise of 'governmental authority other than the power of eminent domain' cannot be attacked as a violation of the Takings Clause in the Fifth Amendment. Subsequent adoption of the Civil Asset Forfeiture Reform Act in 2000 was intended to bring about some reforms in the civil forfeiture process, especially as far as due process was

---

[87] 509 US 602 (1993).

[88] 509 US 602 at 615 (1993). This decision moved away from the *in rem* focus traditionally associated with civil forfeiture by placing the focus on the (vicarious or strict) responsibility and liability of the property owner.

[89] See further *United States v James Daniel Good Real Property* 114 S Ct 492 (1993).

[90] See 5.4 below on constructive expropriation for details.

[91] 518 US 267 (1996).

[92] 516 US 442 (1996). Mr Bennis used the family car to solicit a prostitute in a Detroit suburb and was arrested and convicted for gross indecency for performing a sex act with the prostitute in the car. In addition, the state subsequently sued both Mr and Mrs Bennis in a civil action for forfeiture of the car under a state law that allows forfeiture of property used in a manner constituting a nuisance. The vehicle was declared a nuisance and forfeited. On appeal, the Supreme Court distinguished and implicitly repudiated the *Halper* and *Austin* principles, arguing that in common law the owner is strictly liable for wrongful use of his property, so that innocence plays no role in the justification of the forfeiture. See D Gupta 'Republic of South Africa's Prevention of Organised Crime Act: A comparative bill of rights analysis' (2002) 37 *Harv Civ Rights–Civ Lib LR* 159–183 at 169.

concerned, but some commentators think that these reforms will not make much difference in practice.[93]

The forfeiture cases decided by the European Court of Human Rights in terms of the European Convention on Human Rights and Fundamental Freedoms 1950 point in the same direction as the US cases.[94] Although the Strasbourg Court has not been able to provide a clear answer to the general question whether it is possible to treat regulatory forfeiture as expropriation simply because of its disproportionately burdensome effect, a useful body of case law with regard to seizure and confiscation of private property involved in criminal activity has developed around the property guarantee in article 1 of the First Protocol to the European Convention.[95] In the early *Handyside* case[96] the Court decided that a temporary or provisional seizure of property does not constitute 'deprivation of property'[97] as meant in the second rule,[98] although permanent forfeiture of property could. The Court's attitude is that the expropriation provision in the second rule applies only when someone is deprived of ownership of property and the state acquires the property, and therefore the relevant provision with regard to temporary or regulatory seizure of private property is the third rule,[99] which relates to regulatory control over the use of property (deprivation in the South African sense). Permanent forfeiture of property does deprive its owner of property as envisaged in the second rule and can constitute deprivation as meant in the article (expropriation), but in this case even permanent forfeiture and destruction was regarded as legitimate regulatory action in terms of the third rule, which authorizes the forfeiture and destruction of property deemed illicit and dangerous to the general interest.

In an important decision on forfeiture of property involved in criminal activity but belonging to an innocent third party, the *AGOSI* case,[100] the Court confirmed

---

[93]See D Gupta 'Republic of South Africa's Prevention of Organised Crime Act: A comparative bill of rights analysis' (2002) 37 *Harv Civ Rights–Civ Lib LR* 159–183; B Hadaway 'Executive privateers: A discussion on why the Civil Asset Forfeiture Reform Act will not significantly reform the practice of forfeiture' (2000) 55 *Univ Miami LR* 81–121.

[94]See for further detail F Keyser-Ringnalda 'European integration with regard to the confiscation of the proceeds of crime' (1992) 17 *Eur LR* 499–515.

[95]See AJ van der Walt 'Civil forfeiture of instrumentalities and proceeds of crime and the constitutional property clause' (2000) 16 *SAJHR* 1–45 at 24–31 for more detail.

[96]*Handyside v United Kingdom* [1976] ECHR Series A volume 24.

[97]The property clause in article 1 of the First Protocol uses the term 'deprivation' in the sense of expropriation or compulsory acquisition; see AJ van der Walt *Constitutional property clauses: A comparative analysis* (1999) 110–114 for a general discussion; compare 5.1 above.

[98]The provision dealing with expropriation or 'deprivation' of property in the second sentence of paragraph one of article 1 of the First Protocol is known as 'the second rule'.

[99]The provision dealing with regulatory control over the use of property in the third paragraph of article 1 of the First Protocol is known as the 'third rule'.

[100]*Allgemeine Gold- und Silberscheideanstalt AG v United Kingdom* [1987] ECHR Series A vol 108. The case concerned the confiscation of contraband in terms of the British Customs and Excise Act 1952. AGOSI, a German company, sold South African gold coins to a British citizen. Subsequently,
(continued on next page ...)

that forfeiture was not governed by the deprivation (expropriation) provision in the second rule, but by the regulation provision in the third rule, which recognizes the right of a member state 'to enforce such laws as it deems necessary to control the use of property ... in accordance with the general interest'. According to the established jurisprudence of the Court, regulatory interferences with the peaceful enjoyment of possessions will be valid and legitimate provided they are implemented in terms of valid law and there is 'a reasonable relationship of proportionality between the means employed and the aim sought to be realised'. Member states enjoy a 'wide margin of appreciation' in determining the means of enforcement of these regulatory provisions and ascertaining 'whether the consequences of enforcement are justified in the general interest for the purpose of achieving the object of the law in question', but the Court has the duty and the power to 'determine whether a fair balance has been struck between the demands of the general interest and the interest of the individual or individuals concerned'.[101] Although there is a trend in the practice of member states to take the behaviour of the owner of smuggled goods into account when deciding whether the goods should be forfeited, different standards are used and there is no common practice. Accordingly, forfeiture of innocent owners' property would be acceptable if a member state has struck a fair balance between state interests and the interests of the affected individual. The innocence or the degree of fault or care taken by the innocent owner is no more than one factor to be taken into account when deciding whether a fair balance has indeed been struck.[102]

(... from previous page)
AGOSI found out that the purchaser had dishonoured the cheque with which he had paid for the coins, and also that he had attempted to smuggle the coins into the UK in contravention of customs laws. The customs authorities seized the coins, which still belonged to AGOSI in terms of the contract of sale. Despite representations from AGOSI's lawyers, the British Commissioners of Customs and Excise refused to restore the coins to their lawful owner, and AGOSI lodged a complaint with the Commission in Strasbourg, claiming that the forfeiture of the coins and the refusal of the Commissioners of Customs and Excise to exercise their discretion to return the coins constituted a breach of the property guarantee in article 1 of the First Protocol to the Convention. The applicants did not complain of the original seizure of the coins by the customs authorities; their grievance was directed at the subsequent forfeiture of the coins and the refusal to restore them, despite the fact that AGOSI (the owner) was innocent and unaware of the purchaser's intention or attempt to smuggle the coins into the UK. See JL Pretorius & HA Strydom 'The constitutionality of civil forfeiture' (1998) 13 *SA Public Law* 385–422 at 410–413 for a discussion in view of the comparable South African provisions, and compare AJ van der Walt 'Civil forfeiture of instrumentalities and proceeds of crime and the constitutional property clause' (2000) 16 *SAJHR* 1–45 at 26–28.

[101] *Allgemeine Gold- und Silberscheideanstalt AG v United Kingdom* [1987] ECHR Series A vol 108 par [52] at 18. This test was established and worked out in earlier decisions of the Court such as *Sporrong & Lönnroth v Sweden* [1982] 5 EHRR 35 par [73] at 28; *James v United Kingdom* [1986] 8 EHRR 123 par [50] at 34.
[102] *Allgemeine Gold- und Silberscheideanstalt AG v United Kingdom* [1987] ECHR Series A vol 108 par [54] at 19.

The *AGOSI* decision is based on a fairly narrow procedural approach which resembles the decisions of the US Supreme Court in *Bennis* and the Australian Court in *Lawler*. Despite the Strasbourg Court's avowed use of a proportionality test in evaluating regulatory deprivation of property, the member states are allowed a wide discretion ('margin of appreciation') in deciding what is fair and what is not, and the Court is obviously willing to accept that a fair balance has been struck if the affected individual property owner can take the decision to confiscate or forfeit property on judicial review in terms of municipal law, without much concern for the level of scrutiny that will apply in such a review. Furthermore, given the Court's tendency to restrict the applicability of the deprivation provision in the second rule to instances where the state actually acquired ownership of the property, there does not seem to be much prospect that a disproportionate, excessive or unfair forfeiture of private property would be treated as deprivation (expropriation) as meant in the Protocol. In *Air Canada v United Kingdom*[103] the Court confirmed that seizure and subsequent release of property subject to payment of a sum of money was governed by the regulatory provision in the third rule, as it was 'a measure taken in furtherance of a policy of seeking to prevent carriers from bringing *inter alia* prohibited drugs into the United Kingdom'.[104] Bearing in mind the margin of appreciation given to member states in deciding what is suitable and necessary for the promotion of a regulatory purpose, as well as the size of the consignment of cannabis found on the plane and the importance of the regulatory aim of the legislation, namely to prevent the importation of prohibited drugs into the UK, the majority of the Court held that the requirement to pay the fine was not disproportionate to the aim.

A decision of the European Court that could possibly point the other way is *Raimondo v Italy*.[105] The Court again decided that seizure and confiscation had to be

---

[103] [1995] 20 EHRR 150. After having issued several warnings to Air Canada about apparently lax controls that allowed staff members to smuggle large quantities of illegal drugs into the UK on the airline's aircraft, UK custom officials found a large consignment of cannabis resin on board an airliner owned and operated by Air Canada, and seized the aircraft as liable to forfeiture in terms of the Customs and Excise Management Act 1979. The aircraft was returned to its owner upon payment of $50,000 under circumstances that indicated that the customs authority's intention never was to actually forfeit the aircraft, but rather to use its confiscation powers to enforce payment of the fine. Air Canada accordingly complained that the confiscation amounted to a contravention of the property clause in article 1 of the First Protocol.

[104] [1995] 20 EHRR 150 par [34] at 172.

[105] [1994] 18 EHRR 237. The applicant was arrested, investigated and subjected to house arrest in 1985 on charges relating to his alleged association with a Mafia-type organisation. Some of his movable and immovable property was confiscated as a 'preventive measure' in terms of laws intended to prevent the use of property for illegal purposes. The Italian courts acquitted the applicant of all charges against him and annulled the special supervision order and confiscation orders obtained against him, and eventually all his property was returned to him. However, some properties were only returned to him more than four years after the annulment. The most important characteristic of confiscation under these laws is that the use of the property is merely controlled and restricted temporarily, and the property is not acquired by the state. Property of persons

(continued on next page ...)

judged in terms of the regulation provision in the third rule, and that the seizure and confiscation in this case were implemented in terms of a valid law and struck a fair balance between the individual's property interest and the state's purpose of effectively combating organized crime. However, part of the confiscated property was only returned to the complainant after four years and the Court held that this delay in returning the property constituted interference with the applicant's right to peaceful enjoyment of his possessions that was not provided for by law, not necessary to control the use of property in accordance with the general interest, and therefore in conflict with the property guarantee in the Convention. The Italian government was ordered to pay compensation for the loss suffered by the applicant, but it is not clear whether the compensation was awarded as damages following upon invalid regulatory action or as compensation for constructive expropriation.

5.3.6 Conclusions

In conclusion it can be said that civil forfeiture of property belonging to innocent owners is generally treated as deprivation and not as expropriation: as long as the forfeiture is authorized and governed by general law and not procedurally unfair, courts defer to the decision of the legislature about what is necessary in the fight against crime or the prevention of public harm. Apart from one or two general suggestions that extremely unfair or disproportionate forfeiture of innocent owners' property could be treated as regulatory or constructive expropriation, there is no clear authority for regarding or treating forfeiture as expropriation in any situation. The existing case law suggests that the same approach will be followed in South African law, although the authority is not clear or self-evident on this point. Accordingly, the main test for forfeiture laws and orders will be whether civil forfeiture in terms of these laws constitutes arbitrary deprivation as set out in the Constitutional Court's *FNB* decision,[106] particularly when it is procedurally unfair, excessive, or involves the property of innocent owners and third parties. In view of the *FNB*

(... from previous page)

presenting a danger for security and public morality can be affected by such a confiscation, without that person necessarily having been convicted of a criminal offence, since the idea is not to penalize criminal acts but to prevent future danger to society. The Italian courts have decided in the past that these preventive confiscations do not offend the Italian Constitution, particularly since the protected rights in the Constitution are not absolute, and because the preventive confiscation of property at the disposal of people affected by the laws in question is not transferred to the state by the confiscation order. At 241–244 paras [16]–[20], the Court refers to a comprehensive discussion and explanation of the relevant laws and Italian case law on the subject in the earlier decision of the Court in *Guzzardi v Italy* [1980] 3 EHRR 33 paras [46]–[49].

[106] *First National Bank of SA Ltd t/a Wesbank v Commissioner, South African Revenue Service; First National Bank of SA Ltd t/a Wesbank v Minister of Finance* 2002 (4) SA 768 (CC). See AJ van der Walt 'Civil forfeiture of instrumentalities and proceeds of crime and the constitutional property clause' (2000) 16 *SAJHR* 1–45 at 35–43 for a discussion of the proportionality issues that could be raised in terms of the arbitrary deprivation test.

decision excessively burdensome or unfair forfeiture of property belonging to innocent third parties could possibly be treated as arbitrary deprivation and declared
unconstitutional. The possibility that such excessively burdensome or unfair forfeiture would be treated as constructive expropriation is remote, and depends upon the
general question whether constructive expropriation can and should be recognized
in South African law.

5.4 CONSTRUCTIVE EXPROPRIATION

5.4.1 Introduction

The idea that expropriation must necessarily involve the state acquiring something
is based on the assumption that state limitation of property always amounts to either
non-acquisitive regulatory deprivation or acquisitive expropriation, with no room
for grey areas or overlaps. However, once it is recognized that there are grey areas
between these two categories (or that they just occupy two points on a continuum)
it becomes necessary to consider the possibility that some regulatory state actions
that result in loss for the affected property owner could justify the conclusion that
compensation is required even though the state did not—and did not intend to—
acquire the property. In at least one jurisdiction—Switzerland—this possibility is
built into the property clause, which requires the state to compensate property
owners for certain losses caused by limitation that was not intended but had the
substantive effect of expropriation, even when the state did not acquire the property.
In the Swiss Constitution this middle category of limitation is referred to as 'material
expropriation'.[107] In other jurisdictions a similar middle category of constructive
expropriation is recognized in case law, where it is referred to as 'inverse condemnation', 'regulatory taking' or 'constructive expropriation', which means that the
state does not necessarily acquire property but must nevertheless compensate the
affected owner for her loss as if the property had been expropriated. The notion of
constructive expropriation in these cases is premised on the argument that, when
regulation of the use and enjoyment of property causes excessive and unfair loss for
the owner, even to the extent that the property becomes worthless, the owner
should receive compensation even though the state does not acquire the property
for public use.

The idea of constructive expropriation is usually associated with a claim for
compensation for excessive regulation, but in fact the problems that inspired it can
arise in a number of different situations. One problem situation is the case where the
imposition of a state regulation actually or effectively destroys a private property
interest, without the state acquiring the property, under circumstances where the loss
is not justified by the core police power purpose of protecting public health and

---

[107] Section 26 of the 1999 federal Constitution; see footnotes 115, 137 below and compare further
AJ van der Walt 'The property clause in the new Federal Constitution of the Swiss Confederation
1999' (2004) 15 *Stell LR* 326–332.

safety.[108] This situation must be distinguished from instances where there is no formal expropriation, but the limitation nevertheless results in the state indirectly 'acquiring' the property interest, for example when legislative or administrative action prohibits a private enterprise and simultaneously creates a state monopoly, thereby not so much destroying as practically taking over the business of existing private concerns.[109] The feature which distinguishes these cases from situations where the state merely closes down or prohibits a business as part of the police power, without creating a state monopoly,[110] is that in the former case the state does actually acquire something, at least in the form of the goodwill or the trading opportunities formerly enjoyed and exploited by the property holder.[111] Finally, both previous examples must be distinguished from cases where the limitation destroys property without the state acquiring it, but in such a way that the state derives a benefit from the action, for example when the state cancels a state debt due to a private person, thereby destroying the property interest in payment of the debt and relieving the state from having to make the payment. Although it seems obvious that a creditor has a property interest in payment of a debt,[112] there are a number of foreign cases where the position was taken that the

---

[108] The classic example is the US Supreme Court decision in *Lucas v South Carolina Coastal Council* 505 US 1003 (1992), where it was said that regulatory action that deprived an owner of all economic use of the property has the same effect as a physical invasion and is therefore a *per se* taking. However, when property is destroyed by core police power regulation to protect public health and safety (ie the continued existence or possession of the property is a threat for public health and safety), it is either impossible or very difficult to argue that the owner should be compensated; see eg *Miller v Schoene* 276 US 272 (1928), where it was considered justified to destroy trees, without compensation, to prevent them from spreading a disease. Compare footnotes 114, 119 below.

[109] For examples see *Manitoba Fisheries Ltd v The Queen* (1978) 88 DLR 3d 462 (Canada); *Government of Malaysia and Another v Selangor Pilot Association* (1977) 1 MLJ 133 (Malaysia). Compare *Saghir Ahmad v The State of Uttar Pradesh and Others* 1955 (1) SCR 707 (India), where the private concerns were not prohibited, but state competitors were exempted from controls.

[110] For example see *Hempenstall and Others v The Minister for the Environment* [1994] 2 IR 20 (Ireland). Note that the subjection of a business to controls can amount to the same thing, in that it prohibits or prevents certain people from freely engaging in the business.

[111] In Australian constitutional property case law it is said that the state does not have to acquire the property which the owner lost; all that is required is that the state should acquire some property or benefit, however small or whatever its nature, from the action that caused the owner to lose the property. If the action was undertaken in terms of a power covered by section 51(xxxi) of the Constitution the state would then be obliged to pay compensation; see eg *Georgiadis v Australian and Overseas Telecommunications Corporation* (1994) 179 CLR 297 at 305.

[112] For examples see *Peverill v Health Insurance Commission* (1991) 104 ALR 449 (FC) (Australia); *Nobrega v Attorney-General of Guyana* (1967) 10 WIR 187 (CA G) (Guyana). The most recent illustration is the decision in *In the Matter of Article 26 of The Constitution & In the Matter of the Health (Amendment) (No. 2) Bill 2004* [2005] IESC 7 of 16 Feb 2005, where the Supreme Court of Ireland confirmed that the right of patients to reclaim from the state charges unlawfully imposed upon them for medical services was a constitutionally protected property right known as a chose in action, and that a law purporting to prevent those patients from reclaiming the money by extinguishing the debt retroactively was an unconstitutional 'unjust attack' on property rights. The Irish Court therefore accepted that the person whose claim was extinguished had a property interest in it and that extinguishment of the debt constituted an expropriation of that property by the state.

cancellation of a state debt does not amount to expropriation because the state did not acquire property.[113] If a debt is recognized as property but the courts deny that cancellation of the debt amounts to expropriation they clearly assume that cancellation of the debt amounts to deprivation rather than expropriation, and they therefore do not accept the idea of constructive expropriation.

To accept that excessive or unfair regulatory deprivation could amount to and be treated as constructive expropriation does not mean that a property owner will necessarily succeed with a claim for compensation simply because of the excessive or unfair results of the regulatory action. If regulatory excess is reviewed within the framework of constructive expropriation the process will have to involve a balancing of the interests of the affected owner and the public interest in the regulatory limitation, with due regard for all the relevant circumstances. In principle the excessive results of the limitation could be justifiable and the deprivation would then be valid without compensation.[114]

---

[113] The most important examples are the two Zimbabwean decisions in *Hewlett v Minister of Finance and Another* 1982 (1) SA 490 (ZSC); *Chairman, Public Service Commission, and Others v Zimbabwe Teachers Association and Others* 1997 (1) SA 209 (ZSC).

[114] Depending on the facts and context of each case, the likelihood that regulatory excess would result in a duty to compensate should decrease when the regulatory limitation is closer to the core police power function of protecting public health and safety and increase when the limitation is further removed from that core. The US decision in *Miller v Schoene* 276 US 272 (1928) illustrates the point; see further footnote 119 below. A second consideration that should decrease the likelihood of compensation is when regulatory deprivation occurs in terms of a power that is clearly and rationally distinct from the power of eminent domain, eg the power to regulate civil disputes. The South African case of (but not the decision in) *Harksen v Lane NO* 1998 (1) SA 300 (CC) illustrates this point, as does the German *Contergan* case (again not the decision) *BVerfGE* 42, 263 [1976] and the Australian decision in *Mutual Pools & Staff Pty Limited v The Commonwealth of Australia* (1994) 179 CLR 155. A third consideration that could decrease the likelihood of compensation occurs when the problem with excessive regulation is not only the unfair effect it has for the owner, but also that it is procedurally unfair or otherwise flawed—in such a case the result of review should be that the regulatory action is invalid and not that compensation is due. German case law is particularly instructive on this point, see AJ van der Walt *Constitutional property clauses: A comparative analysis* (1999) 142–145. Finally, at least two considerations should increase the likelihood of compensation. The first is the fact that the state acquires some benefit from the process, even if it does not acquire the affected property. The Zimbabwean decision in *Hewlett v Minister of Finance and Another* 1982 (1) SA 490 (ZSC) went the other way, but the facts illustrate the point. The Australian courts developed the idea of benefit most clearly; see *Georgiadis v Australian and Overseas Telecommunications Corporation* (1994) 179 CLR 297 at 305. A second consideration in favour of compensation is that the affected owner alone (or a small group of owners) is unfairly singled out for the state action that deprives her (or them) of property. The fact that one person is required to bear the cost of state action in the public interest alone indicates that compensation could be in order, especially if compensation is approached from an efficiency point of view (see footnote 126 below). See in this regard the US decisions in *Keystone Bituminous Coal Association v DeBenedictis* 480 US 470 (1987); *Lucas v South Carolina Coastal Council* 505 US 1003 (1992) and compare footnotes 137, 140 below on Swiss law.

All three examples described above involve situations where it is usually said that there was no expropriation because the state did not acquire the property, although it is clear in at least the last two instances that the state derives some benefit from its action. These examples demonstrate the fact that the traditional, conceptually exhaustive view of the distinction between deprivation and expropriation is unrealistic. In view of these examples it becomes necessary to at least consider the possibility that there is a grey area between deprivation and expropriation, and that some limitations in this grey area might require the state to compensate the affected property owner although the state did not acquire the property involved in the narrow sense.

Limitation in the grey area between acquisitive expropriation and non-acquisitive regulatory deprivation of property includes hard cases where it is difficult to identify or classify a specific limitation, usually because it was not intended as but still amounts to or resembles expropriation because of its practical effects. In some jurisdictions this kind of limitation is treated as a special category of expropriation and compensation is required. When this kind of limitation is classified as expropriation it is usually referred to as 'inverse condemnation', 'regulatory taking', 'material expropriation' or 'constructive expropriation'. As was pointed out earlier, section 26 of the Federal Constitution of the Swiss Confederation explicitly makes provision for such a category, referred to as 'material expropriation', and requires compensation for limitations that qualify.[115] The concept of constructive expropriation, its classification and implications and the problems presented by it are discussed further below. Constructive expropriation is distinguished from formal expropriation by the fact that in the latter case the authorizing statutory provision or administrative decision formally declares the state's intention to expropriate, whereas the intention in the former case is not to expropriate but to regulate. Moreover, it is often the case with constructive expropriation that the state does not acquire the affected property or any property, or even that the state does not acquire any benefit from the limitation at all. The question is whether it is necessary and possible to recognize constructive expropriation in South African law to deal with such cases. In the following section jurisdictions where constructive expropriation is either recognized or explicitly rejected are reviewed, followed by an assessment of the need for such a category in South African law and of the chances that it would be recognized in case law.[116]

---

[115] The German term is *materielle Enteignung*. Section 26 was preceded by section 22*ter*(3) of the old Swiss Constitution, which also provided for material expropriation. See the discussion in 5.4.2 below, and compare AJ van der Walt 'The property clause in the new Federal Constitution of the Swiss Confederation 1999' (2004) 15 *Stell LR* 326–332.

[116] The rest of this section relies upon two earlier publications on this topic and resembles parts of them; see AJ van der Walt 'Compensation for excessive or unfair regulation: A comparative overview of constitutional practice relating to regulatory takings' (1999) 14 *SA Public Law* 273–331; AJ van der Walt 'Moving towards recognition of constructive expropriation?' (2002) 65 *THRHR* 459–473. See further A Gildenhuys *Onteieningsreg* (2nd ed 2001) 137–149.

5.4.2 Regulatory taking or constructive expropriation recognized

The notion of constructive expropriation originated in American case law, and US law is still the paradigmatic example of a system in which excessive regulatory deprivation of property is treated as a so-called regulatory taking or inverse condemnation.[117] According to US law, the police power allows the state to regulate and restrict the use of private property, without compensation, provided that the regulation is justified by a rational and legitimate public purpose in the narrow sense of promoting or securing public safety and health and is imposed in accordance with due process of law.[118] A regulatory law or action can be invalidated when it is imposed for an irrational or illegitimate purpose,[119] but the courts will not lightly interfere with a legislative decision to regulate the use of property in the public interest.[120] The Due Process Clause ensures fair procedure in restricting the use of property, but it functions mainly as a purely formal check on the procedure followed in imposing a restriction on the use of property, and when the health or safety of the public is at risk, the courts apply a low level of scrutiny in ensuring the legitimacy of the regulation.[121] Legitimate exercises of the police power to protect public health or safety are not

---

[117]See generally AJ van der Walt 'Compensation for excessive or unfair regulation: A comparative overview of constitutional practice relating to regulatory takings' (1999) 14 *SA Public Law* 273–331 at 280–286; AJ van der Walt *Constitutional property clauses: A comparative analysis* (1999) 427–440.

[118]Mostly public health and safety, although wider regulatory purposes have been recognized, eg town planning and zoning. Compare *Miller v Schoene* 276 US 272 (1928), where it was considered justified to destroy trees, without compensation, to prevent them from spreading a disease.

[119]In the narrow sense, exercise of the police power protects the health, safety and morals of the community; eg fire regulations (*Munn v Illinois* 94 US 113 (1876)); garbage disposal control (*Gardner v Michigan* 199 US 325 (1905)); restrictions upon liquor (*Boston Beer Co v Massachusetts* 97 US 25 (1878)) or prostitution (*L'Hote v City of New Orleans* 177 US 587 (1900)). In *Hadacheck v Sebastian* 239 US 394 (1915) the Supreme Court decided that a brickyard could be closed down without compensation because of residential development, although the brickyard was there before development took place. Compare *Northwestern Fertilizing Co v Hyde Park* 97 US 659 (1878); *Mugler v Kansas* 123 US 623 (1887); *Miller v Schoene* 276 US 272 (1928). See further chapter 4.3.

[120]In *Hawaii Housing Authority v Midkiff* 467 US 229 (1984) the Supreme Court confirmed that a regulatory law has to serve a legitimate government purpose, and that the means selected to serve that purpose must be rational, but reiterated its adherence to the post-*Lochner* tradition of judicial deference to legislative intent on matters of economic policy, indicating that it would review the legislature's judgment as to what constitutes a public use only to ensure that the public use is not 'palpably without reasonable foundation'. The *Lochner* era (referring to *Lochner v New York* 198 US 45 (1905)) started with *Allgeyer v Louisiana* 165 US 578 (1897), where the Supreme Court applied a reasonableness test to review the purpose of regulatory laws and the relationship between the legislative purpose and the means selected to promote it, and ended with *West Coast Hotel Co v Parrish* 300 US 379 (1937).

[121]See the 'new property' cases: *Goldberg v Kelly* 397 US 254 (1970); *Matthews v Eldridge* 424 US 319 (1976): once a person qualifies for social welfare, payments cannot be terminated without a hearing (purely procedural due process protection). A stricter test applies when non-economic rights (liberty, freedom of expression, political participation, privacy, equality) are threatened; see LH Tribe *American constitutional law* (2nd ed 1988) 769ff; *United States v Carolene Products Co* 304 US 144 (1938).

compensated, regardless of the damaging effect they might have on property owners.[122]

Substantive attacks on state interferences with private property are practically always based on the compensation guarantee in the Takings Clause. Taking of property is allowed for public use and against payment of just compensation. Since the Takings Clause requires compensation for 'taking' and not 'expropriation', it is possible to claim compensation even when the state does not acquire property, in other words for regulatory taking imposed to restrict the use of property for a regulatory purpose but with such damaging results that it amounts to taking of the property. Even outside the narrow sphere of using the police power to protect public health and safety the state is not expected to pay compensation for every loss caused by regulatory laws, but compensation is required as soon as a weighing of private and public interests indicates that a regulation has gone too far and that 'the public at large, rather than a single owner, must bear the burden of an exercise of state power in the public interest.'[123] One of the purposes of the Takings Clause is to prevent the state from forcing some people to bear a burden that ought to be shared by the public as a whole, and therefore deprivation of property that forces an individual person or a small group of individuals to bear a regulatory burden on behalf of society at large is illegitimate unless accompanied by just compensation. Consequently, when exercises of the police power move outside the narrow area of protecting public health and safety and into the wider sphere of general regulatory action, the damage imposed on property owners becomes relevant, even when the purpose of regulation is legitimate and it is imposed by valid law. In these cases, an exercise of the police power will require compensation in terms of the Takings Clause if it places a too heavy burden on the property owner. The police power and the power of eminent domain have therefore been portrayed as different positions on a continuum: although the state has wide-ranging police powers to regulate the use of property in the public interest, a regulation that 'goes too far' will be treated as a taking and compensation will be required.[124] Ever since this principle was recognized, the question that dominates the takings debate in US law is: when does a regulation go too far and become a (regulatory) taking that requires compensation in terms of the Takings Clause?

Initially, the Supreme Court declined the use of any set formula in deciding whether a regulation goes too far, preferring to engage in ad hoc, factual inquiries.[125]

---

[122] *Pennsylvania Coal Co v Mahon* 260 US 393 (1922) provides the principle: property may be regulated, because government could hardly go on if values incident to property could not be diminished to a certain extent through regulation without paying for every change in the law. See further *Hadacheck v Sebastian* 239 US 394 (1915).

[123] *Keystone Bituminous Coal Association v DeBenedictis* 480 US 470 (1987).

[124] The classic case in which the principle was formulated and the question stated is *Pennsylvania Coal Co v Mahon* 260 US 393 (1922).

[125] In *Penn Central Transportation Co v City of New York* 438 US 104 (1978) the Supreme Court subscribed to an open-ended, contextual approach: the question whether a regulation goes too far

(continued on next page ...)

The preference for ad hoc, context-sensitive decisions was based on the utilitarian argument that the issue should be decided on efficiency considerations: compensation should be required whenever it would promote efficient (wealth-maximizing) regulation.[126] In later cases,[127] the Supreme Court either subscribed to a stricter, rule-bound approach in which more emphasis was placed on so-called 'per se takings'[128] or restricted the case-specific and context-sensitive test to situations where regulatory action could not be identified 'categorically' as regulatory taking. *In Lucas v South Carolina Coastal Council*[129] the Supreme Court summarized three categories of *per se* takings that are always subject to compensation, without case-specific inquiry into the public interest advanced by the regulation or the effect it has on the property owner:

(... from previous page)
is investigated case by case. The decision referred to FI Michelman 'Property, utility, and fairness: Comments on the ethical foundations of "just compensation" law' (1967) 80 *Harv LR* 1165–1258 and JL Sax 'Takings and the police power' (1964) 74 *Yale LJ* 36–76. See further FI Michelman 'Possession vs. distribution in the constitutional idea of property' (1987) 72 *Iowa LR* 1319–1350 at 1338ff. Compare A Gildenhuys *Onteieningsreg* (2nd ed 2001) 137–138.

[126]FI Michelman 'Property, utility, and fairness: Comments on the ethical foundations of "just compensation" law' (1967) 80 *Harv LR* 1165–1258 argued that the inquiry should take three kinds of costs involved in taking into account: the harm to uncompensated victims of the action; the vesting or administrative cost in compensating those victims; and the demoralisation cost resulting from not compensating them. Michelman's article was cited with approval in *Penn Central Transportation Co v City of New York* 438 US 104 (1978), where the context-sensitive test was worked out by the Supreme Court.

[127]In *Loretto v Teleprompter Manhattan CATV Corp* 458 US 419 (1982) and *Lucas v South Carolina Coastal Council* 505 US 1003 (1992) the context-sensitive ad hoc approach was abandoned. A series of decisions between 1987 *(Keystone Bituminous Coal Association v DeBenedictis* 480 US 470 (1987); *Hodel v Irving* 481 US 704 (1987); *First English Evangelical Lutheran Church of Glendale v County of Los Angeles* 482 US 304 (1987); *Nollan v California Coastal Commission* 483 US 825 (1987)) and the early 1990's (especially *Lucas v South Carolina Coastal Council* 505 US 1003 (1992); *Dolan v City of Tigard* 512 US 374 (1994)) suggest that the tendency to formulate context-neutral (so-called *per se*) rules gathered momentum and became entrenched. FI Michelman 'Takings, 1987' (1988) 88 *Col LR* 1600–1629 at 1622 concluded that the Supreme Court was finding it hard to maintain the open-ended balancing approach and was moving towards a more formalized takings doctrine that relies on a larger number of 'redline' or *per se* rules. See FI Michelman 'Possession vs. distribution in the constitutional idea of property' (1987) 72 *Iowa LR* 1319–1350 at 1338–1339 for a critical comparison of the 'redline exceptions' in *Loretto* and the open-ended, ad hoc approach in *Penn Central*. JW Singer *Property law: Rules, policies, and practices* (1993) at 1185–1187 distinguishes between three positions on what he calls the 'physicalism model', with *Loretto* and *PruneYard Shopping Center v Robins* 447 US 74 (1980) on the extremes, and *Kaiser Aetna v United States* 444 US 164 (1979), *Pennell v City of San Jose* 485 US 1 (1988) and *Yee v City of Escondido* 503 US 519 (1992) in the middle.

[128]Which are identified as takings abstractly, without reference to the actual effect of the interference or the importance of the public interest for which the state action was imposed in the first place: *Loretto v Teleprompter Manhattan CATV Corp* 458 US 419 (1982).

[129]505 US 1003 (1992). Based on the *Lucas* principle of total economic loss, an inverse condemnation claim was dismissed by the US Supreme Court in *Palazzolo v Rhode Island* 533 US 606 (2001); see further DL Callies & CG Chipchase '*Palazzolo v. Rhode Island*: Ripeness and 'notice' rule clarified and statutory "background principles" narrowed' (2001) 33 *The Urban Lawyer* 907–922.

(*a*) regulation that involves permanent physical invasion or occupation of the property;[130] (*b*) regulation that destroys or denies all economically viable use of land;[131] and (*c*) regulation that destroys a core property right, such as the right to exclude others from one's property.[132] When none of the three categories of *per se* takings is present, the ad hoc, open-ended inquiry originally laid down as the baseline test for all takings questions applies,[133] and a three-factor test is used to determine whether regulation nevertheless goes too far and constitutes a taking, based on investigation into the nature of the government action involved;[134] the diminution of value that results from regulation;[135] and the extent to which regulation interferes with reasonable, investment-backed expectations of the property holder.[136]

Based on the principles and logic set out above, US law provides the paradigmatic argument in favour of recognizing constructive expropriation and the method for distinguishing between cases that require compensation and those that don't. However, US law on this topic is quite complex (it is often described as an incomprehensible muddle) and comparative use of it is difficult and fraught with dangers. Because of the age and structure of the Constitution many aspects of the jurisprudence in which the notion of regulatory taking was developed are not relevant to property clauses in more recent constitutions, and the economic efficiency framework within which some of the key developments took place is foreign to many other constitutional property contexts. For all these reasons,

---

[130] *Lucas v South Carolina Coastal Council* 505 US 1003 (1992), referring to *Loretto v Teleprompter Manhattan CATV Corp* 458 US 419 (1982). This category of permanent physical invasions is construed narrowly by the Supreme Court, although there are indications in *Nollan v California Coastal Commission* 483 US 825 (1987); *Dolan v City of Tigard* 512 US 374 (1994) that this doctrine may be expanded. See further *PruneYard Shopping Center v Robins* 447 US 74 (1980); *Yee v City of Escondido* 503 US 519 (1992).

[131] *Lucas v South Carolina Coastal Council* 505 US 1003 (1992). The Court switched from the original phrase 'economically viable use' in *Agins v City of Tiburon* 447 US 255 (1980) to the potentially much wider 'economically beneficial use'; 'economically beneficial or productive use'; and 'economically valuable use'.

[132] *Hodel v Irving* 481 US 704 (1987); compare JW Singer *Property law: Rules, policies, and practices* (1993) at 1223.

[133] *Penn Central Transportation Co v City of New York* 438 US 104 (1978). Very few cases based on the three-factor test have succeeded in extracting compensation; see *Pennsylvania Coal Co v Mahon* 260 US 393 (1922); *Kaiser Aetna v United States* 444 US 164 (1979); *Nollan v California Coastal Commission* 483 US 825 (1987); *Dolan v City of Tigard* 512 US 374 (1994).

[134] The question is whether the action is more closely analogous to a physical invasion or a denial of core property rights than to a widespread and general regime of regulation that protects the public interest from harm: see JW Singer *Property law: Rules, policies, and practices* (1993) 1228.

[135] This aspect differs from the second category of *per se* takings only as a matter of degree (if all economic use is destroyed, it amounts to a *per se* taking; if some economic use is destroyed, it depends on the seriousness of the loss): JW Singer *Property law: Rules, policies, and practices* (1993) 1229.

[136] A regulation is more likely to be a taking if it interferes with reasonable, investment-backed expectations; less likely if it interferes with mere future possibilities and expectations not backed up by investment: Singer *Property law: Rules, policies, and practices* (1993) 1229–1230.

comparison with US law on regulatory taking is complicated, but it nevertheless still sets out the most comprehensive and authoritative set of arguments in favour of constructive expropriation.

The Swiss property clause is unique in that it makes explicit provision for compensation in cases of so-called 'material expropriation'.[137] In addition to formal expropriation, where the property is acquired by the state, regulatory limitation of property qualifies as material expropriation and requires compensation when it places such a heavy burden upon the property owner that the effect is similar to that of expropriation. Only substantive interferences with property are recognized as material expropriation—slight or small interferences have to be accepted by the property holder without compensation.[138] Whether a burden is heavy or slight is determined objectively: a regulation amounts to material expropriation and requires compensation when a property holder is deprived of an existing or foreseeable future use that is an essential entitlement of the property.[139] Secondly, in less burdensome cases a regulation can still amount to material expropriation if one owner (or a small group of owners) is unfairly expected to make an extraordinary sacrifice for the sake of

---

[137]Section 26(3) of the new Constitution of the Swiss Confederation 1999, section 22*ter*(3) of the old Swiss Constitution (1874, but section 22*ter* was inserted only in 1969). See AJ van der Walt 'The property clause in the new Federal Constitution of the Swiss Confederation 1999' (2004) 15 *Stell LR* 326–332, and compare generally AJ van der Walt 'Compensation for excessive or unfair regulation: A comparative overview of constitutional practice relating to regulatory takings' (1999) 14 *SA Public Law* 273–331 at 291–293; AJ van der Walt *Constitutional property clauses: A comparative analysis* (1999) 369–372. It is unlikely that the notion of constructive expropriation derives from Swiss law, as is stated by A Gildenhuys *Onteieningsreg* (2nd ed 2001) 139 with reference to J Murphy 'Interpreting the property clause in the Constitution Act of 1993' (1995) 10 *SA Public Law* 107–130 at 120. Apart from the fact that the idea was already alive in US law by 1922 (see footnote 12 above), it was already mooted and applied by the German civil courts in the 1950s, although the constitutional courts later rejected it (see footnote 159 below), and it was always used in French law (see footnote 151 below). The term 'material expropriation' is unique to Swiss law, but it is possible that Swiss law was influenced by either German or (more likely) French practice. Section 22*ter* was only inserted in the old Swiss Constitution (1874) in 1969, which is too late for it to have influenced early German case law on constructive expropriation. It is much more likely that German law influenced Swiss law initially, although the German Federal Constitutional Court eventually abandoned the idea of constructive expropriation, as is explained below.

[138]*BGE* 110 Ib 340 *(Staat Bern case)* [1984]. Compare the similarities with the French situation discussed in this section below.

[139]For material expropriation in this category the following requirements are laid down by the Swiss Federal Court: only lawful existing uses qualify; future uses have to be foreseeable and probable, not just vague future hopes or possibilities; the legal and economic situation must allow the property holder reasonably to have expected to exploit that use in the near future, the crucial moment for testing the foreseeability and probability of a future use being the moment when the regulation became effective. If the planning situation makes it difficult or improbable that the use will be realized (for example if a rezoning is required) it is not a probable future use which is protected. See *BGE* 101 Ia 224 *(Würth case)* [1975]; *BGE* 105 Ia 330 *(Meier case)* [1979]; *BGE* 106 Ib 336 *(Einwohnergemeinde Aarberg case)* [1980]; *BGE* 110 Ib 340 *(Staat Bern case)* [1984].

society at large, and if it would be inequitable not to compensate her for it.[140] Regulatory interference of this nature does not have to be as extensive or burdensome as is required for the first category, but it must still be so intense that it justifies compensation. Awards of compensation for this category occur very seldom.

Although the Spanish property clause resembles the German provision, an important difference is that the Spanish provision does not require expropriation laws to state the amount or the method of computation of compensation explicitly, and consequently the main reason why the German Federal Constitutional Court has refused to acknowledge that compensation can be required for constructive expropriation does not exist in Spanish law.[141] The Spanish courts do not subscribe to the clear distinction between formal expropriation and regulatory limitation of property that is relied on in the jurisprudence of the German Federal Constitutional Court either, and consequently the Spanish courts were able to recognize that regulatory limitation that places an extraordinarily heavy burden on a property owner is transformed into expropriation, and compensation is required for it.[142]

Although the property clause in the French Declaration of the Rights of Man and the Citizen 1789 refers only to 'deprivation', this term is understood to refer to expropriation rather than regulatory limitation of property.[143] The property guarantee requires that deprivation should be authorized by valid law, justified by public necessity, accompanied by just compensation, and it should include safeguards to minimize the interference it causes.[144] Not all interferences with property are regarded as deprivation: a regulatory interference qualifies as deprivation that requires compensation when the interference is significant, and it is regarded as

---

[140] *BGE* 101 Ia 224 (*Würth* case) [1975]; *BGE* 105 Ia 330 (*Meier* case) [1979]; *BGE* 106 Ib 336 (*Einwohnergemeinde Aarberg* case) [1980]; *BGE* 110 Ib 340 (*Staat Bern* case) [1984]. The *Sonderopfertheorie* is also followed, to a certain extent, in the US in the sense that the effect of regulation on a single owner is important in identifying a regulatory taking. See footnotes 114, 137 above.

[141] The German situation is discussed in 5.4.3 below. Compare article 14.3 of the German Basic Law with article 33.3 of the Spanish Constitution; and see M Ibler 'Der Grundrechtsschutz in der spanischen Verfassung am Beispiele des Eigentumsschutz' (1999) 54 *Juristen-Zeitung* 287–294 at 294. On the Spanish clause in general see AJ van der Walt 'Compensation for excessive or unfair regulation: A comparative overview of constitutional practice relating to regulatory takings' (1999) 14 *SA Public Law* 273–331 at 293–294.

[142] J Barnés 'El Derecho de propiedad en la Constitución Española de 1978' in J Barnés (ed) *Propiedad, expropiación, y responsabilidad: La garantía indemnizatoria en el derecho Europeo y comparado* (1995) 25–66 at 29, 44; M Ibler 'Der Grundrechtsschutz in der spanischen Verfassung am Beispiele des Eigentumsschutz' (1999) 54 *Juristen-Zeitung* 287–294 at 294. Although the Spanish property clause leaves scope for regulatory limitation of property, the intention is also to develop constitutional law in the direction of European law: article 10.2 of the Constitution provides that constitutional rights must be protected in accordance with international conventions ratified by Spain.

[143] See on the French situation generally AJ van der Walt 'Compensation for excessive or unfair regulation: A comparative overview of constitutional practice relating to regulatory takings' (1999) 14 *SA Public Law* 273–331 at 295–299.

[144] *Nationalizations* case (Constitutional Court decision no 81–132 DC of 16 January 1982); *TGV Nord* case (Constitutional Court decision no 89–256 DC of 25 July 1989).

significant when it deprives the property holder of the right itself or of all enjoyment of the right, or if it undermines the meaning of the right, or empties the right of all its content, or when it affects not only the property itself but the persons occupying the property in a significant manner, for instance by threatening their right to liberty as well as their property right.[145]

The principle is illustrated nicely by the constitutional practice with regard to public utility easements. Traditionally,[146] to enable the state to install and maintain public services infrastructure such as telegraph wires and electric cables, restrictions imposed on private property by a public utility easement were not regarded as deprivation for purposes of the property guarantee and compensation was not required unless the law in question specifically provides for compensation. The Constitutional Court's view is that the property guarantee does not prevent the creation of an administrative easement for a public utility, and as long as the easement does not impose more than a bearable burden or 'a tolerable inconvenience', it is not regarded as deprivation of property as meant in the Declaration.[147] The courts have applied the same principle in the field of town planning[148] and with regard to other socio-economic regulatory legislation.[149] In terms of the constitutional provision compensation is therefore only available if the limitation imposed is so significant that it cannot be tolerated without compensation.

Apart from constitutional law, property owners can also claim compensation for loss caused by regulatory action in administrative law.[150] In certain cases compensa-

---

[145]J Bell *French constitutional law* (1994) at 183; F Colly 'Le Conseil Constitutionnel et le droit de propriété' (1988) 104 *Revue du Droit Public* 135–197 at 164–167, 181–185; *Eiffel Tower Amendment* case (Constitutional Court decision 85–198 DC of 13 December 1985). Note the similarities with the Swiss situation discussed in this section above.

[146]This tradition originated in administrative, not constitutional, law: J Bell *French constitutional law* (1994) at 182; F Colly 'Le Conseil Constitutionnel et le droit de propriété' (1988) *Revue du Droit Public* 135–197 at 164–167.

[147]The *Eiffel Tower Amendment* case (Constitutional Court decision 85–198 DC of 13 December 1985). The case dealt with administrative easements, and more specifically the installation of radio and transmitting equipment on the Eiffel Tower, which is private property belonging to the city of Paris. The facts in this case are remarkably similar to those in the US case of *Loretto v Teleprompter Manhattan CATV Corp* 458 US 419 (1982).

[148]See J Bell *French constitutional law* (1994) at 183–184 for a brief discussion.

[149]In the *Democratization in the Public Sector* case (Constitutional Court decision 83–162 of 19–20 July 1983) it was decided that a statute requiring certain firms to have worker-directors was not a significant imposition on the rights of private shareholders, but the requirement that a minister could appoint directors as representatives for private shareholders was a significant imposition because it potentially interfered with their power to have a say in the management of the company. This case shows interesting similarities with the decision of the German Federal Constitutional Court in the *Mitbestimmung* case *BVerfGE* 50, 290 [1979].

[150]Because of the very strict division between French private and public law, compensation will never be available on the basis of private law (contract or delict) when the state is involved, and consequently the compensation claim will always be based either on the Constitution (deprivation

(continued on next page ...)

tion is required for damage caused by state action on the basis of the equality principle: direct, clear, and serious loss resulting from the installation or maintenance of
public works can be compensated even when it is not deprivation for which the
Constitution requires compensation. In this case compensation is based on the administrative law principle of equality before public burdens[151] and not on the constitutional property clause (or on private law). Compensation is also required on the basis
of administrative law for various losses caused by unilateral changes to administrative
contracts.[152] The most important example of this kind of compensation claim is based

---

(... from previous page)
of private property) or on administrative law (equalization compensation for loss caused by unilateral changes in an administrative contract or compensation for loss caused by other state action).
Note the similarities between this administrative compensation and the equalization payment
recognized by German courts (as discussed below). The difference between French and German
law in this regard is that both expropriatory compensation (for a deprivation caused by an unbear-
able burden) and administrative compensation (for unequal burdening) can be available in French
law; in German law only equalization payment (similar to the French administrative compensation)
is possible. Compare chapter 4.2.3 footnotes 50–52 and accompanying text.

[151] See J Bell *French constitutional law* (1994) at 184. Compare A Gildenhuys *Onteieningsreg* (2nd ed
2001) 139, who correctly points out the resulting similarities between current German and French
law. However, it is important to also see the differences. German and French law are similar in that
both allow a non-constitutional claim for compensation (in German law called an equalization
payment and developed in the administrative courts, see the discussion in 5.4.3 below; in French
law called administrative compensation and based on the principle of equality before state burdens).
On the other hand, German law is different from French law, which resembles Swiss and Spanish
(and of course US) law in also allowing another kind of constitutional claim for compensation
based on the idea of constructive or material expropriation. German law does not allow this possibility at all; see the discussion in 5.4.3 below. Swiss and Spanish law are discussed in this section
above. See further footnote 157 below; compare chapter 4.2.3 footnote 50 and accompanying text.

[152] The state is allowed to amend contracts with private parties unilaterally when the public interest
demands it, but the state must compensate the private party for loss resulting from the amendment
(eg when the administration concludes a contract with an investor and then unilaterally imposes
additional burdens on the contracting party because of requirements of the public interest). The
'principe d'équation financière' relates to the one-sided character of administrative contracts and
public authorities' power (particularly in concessions) to redefine the nature of the service to be
performed or the work to be done, in order to meet the changing needs of the public interest, and
thereby imposing additional expenses or cost on the private contractor: LN Brown & JS Bell *French
administrative law* (4th ed 1993) at 196–197. This power to redefine the nature of the service or work
is not reserved for the public authority by the contract, but derives from administrative law. To
protect the private contractor, the law provides for a claim for compensation to preserve the balance
of the contract ('le principe d'équation financière'). The compensation claim is meant as indemnity
for the unilateral disturbance of the balance of the contract. An example is the *Tramways* case (1910),
where the state made a franchise agreement with a transport company that operated the public
transport system in Marseilles, and subsequently insisted on timetable changes to accommodate
public order considerations, thereby causing greater expenditure for the operating company. The
Conseil d'Etat upheld the amendment of the agreement, but required the public authority to
compensate for the extra expenditure. The theory of 'fait du prince' is not necessarily concerned
with public service, but covers the situation where the economic basis of a contract is affected by
(continued on next page ...)

on the doctrine that the 'balance of the contract' was disturbed by unilateral cancellation or amendment, and has to be restored.

In summary it can be said that constructive expropriation is recognized and
compensated in US, Swiss, Spanish and French law. Swiss law is unique in that the
property clause itself guarantees compensation for 'material expropriation'; the others
developed the idea in case law. In each case constructive expropriation is characterized by the fact that regulatory limitation imposed on property causes such an excessive or unfair burden on the property owner that the effect is comparable to
expropriation, and therefore compensation is required as if the property were in fact
expropriated. Important considerations in characterizing a regulatory limitation as
constructive expropriation include the following: that the property is effectively if not
formally acquired by the state; that the state acquires some benefit from the destruction of the property; or that one property owner alone (or a small group of owners)
is expected to bear the burden of police power regulation for the public interest.

5.4.3 Constructive expropriation not recognized

German law is the paradigmatic example of a jurisdiction that refuses to recognize
constructive expropriation.[153] The property clause in article 14 of the German Basic
Law 1949 makes provision for two kinds of legitimate state interference with private
property: regulation of property through legislative provisions which determine the
content and the limits of property rights; and expropriation of private property for a
public purpose and against payment of compensation. Through regulation, the legislature can determine the content and limits of individual property rights by imposing
restrictions on the exercise of individual property rights. Regulatory limitations must
be authorized by valid legislation and must also satisfy the proportionality principle.[154]

(... *from previous page*)
an act of the administration (eg other public powers). If the exercise of public powers upsets the
balance of an administrative contract, and unless the act assumed the form of general legislation
affecting all citizens equally, the private contractor will be entitled to a monetary indemnity or to
increase charges to the consumer. (LN Brown & JS Bell *French administrative law* (4th ed 1993) 198
mention the example of the *Ville de Paris* case (1936).) This theory of 'fait du prince' is in turn
distinguished from the theory of 'force majeuere', which applies to the termination of contracts
(without penalties for the private operator) in cases of unforeseen and unforeseeable occurrences
such as Acts of God; and from the theory of 'imprévision', which allows the private operator or
investor to obtain compensation when abnormal and unforeseeable changes unconnected to the
administration (eg economic crisis resulting from currency devaluations) result in substantial deterioration of the private party's position. Compare the discussion of the South African *Modderklip*
case in chapter 6.3.8 and see chapter 4.2.3 and 4.5.5.
[153] On German law see generally AJ van der Walt 'Compensation for excessive or unfair regulation:
A comparative overview of constitutional practice relating to regulatory takings' (1999) 14 *SA
Public Law* 273–331 at 286–290; AJ van der Walt *Constitutional property clauses: A comparative analysis*
(1999) 141–145.
[154] *BVerfGE* 25, 112 [1969] at 117; *BVerfGE* 50, 290 [1979] (*Mitbestimmung*) at 340; *BVerfGE* 52, 1
[1979] (*Kleingarten*) at 29.

The proportionality principle requires that an equitable balance must be established between the interests of the individual and the social interest, and to satisfy this principle regulation must be strictly necessary; suitable for the purpose it serves; and not impose burdens disproportionate to its benefits.[155] A regulatory measure that is not properly authorized or that goes too far and disturbs the equitable balance between the interests of the individual and the social interest is invalid.[156]

German constitutional law resists the notion of constructive expropriation: the fact that a regulatory limitation of property is excessive means that the action might be invalid, but cannot be used to found a compensation claim.[157] Expropriation is seen as a partial or complete acquisition of concrete individual property holdings for the realization of specific public duties, provided it complies with constitutional and statutory requirements.[158] During the 1950s and 1960s the civil courts[159] awarded expropriatory compensation when a property holder was forced by regulatory action to make an extraordinary sacrifice, thereby extending the compensation requirement for formal expropriation to non-expropriatory sacrifices imposed by excessive regulation. However, in 1981 the Federal Constitutional Court declared unambiguously that unlawful and excessive regulatory action does not satisfy the requirements for valid regulation, and therefore it is invalid, but even when excessive regulation has the same practical result as expropriation it cannot be transformed into expropriation

---

[155]The proportionality principle is applied with attention for the relative proximity between the right and personal liberty: the closer the property right is involved in securing the personal liberty of its holder, the less opportunities there are for the legislature to interfere with it; the further a specific property right is removed from the personal liberty of its holder, the easier it is to regulate it: *BVerfGE* 89, 1 [1993] (*Besitzrecht des Mieters*) (subjective right of a lessee vis-à-vis investment right of the lessor) and *BVerfGE* 50, 290 [1979] (*Mitbestimmung*) (right of employees to participate in the management of a large business concern vis-à-vis investment rights of shareholders); and see the cases on the rights of lessors and lessees of garden allotments (*Kleingarten*): *BVerfGE* 52, 1 [1979]; *BVerfGE* 87, 114 [1992]. When the social interest in the regulation of a certain kind of property is particularly great, it can be subjected to especially strict and far-reaching regulation. Land, being an indispensable and limited resource of great social import, is routinely subjected to social regulation: *BVerfGE* 21, 73 [1967] (*Grundstücksverkehrsgesetz*). Compare chapter 4.2.3.

[156]*BVerfGE* 25, 112 [1969] at 117; *BVerfGE* 50, 290 [1979] (*Mitbestimmung*) at 340; *BVerfGE* 52, 1 [1979] (*Kleingarten*) at 29. In addition, a regulation should not conflict with other constitutional principles such as equality or the protection of trust.

[157]Note the difference between the proportionality argument here and in Swiss, Spanish or French law (see footnote 151 above): in German law excessively unequal treatment (and hence lack of proportionality) can result in the regulation being invalid, whereas in Swiss, Spanish and French law it can found a claim for compensation on the basis of material or constructive expropriation. In French law it can also result in an additional claim for administrative compensation, which is again comparable to the German claim for an equalization payment discussed below.

[158]The requirements are set out in article 14.3 GG: validly authorized by or embodied in a law that specifies the compensation or its manner of computation; imposed for a public purpose; subject to payment of compensation.

[159]Which have jurisdiction in awarding and determining compensation for expropriation; see *BGHZ* 6, 270 [1952]; *BGHZ* 64, 220 [1975]; *BGHZ* 54, 384 [1970]; *BGHZ* 57, 359 [1971].

by the courts.[160] An award of expropriatory compensation for constructive expropriation is therefore impossible in German constitutional law; when someone is detrimentally affected by unlawful or excessive regulatory action, the correct route is to attack the validity of the regulation in the administrative courts and not to claim expropriatory compensation. The courts do not have the power to transform a regulatory action into an expropriation, even when it is excessive or disproportionate and unfair—when a court considers regulatory action excessive it should declare the action invalid.

In subsequent decisions it was accepted that a money award for certain kinds of excessive regulation is sometimes possible; not as compensation for expropriation, but as an equalization payment that 'softens' the impact of the burden which a regulatory measure or action places upon an individual property holder, thereby ensuring that the burden is not invalid for being excessive (in terms of the proportionality principle).[161] Equalization payment resembles private-law compensation for delictual damage and is not constitutional compensation for expropriation, and therefore recognition of this procedure is fundamentally different from expropriatory compensation for regulatory taking in US or Swiss or French law.

In Commonwealth countries, the distinction between deprivation resulting from the regulation of property in terms of the police power and expropriation in terms of the power of eminent domain is important because compensation is required for expropriation, but not for deprivation. The property clause in the Malaysian

---

[160] In the *Naßauskiesung* case *BVerfGE* 58, 300 [1981]. The most obvious requirement not met by regulatory measures is the linking clause in article 14.3.2 GG, which requires that an expropriation should be authorized by a law which provides for the form and extent of compensation. Regulatory laws do not contain such a clause and never satisfy this requirement because they obviously do not foresee payment of compensation, and thus expropriatory compensation cannot be awarded for actions under their authority. This position was confirmed in *BVerfGE* 100, 226 [1999].

[161] In a case which concerned the effect of excessive street noise resulting from the re-planning of a quiet residential street to transform it into a busy thoroughfare, the civil court decided that the planning and development authorities have several choices when attempting to keep the results of development within limits. As a first option, streets which cause excessive noise should be planned for areas where they do not affect property owners. If that is impossible, the developers should erect noise-reducing installations like walls, tunnels and so on. If that is impossible or insufficient, the developer must rely on individual property holders to insulate their properties against noise, and must provide them with the necessary funds to do so. As a last resort, when all else fails, the developer should soften the blow for the complainant by paying suitable compensation for loss of use of or damage to the property. See *BGHZ* 64, 220 [1975]. The notion of equalization payments was developed on the basis of this line of argument, mostly in the civil and administrative courts, and it was confirmed by the Federal Constitutional Court in *BVerfGE* 100, 226 [1999]. Compare the similarities between the German equalization payments and the French administrative compensation for excessive and unequal burdens discussed above: footnotes 151, 157 above; compare chapter 4.2.3 footnote 51 and accompanying text. See further the discussion of the South African *Modderklip* case in chapter 6.3.8.

Constitution is an important source of this distinction.[162] However, Commonwealth case law does not provide authority for the recognition of constructive expropriation. With regard to Malaysian case law the Privy Council confirmed that, while deprivation of private property must be in accordance with a law,[163] only those deprivations that involve the compulsory acquisition or use of property by the state need to be compensated.[164] The Privy Council recognized that a person can be deprived of property by a 'mere negative or restrictive provision', but pointed out that even deprivation that results in complete loss of the property does not constitute compulsory acquisition or use of the property. When the term 'compulsory acquisition or use' is interpreted strictly so that the state should not merely deprive the plaintiff of property but acquire or use it before compensation is required,[165] it is not possible to exact compensation for constructive expropriation.

5.4.4 Recognition of constructive expropriation uncertain

The position in the case law of the European Court of Human Rights is uncertain.[166] The phrase 'deprived of his possessions' in the second rule (the second sentence of the first paragraph of article 1 to the First Protocol) is interpreted as expropriation in

---

[162]See generally AJ van der Walt 'Compensation for excessive or unfair regulation: A comparative overview of constitutional practice relating to regulatory takings' (1999) 14 *SA Public Law* 273–331 at 306–307; AJ van der Walt *Constitutional property clauses: A comparative analysis* (1999) 271–273.

[163]As prescribed by section 13(1). Section 13 bears a close structural and terminological resemblance to the South African section 25(1)–(3). The due-process guarantee in section 13(1) ensures that deprivation (including expropriation) takes place according to law and not arbitrarily. The High Court held that section 13(1) protects private property by preventing the executive from depriving persons of their property unless such deprivation is in accordance with a properly enacted law: *S Kulasingam & Another v Commissioner of Lands, Federal Territory & Others* [1982] 1 MLJ 204.

[164]*Government of Malaysia & Another v Selangor Pilot Association* [1977] 1 MLJ 133. The case, which dealt with the situation where the distinction between 'mere' deprivation and compulsory acquisition of property is most difficult, namely where property is destroyed by state action without actually being taken over, acquired or used by the state, is often referred to in other jurisdictions. The respondents had a monopoly in the provision of pilotage services. Stronger control over pilotage services effectively prohibited the respondents from carrying on their business. The physical assets of the respondents were sold to the government, who paid for them. The respondents claimed compensation for loss of future profits and loss of goodwill, but this was denied. They then applied for a declaration that they were entitled to compensation for loss of goodwill and argued in the alternative that the Act was unconstitutional as it was in conflict with section 13 of the Constitution of Malaysia.

[165]Compare the position in Australia (see this section below), where the term 'compulsory acquisition' is interpreted in the same manner, with similar results. However, in Australia any benefit or gain by the state, however slight or insubstantial, qualifies the deprivation as an acquisition.

[166]See generally AJ van der Walt 'Compensation for excessive or unfair regulation: A comparative overview of constitutional practice relating to regulatory takings' (1999) 14 *SA Public Law* 273–331 at 299–302; AJ van der Walt *Constitutional property clauses: A comparative analysis* (1999) 111–113.

the narrow sense, that is, as acquisition of ownership.[167] The restrictive reading of the second rule created a clear and strict distinction between expropriation of property (second rule) and regulatory limitation of property (third rule). In one or two cases the clarity of this distinction was watered down[168] and the door was left open for the recognition of constructive expropriation when it was said that the Court has a duty to 'investigate behind' the effects of state regulation and ascertain whether there was effective or constructive taking of property. The uncertainty created by this statement was subsequently deepened by seemingly conflicting decisions, some of which suggested quite strongly that excessive regulatory control could be treated as deprivation that requires compensation[169] while others raised doubts about such a possibility.[170] A third group of decisions[171] confirmed the similar-looking but significantly different point that the real rather than the apparent intention of the state has to be considered when deciding whether an interference with private property amounts to deprivation. In at least one case which did not involve formal deprivation (expropri-

---

[167]This emerged from decisions where it was decided that regulatory control measures did not constitute deprivation (expropriation) of property because the applicants retained ownership of the property in question; see *Handyside v United Kingdom* [1976] ECHR Series A volume 24; *X & Y v The Netherlands* [1975] 1 DR 66; *Wiggins v The United Kingdom* [1978] 13 DR 40; *X v Austria* [1980] 17 DR 80; *Tre TraktörerAB v Sweden* [1989] ECHR Series A vol 159; *Mellacher and Others v Austria* [1989] ECHR Series A vol 169; *Gasus Dosier- und Fordertechnik GmbH v The Netherlands* [1995] ECHR Series A vol 306B.
[168] *Sporrong & Lönnroth v Sweden* [1982] 5 EHRR 35.
[169]Some of these cases offer weak support for the notion of regulatory takings: *Erkner and Hofauer v Austria* [1987] ECHR Series A vol 117 39; *Poiss v Austria* [1987] ECHR Series A vol 117 84 create the impression that the Court classified the regulatory provisions as deprivations or regulatory takings, but there was no finding on prejudice in these cases, and they merely held that the effect of the regulations was disproportionate and therefore in conflict with article 1. In *Inze v Austria* [1988] ECHR Series A vol 126 the Court held that a law which prohibited the complainant, because of illegitimacy, from inheritance of land through intestate succession amounted to a disproportionate and invalid deprivation of property, which resembles the *per se* classification of a similar law in the US decision in *Hodel v Irving* 481 US 704 (1987). However, the issue in *Inze* was that the deprivation was excessive and invalid, not whether compensation was required. There are stronger indications that some regulatory controls will be treated as regulatory deprivations that require compensation: in *Sporrong & Lönnroth v Sweden* [1982] 5 EHRR 35 the Court seemingly meant to treat regulatory control of the use of property as a deprivation that required compensation because it went too far. In *Stran Greek Refineries and Stratis Andreadis v Greece* [1995] ECHR Series A vol 301B (particularly par [63] at 85) the Court classified the cancellation of a state debt, arising from a final and binding arbitration award, as a deprivation (expropriation) rather than a regulation of property.
[170] *Tre Traktörer AB v Sweden* [1989] ECHR Series A vol 159; *Mellacher and Others v Austria* [1989] ECHR Series A vol 169.
[171] *Papamichalopoulos v Greece* [1993] ECHR Series A vol 260B; *The Holy Monasteries v Greece* [1995] ECHR Series A vol 301A. The issue in these cases was that the state actually wanted to expropriate property but disguised the action as something else, whereas the regulatory taking issue involves a situation where the state actually wants to regulate, but the effects of the regulation are much harsher than was foreseen.

ation) the Court accepted that 'deprivation' in the second rule includes regulatory measures that deprive the owner of all meaningful use of the property.[172]

The application of the proportionality test to determine whether regulatory control over the use of property establishes and maintains a proper balance between individual and public interests and the small number of individual cases mentioned in the previous paragraph create the impression that it is possible for the European Court to treat a particular regulatory limitation of property as deprivation that requires compensation, simply because it goes too far and imposes and unfair burden on an individual owner. However, this impression is not supported by unequivocal authority and the matter remains unclear.

The recognition of constructive expropriation is equally complex in Australian law.[173] Even regulatory action that involves acquisition of property will not necessarily require compensation when it is an incidental result of the state's regulatory power,[174] particularly when this is not part of the power to acquire property compulsorily in terms of section 51(xxxi) of the Commonwealth Constitution. Only section 51(xxxi) guarantees 'just terms' or compensation, while other 'heads of power' in the Constitution that authorize compulsory acquisition are not subject to the compensation guarantee. For example, a law that adjusts or resolves competing civil claims or that creates, modifies, extinguishes or transfers rights and liabilities as part of the state's general regulation of the conduct, rights and obligations of citizens in relationships or areas that need to be regulated in the common interest, is not a law with respect to the acquisition of property as meant in section 51(xxxi) of the Constitution and is

---

[172] *Fredin v Sweden* [1991] ECHR Series A vol 192 17 (regulation of permits for gravel excavation). The Court decided on the facts that the control measures in question did not take away all meaningful use of the property; consequently, they established regulatory control of the use of property and not deprivation of property. However, the implication is that a regulatory control measure that does take away all meaningful use of the property might be regarded as a deprivation of property and judged in terms of the second rule. Note the similarities between this decision and the US decision in *Lucas v South Carolina Coastal Council* 505 US 1003 (1992) and contrast it with the German decision in the *Naßauskiesung* case *BVerfGE* 58, 300 [1981].

[173] See generally AJ van der Walt 'Compensation for excessive or unfair regulation: A comparative overview of constitutional practice relating to regulatory takings' (1999) 14 *SA Public Law* 273–331 at 304–306; AJ van der Walt *Constitutional property clauses: A comparative analysis* (1999) 51–57. See A Gildenhuys *Onteieningsreg* (2nd ed 2001) 146.

[174] These acquisitions are 'otherwise reasonable and appropriate measures taken in the process of regulatory functions of the state that are unrelated to the acquisition of property', eg the power to impose and regulate the payment of taxes: *Mutual Pools & Staff Pty Limited v The Commonwealth of Australia* (1994) 179 CLR 155. A regulation may also be excluded because exercise of the authorizing power does not permit compensation or just terms, eg the forfeiture of property as a penalty upon conviction of a crime: *Re Director of Public Prosecutions; Ex Parte Lawler and Another* (1994) 179 CLR 270. In *Health Insurance Commission v Peverill* (1994) 179 CLR 226 236 the deprivation 'was effected not only by way of genuine adjustment of competing claims, rights and obligations in the common interests between parties who stand in a particular relationship but also as an element in a regulatory scheme ...'

therefore not subject to the compensation requirement.[175] Construing a compensation duty based on the constructive expropriation argument is therefore difficult if not impossible in these cases. However, it has been decided that incidental acquisition of property is only excluded from the compensation requirement as long as it is appropriate and proportionate to its purpose,[176] which might open the door for imposing the compensation requirement on disproportionate exercise of the regulatory police power in cases not authorized by section 51(xxxi).

Apart from these structural considerations, the issue of constructive expropriation under section 51(xxxi) has not been settled either. Although a few cases suggested that compensation is required when regulatory restriction on the use of land goes too far,[177] the recognition of constructive expropriation in Australian law was qualified in decisions where the High Court adopted the position that regulatory deprivation of property that does not involve some advantage or benefit for the state is excluded from the compensation requirement because there was no 'acquisition'—for an acquisition of property, the state must acquire some benefit or advantage, however slight or insubstantial.[178]

---

[175] *Mutual Pools & Staff Pty Limited v The Commonwealth of Australia* (1994) 179 CLR 155 171.

[176] *Australian Capital Television Pty Ltd and Others v The Commonwealth of Australia; The State of New South Wales v The Commonwealth of Australia and Another* (1992) 177 CLR 106 at 157–162.

[177] Above all *The Commonwealth of Australia and Another v The State of Tasmania and Others* (1983) 158 CLR 1. The case concerned federal legislation which prevented the State of Tasmania from using its land for certain purposes without the consent of the federal authority. The property acquired was described as 'the benefit of a prohibition' of certain actions regarding the use of the land; a benefit which the federal government acquired from the state government. Since the laws in question did not provide just terms, the provisions which effected the acquisition were declared invalid.

[178] *Health Insurance Commission v Peverill* (1994) 179 CLR 226; *Mutual Pools & Staff Pty Limited v The Commonwealth of Australia* (1994) 179 CLR 155; *Re Director of Public Prosecutions; Ex Parte Lawler and Another* (1994) 179 CLR 270; *Georgiadis v Australian and Overseas Telecommunications Corporation* (1994) 179 CLR 297. Not every deprivation of property is an acquisition of property, even if the complainant's property is taken away or extinguished. The Court emphasized the distinction between taking of property (in the US Fifth Amendment) and the compulsory acquisition of property (in section 51(xxxi) of the Australian Constitution) and argued that cases where property is taken from someone without the state acquiring the property or any other benefit do not qualify as acquisitions of property for purposes of the compensation requirement in the Australian property clause. The best example is when a state debt is extinguished not to free the state from the duty to pay, but to ensure that the money is paid to the right person: in *Mutual Pools & Staff Pty Limited v The Commonwealth of Australia* (1994) 179 CLR 155 the state had a contractual obligation to pay a tax refund to X, while it was clear that X had passed the tax on to Y, and the state wanted to ensure that the refund was paid to Y and not to X. In *Australian Capital Television Pty Ltd and Others v The Commonwealth of Australia; The State of New South Wales v The Commonwealth of Australia and Another* (1992) 177 CLR 106 at 165–166, 196–197 it was said that a law which forces broadcasters to provide free time slots for political parties during an election campaign does not effect an acquisition of property for purposes of section 51(xxxi). The free advertising time did not constitute a proprietary benefit or advantage, and therefore there was no acquisition of property, even though the broadcaster suffered a loss in the form of lack of income.

The property clause in the Constitution of Mauritius is a standard example of the 'double' property clause that appears in most postcolonial constitutions drafted on the Lancaster House model. The most important feature of these clauses is that one part of the clause refers to deprivation of property and another to compulsory acquisition of property, and both require compensation.[179] The question is whether this creates one or two independent compensation requirements: if the two parts of the double property clause establish two separate compensation guarantees, all state interventions with private property, including regulatory deprivation, require compensation.[180] In 1985 the Privy Council decided that the introductory provision in such a double property clause does indeed create a separate and independent guarantee of compensation for deprivations of property, in addition to the guarantee of compensation for compulsory acquisition of property.[181] However, in 1995 the Privy Council qualified this position by deciding that certain regulatory controls over the use of property are excluded from the compensation requirement, even when they cause losses for prop-

---

[179]On these property clauses and the interpretation problems associated with them see AJ van der Walt '"Double" property guarantees: A structural and comparative analysis' (1998) 14 *SAJHR* 560–586. See further generally AJ van der Walt 'Compensation for excessive or unfair regulation: A comparative overview of constitutional practice relating to regulatory takings' (1999) 14 *SA Public Law* 273–331 at 308–310; AJ van der Walt *Constitutional property clauses: A comparative analysis* (1999) 301–304.

[180]Apart from Mauritius, this problem has been raised in a number of other jurisdictions: see T Allen 'Commonwealth constitutions and the right not to be deprived of property' (1993) 42 *Int & Comp LQ* 523–552; T Allen 'Commonwealth constitutions and implied social and economic rights' (1994) 6 *Afr J Int & Comp L* 555–570. The Ugandan High Court decided that the two provisions create separate guarantees (*Shah v Attorney-General (No. 2)* [1970] EA 523 (UHC)); the Botswana Court of Appeal held that the introductory section was not a mere preamble, and that separate actions could be brought for breaches of rights mentioned or included in the protection provided by it (*Dow v Attorney General* [1992] LRC (Const) 623 (BCA)); the Court of Appeals of Guyana decided that the two provisions had to be read together, and that they did not create separate guarantees (*Macadeen Ameerally and Aubrey Bentham v Attorney General, Director of Public Prosecutions and Magistrate, Prem Persaud* (1978) 25 WIR 272 (CAG)); and the Zimbabwe Supreme Court held that the introductory section, while being more than a mere preamble, did not create separate rights (*Davies and Others v Minister of Lands, Agriculture and Water Development* 1997 (1) SA 228 (ZSC) 231H–232E).

[181]*Société United Docks and Others v Government of Mauritius* [1985] LRC (Const) 801 (SC, PC). Companies engaged in storing and loading sugar for export by means of dockers and stevedores were affected by a development in the method used to load sugar, shifting from loading in bags to bulk loading. To keep up with this development, legislation established the Mauritius Sugar Terminal Corporation, which had a monopoly on the storing and loading of sugar for export. As a result, the old business became redundant. The Act makes provision for compensation to be paid to the employees of the affected companies, but not to the companies themselves. Some companies claimed compensation on the grounds that the Act amounted to a compulsory acquisition of the property in their businesses, without compensation, but they were unsuccessful. The decision of the Privy Council was based on the consideration that the sugar industry was of vital importance for the economy, which made it necessary to support new and more efficient technology.

erty holders.[182] The lack of compensation for losses caused by regulation of the use of property was said to be justified when a regulation achieved a fair balance between the interests of the community and the interests of the individuals whose property interests have been adversely affected. This balance, according to the Privy Council, was a matter of fact and of degree, and a substantial margin of appreciation would be allowed in adjudicating it:[183] when regulatory deprivation of property goes too far, judging on a proportionality test, it should be compensated, even though it does not amount to compulsory acquisition of the property.[184] This decision confirmed that deprivation

---

[182] *La Compagnie Sucriere de Bel Ombre Ltee and Others v Government of Mauritius* [1995] 3 LRC 494 (PC). The Act concerned the Mauritian land-lease system, applicable to certain marginal parcels of land upon which sugar cane was grown, known as *metayage* (not unlike sharecropping leases of agricultural land); and it gave a *metayer* a statutory right to renew the contract; required the planter-landlord to relet the land to a *metayer* when the contract expires; and confined the use of the land to the growing of sugar cane. A regulatory law (the Sugar Industry Efficiency (Amendment) Act 1993) placed certain restrictions and obligations on contracts with regard to the lease of land on which sugar cane was produced, *inter alia* to provide improved security of tenure to small-scale lessees and producers. The regulatory controls imposed by the Act were clearly intended to improve the security of tenure of small-scale agriculturalists, as part of a larger project aimed at diversifying the already heavily regulated industry and making it more efficient, in the public interest. See the decision at 497c-499a for the background.

[183] The decision whether a particular law strikes this balance is described as 'very much a question of fact and degree', where the Supreme Court would be allowed a margin of appreciation by the Privy Council. The Privy Council based its discussion on the decision of the European Court on Human Rights in *Sporrong & Lönnroth v Sweden* [1982] 5 EHRR 35, the US Supreme Court decision in *Pennsylvania Coal Co v Mahon* 260 US 393 (1922), and the decision of the European Court of Human Rights in *James v United Kingdom* [1986] 8 EHRR 123. The concept of a 'margin of appreciation' derives from international law, and particularly the jurisprudence of the European Court of Human Rights. The Privy Council construed the relationship between the Mauritian Supreme Court and the Privy Council (at least for purposes of the question of a margin of appreciation) as analogous to that between a national court of a member state and the European Court on Human Rights.

[184] Although this decision justifies compensation for regulatory takings that 'go too far' with an appeal to European Convention and US law, the question in Mauritian law is not whether the courts should require compensation for extremely burdensome regulatory interferences with property interests, but whether the courts can disallow compensation for less burdensome regulatory interferences. By introducing a proportionality-based test to distinguish between regulatory interferences that require compensation and regulatory interferences that do not recquire compensation, the Privy Council argued in the opposite direction from either the European Court or the US Supreme Court. In Mauritius, the proportionality test does not justify the inference that some regulations *do* require compensation because they impose an unreasonable burden; it justifies the inference that some regulations do not require compensation because they strike a fair balance between the interests of the affected persons and the public interest. The notion of regulatory takings is taken over from the US Supreme Court and the proportionality test is taken over from the jurisprudence of the European Court on Human Rights, and both are turned upside-down to make sense of the double compensation guarantee in the Mauritian Constitution. It is possible to argue that the effect of the *Bel Ombre* decision is simply to deny that section 3(*c*) presents a separate and independent compensation guarantee, but then one would have expected an explicit rejection of the earlier decision in *Societé United Docks*.

that protects the rights and interests of others and the public interest by establishing or maintaining a fair balance between the interests of property owners and the interests of the community does not require compensation, but deprivation requires compensation, even when it does not involve actual acquisition of property by the state, when it places such a heavy burden upon a property holder that the deprivation fails to establish a fair balance between the interests of the affected person and the public interest. The result is closer to US law than to standard Commonwealth law, but because of the unique structure and language of these double guarantees and conflicting decisions on their interpretation it is uncertain whether constructive expropriation will more generally be recognized by Commonwealth courts in terms of the unique double property provisions in Commonwealth property clauses.[185]

5.4.5 Constructive expropriation in South African law

Although the question whether constructive expropriation is necessary or useful in South African law—and possible in terms of section 25—has not yet been decided authoritatively,[186] it was raised and discussed in *Steinberg v South Peninsula Municipality*.[187] Given the categorical distinction between deprivation and expropriation that was adopted by the Constitutional Court in *Harksen v Lane NO*,[188] the odds were against recognition of constructive expropriation, but the Supreme Court of Appeal

---

[185]Concerning the conflicting case law see footnote 180 above; on different formulations in these clauses see AJ van der Walt '"Double" property guarantees: a structural and comparative analysis' (1998) 14 *SAJHR* 560–586.

[186]The following section is based in part on two earlier publications: AJ van der Walt 'Moving towards recognition of constructive expropriation?' (2002) 65 *THRHR* 459–473; AJ van der Walt 'Overview of developments since the introduction of the constitutional property clause' (2004) 19 *SA Public Law* 46–89. See further A Gildenhuys *Onteieningsreg* (2nd ed 2001) 137–149. Gildenhuys apparently assumes that constructive expropriation is a relevant issue in South African law.

[187]2001 (4) SA 1243 (SCA). The applicant approached the Cape High Court for an order to force the respondent, a local authority, to complete an expropriation process initiated by a road scheme adopted by the respondent. It was alleged that the scheme prevented the applicant from either selling or properly using her land. The fact that the notion of constructive expropriation was relied upon where the applicant was trying to force the local authority to complete an apparently existing expropriation process was perhaps an early sign that the application was misconceived. However, stated somewhat differently, the appellant's case seems to have been that (a) the road scheme proclaimed and approved by the local authority does not constitute a proper expropriation, but (b) it amounts to a constructive expropriation, and (c) as such it entitles her to a remedy in terms of the constitutional property clause. The Cape High Court and the Supreme Court of Appeal dismissed the application for different reasons, but for present purposes the Supreme Court of Appeal's decision is more interesting. See AJ van der Walt 'Moving towards recognition of constructive expropriation?' (2002) 65 *THRHR* 459–473 for a discussion of the decision. The possibility of a constructive expropriation claim was also mooted in *Oudekraal Estates (Pty) Ltd v City of Cape Town* 2002 (6) SA 573 (C) at 595G, but not pursued.

[188]1998 (1) SA 300 (CC); on the basis of the question whether the state actually acquired the property in question; see *Harksen* par [37] at 1505A–B.

conceded that there may be room for constructive expropriation[189] when a regulatory deprivation has the effect, albeit indirectly, of transferring rights to the state.[190]

However, having mooted the point the Court immediately indicated *obiter*[191] that such a development might be undesirable because it could create confusion and adversely affect land reform.[192] The Court raised two arguments against the development of constructive expropriation in South African law: (*a*) the pragmatic reason that it could introduce confusion into the law, and (*b*) the theoretical reason that

---

[189]The Supreme Court of Appeal should be commended for its use of the term 'constructive expropriation', but the Court also uses 'taking', which has no place in the South African constitutional context, loosely in some passages (*Steinberg v South Peninsula Municipality* 2001 (4) SA 1243 (SCA) par [4] at 1246B, par [12] at 1249F). The term 'taking' is also used inconsistently and mistakenly in this case: In US law it would have been correct to ask whether the approval of the road scheme in *Steinberg* amounted to or constituted a (regulatory) taking (*Steinberg* par [12] at 1249F), but it would have been senseless to describe the distinction between deprivation and expropriation in section 25 of the Constitution as 'two kinds of taking' (*Steinberg* par [4] at 1246B)—the point is that US law distinguishes between (regulatory) deprivation of property and the two categories of taking (namely expropriation proper and regulatory taking). See AJ van der Walt 'Moving towards recognition of constructive expropriation?' (2002) 65 *THRHR* 459–473 at 462; A Gildenhuys *Onteieningsreg* (2nd ed 2001) 137.

[190] *Steinberg v South Peninsula Municipality* 2001 (4) SA 1243 (SCA) par [6] at 1246G–1247A: 'The principle of constructive expropriation creates a middle ground, and blurs the distinction, between deprivation and expropriation. According to that principle a deprivation will in certain circumstances attract an obligation to pay compensation even although no right vests in the body effecting the deprivation'; and par [8] at 1247G–H: 'Despite the clear distinction made in s 25 of the Constitution between deprivation and expropriation, there may be room for the development of a doctrine akin to constructive expropriation in South Africa—particularly where a public body utilises a regulatory power in a manner which, taken in isolation, can be categorised as a deprivation of property rights and not an expropriation, but which has the effect, albeit indirectly, of transferring those rights to the public body.'

[191]In this case it was unnecessary to decide the matter one way or the other, because even if the doctrine were recognized, the effect of the road scheme would still not be to establish either expropriation or constructive expropriation—the road scheme had no further purpose or effect than serving as advance notification of a possible intention to construct the road which, if ever implemented, would necessitate expropriation of the property: *Steinberg v South Peninsula Municipality* 2001 (4) SA 1243 (SCA) par [12] at 1249E–F. It was decided that the negative effects complained of were not proven on the facts, and in this view the decision is probably correct. The result also finds support in foreign law; see *Davies and Others v The Minister of Lands, Agriculture and Water Development* 1995 (1) BCLR 83 (ZHC); *Davies and Others v The Minister of Lands, Agriculture and Water Development* 1997 (1) SA 228 (ZSC).

[192] *Steinberg v South Peninsula Municipality* 2001 (4) SA 1243 (SCA) par [8] at 1247G–1248B: 'However, development of a more general doctrine of constructive expropriation, even if permissible in view of the express wording of s 25 of the Constitution, may be undesirable both for the pragmatic reason that it could introduce confusion into the law, and the theoretical reason that emphasis on compensation for the owner of a right which is limited by executive action could for instance adversely affect the constitutional imperative of land reform embodied in ss (4), (6) and (8) of s 25 itself.'

emphasis on compensation for the owner of a right which is limited by executive action could adversely affect land reform. Neither argument is conclusive or convincing.[193]

The first objection creates the impression that the courts have to 'protect' common law and tradition against confusion inspired by foreign constitutional concepts. In view of the relationship between the common law, statute law and the Constitution this would be the wrong approach, because new concepts and ways of thinking introduced by the Constitution, explicitly or by implication, have to be accommodated in common law—constitutional principles or ideals cannot be sacrificed for the sake of clarity and certainty in private law.[194] Tradition-based arguments that rely on settled judicial interpretations of what expropriation meant in the pre-constitutional era cannot carry much weight now that our courts are confronted by a constitutional property clause that regulates expropriation and distinguishes between deprivation and expropriation of property. The authority of pre-constitutional case law on the definition of expropriation is limited,[195] because the continuum approach to the distinction between deprivation and expropriation (regulation and taking) followed by the US Supreme Court in *Mahon*[196] arguably suits the new constitutional order better than the categorical approach favoured by the South African Constitutional Court in *Harksen*.[197] According to the purposive approach accepted by the Court the new constitutional order demands a flexible, context-sensitive interpretation strategy and not an abstract, definitional approach in terms of which the effects of state action are deduced from the category into which it is classified. A continuum approach assumes that the line between deprivation and expropriation is notional and not real, and that cases will inevitably arise in which that line is blurred and impossible to define with clarity or certainty.

The first objection is also open for criticism for assuming that the acceptance of constructive expropriation will cause confusion—it is not the notion of constructive expropriation that muddles the distinction between expropriation and deprivation; the distinction is artificial and confusing from the beginning. Moreover, it is unnecessarily negative to assume that the acceptance of a grey area between deprivation and expropriation will be confusing; a suitable theory (rather than a doctrine) of construc-

---

[193]See AJ van der Walt 'Moving towards recognition of constructive expropriation?' (2002) 65 *THRHR* 459–473 at 468–471, especially at 464–468 on the suitability of the foreign case law referred to in the decision.

[194]On the relationship between common law and Constitution see chapter 7. See further AJ van der Walt 'Tradition on trial: A critical analysis of the civil-law tradition in South African property law' (1995) 11 *SAJHR* 169–206; AJ van der Walt 'Transformative constitutionalism and the development of South African property law' 2005 *TSAR*; 2006 *TSAR* (forthcoming).

[195]Compare MD Southwood *The compulsory acquisition of rights* (2000) 14–15, who seems to favour such a tradition-based argument. A Gildenhuys *Onteieningsreg* (2nd ed 2001) 15, 137–149 (especially at 142) recognizes the possibility of constructive expropriation.

[196]*Pennsylvania Coal Co v Mahon* 260 US 393 (1922); see footnote 122 above.

[197]*Harksen v Lane NO* 1998 (1) SA 300 (CC); see the section on the definition of expropriation in 5.2 above.

tive expropriation will not necessarily make the courts' work easier, but it could provide useful beacons and signposts that can assist the courts in a difficult journey into uncharted terrain.[198]

The Court's second concern is that a general doctrine of constructive expropriation will obstruct or frustrate land reform. This is a serious matter, but perhaps it is overstated, because there are several reasons why the development of a theory of constructive expropriation need not have a detrimental effect on land reform. Firstly, judging from experience elsewhere, constructive expropriation might find less application in land reform cases than in commercial property.[199] Even where constructive expropriation does apply to land reform situations it is not clear why it should frustrate land reform, which is after all clearly sanctioned and authorised by the property clause in the Constitution. The kind of situation where regulatory deprivation imposed by land reform legislation could possibly be construed as constructive expropriation is where landowners' common-law rights or entitlements are curtailed for the sake of land reform objectives such as security of tenure,[200] and then the constructive expropriation question should not raise unnecessary problems. With the assistance of a suitable theoretical model, the courts should be able to work out when regulatory deprivation goes too far and should be treated as expropriation, and in making this decision the land-reform oriented principles and obligations in the Constitution and in land reform legislation should provide guidance to balance the claim for compensation against the public interest in effecting the reforms in question. The fact that constructive expropriation may be used to extract compensation or to invalidate a deprivation does not mean that landowners will always succeed with their claims against land reform laws—it will be up to the courts to interpret and apply the laws, with due recognition of the reform- and transformation-oriented context, in the light of the theory of constructive expropriation, on a case-by-case basis.

A point of some importance is that, although the purpose in raising the constructive expropriation argument is usually to extract compensation for regulatory deprivation that has the same effect as expropriation, it could also be employed to have deprivation invalidated because it has the same effect as expropriation while it does not or cannot provide for compensation. In such a case the answer might sometimes

---

[198]See AJ van der Walt 'Moving towards recognition of constructive expropriation?' (2002) 65 *THRHR* 459–473 at 469.

[199]See AJ van der Walt 'The constitutional property clause and police power regulation of intangible commercial property—A comparative analysis of case law' in P Jackson & DC Wilde *Property law: Current issues and debates* (1999) 208–280 for examples.

[200]Eg restrictions on the right to obtain an eviction order, see AJ van der Walt 'Exclusivity of ownership, security of tenure, and eviction orders: A model to evaluate South African land-reform legislation' 2002 *TSAR* 254–289; AJ van der Walt 'Exclusivity of ownership, security of tenure, and eviction orders: A critical evaluation of recent case law' (2002) 18 *SAJHR* 371–419 for an analysis. See further chapter 6.3.

be simply to amend the authorizing legislation in order to avoid invalidity.[201] The point of attacking regulatory excess is not always to extract expropriation, and even when a landowner should succeed with a claim for compensation the property clause provides adequate guidelines in section 25(3) for the courts to calculate the compensation award with due regard for all the relevant contextual factors, including the importance of the land reform process and the possibility of historical imbalances and inequities.[202] If a particular regulatory deprivation in the land reform legislation is treated as constructive expropriation under circumstances where payment of compensation would be unreasonable and unjust, it should be possible to reach and justify a suitable order in terms of section 25(3); if compensation seems to be required for the sake of fairness, its award and quantum should be calculated and justifiable in the same fashion. In either situation the land reform process need not suffer, because the relevant constitutional and statutory measures already ensure that the importance of land reform is taken into account.

Where the state does not acquire the property (or any property or benefit or advantage)[203] it could be more difficult to succeed with a claim based on constructive expropriation, although it should not be excluded from the realm of possibility too early. It is foreseeable that the state could destroy or extinguish private property, without acquiring the property and without acquiring any advantage or benefit from its extinction, simply to punish or harm existing owners or in circumstances that single a small group of owners out for disproportionately harsh regulation, and then the courts could use the notion of constructive expropriation to ask whether the discrepancy (an action intended and structured as a regulatory deprivation but which has the effect of an expropriation) should be addressed by way of a compensation award or by way of a legitimacy inquiry which could result in the action being invalidated. In a legitimacy inquiry, the question is whether deprivation is valid when it has the same effects as expropriation, under circumstances where it is impossible to view and treat the deprivation as constructive expropriation (eg because a compensation award is out of the question). Such an inquiry need not frustrate legislative purposes, for it may prove that the action is justified by the Constitution or by land reform law.[204] In most cases, this kind of justification would terminate the

---

[201] Either by actual legislative amendment or by the court reading down or reading in. See the examples discussed in chapter 4.5.5; in *Jaftha v Schoeman and Others; Van Rooyen v Stoltz and Others* 2005 (2) SA 140 (CC) the regulatory provision could be salvaged by reading in; in *Zondi v Member of the Executive Council for Traditional and Local Government Affairs and Others* 2005 (3) SA 589 (CC) it could not and the impugned provision was declared invalid.

[202] Compensation is discussed in 5.8 below.

[203] The reference to the 'more general doctrine' of constructive expropriation in *Steinberg v South Peninsula Municipality* 2001 (4) SA 1243 (SCA) par [8] at 1248A probably relates to this situation, where deprivation that does not involve any state acquisition of the property or state benefit would be treated as expropriation if the doctrine was accepted.

[204] Eg when property is seized and forfeited or even destroyed for being dangerous or prohibited contraband; see the section on forfeiture in 5.3 above.

inquiry, but the benefit of a theory of constructive expropriation is that it may prove useful in more difficult cases, for instance where seizure and forfeiture of property is apparently authorised by law, but the matter is complicated because the property belongs to an innocent third party, or because the state benefits from the use or sale of the seized and forfeited property.[205] In these circumstances a balanced and subtle theory of constructive expropriation could assist the courts in distinguishing between different situations and contexts in order to reach a context-sensitive and justifiable outcome.

It might be said that the same result could be reached without involving the theory of constructive expropriation, by inquiring whether a particular deprivation (which is deemed excessive because it has the effects of an expropriation, but without compensation) is arbitrary as meant in section 25(1), and therefore unconstitutional and invalid. Of course this is the result that one would probably expect in view of the Constitutional Court decision in *FNB*,[206] but the problem with this approach is that it is inflexible: if the regulatory limitation is arbitrary it is invalid and there is little chance that it could be saved through the limitation inquiry.[207] By comparison, the constructive expropriation approach is more flexible: when a particular regulatory limitation is excessive it could either be invalidated (because it has the effects of expropriation but does not make provision for compensation), or it could be upheld against payment of compensation, even though expropriation and compensation were not originally foreseen and the state does not acquire the property.[208] The question is whether it is necessary to keep open the possibility to argue that a seemingly arbitrary deprivation is in fact expropriation that requires compensation. Perhaps this door should not be shut too quickly, as I can think of at least one hypothetical situation where it would be useful to have this construction for the court to fall back on for the benefit of land reform.

The situation I have in mind is where a limitation is imposed as a regulatory measure and not as expropriation, but the effects of the limitation on the affected property holder are so excessive and unfair or disproportionate (compared to others in a similar position) that a court would be tempted to strike it down for being

---

[205]See AJ van der Walt 'Civil forfeiture of instrumentalities and proceeds of crime and the constitutional property clause' (2000) 16 *SAJHR* 1–45 for a discussion and examples, and compare the section on forfeiture in 5.3 above.

[206] *First National Bank of SA Ltd t/a Wesbank v Commissioner, South African Revenue Service; First National Bank of SA Ltd t/a Wesbank v Minister of Finance* 2002 (4) SA 768 (CC).

[207]See T Roux 'Property' in MH Cheadle, DM Davis & NRL Haysom *South African constitutional law: The bill of rights* (2002) 429–472 at 461–462, and compare the discussion below.

[208]Of course, when compensation is actually really out of the question for some reason this possibility will not be available. Similarly, if the limitation is simply irredeemably tainted by corruption or lack of authority the obvious solution is to invalidate it. The point here is that there are cases where that is not the problem, eg where the limitation is authorized and legitimate in view of the land reform laws, but its effects are simply excessively and indefensibly harsh, disproportionate or unequally distributed.

arbitrary in the sense developed in *FNB*.[209] However, when the limitation and the regulatory scheme that it forms part of are authorized by a legitimate and important (land reform-related) public purpose, the court may be unwilling to strike down the legislation or invalidate the deprivation. In such a situation the notion of constructive expropriation could be used not to frustrate land reform, but to facilitate land reform by saving a legitimate and important but harsh regulatory measure from being struck down. Rather than losing the regulatory scheme with its reform benefits, one might want to soften the blow for the affected person and pay compensation. To me, this looks like an eminently sensible solution for a hypothetical situation that may one day arise, and I would prefer to keep the possibility open.[210]

The question is, is this still possible in view of the decisions of the Constitutional Court in *Harksen*[211] and *FNB*?[212] The situation with *Harksen* is not so difficult: even though the Court drew a strict, conceptual distinction between deprivation and expropriation it never entertained the possibility of a third category and it cannot be said that *Harksen* necessarily excluded the possibility of a middle category. The situation in *FNB* is somewhat more complex. In *FNB*, the Court explained the distinction between deprivation and expropriation in hierarchical terms, so that deprivation and expropriation were not so much conceptually distinguished from each other, but rather set up as a wider and a smaller category, the one including the other. This makes it difficult to explain where and how a third, middle category would be placed. The Court also construed an analytical method on the basis of the distinction, and indicated that review in terms of section 25 must start with the requirements pertaining to the wider category of deprivations, and that it will proceed to the narrower category of expropriations only when the requirements for a deprivation were either satisfied or, failing that, if any limitation was justified in terms of section 36. Practically,

---

[209] Ie that there is insufficient reason for that effect under those circumstances; see *First National Bank of SA Ltd t/a Wesbank v Commissioner, South African Revenue Service; First National Bank of SA Ltd t/a Wesbank v Minister of Finance* 2002 (4) SA 768 (CC) and compare the discussion in chapter 4.5. An example is explained in chapter 4.6, text accompanying footnote 158.

[210] The solution could also be construed in a different direction, namely in line with the German practice of paying so-called equalization compensation to soften the blow of extremely harsh regulatory deprivation, see AJ van der Walt *Constitutional property clauses: A comparative analysis* (1999) 150–151; and with the similar French practice of paying non-expropriatory compensation for loss caused by harsh or unfair regulatory limitations (see footnotes 151, 157 above and the discussion of German and French law in 5.4.2 and 5.4.3 above). In that case the regulatory action is not transformed into expropriation to save it, but saved from being excessive through payment of equalization money. Compare further the injunction in section 25(8) to save land reform measures from invalidity if possible.

[211] *Harksen v Lane NO* 1998 (1) SA 300 (CC).

[212] *First National Bank of SA Ltd t/a Wesbank v Commissioner, South African Revenue Service; First National Bank of SA Ltd t/a Wesbank v Minister of Finance* 2002 (4) SA 768 (CC); see the discussion in chapter 4.5.

this 'telescoping' effect[213] might exclude the possibility of arguing a constructive expropriation case in most if not all situations. If the deprivation satisfies the requirements in section 25(1) the applicant may get the opportunity to argue that the deprivation is so unreasonably disproportionate that it amounts to expropriation that requires compensation, even though it was intended and set up as a regulatory deprivation and not as an expropriation. However, it seems unlikely that this will be possible in many cases, because unreasonable and disproportionate deprivation will more often than not already be struck down as arbitrary during the initial deprivation analysis as set out in *FNB*.

Once a deprivation has been declared arbitrary, it is highly unlikely that it will be justifiable in terms of section 36, which means that the inquiry will often end there. The opportunity to argue that the deprivation could or should be treated as an expropriation that requires compensation might therefore never arise, if the *FNB* logic is followed strictly. The result is that the possibility of arguing that a particular deprivation should be saved from invalidity but treated as constructive expropriation has become remote because of the methodology proposed in *FNB*. For the sake of important land reform laws or initiatives that could be saved in this way one hopes that the Constitutional Court is willing in future to deviate from this method in suitable cases.

5.5 FORMAL REQUIREMENTS: INTRODUCTION

Section 25(2) sets out three requirements: expropriation must (*a*) take place in terms of law of general application; (*b*) be for a public purpose or in the public interest (as further defined in subsection 25(4)); and (*c*) be accompanied by compensation (as further specified in subsection 25(3)). Each of these requirements is discussed separately below.

In reality the test for valid expropriation could look very different from what is suggested by these requirements. If the courts should adhere to the methodology set out in the Constitutional Court's *FNB* decision,[214] and if Theunis Roux's prediction about the 'telescoping' or 'vortex' effect of this methodology should come true,[215] it

---

[213] Theunis Roux identified the fact that the *FNB* decision results in all property issues being 'telescoped' or—in his later metaphor—being sucked in by the 'arbitrariness vortex'. See T Roux 'Section 25' in S Woolman et al (eds) *Constitutional law of South Africa* (2nd ed 2003 original service Dec 2003) 46-2–46-5. See the discussion in chapter 4.5.

[214] *First National Bank of SA Ltd t/a Wesbank v Commissioner, South African Revenue Service; First National Bank of SA Ltd t/a Wesbank v Minister of Finance* 2002 (4) SA 768 (CC). See the discussion in chapter 4.5 and 4.6.

[215] T Roux 'Section 25' in S Woolman et al (eds) *Constitutional law of South Africa* (2nd ed 2003 original service Dec 2003) 46-2–46-5 argued that the 'telescoping' effect of the *FNB* approach is that all property cases will be treated as deprivations first, which means that the law of general application issue will be decided during the deprivation analysis, and that most if not all irregularities that might disqualify an expropriation under section 25(2) or (3) would probably already taint it as an arbitrary deprivation in terms of section 25(1). See the discussion in 5.4.5 above and chapter 4.5, 4.6.

is highly unlikely that any property case would ever be subjected to analysis in terms of the requirements in subsections 25(2) and 25(3). According to the *FNB* decision and Roux's astute interpretation of it, property cases would only ever reach section 25(2) analysis once they have passed the section 25(1) arbitrariness test, and the cases that pass that test are not very likely to present any problems with the section 25(2) test.[216] However, it is still necessary to discuss the requirements in subsections 25(2) and 25(3) on their own merit, even if only on the off chance that the courts might decide to deviate from the *FNB* methodology and treat a specific expropriation case as such without allowing it to get bogged down in the arbitrary deprivation issue.

5.6 LAW OF GENERAL APPLICATION

Section 25(2) states that property may be expropriated in terms of law of general application, echoing the similar requirements in section 25(1) (no one may be deprived of property except in terms of law of general application) and in section 36(1) (the rights in the Bill of Rights may be limited only in terms of law of general application). Consequently, many of the same considerations apply in all three cases.[217] In fact, in view of the approach adopted in the Constitutional Court's *FNB* decision[218] it is highly likely that when the law of general application issue crops up for adjudication it will already be dealt with conclusively during the deprivation analysis stage, so that it will not be necessary to raise it again if the issue should proceed to the expropriation analysis stage.[219] Even if and when the section 25(2) law of general application issue should ever come up the issues should be very similar to those that apply in the case of section 25(1).

The requirement in section 25(2) that property may only be expropriated in terms of law of general application is wider than section 28(2) of the interim Constitution, which stated that property may be expropriated 'in accordance with a law'.[220] In *Park-*

---

[216]See the discussion in 5.4.5 above and chapter 4.5, 4.6. To summarize: the law of general application issue would have been dealt with under section 25(2) already; and expropriations that do not meet the public purpose or compensation requirements are very unlikely to pass the arbitrariness test in the first place.

[217]See chapters 2.5 and 4.4 respectively.

[218]*First National Bank of SA Ltd t/a Wesbank v Commissioner, South African Revenue Service; First National Bank of SA Ltd t/a Wesbank v Minister of Finance* 2002 (4) SA 768 (CC). See the discussion in chapter 4.5, 4.6.

[219]The argument is based upon the analysis of T Roux 'Section 25' in S Woolman et al (eds) *Constitutional law of South Africa* (2nd ed 2003 original service Dec 2003) 46-2–46-5, who pointed out that the 'telescoping' effect of the *FNB* approach is that all property cases will be treated as deprivations first; see chapter 4.5, 4.6. Since section 25(1) also includes a law of general application requirement the question whether a particular limitation on property was authorized by a law of general application will already be asked with regard to section 25(1), and the chances are slim that the same question will be answered differently if and when the section 25(2) test comes up.

[220]See AJ van der Walt *Constitutional property clauses: A comparative analysis* (1999) 341.

Ross and Another v The Director, Office for Serious Economic Offences[221] the Cape High Court decided that section 6 of the Investigation of Serious Offences Act 117 of 1991 (which authorizes certain search and seizure procedures) was 'a law' as meant in section 28(2). Roux[222] argues that this decision will be followed in cases decided under section 25 of the 1996 Constitution, and that all original and delegated legislation will accordingly qualify as 'law of general application' for this purpose. Accordingly, internal administrative policy documents will probably not qualify.[223] Roux is probably correct in stating that, although the rules of common law should in principle also qualify as 'law of general application', it is unlikely that those rules will be invoked or become the source of controversy in expropriation cases, because as far as South African law is concerned expropriation is a state action always carried out in terms of statutory authorization.[224]

---

[221] 1995 (2) SA 148 (C) at 167B. See further T Roux 'Property' in MH Cheadle, DM Davis & NRL Haysom *South African constitutional law: The bill of rights* (2002) 429–472 at 458–460; and compare with regard to the law of general application requirement in section 25(1) *Deutschmann NO and Others v Commissioner for the South African Revenue Service; Shelton v Commissioner for the South African Revenue Service* 2000 (2) SA 106 (E) at 124A (regarding the Income Tax Act 58 of 1962 and the Value-Added Tax Act 89 of 1991).

[222] T Roux 'Property' in MH Cheadle, DM Davis & NRL Haysom *South African constitutional law: The bill of rights* (2002) 429–472 at 458.

[223] A Gildenhuys *Onteieningsreg* (2nd ed 2001) 93. The general analysis of the law of general application requirement in section 36(1) by S Woolman 'Limitation' in M Chaskalson et al (eds) *Constitutional law of South Africa* (1st ed 5th rev service 1999) 12-28–12-32 is useful in this regard as well; see further chapter 2.5. At 12–29 footnote 3 Woolman points out that Canadian case law is divided on the question whether government policy directives or guidelines are to be regarded as law of general application. In *De Lille and Another v Speaker of the National Assembly* 1998 (3) SA 430 (C) 454I–455C the Cape High Court held that the rule of parliamentary privilege does not qualify as law of general application, particularly because it was neither published or accessible nor precise or certain.

[224] A Gildenhuys *Onteieningsreg* (2nd ed 2001) 93; T Roux 'Property' in MH Cheadle, DM Davis & NRL Haysom *South African constitutional law: The bill of rights* (2002) 429–472 at 458–459; T Roux 'Section 25' in S Woolman et al (eds) *Constitutional law of South Africa* (2nd ed 2003 original service Dec 2003) 46–33. In the former publication at 458 footnote 144 Roux refers to the Canadian decision in *Retail, Wholesale & Department Store Union, Local 580 et al v Dolphin Delivery Ltd et al* (1987) 33 DLR (4th) 174 at 188–190 as authority for the proposition that a rule of Canadian common law is 'law' as contemplated in section 1 of the Canadian Charter of Human Rights and Freedoms 1982. The common law rules pertaining to the establishment of a right of way of necessity (mentioned by Gildenhuys (2001) at 93) certainly effect a loss of property (free or unburdened ownership) by one person (owner of the servient tenement) and an original acquisition of property (the right of way) by another (owner of the dominant tenement), but this cannot be characterized as expropriation because it does not involve the element of public purpose, even in its wider form that allows a private person to benefit—the purpose of the rule is purely to improve the use of private land. Another, similarly problematic, example is the common law rules in terms of which land may be transferred (against compensation awarded by the court) to a neighbour whose building encroaches upon another neighbour's land; see in this regard *Rand Waterraad v Bothma* 1997 (3) SA 120 (O); *Trustees of the Brian Lackey Trust v Annandale* [2003] 4 All SA 528 (C); *Lombard v Fischer* [2003] 1 All SA 698 (O).

The fact that a law was formally promulgated and is valid law will not necessarily satisfy the law of general application requirement—the law must also apply generally, which excludes so-called bills of attainder.[225] Laws that are made to target a specific, named or easily identifiable individual or property will fall foul of the general application requirement when they single specific persons out for discriminatory treatment.[226] This principle cannot be applied too generally, because many if not all laws apply to classes of people rather than universally, even if only in effect. Therefore, the fact that a law affects one class of people or one class of property to the exclusion of others will generally not mean that this requirement is not met.[227] The 'singling out for discriminatory treatment' test applied in *Lebowa Mineral Trust Beneficiaries Forum*[228] could be handy in distinguishing between laws that merely apply to a small class of persons or instances and true bills of attainder.

Apart from its formal validity and general application, the law of general application requirement also means that laws should be published officially and accessible to citizens; not arbitrary in the sense that they do not depend on the exercise of discretionary powers; and clear in the sense that people should be able to infer from them how to arrange their own actions and their affairs.[229] The general application requirement therefore includes the requirement that laws be accessible and clear to citizens.

Comparatively speaking, German law is perhaps the strictest example of the requirement that expropriations have to be authorized by law of general application. Article 14.3.2 GG provides that expropriation may only take place by or on the

---

[225]T Roux 'Property' in MH Cheadle, DM Davis & NRL Haysom *South African constitutional law: The bill of rights* (2002) 429–472 at 459 refers to the case of *Attorney-General of Lesotho and Another v Swissborough Diamond Mines (Pty) Ltd and Others* 1997 (8) BCLR 1122 (Les CA) as an example of a military decree that was aimed at revoking very specific mining leases and at evicting the leaseholders, and which was therefore declared inconsistent with the Lesotho Human Rights Act 24 of 1983. Another example is *Cultura 2000 and Another v Government of the Republic of Namibia and Others* 1993 (2) SA 12 (Nam HC); see AJ van der Walt *Constitutional property clauses: A comparative analysis* (1999) at 317–318. See further S Woolman 'Limitation' in M Chaskalson et al (eds) *Constitutional law of South Africa* (1st ed 5th rev service 1999) 12-28–12-32.
[226]*Lebowa Mineral Trust Beneficiaries Forum v President of the Republic of South Africa* 2002 (1) BCLR 23 (T) at 29H. See further T Roux 'Section 25' in S Woolman et al (eds) *Constitutional law of South Africa* (2nd ed 2003 original service Dec 2003) at 46–21.
[227]T Roux 'Property' in MH Cheadle, DM Davis & NRL Haysom *South African constitutional law: The bill of rights* (2002) 429–472 at 459 correctly points out that the *obiter dictum* in *Joubert and Others v Van Rensburg and Others* 2001 (1) SA 753 (W) par [42.1] at 797C–D (that the Extension of Security of Tenure Act 62 of 1997 applies only to agricultural land and is therefore not of general application) is certainly wrong. See chapter 6.3.8 on this decision.
[228]*Lebowa Mineral Trust Beneficiaries Forum v President of the Republic of South Africa* 2002 (1) BCLR 23 (T) at 29H. S Woolman 'Limitation' in M Chaskalson et al (eds) *Constitutional law of South Africa* (1st ed 5th rev service 1999) 12-28–12-32 at 12–28 points out that discriminatory treatment is precluded by this requirement.
[229]S Woolman 'Limitation' in M Chaskalson et al (eds) *Constitutional law of South Africa* (1st ed 5th rev service 1999) 12-28–12-32 at 12.28; A Gildenhuys *Onteieningsreg* (2nd ed 2001) 93.

authority of a law[230] that also provides for the nature and measure of compensation. This provision is extremely important in German law because it informs the Federal Constitutional Court's decision[231] that a court cannot transform an excessive regulatory deprivation into an expropriation that requires compensation: since expropriation is such an extreme infringement upon private property, it is only possible if it is effected or authorized explicitly or clearly by a statute that foresees and authorizes the expropriation and the compensation to be paid for it.[232] Expropriation is therefore impossible in German law without direct and explicit statutory authorization for both the expropriation and the compensation to be paid for it. The strict control over authorization that is read into article 14.3.2 GG also affects the German courts' interpretation of the public purpose requirement,[233] because it means that expropriation is only possible if it is justified by its public purpose and if both the purpose and expropriation for that purpose are foreseen and authorized by a law that also sets out the nature and scope of compensation to be paid for it. The existence of an authorizing statute that complies with certain strict requirements is therefore at the heart of the power of expropriation.

The European Convention on Human Rights also requires that expropriation should take place in terms of law.[234] This requirement is interpreted formally in the sense that the expropriation must be authorized by a law, which could be either a statute or a legal rule; and qualitatively in the sense that the legal rule that authorizes the expropriation must be constitutional, valid, accessible, not arbitrary and clear.[235] Roux[236] points out that the requirement that fundamental rights may only be limited

---

[230]German law recognizes both administrative and statutory expropriations, the latter of which takes place or is effected directly by law. Because this obviously excludes the possibility of preventing bills of attainder and increases the possibility of injustice, statutory expropriation is treated as an exception and a high standard of scrutiny is applied; see R Wendt 'Eigentum, Erbrecht und Enteignung' in M Sachs (ed) *Grundgesetz Kommentar* (3rd ed 2002) 654 Rdn 159.

[231]The classic decision is *BVerfGE* 58, 300 [1981] (*Naßauskiesung*); see the discussion in 5.3 above. The position was confirmed in *BVerfGE* 100, 226 [1999].

[232]See R Wendt 'Eigentum, Erbrecht und Enteignung' in M Sachs (ed) *Grundgesetz Kommentar* (3rd ed 2002) 654 Rdn 158–159. On the non-availability of regulatory takings or constructive expropriation in German law see 5.3 above.

[233]See 5.7 below.

[234]Article 1 of the First Protocol to the European Convention, which provides that '[n]o one shall be deprived of his possessions except in the public interest and subject to the conditions provided for by law and by the general principles of international law.' See further J Meyer-Ladewig *Konvention zum Schutz der Menschenrechte und Grundfreiheiten Handkommentar* (2003) 332–333 Rdn 24–25.

[235]J Meyer-Ladewig *Konvention zum Schutz der Menschenrechte und Grundfreiheiten Handkommentar* (2003) 332 Rdn 25. See further S Woolman 'Limitation' in M Chaskalson et al (eds) *Constitutional law of South Africa* (1st ed 5th rev service 1999) 12-28–12-32 at 12.28; A Gildenhuys *Onteieningsreg* (2nd ed 2001) 93.

[236]T Roux 'Property' in MH Cheadle, DM Davis & NRL Haysom *South African constitutional law: The bill of rights* (2002) 429–472 at 459–460, 459 footnote 150, with reference to EHRR cases cited there. S Woolman 'Limitation' in M Chaskalson et al (eds) *Constitutional law of South Africa* (1st ed 5th rev service 1999) 12-28–12-32 at 12–28 points out that the law of general application requirement serves two purposes, ie to 'filter out bills of attainder' and to 'promote and give effect to the rule of law'.

in terms of law has been interpreted in the European Court of Human Rights as if it may only be limited in terms of the rule of law, which *inter alia* means that it may not be applied retrospectively. If this interpretation were followed in South Africa it could affect the validity of land reform laws that are made applicable to a date before the first publication of the law.[237] On the other hand the land reform provisions that have retrospective effect are usually aimed at evictions and not expropriation, and hence this should not pose a problem. The land reform laws are discussed in chapter 6.

5.7 PUBLIC PURPOSE OR PUBLIC INTEREST

5.7.1 Introduction

Section 25(2) states that property may be expropriated for a public purpose or in the public interest, and section 25(4)(*a*) explains that the public interest includes 'the nation's commitment to land reform and to reforms to bring about equitable access to all South Africa's natural resources'.

Constitutional property clauses include public purpose requirements to ensure that expropriations are strictly necessary and to prevent frivolous or arbitrary use of the state's power of eminent domain. These requirements have two related effects: to prevent or stop expropriations of private property for improper, unlawful purposes; and to control legitimate exercises of the power to expropriate. The foundation of the requirement is the classic liberal view that state infringements of private property—and particularly expropriation—should be restricted to instances where the relevant action is unavoidable. In this sense, the public purpose requirement is a remnant of the traditional, liberal character of the constitutional property guarantee as a defensive shield against unwarranted state interference in the private domain. As will appear from the discussion below, the public purpose requirement has lost much of its original purely defensive flavour in the postliberal era, although both the preventive and control functions of this requirement are still relevant. The public purpose requirement in the South African Constitution illustrates the point very well.

Section 25(2)(*a*) provides that property may be expropriated 'for a public purpose or in the public interest', and section 25(4)(*a*) adds that 'the public interest' includes land reform and other reforms to bring about equitable access to South Africa's natural resources. There is authority in South African law to the effect that the public purpose requirement should not be construed too narrowly,[238] but the double

---

[237] T Roux 'Property' in MH Cheadle, DM Davis & NRL Haysom *South African constitutional law: The bill of rights* (2002) 429–472 at 460 refers to an example from the Extension of Security of Tenure Act 62 of 1997.

[238] A Eisenberg '"Public purpose" and expropriation: Some comparative insights and the South African bill of rights' (1995) 11 *SAJHR* 207–221 provides a very useful overview. See M Jacobs *The law of expropriation in South Africa* (1982) 15–16; A Gildenhuys *Onteieningsreg* (2nd ed 2001) 89–92, 94–99; *Fourie v Minister van Lande en 'n Ander* 1970 (4) SA 165 (O); *Administrator Transvaal v J van Streepen (Kempton Park) (Pty) Ltd* 1990 (4) SA 644 (A) for existing South African law, and compare
(continued on next page ...)

reference to 'public purpose' and 'public interest' in section 25(2)(a) was probably nevertheless inserted—and the wide definition in section 25(4)(a) added—in a belt-and-braces effort to prevent expropriations for land reform from being invalidated for not being in the public interest purely because they involve transfer of the expropriated property to private beneficiaries.[239] Concern that the provision could be interpreted this narrowly is not unfounded, because at least two foreign courts have indeed decided that an expropriation was not for a public purpose if the property was transferred to another private person.[240]

The public purpose requirement can be interpreted in at least three different ways: very narrowly to restrict expropriations to actual public use;[241] slightly wider to include some public benefits that exceed actual public use; or very widely to include almost any purpose that is vaguely beneficial to the public weal. According to the narrow view, expropriation only serves a public purpose if the property is acquired by the state for actual use by the state or the public;[242] in this view transfer of the

(...from previous page)
G Budlender 'The constitutional protection of property rights' in G Budlender, J Latsky & T Roux *Juta's new land law* (original service 1998) 1-48–1-55; T Roux 'Property' in MH Cheadle, DM Davis & NRL Haysom *South African constitutional law: The bill of rights* (2002) 429–472 at 463–464; T Roux 'Section 25' in S Woolman et al (eds) *Constitutional law of South Africa* (2nd ed 2003 original service Dec 2003) 46–33; DG Kleyn 'The constitutional protection of property: A comparison between the German and the South African approach' (1996) 11 *SA Public Law* 402–445 at 434ff on the new constitutional requirement in section 25(2).
[239] In *Administrator, Transvaal and Another v J van Streepen (Kempton Park) (Pty) Ltd* 1990 (4) SA 644 (A) the former Appellate Division of the Supreme Court distinguished (at 661C–D) between expropriation in the public interest and expropriation for a public purpose, and argued that expropriation for the benefit of a private person cannot be for a public purpose; however, it could be in the public interest (e g to facilitate private provision of public electricity) and as such it could satisfy the requirement, depending on how it is formulated in the authorizing legislation. A Gildenhuys *Onteieningsreg* (2nd ed 2001) 98 points out that this has become a false distinction in view of the double-barrelled provision in section 25(2), which was no doubt intended to have exactly that effect. See further M Chaskalson 'Stumbling towards section 28: Negotiations over the protection of property rights in the Interim Constitution' (1995) 11 *SAJHR* 222–240 at 237–238; and see G Budlender 'The constitutional protection of property rights' in G Budlender, J Latsky & T Roux *Juta's new land law* (original service 1998) 1-48–1-55.
[240] *Trinidad Island-Wide Cane Farmers' Association Inc and Attorney General v Prakash Seereeram* (1975) 27 WIR 329 (CA) (Trinidad & Tobago); *Clunies-Ross v Commonwealth* (1984) 155 CLR 193 (Australia). See further A Eisenberg '"Public purpose" and expropriation: Some comparative insights and the South African bill of rights' (1995) 11 *SAJHR* 207–221; and compare the discussion below.
[241] An argument in favour of this interpretation of the American clause, which reads 'for public use', is made by J Rubenfeld 'Usings' (1993) 102 *Yale LJ* 1077–1163. This interpretation is not shared by many other academics, nor is it followed by the US courts; see the discussion below.
[242] Compare the discussion and references below. See DG Kleyn 'The constitutional protection of property: A comparison between the German and the South African approach' (1996) 11 *SA Public Law* 402–445 at 434 for a brief discussion; and see G Peller 'The metaphysics of American law' (1985) 73 *Cal LR* 1151–1290 at 1194–1207, especially at 1197, for an interesting theoretical perspective on this view.

property to private beneficiaries is an improper, non-public purpose that would render the expropriation unconstitutional. In view of the potential irregularities that could occur in a system that allows for private property to be expropriated for the benefit of private persons a narrow attitude towards the public purpose requirement may be commendable, but in a transformative setting where reforms are authorized by the constitution it can also impede or frustrate land reform efforts.[243] The narrow view has accordingly been rejected in foreign cases where it was accepted that expropriation for land reform purposes was in the public interest even when the land was transferred to private beneficiaries.[244] However, the narrow view was upheld in other cases,[245] while it caused at least some concern about transfer of expropriated property to private beneficiaries in a third group of cases.[246] It was therefore important to ensure that the narrow approach would not be followed blindly in South Africa, and the provision in section 25(2) was framed to make this abundantly clear.[247] For practical purposes the narrow approach to the public purpose requirement can therefore mostly be ignored, and the only question is whether the remaining, more accommodating approach should be cast in a lenient but reasonably strict or in a totally deferent mould. The comparative analysis below sets out examples of each of these possibilities and points out the differences between them and the problems associated with them.

---

[243] A Eisenberg '"Public purpose" and expropriation: Some comparative insights and the South African bill of rights' (1995) 11 *SAJHR* 207–221 at 207–208; G Budlender 'The constitutional protection of property rights' in G Budlender, J Latsky & T Roux *Juta's new land law* (original service 1998) 1-48–1-55.

[244] See *Clunies-Ross v Commonwealth* (1984) 155 CLR 193 (dissenting judgment of Murphy J) (Australia); *Grand Bench 23 December 1953* in JM Maki *Court and constitution in Japan: Selected Supreme Court decisions, 1948–1960* (1964) 228–252 at 238ff (Japan); *Hawaii Housing Authority v Midkiff* 467 US 229 (1984) (United States). Since the introduction of the Constitution of Zimbabwe (Amendment No 11) Act 1990, section 16(1)(a)(i) of the Zimbabwe Constitution provides explicitly for expropriation of land for purposes of land reform. Compare further *James v United Kingdom* [1986] 8 EHRR 123 (European Convention on Human Rights 1950), where it was decided that an expropriation for the purpose of transferring property from one private person to another generally was not in the public interest, but if the property was expropriated from one private person and transferred to another in pursuance of legitimate social, economic or other policies it might be in the public interest. Compare further *X & Y v The Netherlands* [1975] 1 DR 66; *X and Others v Belgium* [1976] 3 DR 135; *Wiggins v The United Kingdom* [1978] 13 DR 40; *X v Austria* [1980] 17 DR 80 (all decisions of the European Commission of Human Rights). In both Germany and Switzerland it is accepted that private persons or businesses may benefit from an expropriation if it is clear that they are acting in or otherwise empowered to promote the public interest, eg a private company which provides electricity: see *BVerfGE* 66, 248 [1984]; *BVerfGE* 68, 193 [1984]; *BVerfGE* 74, 264 [1986] (*Boxberg*) (all Germany). See the discussion below.

[245] See *Trinidad Island-Wide Cane Farmers' Association Inc and Attorney General v Prakash Seereeram* (1975) 27 WIR 329 (CA) (Trinidad & Tobago); *Clunies-Ross v Commonwealth* (1984) 155 CLR 193 (majority judgment) (Australia); *VfSlg 8981/1980* (Austria); *BVerfGE* 74, 264 [1986] (*Boxberg*) (Germany); *Government of Malaysia & Another v Selangor Pilot Association* (1977) 1 MLJ 133 (Malaysia).

[246] See *Bank of New South Wales v The Commonwealth* (1948) 76 CLR 1 at 206; *PJ Magennis Pty Ltd v Commonwealth* (1949) 80 CLR 382 (Australia).

[247] See footnote 238 above.

If one accepts that the approach should not be narrow, it could be said that the public purpose requirement in section 25(2) has a double function, namely to control the justification and authority for expropriations in the way that constitutional property clauses usually do, and further to ensure that this 'normal' function of the property clause does not impede or frustrate expropriations that form part of land and other, similar reforms to which the Constitution commits itself.[248] This double function of the public purpose requirement reflects the tension that characterizes the whole of section 25, which provides a constitutional property guarantee while simultaneously promoting and legitimising land reforms that could involve state infringements of existing property holdings. To serve this double function, the public purpose requirement in section 25(2) should be interpreted strictly to ensure that the power of expropriation is not abused, but it also has to be interpreted leniently in recognition of the fact that much-needed and constitutionally legitimated land reform may require expropriation of private property in favour of other private beneficiaries. In this section such a double-sided interpretation of the public purpose requirement is described as a lenient but fairly strict approach to indicate that it allows for expropriations that involve transfers to private beneficiaries in the public interest, but nevertheless requires fairly strict control over the legitimacy of the public purpose and over the lawfulness and authority of expropriation as a means to serve that particular public purpose. In other words, this approach does not involve complete deference to legislative or executive decisions with regard to the public purpose of expropriation, but it does not frustrate land reform on a narrow liberal interpretation either.[249] Comparative law is quite useful in developing such a double-sided interpretation.

---

[248]T Roux 'Section 25' in S Woolman et al (eds) *Constitutional law of South Africa* (2nd ed 2003 original service Dec 2003) 46–33; A Eisenberg '"Public purpose" and expropriation: Some comparative insights and the South African bill of rights' (1995) 11 *SAJHR* 207–221; T Roux 'Property' in MH Cheadle, DM Davis & NRL Haysom *South African constitutional law: The bill of rights* (2002) 429–472 at 464. Compare (with reference to the 1993 Constitution) G Budlender 'The constitutional protection of property rights' in G Budlender, J Latsky & T Roux *Juta's new land law* (original service 1998) 1-48−1-55.

[249]In many ways this approach is perhaps typical of what Karl Klare 'Legal culture and transformative constitutionalism' (1998) 14 *SAJHR* 146–188 at 150 described as 'transformative constitutionalism': 'a long-term project of constitutional enactment, interpretation, and enforcement committed [...] to transforming a country's political and social institutions and power relationships in a democratic, participatory, and egalitarian direction.' In this instance, the transformative aspirations of a legitimate land reform programme are served by a lenient interpretation of the public purpose requirement, while the constitutional controls of legitimacy and proper authorization are applied more strictly. For further explorations of the theme see H Botha 'Metaphoric reasoning and transformative constitutionalism' 2002 *TSAR* 612–627; 2003 *TSAR* 20–36; D Moseneke 'The fourth Bram Fischer memorial lecture: Transformative adjudication' (2002) 18 *SAJHR* 309–319; H Botha 'Freedom and constraint in constitutional adjudication' (2004) 20 *SAJHR* 249–283.

5.7.2 Pre-constitutional expropriation law

Gildenhuys[250] points out that a lenient (but reasonably strict) approach was already favoured in pre-constitutional expropriation law, albeit only in instances where such an approach was indicated by the phraseology of the authorizing statute.[251] In *Administrator, Transvaal and Another v J van Streepen (Kempton Park) (Pty) Ltd*[252] the court distinguished between expropriation in the public interest (which could accommodate the lenient interpretation) and expropriation for a public purpose (which would not), pointing out that the correct approach in each case depends upon the wording of the statutory provision that authorizes the expropriation. This decision confirms that, during the pre-constitutional era, the courts were willing to follow a lenient interpretation that corresponds with the wider notion of public interest or a narrower interpretation that corresponds with the notion of public purpose, depending upon the authorizing statute and the context.

However, in view of the double-barrelled provision in section 25(2) of the Constitution (that includes both phrases), this distinction has lost all meaning in the constitutional era: in view of the formal, normative and interpretive superiority of the Constitution and the obvious effort to frame the constitutional requirement purposefully to leave room for land-reform related expropriation, the lenient approach should now always prevail when a statute authorizes expropriation in terms of either 'public purpose' or 'public interest.'[253] It is of course possible that an enabling statute could explicitly impose a stricter or narrower public purpose requirement, but in view of the *Van Streepen* decision and the subsequent constitutional requirement use of the phrases 'public purpose' and/or 'public interest' that should no longer make any difference in principle.

---

[250] A Gildenhuys *Onteieningsreg* (2nd ed 2001) 94–99. See further G Budlender 'The constitutional protection of property rights' in G Budlender, J Latsky & T Roux *Juta's new land law* (original service 1998) 1-48–1-50.

[251] This seems to be borne out by the most important pre-constitutional decisions. The most important decisions referred to by A Gildenhuys *Onteieningsreg* (2nd ed 2001) 95 are *Slabbert v Minister van Lande* 1963 (3) SA 620 (T); *African Farms and Townships v Cape Town Municipality* 1961 (3) SA 392 (C); *Fourie v Minister van Lande en 'n Ander* 1970 (4) SA 165 (O), but the most significant decision that is also cited by international sources such as T Allen *The right to property in Commonwealth constitutions* (2000) is *Administrator, Transvaal and Another v J van Streepen (Kempton Park) (Pty) Ltd* 1990 (4) SA 644 (A). In the *Van Streepen* case the former Appellate Division of the Supreme Court (at 660I–661I) explicitly accepted the lenient approach with reference to the private electricity supplier example that is also referred to in the section on German law below (*BVerfGE* 66, 248 [1984]); see footnote 287 below. Section 2(1) of the Expropriation Act 63 of 1975 authorizes expropriation for public purposes, and section 1 defines 'public purposes' as including 'any purposes connected with the administration of any law by an organ of State'.

[252] 1990 (4) SA 644 (A) at 660I–661I.

[253] A Gildenhuys *Onteieningsreg* (2nd ed 2001) 98. See also to the same effect and with reference to the same cases G Budlender 'The constitutional protection of property rights' in G Budlender, J Latsky & T Roux *Juta's new land law* (original service 1998) 1-48–1-50.

5.7.3 Comparative perspective: General remarks

Thorough and sensible comparative analysis requires careful reflection about the comparative sources to be used, and this is particularly true with regard to the public purpose requirement. In the final analysis only a few jurisdictions offer useful comparative information and argument for the South African context in this particular sphere. English law is largely irrelevant with regard to the public purpose requirement[254] because debate about the legitimacy of the purpose of any expropriation takes place in parliament (when the law is made) and not in court.[255] Extra-parliamentary control to ensure that expropriations would not be unlawful and arbitrary has therefore always been served by other legal methods such as administrative review and the interpretation of the authorizing statute[256] and not by constitutional review.[257] The introduction of the Human Rights Act 1998 changed this position in so far as the European Convention now applies in the UK.[258]

In fact, there is very little by way of Commonwealth case law that can cast any useful light on the public purpose requirement. The Irish property clause is phrased and interpreted in such a unique way that case law dealing with the limitation of property based on 'the exigencies of the common good' can hardly be compared meaningfully with the public purpose requirement in section 25(2), particularly because the requirement relates to both deprivation and expropriation of property. However, probably at least partly under the influence of European law the High Court of Ireland surprisingly did give an important and applicable decision on the public purpose requirement recently.[259] The Court of Appeal of Trinidad and

[254]This conclusion should be relatively obvious in view of the doctrine of parliamentary sovereignty and the lack of constitutional review based on a written supreme constitution. These considerations have changed to an extent because of the introduction of the Human Rights Act 1998; see the discussion below.

[255]See T Allen *The right to property in Commonwealth constitutions* (2000) 201, 204; M Taggart 'Expropriation, public purpose and the Constitution' in C Forsyth & I Hare (eds) *The golden metwand and the crooked cord: Essays on public law in honour of Sir William Wade QC* (1998) 91–112 at 101–112, particularly 101–103.

[256]In this respect English law does resemble German law; see the discussion in 5.6 above. However, in addition to control over the authorization of expropriation German law also allows for judicial control over the justification of expropriation, and that is where English law is different and of less significance in a comparative perspective.

[257]Other procedures include parliamentary private bill procedures, administrative law, the *ultra vires* doctrine, and the rules of statutory interpretation.

[258]The European Convention law is discussed in 5.7.5 below.

[259]The phrase 'the exigencies of the common good' appears in article 43(2) of the Constitution of Ireland 1937. For more detail see G Hogan & G Whyte (eds) *JM Kelly: The Irish Constitution* (4th ed 2003) paras [7.7.20]—[7.7.47], [7.7.78]—[7.7.81]. Although there are cases in which the Irish courts have treated this requirement with varying degrees of deference, many of the early cases concern the legitimacy of regulatory laws and not expropriations, and therefore it does not seem useful to pursue this comparison. See AJ van der Walt *Constitutional property clauses: A comparative analysis* (1999) 229–244, particularly 238–239. In a recent decision of the Irish Supreme Court it
(continued on next page ...)

Tobago[260] and the Australian High Court[261] have decided in one case each that expropriation aimed at land restitution was unconstitutional because it was not for a public purpose but, as will be argued below, these two decisions offer poor authority for that proposition. A number of Indian cases upheld redistributory laws that authorized expropriation of private land in order to provide housing, thereby continuing an earlier trend to read the public interest requirement quite broadly, arguing that the public interest was served in the process. However, these cases formed part of a battle between the Indian legislature and the courts that ended with the property clause being scrapped from the Indian Bill of Rights in 1978, and consequently the case law is conflicting and of limited comparative value, apart from establishing the possibility that the public purpose requirement could be interpreted widely in a setting where land reform is an important social, economic and political goal.[262]

(... from previous page)
was held (arguably with regard to deprivation rather than expropriation of private property) that statutory measures that abrogate property rights purely for state financial reasons could only be justified with reference to the common good if those measures were required objectively to avoid an extreme financial crisis or a fundamental disequilibrium in public finances: *In the Matter of Article 26 of The Constitution & In the Matter of the Health (Amendment) (No. 2) Bill 2004* [2005] IESC 7 (Supreme Court of Ireland 16 Feb 2005). In another recent decision that dealt with compulsory purchase (expropriation), the High Court of Ireland adopted a fairly strict attitude with regard to the public purpose requirement: compulsory purchase is a serious invasion of property rights that cannot be justified simply by payment of compensation, because the right to private property cannot be equated with the right to compensation. Therefore the decision to expropriate must be reconcilable with the exigencies of the common good and the principles of social justice, and there must be a sufficient and proper public purpose, that cannot be achieved by lesser means, for a compulsory acquisition. Furthermore, the margin of appreciation allowed for the legislature with regard to fundamental rights is not as wide in cases of compulsory acquisition as it may be in cases of social welfare benefits or taxation; both the relevant statutory provisions that authorise the acquisition and the manner in and purpose for which they are exercised are subject to heightened scrutiny: *Clinton v an Bord Pleanála and Others* [2005] IEHC 84. I am indebted to Gerry Whyte for bringing these decisions to my attention.

[260] *Trinidad Island-Wide Cane Farmers' Association Inc and Attorney General v Prakash Seereeram* (1975) 27 WIR 329 (CA). See T Allen *The right to property in Commonwealth constitutions* (2000) 210–211 and compare the discussion below. See also AJ van der Walt *Constitutional property clauses: A comparative analysis* (1999) 391–394. For the contrary position see the discussion and references below.

[261] *Clunies-Ross v The Commonwealth of Australia and Others* (1984) 155 CLR 193. See AJ van der Walt *Constitutional property clauses: A comparative analysis* (1999) 57–58.

[262] See T Allen *The right to property in Commonwealth constitutions* (2000) 204–210; *Hamabai Framjee Petit v Secretary of State for India* (1914) 42 IA 44; *Bihar v Singh* AIR 1952 SC 252; *Babu Barkya Thakur v State of Bombay* AIR 1960 SC 1203, [1961] 1 SCR 128; *Arnold Rodricks v Maharashtra* AIR 1966 SC 1788, [1966] 3 SCR 885. Allen (2000) refers to other housing cases at 207 footnotes 28–30. A Eisenberg '"Public purpose" and expropriation: Some comparative insights and the South African bill of rights' (1995) 11 *SAJHR* 207–221 at 216–218 discusses the same cases and points out that they gave the public purpose requirement a liberal interpretation. See AJ van der Walt *Constitutional property clauses: A comparative analysis* (1999) 188–228, particularly 192–206 on the Indian history that resulted in the scrapping of the property clause.

Despite the absence of a 'normal' public purpose requirement in section 51 of the Australian Commonwealth Constitution Act of 1900,[263] there are a number of Australian decisions on public purpose issues, but upon closer scrutiny most of them turn out to be less applicacable than they appear.[264] In an early case,[265] the Australian court confirmed that compulsory acquisition must be undertaken for a purpose in respect of which the federal government is empowered to make laws in terms of section 51. Superficially this phrase resembles the 'normal' public purpose require-ment, but in fact it underlines the uniqueness of the Australian provision: compulsory acquisition is subject to a control requirement that is less concerned with the public purpose of compulsory acquisition than with the division of state and federal legisla-tive powers in section 51. In addition to a number of other factors,[266] the focus on federal and state powers in the Australian Constitution means that case law dealing

---

[263] Section 51(xxxi) of the Australian Commonwealth Constitution Act (1900) reads as follows:
'Section 9; Part V: Powers of the Parliament, section 51 (xxxi)
51. The Parliament shall, subject to this Constitution, have power to make laws for the peace, order and good government of the Commonwealth with respect to:—
[...]
(xxxi) The acquisition of property on just terms from any State or person for any purpose in respect of which the Parliament has the power to make laws;
[...]'

[264] Although some of them illustrate the difference between public purpose issues revolving around third party expropriations with a redistributory purpose (which is usually accepted as being in the public interest or for a public purpose) and other third party expropriations involving what Tom Allen *The right to property in Commonwealth constitutions* (2000) at 212 calls 'the holdout problem' (contrasting it with the more straightforward redistribution problem), where the state is forced to expropriate one private person for the benefit of another private person who is undertaking a private development considered to be in the public interest, but whose development is frustrated or held up by the one owner who does not want to sell or negotiate on any reasonable terms. See the discussion below for details and references, and compare the German *Dürkheimer Gondelbahn* and *Boxberg* cases discussed in 5.7.4 below.

[265] *Bank of New South Wales v The Commonwealth* (1948) 76 CLR 1 at 300–301.

[266] One important consideration is that the Australian Commonwealth Constitution Act 1900 does not include a classic bill of rights, and although section 51(xxxi) of the Constitution has acquired something of the status of a property clause in case law, there are still many differences. Another, related consideration is that the Constitution in general and section 51(xxxi) in particular are more concerned with the articulation between federal and state powers than with individual rights. Thirdly, in terms of the Australian Commonwealth Constitution expropriation is possible under various constitutional heads of power, but compensation (just terms) is required only by section 51(xxxi), and consequently many cases are concerned with deciding when a compulsory acquisi-tion falls under this section and when not. A fourth consideration is that section 51(xxxi) is struc-tured and phrased in such a unique fashion that many decisions are concerned with clarification of issues that would not have featured or would have adopted a different shape in other jurisdictions with a classic property clause. This last observation is specifically true with regard to the traditional distinction between regulation (and deprivation) of property and expropriation (or compulsory acquisition)—since only the latter is mentioned in section 51(xxxi), many cases are concerned with the distinction between these categories and determining when compensation (just terms) is required. All of these considerations have a direct bearing on case law concerning the public purpose requirement, and as a result some care is required when referring to Australian case law in this context. See AJ van der Walt *Constitutional property clauses: A comparative analysis* (1999) 39–46, 48–57; T Allen 'The acquisition of property on just terms' (2000) 22 *Sydney LR* 351–380 at 352–358, 362–371, 375–379.

with this aspect has limited comparative value for the South African context. It is difficult to ignore Australian case law altogether, since at least one case (*Clunies-Ross v The Commonwealth of Australia and Others*)[267] is directly important for comparative analysis, but apart from that even the decisions that look interesting are not really significant for a comparative analysis of public purpose issues.[268] Australian case law is

---

[267](1984) 155 CLR 193. This case is discussed in the section on strict interpretation of the public purpose requirement in 5.7.4 below.

[268]The reasons why promising looking cases are not relevant can be summarized as follows: (*a*) One group of Australian cases seem to establish that compulsory acquisitions are valid even if the property was expropriated for and transferred to another private person. However, these cases in fact establish that the compensation duty imposed by section 51(xxxi) applies even when the state itself does not acquire or use the property, provided it was clear from the outset that the property was acquired under and in accordance with powers granted in section 51(xxxi). These decisions are therefore coloured by the focus on federal and state powers in section 51 and not by public purpose considerations. See *PJ Magennis Pty Ltd v The Commonwealth* (1949) 80 CLR 382 (an acquisition in terms of section 51(xxxi) is involved even if the property was not acquired by the federal government itself, but by another organ of state or even another person; the identity of the eventual acquirer was irrelevant, and the acquisition would be subject to the just terms requirement in section 51(xxxi) as long as it was done in terms of a law of the Commonwealth concerned with the acquisition of property for a Commonwealth purpose); *Australian Tape Manufacturers Association Ltd and Others v The Commonwealth of Australia* (1993) 177 CLR 480 at 508–511 (*obiter*: a statutory obligation to pay a sum of money may amount to an acquisition of property even if the money is to be paid to someone else than the Commonwealth). Compare AJ van der Walt *Constitutional property clauses: A comparative analysis* (1999) 39–46, 48–57; T Allen 'The acquisition of property on just terms' (2000) 22 *Sydney LR* 351–380 at 376–377. (*b*) In two sets of cases that seem to deal with the public purpose issue the Australian courts decided that the compensation duty does not apply to interferences with private property that fall outside of the scope of compulsory acquisition in terms of section 51(xxxi). (i) The issue in the first set of cases was that, even when the state does acquire private property compulsorily, this does not require compensation unless the acquisition was specifically made under the power granted in section 51(xxxi)—in terms of the Australian Constitution, the state can compulsorily acquire property under various heads of constitutional power, and it is only section 51(xxxi) that requires compensation. The cases dealing with this issue of state powers establish that the compulsory acquisitions in question were not carried out in terms of section 51(xxxi) and therefore do not provide useful comparative material for the public purpose requirement, even though they seem to deal with public purpose. See *Attorney-General (Commonwealth) v Schmidt* (1961) 105 CLR 361 at 372 (section 51(xxxi) should be restricted to government procurement cases, where the Commonwealth acquires property for its own use in the execution of its duties; this does not apply to seizure of enemy property); *Burton v Honan* (1952) 86 CLR 169 (seizure of goods in terms of customs legislation); *Re Director of Public Prosecutions; ex parte Lawler* (1994) 179 CLR 270 (forfeiture of property in terms of customs legislation). See further T Allen 'The acquisition of property on just terms' (2000) 22 *Sydney LR* 351–380 at 377–379. (ii) The second set of cases excluded certain limitations of private property from the compensation duty in section 51(xxxi) on the basis that they were not compulsory acquisitions at all. Section 51(xxxi) mentions only compulsory acquisitions, and the courts had to fashion their own criteria for distinguishing between compensable expropriations and noncompensable deprivations of property. Many of these decisions create the impression that they involve the public purpose issue in the sense that they concern transfers of expropriated property to a private party, but in fact they establish that

(continued on next page ...)

therefore of limited interest in discussing the public purpose issue in the South African context, and therefore the discussion below refers only to the decision in *Clunies-Ross v The Commonwealth of Australia and Others*,[269] where it was explicitly held that compulsory acquisition for land reform purposes was unconstitutional because it was not carried out for a public purpose.

German law is a much more important source for comparative analysis because the German courts interpret the public purpose requirement in the German constitution (Basic Law 1949) leniently enough to allow expropriation that benefits private persons in some cases. However, despite the lenient approach the requirement is interpreted and enforced fairly strictly, with the courts giving a detailed account of how the requirement should be applied in different contexts. German law is discussed in 5.7.4 below.

The US courts have applied the public use requirement in the Fifth Amendment to the US Constitution very leniently, even in situations where private property was expropriated for the benefit of a private person. These cases offer good possibilities for comparative analysis, because they illustrate an approach of almost extreme deference with regard to the public purpose requirement. The public use requirement in the European Convention on Human Rights is stated in a unique and problematic format, but the European Court of Human Rights also defers largely to state governments' choices and decisions regarding the public interest in expropriation. US and European Convention law is discussed in 5.7.5 below.

In the rest of this section comparative analysis will therefore focus on German law and US law as the two examples of strict and deferent interpretations of the public purpose requirement respectively, with additional references to the jurisprudence of the European Court of Human Rights and to single cases from Australia and Trinidad and Tobago.

(... from previous page)
state actions that interfere with private property (even up to the point of extinguishing property interests, especially in the form of debts) in the process of regulating competing and conflicting private interests do not qualify as compulsory acquisitions of property in terms of section 51(xxxi), unless the state itself acquires some benefit from them. Consequently, section 51(xxxi) and the compensation duty only apply when there is not only a taking away or deprivation of property but also some indication of benefit or advantage for the state. Once again, the cases establishing this point are of limited comparative interest in the South African context because they do not address the public purpose issue as such. See *Trade Practices Commission and Another v Tooth & Co Ltd and Another* (1979) 142 CLR 397 (regulatory deprivations of property do not involve acquisitions in the broad sense and therefore did not require compensation in terms of section 51(xxxi)); *Mutual Pools and Staff Pty Ltd v The Commonwealth of Australia* (1994) 179 CLR 155 at 223; *Georgiades v Australian and Overseas Telecommunications Corporation* (1994) 179 CLR 297 at 305; *Nintendo Co Ltd v Centronics Systems Pty Ltd* (1994) 181 CLR 134; AJ van der Walt *Constitutional property clauses: A comparative analysis* (1999) 46–48; T Allen 'The acquisition of property on just terms' (2000) 22 *Sydney Law Review* 351–380 at 375–379.

[269](1984) 155 CLR 193. This case is discussed in the section on strict interpretation of the public purpose requirement in 5.7.4 below.

5.7.4 Strict interpretation of the public purpose requirement

It has been said above that a public purpose requirement can be interpreted narrowly to restrict expropriations to instances where the state actually acquires the property for public or state use, or more widely. Expropriation for a purpose that is not properly authorized, frivolous, arbitrary or corrupt will be invalid regardless of the approach followed, but a very narrow interpretation would also exclude (or invalidate) instances where the property is transferred—directly or in due course—to another private person as part of a legitimate state programme such as land reform, provision of public housing or private provision of public utilities.[270] Such a narrow interpretation, according to which expropriation for transfer to a private person is fundamentally not for a public purpose and therefore unconstitutional, was adopted in two significant decisions.

In *Trinidad Island-Wide Cane Farmers' Association Inc and Attorney General v Prakash Seereeram*[271] the Trinidad and Tobago Court of Appeal decided that a statutory provision that imposed the obligation to pay a certain sum of money to the state, who then pays the money to a private corporation, was neither a legitimate tax nor a valid expropriation, because it was not for a public purpose. The fact that the money was taken from one private person to be given to another was central in the decision that the imposition did not serve a public purpose, and several of the judges stated explicitly in their opinions that property cannot legitimately be expropriated from one private person to be given to another. Allen points out that the decision cannot be regarded as good authority since it relied on US case law but ignored the US Supreme Court's repudiation of its own older, narrow public use doctrine.[272] As Allen explains, the more expansive view that—all other things being equal—expropriation for land reform could satisfy the public purpose requirement was accepted in most Commonwealth jurisdictions even before the Trinidad & Tobago case was decided.[273]

The second case in which the narrow interpretation was adopted is *Clunies-Ross v The Commonwealth of Australia and Others*,[274] which involved a compulsory acquisition of land that the government acquired to break down the social and political relation-

---

[270] As will appear from the discussion below this can assume different forms. One possibility is that the state expropriates property from A in order to give it to B for some public purpose such as land redistribution. A second possibility is that the state expropriates property from A to give it to B, who needs it to fulfil a privatized state purpose such as delivery of electricity. A third possibility is that the state expropriates property from A to give it to B for a private purpose (such as economic development) or job creation that would benefit the public in general without serving a narrow public purpose.

[271] (1975) 27 WIR 329 (CA). Compare AJ van der Walt *Constitutional property clauses: A comparative analysis* (1999) 391–394.

[272] For a discussion of later US law see 5.7.5 below.

[273] T Allen *The right to property in Commonwealth constitutions* (2000) 210–211.

[274] (1984) 155 CLR 193. See AJ van der Walt *Constitutional property clauses: A comparative analysis* (1999) 57–58; G Budlender 'The constitutional protection of property rights' in G Budlender, J Latsky & T Roux *Juta's new land law* (original service 1998) 1-53–1-54.

ship (described as 'feudal') between the plaintiff and the rest of the community of the Cocos Island. The majority in *Clunies-Ross* took the view that the social and political wisdom of the reasons why the government wanted to expropriate land was irrelevant, and that the limits of public purpose in the context of expropriation are indicated simply by considerations of law. The majority construed the power to expropriate narrowly to acquisitions of land needed or to be used, applied or preserved for the advancement or achievement of a specific public purpose; excluding expropriations for other purposes such as land reform, regardless of their social or political merits.[275]

Generally speaking the Australian court in *Clunies-Ross* and the Trinidad and Tobago court in *Trinidad Island-Wide Cane Farmers' Association* applied the public purpose requirement extremely conservatively—as is indicated below, most courts now favour a more lenient approach according to which expropriation for the benefit of a private person may sometimes be justified as being for a public purpose.

Even the German courts, while favouring fairly strict scrutiny of the public purpose requirement in article 14.3.1 of the Basic Law,[276] nevertheless allow room for situations where expropriation could be justified as being for a public purpose although a private person benefits from it in some way. In this regard the German application of this requirement is more sophisticated than the two cases discussed above. The German approach can be characterized as strict rather than narrow, in the sense that it allows for a more lenient interpretation of the public purpose requirement but still insists upon a reasonably high level of scrutiny in applying the public purpose standard. This lenient but fairly strict approach enables the German courts to control the public purpose limits of the state's power of expropriation without necessarily frustrating social or economic reforms that require expropriation and redistribution of private property or the promotion of private property interests that also serve the public purpose.

---

[275] In a dissenting judgment Murphy J agreed that capricious acquisition of land would not be for a public purpose, but he did not think that the social considerations in this case indicated such capricious acquisition and he considered the context relevant. In this instance the history and surrounding circumstances indicated, in his view, that the expropriation of the plaintiff's property was necessary for the process of breaking down the existing feudal relationship between the plaintiff and the other inhabitants of the Cocos (Keeling) Islands. In this context Murphy J referred to the US decision in *Hawaii Housing Authority v Midkiff* 467 US 229 (1984) (see the discussion below) as authority for the view that compulsory acquisitions meant to break down existing unhealthy land distribution patterns was valid state action for a public purpose.

[276] The Basic Law for the Federal Republic of Germany 1949 (*Grundgesetz für die Bundesrepublik Deutschland*; GG) provides as follows in article 14.3.1: 'Expropriation shall only be permissible in the public interest. […]'

The German Federal Constitutional Court[277] treats the public purpose requirement as an open-ended but justiciable constitutional requirement that cannot be
amended by normal legislation or by administrative decision.[278] Any law or administrative action that does not comply with this requirement is in conflict with the Basic
Law and unconstitutional. The courts have the duty and the jurisdiction to test
whether every individual expropriation is justified by the public interest it is meant
to serve and authorized (by legislation) for that public purpose. The heart of the
German courts' treatment of this requirement is located in the double-barrelled
control over the justification of the expropriation by the public purpose it serves and
the authorization of the expropriation for that purpose. In other words, even when
the expropriation is clearly justified by the public purpose it still needs to be authorized as a valid means to attain or promote that particular end.

In German law, expropriation is justified in a given case if it is the only possible
way (*ultima ratio*) in which the specific public need or purpose can be satisfied, and (in
terms of the proportionality principle) if the expropriation is strictly necessary (*erforderlich*) to fulfil that purpose.[279] The public interest that justifies a specific expropriation
has to be sufficiently important to justify the extraordinary disturbance that expropriation brings about in the normal constitutional balance between the interests of the
individual and of society, and must justify subjecting the individual interest to those of
society in that specific case (referred to as the justification aspect of the public purposes

---

[277] *Bundesverfassungsgericht—BVerfG.* See footnote 296 below. In a recent decision the High Court
of Ireland followed a remarkably similar approach with regard to the public purpose requirement,
saying that compulsory purchase is a serious invasion of property rights that cannot be justified
simply by payment of compensation, because the right to private property cannot be equated with
the right to compensation. Therefore the decision to expropriate must be reconcilable with the
exigencies of the common good and the principles of social justice, and there must be a sufficient
and proper public purpose, that cannot be achieved by lesser means, for a compulsory acquisition.
Furthermore, the margin of appreciation allowed for the legislature with regard to fundamental
rights is not as wide in cases of compulsory acquisition as it may be in cases of social welfare benefits
or taxation; both the relevant statutory provisions that authorise the acquisition and the manner in
and purpose for which they are exercised are subject to heightened scrutiny: *Clinton v an Bord
Pleanála and Others* [2005] IEHC 84. The similarities with German law are explained by the fact
that Finnegan P in *Clinton* referred to a passage in G Hogan & G Whyte (eds) *JM Kelly: The Irish
Constitution* (4th ed 2003) par [7.7.88] where the authors argue in favour of following the German
approach to compensation in Irish law.

[278] The legislator can require stricter compliance in certain cases, but cannot overrule or weaken
the public purpose requirement. See in general HJ Papier 'Art. 14' in T Maunz, G Dürig et al (eds)
Grundgesetz Kommentar vol II (40th update 2002) 303; R Wendt 'Eigentum, Erbrecht und
Enteignung' in M Sachs (ed) *Grundgesetz Kommentar* (3rd ed 2002) 654–656 Rdn 160–165; B
Schmidt-Bleibtreu 'Art. 14' in B Schmidt-Bleibtreu & F Klein *Kommentar zum Grundgesetz* (9th ed
1999) 401–402 Rdn 13; *BVerfGE* 56, 249 [1981] (*Dürkheimer Gondelbahn*; especially the separate
concurring judgment of Böhmer J at 266ff); *BVerwGE* 3, 332 [1957] at 334. See further AJ van der
Walt *Constitutional property clauses: A comparative analysis* (1999) 147–149.

[279] If the public purpose could also be served by another measure (eg purchase of the land or use
of other land) the expropriation may be in conflict with the proportionality principle and unjustified. A similar attitude was recently followed by the High Court of Ireland; see footnote 277 above.

requirement).[280] Expropriations are not automatically validated when they are generally or loosely associated with some public purpose; each case has to be tested individually to establish that the expropriation actually serves a specific public purpose and is
justified by it in the sense that the public purpose is a more important or overriding
interest compared to the private interest that is affected by the expropriation.[281]

In addition to the justification of the expropriation, the public purpose relating to
a particular expropriation has to be established in every individual case with regard to
the authorizing legislation. The Federal Constitutional Court requires rigorous
control to see whether the goal of the expropriation—as set out in the authorizing
legislation—corresponds with a public purpose and whether that goal is in fact
concretely realized. In other words, apart from the requirement that its public
purpose should be important enough to justify an expropriation, the authorizing legislation must also authorize and enable the state to pursue or promote the specific
public purpose by means of the expropriation[282] (this is referred to as the authorizing
aspect of the public purpose requirement).

In line with the justification aspect of the public purpose requirement, German
courts agree that expropriation cannot be undertaken for improper purposes. More

---

[280] This interpretation confirms earlier German constitutional case law, where it was said that the
property guarantee was not a simple guarantee of compensation (*Wertgarantie*) upon expropriation:
the property holder is entitled to the property as such and not just to its value by way of compensation. Therefore, expropriation is not justified simply because the owner receives compensation—
compensation is the result of a legitimate expropriation and not a justification for expropriation.
Justification for each expropriation has to be established independently on the basis of the public
purpose requirement. See HJ Papier 'Art. 14' in T Maunz, G Dürig et al (eds) *Grundgesetz
Kommentar* vol II (40th update 2002) 309–310; R Wendt 'Eigentum, Erbrecht und Enteignung' in
M Sachs (ed) *Grundgesetz Kommentar* (3rd ed 2002) 655 Rdn 164; B Schmidt-Bleibtreu 'Art. 14' in
B Schmidt-Bleibtreu & F Klein *Kommentar zum Grundgesetz* (9th ed 1999) 401–402 Rdn 13;
BVerfGE 24, 367 [1968] *(Deichordnung)* at 404; *BVerfGE* 38, 175 [1974] at 179ff; *BVerfGE* 56, 249
[1981] *(Dürkheimer Gondelbahn)]* at 261; *BVerfGE* 74, 264 [1986] *(Boxberg)* at 296–297. See further
AJ van der Walt *Constitutional property clauses: A comparative analysis* (1999) 147–149. A similar attitude was recently followed by the High Court of Ireland; see footnote 277 above.
[281] This principle is especially relevant when the purpose of the expropriation is said to be planning
or building regulation in general—land use planning and building regulation are categories of state
action that are usually regarded as for a valid public purpose, but the mere fact that it forms part of
a larger scheme generally connected with land-use planning or building regulation does not automatically validate a particular expropriation. However, having said that, due regard is also to be had
for the powers of planning authorities to make planning decisions, and therefore the public purpose
that justifies a particular expropriation has to be established in every individual case with regard to
the authorizing legislation. See the decision of the High Court of Ireland referred to in footnote
277 above.
[282] See HJ Papier 'Art. 14' in T Maunz, G Dürig et al (eds) *Grundgesetz Kommentar* vol II (40th
update 2002) 304; B Schmidt-Bleibtreu 'Art. 14' in B Schmidt-Bleibtreu & F Klein *Kommentar zum
Grundgesetz* (9th ed 1999) 401–402 Rdn 13; *BVerfGE* 45, 297 [1977] at 321ff; *BVerfGE* 74, 264
[1987] 287ff; Böhmer J in the *Dürkheimer Gondelbahn* case (*BVerfGE* 56, 249 [1981]) 276, 277ff;
confirmed in *BVerfG,* 1 BvR 390/01 of 4.7.2001. See further AJ van der Walt *Constitutional property
clauses: A comparative analysis* (1999) 147–149.

specifically, expropriation cannot be justified for the general purpose of improving or increasing state property or wealth, since the purpose of the power to expropriate is not to enrich the state but to serve specific public purposes that cannot be fulfilled otherwise.[283] The same argument implies that property that was expropriated for a public purpose that was never realized (or for a purpose that ceased to exist) should be returned to the original owner, even if compensation was paid for it: if the public purpose in question is abandoned or never realized, the justification for the expropriation falls away and then there is no justification for the state retaining the property.[284] The public purpose that justifies expropriation has to endure beyond the act of expropriation and must have a lasting rather than fleeting or temporary quality to secure the interest of the public in the fulfilment of that purpose.[285]

Because expropriation cannot be undertaken for improper purposes, expropriation of one person's property to enrich or benefit another private person is generally not justifiable. The power of expropriation is particularly not intended to decide property disputes between private parties in favour of one of them.[286] However, that does not mean that the German courts will strike down an expropriation simply because a private person (such as a business concern) benefits from (or even undertakes) it—as long as it is clear that the expropriation is undertaken in pursuance of a public purpose or in the public interest, and not purely for personal gain, it could still satisfy the public purpose requirement. The textbook example is an expropriation of property that is required by a private person or institution that supplies public services in accordance with a contract with the responsible state authority: when the provision of services requires that private property be expropriated the public purpose require-

[283]See HJ Papier 'Art. 14' in T Maunz, G Dürig et al (eds) Grundgesetz Kommentar vol II (40th update 2002) 304; R Wendt 'Eigentum, Erbrecht und Enteignung' in M Sachs (ed) Grundgesetz Kommentar (3rd ed 2002) 655 Rdn 165; B Schmidt-Bleibtreu 'Art. 14' in B Schmidt-Bleibtreu & F Klein Kommentar zum Grundgesetz (9th ed 1999) 401–402 Rdn 13; BVerfGE 38, 175 [1974] 180; confirmed in BVerfG, 1 BvR 21/97 of 18.11.98.

[284]See HJ Papier 'Art. 14' in T Maunz, G Dürig et al (eds) Grundgesetz Kommentar vol II (40th update 2002) 310–311; R Wendt 'Eigentum, Erbrecht und Enteignung' in M Sachs (ed) Grundgesetz Kommentar (3rd ed 2002) 655–656 Rdn 165; BVerfGE 38, 175 [1974] 181ff; BVerfGE 56, 249 [1981] (Dürkheimer Gondelbahn) 260–261, 271; confirmed in BVerfGE 97, 89 [1997] at 89. See further AJ van der Walt Constitutional property clauses: A comparative analysis (1999) 147–149.

[285]See HJ Papier 'Art. 14' in T Maunz, G Dürig et al (eds) Grundgesetz Kommentar vol II (40th update 2002) 308; BVerfGE 56, 249 [1981] (Dürkheimer Gondelbahn) 271; confirmed in BVerfGE 97, 89 [1997] 89. See further AJ van der Walt Constitutional property clauses: A comparative analysis (1999) 147–149.

[286]See HJ Papier 'Art. 14' in T Maunz, G Dürig et al (eds) Grundgesetz Kommentar vol II (40th update 2002) 304; BVerfGE 56, 249 [1981] (Dürkheimer Gondelbahn) 270–271; BVerfGE 66, 248 [1984] 257; BVerfGE 74, 264 [1986] (Boxberg) 279ff. See further AJ van der Walt Constitutional property clauses: A comparative analysis (1999) 147–149.

ment is satisfied even though the private provider also makes a profit from the transaction and so benefits from the expropriation.[287]

Despite recognition of the possibility that expropriation for the benefit of a private person might in some cases satisfy the public purposes requirement, the German courts tend to apply the requirement rather strictly, and in a few cases expropriations that superficially seemed to satisfy the test were held to be unconstitutional. In the *Dürkheimer Gondelbahn* case[288] Böhmer J summarized the principles as follows: the public interest requirement means that expropriation has to be strictly necessary for some public duty that has to be carried out or undertaken; not every public action which serves the public interest in general or benefits the public in some general way is in the public interest as intended in article 14.3.1; 'public purpose' is a narrower category than 'public benefit'; and the mere fact that a development benefits the public is insufficient to satisfy the public purpose requirement in article 14.3.1.[289] Moreover, even when the expropriation does serve a legitimate public purpose the expropriating authority has to be properly authorized by legislation to expropriate in pursuit of that purpose.[290]

---

[287]The classic example is *BVerfGE* 66, 248 [1984], in which expropriation of property for the purpose of enabling a private person to provide electricity (on contract) was judged to be constitutional, even though the expropriated property was used by the private company to make a profit from the provision of services contract with the state. This case is regarded as authority for the proposition that expropriations for the benefit of private persons or entities that provide public services may be in accordance with the public purpose requirement. See HJ Papier 'Art. 14' in T Maunz, G Dürig et al (eds) *Grundgesetz Kommentar* vol II (40th update 2002) 304; B Schmidt-Bleibtreu 'Art. 14' in B Schmidt-Bleibtreu & F Klein *Kommentar zum Grundgesetz* (9th ed 1999) 401–402 Rdn 13; *BVerfGE* 56, 249 [1981] *(Dürkheimer Gondelbahn)* 279; *BVerfGE* 66, 248 [1984] 257ff; *BVerfGE* 74, 264 [1986] *(Boxberg)* 284ff. See further AJ van der Walt *Constitutional property clauses: A comparative analysis* (1999) 147–149.

[288] *BVerfGE* 56, 249 [1981] 266ff.

[289]See *BVerfGE* 56, 249 [1981] *(Dürkheimer Gondelbahn)* 266ff, especially 277ff. See further AJ van der Walt *Constitutional property clauses: A comparative analysis* (1999) 147–149.

[290] *BVerfGE* 56, 249 [1981]. The Federal Constitutional Court declared the expropriation in this case invalid because of a technical point regarding the powers of the local authority to authorize the expropriation and not on the basis of the public purpose requirement. Böhmer J set out his analysis and conclusions in a separate concurring judgment. A local entrepreneur and the local authority of the city of Dürkheim established a limited company with the purpose of building and managing a cable-car installation from the city to the nearby nature area Teufelstein. The company attempted unsuccessfully to purchase or acquire servitudes over the private properties over which the cable car would have to travel. An application of the company to have the properties (or servitudes over them) expropriated for the purpose was denied by the provincial authorities. The local authority then prepared a development plan for the city in which the expropriation of the necessary servitudes could be undertaken in terms of legislation pertaining to the building of public railroads, arguing that the cable car would serve the public transport interest by establishing access to the Teufelstein, which is a popular holiday area. The expropriation for the cable car system was held to be unconstitutional because the local authority lacked the necessary powers to expropriate private land for purposes of the development, even though the development would have introduced a generally beneficial addition to the public transport system.

In the subsequent *Boxberg* case[291] the Federal Constitutional Court held that the 'private' expropriation in question was unconstitutional because the authorizing legislation did not include a general expropriation power, but it pointed out that such an expropriation could be valid in other instances.[292] The case illustrates the way in which the courts apply different levels of scrutiny when considering the public purpose requirement, depending upon the context and the question whether the justification aspect or the authorization aspect of the requirement is at stake in a particular case. In each case where an expropriation benefits a private person, the courts will take particular note of the nature of the beneficiary's business, the purpose for which the expropriation is undertaken, and the provisions of the authorizing legislation. In general an expropriation in favour of a private person cannot be justified by vague and general claims that the expropriation also serves the general interests of the public, and consequently the possibility that a particular expropriation could benefit the economy or the labour market of the region would not justify a 'private' expropriation. However, general public benefit considerations of that nature could justify an expropriation when the economic or labour benefits were foreseen and set out concretely in the authorizing legislation.[293] In explaining this principle, the court emphasized that the person who benefits from an expropriation is not the decisive consideration in deciding whether the expropriation was constitutional. Article 14.3.1 requires that the expropriation should serve a public purpose, and that purpose must find its concrete embodiment in or on the basis of the authorizing statute. The clarity and concreteness with which such a benefit for the general economic or other aspects of regional welfare was foreseen and set out in the authorizing statute will be decisive in determining whether there was a sufficient foundation for accepting that the public purpose justified the expropriation in such a case. The courts seem willing to defer on the importance and justification of the expropriation when the private concern is obviously involved in a business venture or sphere of business that primarily delivers public services, but will apply stricter scrutiny on the justification aspect in all other cases, and will strictly scrutinize the authorization aspect in all cases.[294]

---

[291] *BVerfGE* 74, 264 [1986]. Expropriation of land to facilitate the establishment of a testing ground for a motor-car company was unconstitutional, even though the whole region would have benefited from the ensuing development, which would have created much-needed jobs and stimulated the economy. It was held in this case that the public purpose of the expropriation was not sufficiently established in the authorizing statute. Compare the US *Poletown* decision discussed in 5.7.5 text accompanying footnote 310 below.

[292] The indications that would support the validity of such an expropriation for the benefit of a private person as set out in this decision were confirmed in *BVerfG*, 1 BvR 1367/88 of 18.2.99.

[293] The same approach explains why regulatory or indirect expropriations are not recognized by the German Federal Constitutional Court: a valid expropriation is only possible if the expropriation, the public purpose it serves, and the compensation to be paid for it were foreseen and authorized in the authorizing legislation. See the discussion in 5.6 and in this section above.

[294] See HJ Papier 'Art. 14' in T Maunz, G Dürig et al (eds) *Grundgesetz Kommentar* vol II (40th update 2002) 306; R Wendt 'Eigentum, Erbrecht und Enteignung' in M Sachs (ed) *Grundgesetz Kommentar* (3rd ed 2002) 656 Rdn 161–162; *BVerfGE* 74, 264 [1986] *(Boxberg)* 284ff; confirmed in *BVerfG*, 1 BvR 1367/88 of 18.2.99.

Expropriation for the benefit of private persons was historically possible in Germany (and elsewhere), for instance in the establishment and development of the railway system. These developments were mostly undertaken by private entrepreneurs, and they have always been supported by expropriation powers. Moreover, it is now more and more common for entrepreneurs to do business in fields where they provide public services, especially with regard to public transport and provision of water and electricity, sanitation and other public utility services. In view of the Federal Constitutional Court's decisions in *Boxberg* and other similar cases it is not a problem to justify expropriation that benefits these private business concerns with reference to the public purpose requirement. When the normal business activity of a private concern takes place in the sphere of public service (eg businesses purely involved in provision of public transport or public services) expropriation for the benefit of such a concern would generally be admissible, provided that suitable provision has been made in the authorizing legislation to control the lawful fulfilment of that public purpose by the private concern. In these cases the courts will defer to the legislature's indication that expropriation is for a public purpose as far as justification of the expropriation is concerned. However, the authority to expropriate private property for the purpose in question will still be scrutinized strictly even in these cases, and the courts could still declare the expropriation invalid if the statutory authorization for the expropriation is deficient (as in the *Boxberg* case).

When the business sphere of the private concern is not in itself sufficient to indicate that a public purpose is served by the expropriation in favour of that concern, stricter controls are imposed even with regard to the justification aspect. In such a case an authorizing law is required that clearly describes the public purpose that is indirectly served by expropriation in favour of the private concern; sets out the expropriation requirements and procedures; and regulates control measures to ensure that the public purpose is indeed served. In these cases the courts will apply a higher level of scrutiny on the level of both the justification and the authorization aspects of the requirement.[295]

In view of the approach set out above, the public purpose requirement makes it difficult to justify expropriation that benefits private business concerns that do not provide public services on behalf of the state, although their activities might have indirect benefits for the public (eg in stimulating the economy, creating jobs etc). In

---

[295]Recently an expropriation was justified, following the *Boxberg* approach, in a case where the expropriated property was let on a long lease to a private school, arguing that the establishment of schools was an important public purpose that directly benefited the city. This public purpose justified the expropriation even though the school in question was a private school. The Court was also satisfied that the purpose for the expropriation and control mechanisms were set out clearly in the authorizing legislation, and that the state had the necessary expropriation power. See *BVerfG*, 1 BvR 1367/88 of 18.2.99.

this respect, the German Federal Administrative Court[296] has held that expropriation can satisfy the public purpose requirement when it forms part of a development scheme specifically intended to create jobs, even when private developers also benefit from the development. In the view of commentators, this justification is similar to situations where expropriation serves other socio-political purposes such as improvement of the distribution of land or other property. Recently a similar expropriation was held to be justified in a case where the expropriated property was let on a long lease to a private school, arguing that the establishment of schools was an important and concrete public purpose that directly benefited the city and the public interest.[297] The courts will scrutinize both the justification for expropriation and the authority aspects strictly in these circumstances, but in this case the purpose and control mechanisms were set out clearly in the authorizing legislation.

Despite these expanding arguments, not every public benefit would justify expropriation (in general or in favour of a private person). In the final analysis, the public purpose that is supposed to justify any expropriation has to embody a particularly important, urgent need of the public, and it has to be rooted in the authorizing legislation.[298] It has recently again been confirmed that the general justification of socially and economically needed housing development might justify a development plan in general, but it has to be established for every individual property that is expropriated whether the expropriation of that property is necessary for the public purpose.[299]

In conclusion, the narrow interpretation of the public purpose requirement that would exclude expropriations for land reform and similar purposes simply because the property is transferred to private beneficiaries seems to be outdated. In German law the public purpose requirement is taken very seriously and applied fairly strictly, but even then there is room for expropriation that serves a public purpose even though it also benefits private persons in some way. Accordingly, the public purpose requirement need not stand in the way of land reform and similar initiatives that require expropriation from which private persons will benefit, even when interpreted reasonably strictly. At the same time, strict scrutiny of the authority for expropriation and (in some cases) the justification for its purpose means that German courts retain a large measure of control over the state's exercise of its power of expropriation, both with

---

[296] *Bundesverwaltungsgericht—BVerwG*. The German administrative courts have jurisdiction with regard to the administrative aspects of expropriation, while the civil courts (of which the highest is the *Bundesgerichtshof in Zivilsachen—BGHZ*) has jurisdiction regarding compensation; the constitutional courts (of which the highest is the *Bundesverfassungsgericht—BVerfG*) have jurisdiction regarding constitutional validity. See AJ van der Walt *Constitutional property clauses: A comparative analysis* (1999) 122–123.

[297] See HJ Papier 'Art. 14' in T Maunz, G Dürig et al (eds) *Grundgesetz Kommentar* vol II (40th update 2002) 307–308; confirmed in *BVerfG*, 1 BvR 1367/88 of 18.2.99.

[298] See *BVerfGE* 56, 249 [1981] (*Dürkheimer Gondelbahn*) 266ff, especially 277ff. See further AJ van der Walt *Constitutional property clauses: A comparative analysis* (1999) 147–149.

[299] See HJ Papier 'Art. 14' in T Maunz, G Dürig et al (eds) *Grundgesetz Kommentar* vol II (40th update 2002) 307–308; Böhmer J in the *Dürkheimer Gondelbahn* case (*BVerfGE* 56, 249 [1981]) 284ff; confirmed in *BVerfG*, 1 BvR 390/01 of 4.7.2001.

regard to the justification for each expropriation in terms of the public purpose it is supposed to serve and the actual statutory authorization for and realization of that purpose through the expropriation.

The most significant results of the German approach are that (*a*) expropriation for improper, arbitrary and frivolous purposes will never be valid; (*b*) expropriation can be valid despite the fact that it also benefits private persons, provided it serves a legitimate public purpose; (*c*) in testing for the public purpose requirement the courts use different levels of scrutiny regarding the justification of expropriation, depending upon the nature of the beneficiary's business and the context, but they always test strictly as far as the authorization of expropriation for its specific purpose and the actual realization of the goal are concerned; and (*d*) expropriation that does not realize (or continue to realize) its goals may be reversed.

5.7.5 Lenient interpretation of the public purpose requirement

In contrast with German law, which allows for expropriation that benefits private persons but still apply relatively strict review controls through selective heightened scrutiny, the US Supreme Court and the European Court of Human Rights simply defer to the legislature and executive with regard to the public purpose requirement. In both cases the role of the courts is extremely restricted and the legislature is given a wide scope in determining what is or is not a public purpose for purposes of expropriation. The property clause in the US Constitution requires that expropriation must be for public use,[300] and after an initial phase during which this requirement was applied narrowly, the US courts have developed what could be described as a thin, deferent interpretation of the public purpose requirement.[301] This approach to the public use requirement was set out in a line of case law that runs from *Berman v Parker* through to *Hawaii Housing Authority v Midkiff*.[302] The point of departure is that the

---

[300] The Takings Clause in the last part of the Fifth Amendment to the US Constitution provides that '... nor shall private property be taken for public use without just compensation.'

[301] Authorities agree that the US Supreme Court 'does not give teeth' to this provision, preferring to adopt an attitude of extreme deference towards the legislator in determining what is or is not for the public good in general or a public use in particular. Generally speaking it is said that the Court lacks 'any coherent and broadly accepted theory of the public good as more than an aggregate of private needs and wants': see LH Tribe *American constitutional law* (3rd ed 2000) at 837, referring to judicial review of federal spending powers, but linking it to the public use requirement in the Takings Clause. See further A Eisenberg '"Public purpose" and expropriation: Some comparative insights and the South African bill of rights' (1995) 11 *SAJHR* 207–221 at 209–216.

[302] This attitude has been confirmed in the most important decisions of the US Supreme Court dealing with the public use requirement, going back to *Miller v Schoene* 276 US 272 (1928) at 279 and continuing through the landmark decisions in *Berman v Parker* 348 US 26 (1954) at 32–35 and *Hawaii Housing Authority v Midkiff* 467 US 229 (1984) at 239–243, up to the most recent decisions in *Brown v Legal Foundation of Washington* 538 US 216 (2003), where the general attitude was again confirmed (albeit probably *obiter*), and *Kelo v City of New London* US S Ct 23/06/2005. Compare AJ van der Walt *Constitutional property clauses: A comparative analysis* (1999) 424–427; M Taggart
(continued on next page ...)

state may only exercise its power of eminent domain to take private property if it does so for a public use, even if it pays compensation. Even compensated taking of property for an illegitimate (eg purely private) use is unconstitutional.[303] However, in *Berman v Parker*[304] the Supreme Court accepted that the courts would defer to the wide discretion of the legislator in determining what was a public purpose—legislative declarations of what is in the public interest were said to be 'well-nigh conclusive.' Accordingly, the Court accepted that a taking of private land for resale to a private developer in terms of a general slum-clearance and land development plan was in the public interest because the authorizing legislation declared it so:

> 'Subject to specific constitutional limitations, when the legislature has spoken, the public interest has been declared in terms well-nigh conclusive. In such cases the legislature, not the judiciary, is the main guardian of the public needs to be served by social legislation [...]'[305]

This approach was continued and explicated further in *Hawaii Housing Authority v Midkiff*.[306] At stake in this case was a state law that authorized taking of private land for redistribution to other private owners, in order to break up a traditional, feudal and economically unhealthy pattern of land holdings and to replace it with a more equitable and open system of land holdings. The Supreme Court reiterated that the courts would defer to the wide legislative discretion in deciding what is in the public

---

(... from previous page)
'Expropriation, public purpose and the Constitution' in C Forsyth & I Hare (eds) *The golden metwand and the crooked cord: Essays on public law in honour of Sir William Wade QC* (1998) 91–112 at 99–101; L Berger 'The public use requirement in eminent domain' (1978) 57 *Oregon LR* 203–246 at 216–217 (up to *Berman*); TW Merrill 'The economics of public use' (1986) 72 *Cornell LR* 61–116 at 62–64, 95–97, 109–116. I am indebted to Greg Alexander and Kevin Gray for assistance and discussions with regard to the sources in this section.
[303] See *Missouri Pacific Railway Co v Nebraska* 164 US 403 (1896) at 416–417 (where the US Supreme Court held for the first time that a state exercise of the power of eminent domain for a private use was a violation of the Due Process Clause in the Fourteenth Amendment, which is the route through which the Fifth Amendment is made binding on the states); L Berger 'The public use requirement in eminent domain' (1978) 57 *Oregon LR* 203–246 at 213. Compare *Miller v Schoene* 276 US 272 (1928) at 279, where it was said that what looked like the state choosing sides in a conflict between two private property owners was in fact something else, because there was a serious and urgent public interest in the state choosing one side above the other.
[304] 348 US 26 (1954).
[305] *Berman v Parker* 348 US 26 (1954) at 32–33. Although the attitude of extreme judicial deference was formulated with reference to the state's regulatory police powers in *Berman v Parker*, the Supreme Court held in *Hawaii Housing Authority v Midkiff* 467 US 229 (1984) at 240 that the public use requirement in the Takings Clause is 'coterminous with the scope of a sovereign's police powers'. See further AJ van der Walt *Constitutional property clauses: A comparative analysis* (1999) 425; M Taggart 'Expropriation, public purpose and the Constitution' in C Forsyth & I Hare (eds) *The golden metwand and the crooked cord: Essays on public law in honour of Sir William Wade QC* (1998) 91–112 at 99–100.
[306] 467 US 229 (1984). See also G Budlender 'The constitutional protection of property rights' in G Budlender, J Latsky & T Roux *Juta's new land law* (original service 1998) 1-50–1-51.

interest, and indicated that mere rationality control is the only test that the courts will use with regard to this discretion:

> '[W]here the exercise of the eminent domain power is rationally related to a conceivable public purpose, the Court has never held a compensated taking to be proscribed by the Public Use Clause.'[307]

Despite the assumption that deference was the correct judicial attitude towards legislative determinations of the public use in takings cases, the Supreme Court confirmed that the courts did have a role to play in reviewing the legislature's judgment of what constitutes a public use, but—and this is the important qualification—that role is the 'extremely narrow one' of ensuring that the legislature's determination 'does not involve an impossibility':

> 'In short, the Court has made clear that it will not substitute its judgment for a legislature's judgment as to what constitutes a public use 'unless the use be palpably without reasonable foundation".[308]

The Supreme Court has previously decided that one person's property may not be taken for the benefit of another private person, even when compensation is paid, but that decision was qualified by the proviso that such a taking for the benefit of another private person may be justified by 'being rationally related to a conceivable public purpose'. On that basis, the Court had no trouble in finding that the purpose of the taking for redistribution to private persons in the *Hawaii Housing Authority* case was justified by the purpose of the authorizing statute, namely to break up the land oligopoly that was a remnant of feudal land holdings and that damaged the land market and the economy. Rectifying imbalances in the land holding regime was seen as a legitimate state action that is rationally related to a conceivable public purpose; it cannot be described as irrational; and therefore the Court would not second-guess the legislature's decision in this regard.[309]

The *Berman* line of argument, according to which the courts would defer to the wide discretion of the legislator in determining what was a public purpose, found a rather striking result in a state court decision. In *Poletown Neighbourhood Council v City*

---

[307] *Hawaii Housing Authority v Midkiff* 467 US 229 (1984) at 241.

[308] *Hawaii Housing Authority v Midkiff* 467 US 229 (1984) at 241. The approach adopted in *Hawaii Housing Authority v Midkiff* was confirmed (albeit probably *obiter*) recently in *Brown v Legal Foundation of Washington* 538 US 216 (2003), where it was said that the state could just as well have served the same public purpose (providing free legal services for the needy) by imposing a tax, which proved that the taking in question (state use of interest on lawyers' trusts accounts) was for a public use. It was again confirmed in *Kelo v City of New London* US S Ct 23/06/2005.

[309] See *Hawaii Housing Authority v Midkiff* 467 US 229 (1984) at 239–244; compare further AJ van der Walt *Constitutional property clauses: A comparative analysis* (1999) 424–427; G Budlender 'The constitutional protection of property rights' in G Budlender, J Latsky & T Roux *Juta's new land law* (original service 1998) 1-50–1-51; M Taggart 'Expropriation, public purpose and the Constitution' in C Forsyth & I Hare (eds) *The golden metwand and the crooked cord: Essays on public law in honour of Sir William Wade QC* (1998) 91–112 at 100–101.

of Detroit[310] the Supreme Court of Michigan held that the expropriation of residential land in a Polish-American suburb of Detroit, aimed at clearing a site for a new assembly plant for the General Motors Corporation, satisfied the public use requirement. This application of the public use requirement accommodated private development interests to such an extent that the requirement has been declared a dead letter by commentators.[311] The by now infamous *Poletown* decision was subsequently overruled by the Michigan Supreme Court in a decision that seems to revert to a somewhat stricter public purposes test when private land is expropriated for the benefit of a private enterprise that wants to develop it for the public benefit.[312] However, the Supreme Court again confirmed its earlier, deferent approach in a case where private residential property is to be expropriated in favour and for the exclusive benefit of a private development company that wants to build a hotel, conference centre, retail outlets, office space, parking and luxury residential condominiums on the land.[313] In other words, one group of homeowners are expropriated so that a

---

[310] 304 NW2d 455 (Mich 1981). For an insightful discussion of this decision and the *Kelo* case referred to below see Kevin Gray 'Human property rights in land: The propriety of expropriation' (2005) 16 *Stell LR* (forthcoming). Compare the German *Boxberg* decision discussed in 5.7.4 text accompanying footnote 291 above.

[311] See TW Merrill 'The economics of public use' (1986) 72 *Cornell LR* 61–116; compare Kevin Gray 'Human property rights in land: The propriety of expropriation' (2005) 16 *Stell LR* (forthcoming) footnote 29.

[312] In *County of Wayne v Hathcock* 685 NW2d 765 at 786–787 (Mich 2004). The Court held that a public agency may use the power of eminent domain to acquire property for economic development purposes subject to three requirements (1) the exercise of eminent domain powers for the benefit of private corporations is limited to enterprises that generate public benefits whose existence depends upon the use of land that can only be assembled by coordination that only central government can achieve; (2) the private entity that acquires the land must remain accountable to the public in its use of the condemned land; and (3) the acquisition must satisfy a special public concern test, which means that the selection of the land to be condemned and the decision to resort to condemnation must in themselves satisfy the (state) constitutional public use requirement. In other words, not only the subsequent use of the land but the selection of the land and the decision to expropriate must also satisfy the public purposes rule. I am indebted to Gregory Alexander for bringing this case to my attention. See further *Casino Reinvestment Development Authority v Banin* 727 A2d 102 at 111 (NJ Super L 1998).

[313] *Kelo v City of New London* US S Ct 23/06/2005. The Supreme Court argued that (*a*) the notion that expropriated property had to be open for use by the public was abandoned long ago; (*b*) the city could not take private land simply to confer a private benefit on a particular private person, but that is not the case here, as the taking forms part of a carefully considered development plan that does not benefit a particular class of identifiable individuals; (*c*) the city's determination that the area required rejuvenation was entitled to deference; and (*d*) the proposal that economic development should not qualify as public purpose was not supported by precedent or logic. Economic development is a traditional and long accepted governmental function that could not easily be distinguished from other public purposes already recognized. The case was decided in favour of the developer in the state court: *Kelo v City of New London* 843 A2d 500 (Conn 2004). For a discussion and analysis of the oral argument before the Supreme Court see Kevin Gray 'Human property rights in land: The propriety of expropriation' (2005) 16 *Stell LR* (forthcoming) text accompanying footnotes 10–20.

developer can build new luxury homes for another group of private beneficiaries. The Supreme Court reiterated in *Kelo* that rational government decisions to expropriate for a public purpose deserved deference, even (or perhaps particularly) when they concerned state promotion of economic development.

The European Convention on Human Rights requires in article 1 of the First Protocol that legitimate expropriation should be in the public interest.[314] In the majority of recent cases on article 1 the European Court of Human Rights[315] reiterated almost formulaically that, in applying the property clause in article 1, it will first check whether there has been an interference with the right of property as it is understood under article 1; whether the interference was provided for by law (properly authorized); whether the interference was in the public interest; and finally whether the interference was proportional.[316] Although the Court indicated that it will investigate the authority for expropriation to ensure that the action was authorized properly and that there was a legitimate public purpose involved, it has in fact generally followed the same lenient approach as the US Supreme Court and consistently interpreted the public interest requirement sympathetically to leave the signatory states the widest possible 'margin of appreciation'.[317]

This deferent attitude dates from the very earliest cases considered or heard in terms of the Convention. In two early cases considered by the former European Commission of Human Rights,[318] the Commission stated that land reform measures

---

[314] Article 1 of the First Protocol to the European Convention on Human Rights and Fundamental Freedoms (1950) provides as follows (in this section 'deprived' is read as 'expropriated'; see the next footnote below):

'First Protocol; Article 1

Every natural or legal person is entitled to the peaceful enjoyment of his possessions. No one shall be deprived of his possessions except in the public interest and subject to the conditions provided for by law and by the general principles of international law.

[...]'

[315] Case law on the property clause in the European Convention on Human Rights 1950 must be read with care, since the unique nature and the extraordinary structural and terminological characteristics of this clause render comparison with case law from domestic constitutional cases difficult. Even before the influential decision in *Sporrong & Lönnroth v Sweden* [1982] 5 EHRR 35 the expropriation clause in the First Protocol to the Convention was associated with the second rule (the second sentence of the first paragraph of article 1), which states that no one shall be deprived of his possessions except in the public interest and subject to the conditions provided for by law and by the general principles of international law. For purposes of the Convention it is assumed that 'possessions' should be read as 'property' and 'deprived' as 'expropriated'; see AJ van der Walt *Constitutional property clauses: A comparative analysis* (1999) 110.

[316] See generally AJ van der Walt *Constitutional property clauses: A comparative analysis* (1999) 113; DJ Harris, M O'Boyle & C Warbrick *Law of the European Convention on Human Rights* (1995) 529–530.

[317] For the approach followed in recent case law see *Former King of Greece and Others v Greece* (2001) 33 EHRR 21 paras 67–99; *Pincova and Pinc v Czech Republic* (36548/97) [2002] ECHR 706 paras 43–63; *Zvolsky and Zvolska v Czech Republic* (46129/99) [2002] ECHR 732 paras 63–74; *Jahn and Others v Germany* (46720/99) [2004] ECHR 36 par 80.

[318] Abolished in the new adjudication structure since 2000.

(a scheme for the redistribution of agricultural land and a permit system imposed to regulate a housing crisis respectively) fall within the scope of the regulatory powers of states as envisaged in the second paragraph of article 1 of the First Protocol. In other words, land reform and land redistribution programmes can, in principle, justify expropriation of property 'in the public interest and subject to the principles provided for by law' without violating the guarantee in article 1 of the First Protocol. The willingness to bow to the decision of the states as far as the question of necessity in the control of property is concerned must be seen in the light of the Commission's approach to the second paragraph of article 1—in these decisions the Commission consistently repeated that its role was limited to supervising the lawfulness and public purpose of the restrictions in question, but the level of scrutiny was very low, review being limited to instances where the state's purpose was obviously without any reasonable foundation.[319]

The same trend was continued in more recent cases, where the Court's attitude has been that the national authorities are better placed than the international Court to appreciate what is in the public interest because of their direct knowledge of their society and its needs. It is for the national authorities to assess the existence of a problem of public concern warranting deprivations of property, and in this respect the national authorities must enjoy a certain margin of appreciation. The notion of public interest is necessarily extensive, and the decision to expropriate property in the public interest will commonly involve consideration of political, economic and social issues. The Court appreciates that the margin of appreciation available to national legislatures in implementing social and political policies should be a wide one and respects the legislature's judgment as to what is in the public interest unless that judgment is manifestly without reasonable foundation.[320]

The most important case in which the European Court of Human Rights confirmed this position is *James v United Kingdom*.[321] It was alleged that the expropriation in question—part of a land reform programme introduced by the Leasehold Reform Act 1967—was illegitimate because the property was to be transferred to another private person. The Court accepted that depriving one person of his property for the sole purpose of conferring a private benefit on another private person cannot

---

[319] See *X & Others v Belgium* [1976] 3 DR 135; *Wiggins v The United Kingdom* [1978] 13 DR 40; AJ van der Walt *Constitutional property clauses: A comparative analysis* (1999) 109, 113.

[320] See *James v United Kingdom* [1986] 8 EHRR 123 par 46; *Former King of Greece and Others v Greece* (2001) 33 EHRR 21 paras 86–87; *Pincova and Pinc v Czech Republic* (36548/97) [2002] ECHR 706 paras 47–48; *Zvolsky and Zvolska v Czech Republic* (46129/99) [2002] ECHR 732 paras 67–68; *Jahn and Others v Germany* (46720/99) [2004] ECHR 36 par 80. In *Zwierzynski v Poland* (34049/96) [2001] ECHR 39 paras 71–72 the Court decided that there was no public interest involved when a public authority refused to vacate property of which the complainant could prove ownership. In the other cases the Court bowed to the national authority's judgment on the public interest issue, even when it had slight doubts. See further J Meyer-Ladewig *Konvention zum Schutz der Menschenrechte und Grundfreiheiten: Handkommentar* (2003) 333 Rdn 26.

[321] [1986] 8 EHRR 123. See also G Budlender 'The constitutional protection of property rights' in G Budlender, J Latsky & T Roux *Juta's new land law* (original service 1998) 1-52–1-53.

be in the public interest, but pointed out that compulsory transfer of property from one individual to another may, depending on the circumstances, constitute a legitimate means of promoting the public interest: a taking of property effected in pursuance of legitimate social, economic or other policies may be in the public interest even if the community at large has no direct use or enjoyment of the property taken. In investigating whether the reforms were in fact aimed at a legitimate public purpose in this case, the Court considered the historical and social circumstances that can indicate, on the facts as well as in principle, whether the aim was to promote a legitimate purpose in the public interest. In the *Holy Monasteries* case,[322] the Court expressed doubt about the actual intention and the seriousness of the land reforms that were claimed to have been the purpose of the actions complained of, but nevertheless held that these doubts were insufficient to deprive the overall objective of the law in question of its legitimacy as being in the public interest. This approach was consistently followed in recent cases, although none of them dealt with expropriations for the benefit of another private person as clearly as the *James* case did.

5.7.6 Concluding remarks on the public purpose requirement

Foreign courts dealing with the public purpose requirement tend to distinguish two separate issues. The first is whether the expropriation in fact serves a legitimate public purpose in the sense that it satisfies an important public need. On this issue the US Supreme Court and the European Court of Human Rights defer almost absolutely to the legislature in defining what is in the public interest, restricting their control to the lowest level of scrutiny and ensuring only that there is some rational foundation for the expropriation. The German courts apply a stricter level of scrutiny on this issue, although they will also relax their scrutiny when the expropriation is carried out by or on behalf of a private person or institution obviously and exclusively engaged in the business of serving public needs or delivering public services on behalf of the state.

The second issue is whether there is proper legislative authority for the expropriation as a way to serve the stated purpose. On this issue the German courts are the strictest in that they require that the authorizing statute must authorize expropriation for the specific public purpose; although the US courts and the European Court of Human Rights also ensure that there is proper legal authority for the expropriation and that the expropriation has some rational connection to a public purpose, they apply a much lower level of scrutiny on this issue. In Australian law (and in English law) legislative authority is the main issue in controlling the legitimacy of expropriation; much more important than the legitimacy of the public purpose served by it (which is assumed to have been debated in parliament when the authorizing statute was made, and it is therefore not usually controlled judicially); but usually this is

---

[322] *The Holy Monasteries v Greece* [1995] ECHR Series A vol 301A; see further *Jahn and Others v Germany* (46720/99) [2004] ECHR 36 par 80.

treated as a matter of administrative rather than constitutional review. On this issue the degree of deference is markedly lower and scrutiny stricter than in defining what is in the public interest, especially in German law.

The comparative overview suggests that expropriation that serves a public purpose even while benefiting a private person is most easily and widely accepted in cases involving general programmes of land reform or redistribution. The two decisions that conflict with this view seem to be outdated and unsubstantiated by authority. The more lenient view has been accepted even when the only public benefit of the scheme was to create jobs or stimulate the local economy through private development schemes, provided there was sufficient authority for serving that purpose through expropriation. There is no clear comparative authority for the view that the same lenient approach should also be valid for holdout cases, where one individual unreasonably holds up a private development scheme that involves a general public benefit such as creating jobs or stimulating the economy. However, in suitable cases expropriation could be justified in such a case for the same reasons as have been accepted in the redistribution situations.

The public purpose requirement in section 25(2) of the South African Constitution should be interpreted leniently rather than narrowly, and the possibility that it would be interpreted so narrowly as to frustrate or impede expropriations for purposes of land reform can probably be discounted.[323] It is in fact more likely than not that this requirement will play a relatively insignificant role in most if not all constitutional property cases dealing with expropriation, especially if Roux's prediction about the 'telescoping' effect of the *FNB* decision[324] comes true and all property issues are decided on the basis of the arbitrary deprivation test.[325] In that case, issues about the public purpose of an expropriation might perhaps never come to the court's attention in terms of section 25(2), as they would be decided at an earlier stage as arbitrary deprivation issues in terms of section 25(1). However, if the public purpose issue is decided on its own merit in terms of section 25(2) all indications are that the courts will follow either the deferent attitude of the US Supreme Court and the European Court of Human Rights or a variation of the stricter but lenient approach of the German courts.

---

[323] T Roux 'Section 25' in S Woolman et al (eds) *Constitutional law of South Africa* (2nd ed 2003 original service Dec 2003) 46–33; A Eisenberg '"Public purpose" and expropriation: Some comparative insights and the South African bill of rights' (1995) 11 *SAJHR* 207–221; G Budlender 'The constitutional protection of property rights' in G Budlender, J Latsky & T Roux *Juta's new land law* (original service 1998) 1-48–1-55; T Roux 'Property' in MH Cheadle, DM Davis & NRL Haysom *South African constitutional law: The bill of rights* (2002) 429–472 at 464.

[324] *First National Bank of SA Ltd t/a Wesbank v Commissioner, South African Revenue Service; First National bank of SA Ltd t/a Wesbank v Minister of Finance* 2002 (4) SA 768 (CC). See the discussion in 5.4 above and in chapter 4.5, 4.6.

[325] T Roux 'Section 25' in S Woolman et al (eds) *Constitutional law of South Africa* (2nd ed 2003 original service Dec 2003) 46-2–46-5.

In any event the outcome should be that (*a*) expropriation for arbitrary, capricious or improper purposes are always invalid; and (*b*) expropriation could satisfy the public purpose requirement even when it benefits private persons, provided that it primarily serves a legitimate public purpose such as land reform or the provision of public utilities and services. Whether the courts apply a low or a stricter level of scrutiny and whether they distinguish between justification aspects and authorization aspects of the public purpose requirement remains to be seen.

5.8 COMPENSATION

5.8.1 Overview

Section 25(3) provides a new, overriding framework within which the duty to compensate, the amount of compensation and the manner and time of payment have to be determined. The Expropriation Act 63 of 1975 is still valid and relevant in deciding compensation issues,[326] but the point of departure is now that the Act—just like other statutes that provide for, authorize or deal with expropriation and the pre-constitutional body of case law on related matters—is subject to the constitutional provisions and valid only in so far as it does not conflict with those provisions. Furthermore, the 1975 Act—like all other statutes and case law dealing with expropriation—must be interpreted and applied in view of the new conceptual and aspirational framework embodied in the Constitution. It is commonly accepted that certain parts of the 1975 Act will have to be amended to facilitate adjudication in the new era, but so far this has not been done.[327] The 1975 Expropriation Act and case law dealing with it are not discussed here, since it is dealt with more than adequately elsewhere.[328] Instead, this

---

[326]The 1975 Act still provides the general procedural and compensation principles that regulate expropriation when the authorizing statute does not do so, but of course now the 1975 Act is seen within the constitutional framework. See T Roux 'Property' in MH Cheadle, DM Davis & NRL Haysom *South African constitutional law: The bill of rights* (2002) 429–472 at 465.

[327]See A Gildenhuys *Onteieningsreg* (2nd ed 2001) 164.

[328]The most important post-constitutional source is A Gildenhuys *Onteieningsreg* (2nd ed 2001), especially chapters 8–15. Other useful sources on the new compensation requirement are G Budlender 'The constitutional protection of property rights' in G Budlender, J Latsky & T Roux *Juta's new land law* (original service 1998) 1-48–1-55 at 1-56–1-66; AJ van der Walt *Constitutional property clauses: A comparative analysis* (1999) 345–348; T Roux 'Section 25' in S Woolman et al (eds) *Constitutional law of South Africa* (2nd ed 2003 original service Dec 2003) 46-34–46-36. See further in general AJ van der Walt 'Towards a theory of rights in property: Exploratory observations on the paradigm of post-apartheid property law' (1995) 10 *SA Public Law* 298–345; DG Kleyn 'The constitutional protection of property: A comparison between the German and the South African approach' (1996) 11 *SA Public Law* 402–445 at 441ff; M Chaskalson 'The property clause: Section 28 of the Constitution' (1994) 10 *SAJHR* 131–139 at 138; AJ van der Walt 'Notes on the interpretation of the property clause in the new Constitution' (1994) 57 *THRHR* 181–203 at 195ff; A Claassens 'Compensation for expropriation: The political and economic parameters of market value compensation' (1993) 9 *SAJHR* 422–427; A Eisenberg 'Different constitutional formulations of compensation clauses' (1993) 9 *SAJHR* 412–421; J Murphy 'Compensation for nationalization in international law' (1993) 110 *SALJ* 79–99.

section provides a general overview of and introduction to the constitutional compensation provisions in subsections 25(2) and 25(3). In summarized form, section 25 contains the following general provisions regarding compensation for expropriation:

- Property may be expropriated only subject to compensation (section 25(2)(*b*)).
- The amount of compensation and the time and the manner of payment have to be either agreed to by those affected or decided or approved by a court (section 25(2)(*b*)).
- The amount of compensation and the time and manner of payment must be just and equitable, reflecting an equitable balance between the public interest and the interests of those affected, having regard to all relevant circumstances, including those listed in section 25(3)(*a*)–(*e*).
- The circumstances listed in section 25(3)(*a*)–(*e*) are: the current use of the property, the history of the acquisition and use of the property, the market value of the property, the extent of direct state investment and subsidy in the acquisition and beneficial capital development of the property, and the purpose of the expropriation. Enumeration of these considerations was intended to contextualize decisions about compensation to ensure that they reflect what is just and equitable in the complex social, economic and political history of land during and since the end of the apartheid era.
- In calculating the amount of compensation and determining the equitable balance between the interests of those affected and the public interest, the public interest includes the nation's commitment to land reform and reforms to bring about equitable access to all the country's assets (section 25(4)(*a*)). This provision serves the same purpose as the list of considerations in section 25(3)(*a*)–(*e*).

5.8.2 The duty to compensate

In foreign case law the tendency is to accept that there is a general duty to pay compensation for expropriation.[329] The classic authority for this proposition, as far as Commonwealth jurisdictions are concerned, is the decision in *Attorney-General v De Keyser's Royal Hotel, Ltd*,[330] where the House of Lords confirmed that there is a general, common-law right to receive compensation for expropriation, even in a war situation and even if the property is only used for a limited period of time and not acquired permanently.

Compensation is required for expropriation in most constitutional property clauses in foreign law, and the duty to compensate is even confirmed by the case law of the European Court of Human Rights, despite the fact that Article 1 of the First Protocol to the European Convention on Human Rights 1950 does not specify compensation as a requirement for expropriation (in fact, expropriation as a specific

---

[329]T Allen *The right to property in Commonwealth constitutions* (2000) 224.
[330][1920] AC 508 (HL). See in general GR Rubin *Private property, government requisition and the constitution, 1914–1927* (1994) chapter 6; compare A Gildenhuys *Onteieningsreg* (2nd ed 2001) 143.

category of limitation of property is read into the so-called second rule of the property clause in the European Convention and not mentioned explicitly). Since the 1980s the European Court of Human Rights has developed jurisprudence in terms of which compensation is required for expropriation on the basis of the proportionality principle. In *James v United Kingdom*[331] the following principles were laid down: article 1 impliedly requires compensation as a necessary condition for the taking of property, except in certain circumstances; compensation is a material element in determining whether the burden placed upon a person is disproportionate and therefore in conflict with article 1; article 1 does not guarantee a specific amount of compensation or full compensation, since circumstances and public interest may influence the calculation of what is just and equitable; and the taking of property without any compensation would normally constitute a disproportionate interference with property that could not be justified under article 1 and would therefore be invalid.

The European Court left the possibility open that compensation might not be required in exceptional circumstances. In terms of section 25(3)(a)–(e) of the South African Constitution it is also possible, in suitable cases, that expropriation may be just and equitable without compensation. This will especially be the case when the property was acquired in an inequitable manner in the first place, or where the state funded or subsidized the acquisition and development of the property to such an extent that it would be inequitable to require compensation. These cases fit in with the general requirements of section 25(3), since the compensation provision and the 'equitable balance' test applied in it allow for situations where the circumstances indicate that no compensation is necessary.

A related question is whether the mere fact that the expropriation is undertaken for purposes of land reform will justify the absence of compensation (section 25(3)(e)). In the context of section 25 as a whole the answer seems to be that one factor, such as the purpose of the expropriation, should not be sufficient on its own to justify the absence of compensation, just as one factor (like the market value of the property) should not be sufficient on its own to determine the necessity or amount of compensation. Instead, all the relevant circumstances (including the ones mentioned in section 25(3)(a)–(e) but not restricted to them) should be considered together in deciding whether it would be just and equitable to pay no compensation (or extremely low compensation, compared to market value) in a specific case.

The tenor of these decisions is that the duty to compensate for expropriation has to be taken seriously, and it is possible that expropriation without compensation would generally be considered arbitrary in terms of section 25(1); but in view of the land reform context and the considerations enumerated in section 25(3) it is also possible that expropriation without compensation may be justifiable in certain circumstances.

---

[331] [1986] 8 EHRR 123. The proportionality test was already developed in *Sporrong and Lönnroth v Sweden* [1982] 5 EHRR 35.

5.8.3 Time and manner of payment

According to section 25(2) the amount of compensation and the time and manner of payment have to be determined as prescribed in section 25(2) and 25(3). As with the amount of compensation, the time and manner of payment must be either agreed to by those affected or decided or approved by a court.[332] The general principle is, as in the case of the amount of compensation, that the time and manner of payment of compensation should be just and equitable, taking into account all the relevant circumstances. It is accepted in foreign jurisdictions that the time and manner of payment of compensation may vary: compensation need not be paid in money, nor is it necessary that it be paid immediately. However, prompt payment is usually expected,[333] and in view of the just and equitable requirement it is likely that overly long and unjustified delays in making payment would be considered unacceptable, as they have been in other jurisdictions.[334]

5.8.4 Amount of compensation I: Equitable balance

Section 25(2)(b) provides that the amount of compensation for expropriation must either be agreed to by those affected or decided or approved by a court. In the first place compensation could therefore be determined by agreement between the state and those affected; in the absence of agreement a court can determine the amount of compensation or approve it (probably upon proposal by one or more of the parties). In the absence of agreement section 25(3) provides the principles according to which compensation has to be calculated.

The basic principle for the calculation of the amount of compensation is that it must reflect an equitable balance between the public interest and the interests of those affected by expropriation, having regard to all relevant circumstances, including the (non-exhaustive) list of circumstances enumerated in section 25(3)(a)–(e). It is clear from the structure and tone of the provision as a whole that the calculation of the amount of compensation requires a contextualized judgment with due regard for individual property interests but also for the history of land rights in the pre-constitutional era, the new constitutional framework and the legitimate land reform efforts of the state. What is adjudged just and equitable has to reflect sensitivity for that context, and cannot simply be based on abstract value attached to the property in question.[335] In general the amount of compensation should be determined within the broad

---

[332]Section 25(2)(b).
[333]See T Roux 'Section 25' in S Woolman et al (eds) *Constitutional law of South Africa* (2nd ed 2003 original service Dec 2003) 46-34–46-36 at 46–35.
[334]See *Pemungut Hasil Tanah, Daerah Barat Daya, Pulau Pinang v Ong Gaik Kee* (1983) 3 MLJ 35 (Malaysia), where the Malaysian High Court decided that a hearing to determine compensation should be held with 'all convenient speed', although the same court had held in *Tan Boon Bak & Sons Ltd v Government of the State of Peral and Another* (1983) 1 MLJ 117 that a delay of seven years in making the payment was not unacceptable.
[335]G Budlender 'The constitutional protection of property rights' in G Budlender, J Latsky & T Roux *Juta's new land law* (original service 1998) 1-48–1-55 at 1–57.

scheme and purpose of the Constitution,[336] with special attention for land reform aspirations. Although the flexible and contextualized standard set out in this provision certainly signals a departure from the uncompromising full market value standard of the liberal tradition, it is not uncommon; a similar approach is followed in certain foreign jurisdictions and it is broadly in line with the standards of international law.[337]

To determine the amount of compensation within this general constitutional framework, the courts have to have regard to all relevant circumstances. These circumstances include but are not restricted to the factors enumerated in section 25(3)(a)–(e).

5.8.5 Amount of compensation II: All relevant circumstances

It is clear that the amount of compensation is not primarily informed by full or market value, as it used to be in the liberal tradition, but rather by the constitutional notion of just and equitable compensation that reflects an equitable balance between the interests of those affected by the expropriation and the public interest, taking into account all the relevant circumstances. This approach is in line with the tendency in foreign jurisdictions. The fact that compensation may, but need not, equal market value is not startling; a similar conclusion has been reached in other jurisdictions,[338] particularly in Germany, on the basis of a similar kind of compensation provision. Like the South African subsection 25(3), article 14.3 of the German Basic Law also demands that compensation should reflect an equitable balance between the interests of those affected and the public interest, and the German courts have in the past indicated that

---

[336] G Budlender 'The constitutional protection of property rights' in G Budlender, J Latsky & T Roux *Juta's new land law* (original service 1998) 1-48–1-55 at 1–58.

[337] A Gildenhuys *Onteieningsreg* (2nd ed 2001) 169; G Budlender 'The constitutional protection of property rights' in G Budlender, J Latsky & T Roux *Juta's new land law* (original service 1998) 1-48–1-55 at 1-57–1-58; A Claassens 'Compensation for expropriation: The political and economic parameters of market value compensation' (1993) 9 *SAJHR* 422–427; A Eisenberg 'Different constitutional formulations of compensation clauses' (1993) 9 *SAJHR* 412–421. See further T Allen *The right to property in Commonwealth constitutions* (2000) 242–243, read with 224–240, where the liberal full market value attitude of earlier Commonwealth courts is set out.

[338] See for example *BVerfGE* 24, 367 [1968] (*Deichordnung*). Article 14(3) of the German *GG* stipulates that compensation shall be determined by establishing an equitable balance between the public interest and the interests of those affected, very similar to section 25(3) of the South African property clause. The principle that compensation has to be determined by establishing an equitable balance, and that it can therefore deviate from market value, was also accepted in *Sporrong and Lönnroth v Sweden* [1985] 5 EHRR 35; *James v United Kingdom* [1986] 8 EHRR 123 (European Convention on Human Rights 1950); *Dreher v Irish Land Commission and Others* [1984] ILRM 94 (Ireland); *Grace Brothers Pty Ltd v The Commonwealth* (1946) 72 CLR 269; *Nelungaloo Pty Ltd v The Commonwealth and Others* (1948) 75 CLR 495 at 569 (Australia); *Grand Bench 23 December 1953* in JM Maki *Court and constitution in Japan: Selected Supreme Court decisions, 1948–1960* (1964) 228–252 (Japan). Van Dijkhorst J rejected the traditional view that the current South African Expropriation Act 63 of 1975 uses market value as the standard for compensation, and stated that even in that Act market value was the exception rather than the rule: *Kerksay Investments (Pty) Ltd v Randburg Town Council* 1997 (1) SA 511(T) at 522E–G. A Gildenhuys *Onteieningsreg* (2nd ed 2001) 156–161 gives an overview of compensation principles in other jurisdictions.

compensation need not be equal to market value.[339] Market value was presented as the one and only measure of just compensation in some older foreign decisions,[340] but they are no longer accepted as sound authority, except perhaps in the Commonwealth.[341] In the *First Certification Case*[342] the South African Constitutional Court also concluded that there was no evidence that market value was the accepted international standard for compensation. In calculating the amount of compensation the considerations in section 25(3) have to be taken into account, and that should ensure that the compensation is just and equitable even when it is lower than market value.

Section 25(3) enumerates the considerations that have to be taken into account when calculating the amount of just and equitable compensation in an effort to establish an equitable balance between the public interest and the interests of those affected by expropriation. These considerations are the current use of the property; the history of the acquisition and use of the property; the market value of the property; the extent of direct state investment and subsidy in the acquisition and beneficial improvement of the property; and the purpose of the expropriation.[343]

Budlender argues that the first consideration, the current use of the property, is particularly significant to justify expropriation of a scarce resource (such as residential or agricultural land in areas where land is required for housing or the establishment of newcomer farmers) that is currently not being used productively. He adds that this consideration in section 25(3) should not be used to punish someone for socially undesirable use of land, because doing so would not constitute a public purpose. However, as is the case with current non-use or non-productive use of a scarce resource, use of land for a socially undesirable purpose and the purpose of expropriation in a specific case could affect the determination of the amount of compensation without amounting to a purely punitive measure.[344]

---

[339]See *BVerfGE* 24, 367 [1968] (*Deichordnung*). See AJ van der Walt *Constitutional property clauses: A comparative analysis* (1999) 150–151; DG Kleyn 'The constitutional protection of property: A comparison between the German and the South African approach' (1996) 11 *SA Public Law* 402–445 at 441ff.

[340]Such as the Indian decision in *State of West Bengal v Mrs Bella Banerjee and Others* AIR 1954 SC 170. See T Allen *The right to property in Commonwealth constitutions* (2000) 224; AJ van der Walt *Constitutional property clauses: A comparative analysis* (1999) 219–221.

[341]T Allen *The right to property in Commonwealth constitutions* (2000) 242–243, read with 224–240, sets out the liberal full market value attitude of earlier Commonwealth courts and contrasts it with more recent developments in the European Court of Human Rights.

[342]*Ex Parte Chairperson of the Constitutional Assembly: In re Certification of the Constitution of the Republic of South Africa, 1996* 1996 (4) SA 744 (CC) par [73] at 799B–D.

[343]On the interpretation of these considerations see particularly A Gildenhuys *Onteieningsreg* (2nd ed 2001) 170–179; G Budlender 'The constitutional protection of property rights' in G Budlender, J Latsky & T Roux *Juta's new land law* (original service 1998) 1-48–1-55 at 1-56–1-64.

[344]G Budlender 'The constitutional protection of property rights' in G Budlender, J Latsky & T Roux *Juta's new land law* (original service 1998) 1-48–1-55 at 1–59. See further A Gildenhuys *Onteieningsreg* (2nd ed 2001) 172. The suggestion of MD Southwood *The compulsory acquisition of rights* (2000) 80, that purely philanthropic use of property should also allow an upward adjustment in favour of the owner, looks doubtful.

The second factor is the history of the acquisition and use of the property; a consideration that was clearly inserted to allow the court to consider the effect that previous apartheid-related expropriation might have on the compensation award. Gildenhuys[345] reminds us that land was often sold or rented out to white farmers for less than market value after having been expropriated from black and white land-owners during the apartheid era; if such an owner were now to be expropriated for land restitution it would be unfair to compensate him at full market value, although one obviously has to be careful not to let context-sensitive adjustment slip into punitive denial of just and equitable compensation. Budlender[346] gives a good example of a situation in which the history of the use of the property could affect the award of compensation: when land was occupied unlawfully and the market value is consequently depressed, a court could adjust the compensation upward to cancel out the negative effect of the occupation. The *Modderklip* case[347] is a good example where exactly such an argument could have been valuable if the land were to be expropriated.

Market value is still a factor to be taken into account when calculating just and equitable compensation, but it is no longer the only or the main consideration.[348] Market value can be determined with some measure of accuracy with the use of traditional valuation methods, and the Expropriation Act 1975 relies upon market value, calculated with reference to these methods, as the starting point for the determination of compensation. This factor should therefore not pose new challenges beyond placing it into the correct new perspective as one factor amongst others.[349]

The factor relating to the extent of direct state investment and subsidy in the acquisition and beneficial capital development of the property allows the courts to adjust the amount of compensation when the state has made a direct investment or granted a subsidy for the acquisition or beneficial capital investment of the property

---

[345] A Gildenhuys *Onteieningsreg* (2nd ed 2001) 172; see further G Budlender 'The constitutional protection of property rights' in G Budlender, J Latsky & T Roux *Juta's new land law* (original service 1998) 1-48–1-55 at 1-59–1-60.

[346] G Budlender 'The constitutional protection of property rights' in G Budlender, J Latsky & T Roux *Juta's new land law* (original service 1998) 1-48–1-55 at 1–60.

[347] *Modderfontein Squatters, Greater Benoni City Council v Modderklip Boerdery (Pty) Ltd; (Agri SA and Legal Resources Centre, Amici Curiae); President of the Republic of South Africa and Others v Modderklip Boerdery (Pty) Ltd (Agri SA and Legal Resources Centre, Amici Curiae)* 2004 (6) SA 40 (SCA); *President of the Republic of South Africa and Another v Modderklip Boerdery (Pty) Ltd (Agri SA and Others, Amici Curiae)* 2005 (5) SA 3 (CC). See chapters 4.5.5 and 6.4 for a discussion.

[348] In *Kerksay Investments (Pty) Ltd v Randburg Town Council* 1997 (1) SA 511(T) at 522E–G van Dijkhorst J rejected the traditional view that the current South African Expropriation Act 63 of 1975 uses market value as the standard for compensation, and stated that even in that Act market value was the exception rather than the rule.

[349] A Gildenhuys *Onteieningsreg* (2nd ed 2001) 174–176; see further G Budlender 'The constitutional protection of property rights' in G Budlender, J Latsky & T Roux *Juta's new land law* (original service 1998) 1-48–1-55 at 1-61–1-63.

by the current owner.[350] This factor again refers to the practice of the apartheid state assisting white farmers to acquire and develop land that was previously expropriated from black or white farmers under the apartheid land laws. Obviously it would make no sense to compensate someone at full market value for land that was originally acquired or subsequently developed with state assistance. The scope of the negative effect that this factor might have on the amount of compensation is restricted by the requirements that state investments must be direct[351] and that only beneficial capital improvement is taken into consideration.

The final factor that is enumerated in section 25(3) is the purpose of the expropriation. This factor raises several difficult questions. Budlender[352] is probably right in identifying the only rational interpretation of this provision in ensuring that the compensation award does not unjustifiably frustrate expropriation that is aimed at serving a 'pressing social necessity'. In this respect this factor should be understood directly in the context of the reformist agenda of section 25 and not outside it. A decision of the Cape High Court illustrates the questionable result of applying this factor too widely.

In *Du Toit v Minister of Transport*[353] gravel was removed from private land for public road building; land reform was not in issue. The Cape High Court correctly approached the matter from the point of view that the 1975 Expropriation Act was relevant but had to be applied with due regard for section 25 of the Constitution,[354] and decided that the best way to do the calculation was according to the approach followed by Gildenhuys J in *Khumalo*.[355] Based on this approach the court decided that the public interest in the building of roads would be prejudiced if the owner were to be paid full market value for the expropriated gravel, and in its award the court therefore reduced the market value quite significantly.[356] It is doubtful whether this is what is referred to as 'just and equitable compensation that reflects an equitable

---

[350]A Gildenhuys *Onteieningsreg* (2nd ed 2001) 176–177; see further G Budlender 'The constitutional protection of property rights' in G Budlender, J Latsky & T Roux *Juta's new land law* (original service 1998) 1-48–1-55 at 1–65.

[351]Indirect investments through tax benefits etc are probably excluded because they are too difficult to calculate.

[352]G Budlender 'The constitutional protection of property rights' in G Budlender, J Latsky & T Roux *Juta's new land law* (original service 1998) 1-48–1-55 at 1–66. See further A Gildenhuys *Onteieningsreg* (2nd ed 2001) 178.

[353]2003 (1) SA 586 (C), especially paras [23]–[52] at 596C–606I. The discussion of this decision below is based in part on AJ van der Walt 'Overview of developments since the introduction of the constitutional property clause' (2004) 19 *SA Public Law* 46–89.

[354]*Du Toit v Minister of Transport* 2003 (1) SA 586 (C) par [14] at 594B–C, read with par [27] at 597J–598D.

[355]*Du Toit v Minister of Transport* 2003 (1) SA 586 (C) par [23] at 596C–H and par [28] at 598E–G, referring to *Khumalo and Others v Potgieter and Others* [2000] 2 All SA 456 (LCC) paras [26]–[31]. According to Jamie AJ, this approach could be followed in applying section 12(1)(bb) of the 1975 Expropriation Act.

[356]*Du Toit v Minister of Transport* 2003 (1) SA 586 (C) par [51] at 606G.

balance between the interests of those affected by the expropriation and the public interest, taking into account all the relevant circumstances'—ultimately, the court's understanding in this case of its duty to take into account the purpose of the expropriation is unconvincing.[357] Section 25(3) is used as the basis for the argument that property owners should receive significantly less than market value for expropriated property that is to be used for maintenance of a national asset, because that would reflect a fairer balance between the public interest and the interest of the expropriated owner than paying full market price would, even in a case that has no bearing on land reform or the transformation of land rights or greater access to land rights. If one were to accept that different levels of scrutiny apply to different contexts within which property rights are affected by expropriation, it might well be possible to argue that expropriation related to land reform should or could be treated with greater understanding and accommodation, but in this particular case that argument does not apply.

The court's approach does not make sense economically either. Economic principles require that the burden of road maintenance (like all other 'business as usual' regulatory state expenditure) should be spread more or less equally among citizens through taxation and other measures, from which compensation can be paid for unequally distributed burdens (such as expropriation of gravel from private commercial gravel pits). However, regardless of economic principles the decision still begs the question whether section 25(3) really means that compensation should be significantly below market value simply because the public interest in expropriated property is higher than the private interest of the property holder. Would the same principle not justify not paying any compensation at all? Or does it imply that the same significant deduction must apply to all expropriations for a public purpose, in other words, all lawful expropriations? The last question identifies the problem with this decision: the public interest justifies expropriation in the first place, but should not also justify a reduction of the compensation amount unless there is a special reason such as land reform involved. Section 25(3) instructs courts to find a fair balance between the public interest and the interests of those affected by expropriation, but the decision attached too much weight to the public interest and too little to the interests of the affected owner, without a special justification for doing so in the specific case. In certain cases the considerations listed in section 25(3) could and would undoubtedly require and justify a significant reduction of market value to reach the appropriate balance, but those circumstances cannot be identified on the basis of the greater public interest in the use of the property alone; something more would be required, particularly related to the other factors in section 25(3) and to the unfair balance that characterized land rights and land holdings in the apartheid system. In an expropriation of farmland for redistribution purposes, the fact that a large number of workers already lived on the land with the previous owner's permission might justify a signif-

---

[357]Section 25(3)(e) provides that, in calculating the amount of expropriation, the court should take into account the purpose of the expropriation.

icant deduction in establishing the kind of balance that is required. In *Du Toit*, the court's argument and interpretation of these provisions do not convince.

When the case went on appeal the Supreme Court of Appeal held that the matter should have been decided exclusively with reference to section 12(1)(*b*) of the Expropriation Act 63 of 1975, which deals with the (permanent) expropriation of rights and temporary takings of a right to use property (as opposed to expropriation of property).[358] In the SCA's view, this case concerned only a temporary taking of a right to use property and therefore compensation is only payable if the taking has caused actual financial loss that results directly from the taking.[359] In order to obtain any compensation, the plaintiff in this case should have proven his actual financial loss directly resulting from the taking of the right to use the property, but since he argued that the taking of the gravel amounted to an expropriation proper he claimed compensation for the market value of the gravel that was taken and said nothing about loss caused by the taking of the use right. Accordingly, he failed to prove actual financial loss caused by the taking and was awarded a small sum of compensation for the use of the land during the period in question, calculated on the basis of the market value of temporary use of agricultural land.[360] The SCA completely ignored the loss of the gravel taken by the state, discounting it in view of the large volumes of gravel still available to the plaintiff, and concentrated purely on the temporary taking of the use of plaintiff's land.[361] It also accepted, without much discussion, that this application of the power of temporary taking in section 12(1)(*b*) of the Expropriation Act was justified and unassailable in view of section 25(1) of the Constitution.[362] However, the Court never asked whether the particular application of the power of temporary taking amounted to an expropriation that might be open to attack in terms of section 25(2) because it allows, above and beyond the temporary use of property obviously foreseen and authorised by section 12(1)(*b*), actual removal or taking of parts of the owner's property.

The problem is perhaps uniquely restricted to non-essential extraction of minerals or other materials from land while temporarily 'using' it. One can easily see how temporary use of land (or other property) could be required and justified when the state has to deal with emergencies caused by natural disasters or public threats such as war, and in cases like that it would obviously usually be sufficient to compensate the owner for direct loss caused by the requisitioning. However, if the military personnel temporarily occupying a farmer's land for military operations should also remove his vegetable crop or slaughter his cattle for food the loss caused by such actions would clearly be included in the possible claim he might have afterwards. Moreover, his loss of vegetables or cattle could probably not be calculated with reference to how much he has

[358] *Minister of Transport v Du Toit* 2005 (1) SA 16 (SCA) paras [6] at 22D–F, [7] at 22F. The relevant parts of the Act are cited in par [6] at 21I–22D.
[359] Par [8] at 22G–H.
[360] Par [16] at 25G–H.
[361] Par [14] at 24D–I.
[362] Par [8] at 22H–I.

left—the issue is how much was taken. The purpose of the requisitioning of the land, namely a military operation necessitated by the public threat, covers the requisitioning of food as well, and the compensation provision would include all the losses. The picture changes when the state requisitions private land for temporary use not to deal with or avert a particular public threat, but specifically to remove valuable assets from the land that it would otherwise have had to purchase in the open market. To exclude compensation for the gravel removed in the *Du Toit* case and compensate him for the temporary 'use' of his land only amounts to sophistry, because the whole purpose of the temporary use was exclusively to remove the gravel free of charge—the state had no other use for the land and cynically employed the temporary use construction to avoid paying for the gravel. If this construction was accepted and declared constitutionally valid the state would never again have to pay for gravel or sand extracted from private land—in fact, it could also use the same construction to fill its coffers by removing minerals and oil through temporary use of private mines and extraction wells, provided that a large reserve of the relevant asset remains for the owner.

The plaintiff in the *Du Toit* case appealed against the SCA order, but the Constitutional Court upheld the SCA decision.[363] The majority of the Constitutional Court accepted the SCA's argument that it was compensation for temporary use that had to be established, and by and large confirmed the SCA's decision on this point. The majority also mentioned the public purpose argument used earlier in the Cape High Court decision and seemingly adopted it without discussion. In the majority's view, the compensation award by the SCA was indeed just and equitable. The minority rejected the focus on the right of temporary use and argued that what was expropriated was the gravel itself, but concluded that the compensation award was nevertheless just and equitable. The minority also rejected the approach of first determining the compensation award and then asking whether it complied with the just and equitable standard in section 25—in the minority's view this approach would entrench the centrality of market value.

A related question is whether expropriation without compensation (or against very low or nominal compensation) is or can in general be justified merely because the expropriation is aimed at land reform. This question also involves the meaning of section 25(8), which states that no provision of section 25 may impede land and related reforms to redress the results of past imbalances, provided that any departure from the provisions of section 25 is still in accordance with section 36. This raises a number of questions, the first of which is whether section 25(8) in fact means that the compensation requirement is the one provision in section 25 that can be deviated from for the sake of land reform.[364] The explicit enumeration of the purpose of the expropriation in section 25(3)(e) seems to strengthen the impression that the purpose of the expropriation, and specifically land reform, could justify not paying compensation or paying

[363] *Du Toit v Minister of Transport* CCT 22/04 8 September 2005 (CC).
[364] This issue is discussed in more detail in chapter 2.5. It boils down to the fact that any other deviation from the requirements in section 25 will inevitably fall foul of section 36(1) anyway.

compensation at a discounted rate. However, this impression is misleading and does not reflect a convincing interpretation of either subsection 25(3)(e) or subsection 25(8). Even in jurisdictions where the property clause does not require compensation explicitly[365] the principle is that expropriation will be unfair in the absence of compensation.[366] On the same basis, expropriation would probably be unconstitutional in most cases if it is not compensated at all or at a lower value than indicated by the considerations in section 25(3), simply because it concerns land reform. Of course the considerations in subsection 25(3) may well indicate, in a specific case, that no compensation or a very low measure of compensation is just and equitable, but that would have been the case even in the absence of section 25(8). The fact that the purpose of expropriation is land reform should therefore not on its own imply that compensation is not required or that it can be calculated at a special discounted rate, although this conclusion could follow from consideration of all the relevant circumstances.

An interesting illustration of the way in which consideration of all the circumstances together could indicate that expropriation of a right without any compensation might be justified appears in a case that does involve land reform. *Nhlabati and Others v Fick*[367] dealt with the constitutional validity of section 6(2)(dA), which was inserted into the Extension of Security of Tenure Act 62 of 1997 to grant a right to bury a deceased occupier or member of the occupier's family on agricultural land, without the consent and even against the will of the landowner, in accordance with their religion or cultural belief, if an established practice in respect of such burials on the land exists. In deciding that the provision was not unconstitutional the Land Claims Court acknowledged, without deciding the point, that granting of a right to establish a grave as of right could amount to the granting of a servitude, which would amount to a *de facto* expropriation of a servitude without compensation.[368] The court pointed out that statutory permission for what might amount to an expropriation of a right could either imply that compensation was due or that the absence of compensation was justifiable under section 36 of the Constitution, and concluded that the statutory obligation of a landowner to allow an occupier to appropriate a gravesite on

---

[365] Article 5 of the Austrian Bill of Rights; articles 40, 43 of the Irish Constitution. Since 1990 section 16(2) of the Zimbabwean Constitution has ousted the jurisdiction of the courts to question the fairness of compensation, but compensation is still required.

[366] In Austria the courts are not quite willing to accept a general compensation duty, but they are forced by the European Convention on Human Rights 1950, which is interpreted as if it required compensation, to fall into line with the rest of the European Union. The same applies to Ireland since it became a member. See 5.2.1 above.

[367] 2003 (7) BCLR 806 (LCC); see W du Plessis, N Olivier & J Pienaar 'Expropriation, restitution and land redistribution: An answer to land problems in South Africa?' (2003) 18 *SA Public Law* 491–514 at 501–504. The alternative is that section 6(2)(dA) brings about a deprivation of property and not an expropriation of a right. In that case the compensation question does not arise; see chapter 4.7.3 for a discussion of the case in that context. In the present context the possibility that the effect of the section can be seen as expropriation of a right is taken as the point of departure for analysis, even though the court did not decide the matter either way.

[368] *Nhlabati and Others v Fick* 2003 (7) BCLR 806 (LCC) paras [32]–[35] at 817D–819E.

his or her land without compensation is reasonable and justifiable as meant in section 36, having regard to the following circumstances: (*a*) the right does not constitute a major intrusion on the landowner's property rights; (*b*) the right is subject to balancing with the landowner's property right and may sometimes be subject to it; (*c*) the right exists only where there is an established past practice with regard to grave sites; and (*d*) the right will enable occupiers to comply with religious or cultural beliefs that forms an important part of their security of tenure, and giving statutory recognition to their security of tenure is in accordance with the constitutional mandate.[369] Accordingly, even if one accepted that section 6(2)(*d*A) authorized expropriation of grave sites without compensation, in conflict with section 25 of the Constitution,[370] this result would be reasonable and justifiable under section 36 of the Constitution.

The factors enumerated in section 25(3) are not exhaustive, and the courts should consider other factors where they are relevant. Gildenhuys[371] points out that specific considerations enumerated or specified in the authorizing statute would also be relevant, unless they are in conflict with the Constitution and therefore invalid.

5.8.6 Amount of compensation III: Making the determination

Theunis Roux[372] argues that the courts, including the Constitutional Court, have not considered section 25(3) extensively so far and might therefore approach the calculation of the amount of compensation in terms of section 25(3) in the way that was proposed by Gildenhuys J in the Land Claims Court in *Khumalo and Others v Potgieter and Others*.[373] In the *Khumalo* case Gildenhuys J applied the constitutional compensation standard as it was incorporated in section 23(1) of the Land Reform (Labour Tenants) Act 3 of 1996, and he decided that the court should determine the amount of just and equitable compensation in two stages. First, the court has to determine the market value of the property according to the established principles and valuation methods; and subsequently the court must consider to what extent the market value should be adjusted according to the considerations enumerated in section 25(3).[374] In

---

[369] Par [35] at 819A–E.

[370] The court made no finding on this point, merely accepting the possibility for argument's sake: par [32] at 817F.

[371] A Gildenhuys *Onteieningsreg* (2nd ed 2001) 170. See further G Budlender 'The constitutional protection of property rights' in G Budlender, J Latsky & T Roux *Juta's new land law* (original service 1998) 1-48–1-55 at 1–64.

[372] T Roux 'Property' in MH Cheadle, DM Davis & NRL Haysom *South African constitutional law: The bill of rights* (2002) 429–472 at 464.

[373] [2000] 2 All SA 456 (LCC).

[374] *Khumalo and Others v Potgieter and Others* [2000] 2 All SA 456 (LCC) par [93]. T Roux 'Property' in MH Cheadle, DM Davis & NRL Haysom *South African constitutional law: The bill of rights* (2002) 429–472 at 464 footnote 174 points out that the LCC followed the same approach in another case where it had to assess just and equitable compensation in terms of the Restitution of Land Rights Act 2 of 1994: *Ex parte Former Highland Residents; In re: Ash and Others v Department of Land Affairs* [2002] 2 All SA 26 (LCC) paras [25]–[38].

Roux's view the two-stage approach looks like a sound and reliable method of calculating the amount of compensation in terms of section 25(3), the only problem being that, with the exception of 'the extent of direct state investment' in section 25(3)(d) and the market value in section 25(3)(c), the factors enumerated in section 25(3) are not readily quantifiable in money terms.[375] However, the Cape High Court followed this approach in *Du Toit v Minister of Transport*[376] with questionable results, attaching too much weight to the public purpose of the expropriation and not enough to the individual interests of the affected owner, in circumstances where land reform and prior injustices played no role. As was indicated above, the minority of the Constitutional Court questioned the roughly comparable approach that was followed by the majority in *Du Toit*, pointing out that it will entrench the centrality of market value. In view of this dissent the *Khumalo* methodology may have to be reconsidered in future.

Gildenhuys[377] raises the question whether the state can also use the considerations enumerated in section 25(3)(a)–(e) to reduce the amount of compensation when the authorizing legislation provides for compensation that is higher than the standard set by section 25(3). Chaskalson & Lewis[378] and Budlender[379] argued that the Constitution sets minimum standards from which the legislature can deviate, and therefore the higher standard provided for in legislation should be adhered to when the legislature chooses to compensate at a higher rate than the Constitution. Gildenhuys argues that the state should not pay more compensation than is necessary, and that the Constitution should therefore always be followed, also when legislation provides for a higher standard of compensation.

The general attitude that the Constitution should always determine the direction and spirit in which compensation is calculated seems to be correct, and in that sense Gildenhuys' argument is more convincing. On the other hand, it is true that the legislature is free to deviate from the minimum standards in the Constitution, and this freedom of political choice should not be restricted unnecessarily by the courts. It therefore seems best to say that, whenever legislation provides a higher standard of compensation than section 25(3), the question should first be whether the legislation pre- or post-dates the Constitution; in the former case the presumption should be against compensation that deviates from the constitutional standard. The second question should be whether a deviation from the constitutional standard would directly contradict the purport, object and spirit of the compensation provision and the property clause as a whole or frustrate the land reform effort; if it does, the constitutional

---

[375] T Roux 'Property' in MH Cheadle, DM Davis & NRL Haysom *South African constitutional law: The bill of rights* (2002) 429–472 at 465.

[376] 2003 (1) SA 586 (C), especially paras [23]–[52] at 596C–606I. See the discussion in 5.8.5 above.

[377] A Gildenhuys *Onteieningsreg* (2nd ed 2001) 164–165.

[378] M Chaskalson & C Lewis 'Property' in M Chaskalson et al (eds) *Constitutional law of South Africa* (1st ed 1996) at 31–33.

[379] G Budlender 'The constitutional protection of property rights' in G Budlender, J Latsky & T Roux *Juta's new land law* (original service 1998) 1-48–1-55 at 1–66.

standard should prevail. In all other cases it should in principle be possible to deviate from the constitutional standard and award higher compensation if the authorizing legislation clearly provides for it, provided that doing so is not otherwise unlawful, arbitrary or capricious and will not conflict with any other constitutional or statutory provision or principle.

CHAPTER 6

Land Reform and Equitable Access to Natural Resources

6.1 INTRODUCTION

The need to simultaneously secure vested property interests and promote investment confidence and, conversely, fears that the constitutionalization of property could insulate existing property holdings and frustrate necessary land reforms dominated early debates about the inclusion of a property clause in the Constitution. Consequently, the legitimacy of land reform initiatives was particularly important in the early debates about the 1993 and 1996 constitutions.[1] Although these concerns still feature in the background of the constitutional property debate,[2] academic discussion about finding the constitutionally legitimate and politically appropriate balance between the preservation of existing rights and the promotion of land reform has lost some of its original air of transformation anxiety and developed into a more rigorous, practical and occasionally critical debate about the respective places and functions of land rights and land reform—and the relationship between land rights and land reform—in South African society in the post-apartheid era.[3]

It was always clear that land reform would necessarily have to feature in any legitimate and sustainable transformation process in South Africa, if only because the injustices of apartheid were manifested and entrenched so deeply in the unequal distribution of land and the legal insecurity of race-determined 'black' land holdings.[4] It should therefore not have come as a surprise when the last pre-1994 De Klerk government introduced a limited range of land reforms in response to increasing pressure for political and social transformation during the late 1980s.[5] The reforms

---

[1] See generally AJ van der Walt 'Overview of developments since the introduction of the constitutional property clause' (2004) 19 *SA Public Law* 46–89; this section is based on and in part resembles sections of the article. The constitutionalization debate is discussed in chapter 2.3.4.

[2] An issue that still bothers some commentators is the place and use of comparative law in interpreting section 25. The use of international and foreign law is discussed in chapter 2.3.2.

[3] See AJ van der Walt 'Overview of developments since the introduction of the constitutional property clause' (2004) 19 *SA Public Law* 46–89 for a general evaluation of the current state of the debate.

[4] See generally TRH Davenport 'Some reflections on the history of land tenure in South Africa, seen in the light of attempts by the state to impose political and economic control' 1985 *Acta Juridica* 53 76; JT Schoombee 'Group areas legislation—The political control of ownership and occupation of land' 1985 *Acta Juridica* 77–118; R Haines & CR Cross 'An historical overview of land policy and tenure in South Africa's black areas' in CR Cross & R Haines (eds) *Towards freehold—Options for land and development in South Africa's black rural areas* (1988) 73–92; AJ van der Walt 'Towards the development of post-apartheid land law: An exploratory survey' (1990) 23 *De Jure* 1–45; AJ van der Walt 'Land reform in South Africa since 1990—An overview' (1995) 10 *SA Public Law* 1–30; AJ van der Walt 'Property rights and hierarchies of power: A critical evaluation of land-reform policy in South Africa' (1999) 64 *Koers* 259–294 at 260–269 for an impression of the effect that apartheid land law had on the racially determined distribution of land, access to land and the security of land rights. Compare further PJ Badenhorst, JM Pienaar & H Mostert (assisted by M van Rooyen) *Silberberg and Schoeman's The law of property* (4th ed 2003) 485.

[5] Most (mainly white) lawyers were nevertheless surprised by the scope and the speed of changes in property law, and in a sense it is only now, 15 years later, that the majority of lawyers can be said

(continued on next page ...)

proposed by the De Klerk government were introduced by way of a *White Paper on land reform* in March 1991, followed by a series of legislative measures[6] that abolished racially-based land laws;[7] provided for restitution of land that was dispossessed under apartheid;[8] upgraded the security of tenure of certain categories of black land holders;[9] and facilitated the establishment of black townships in former white areas to ease the burden of urban homelessness.[10] The central feature of these early reforms was

----

(... from previous page)

to be reasonably well aware of the transformation brought about by land reform. See AJ van der Walt 'Land reform in South Africa since 1990—An overview' (1995) 10 *SA Public Law* 1–30 at 10–11 and compare AJ van der Walt 'Overview of developments since the introduction of the constitutional property clause' (2004) 19 *SA Public Law* 46–89 at 46–47. PJ Badenhorst, JM Pienaar & H Mostert (assisted by M van Rooyen) *Silberberg and Schoeman's The law of property* (4th ed 2003) 482 point out (with reference to the applicable legislation) that certain reforms preceded the 1991 White Paper: forced removal of non-urban blacks was suspended in 1984 and the enabling legislation was repealed in 1986, blacks could acquire leasehold and ownership of urban land under certain conditions since 1986, and since 1986 provision was made for conversion of leasehold into full ownership. In the rural areas leasehold became available from 1983 and ownership from 1988.

[6] The most important statutes were the Abolition of Racially Based Land Measures Act 108 of 1991, the Upgrading of Land Tenure Rights Act 112 of 1991 and the Less Formal Township Establishment Act 113 of 1991. See AJ van der Walt 'Land reform in South Africa since 1990—An overview' (1995) 10 *SA Public Law* 1–30 at 11–12; PJ Badenhorst, JM Pienaar & H Mostert (assisted by M van Rooyen) *Silberberg and Schoeman's The law of property* (4th ed 2003) 483–485 for a brief overview, and see DL Carey Miller (with A Pope) *Land title in South Africa* (2000) 241–281 for a fuller discussion.

[7] The so-called Land Acts—the Black Land Act 27 of 1913 and the Development and Trust Land Act 18 of 1936—established 'grand apartheid' or spatial race-based segregation by dividing the country into white and non-white areas, but apart from them both 'grand apartheid' and 'petty apartheid' were entrenched in a host of other laws and legally created and sanctioned practices. See the sources in footnote 4 above for further references.

[8] The creation of white and non-white areas involved large-scale forced removals, sometimes but not always based on legal processes of expropriation and compensation. See the sources in footnote 4 above for further references.

[9] One of the strategies involved in establishing apartheid land law was to weaken black land rights, which facilitated forced removals. The establishment of white and 'non-white' areas meant that 'non-white' persons were in principle not allowed to settle in white urban areas, and their position there was always either illegal or tenuous in so far as they were temporarily allowed to live in black, coloured or Indian townships near the white urban areas to provide labour. In black tribal areas land rights of individuals were subject to tribal authority structures, which were in turn often corrupted by political interference and hence rendered insecure. In either event the mainly white law never developed suitable protection for these weak land rights and focused on traditional or new white land holding patterns. See the sources in footnote 4 above for further references, particularly AJ van der Walt 'Towards the development of post-apartheid land law: An exploratory survey' (1990) 23 *De Jure* 1–45 at 1–34; and see further AJ van der Walt 'Property rights and hierarchies of power: A critical evaluation of land-reform policy in South Africa' (1999) 64 *Koers* 259–294 at 259–267.

[10] The unfair division of white and black land (it is usually said that under apartheid more than 80% of the people were restricted to less than 13% of the land), combined with apartheid homeland and urbanization policy, implied that access to land and housing (especially in urban areas, but also

(continued on next page ...)

obviously the abolition of the apartheid land laws but, limited as they were,[11] these reforms already anticipated the direction of the more comprehensive land reform programme that would eventually be established by the new democratic government. The direction of land reform was characterized by its focus on three main areas: restitution of land rights that had been dispossessed in terms of apartheid laws and practices;[12] improvement of security of tenure for those whose land rights were weakened by apartheid land laws and practices;[13] and introduction of measures to increase and facilitate access to land and housing for individuals and communities who have been deprived of it during or because of apartheid.[14] The distinction between the three focus areas of land reform, namely restitution, improved security of tenure and increased access to land and housing (redistribution), is still reflected in the new government's official land policy and land reform programme.[15]

The 1993 Constitution explicitly provided for land reform and attempted to establish a balance between the promotion of land reform and the protection of existing property rights by way of two separate provisions with regard to property. Section 28, which was a more or less conventional property clause, was included in the entrenched Bill of Rights and guaranteed existing property rights, while sections 121–123 provided for land reform—specifically restitution of land—separately. The fact that the land reform provisions did not form part of the Bill of Rights, possibly because of their intended limited lifespan,[16] attracted criticism because it created an imbalance (or even a dichotomy) between the protective and the reformist aspects of the property provisions.[17] In the 1996 Constitution both sets of provisions were united in a single, double-sided property clause that is unique in its evident effort to

---

(... from previous page)
in overcrowded rural areas) was always a huge problem. Racially determined housing policy meant that access to housing was a critical problem in black communities, especially in urban areas. See the sources in footnote 4 above for further references, especially AJ van der Walt 'Towards the development of post-apartheid land law: An exploratory survey' (1990) 23 *De Jure* 1–45 at 1–34.

[11] The 1991 reforms were largely hesitant and limited in scope. For example, the possibilities for restitution of land in the Abolition of Racially Based Land Measures Act 108 of 1991 were much more limited (even after amendments) than the restitution process eventually introduced by the Restitution of Land Rights Act 22 of 1994 (on which see 6.2 below); see AJ van der Walt 'Land reform in South Africa since 1990—An overview' (1995) 10 *SA Public Law* 1–30 at 12–15. Moreover, these early reforms never addressed the central issues of access to limited natural resources such as water and minerals (about which see 6.5 below).

[12] See 6.2 below.

[13] See 6.3 below.

[14] See 6.4 below.

[15] See the official policy explanation of the Department of Land Affairs *White Paper on South African land policy* (1997) heading 2.3 'The three elements of the land reform programme' at http://land.pwv.gov.za/legislation_policies/white_papers.htm.

[16] See AJ van der Walt 'Land reform in South Africa since 1990—An overview' (1995) 10 *SA Public Law* 1–30 at 15–17.

[17] See PJ Badenhorst, JM Pienaar & H Mostert (assisted by M van Rooyen) *Silberberg and Schoeman's The law of property* (4th ed 2003) 488.

combine the protection of existing rights with a strong commitment to and detailed provision for land reform. Subsections 25(1)–(3) now contain the more or less conventional constitutional provisions that deal with state powers for and the constitutional validity of deprivation and expropriation of property, while subsections 25(4)–(9) legitimize land reform and place specific duties upon the state to legislate for, administer and promote various land reform initiatives in the three categories already mentioned.[18] The land reform provisions in section 25 again reflect the distinction between reforms aimed at restitution (subsection 25(7)), improved security of tenure (subsection 25(6)) and access to land (subsection 25(5)). In addition, section 26 provides for access to housing, while sections 24 and 27 provide for access to natural resources such as a clean environment and water.

The combination in section 25 of conventional protective provisions and land reform provisions in the same constitutional property clause is of the greatest political, legal and social interest. Obviously the property clause was drafted in this way to legitimize land reform and to ensure that the constitutional protection of existing rights should not exclude or frustrate necessary land reforms, but at the same time the intention was also to ensure that land reforms do not simply obviate the protection of existing property rights.[19] This creates difficult issues of interpretation in at least two areas. Firstly, the structure of section 25 raises internal interpretation issues in the sense that the interpretation and application of the section need to reflect a proper balance between the two seemingly different and even conflicting goals or purposes. In view of criticism leveled against the split property provisions in the 1993 Constitution it seems clear that an interpretation that treats the two aspects of section 25 as parts of one integrated guarantee is preferable to one that treats them as two separate and conflicting duties, but such an integrated interpretive strategy is difficult to develop. This aspect is discussed in chapter 2.3. Apart from the internal interpretation issue the structure of section 25 also raises external problems with regard to the relationship between section 25 and the rest of property law, especially in as far as land reform initiatives and laws and their constitutionally sanctioned impact on existing property interests tend to conflict with common law rules and principles. This issue is discussed in chapter 7 in the context of the development of the common law.

---

[18]See chapter 2.2. Compare Department of Land Affairs *White Paper on South African land policy* (1997) subheading '5. Property clause' under heading 'Constitutional issues' in Section III 'Land policy issues' at http://land.pwv.gov.za/legislation_policies/white_papers.htm: 'The new Constitution seeks to achieve a balance between the protection of existing property rights on the one hand, and constitutional guarantees of land reform on the other hand. The property clause itself now provides clear constitutional authority for land reform. The equality clause also provides clear authority for a programme aimed at achieving substantive equality.' Subsection 25(4) is an interpretation provision, 25(8) is a limitation provision, and 25(9) ensures that the state shall legislate to comply with 25(6). Subsections 25(5), 25(6) and 25(7) provide for reform initiatives to ensure access to land, greater security of tenure and restitution of land rights respectively. See further PJ Badenhorst, JM Pienaar & H Mostert (assisted by M van Rooyen) *Silberberg and Schoeman's The law of property* (4th ed 2003) 488.

[19]See footnote 18 above.

In addition to the land reform provisions in section 25 this chapter also includes a review of related constitutional provisions, such as sections 24, 26 and 27, in which access to other natural resources is guaranteed or referred to. Read together with section 25 these provisions make it clear that property reform involves not only the promotion of more equitable access to land, but also more equitable access to housing, water, mineral and petroleum resources and other natural resources. The wider access issues are considered in 6.4 and 6.5 below.

6.2 RESTITUTION OF LAND RIGHTS

25. Property

(4) For the purposes of this section—
   (a) ...
   (b) property is not limited to land.
(7) A person or community dispossessed of property after 19 June 1913 as a result of past discriminatory laws or practices is entitled, to the extent provided by an Act of Parliament, either to restitution of that property, or to equitable redress.

6.2.1 Introduction

Given the scale and central function of forced removals and evictions during the establishment and entrenchment of apartheid land law, restitution clearly had to be a central aspect of the land reform process regardless of its economic or social efficiency.[20] Consequently, restitution of land rights is one of the three key areas on which land reform initiatives have been focused from the outset. The De Klerk government's Abolition of Racially Based Land Measures Act 108 of 1991 already provided for a limited land claims process[21] and the current—much more extensive and refined—Restitution of Land Rights Act 2 of 1994 remains one of the main pillars of land reform.[22]

The essence of the restitution process is that individuals and communities who have been deprived of land rights as a result of apartheid land laws and practices (and who qualify in terms of the requirements set out in the Act) are entitled to claim restitution of their land rights or other equitable redress.

---

[20]See AJ van der Walt 'Towards the development of post-apartheid land law: An exploratory survey' (1990) 23 *De Jure* 1–45; PJ Badenhorst, JM Pienaar & H Mostert (assisted by M van Rooyen) *Silberberg and Schoeman's The law of property* (4th ed 2003) 485. Compare Department of Land Affairs *White Paper on South African land policy* (1997) heading 3.17 'The need for restitution' at http://land.pwv.gov.za/legislation_policies/white_papers.htm.

[21]See DL Carey Miller (with A Pope) *Land title in South Africa* (2000) 249–251 on the restitution process in terms of the Abolition of Racially Based Land Measures Act 108 of 1991. Compare footnote 23 below.

[22]The three areas are restitution, improved security of tenure and access to land and housing; see text accompanying footnotes 12–14 above.

The Restitution Act—the earliest land reform law promulgated by the new government—was initially authorized by sections 121–123 of the 1993 Constitution and came into operation on 2 December 1994.[23] The speed with which the Act was promulgated was an indication of the high priority of the restitution process for the newly elected ANC government.[24] When the 1996 Constitution became operative on 4 February 1997 section 25(7), which is framed slightly wider than the 1993 provisions, became the new source of constitutional authority for the restitution process; this section now authorizes restitution of land rights in terms of the Restitution of Land Rights Act 2 of 1994, providing that persons who have been dispossessed of land rights as a result of apartheid laws and practices and who qualify in terms of the Act may claim restitution or other equitable redress.[25] Since 1994 the Act has been amended several times to streamline and facilitate the process and to bring it in line with the 1996 Constitution.

6.2.2 Requirements framework of the restitution process

The Act sets out the requirements for restitution claims in section 2. The essential requirements are that a person or community can institute a restitution claim if that (a) person or community (b) was dispossessed (c) of a right in land (d) after 19 June

---

[23] Section 121 of the 1993 Constitution set out an entitlement to claim restitution, while sections 122–123 established a Commission on Restitution of Land Rights and vested certain powers in the courts to grant consequential relief. See T Roux 'Chapter 3: The Restitution of Land Rights Act' in G Budlender, J Latsky & T Roux *Juta's new land law* (1998); DL Carey Miller (with A Pope) *Land title in South Africa* (2000) 249–251 (on the Abolition of Racially Based Land Measures Act 108 of 1991), 313–397 (on restitution in terms of the Restitution of Land Rights Act 2 of 1994). See further W du Plessis, N Olivier & J Pienaar 'The ever-changing land law—1994–1995 reforms' (1995) 10 *SA Public Law* 145–167 at 147–154 for an analysis of the Act in its initial form, and PJ Badenhorst, JM Pienaar & H Mostert (assisted by M van Rooyen) *Silberberg and Schoeman's The law of property* (4th ed 2003) 512–527 for a discussion of the position as it stood in 2003.

[24] Theunis Roux 'Chapter 3: The Restitution of Land Rights Act' in G Budlender, J Latsky & T Roux *Juta's new land law* (1998) 3A–4 footnote 3 explains how the Act was promulgated within 7 months of the new government taking office in 1994.

[25] See the Restitution of Land Rights Amendment Act 84 of 1995, the Land Restitution and Reforms Laws Amendment Act 78 of 1996, especially the Land Restitution and Reform Laws Amendment Act 63 of 1997, the Land Restitution and Reform Laws Amendment Act 63 of 1997, the Land Restitution and Reform Laws Amendment Act 18 of 1999 and the Restitution of Land Rights Amendment Act 48 of 2003. Compare W du Plessis, N Olivier & J Pienaar 'Land reform gains momentum during 1996' (1997) 12 *SA Public Law* 251–273 at 251–252 on the 1997 Amendment Act. The principal Act was again amended by the Restitution of Land Rights Amendment Act 48 of 2003 to extend the powers of the Minister of Land Affairs to expropriate private land for restitution purposes and to bring those powers into line with section 25 of the Constitution; see W du Plessis, N Olivier & J Pienaar 'Land matters: New developments 2004 (1)' (2004) 19 *SA Public Law* 212–229 at 213. At the time of finalizing this chapter (June 2005) news reports started indicating that the minister was preparing to use these powers of expropriation for the first time to acquire land for restitution purposes compulsorily. Obviously such expropriations would be subject to the overarching requirements in section 25(2) and (3); see further chapter 5.

1913 (e) as a result of a past racially discriminatory law or practice and (f) did not receive just and equitable compensation or consideration; (g) provided the claim was lodged in time.[26]

Both natural and legal persons can claim; the latter applies especially in cases where communities are represented by trusts or property development companies.[27] A direct descendant (including a spouse or partner in a customary union) of a person who otherwise qualifies but has not claimed restitution is allowed to claim under certain circumstances.[28] It is not necessary that a community intending to claim should survive intact or that all members of the community should still be living together as a group or continue to hold land on a communal basis,[29] and there is provision for rival groups within a community to lodge separate claims.[30]

Claimants must have been dispossessed of a right in land, but do not have to prove actual physical dispossession of the land. The decision in *Dulabh and Another v The Department of Land Affairs*[31] implies that loss of a land right that accompanied the

---

[26]Section 2 of the 1994 Act as amended; compare section 25(7) of the 1996 Constitution.

[27]See DL Carey Miller (with A Pope) *Land title in South Africa* (2000) 329; T Roux 'Chapter 3: The Restitution of Land Rights Act' in G Budlender, J Latsky & T Roux *Juta's new land law* (1998) 3A–11; PJ Badenhorst, JM Pienaar & H Mostert (assisted by M van Rooyen) *Silberberg and Schoeman's The law of property* (4th ed 2003) 512–513; compare *Chief Nchabeleng v Chief Phasha* 1998 (3) SA 579 (LCC) par [22] at 589F–590C (accepted that the chief claims for the tribe, who has to satisfy the requirement of a community); *Farjas (Pty) Ltd v Regional Land Claims Commissioner, KwaZulu-Natal* 1998 (2) SA 900 (LCC) (the case concerned the nature and scope of the regional commissioner's powers in accepting or rejecting claims, and in the case the rejection was based purely on the question whether the community had been deprived of a right in land and whether the dispossession was effected under or for the purpose of furthering the objects of a racially discriminatory law, which suggests that it was accepted that the development company's representation of the group was in order).

[28]Section 2(1)(c) read with section 1 of the 1994 Act. See DL Carey Miller (with A Pope) *Land title in South Africa* (2000) 327–329; T Roux 'Chapter 3: The Restitution of Land Rights Act' in G Budlender, J Latsky & T Roux *Juta's new land law* (1998) 3A–9, 3A–12; PJ Badenhorst, JM Pienaar & H Mostert (assisted by M van Rooyen) *Silberberg and Schoeman's The law of property* (4th ed 2003) 512–513. See further *In re Moodley NO* 2002 (3) SA 846 (LCC), compare W du Plessis, N Olivier & J Pienaar 'A new dispensation for communal land and minerals' (2002) 17 *SA Public Law* 409–439 at 412.

[29]See *Ndebele-Ndzundza Community v Farm Kafferskraal No 181 JS* 2003 (5) SA 375 (LCC) paras [6]–[18] at 380B–389C; compare PJ Badenhorst, JM Pienaar & H Mostert (assisted by M van Rooyen) *Silberberg and Schoeman's The law of property* (4th ed 2003) 513; W du Plessis, N Olivier & J Pienaar '"Your land is safe in South Africa"?' (2003) 18 *SA Public Law* 229–250 at 231–233.

[30]See PJ Badenhorst, JM Pienaar & H Mostert (assisted by M van Rooyen) *Silberberg and Schoeman's The law of property* (4th ed 2003) 513; T Roux 'Chapter 3: The Restitution of Land Rights Act' in G Budlender, J Latsky & T Roux *Juta's new land law* (1998) 3A–11–3A–12, referring to the definition of 'community' in section 1 read with sections 13(1)(b) and 35(3) of the 1994 Act.

[31]1997 (4) SA 1108 (LCC) par [31] at 1120C–E. See DL Carey Miller (with A Pope) *Land title in South Africa* (2000) 329; T Roux 'Chapter 3: The Restitution of Land Rights Act' in G Budlender, J Latsky & T Roux *Juta's new land law* (1998) 3A–13; PJ Badenhorst, JM Pienaar & H Mostert (assisted by M van Rooyen) *Silberberg and Schoeman's The law of property* (4th ed 2003) 513.

downgrading of the landholder's right, preventing her from inheriting and taking transfer of the property, was enough to conclude that she was dispossessed of a right in property, even though she continued to rent the property and was therefore not physically dispossessed. Although mere downgrading of a right does not necessarily amount to dispossession, compulsory loss of a stronger right in order to retain a weaker right can qualify as dispossession for purposes of the Act. The Supreme Court of Appeal has held that, although it was necessary to establish that a dispossession took place because of some compulsory action by an outside agency, the fact that a claimant sold the land did not necessarily preclude a claim because sales of land often took place because of the political pressure upon owners who were no longer allowed to occupy or use their own land after its racial reclassification.[32]

Section 1 of the Act defines 'right in land' as any right in land whether registered or not, including the interests of a labour tenant or a sharecropper, a customary law interest, the interest of a beneficiary under a trust arrangement and beneficial occupation for a continuous period of not less than 10 years prior to the dispossession in question.[33] By defining a right in land as widely as possible the Act extends the restitution process to all persons and groups who have been negatively affected by apartheid land laws and practices, as opposed to just those who lost ownership or other registered rights in land.[34] The reference to the interests of labour tenants, sharecrop-

---

[32]See *Abrams v Allie NO and Others* 2004 (4) SA 534 (SCA) paras [11]–[12] at 541B–542B. The claimant sold the land to the state only because it became clear that he no longer qualified to live there once the land was classified white. In *Khumalo NO v Minister of Land Affairs and Another* 2005 (2) SA 618 (LCC) paras [19] at 627B–D, [21] at 627H–628B it was decided that the administrative act by which black persons could be deprived of their ownership by a commissioner acting in terms of section 8(7) of the Black Administration Act 33 of 1927 (issuing a certificate naming the person entitled to be registered as holder of the land) deprived the previous holder of land and was racially discriminatory, and therefore qualified for a restitution claim.

[33]Theunis Roux 'Chapter 3: The Restitution of Land Rights Act' in G Budlender, J Latsky & T Roux *Juta's new land law* (1998) 3A–15 argues that the reference to 'beneficial occupation' in the definition of rights in land in the 1994 Act, read together with similar definitions of the term in the Development Facilitation Act 67 of 1995 and the Interim Protection of Informal Land Rights Act 31 of 1996, suggests that this term might be 'gradually taking on a meaning similar to "statutory prescriptive title"'. In suggesting that beneficial occupation is developing in this direction Roux refers to the similarities between the definitions of beneficial occupation and the statutory requirements for original acquisition of property through prescription; see the Prescription Act 18 of 1943 section 2(1) and the Prescription Act 68 of 1969 section 1. The prescription period in both acts is 30 years. PJ Badenhorst, JM Pienaar & H Mostert (assisted by M van Rooyen) *Silberberg and Schoeman's The law of property* (4th ed 2003) 514 point out, with reference to *Richtersveld Community v Alexkor Ltd* 2001 (3) SA 1293 (LCC) at 1331E–1332C, that some benefit must be derived from beneficial occupation and that the occupiers must have had the intention to derive such benefit from their occupation.

[34]See DL Carey Miller (with A Pope) *Land title in South Africa* (2000) 330–331, 323–326; who argues at 323 that there is no reason why the traditional real vs personal rights distinction should play any role in the restitution context; all rights should qualify. See further T Roux 'Chapter 3: The Restitution of Land Rights Act' in G Budlender, J Latsky & T Roux *Juta's new land law* (1998)

(continued on next page ...)

pers, beneficiaries under a trust and beneficial occupiers is not exhaustive and the courts could extend the concept of a right in property to include other so-called 'informal' interests as well.[35] In *Dulabh and Another v The Department of Land Affairs*[36] the Land Claims Court decided that the right to inherit and take transfer of property was included in the Act's concept of a right in property. In the *Richtersveld* case the Supreme Court of Appeal held that a customary law interest in land that survived annexation by a colonial power qualified as a right in land for purposes of the Act, even if that right involved no more than seasonal, sparse and intermittent use of the land.[37] In the *Kranspoort Community* case[38] the Land Claims Court analyse and discussed the notion of beneficial occupation extensively and concluded that even non-exclusive, seasonal use of land by agreement with the registered landowner (a church) would qualify for a restitution claim; in the event the community was awarded stronger rights (full ownership) of the land than it had lost originally.

Restitution claims are restricted to dispossessions that took place after 19 June 1913, which is the date on which the Black Land Act 27 of 1913 became law.[39]

(*... from previous page*)

3A–13–3A–16; PJ Badenhorst, JM Pienaar & H Mostert (assisted by M van Rooyen) *Silberberg and Schoeman's The law of property* (4th ed 2003) 514. Roux at 3A–14 argues that in practice the term will not be interpreted as widely as possible and that certain categories of potential claimants will receive alternative redress through land redistribution and tenure reform programmes instead.

[35] T Roux 'Chapter 3: The Restitution of Land Rights Act' in G Budlender, J Latsky & T Roux *Juta's new land law* (1998) 3A–15 refers to *Dulabh and Another v The Department of Land Affairs* 1997 (4) SA 1108 (LCC) par [31] at 1120C–E as an example where the Land Claims Court extended the concept of a right in property to include the right to inherit and take transfer of property.

[36] 1997 (4) SA 1108 (LCC) par [31] at 1120C–E. See DL Carey Miller (with A Pope) *Land title in South Africa* (2000) 329; T Roux 'Chapter 3: The Restitution of Land Rights Act' in G Budlender, J Latsky & T Roux *Juta's new land law* (1998) 3A–13.

[37] *Richtersveld Community and Others v Alexkor Ltd and Another* 2003 (6) SA 104 (SCA) par [24] at 117G–H. The Constitutional Court confirmed this decision in *Alexkor Ltd and Another v The Richtersveld Community and Others* 2004 (5) SA 460 (CC) par [62] at 482D–F, paras [68]–[69] at 483H–484E, although it scrapped the SCA's finding that the community's customary law interest was 'akin to that held under common law ownership' (SCA judgment par [26] at 118F, CC decision paras [49]–[50] at 478E–G).

[38] *In re Kranspoort Community* 2002 (2) SA 124 (LCC) paras [52]–[69] at 153F–162F, par [103] at 177E–J. See PJ Badenhorst, JM Pienaar & H Mostert (assisted by M van Rooyen) *Silberberg and Schoeman's The law of property* (4th ed 2003) 514; W du Plessis, N Olivier & J Pienaar 'Land reform: A never-ending process' (2000) 15 *SA Public Law* 230–254 at 234. See further *Ndebele-Ndzundza Community v Farm Kafferskraal No 181 JS* 2003 (5) SA 375 (LCC) paras [6]–[18] at 380B–389C; compare W du Plessis, N Olivier & J Pienaar '"Your land is safe in South Africa"?' (2003) 18 *SA Public Law* 229–250 at 231–233.

[39] See *Alexkor Ltd and Another v The Richtersveld Community and Others* 2004 (5) SA 460 (CC) par [37] at 475C–D. The Court decided in paras [38] at 475G–H, [40] at 476C that the case could be disposed of effectively on the assumption, without deciding the issue, that none of the relevant provisions of the Act had retrospective effect before 19 June 1913.

Roux[40] points out that this date is arbitrary because colonial land dispossession preceded the promulgation of the Black Land Act, and adds that although the choice of a cutoff date was inspired by a political compromise during the constitutional settlement and by the historical context of land occupation in South Africa,[41] the arbitrary choice of a date could nevertheless cause severe hardship in cases where potential claimants are excluded narrowly and formalistically. The most obvious effect of the 1913 cutoff date is that historical, so-called aboriginal or native land claims against pre-1913 colonial powers or settlers are apparently excluded from the restitution process (although the issue remains controversial). For the same reasons that inspired the constitutional settlement and the choice of a relatively late cutoff date the Department of Land Affairs is against open-ended historical land claims,[42] and consequently it has been necessary for restitution claimants to prove that a particular dispossession took place after the cutoff date.[43]

---

[40]T Roux 'Chapter 3: The Restitution of Land Rights Act' in G Budlender, J Latsky & T Roux *Juta's new land law* (1998) 3A–16. The reference to the historical context alludes to the fact that historical land claims in South Africa would have opened up a vast number of old and overlapping land disputes with serious ethnic implications. Accordingly the situation has to be distinguished from the position in other countries such as Australia, New Zealand and Canada, where restitutions based on so-called aboriginal title can be allowed right back to the date of colonial settlement because of the relatively small areas of land and the relatively small number of potential claimants involved. Roux therefore suggests that the decision to exclude restitution claims based on original title was based on policy grounds that involve a number of considerations: the undesirability of opening up old ethnic conflicts about land, the lack of clear and uncontested evidence about early land rights, the practical feasibility of administering and adjudicating basically all-encompassing conflicting historical land claims, and the wish to facilitate a workable constitutional settlement. See further DL Carey Miller (with A Pope) *Land title in South Africa* (2000) 316, 318, 319–320, 332; compare TW Bennett 'Restitution of land and the doctrine of aboriginal title in South Africa' (1993) 9 *SAJHR* 443–476; TW Bennett *Human rights and African customary law under the South African Constitution* (1995) 148–150; TW Bennett & CH Powell 'Aboriginal title in South Africa revisited' (1999) 15 *SAJHR* 449–485.

[41]On the political compromise see Geoff Budlender 'The constitutional protection of property rights' in G Budlender, J Latsky & T Roux *Juta's new land law* (1998) 1–4.

[42]See Department of Land Affairs *White Paper on South African land policy* (1997) par 4.14.2; compare T Roux 'Chapter 3: The Restitution of Land Rights Act' in G Budlender, J Latsky & T Roux *Juta's new land law* (1998) 3A–17. For the counter-arguments in favour of restitution claims based on aboriginal title doctrine see TW Bennett 'Restitution of land and the doctrine of aboriginal title in South Africa' (1993) 9 *SAJHR* 443–476; TW Bennett *Human rights and African customary law under the South African Constitution* (1995) 148–150; TW Bennett & CH Powell 'Aboriginal title in South Africa revisited' (1999) 15 *SAJHR* 449–485.

[43]The *Richtersveld* case is an interesting example. In *Richtersveld Community and Others v Alexkor Ltd and Another* 2001 (3) SA 1293 (LCC) par [117] at 1349A–B the Land Claims Court noted that it had no jurisdiction to adjudicate a restitution claim based on native title: 'I regret that the limited jurisdiction of this Court makes it impossible for me to decide on the issue of the realization of indigenous title, ...' The Court previously held that the plaintiffs had not succeeded in proving that it was dispossessed as a result of a racially discriminatory law or practice because the original legal dispossession was effected by annexation in 1847 by the British colonial powers, while the actual

(continued on next page ...)

The dispossession must have been the result of past racially discriminatory laws or practices.[44] Many apartheid land dispossessions took place in terms of apparently race neutral laws,[45] and therefore the dispossession requirement was framed widely to ensure that even dispossessions that look race neutral superficially would be included if the dispossession furthered the object of racially discriminatory laws or practices. Initially the courts tended to read this requirement narrowly, rejecting restitution claims in cases where it could feasibly be said that the dispossession was justified by

---

(... from previous page)
physical dispossession after 1913 (when, according to the decision, the community had enjoyed beneficial occupation for longer than ten years) was not effected for a racially discriminatory purpose but in order to facilitate the diamond mining operation that required everybody (not only the black community) to be removed from the land (see paras [106] at 1344H, [110] at 1346C). In *Richtersveld Community and Others v Alexkor Ltd and Another* 2003 (6) SA 104 (SCA) the Supreme Court of Appeal reversed the Land Claims Court's decision, first holding that the community's customary law interest in the land survived annexation by the British colonial powers (paras [23]–[29] at 17E–119D, [34]–[62] at 120F–128I); then holding that the relevant dispossession was the actual physical removal of the community from the land, which took place through the promulgation and implementation of a series of mining and minerals legislation after the cutoff date of 19 June 1913 (paras [90]–[95] at 135H–136J); and finally deciding that the dispossession was clearly inspired by racial discrimination (paras [96]–[110] at 137A–139I). On appeal to the Constitutional Court the SCA decision was upheld: *Alexkor Ltd and Another v The Richtersveld Community and Others* 2003 (5) SA 460 (CC). On the *Richtersveld* cases see PJ Badenhorst, JM Pienaar & H Mostert (assisted by M van Rooyen) *Silberberg and Schoeman's The law of property* (4th ed 2003) 514; W du Plessis, N Olivier & J Pienaar 'Evictions, restitution, spatial information, the right to housing and minerals: New approaches from the government and the courts' (2001) 16 *SA Public Law* 181–216 at 190–193; W du Plessis, N Olivier & J Pienaar 'Expropriation, restitution and land redistribution: An answer to land problems in South Africa?' (2003) 18 *SA Public Law* 491-514 at 496–498; W du Plessis, N Olivier & J Pienaar 'Land matters: New developments 2004 (1)' (2004) 19 *SA Public Law* 212–229 at 215–216; H Mostert & P Fitzpatrick '"Living in the margins of history on the edge of the country"—Legal foundation and the Richtersveld community's title to land' 2004 *TSAR* 309–323, 498–510; M Barry 'Now something else must happen: *Richtersveld* and the dilemmas of land reform in post-apartheid South Africa' (2004) 20 *SAJHR* 355–382.

[44]Originally the 1994 Act provided that the dispossession must have taken place under or in furtherance of the objects of a racially discriminatory law, but this requirement was simplified in the current provision. See section 25(7) of the 1996 Constitution; section 2(1)(a) of the 1994 Act. Compare DL Carey Miller (with A Pope) *Land title in South Africa* (2000) 331–332; T Roux 'Chapter 3: The Restitution of Land Rights Act' in G Budlender, J Latsky & T Roux *Juta's new land law* (1998) 3A–17–3A–20; PJ Badenhorst, JM Pienaar & H Mostert (assisted by M van Rooyen) *Silberberg and Schoeman's The law of property* (4th ed 2003) 514–516. In the case of *In re Macleantown Residents Association: Re Certain Erven and Commonage in Macleantown* 1996 (4) SA 1272 (LCC) at 1277E–F the Land Claims Court held that the Group Areas Act 36 of 1996 'clearly offends the provisions of s 8(2) of the interim Constitution'.

[45]T Roux 'Chapter 3: The Restitution of Land Rights Act' in G Budlender, J Latsky & T Roux *Juta's new land law* (1998) 3A–18 at 3A–20 lists some of the apparently race neutral laws that were used to further the objects of racially discriminatory laws and practices. PJ Badenhorst, JM Pienaar & H Mostert (assisted by M van Rooyen) *Silberberg and Schoeman's The law of property* (4th ed 2003) 516 refer to cases dealing with the question whether practices followed in the (area-specific and thus in fact racially separated) deeds registry offices were racially discriminatory.

apparently race-neutral state goals such as the building of schools, slum clearance and urban renewal or economic development,[46] but more recently it was accepted that the real racially inspired intention behind ostensibly race-neutral laws and practices should be taken into account when deciding whether a specific dispossession was tainted.[47] In its current form the requirement avoids the problem of deciding whether the dispossession was authorized by or promoted the objects of a racially discrimina-tory law, and it is only necessary to show that it was the result of a racially discrimi-natory law or practice. The requirement is wide enough to include both state and

---

[46] In *Minister of Land Affairs v Slamdien* 1999 (4) BCLR 413 (LCC) the Land Claims Court decided that forced removals for the purpose of building a school for coloured children in a coloured township did not qualify for restitution because it was not the type of racially discriminatory prac-tice contemplated in the Act (specifically in creating spatial segregation); see PJ Badenhorst, JM Pienaar & H Mostert (assisted by M van Rooyen) *Silberberg and Schoeman's The law of property* (4th ed 2003) 515; W du Plessis, N Olivier & J Pienaar 'Land issues: An assessment of the failures and successes' (1999) 14 *SA Public* Law 241–270 at 245; W du Plessis, N Olivier & J Pienaar 'Evictions, restitution, spatial information, the right to housing and minerals: New approaches from the government and the courts' (2001) 16 *SA Public Law* 181–216 at 183. In *Richtersveld Community and Others v Alexkor Ltd and Another* 2001 (3) SA 1293 (LCC) the Court applied this test to find that the mining laws that authorized the dispossession of the Richtersveld community were not racially inspired and that the community could therefore not succeed with a restitution claim. This decision was overturned by the Supreme Court of Appeal and the Constitutional Court; see footnote 43 above and footnote 47 below. On the LCC decision see T Roux 'Pro-poor court, anti-poor outcomes: Explaining the performance of the South African Land Claims Court' (2004) 20 *SAJHR* 511–543 at 522–525. The narrow LCC approach was not followed consistently in early decisions, though: *Farjas (Pty) Ltd v Regional Land Claims Commissioner, KwaZulu-Natal* 1998 (2) SA 900 (LCC) dealt with a land claims commissioner's decision that a claim was precluded, *inter alia* because she was unconvinced that the land was dispossessed under or in furtherance of a racially discrimi-natory law. The Land Claims Court held (paras [33]–[42] at 920I–925B) that the commissioner was mistaken about the statute under which the dispossession was undertaken and about the racially discriminatory nature of the objects served by that statute. In the Court's view there was an arguable case that the Housing Development Act (House of Delegates) 4 of 1987, under which the dispos-session took place, would not survive scrutiny under section 8(2) of the 1993 Constitution (equality and non-discrimination).

[47] In *Richtersveld Community and Others v Alexkor Ltd and Another* 2001 (3) SA 1293 (LCC) the Land Claims Court initially applied the narrow test to find that the mining laws that authorized the dispossession of the Richtersveld community were not racially inspired and that the community could therefore not succeed with a restitution claim, but this interpretation was reversed by the Supreme Court of Appeal in *Richtersveld Community and Others v Alexkor Ltd and Another* 2003 (6) SA 104 (SCA) paras [97]–[105] at 137C–139B; the latter decision being confirmed by the Consti-tutional Court in *Alexkor Ltd and the Government of the Republic of South Africa v Richtersveld Commu-nity* 2004 (5) SA 460 (CC). Since then the broader approach that was followed in some early decisions became the norm. In *Abrams v Allie NO and Others* 2004 (4) SA 534 (SCA) par [14] at 542F–543D the Supreme Court of Appeal again overturned a narrow Land Claims Court interpre-tation and confirmed that, although the removal was ostensibly justified by slum clearance and urban renewal purposes under the Community Development Act 3 of 1966, the principal object was actually to facilitate the resettlement of specific race groups.

private dispossessions as well as disposal of the land that appears voluntary but that was in fact not entirely voluntary.[48]

Restitution claims are only possible if the dispossessed did not receive just and equitable compensation or consideration for the loss.[49] In terms of the amended 1994 Act a restitution claim is barred when the dispossessed person or community either received just and equitable compensation as contemplated in section 25(3) of the 1996 Constitution or received any other consideration which is just and equitable, calculated at the time of the dispossession.[50] Even claimants who did receive compensation for the dispossession could be entitled to a restitution claim if they can prove that the compensation was inadequate, and the Land Claims Court has decided that a compensation claim for financial loss directly caused by the dispossession and for non-financial hardship is not excluded.[51]

Restitution claims had to be lodged before 31 December 1998.[52] The thinking behind this deadline was to place a sunset limit on restitution claims for the sake of

---

[48]T Roux 'Chapter 3: The Restitution of Land Rights Act' in G Budlender, J Latsky & T Roux *Juta's new land law* (1998) 3A–20. See *Abrams v Allie NO and Others* 2004 (4) SA 534 (SCA) paras [11]–[12] at 541B–542B; compare footnotes 46, 47 above.

[49]Section 2(2) of the 1994 Act. See further T Roux 'Chapter 3: The Restitution of Land Rights Act' in G Budlender, J Latsky & T Roux *Juta's new land law* (1998) 3A–20–3A–2; DL Carey Miller (with A Pope) *Land title in South Africa* (2000) 333; PJ Badenhorst, JM Pienaar & H Mostert (assisted by M van Rooyen) *Silberberg and Schoeman's The law of property* (4th ed 2003) 512. In *Abrams v Allie NO and Others* 2004 (4) SA 534 (SCA) paras [25]–[27] at 543G–547J it was held that a difference of less than 2% between the estimated market value at the time of dispossession and the compensation received was insufficient to satisfy the threshold inadequate-compensation requirement; since valuation is an inexact science and values are always approximate such as small difference could not justify a restitution claim.

[50]Section 2(2) as it was amended by the Land Restitution and Reform Laws Amendment Act 18 of 1999. See T Roux 'Chapter 3: The Restitution of Land Rights Act' in G Budlender, J Latsky & T Roux *Juta's new land law* (1998) 3A–20ff for the previous position.

[51]See *Hermanus v Department of Land Affairs: In re Erven 3535 and 3536, Goodwood* 2001 (1) SA 1030 (LCC) (concerning additional compensation apart from restitution of the land or restitutionary compensation, in the form of a *solatium* or compensation for suffering); W du Plessis, N Olivier & J Pienaar 'Evictions, restitution, spatial information, the right to housing and minerals: New approaches from the government and the courts' (2001) 16 *SA Public Law* 181–216 at 187–189. In *Abrams v Allie NO and Others* 2004 (4) SA 534 (SCA) paras [25]–[27] at 543G–547J it was held that a difference of less than 2% between the estimated market value at the time of dispossession and the compensation received did not justify a restitution claim.

[52]The original deadline of 30 April 1998 (within 3 years of the date, 1 May 1995, fixed by the Minister of Land Affairs by notice in the *Gazette* GN 575 in GG 16370 of 21 April 1995, as initially required by section 2(1)(c) of the 1994 Act) was extended to 31 December 1998 by the Land Restitution and Reform Laws Amendment Act 63 of 1997 (which replaced section 2(1)(c) with the new section 2(1)(e)). See DL Carey Miller (with A Pope) *Land title in South Africa* (2000) 326, 332; T Roux 'Chapter 3: The Restitution of Land Rights Act' in G Budlender, J Latsky & T Roux *Juta's new land law* (1998) 3A–9, 3A–22; PJ Badenhorst, JM Pienaar & H Mostert (assisted by M van Rooyen) *Silberberg and Schoeman's The law of property* (4th ed 2003) 512.

economic and legal certainty and social and political closure.[53] In addition, it has been decided that all claims have to be processed and dealt with by 31 December 2005 (subsequently extended to 31 December 2007).[54]

6.2.3 Institutional and procedural framework[55]

Chapter II of the 1994 Act provides for the establishment and functions of the Commission on Restitution of Land Rights, consisting of a Chief Land Claims Commissioner, a Deputy Commissioner and a number of regional commissioners. The Commission is charged with a number of mandatory functions related to the restitution process: regular publication of information regarding the right to claim restitution and the procedure involved, providing assistance with the preparation and

---

[53] See eg Department of Land Affairs *White Paper on South African land policy* (1997) heading 3.2 'The role of the market and the state in land reform': 'The challenge is to find a way of redistributing land to the needy, and at the same time maintaining public confidence in the land market'; and Box 4.7 heading 'Land restitution strategy': 'The programme will be judged to be successful if land restitution is attained while maintaining public confidence in the land market'; at http://land.pwv.gov.za/legislation_policies/white_papers.htm.

[54] In the Department of Land Affairs *White Paper on South African land policy* (1997) (heading 4.13 'Purpose of land restitution') it was stated that the government had set itself the following targets with regard to restitution claims: a three-year period for the lodgement of claims, from 1 May 1995 (ie 1 May 1998, later extended to 31 December 1998); a five-year period for the Commission and the Court to finalize all claims (ie 31 December 2000, extended to 31 December 2005 and again to 31 December 2007); and a ten-year period for the implementation of all Court orders (ie 31 December 2005). The 31 December 2005 date for completion of restitution claims, which coincides with the five year target after the extended lodgement date for claims, was announced by State President Mbeki in his *State of the nation address* of 8 February 2002 at http://www.info.gov.za/speeches/2002/0202281146a1001.htm: 'We intend, within the next three years, to complete the land restitution process, which is a critical part of our land reform programme ...' By early January 2005 it was reported that the Commission on Land Rights has processed 52 247 claims, involving more than 26 000 households and 160 000 beneficiaries, at a cost of more than R4.4 billion. At that point a further 22 447 unresolved claims remained, 13 247 of which involved urban land and 9 200 rural land. In early 2005 the Commission still expected to finalize all urban claims by the end of March 2005 and the rest by the end of 2005. Source: *Legalbrief* Thursday 20 January 2005 at www.legalbrief.co.za, citing Chief Land Claims Commissioner Tozi Gwayana from the *Eastern Province Herald* of 19 January 2005 at www.epherald.co.za/herald/2005/01/19/news/. See further W Mbhele et al 'The state of delivery' *SA Sunday Times* 13 February 2005 p 4, with reference to President Mbeki's *State of the nation address* of 11 February 2005: 'Teikens vir besit van grond nie gehaal' *Die Burger* 11 February 2005 S2. The 31 December 2005 date was again postponed to 31 December; see Anon 'Manuel injects R6-billion into land restitution' *Mail & Guardian* 23 February 2005 at http://www.mg.co.za/articlePage.aspx?articleid=198176&area=/budget_2005/budget_news/.

[55] See sections 4–21 of the 1994 Act, and compare T Roux 'Chapter 3: The Restitution of Land Rights Act' in G Budlender, J Latsky & T Roux *Juta's new land law* (1998) 3A–24–3A–48; DL Carey Miller (with A Pope) *Land title in South Africa* (2000) 334–362; PJ Badenhorst, JM Pienaar & H Mostert (assisted by M van Rooyen) *Silberberg and Schoeman's The law of property* (4th ed 2003) 516–527; W du Plessis, N Olivier & J Pienaar 'The ever-changing land law—1994–1995 reforms' (1995) 10 *SA Public Law* 145–167 at 148–150 for an overview.

submission of claims, reception and acknowledgement of claims received, regular reports on the progress of claims received, investigation of claims, mediation and settlement of disputes arising from claims, referral of claims to the Land Claims Court and regular reporting to the Court on the terms of settlement of successfully mediated claims, and preparation and submission of evidence and other materials relating to claims that are proceeding to the Court for a determination on the merits. Apart from these mandatory duties the Commission is also empowered to carry out certain optional duties, including doing anything connected with or incidental to the expeditious finalization of claims, prioritizing claims affecting a substantial number of persons or persons who have suffered substantial losses or with pressing needs, making recommendations to the Minister of Land Affairs on appropriate relief for claimants who fail to satisfy the criteria for restitution claims, cooperation in the implementation of specific restitution orders, and application to the Court for a declaratory order on questions of law. The Commission is further allowed to apply for a prohibitive interdict to prevent the sale, exchange, donation, lease, subdivision, rezoning or development of land subject to a restitution claim.[56]

---

[56]The Supreme Court of Appeal decided in *Gamevest (Pty) Ltd v Regional Land Claims Commissioner, Northern Province and Mpumalanga, and Others* 2003 (1) SA 373 (SCA) par [7] at 379B–380H that the procedure for the lodgement, consideration and final determination of a restitution claim may be divided into four phases: (*a*) lodgement; (*b*) consideration, acceptance and publication; (*c*) investigation and (*d*) referral to the Land Claims Court. The SCA further held that the Promotion of Administrative Justice Act 3 of 2000 did not apply to the case because it came into effect after the particular claim was lodged, and that the common law therefore applied. For purposes of the common law an administrative act was described by the Court as 'non-performance or wrong performance of a statutory duty or power; where the duty/power is essentially a decision-making one and the person or body concerned has taken a decision' (par [12] at 382D). The Court then held that actions taken or advice given by the regional commissioner before lodgement of a restitution claim was not administrative action and hence not subject to review. One could argue that the Court's common law definition of administrative action was too narrow, perhaps confusing administrative action with the narrower category of discretionary administrative action. See further W du Plessis, N Olivier & J Pienaar '"Your land is safe in South Africa"?' (2003) 18 *SA Public Law* 229–250 at 234. In any event it has to be said that the issue would probably be decided differently under the 2000 Act, which defines administrative action as:

'any decision taken, or any failure to take a decision, by

(*a*) an organ of State, when—

(i) exercising a power in terms of the Constitution or a provincial constitution; or

(ii) exercising a public power or performing a public function in terms of any legislation; or

(*b*) a natural or juristic person, other than an organ of State, when exercising a public power or performing a public function in terms of an empowering provision, which adversely affects the rights of any person and which has a direct, external legal effect, ..."

See the discussion of the definition in *South African Jewish Board of Deputies v Sutherland NO and Others* 2004 (4) SA 368 (W) par [21] at 382D–H; compare further C Hoexter (with R Lyster) *The new constitutional and administrative law Vol 2: Administrative law* (2002) 99–113. A second point in the *Gamevest* decision that might be controversial is that there was no room for review in the absence of administrative action; in *Fedsure Life Assurance Ltd and Others v Greater Johannesburg Transitional*

(continued on next page ...)

The procedure regarding the lodgement and processing of restitution claims is set out in the Act, read together with the rules of procedure published in 1995 in terms of section 16. A claim is lodged on a prescribed form, together with additional substantiating documents.[57] Once a claim has been lodged the relevant regional commissioner must ensure that it meets the qualifying criteria in section 2 of the Act,[58] that the claim has been lodged in the prescribed manner and that it is not frivolous or vexatious.[59] Acceptance or entry-level scrutiny of claims does not involve the same strict proof of the substantive requirements that applies to establishing a right to relief under the Act.[60]

Once a regional commissioner has accepted a claim it must be published in the *Government Gazette*. Such publication has important implications: no person may improperly obstruct the passage of the claim through the process; no person may sell, exchange, donate, lease, subdivide, rezone or develop the land without giving the commissioner prescribed notice; no claimant who had occupied the land may be evicted without prescribed notice to the commissioner; no person may remove,

---

(... from previous page)

Metropolitan Council and Others 1999 (1) SA 374 (CC) paras [53], [54] and [59] at 398G–I, 400F–401B; *Pharmaceutical Manufacturers Association of SA and Another: In re Ex parte President of the Republic of South Africa and Others* 2000 (2) SA 674 (CC) par [17] at 687B–E, par [20] at 687H–688A it was made clear that all state action, whether administrative action or not, had to comply with (and could be reviewed with reference to) the requirement of legality and other constitutional requirements, even if it should not qualify as administrative action in the narrow sense.

[57] The form and required documentation are prescribed in Annexure A to the Act. See DL Carey Miller (with A Pope) *Land title in South Africa* (2000) 340–362; T Roux 'Chapter 3: The Restitution of Land Rights Act' in G Budlender, J Latsky & T Roux *Juta's new land law* (1998) 3A–24–3A–48; PJ Badenhorst, JM Pienaar & H Mostert (assisted by M van Rooyen) *Silberberg and Schoeman's The law of property* (4th ed 2003) 516–527; W du Plessis, N Olivier & J Pienaar 'The ever-changing land law—1994–1995 reforms' (1995) 10 *SA Public Law* 145–167 at 145–150.

[58] As discussed above. This mainly involves the requirements that the dispossession must have taken place after 19 June 1913, that it involved a dispossession of a right in land, and that the dispossession was a result of a racially discriminatory law or practice. Finally, the claim must have been lodged before the cutoff date of 31 December 1998. See DL Carey Miller (with A Pope) *Land title in South Africa* (2000) 341 footnote 212.

[59] Section 11. In *Farjas (Pty) Ltd v Regional Land Claims Commissioner, KwaZulu-Natal* 1998 (2) SA 900 (LCC) the Land Claims Court held that the questions whether the claim was lodged in the prescribed manner and whether dispossession had occurred on or after 19 June 1913 involved no independent discretion of the commissioner and that they were purely mechanical. See DL Carey Miller (with A Pope) *Land title in South Africa* (2000) 341–342; PJ Badenhorst, JM Pienaar & H Mostert (assisted by M van Rooyen) *Silberberg and Schoeman's The law of property* (4th ed 2003) 517; W du Plessis, N Olivier & J Pienaar 'Land: Still a contentious issue' (1998) 13 *SA Public Law* 149–169 at 153.

[60] *Farjas (Pty) Ltd v Regional Land Claims Commissioner, KwaZulu-Natal* 1998 (2) SA 900 (LCC) par [41] at 923I–924F; see DL Carey Miller (with A Pope) *Land title in South Africa* (2000) 345; PJ Badenhorst, JM Pienaar & H Mostert (assisted by M van Rooyen) *Silberberg and Schoeman's The law of property* (4th ed 2003) 517; W du Plessis, N Olivier & J Pienaar 'Land: Still a contentious issue' (1998) 13 *SA Public Law* 149–169 at 153.

destroy or damage any improvement on the land without prescribed notice; no claimant or other person may enter upon the land without permission from the owner or lawful occupier; and the regional commissioner acquires certain powers to act if he or she believes that any improvement on the land is about to be removed, destroyed or damaged or that any person on the land is likely to be adversely affected by actions pursuant to publication of the notice of claim.[61] In *Transvaal Agricultural Union v Minister of Land Affairs and Another*[62] the Transvaal Agricultural Union alleged that certain provisions of section 11 were unconstitutional for contravening the administrative justice guarantee in section 24(*b*) and the property and free economic activity guarantees in sections 28 and 26 respectively of the 1993 Constitution. The application was dismissed on procedural grounds relating to direct access to the Constitutional Court,[63] but the Act was amended at the same time when the case was heard, and some of the objections relating to administrative justice were removed by the amendments, particularly with regard to notification of the owner and other interested parties of a restitution claim and giving them the possibility to oppose publication of such a claim. In the amended version of section 11 a person affected by publication of the notice of claim may make representations to the relevant regional commissioner for withdrawal or amendment of the notice, and if the commissioner is convinced after consideration of the representations that any of the required criteria had not been met he or she can take steps to cancel or amend the notice.[64]

---

[61] Section 11 of the 1994 Act. See DL Carey Miller (with A Pope) *Land title in South Africa* (2000) 348; PJ Badenhorst, JM Pienaar & H Mostert (assisted by M van Rooyen) *Silberberg and Schoeman's The law of property* (4th ed 2003) 518–519 for a more detailed discussion.

[62] 1997 (2) SA 621 (CC). For a discussion and criticism of the decision see T Roux 'Turning a deaf ear: The right to be heard by the Constitutional Court' (1997) 13 *SAJHR* 216–227. Compare W du Plessis, N Olivier & J Pienaar 'Land reform gains momentum during 1996' (1997) 12 *SA Public Law* 251–273 at 252; T Roux 'Chapter 3: The Restitution of Land Rights Act' in G Budlender, J Latsky & T Roux *Juta's new land law* (1998) 3A–30–3A–34.

[63] T Roux 'Chapter 3: The Restitution of Land Rights Act' in G Budlender, J Latsky & T Roux *Juta's new land law* (1998) 3A–30 argues that, although the Court declined to consider the claims on their merit, there are indications that the Court might have upheld the relevant provisions had they been tested for constitutional validity. See further T Roux 'Turning a deaf ear: The right to be heard by the Constitutional Court' (1997) 13 *SAJHR* 216–227. In *Transvaal Agricultural Union v Minister of Agriculture and Land Affairs and Others* 2005 (4) SA 212 (SCA), the Supreme Court of Appeal confirmed a decision in which the Land Claims Court refused to make a long list of requested declaratory orders regarding the rights of landowners under the Act (largely with regard to the procedure followed by the commission in investigating a claim before it was published) because the orders would be academic and non-binding upon persons whose rights would be set out in the order, but who were not parties.

[64] Section 6 of the Land Restitution and Reform Laws Amendment Act 78 of 1996 and section 5 of the Land Restitution and Reform Laws Amendment Act 18 of 1999 amended the Act by inserting section 11A(1). On the amendments see T Roux 'Chapter 3: The Restitution of Land Rights Act' in G Budlender, J Latsky & T Roux *Juta's new land law* (1998) 3A–30–3A34; PJ Badenhorst, JM Pienaar & H Mostert (assisted by M van Rooyen) *Silberberg and Schoeman's The law of property* (4th ed 2003) 519; W du Plessis, N Olivier & J Pienaar 'Land reform continues during
(continued on next page …)

Admitted and published claims are administered in accordance with the Act. To ensure that all the requirements are met the Act and the Rules provide the Commission with wide powers to find and establish information regarding the claim that could not be provided by the claimant.[65] If it should appear that there are two or more competing claims in respect of the same land, or that there are competing groups within a community that lodged a claim, or that the land is not state owned and the owner opposes the claim, the Chief Land Claims Commissioner may direct the parties to attempt to settle their dispute through mediation and negotiation.[66] Once a claim has been investigated the matter may be referred to the Land Claims Court if the parties agree that their disputes cannot be solved through mediation, or if the regional commissioner is convinced either that the existing disputes cannot be solved through mediation or that the claim is ready for hearing by the Court.[67] Initially cases settled by agreement were also referred to the Court, but this was changed by a 1999 amendment and such cases can now be concluded when the relevant regional commissioner certifies the agreement, although the commissioner can still refer settlement agreements to the Court in certain circumstances.[68]

The Land Claims Court was established by section 22 of the 1994 Act, which also provides for the appointment of a President and a number of judges.[69] The Court has

---

(... from previous page)

1997' (1997) 12 SA Public Law 531–550 at 532–534; W du Plessis, N Olivier & J Pienaar 'Land reform—Trends developing in case law' (1999) 14 SA Public Law 528–553 at 530. A further challenge to the relevant functionaries' exercise of their statutory powers in receiving and processing restitution claims was dismissed by the Supreme Court of Appeal: Transvaal Agricultural Union v Minister of Agriculture and Land Affairs and Others 2005 (4) SA 212 (SCA).

[65] See DL Carey Miller (with A Pope) Land title in South Africa (2000) 350–254 for an overview; compare T Roux 'Chapter 3: The Restitution of Land Rights Act' in G Budlender, J Latsky & T Roux Juta's new land law (1998) 3A–24–3A–42.

[66] Section 13; see DL Carey Miller (with A Pope) Land title in South Africa (2000) 354–355. Section 35(A) also allows the Land Claims Court to direct parties to try and settle their dispute through mediation.

[67] Section 14; see DL Carey Miller (with A Pope) Land title in South Africa (2000) 356; PJ Badenhorst, JM Pienaar & H Mostert (assisted by M van Rooyen) Silberberg and Schoeman's The law of property (4th ed 2003) 519.

[68] Section 14 as amended by the Land Restitution and Reform Laws Amendment Act 18 of 1999; see DL Carey Miller (with A Pope) Land title in South Africa (2000) 357.

[69] See DL Carey Miller (with A Pope) Land title in South Africa (2000) 364; PJ Badenhorst, JM Pienaar & H Mostert (assisted by M van Rooyen) Silberberg and Schoeman's The law of property (4th ed 2003) 520–527; W du Plessis, N Olivier & J Pienaar 'The ever-changing land law—1994–1995 reforms' (1995) 10 SA Public Law 145–167 at 150–154. The Court's procedure is governed by rules made in terms of section 32; see DL Carey Miller (with A Pope) Land title in South Africa (2000) 382–386. The Court has appellate jurisdiction over orders and determinations made by magistrates, other divisions of the High Court and arbitrators in terms of the Land Reform (Labour Tenants) Act 3 of 1996: section 28N of the 1994 Act; LCC Rule 71; section 33 of the 1996 Act. Appeals from the Land Claims Court lie to the Supreme Court of Appeal and the Constitutional Court: section 37 of the 1994 Act. For a critical evaluation of the Land Claims Court's role in social and economic transformation see T Roux 'Pro-poor court, anti-poor outcomes: Explaining the performance of the South African Land Claims Court' (2004) 20 SAJHR 511–543.

the status and powers of a High Court within its sphere of jurisdiction. The Court has exclusive jurisdiction with regard to restitution of any right in land, compensation in respect of land privately owned and expropriated under the Act, and certain other related matters.[70] In order to fulfill its role the Court is empowered to order the restoration of land, a portion of land or a right in land to a claimant or to award any land, portion of land or right in land to the claimant in full or partial settlement of the claim.[71] The Court can also order the state to grant the claimant a right in alternative state land; to pay the claimant compensation;[72] to include the claimant as beneficiary in a state-support programme for allocation of housing or development of rural land; or to grant alternative relief.[73] In addition, the Court can make a range of additional orders regarding the conditions to be met before a right in land can be restored, the amount, manner and time of payments, the manner in which communities are to hold the restored land or receive compensation, time limits, costs and other ancillary matters.[74] The Court is also empowered to consider applications by national, provincial

---

[70]The related matters are the discretionary power to grant a declaratory order on a question of law with regard to section 25(7) of the Constitution, the 1994 Act or any other matter or law in its jurisdiction, the power to determine whether compensation or consideration in lieu of compensation for a dispossession under the Act was just and equitable, the power to determine the validity, enforceability, interpretation and implementation of settlement agreements under the Act, the power to determine all other matters that require determination under the Act, and the power to determine any matter involving the interpretation or application of the 1994 Act or the Land Reform (Labour Tenants) Act 3 of 1996: section 22. Compare DL Carey Miller (with A Pope) *Land title in South Africa* (2000) 369.

[71]Where necessary the Court can order prior acquisition or expropriation of the land, portion of land or right in land; provided that land, a portion of land or a right of land shall not be awarded to the claimant if it had been dispossessed from another claimant, unless the other claimant is or has been granted restitution or waives his right to restoration or the Court is satisfied that other satisfactory arrangements have been or will be made to grant the other claimant restitution: section 35. See DL Carey Miller (with A Pope) *Land title in South Africa* (2000) 370.

[72]See eg *Ex parte Former Highlands Residents: In re Ash v Department of Land Affairs* [2002] 2 All SA 26 (LCC); compare W du Plessis, N Olivier & J Pienaar 'New measures to expedite land reform' (2000) 15 *SA Public Law* 549–573 at 553. See further *Hermanus v Department of Land Affairs: In re Erven 3535 and 3536, Goodwood* 2001 (1) SA 1030 (LCC) (concerning additional compensation apart from restitution of the land or restitutionary compensation, in the form of *solatium* or compensation for suffering); W du Plessis, N Olivier & J Pienaar 'Evictions, restitution, spatial information, the right to housing and minerals: New approaches from the government and the courts' (2001) 16 *SA Public Law* 181–216 at 187–189.

[73]Section 35; see DL Carey Miller (with A Pope) *Land title in South Africa* (2000) 370; W du Plessis, N Olivier & J Pienaar 'The ever-changing land law—1994–1995 reforms' (1995) 10 *SA Public Law* 145–167 at 152–153.

[74]Section 35; see DL Carey Miller (with A Pope) *Land title in South Africa* (2000) 370–371; W du Plessis, N Olivier & J Pienaar 'The ever-changing land law—1994–1995 reforms' (1995) 10 *SA Public Law* 145–167 at 152–153.

or local government bodies to bar specific pieces of land from restoration orders,[75] and it has the power to review actions or decision of the minister, the Commission or any functionary acting in terms of the Act.[76]

Of particular significance is the power that the Court has to specify the conditions under which land or compensation is awarded to a community to ensure that all members of the dispossessed community share in the land or compensation on a fair and non-discriminatory basis, and to adjust the nature of a right previously held by the claimant when awarding restitution to ensure that the form of title under which the restored land right is held suits the circumstances.[77] In making its decisions the Court must have regard to a number of considerations relating to the desirability of providing restitution for persons previously dispossessed as a result of discriminatory laws and practices, the desirability of remedying past violations of human rights, the requirements of equity and justice and the desirability of avoiding major social conflict. In addition, the Court is required to consider the feasibility of restoration of a particular portion of land, any existing provision applying to the land in question and directed towards the protection of previously disadvantaged persons or groups and the advancement of equality and redress, the amount of compensation or other consideration received in respect of the dispossession and the circumstances prevailing at the time, the history of the land, the hardship caused by the dispossession, the current use of the land and the history of the acquisition and use of the land, changes over time in the value of money, and any other consideration judged to be relevant and consistent with the Court's function in this regard.

Since about 2001 the role of the Land Claims Court in restitution cases has changed, and the Court now hears fewer cases than before; most cases are finalized administratively in an effort to speed up the restitution process.[78]

---

[75]Section 34; see DL Carey Miller (with A Pope) *Land title in South Africa* (2000) 375. See in this regard also PJ Badenhorst, JM Pienaar & H Mostert (assisted by M van Rooyen) *Silberberg and Schoeman's The law of property* (4th ed 2003) 523; W du Plessis, N Olivier & J Pienaar '"Your land is safe in South Africa"?' (2003) 18 *SA Public Law* 229–250 at 235; W du Plessis, N Olivier & J Pienaar 'Land matters: New developments 2004 (1)' (2004) 19 *SA Public Law* 212–229 at 216. Compare *Ex parte North Central and South Central Metropolitan Substructure Councils of the Durban Metropolitan Area* 1998 (1) SA 78 (LCC). In *Khosis Community, Lohatla, and Others v Minister of Defence and Others* 2004 (5) SA 494 (SCA) the Supreme Court of Appeal upheld a decision of the Land Claims Court in which it was decided in terms of section 34 that it was not in the public interest to restore an area used by the SA National Defence Force to the claimants.

[76]Section 36; see DL Carey Miller (with A Pope) *Land title in South Africa* (2000) 377; PJ Badenhorst, JM Pienaar & H Mostert (assisted by M van Rooyen) *Silberberg and Schoeman's The law of property* (4th ed 2003) 524–525.

[77]Section 35; see DL Carey Miller (with A Pope) *Land title in South Africa* (2000) 371; PJ Badenhorst, JM Pienaar & H Mostert (assisted by M van Rooyen) *Silberberg and Schoeman's The law of property* (4th ed 2003) 524–525.

[78]See in this regard W du Plessis, N Olivier & J Pienaar 'Delays in land reform—South Africa emulating Zimbabwe?' (2001) 16 *SA Public Law* 432–457 at 435–436.

6.2.4 Constitutional issues

In its 1997 *White Paper on land policy* the Department of Land Affairs already indicated that it was sensitive to the double nature of its constitutional duties: 'The Bill of Rights in the new Constitution guarantees existing property rights; but it simultaneously places the state under a constitutional duty to take reasonable steps to enable citizens to gain equitable access to land, to promote security of tenure, and to provide redress to those who were dispossessed of property after 19 June 1913 as a result of past discriminatory laws or practices.'[79] It therefore comes as no surprise that the biggest substantive constitutional issue raised by the restitution process would involve conflicts of interest between those who benefit from restitution claims and those whose existing rights are affected (and potentially threatened) by such claims.

The first case in which the constitutional validity of the 1994 Restitution Act was attacked involved just such a conflict between vested property interests and the publication of a restitution claim, but the case was dismissed by the Constitutional Court on procedural grounds.[80] Even then it could perhaps be said that the constitutional argument against the Act, had it been heard and decided on its merits, would probably not have succeeded. Moreover, the administrative justice issues that were raised in that case have largely been solved by subsequent amendments to the Act.[81]

It has been pointed out that there may be some confusion about the scope of the rights that could be claimed in terms of the Act, given the differences in formulation of 'rights in property' (section 28 of the 1993 Constitution), 'property' (section 25(7) of the 1996 Constitution) and 'right in land' (as defined in the Act).[82] However, despite the wider authorizing provision in section 25(7) and the narrower phrase-

---

[79]Department of Land Affairs *White Paper on South African land policy* (1997); see the subheading 'Constitutional issues' under Section III entitled 'Land policy issues' at http://land.pwv.gov.za/legislation_policies/white_papers.htm. See further text accompanying footnote 18 above.

[80]*Transvaal Agricultural Union v Minister of Land Affairs and Another* 1996 (12) BCLR 1573 (CC); see text accompanying footnotes 62–64 above. For a discussion of the decision compare T Roux 'Turning a deaf ear: The right to be heard by the Constitutional Court' (1997) 13 *SAJHR* 216–227; T Roux 'Chapter 3: The Restitution of Land Rights Act' in G Budlender, J Latsky & T Roux *Juta's new land law* (1998) 3A–30; W du Plessis, N Olivier & J Pienaar 'Land reform gains momentum during 1996' (1997) 12 *SA Public Law* 251–273 at 252. In *Transvaal Agricultural Union v Minister of Agriculture and Land Affairs and Others* 2005 (4) SA 212 (SCA) the Supreme Court of Appeal confirmed a decision in which the Land Claims Court refused to make a long list of requested declaratory orders regarding the rights of landowners under the Act (largely with regard to the procedure followed by the commission in investigating a claim before it was published) because the orders would be academic and non-binding upon persons whose rights would be set out in the order, but who were not parties.

[81]T Roux 'Chapter 3: The Restitution of Land Rights Act' in G Budlender, J Latsky & T Roux *Juta's new land law* (1998) 3A–30 argues that, although the Court declined to consider the claims on their merit, there are indications that the Court might have upheld the relevant provisions had they been tested for constitutional validity.

[82]On this issue see Geoff Budlender 'The constitutional protection of property rights' in G Budlender, J Latsky & T Roux *Juta's new land law* (1998) 1–71; DL Carey Miller (with A Pope) *Land title in South Africa* (2000) 322.

ology used in the Act it is clear that the Act creates a very broad right,[83] rendering it unlikely that there will be any constitutionally relevant confusion in practice about the scope of restitution.

The main constitutional issue is the effect that lodgement, acceptance and publication of a restitution claim have on the rights of the landowner and others who have legal and financial interests in the land. In terms of section 11 of the Act publication places severe restrictions on the landowner and other interested parties such as lessees or mortgagees, particularly by preventing them from certain actions with regard to the land that might otherwise have been considered normal land-use activities: sale, exchange, donation, lease, subdivision or rezoning of the land and development of the land are not allowed without prior written notice to the regional land commissioner; eviction of claimants who occupied the land at the date of commencement of the Act and removal, destruction or damaging of improvements on the land are not allowed without prior written permission from the Chief Land Claims Commissioner.[84] The burden that these provisions no doubt place upon the landowner and other interested parties is alleviated by the provisions of sections 11(6) and 11A, which were inserted into the Act by the 1999 and 1996 amendments so as to give affected persons the opportunity to have the notice amended or withdrawn upon application to the regional commissioner.[85]

In addition to the improvement of administrative processes surrounding the publication of the notice of claim, it also has to be said that the effect of such publication is probably not excessive, even if it does restrict the landowner and other interested parties to a certain extent in their use and enjoyment of the land. In terms of comparative law the restrictions imposed by such a preservation order could probably be regarded as constitutionally valid regulatory deprivation of property as long as the limitations imposed are reasonable and proportionate in their implementation and effect. In terms of section 25 they should therefore attract neither a constitutional validity attack nor a claim for compensation.[86] Of course it would always be possible to attack a notice of claim or a related administrative action on the basis that the effect of the preservation order on the landowner or another interested party was unreasonable or disproportionate in the particular case, but in view of the Constitutional Court's approach in *First National Bank of SA Ltd t/a Wesbank v Commissioner, South*

---

[83] Geoff Budlender 'The constitutional protection of property rights' in G Budlender, J Latsky & T Roux *Juta's new land law* (1998) 1–71.

[84] Section 11(7).

[85] Section 1(6) requires the regional land claims commissioner to advise the owner and other interested parties of the publication of the notice. Section 1A makes provision for withdrawal or amendment of the notice of claim upon representations made to the regional commissioner. See the text accompanying footnotes 61, 62 above.

[86] See the Zimbabwean decision in *Davies and Others v The Minister of Lands, Agriculture and Water Development* 1997 (1) BCLR 83 (ZHC); confirmed on appeal in *Davies and Others v Minister of Lands, Agriculture and Water Development* 1997 (1) SA 228 (ZSC). Compare AJ van der Walt *Constitutional property clauses: A comparative analysis* (1999) 484–485.

African Revenue Service; First National Bank of SA Ltd t/a Wesbank v Minister of Finance[87] it seems unlikely that these restrictions would easily be regarded as arbitrary deprivation as described in section 25(1) and interpreted in the *FNB* decision, unless the action was tainted by procedural impropriety or unfairness or unless it had excessively unfair, disproportionate effects.

Expropriation of private land for purposes of restitution has been authorized explicitly in amendments to the 1994 Act; once implemented, these expropriations would be undertaken in terms of the provisions of section 25 of the Constitution and the Expropriation Act 63 of 1975.[88] Although the popular press sometimes blames the 'velvet glove' approach of preferring to purchase rather than expropriate land for restitution purposes for slow progress with restitution claims, the slow pace of reform cannot be blamed purely on lack of expropriation powers; in so far as legal uncertainty, administrative difficulties and lack of capacity prevented the state from using expropriation to acquire land for redistribution in the past, recent amendments to the Act and changes in departmental policies and procedures should overcome that problem. When the expropriation route is followed it should not cause any special or unique problems simply because the end goal is to transfer the property to another private person or group for restitution purposes, because there is authority in comparative case law for the proposition that expropriation of private land could still be for a public purpose if the end goal is to transfer the land to another private person, provided the expropriation and transfer form part of a legitimate land reform process or programme. This aspect is discussed in chapter 5.7. Even though there is also authority in comparative case law for the narrower proposition that expropriation may not take place for the benefit of another private person, the framing of section 25(2) (read with section 25(4)) leaves little doubt that the restitution process, including transfer of the property to another private person, is authorized by the Constitution and that land may be expropriated for it. In this perspective expropriation should not in principle cause any new or special problems regarding the constitutional validity of the restitution process.

---

[87] 2002 (4) SA 768 (CC). See the discussion of the case in chapter 4.5 and 4.6 and compare chapter 5.4. See further on the *FNB* decision T Roux 'Section 25' in S Woolman et al (eds) *Constitutional law of South Africa* (2nd ed 2003 original service Dec 2003) 46-2–46-5 at 46-2–46-5, 46-21–46-25.

[88] The Restitution of Land Rights Amendment Act 48 of 2003 inserted section 42E into the main Act of 1994 to authorize the minister to purchase, acquire or expropriate land and rights in land for restitution purposes. At the time of finalizing this chapter the minister of land affairs gave indications that she was about to use these powers for the first time to expropriate agricultural land for restitution.

6.3 SECURITY OF TENURE

25. Property

(6) A person or community whose tenure of land is legally insecure as a result of past racially discriminatory laws or practices is entitled, to the extent provided by an Act of Parliament, either to tenure which is legally secure, or to comparable redress.

(7) ...

(8) ...

(9) Parliament must enact the legislation referred to in subsection (6).

26. Housing

(1) ...

(2) ...

(3) No one may be evicted from their home, or have their home demolished, without an order of court made after considering all the relevant circumstances. No legislation may permit arbitrary evictions.

6.3.1 Introduction

David Carey Miller has described tenure reform as 'the reform of the legal basis of landholding, usually directed towards the implementation of social change', noting that apartheid land law was a system of land tenure in this sense and thus implying that the abolition of apartheid per definition necessitated tenure reform to rectify social imbalances in the land tenure system that were brought about by apartheid.[89] In the same vein it has been pointed out that land law, described as 'legal rules which govern the content, acquisition and protection of various rights to own, use or exploit land and natural resources', has been employed in apartheid South Africa to 'entrench the political ideology of racial segregation', which again means that tenure reform is necessary to help dismantle the legacy of apartheid land law and establish a new, post-apartheid land law based on non-discrimination and equal access to land, housing and other natural resources.[90]

Tenure reform can be described as the non-redistributory part of land reform that remains necessary even when the apartheid laws have been abolished. When talking about the abolition of apartheid land law one tends to think mainly of the infamous apartheid statutes such as the Land Act 27 of 1913, the Population Registration Act 30 of 1950, the Reservation of Separate Amenities Act 49 of 1953 and the Group Areas Act 36 of 1966, but in fact apartheid was much more deeply embedded in the tissue of the law than is reflected by these laws, and consequently it has been recognized that the mere abolition of the racially based statutes will not succeed in eradicating apartheid land law and establishing a more just and equitable post-apartheid

---

[89] DL Carey Miller (with A Pope) *Land title in South Africa* (2000) 456.

[90] AJ van der Walt 'Towards the development of post-apartheid land law: An exploratory survey' (1990) 23 *De Jure* 1–45 at 2.

land law.[91] Instead, the establishment of post-apartheid land law through land reform requires at least five interrelated steps: (a) the abolition of apartheid statutes (which has been accomplished fairly early), (b) steps to ensure restorative justice (mainly through the restitution process described in 6.2 above), (c) the improvement of greater and more equitable access to land and natural resources through redistribution programmes and initiatives (discussed in 6.4 and 6.5 below), (d) the development of the common law and customary law to fit in with the new constitutionally driven land law system (discussed in chapter 7), and (e) the strengthening, through tenure reform, of existing land rights and interests that give people access to land and housing but have been weakened and legally undermined by apartheid laws and practices. In this sense, tenure reform is a technical legal process through which the legal status and protection of existing land interests and rights are upgraded and strengthened. This section is specifically concerned with the last-mentioned process.

Tenure reform is necessary because apartheid land law had effects on the land rights and interests of black land users that cannot be rectified by the abolition of the apartheid land statutes, by restitution or by improved access to land only. Described in this way, tenure reform is aimed at land users who already have access to land, but whose land rights and interests are and remain weak or insecure because of apartheid laws and practices, including apartheid laws and policies that created or deepened problematic power structures in communal land use systems. These land users require neither restitution of land rights that were lost nor access to new land—their problem is legal redefinition and increased security and protection of the land rights they already have. The biggest problem is that most black land rights and interests lack proper legal recognition and protection, even now that the underlying apartheid land laws have been abolished,[92] because these rights and interests in land have been rendered vulnerable by apartheid land laws that denied them appropriate legal recognition and protection, especially when they come into conflict with state power or with

---

[91] See eg DL Carey Miller (with A Pope) *Land title in South Africa* (2000) 456–461, 556–567; AJ van der Walt 'Towards the development of post-apartheid land law: An exploratory survey' (1990) 23 *De Jure* 1–45 at 4; AJ van der Walt 'Property rights and hierarchies of power: A critical evaluation of land-reform policy in South Africa' (1999) 64 *Koers* 259–294 at 262–265. See further the explanation in *Port Elizabeth Municipality v Various Occupiers* 2005 (1) SA 217 (CC) paras [8]–[23] at 222A–229G, setting out the historical context of discriminatory land law and the new constitutional context within which conflicting land rights have to be adjudicated.

[92] See DL Carey Miller (with A Pope) *Land title in South Africa* (2000) 456, 458. PJ Badenhorst, JM Pienaar & H Mostert (assisted by M van Rooyen) *Silberberg and Schoeman's The law of property* (4th ed 2003) at 499 seem to link the need for tenure reform to the fact that the South African land tenure system is diversified, but the problem is not diversification or fragmentation of tenure as such — the real problem is the hierarchical structuring of land rights brought about during the apartheid era and the weakening of certain rights that resulted from it; see AJ van der Walt 'Property rights and hierarchies of power: A critical evaluation of land-reform policy in South Africa' (1999) 64 *Koers* 259–294. Diversification of land rights and tenure forms can, in a non-discriminatory context, promote rather than threaten security of tenure; see AJ van der Walt 'The fragmentation of land rights' (1992) 8 *SAJHR* 431–450.

the privileged, strong land rights that white land users have traditionally enjoyed and that still form the backbone of mainstream property rights in South African private law. Tenure reform is aimed at filling that gap by providing temporary or permanent protection for vulnerable land users, or by restructuring their rights to make them stronger and less vulnerable, or by establishing new, suitably protected rights for specific needs and situations by way of legislation.[93]

The necessity for and significance of tenure reform is most clearly illustrated by the phenomenon of eviction (discussed in 6.3.8 below). The evictions and forced removals that characterized apartheid land law were made possible by—amongst other things—the systematic and structural weakening of black land users' rights, and the resulting weakness and vulnerability of black land users remained in place even after the abolition of apartheid land statutes, unless they are strengthened by equally systematic and structural reforms in the Constitution and various land reform laws. The tenure reform process adopted two main strategies, namely the introduction of anti-eviction provisions to prevent apartheid-style evictions and forced removals in general; and the implementation of individualized structural reforms to strengthen and support specific weak and unsuitable tenure forms. The anti-eviction strategy is based on the authority of section 26(3) of the Constitution, which provides that no one may be evicted from their home without a court order, that such a court order shall not be granted without considering all the relevant circumstances, and that no law shall permit arbitrary evictions. In accordance with section 26(3) anti-eviction provisions appear in various land reform laws.[94]

The structural reinforcement and support strategy is based on the authority of section 25(6) and 25(9), according to which Parliament must enact laws that will provide those whose tenure is insecure because of past discriminatory laws and practices with security of tenure or equitable redress. In compliance with section 25(9) a range of laws have been promulgated since 1996 to promote these purposes. The following overview covers the most important tenure reform legislation briefly, with

---

[93] See the previous footnote above. Apart from the legislation discussed below, various other laws have been promulgated in the state's effort to improve security of tenure, as appears from the discussion below. See eg *Nzimande v Nzimande and Another* 2005 (1) SA 83 (W) on the pre-1994 (subsequently amended) Conversion of Certain Rights into Leasehold or Ownership Act 81 of 1988, which is aimed at converting some of the old apartheid-style occupation permits into a stronger form of tenure, namely leasehold or ownership. See further DL Carey Miller (with A Pope) *Land title in South Africa* (2000) 155.

[94] In *Port Elizabeth Municipality v Various Occupiers* 2005 (1) SA 217 (CC) par [19] at 228B–D Sachs J indicated that the provisions of sections 25 and 26 had to be read together when interpreting the anti-eviction laws. The eviction issue is discussed separately in 6.3.8 below, but see 6.3.5 and 6.3.6 and compare chapter 7.3. See further AJ van der Walt 'Towards the development of post-apartheid land law: An exploratory survey' (1990) 23 *De Jure* 1–45 at 4; AJ van der Walt 'Property rights and hierarchies of power: A critical evaluation of land-reform policy in South Africa' (1999) 64 *Koers* 259–294 at 262. For a systematic analysis of the anti-eviction measures in the Constitution and land laws see AJ van der Walt 'Exclusivity of ownership, security of tenure, and eviction orders: A model to evaluate South African land-reform legislation' 2002 *TSAR* 254–289.

special attention for those laws that have the greatest constitutional significance, namely the Land Reform (Labour Tenants) Act 3 of 1996, the Extension of Security of Tenure Act 62 of 1997 and the Prevention of Illegal Eviction from and Unlawful Occupation of Land Act 18 of 1998.

6.3.2 Interim Protection of Informal Land Rights Act 31 of 1996

The Interim Protection of Informal Land Rights Act 31 of 1996 was initially regarded as a temporary measure and was meant to have lapsed on 31 December 1997, but in fact it is still in operation and its validity has been extended on an annual basis.[95] The Act's purpose is to protect insecure land rights, described as 'informal land rights', on the same basis as acknowledged property rights—in effect these rights are protected as if they were real rights, even though they are not recognized as such or reflected in the relevant deeds registries records.[96] The rights that enjoy this protection are described in wide terms in section 1(1) of the Act and include the use and occupation of or access to land in terms of tribal, customary or indigenous laws or practices; customs, use or administrative practice in a particular area; rights and interests of beneficiaries under a trust arrangement established by statute; beneficial occupation of land for not less than five years prior to 31 December 1997; and use or occupation of land as if the person were a holder under the Upgrading of Land Tenure Rights Act 112 of 1991, although not formally recorded as such.[97]

In effect, the Act provides interim protection for a large range of land holdings and interests that enjoyed little or no legal recognition and protection because of their low status in the system of apartheid land law, without effecting any permanent or structural changes to any of these interests. The Act protects these rights by providing that the relevant holders or occupiers may not be deprived of their land rights without their consent.[98] Although a person may in terms of the Act be deprived of his or her right in communal land in accordance with the customs of the particular community,

---

[95]See the Schedule to the Communal Land Rights Act 11 of 2004; compare PJ Badenhorst, JM Pienaar & H Mostert (assisted by M van Rooyen) *Silberberg and Schoeman's The law of property* (4th ed 2003) 508; DL Carey Miller (with A Pope) *Land title in South Africa* (2000) 466.

[96]PJ Badenhorst, JM Pienaar & H Mostert (assisted by M van Rooyen) *Silberberg and Schoeman's The law of property* (4th ed 2003) 509; DL Carey Miller (with A Pope) *Land title in South Africa* (2000) 461; AJ van der Walt 'Exclusivity of ownership, security of tenure, and eviction orders: A model to evaluate South African land-reform legislation' 2002 *TSAR* 254–289 at 282–283.

[97]Section 1(1) of the Act; see DL Carey Miller (with A Pope) *Land title in South Africa* (2000) 462–463; PJ Badenhorst, JM Pienaar & H Mostert (assisted by M van Rooyen) *Silberberg and Schoeman's The law of property* (4th ed 2003) 509; AJ van der Walt 'Exclusivity of ownership, security of tenure, and eviction orders: A model to evaluate South African land-reform legislation' 2002 *TSAR* 254–289 at 282.

[98]See AJ van der Walt 'Exclusivity of ownership, security of tenure, and eviction orders: A model to evaluate South African land-reform legislation' 2002 *TSAR* 254–289 at 282–283. The Communal Land Rights Act 11 of 2004 amended the situation as far as communal land is concerned; see 6.3.7 below.

certain restrictions are placed upon sale and other dispositions of communal land.[99] In the final analysis the Act functions as and resembles nothing more than a temporary, catch-all stop-gap instrument without any permanent or systemic aspirations or pretensions. It was always assumed that the necessity for the Act would wither away as new, focused legislation provides for the specific interests of various urban and rural land users, but the Communal Land Rights Act 11 of 2004 did not repeal the 1996 Act and it looks as if it will remain in force more or less permanently.[100]

6.3.3 Land Reform (Labour Tenants) Act 3 of 1996

The Land Reform (Labour Tenants) Act 31 of 1996 is meant to strengthen labour tenants' land rights and to increase access to agricultural land.[101] The Act is restricted to a very specific and circumscribed category of rural land users known as labour tenants (as opposed to farm workers). Generally speaking labour tenants are distinguished from farm workers on the basis that labour tenants are not primarily salaried labourers—they provide labour (in person or by way of nominees) to the landowner or lessee in exchange for the right to occupy and use certain parts of the land (for residential purposes as well as cropping or grazing).[102] In order to qualify for any of the protective measures in the Act a prospective applicant therefore first has to prove that he or she is a labour tenant as defined in the Act.

Section 1 of the Act defines a labour tenant as someone (a) who is residing or has the right to reside on a farm; (b) who has or has had the right to use cropping or grazing land on the farm (or on another farm of the same owner) in exchange for labour provided to the landowner or lessee; and (c) whose parent or grandparent resides or resided on a farm or had the use of cropping or grazing land on such farm

---

[99]Section 2 of the Act; see further PJ Badenhorst, JM Pienaar & H Mostert (assisted by M van Rooyen) *Silberberg and Schoeman's The law of property* (4th ed 2003) 509; DL Carey Miller (with A Pope) *Land title in South Africa* (2000) 465–466.

[100]Promulgation of the Extension of Security of Tenure Act 62 of 1997 and the Prevention of Illegal Eviction from and Unlawful Occupation of Land Act 18 of 1998 diminished the necessity for the Act, but the Communal Land Rights Act 11 of 2004 did not repeal the Act; see the schedule to the 2004 Act. See the discussion in 6.3.5, 6.3.6 and 6.3.7 below.

[101]In this regard the Act has both restitution and tenure reform facets to it; see DL Carey Miller (with A Pope) *Land title in South Africa* (2000) 525; PJ Badenhorst, JM Pienaar & H Mostert (assisted by M van Rooyen) *Silberberg and Schoeman's The law of property* (4th ed 2003) 490; AJ van der Walt 'Property rights and hierarchies of power: A critical evaluation of land-reform policy in South Africa' (1999) 64 *Koers* 259–294 at 279.

[102]Labour tenancy has a long and sad history in South African land politics. Charles van Onselen *The seed is mine: The life of Kas Maine, A South-African sharecropper 1894–1985* (1996) described a case study that exemplifies this history in a powerful and evocative manner. See further on the history of labour tenancy M Hathorn & D Hutchinson 'Labour tenants and the law' in C Murray & C O'Regan *No place to rest: Forced removals and the law in South Africa* (1990) 194–213; DL Carey Miller (with A Pope) *Land title in South Africa* (2000) 526. On the distinction between farm workers and labour tenants see most recently *Msiza and Others v Uys and Others* 2005 (2) SA 456 (LCC); *Landman and Another v Ndlozi* 2005 (4) SA 89 (LCC).

(or on another farm of the same landowner) in exchange for labour provided to the owner or lessee. This definition includes a person who has been appointed a successor to a labour tenant in accordance with sections 3(4) and 3(5) of the Act,[103] but excludes a farm worker.[104] Initially there were conflicting decisions on the correct interpretation of this definition: the Transvaal High Court and the Land Claims Court preferred a conjunctive interpretation of section 1 in terms of which an applicant has to comply with the requirements in (a), (b) and (c)[105] while the Natal High Court favoured the less restrictive approach that it would suffice if the applicant satisfied either requirements (a) and (b) or (a) and (c).[106] If the conjunctive interpretation is followed it is more difficult to satisfy the threshold requirements and a number of prospective beneficiaries are excluded, while the disjunctive reading of the definition allows more beneficiaries to claim protection under the Act. The Supreme Court of Appeal settled the dispute by deciding that the more restrictive conjunctive approach is correct.[107]

---

[103] Section 3(4) provides that when a labour tenant dies, becomes mentally ill or is unable to manage his or her own affairs or leaves the farm voluntarily without appointing a successor his or her family may appoint a successor and shall inform the owner of the appointment. Section 3(5) provides that a person who is not a family member may only be appointed a successor if he or she is reasonably acceptable to the owner. See further DL Carey Miller (with A Pope) *Land title in South Africa* (2000) 528–529; PJ Badenhorst, JM Pienaar & H Mostert (assisted by M van Rooyen) *Silberberg and Schoeman's The law of property* (4th ed 2003) 490.

[104] Section 1, read with section 3. Section 1 defines a farm worker as someone who is employed on a farm and who is paid predominantly in cash or other forms of remuneration and not predominantly in the right to occupy and use land, and who has to provide the labour personally. On the distinction between farm workers and labour tenants see most recently *Msiza and Others v Uys and Others* 2005 (2) SA 456 (LCC); *Landman and Another v Ndlozi* 2005 (4) SA 89 (LCC).

[105] *Mahlangu v De Jager* 1996 (3) SA 235 (LCC); *Zulu v Van Rensburg* 1996 (4) SA 1236 (LCC); *Mosehla v Sancor* 1999 (1) SA 614 (T); *Ngcobo v Van Rensburg* 1999 (2) SA 525 (LCC); *Mahlangu v De Jager* 2000 (3) SA 145 (LCC). See further JM Pienaar 'Land reform, labour tenants and the application of the Land Reform (Labour Tenants) Act 3 of 1996' 1997 *TSAR* 538–548; JM Pienaar 'Labour tenancy: Recent developments in case law' (1998) 9 *Stell LR* 311–325; PJ Badenhorst, JM Pienaar & H Mostert (assisted by M van Rooyen) *Silberberg and Schoeman's The law of property* (4th ed 2003) 491; DL Carey Miller (with A Pope) *Land title in South Africa* (2000) 529–532.

[106] *Klopper v Mkhize* 1998 (1) SA 406 (N); *Tselentis Mining (Pty) Ltd v Mdlalose* 1998 (1) SA 411 (N). See further JM Pienaar 'Land reform, labour tenants and the application of the Land Reform (Labour Tenants) Act 3 of 1996' 1997 *TSAR* 538–548; JM Pienaar 'Labour tenancy: Recent developments in case law' (1998) 9 *Stell LR* 311–325; PJ Badenhorst, JM Pienaar & H Mostert (assisted by M van Rooyen) *Silberberg and Schoeman's The law of property* (4th ed 2003) 491; DL Carey Miller (with A Pope) *Land title in South Africa* (2000) 529–532; W du Plessis, N Olivier & J Pienaar 'Land reform surging forward' (1998) 13 *SA Public Law* 470–489 at 474–477; W du Plessis, N Olivier & J Pienaar 'Land issues: An assessment of the failures and successes' (1999) 14 *SA Public Law* 240–270 at 248, 250.

[107] *Ngcobo and Others v Salimba CC; Ngcobo v Van Rensburg* 1999 (2) SA 1057 (SCA); see W du Plessis, N Olivier & J Pienaar 'Land reform: Trends developing in case law' (1999) 14 *SA Public Law* 528–553 at 536.

The protection envisaged by the Act works in two directions. On the one hand the Act provides tenure security for labour tenants by confirming their right to occupy the land in question and ensuring that they cannot be evicted from the land. Once a person qualifies as a labour tenant the right to occupy the land with his or her family may only be terminated in accordance with the Act, while the labour tenant is in turn obliged to provide or carry on providing labour to the owner or lessee in exchange for the right to occupy. In terms of the Act the owner or lessee may only evict labour tenants if it is fair and equitable to do so and once it is proved that the labour tenant or a nominee or associate has committed a material breach of the duty to provide labour and has failed to rectify that breach, or has committed some other act that amounts to a fundamental breach of the relationship with the owner or lessee and that cannot be rectified.[108] The Act precludes evictions against labour tenants who are older than 60 or who cannot provide labour personally and have not appointed successors; family members are allowed to continue living on the land for 12 calendar months after the death of such a labour tenant.[109] Provision is made for the reinstatement of labour tenants who have been evicted or relocated during the period immediately preceding the commencement of the Act and who would otherwise have benefited from the Act.[110]

The second reform brought about by the Act is that labour tenants are enabled to acquire ownership and/or other rights in land. Labour tenants who satisfy all the requirements in section 1 may apply for an award of land or land rights and for financial assistance.[111] If land is awarded to the claimant the landowner receives compensation in accordance the Act and with section 25(3) of the Constitution for land and

---

[108] Section 7. Urgent evictions are possible in accordance with section 15, which requires that there should be a real and imminent danger for the owner or lessee, that no other effective remedy is available, that the balance of likely harm favours the owner or lessee, and that adequate arrangements for reinstatement exist should the order not be made final. See PJ Badenhorst, JM Pienaar & H Mostert (assisted by M van Rooyen) *Silberberg and Schoeman's The law of property* (4th ed 2003) 493; DL Carey Miller (with A Pope) *Land title in South Africa* (2000) 532–537; W du Plessis, N Olivier & J Pienaar 'Land reform: Trends developing in case law' (1999) 14 *SA Public Law* 528–553 at 536. On evictions under the Act see in general AJ van der Walt 'Exclusivity of ownership, security of tenure, and eviction orders: A model to evaluate South African land-reform legislation' 2002 *TSAR* 254–289 at 271–274.

[109] Section 9. The initial age limit of 65 was lowered to 60 by a 2001 amendment to bring this Act in line with the Extension of Security of Tenure Act 62 of 1997. See PJ Badenhorst, JM Pienaar & H Mostert (assisted by M van Rooyen) *Silberberg and Schoeman's The law of property* (4th ed 2003) 493.

[110] Section 12. This provision was intended to counter cynical evictions undertaken in anticipation of the Act. See *Mlifi v Klingenberg* 1999 (2) SA 647 (LCC) and compare further PJ Badenhorst, JM Pienaar & H Mostert (assisted by M van Rooyen) *Silberberg and Schoeman's The law of property* (4th ed 2003) 494.

[111] Section 16. See PJ Badenhorst, JM Pienaar & H Mostert (assisted by M van Rooyen) *Silberberg and Schoeman's The law of property* (4th ed 2003) 496; DL Carey Miller (with A Pope) *Land title in South Africa* (2000) 537–544; AJ van der Walt 'Property rights and hierarchies of power: A critical evaluation of land-reform policy in South Africa' (1999) 64 *Koers* 259–294 at 280.

land rights transferred to a labour tenant.[112] Obviously this aspect of the Act tends more towards redistribution or access to land than tenure reform and therefore it is discussed further in 6.4.2 below.

Juanita Pienaar[113] pointed out that the Act changed the nature of labour tenancy. Obviously labour tenants who successfully applied for acquisition of land become landowners (or holders of other land rights, depending upon what has been awarded) and their rights with regard to the acquired land are thereafter no longer labour tenancy rights (although they may still conclude or maintain labour tenancy contracts with the landowner). Labour tenants who failed to apply for land (or whose applications failed) will maintain their status as labour tenants, but their position is thereafter statutorily secured and protected under the Act.[114]

6.3.4 Communal Property Associations Act 28 of 1996

Whereas some of the other tenure reform laws have been promulgated to reinforce existing but vulnerable or weak land rights, the Communal Property Associations Act 28 of 1996 was intended to serve a related but slightly different purpose, namely to create a legal framework within which communities can acquire a newly created, legislatively designed form of secure and appropriate tenure of communally held land. The Act provides for the establishment of communal property associations through which communities can acquire well-protected communal land rights that are simultaneously aligned with the new constitutional values of equality and non-discrimination and also suited to and accommodating of community customs, values and traditions.[115]

The tenure framework created by the Act relies on the formation and registration of communal property associations in accordance with the requirements and procedures laid down in the Act. A communal property association is registered provisionally at first,[116] whereafter it has to comply with certain prescribed requirements before final registration can take place. The most significant requirement is the drafting of a constitution for the association in accordance with the following principles: fair and inclusive decision-making processes; equality of membership; democratic processes;

---

[112]DL Carey Miller (with A Pope) *Land title in South Africa* (2000) 544–546; see further W du Plessis, N Olivier & J Pienaar 'Land reform: A never-ending process' (2000) 15 *SA Public Law* 230–254 at 240.
[113]JM Pienaar 'Labour tenancy: Recent developments in case law' (1998) 9 *Stell LR* 311–325; see further PJ Badenhorst, JM Pienaar & H Mostert (assisted by M van Rooyen) *Silberberg and Schoeman's The law of property* (4th ed 2003) 497.
[114]The cutoff date for the registration of labour tenants was 31 March 2001: JM Pienaar 'Labour tenancy: Recent developments in case law' (1998) 9 *Stell LR* 311–325; PJ Badenhorst, JM Pienaar & H Mostert (assisted by M van Rooyen) *Silberberg and Schoeman's The law of property* (4th ed 2003) 497.
[115]PJ Badenhorst, JM Pienaar & H Mostert (assisted by M van Rooyen) *Silberberg and Schoeman's The law of property* (4th ed 2003) 509 point out that the tenure option created in the Act is also used in other land reform contexts, eg for communities that succeed with restitution claims—the award of restitution land is often made on the basis of a communal property association being established. See further DL Carey Miller (with A Pope) *Land title in South Africa* (2000) 467.
[116]See DL Carey Miller (with A Pope) *Land title in South Africa* (2000) 4470–473.

fair access to the property held by the association; and accountability and transparency.[117] These requirements ensure that members of the communal property association—and especially traditionally weak and marginalized members such as women—are treated fairly and protected in accordance with the constitutional requirement of equality and non-discrimination. Security of tenure therefore assumes a form within which both the new constitutional values and traditional communal values are accommodated.

The Act ensures the security of land tenure within a communal property association by prescribing rules and processes that govern the internal relationships between members and the association as well as external relationships with regard to third parties. Within the association the most significant protective measure is that the communally held property may not be disposed of or encumbered without majority consent,[118] combined with the fact that the constitution of the association should ensure that members have equal and fair access to the land and are ensured that they have a democratic and equal role in decision-making with regard to the property.[119] Externally the main source of protection and security is registration, which places the value of land tenure in property held by a communal property association on par with western-style registered land rights.[120]

6.3.5 Extension of Security of Tenure Act 62 of 1997

The Extension of Security of Tenure Act 62 of 1997 is one of the most controversial and heavily litigated land reform laws to date. According to its long title the Act is aimed at promoting long-term security of tenure for lawful occupiers of rural land and protecting them against unfair eviction. As Roux correctly points out,[121] the Act is to be understood and interpreted as a political intervention that forms a very specific part of the government's land reform strategy. One part of the historical context of the Act is of course the history of eviction and forced removals during the apartheid era, but the Act must also be seen against the background of what Roux describes as 'the notable upsurge in the number of unfair evictions in the first half of the 1990s',[122]

---

[117]Section 9 of the Act. See further DL Carey Miller (with A Pope) *Land title in South Africa* (2000) 473–477; PJ Badenhorst, JM Pienaar & H Mostert (assisted by M van Rooyen) *Silberberg and Schoeman's The law of property* (4th ed 2003) 510.

[118]Section 12; see further PJ Badenhorst, JM Pienaar & H Mostert (assisted by M van Rooyen) *Silberberg and Schoeman's The law of property* (4th ed 2003) 511; DL Carey Miller (with A Pope) *Land title in South Africa* (2000) 473–474, 476–477.

[119]Section 6; see further PJ Badenhorst, JM Pienaar & H Mostert (assisted by M van Rooyen) *Silberberg and Schoeman's The law of property* (4th ed 2003) 510–51; DL Carey Miller (with A Pope) *Land title in South Africa* (2000) 474.

[120]DL Carey Miller (with A Pope) *Land title in South Africa* (2000) 483.

[121]T Roux 'Chapter 7: The Extension of Security of Tenure Act' in G Budlender, J Latsky & T Roux *Juta's new land law* (1998) 7A–4.

[122]T Roux 'Chapter 7: The Extension of Security of Tenure Act' in G Budlender, J Latsky & T Roux *Juta's new land law* (1998) 7A–5.

resulting from anxiety amongst white landowners in the face of uncertainty about the nature and scope of inevitable land reforms. The purpose of the Act is to bring certainty and stability in the land tenure situation of lawful occupiers of rural land by (*a*) establishing a mechanism by which these occupiers can obtain independent land rights (sections 4 and 6); (*b*) stabilizing the day-to-day relationship between landowners and lawful occupiers of rural land (sections 5–7); and (*c*) protecting lawful occupiers against unfair eviction (sections 1–3 and 8–25).

The scope of the Act is restricted in that it applies mainly to rural and peri-urban areas. Its scope is also restricted in that it is intended to benefit just one clearly defined category of occupiers of rural land, namely lawful occupiers who have permission (or on 4 February 1997 or thereafter have had permission)[123] to occupy land belonging to someone else.[124] Finally, the scope of the Act is restricted in that it excludes labour

---

[123]Both explicit and tacit consent constitute permission for purposes of the Act: *Atkinson v Van Wyk* 1999 (1) SA 1080 (LCC); *Rademeyer v Western Districts Council* 1998 (3) SA 101 (SE); see further W du Plessis, N Olivier & J Pienaar 'Land reform: Trends developing in case law' (1999) 14 *SA Public Law* 528–553 at 540; DL Carey Miller (with A Pope) *Land title in South Africa* (2000) 493; PJ Badenhorst, JM Pienaar & H Mostert (assisted by M van Rooyen) *Silberberg and Schoeman's The law of property* (4th ed 2003) 500–501; T Roux 'Chapter 7: The Extension of Security of Tenure Act' in G Budlender, J Latsky & T Roux *Juta's new land law* (1998) 7A–7–7A–15. See further *Venter NO v Claasen en Andere* 2001 (1) SA 720 (LCC); W du Plessis, N Olivier & J Pienaar 'Evictions, restitution, spatial information, the right to housing and minerals: New approaches from the government and the courts' (2001) 16 *SA Public Law* 181–216 at 196.

[124]The burden of proof in establishing permission is controversial because the effect of section 26(3) of the Constitution on the common law is unclear; see text accompanying footnote 149 below. In *Skhosana v Roos t/a Roos se Oord* 2000 (4) SA 561 (LCC) par [26] at 573A–B the Land Claims Court held that a person who claims to be an occupier must prove that he or she complies with all components of the definition in the Act, although there are presumptions that will assist him or her. (Section 3(4) for example provides that for purposes of civil proceedings under the Act a person who has continuously and openly resided on land for a period of one year shall be presumed to have had permission unless the contrary is proved.) This decision means, as T Roux 'Chapter 7: The Extension of Security of Tenure Act' in G Budlender, J Latsky & T Roux *Juta's new land law* (1998) 7A– 8 points out, that the defendant-occupier in an eviction case bears the normal common law burden of proof to establish a right to occupy, as it was established in *Chetty v Naidoo* 1974 (3) SA 13A at 20C. In *Ross v South Peninsula Municipality* 2000 (1) SA 589 (C) at 596H the Cape High Court held that the common law situation was modified by section 26(3) of the Constitution, which means that the plaintiff would bear the burden of proof to show relevant circumstances that would justify the granting of the eviction order. In *Betta Eiendomme (Pty) Ltd v Ekple-Epoh* 2000 (4) SA 468 (W) the Witwatersrand High Court rejected the approach in *Ross*, holding that 'normal' landlord-tenant relationships have not at all been affected by section 26(3) of the Constitution and that the common law situation applied unchanged. The same approach was later followed in *Ellis v Viljoen* 2001 (4) SA 795 (C). (The *Betta Eiendomme* decision is discussed again in 6.3.8 below.) Eventually the Supreme Court of Appeal overturned both *Ross* and *Betta Eiendomme* in *Brisley v Drotsky* 2002 (4) SA 1 (SCA) paras [35]–[46] at 19C–22E by deciding that section 26(3) of the Constitution did in fact apply horizontally (and could therefore amend the common law), but that in fact it did not have this effect in the case before the SCA because of the absence of clear indications of the kind of considerations upon which the courts could legitimately depart from the common law privileged position of the plaintiff-landowner. See AJ van der Walt 'Exclusivity of ownership, security of tenure and eviction orders: A critical evaluation of recent case law' (2002) 18 *SAJHR* 372–420 at 394–404 for a discussion of the case law mentioned above, and see 6.3.8 below.

tenants; persons who use or intend to use the land in question mainly for industrial, mining, commercial or commercial farming purposes; and persons with an income exceeding R5000 per month.[125]

The Act stabilizes the relationship between landowner and occupiers.[126] Chapter III sets out the general rights and duties of landowners and occupiers. Section 5 lists the general fundamental rights that both landowners and occupiers have: the right to human dignity, freedom and security of the person, privacy, freedom of religion, belief and opinion and of expression, freedom of association and freedom of movement. Section 6 lists the rights and duties of occupiers of land, while section 7 sets out the rights and duties of owners and persons in charge of land. In terms of the general reciprocal rights and duties set out in the Act the landowner or person in charge has the right to terminate occupation rights and to institute action for eviction in accordance with the provisions of the Act,[127] while the occupier is entitled to security of tenure, to receive bona fide visitors, to receive postal and other communication, to enjoy a family life in accordance with the culture of his or her family and not to be deprived of access to water, education and health services.[128] The landowner or person in charge may not prejudice the occupier's rights, while the occupier may not intentionally and unlawfully harm any other person occupying the land or cause damage to property; threaten or intimidate others who occupy the land or other land; or enable and assist unauthorized persons to establish new dwellings on the land.[129]

---

[125]Section 1(1) of the Act. See PJ Badenhorst, JM Pienaar & H Mostert (assisted by M van Rooyen) *Silberberg and Schoeman's The law of property* (4th ed 2003) 500–501; DL Carey Miller (with A Pope) *Land title in South Africa* (2000) 493; T Roux 'Chapter 7: The Extension of Security of Tenure Act' in G Budlender, J Latsky & T Roux *Juta's new land law* (1998) 7A–14; W du Plessis, N Olivier & J Pienaar 'Land reform surging forward' (1998) 13 *SA Public Law* 474–489 at 478. See further Roux at 7A–15–7A–16 on the question whether the occupier's dependents are protected.

[126]Chapter II (section 4) of the Act provides for long-term security of tenure in on-site or off-site developments for the occupiers involved. This section involves redistribution or access to land rather than tenure reform and is discussed in 6.4.2 below. See PJ Badenhorst, JM Pienaar & H Mostert (assisted by M van Rooyen) *Silberberg and Schoeman's The law of property* (4th ed 2003) 501–502; DL Carey Miller (with A Pope) *Land title in South Africa* (2000) 514–516; T Roux 'Chapter 7: The Extension of Security of Tenure Act' in G Budlender, J Latsky & T Roux *Juta's new land law* (1998) 7A–6; W du Plessis, N Olivier & J Pienaar 'Land: Still a contentious issue' (1998) 13 *SA Public Law* 149–169 at 158.

[127]Sections 7, 8, 9 of the Act. See PJ Badenhorst, JM Pienaar & H Mostert (assisted by M van Rooyen) *Silberberg and Schoeman's The law of property* (4th ed 2003) 502; DL Carey Miller (with A Pope) *Land title in South Africa* (2000) 495–497; T Roux 'Chapter 7: The Extension of Security of Tenure Act' in G Budlender, J Latsky & T Roux *Juta's new land law* (1998) 7A–17–7A–19.

[128]Section 6. See PJ Badenhorst, JM Pienaar & H Mostert (assisted by M van Rooyen) *Silberberg and Schoeman's The law of property* (4th ed 2003) 502–503; DL Carey Miller (with A Pope) *Land title in South Africa* (2000) 495–497; T Roux 'Chapter 7: The Extension of Security of Tenure Act' in G Budlender, J Latsky & T Roux *Juta's new land law* (1998) 7A–17–7A–19.

[129]DL Carey Miller (with A Pope) *Land title in South Africa* (2000) 495–497; T Roux 'Chapter 7: The Extension of Security of Tenure Act' in G Budlender, J Latsky & T Roux *Juta's new land law* (1998) 7A–17.

Apart from the two sets of long-term and day-to-day stabilizing provisions set out above, the Act's main thrust is to protect lawful occupiers of rural land against unfair evictions. Consequently, a large and important part of the Act deals with termination of the occupation rights of lawful occupiers of rural land and, once permission has been terminated lawfully, their eviction.[130] The major premise of this part of the Act is that eviction is allowed only in accordance with the strict requirements and procedures set out in the Act, and then (since the Act deals with occupiers who have permission to occupy) only once existing rights to occupy have been terminated lawfully and in accordance with the Act.[131] The Act therefore presupposes a procedure that consists of two distinct and consecutive phases: lawful and fair termination of lawful occupation rights must precede lawful and fair eviction of occupiers. Two separate sets of provisions and requirements apply to the two phases.

Section 6 of the Act stabilizes the right of residence of occupiers who resided on and used land on 4 February 1997 and ensures that they can continue exercising that right unless it is terminated in accordance with the Act. The tenure reform effect of the Act is attained, as far as this aspect is concerned, by elevating what was a weak and vulnerable lesser land right into a secure and well-protected real right.[132] Existing occupation rights may be terminated on any lawful ground provided that contractual requirements and the fairness requirements in the Act are complied with.[133] Factors that should be taken into account in deciding whether termination of an occupation

---

[130]Chapter IV. See in general AJ van der Walt 'Exclusivity of ownership, security of tenure, and eviction orders: A model to evaluate South African land-reform legislation' 2002 *TSAR* 254–289 at 275–282; PJ Badenhorst, JM Pienaar & H Mostert (assisted by M van Rooyen) *Silberberg and Schoeman's The law of property* (4th ed 2003) 503–507; DL Carey Miller (with A Pope) *Land title in South Africa* (2000) 499–510; T Roux 'Chapter 7: The Extension of Security of Tenure Act' in G Budlender, J Latsky & T Roux *Juta's new land law* (1998) 7A–17–7A–48; W du Plessis, N Olivier & J Pienaar 'Land: Still a contentious issue' (1998) 13 *SA Public Law* 149–169 at 157.

[131]See footnote 133 below.

[132]T Roux 'Chapter 7: The Extension of Security of Tenure Act' in G Budlender, J Latsky & T Roux *Juta's new land law* (1998) 7A–18 (with references in footnote 2) points out that the thrust of the Act is to treat the relationship between owners and occupiers as though it were an ordinary landlord-tenant relationship (at 7A–3) and that the position of the occupier is basically secured by elevating it to the status of a limited real right in land (at 7A–18). In this sense, with reference to the classic common law cases such as *Ex parte Geldenhuys* 1926 OPD 155 at 164; *Lorentz v Melle and Others* 1978 (3) SA 1044 (T); *Pearly Beach Trust v Registrar of Deeds* 1990 (4) SA 614 (C) and *Erlax Properties (Pty) Ltd v Registrar of Deeds and Others* 1992 (1) SA 879 (A), the Act indeed causes a diminution of the landowner's ownership, a subtraction from the *dominium*, which could be and indeed has been the cause of constitutional controversy; see 6.3.8 below.

[133]Section 8. See AJ van der Walt 'Exclusivity of ownership, security of tenure, and eviction orders: A model to evaluate South African land-reform legislation' 2002 *TSAR* 254–289 at 276; PJ Badenhorst, JM Pienaar & H Mostert (assisted by M van Rooyen) *Silberberg and Schoeman's The law of property* (4th ed 2003) 503–504; DL Carey Miller (with A Pope) *Land title in South Africa* (2000) 500; T Roux 'Chapter 7: The Extension of Security of Tenure Act' in G Budlender, J Latsky & T Roux *Juta's new land law* (1998) 7A–19.

right is fair are specified in the Act,[134] and special requirements apply to certain categories such as occupiers whose rights of residence arise solely from employment contracts; long-term protected occupiers;[135] and family members and dependents of long-term protected occupiers.[136]

Once occupation rights have been terminated lawfully and in accordance with the Act it becomes possible for the landowner or person in charge of the land to evict the occupiers, but only on the authority of a court order. Even then the eviction process is subjected to strict fairness requirements in the Act.[137] Four requirements are laid down for an eviction under the Act: the occupier's occupation right must have been terminated lawfully and in accordance with the Act; the occupier must not have vacated the premises voluntarily; the substantive grounds for an eviction in the Act must be satisfied; and the mandatory notice and other due process requirements must have been met.[138]

---

[134]PJ Badenhorst, JM Pienaar & H Mostert (assisted by M van Rooyen) *Silberberg and Schoeman's The law of property* (4th ed 2003) 503–504; DL Carey Miller (with A Pope) *Land title in South Africa* (2000) 501–502; T Roux 'Chapter 7: The Extension of Security of Tenure Act' in G Budlender, J Latsky & T Roux *Juta's new land law* (1998) 7A–19.

[135]This category consists of persons who have resided on the land in question or other land belonging to the same owner for at least 10 years and who have either reached the age of 60 or are employees or former employees who have become unable to supply labour because of ill health or disability. See T Roux 'Chapter 7: The Extension of Security of Tenure Act' in G Budlender, J Latsky & T Roux *Juta's new land law* (1998) 7A–23; AJ van der Walt 'Exclusivity of ownership, security of tenure, and eviction orders: A model to evaluate South African land-reform legislation' 2002 *TSAR* 254–289 at 276–277 footnote 113.

[136]On the special requirements see T Roux 'Chapter 7: The Extension of Security of Tenure Act' in G Budlender, J Latsky & T Roux *Juta's new land law* (1998) 7A–20–7A–27. On the position of family members see *Conradie v Hanekom* 1999 (4) SA 491 (LCC); *Dique NO v Van der Merwe* 2001 (2) SA 1006 (T); W du Plessis, N Olivier & J Pienaar 'Land reform: Trends developing in case law' (1999) 14 *SA Public Law* 528–553 at 544; W du Plessis, N Olivier & J Pienaar 'Evictions, restitution, spatial information, the right to housing and minerals: New approaches from the government and the courts' (2001) 16 *SA Public Law* 181–216 at 442; T Roux 'Pro-poor court, anti-poor outcomes: Explaining the performance of the South African Land Claims Court' (2004) 20 *SAJHR* 511–543 at 525–527.

[137]Section 9. The Supreme Court of Appeal held in *Mpedi and Others v Swanevelder and Another* 2004 (4) 344 (SCA) par [1] at 348D that even lawful termination of the right of residence does not entail availability of an eviction order as of right; the court must still determine whether the requirements for granting an eviction order have been satisfied. See further AJ van der Walt 'Exclusivity of ownership, security of tenure, and eviction orders: A model to evaluate South African land-reform legislation' 2002 *TSAR* 254–289 at 277; PJ Badenhorst, JM Pienaar & H Mostert (assisted by M van Rooyen) *Silberberg and Schoeman's The law of property* (4th ed 2003) 503–504; DL Carey Miller (with A Pope) *Land title in South Africa* (2000) 502; T Roux 'Chapter 7: The Extension of Security of Tenure Act' in G Budlender, J Latsky & T Roux *Juta's new land law* (1998) 7A–27.

[138]Section 9; see AJ van der Walt 'Exclusivity of ownership, security of tenure, and eviction orders: A model to evaluate South African land-reform legislation' 2002 *TSAR* 254–289 at 277; PJ Badenhorst, JM Pienaar & H Mostert (assisted by M van Rooyen) *Silberberg and Schoeman's The law of property* (4th ed 2003) 505–507; DL Carey Miller (with A Pope) *Land title in South Africa* (2000)
(continued on next page …)

For purposes of the third requirement, namely substantive reasons for an eviction, the Act differentiates between those who occupied the land in question on 4 February 1997 and those who became occupiers subsequently. The former group, who had permission to occupy on 4 February 1997, are again divided into four categories for purposes of determining a substantive ground for eviction: those who have done something wrong to trigger eviction; those who triggered eviction by voluntarily resigning from their employment; those who have neither done anything wrong nor voluntarily resigned from their employment; and a fourth special category of instances which do not satisfy any of the first three possibilities but where continued occupation poses a serious threat to the owner's interests or business.[139] In the first of these cases breach of a material and fair term of the occupation agreement which the occupier could have but failed to comply with and failed to remedy after fair notice can establish a ground for eviction, provided all the other requirements in the Act have been complied with. Similarly, a fundamental and irremediable breach of an employment contract that formed the basis of a residence agreement, followed by voluntary resignation from the employment contract, can establish a ground for eviction provided that all other requirements have been complied with. In the third situation, where the occupier has not done anything to trigger the eviction procedure, the landowner can obtain an eviction order if the court is satisfied that suitable alternative accommodation is available. Finally, if the owner provided the accommodation in the first place and continued occupation poses a serious threat of prejudice to the owner's operation or business, the owner can obtain an eviction order subject to a less onerous

---

(... from previous page)

502–508; T Roux 'Chapter 7: The Extension of Security of Tenure Act' in G Budlender, J Latsky & T Roux *Juta's new land law* (1998) 7A–27–7A–31. Roux at 7A–29–7A–31 points out that the formal notice requirement has received lots of attention in case law and he discusses some of the earlier cases; see *Karabo v Kok* 1998 (4) SA 1014 (LCC); *Lategan v Koopman* 1998 (3) SA 457 (LCC); *Dlamini v Mthembu* 1999 (3) SA 1030 (LCC); see further W du Plessis, N Olivier & J Pienaar 'Land issues: An assessment of the failures and successes' (1999) 14 *SA Public Law* 240–270 at 253; W du Plessis, N Olivier & J Pienaar 'Land reform: Trends developing in case law' (1999) 14 *SA Public Law* 528–553 at 540; W du Plessis, N Olivier & J Pienaar 'Evictions, restitution, spatial information, the right to housing and minerals: New approaches from the government and the courts' (2001) 16 *SA Public Law* 181–216 at 197–203. Compare Badenhorst, Pienaar & Mostert (assisted by M van Rooyen) *Silberberg and Schoeman's The law of property* (4th ed 2003) at 505 for more references.

[139] Section 10. See AJ van der Walt 'Exclusivity of ownership, security of tenure, and eviction orders: A model to evaluate South African land-reform legislation' 2002 *TSAR* 254–289 at 278–281; PJ Badenhorst, JM Pienaar & H Mostert (assisted by M van Rooyen) *Silberberg and Schoeman's The law of property* (4th ed 2003) 505–506; DL Carey Miller (with A Pope) *Land title in South Africa* (2000) 503–505; T Roux 'Chapter 7: The Extension of Security of Tenure Act' in G Budlender, J Latsky & T Roux *Juta's new land law* (1998) 7A–31–7A–39.

duty to help find suitable alternative accommodation and may be exempted from it after a certain period of time.[140]

Occupation rights obtained after 4 February 1997 enjoy slightly less protection against eviction. In this case the Act does not distinguish between those who have done anything to trigger eviction proceedings and those who have not, simply providing that eviction becomes possible when it was an express, material and fair term of the occupation agreement that the owner's consent would terminate on a certain fixed or determinable date (which has arrived) or when it is otherwise fair and just to grant the eviction order.[141] The Act provides for urgent evictions in cases in exceptional circumstances.[142]

The courts have struggled to find a suitable interpretation and application framework for evictions under the Act. On the one hand the Act obviously provides protection for occupiers, but on the other hand the rights of landowners—traditionally protected very strongly by the common law—also have to be taken into account, resulting in a conflict between the protection of landowners' rights under the common law and the protection of occupiers' rights in the Act. The fact that the property clause in section 25 can be said to support both sets of protective measures complicates matters further.[143] The first issue arising from this conflict concerns the format of an eviction application, the applicable source of law that determines its

---

[140]See *Theewaterskloof Holdings (Pty) Ltd, Glaser Division v Jacobs* 2002 (3) SA 401 (LCC); W du Plessis, N Olivier & J Pienaar 'Progress in land reform, illegal occupation of land and judicial interpretation' (2002) 17 *SA Public Law* 178–209 at 189–190. See further T Roux 'Chapter 7: The Extension of Security of Tenure Act' in G Budlender, J Latsky & T Roux *Juta's new land law* (1998) 7A–31–7A–38; PJ Badenhorst, JM Pienaar & H Mostert (assisted by M van Rooyen) *Silberberg and Schoeman's The law of property* (4th ed 2003) 505–506; AJ van der Walt 'Exclusivity of ownership, security of tenure, and eviction orders: A model to evaluate South African land-reform legislation' 2002 *TSAR* 254–289 at 275–282; AJ van der Walt 'Exclusivity of ownership, security of tenure and eviction orders: A critical evaluation of recent case law' (2002) 18 *SAJHR* 372–420 for a discussion of case law on these requirements.

[141]Section 1. See AJ van der Walt 'Exclusivity of ownership, security of tenure, and eviction orders: A model to evaluate South African land-reform legislation' 2002 *TSAR* 254–289 at 281; PJ Badenhorst, JM Pienaar & H Mostert (assisted by M van Rooyen) *Silberberg and Schoeman's The law of property* (4th ed 2003) 505–506; DL Carey Miller (with A Pope) *Land title in South Africa* (2000) 503–505; T Roux 'Chapter 7: The Extension of Security of Tenure Act' in G Budlender, J Latsky & T Roux *Juta's new land law* (1998) 7A–31–7A–39.

[142]Section 15. See *Malan v Gordon* 1999 (3) SA 103 (LCC); W du Plessis, N Olivier & J Pienaar 'Land reform: Trends developing in case law' (1999) 14 *SA Public Law* 528–553 at 541; AJ van der Walt 'Exclusivity of ownership, security of tenure, and eviction orders: A model to evaluate South African land-reform legislation' 2002 *TSAR* 254–289 at 282; PJ Badenhorst, JM Pienaar & H Mostert (assisted by M van Rooyen) *Silberberg and Schoeman's The law of property* (4th ed 2003) 507; DL Carey Miller (with A Pope) *Land title in South Africa* (2000) 509; T Roux 'Chapter 7: The Extension of Security of Tenure Act' in G Budlender, J Latsky & T Roux *Juta's new land law* (1998) 7A–44–7A–48.

[143]On case law concerning evictions in terms of the Act see generally AJ van der Walt 'Exclusivity of ownership, security of tenure and eviction orders: A critical evaluation of recent case law' (2002) 18 *SAJHR* 372–420 at 390–409.

adjudication, and related matters of procedure such as the burden of proof.[144] Raylene Keightley[145] has distinguished between two approaches. The first view is that the common law is the starting point, which means that the owner can decide to apply for an eviction order under common law, leaving it to the occupier to plead and prove that one of the land reform laws is applicable and that it provides additional protection or that it changes the burden of proof. The advantage of this approach is that the landowner, who initiates the procedure, knows what is required because the burden of proof is determined by common law. The disadvantage is that it elevates the common law to the default position, which is not only counterintuitive in view of the superior status of the Constitution[146] and the track record of evictions under the common law,[147] but may relegate land reform to a position of lower priority and thus frustrate transformation efforts.

---

[144]Case law indicates that a significant aspect relating to burden of proof involves the onus to provide the court with additional information that is not required or considered in a common law eviction case. At common law an eviction order merely requires the owner to prove his or her ownership and that the property is occupied by the respondent, leaving it to the respondent to raise and prove a possible defence such as a valid lease: *Graham v Ridley* 1931 TPD 476; *Chetty v Naidoo* 1974 (3) SA 13 (A); compare AJ van der Walt 'Exclusivity of ownership, security of tenure, and eviction orders: A model to evaluate South African land-reform legislation' 2002 *TSAR* 254–289 at 256–258. In terms of the land reform laws the courts often have to consider either certain specific circumstances (such as the position of elderly people and children amongst the occupiers or the availability of alternative accommodation) or the relevant circumstances and what is just and fair in the circumstances more generally. When owners initiate eviction proceedings under the common law they do not have to place evidence relating to these additional factors before the court, and they often claim not to have access to the relevant information; see AJ van der Walt 'Exclusivity of ownership, security of tenure and eviction orders: A critical evaluation of recent case law' (2002) 18 *SAJHR* 372–420 at 405–409 and the discussion below. In *Port Elizabeth Municipality v Various Occupiers* 2005 (1) SA 217 (CC) paras [32] and [36] at 235F–236C and 237C–D the Constitutional Court held that courts had to take steps according to their own initiative to ensure that all relevant information was available before granting an eviction order (the case dealt with another land reform law, namely the Prevention of Illegal Eviction from and Unlawful Occupation of Land Act 18 of 1998, which is clearer on relevant circumstances, but the sentiment expressed in this case probably applies more generally).

[145]'The impact of the Extension of Security of Tenure Act on an owner's right to vindicate immovable property' (1999) 15 *SAJHR* 277–307 at 288–292. See further AJ van der Walt 'Exclusivity of ownership, security of tenure and eviction orders: A critical evaluation of recent case law' (2002) 18 *SAJHR* 372–420 at 390–409.

[146]Which proclaims itself the highest law in the land (section 2) and contains an anti-eviction provision (section 26(3)) that authorizes and supports the position adopted in the land reform laws rather than the common law position; compare AJ van der Walt 'Exclusivity of ownership, security of tenure, and eviction orders: A model to evaluate South African land-reform legislation' 2002 *TSAR* 254–289 at 268–269; AJ van der Walt 'Exclusivity of ownership, security of tenure and eviction orders: A critical evaluation of recent case law' (2002) 18 *SAJHR* 372–420 at 391, 394–404; T Roux 'Continuity and change in a transforming legal order: The impact of section 26(3) of the Constitution on South African law' (2004) 121 *SALJ* 466–492.

[147]AJ van der Walt 'Exclusivity of ownership, security of tenure, and eviction orders: A model to evaluate South African land-reform legislation' 2002 *TSAR* 254–289 at 259–263 argues that the strong eviction remedy of the common law was abused during the apartheid era to facilitate forced removals. On that basis it may be argued that common law evictions should now be treated with care, subject to the clear reformist intentions of the anti-eviction provisions in the Constitution and land reform laws.

The second approach is to see land reform laws and control over evictions as the point of departure, which would mean that the onus is on the owner to bring the eviction application within the framework of the Constitution and the applicable land reform legislation. The advantage of this approach is that it foregrounds the anti-eviction provisions in the Constitution and land reform laws, making it less probable that evictions would simply continue more or less as before under the common law. The disadvantage is that owners might through no fault of their own find themselves in an impossible situation because they do not know whether they should bring an application under one land reform law (for example the Extension of Security of Tenure Act 62 of 1997) or another (for example the Land Reform (Labour Tenants) Act 3 of 1996) because they cannot anticipate the occupier's defence—the court that has jurisdiction, the correct statutory framework and the relevant burden of proof with regard to additional information will in each case be determined by the status that the respondent elects to claim, and often the landowner may be unaware of and in no position to establish that status beforehand. In some cases this might result in an eviction application being dismissed although the landowner has satisfied the common law requirements for an eviction and the respondent has not entered any defence, simply because the court decides that a specific land reform law was applicable and the landowner failed to satisfy the additional requirements.[148]

Both approaches are problematic, and the Land Claims Court has by and large preferred to follow the common law approach rather than bring about substantive reforms itself.[149] Keightley suggested that the problem should be solved by legislative

---

[148] See AJ van der Walt 'Exclusivity of ownership, security of tenure and eviction orders: A critical evaluation of recent case law' (2002) 18 *SAJHR* 372–420 at 392, and compare footnote 144 above.

[149] The Land Claims Court followed the common law approach in *Skhosana v Roos t/a Roos se Oord* 2000 (4) SA 561 (LCC); *Khuzwayo v Dludla* 2001 (1) 714 (LCC). In the latter case the Court explicitly refused to solve the problem and subscribed to Keightley's view that legislative intervention was required. See the next two footnotes below and footnote 124 above. In *De Kock v Juggels* 1999 (4) SA 43 (LCC) the court placed the responsibility to place additional information regarding the fairness of the employment agreement and the availability of alternative accommodation on the landowner who brought the application. Similarly, in *Theewaterskloof Holdings (Edms) Bpk, Glaser Afdeling v Jacobs* 2002 (3) SA 401 (LCC) the court required proof from the landowner of the effect of further occupation on the owner's business. However, in both these cases the eviction application was explicitly brought under the Act, and the court therefore merely required compliance with the additional requirements that apply under it, without changing its position on the burden of proof if the application is brought under common law. See further T Roux 'Continuity and change in a transforming legal order: The impact of section 26(3) of the Constitution on South African law' (2004) 121 *SALJ* 466–492; T Roux 'Pro-poor court, anti-poor outcomes: Explaining the perform-ance of the South African Land Claims Court' (2004) 20 *SAJHR* 511–543. In the latter article Roux explains the relatively poor transformation record of the Land Claims Court with reference to the continuing and pervasive influence of South African legal culture; an influence that explains South African courts' relative non-activism more generally: see K Klare 'Legal culture and trans-formative constitutionalism' (1998) 14 *SAJHR* 146–188.

intervention.[150] In a recent case (decided with reference to a different land reform law) the Constitutional Court adopted the view that it is the responsibility of the courts to ensure that they have all the relevant information available when considering an eviction application, and that the courts should take the initiative and make arrangements to obtain that information.[151] This could relieve the applicant-landowner of unfair or impossible burdens of proof in some cases, although it seems fair to assume that applicants would still be expected to place information that is reasonably expected to be in their knowledge before the court upon application.

A second problem deriving from eviction of lawful occupiers under the Act is the question whether occupiers who originally did have permission or another valid legal ground to occupy, but whose occupation became unlawful because of lapse of time or lawful termination of permission should be evicted in accordance with the requirements of the Extension of Security of Tenure Act 62 of 1997 (which applies to occupiers with permission, but only in rural areas); or in terms of the Prevention of Illegal Eviction from and Unlawful Occupation of Land Act 18 of 1998 (which applies to unlawful occupiers of both rural and urban land);[152] or in terms of the common law (or another law altogether). What happens when a landowner wants to evict an occupier who refuses to vacate the premises after his or her right to occupy has been lawfully terminated? If the occupier claims the protection of a land reform law such as the Land Reform (Labour Tenants) Act 3 of 1996 or the Extension of Security of Tenure Act 62 of 1997 and the owner denies the existence of a labour tenancy agreement or permission to occupy it could become very confusing, especially if the owner is uncertain whether to institute the eviction application in the Land Claims Court or the High Court.[153] Since most cases dealing with this problem also involve the applicability of the Prevention of Illegal Eviction from and Unlawful Occupation of Land Act 18 of 1998 this problem is discussed in 6.3.6 below.

Another controversial aspect of the protection that the Act offers to occupiers is the right to bury family members on the land without permission or against the will of the landowner. The Act provides the right to visit and maintain family graves on the land,[154] but until 2001 this did not include the right to bury occupiers or their family members. Initially, the courts interpreted the Act conservatively and held that, without clear authority, enforcement of such a right would imply too much of an encroachment on the right of the landowner without sufficiently clear consti-

---

[150] R Keightley 'The impact of the Extension of Security of Tenure Act on an owner's right to vindicate immovable property' (1999) 15 *SAJHR* 277–307 at 295–302, 306–307. See the previous footnote above and the next footnote below.

[151] *Port Elizabeth Municipality v Various Occupiers* 2005 (1) SA 217 (CC) paras [32] and [36] at 235F–236C and 237C–D. The case dealt with the Prevention of Illegal Eviction from and Unlawful Occupation of Land Act 19 of 1998, but the general thinking of the Court could well apply to other land reform laws as well. See the previous two footnotes above and compare chapter 7.3.4.

[152] This Act is discussed in 6.3.6 below.

[153] The Land Claims Court has exclusive jurisdiction over evictions of labour tenants in terms of the Land Reform (Labour Tenants) Act 3 of 1996; see 6.3.3 above.

[154] Section 6(4).

tutional or legislative authority. Consequently, it was assumed that occupiers and
their family members could not be buried without the landowner's permission and
that the landowner could withhold permission.[155] In this respect it could therefore
be said that the courts declined the opportunity to develop the common law and
the customary law to promote the spirit, purport and objects of the Constitution as
meant in section 39(2). Eventually the Act was amended by inserting a provision
that now allows burial of occupiers and their family members on the land in accordance with the occupiers' religious and cultural beliefs, provided that an established
practice exists in that the landowner previously routinely gave permission for
burials, subject to reasonable conditions.[156] The constitutional validity of this new
provision was attacked but upheld in *Nhlabati and Others v Fick*,[157] the landowner
arguing that section 6(2)(dA) was unconstitutional because it violated the protection
of the landowner's right in section 25 of the Constitution and because it intruded
upon a functional area of exclusive provincial legislative competence. The Land
Claims Court rejected the property argument based on section 25, concluding that
section 6(2)(dA) did not authorize an arbitrary deprivation of property because it
struck the required balance between the rights of the landowner and the rights of
the occupiers. The case is discussed in more detail in 6.3.8 below and in
chapter 4.7.3.

6.3.6 Prevention of Illegal Eviction from and Unlawful Occupation of Land Act 18 of 1998

The Prevention of Illegal Eviction from and Unlawful Occupation of Land Act 18 of
1998 applies specifically to unlawful occupiers of land and therefore does not require
a right to occupy. The Act is primarily concerned with the proper regulation of
eviction procedures as they apply to unlawful occupiers. Accordingly, the strategy of
the Act is not (as in the case of the Extension of Security of Tenure Act 62 of 1997
and other land reform statutes) to stabilize, reinforce or strengthen weak and insecure
existing land rights, but rather (since there are per definition no rights to work with

---

[155]See *Serole and Another v Pienaar* 2000 (1) SA 328 (LCC); *Bührmann v Nkosi* 2000 (1) SA 145 (T);
the latter confirmed by the SCA in *Nkosi and Another v Bührmann* 2002 (1) SA 372 (SCA); W du
Plessis, N Olivier & J Pienaar 'Land reform: A never-ending process' (2000) 15 *SA Public Law* 230–
254 at 241–243. On the SCA judgment see AJ van der Walt 'Property rights v religious rights:
Bührmann v Nkosi' (2002) 13 *Stell LR* 394–414; W du Plessis, N Olivier & J Pienaar 'Progress in
land reform, illegal occupation of land and judicial interpretation' (2002) 17 *SA Public Law* 178–
209 at 186–187. See further PJ Badenhorst, JM Pienaar & H Mostert (assisted by M van Rooyen)
Silberberg and Schoeman's The law of property (4th ed 2003) 503.
[156]Section 6(2)(dA) as amended by the Land Affairs General Amendment Act 51 of 2001; see PJ
Badenhorst, JM Pienaar & H Mostert (assisted by M van Rooyen) *Silberberg and Schoeman's The law
of property* (4th ed 2003) 503.
[157]2003 (7) BCLR 806 (LCC); see W du Plessis, N Olivier & J Pienaar 'Expropriation, restitution
and land redistribution: An answer to land problems in South Africa?' (2003) 18 *SA Public Law* 491–
514 at 501–504. The case is discussed in 6.3.8 below and in chapter 4.7.3.

in this instance) to stabilize existing unlawful occupation of land in order to ensure that eviction of unlawful occupiers takes place only when it is fair and equitable to do so and then only in a fair, equitable and controlled manner. No rights are created or strengthened, but the Act ensures that unlawful occupiers are only evicted by way of proper legal procedure that takes due notice of historical, social and human factors that might influence the fairness of evicting a specific person or group in a specific manner or at a specific time (or at all).

The most significant characteristic of the Act is that, by forcing owners to evict by way of a prescribed legal procedure that requires the courts to take notice of the historical, social and human weaknesses and vulnerabilities of even unlawful occupiers of land, an additional burden is placed upon landowners' traditionally very strong and simple right to evict unlawful occupiers summarily and without any regard for their personal circumstances. This effect can only be described as a very calculated reaction to the role of unfair evictions and forced removals during apartheid and to the current situation of large-scale land- and homelessness; it brings about a considerable limitation on the rights of landowners as they were traditionally seen and understood. As will appear in the course of the discussion this fact has significant constitutional implications.

According to the Act unlawful occupiers can only be evicted with due regard for the prescribed limitations and requirements. The main protective measure prescribed by the Act is that evictions have to be authorized by court order, and that the courts should only allow evictions subject to the fairness requirements laid down in the Act.[158] In considering an application for eviction the courts must determine whether the occupier has a valid defence, take into account the duration of the occupation[159] and decide whether it would be just and equitable to grant the eviction order considering all relevant circumstances. The Act prescribes different criteria and procedures for instances where the eviction is to take place at the instance

---

[158]Section 8 read with section 4. See AJ van der Walt 'Exclusivity of ownership, security of tenure, and eviction orders: A model to evaluate South African land-reform legislation' 2002 *TSAR* 254–289 at 285–287; PJ Badenhorst, JM Pienaar & H Mostert (assisted by M van Rooyen) *Silberberg and Schoeman's The law of property* (4th ed 2003) 527–533; DL Carey Miller (with A Pope) *Land title in South Africa* (2000) 516–524; W du Plessis, N Olivier & J Pienaar 'Land reform surging forward' (1998) 13 *SA Public Law* 474–489 at 484–486 for a discussion of the most important provisions.

[159]If the occupation lasted for less than six months the court can grant the eviction order if it is just and equitable to do so, taking into account all relevant circumstances, including the rights and needs of elderly persons, children, disabled persons and households headed by women. If the occupation lasted for more than six months the court must also consider the availability of alternative land. See subsections 4(6) and 4(7). Compare PJ Badenhorst, JM Pienaar & H Mostert (assisted by M van Rooyen) *Silberberg and Schoeman's The law of property* (4th ed 2003) 530; DL Carey Miller (with A Pope) *Land title in South Africa* (2000) 522.

of an organ of state, as opposed to 'normal' private evictions.[160] Special provision is made for urgent evictions.[161]

The Act explicitly overrides the common law with regard to the right to evict,[162] but in case law the reformist effect of the Act has been restricted to a certain extent. In *ABSA Bank Ltd v Amod*[163] the High Court decided that the Act applies to unlawful invasions of vacant land and to occupation of structures erected unlawfully, but not to formalized housing or to 'normal' common law landlord-tenant situations, which were therefore said still to be governed by the common law with regard to evictions. This approach is apparently based on the rather surprising and clearly fallacious view that apartheid land law was characterized by unfair evictions only in the area of unlawful land invasions and not in so-called 'normal' landlord-tenant situations. The courts' uncritical acceptance of this approach resulted in judgments where unlawful occupiers of land, who should arguably have enjoyed the protection of the Act, were evicted in

---

[160] Section 6, as opposed to 'normal' evictions by the owner in terms of section 4. In the case of public evictions, the relevant considerations include questions such as whether the defendant occupies land or has erected a structure without the necessary consent and whether it is in the public interest (including the health and safety of the occupiers and of the public in general) to grant the order. The circumstances of the original occupation and the duration of occupation are also considered. Furthermore, the availability of alternative accommodation is considered relevant in public evictions regardless of the period of occupation (in private evictions this only becomes relevant if occupation exceeded six months). See *Baartman v Port Elizabeth Municipality* 2004 (1) SA 560 (SCA); W du Plessis, N Olivier & J Pienaar 'Land matters: New developments 2004(1)' (2004) 19 *SA Public Law* 212–229 at 225. See further PJ Badenhorst, JM Pienaar & H Mostert (assisted by M van Rooyen) *Silberberg and Schoeman's The law of property* (4th ed 2003) 527–533; DL Carey Miller (with A Pope) *Land title in South Africa* (2000) 516–524; W du Plessis, N Olivier & J Pienaar 'Progress in land reform, illegal occupation of land and judicial interpretation' (2002) 17 *SA Public Law* 178–209 at 207.

[161] Section 5. See AJ van der Walt 'Exclusivity of ownership, security of tenure, and eviction orders: A model to evaluate South African land-reform legislation' 2002 *TSAR* 254–289 at 287; W du Plessis, N Olivier & J Pienaar 'Progress in land reform, illegal occupation of land and judicial interpretation' (2002) 17 *SA Public Law* 178–209 at 204; PJ Badenhorst, JM Pienaar & H Mostert (assisted by M van Rooyen) *Silberberg and Schoeman's The law of property* (4th ed 2003) 530; DL Carey Miller (with A Pope) *Land title in South Africa* (2000) 522.

[162] Section 4(1): 'Notwithstanding anything to the contrary contained in any law or the common law, the provisions of this section apply to proceedings by an owner or person in charge of land for the eviction of an unlawful occupier.'

[163] [1999] 2 All SA 423 (W). In cases where the occupiers were clearly unlawful land invaders the courts have had no problem in applying the Act; see eg *Port Elizabeth Municipality v Peoples Dialogue on Land and Shelter* 2000 (2) SA 1074 (SEC), confirmed in part and overturned in part in *Port Elizabeth Municipality v Peoples Dialogue on Land and Shelter* 2001 (4) SA 759 (E). For a discussion of the *ABSA* case and subsequent decisions see AJ van der Walt 'Exclusivity of ownership, security of tenure and eviction orders: A critical evaluation of recent case law' (2002) 18 *SAJHR* 372–420 at 386–390; W du Plessis, N Olivier & J Pienaar 'Land reform: A never-ending process' (2000) 15 *SA Public Law* 230–254 at 246–248; W du Plessis, N Olivier & J Pienaar 'Progress in land reform, illegal occupation of land and judicial interpretation' (2002) 17 *SA Public Law* 178–209 at 202–206.

terms of the common law and therefore left unprotected.[164] In one case the High Court even found it necessary to voice certain very negative remarks about the nature and suitability of the reform measures introduced by the Act, invoking the displeasure of and a sharp rebuke from the Supreme Court of Appeal.[165] Generally speaking case law has been characterized by uncertainty about the scope of the Act's explicit intention to override the common law—the intention is clearly that the common law should be changed when the Act applies, but should the whole common law of eviction be overhauled, or should the application of the Act be restricted to mitigate its effect on the common law, in line with the presumption that legislation should be interpreted so as to change the common law as little as possible?[166]

In the final result most courts opted for the view that the Act should be applied restrictively so as to limit its effect on existing law. Although this rather conservative-looking proposal finds support in the notion that legal certainty should be preserved in the absence of a clear intention to amend existing law, it could be countered that the constitutional imperative to develop the common law in line with the spirit,

---

[164] In *Joubert v Van Rensburg* 2001 (1) SA 753 (W) a group of unlawful occupiers had been resettled on land purchased for the purpose in terms of a trust arrangement set up with the assistance of neighbours. When it appeared that the new settlement was also occupied unlawfully because of lack of compliance with planning and development laws, other neighbours applied for an eviction order. The High Court initially granted an order, based on the common law, that was said not to be an eviction order since it merely required the owners of the land to abate a nuisance caused by the settlement, but in effect the order was an eviction order that circumvented the requirements of the Act. The Constitutional Court refused to allow a direct appeal and referred the appealing occupiers to the Supreme Court of Appeal, although it was clear that the Constitutional Court was critical of certain statements made by the High Court: *Mkangeli v Joubert* 2001 (2) SA 191 (CC). On appeal the Supreme Court of Appeal overturned the High Court decision, deciding that the High Court had no jurisdiction to grant an eviction order in the case because the Extension of Security of Tenure Act 62 of 1997 should have found application on the basis that the occupiers had permission from the landowners (the trust) to occupy the land: *Mkangeli v Joubert* 2002 (4) SA 36 (SCA). See further AJ van der Walt 'Exclusivity of ownership, security of tenure and eviction orders: A critical evaluation of recent case law' (2002) 18 *SAJHR* 372–420 at 379–385. These cases are also discussed in 6.3.8 below; see footnote 206 and accompanying text.

[165] *Mkangeli v Joubert* 2002 (4) SA 36 (SCA) paras [26]–[27] at 47G–48E. See AJ van der Walt 'Exclusivity of ownership, security of tenure and eviction orders: A critical evaluation of recent case law' (2002) 18 *SAJHR* 372–420 at 379–385.

[166] See L du Plessis *Re-interpretation of statutes* (2002) 179–181: the common law is not an impenetrable obstacle and, although the presumption preserves legal certainty, the Constitution has changed perceptions of what is necessary and what not. From du Plessis' explanation one could infer that the presumption should not be used to avoid the constitutional obligation to develop the common law so as to reflect and promote the spirit, purport and objects of the Constitution (section 39(2)). See further JR de Ville *Constitutional and statutory interpretation* (2000) 170; PJ Badenhorst, JM Pienaar & H Mostert (assisted by M van Rooyen) *Silberberg and Schoeman's The law of property* (4th ed 2003) 530; and compare *Port Elizabeth Municipality v Peoples Dialogue on Land and Shelter* 2000 (2) SA 1074 (SE). The effect of section 39(2) and the development of the common law are discussed specifically with reference to evictions in chapter 7.3 and the *Port Elizabeth* decision's role in the process is discussed in chapter 7.3.4.

purport and objects of the Constitution (section 39(2)) supports a more generous approach to the interpretation of legislation with a constitutionally mandated and clearly intended reformist agenda.[167]

In *Ndlovu v Ngcobo; Bekker v Jika*[168] the Supreme Court of Appeal settled one aspect of this problem by deciding that the burden of proof rests on the owner-applicant to prove that he or she is the owner and that the occupier-respondent is in unlawful occupation of the land, after which the occupier-respondent could present evidence with regard to special circumstances such as the gender, age and vulnerability of the occupiers. Considering that the owner only had to prove ownership and occupation at common law, this might look like an amended version that requires some additional proof (namely that occupation is unlawful) from the owner, but it is not quite clear that this is what the Court intended, especially in view of the fact that the occupier is still left with the burden to prove any ground for lawful occupation.[169] The only reason why the owner would raise the unlawfulness of the occupation would be to bring the action under the auspices of the Act; and even then it is unclear whether it would not be better (and permissible) to simply bring the eviction application in terms of the common law. The *Ngcobo/Jika* decision of the Supreme Court nevertheless extended the previously limited area of application of the Act by indicating that the Act does apply to situations of holding over and not only to land invasions.[170] At the time of writing the state was considering an amendment of the

---

[167] See further chapter 2.3, chapter 4.7.3 and chapter 7.3 and compare footnote 166 above.

[168] 2003 (1) SA 113 (SCA) par [19] at 124E–F. On this decision see W du Plessis, N Olivier & J Pienaar 'A new dispensation for communal land and minerals' (2002) 17 *SA Public Law* 409–439 at 427–430. See also *FHP Management (Pty) Ltd v Theron NO and Another* 2004 (3) SA 392 (C) at 404I–405B, 406G–I. See further AJ van der Walt 'Ownership and eviction: Constitutional rights in private law' (2005) 9 *Edinburgh LR* 32–64 (comparing German and South African case law); R Youngs 'Human rights in the housing sphere: German comparisons' (2004) 15 *The King's College LJ* 145–158 (comparing German with English case law).

[169] At common law, as explained in *Chetty v Naidoo* 1974 (3) SA 13 (A), the owner did not have to allege or prove that occupation was unlawful but, if he did raise a potential ground for lawful occupation such as lease, he also had to prove that the lease had expired.

[170] This should have ended a series of conflicting decisions; see AJ van der Walt 'Exclusivity of ownership, security of tenure and eviction orders: A critical evaluation of recent case law' (2002) 18 *SAJHR* 372–420 at 385–390; PJ Badenhorst, JM Pienaar & H Mostert (assisted by M van Rooyen) *Silberberg and Schoeman's The law of property* (4th ed 2003) 528. Initially the Witwatersrand High Court held that the Act did not apply to holding over (where the occupation becomes unlawful when a previous ground for occupation lapses or is cancelled): *ABSA Bank Ltd v Amod* [1999] 2 All SA 423 (W). This approach was followed by the Cape High Court in *Ellis v Viljoen* 2001 (4) SA 795 (C), but not in *Bekker v Jika* [2001] 4 All SA 573 (SE), which was one of the cases on appeal in *Ngcobo/Bekker*. See W du Plessis, N Olivier & J Pienaar 'Delays in land reform—South Africa emulating Zimbabwe?' (2001) 16 *SA Public Law* 432–457 at 449. In *ABSA Bank Ltd v Murray and Another* 2004 (2) SA 15 (C) paras [10] and [13]–[16] at 21F–G and 22A–H the Cape High Court followed *Ngcobo/Jika* and applied the requirements of the Act when considering an eviction application under the Act. However, in *FHP Management (Pty) Ltd v Theron and Another* 2004 (3) SA 392

(continued on next page ...)

Act to reverse the effect of the *Ngcobo/Jika* decision in this regard.[171] However, apart from the applicability of the Act to instances of holding over, it seems as if the courts are happy to interpret the *Ngcobo/Jika* decision as if it did not change the burden of proof in any way, so that applicants in an eviction application under the Act can simply place before the court the fact that the applicant is owner of the property and that the respondent is an unlawful occupier, leaving it to the occupier to disclose relevant circumstances to show why the eviction order should not be granted.[172] This amounts to retention of the common law burden of proof, despite the fact that the Act explicitly overrides the common law in requiring that the courts, in considering an application for eviction, must determine whether the occupier has a valid defence, take into account the duration of the occupation and decide whether it would be just and equitable to grant the eviction order considering all relevant circumstances.

The Constitutional Court has answered some of the remaining questions sur-rounding the interpretation and application of the Act in an authoritative judgment that sets out its view of post-apartheid law with regard to evictions in a much clearer and more satisfactory way. In *Port Elizabeth Municipality v Various Occupiers*[173] there was no doubt that the Act applied, because the defendants were clearly unlawful

---

(... from previous page)
(C) at 404I–405B the same court considered the eviction order in terms of the common law, leaving it to the occupier to adduce evidence that would allow the court to consider another conclusion. In *Ndlovu v Ngcobo; Bekker v Jika* 2003 1 SA 113 (SCA) par [21]–[23] at 125B–H the SCA said that PIE had to apply to cases of holding over because it could not be discounted that the legislature intended to extend the applicability of PIE to holding over by tenants and similar occupiers whose right of occupation had been terminated or expired. In the latest decision on this matter (at the time of writing), *Davids and Others v Van Straaten and Others* 2005 (4) SA 468 (C), the Cape High Court followed the *Ndlovu/Bekker* judgment and decided a holding over case in terms of PIE. The court considered the personal circumstances of the majority of occupiers to be such that it would not be unfair to grant the eviction order against them. The most interesting aspect of the decision involved a 77 year old woman who had no income; she was allowed to stay on in the apartment on the strength of a settlement offer from the owner, but the court obviously regarded the settlement as a fair one. It remains unclear whether she would also have been allowed to stay on in the absence of the settlement. The question is, of course, whether the court order means that it is expected, in terms of PIE, that private property owners should bear the burden of the duty to provide access to housing for those whose personal and social position do not allow them to gain access on their own.
[171] Prevention of Illegal Eviction from and Unlawful Occupation of Land Amendment Bill B 1–2005, *Government Gazette No 27370* of 18 March 2005. See W du Plessis, N Olivier & J Pienaar 'Expropriation, restitution and land redistribution: An answer to land problems in South Africa?' (2003) 18 *SA Public Law* 491–514 at 507; AJ van der Walt 'Ownership and eviction: Constitutional rights in private law' (2005) 9 *Edinburgh LR* 32–64 at 41.
[172] See *FHP Management (Pty) Ltd v Theron and Another* 2004 (3) SA 392 (C) at 404I–405B. Apart from the misstatement of the common law, which in fact merely requires proof of occupation by the respondent and not of unlawful occupation, this looks like the common law burden of proof pure and simple, despite the fact that the Act explicitly overrides the common law as explained above.
[173] 2005 (1) SA 217 (CC).

occupiers of vacant land in the municipality's area of jurisdiction. The occupiers indicated that they were willing to vacate the land voluntarily if alternative land was made available to them, and the municipality sought an order to confirm that, in applying for an eviction order, it was not automatically constitutionally bound to provide the occupiers with alternative accommodation or land. The Constitutional Court confirmed that a court exercises a discretion under section 6 of the Act to grant an eviction order if it is just and equitable to do so and that, although the court was bound to take into account all considerations, including the availability of alternative accommodation, there was no unqualified constitutional duty on local authorities to ensure that an eviction is executed only when alternative accommodation or land is available.[174] However, the Court added that courts should generally be reluctant to grant eviction orders against relatively settled occupiers unless alternative accommodation was available, even if only as an interim measure pending availability of housing in the formal housing programme.[175]

The Court analysed and discussed the various factors and considerations that had to be taken into account when considering an eviction application by a state organ, emphasizing the fact that the considerations in section 6(3) of the Act were peremptory but not exhaustive and that the courts should be willing to devise their own steps to ensure that all relevant information was available to them, rather than relying on or placing the whole burden of proof with regard to the facts concerning additional considerations such as availability of alternative accommodation and the interests of vulnerable persons and groups on the parties or even just one party to the dispute.[176]

An important aspect of this decision was that the Constitutional Court explicitly stated that the Act, like all land reform laws, should be interpreted within the proper historical and constitutional framework, which the Court worked out and explained with reference to the historical background of evictions and forced removals under apartheid laws and the transformative purpose of the Constitution and land reform laws.[177] The Court pointed out that section 26(3) of the Constitution and its accompanying anti-eviction provisions in the land reform legislation are specifically aimed at rectifying eviction abuses of the apartheid past and to prevent their recurrence, with the result that the Act has to be interpreted with due regard for its historical and constitutional context.[178] In the historical and constitutional context the protection

---

[174] *Port Elizabeth Municipality v Various Occupiers* 2005 (1) SA 217 (CC) par [29] at 234A–E.

[175] Par [28] at 23G–H. To this could arguably have been added that courts should be more reluctant to grant such an eviction order when the applicant is a local authority (or any other state organ) than when the applicant is a private landowner. The state was the applicant in this case, although the land was private.

[176] See paras [29] at 234D–E (existence of a formal housing programme as a consideration); [30] at 234F (peremptory factors in section 6(1) of the Act); [32] and [36] at 235F–236C and 237C–D (courts to take steps to ensure that all relevant information was available); [43] and [45] at 240E and 241E–242A (whether mediation was attempted as a consideration).

[177] Paras [8]–[23] at 222A–229G.

[178] Paras [10] at 24A–B, [14] at 25A–B.

of property rights and the protection of a person's home are equally important, and accordingly it is necessary to establish an appropriate constitutional relationship between section 25's protection of property rights and section 26's protection of housing rights.[179] The Constitution places new obligations on the courts to avoid a hierarchical view of property and housing rights and to balance and reconcile them in as just a manner as possible, taking into account all the interests involved and the circumstances of each case.[180]

A further significant aspect concerning eviction of unlawful occupiers emerged from the *Modderklip* decision of the Constitutional Court.[181] By holding the state responsible to pay compensation to the landowner for the loss that he suffered as a result of the unlawful invasion and occupation of his land and the lack of state provision for efficient enforcement procedures the Court indicated that the protection of occupiers against eviction will not necessarily or always take place at the cost of the landowner—in suitable instances the landowner will have to be compensated for his loss. Judging from the decision it seems as if one could formulate the principle as follows: when a landowner is entitled to an eviction against unlawful occupiers but prevented from obtaining and executing the eviction order because of the sheer number and the personal circumstances of the occupiers, it is unacceptable for the state to just stand by and leave it to the owner to solve the problem. If the landowner is then expected to bear the continued unlawful occupation of her land until the state can provide an effective remedy (*inter alia* by providing alternative accommodation for the occupiers), the owner might have a claim for compensation against the state.

It could perhaps be said that the owner's compensation claim in the *Modderklip* case is similar to the equalization payments that German and French courts allow in cases where one or a small group of owners are expected to bear an extraordinarily and unfairly heavy burden because of otherwise legitimate and lawful state regulatory action.[182] These payments are not regarded as compensation for expropriation, but as compensation for loss that the owner suffers in bearing the burden of a quite legitimate regulatory action that has an unacceptably heavy impact on just one or a small number of property owners.

---

[179] Par [19] at 28B–D. See further the discussion of access to housing in 6.4 below and compare chapter 4.7.3 and chapter 7.3.

[180] Par [23] at 29E–G.

[181] The Constitutional Court decision is reported as *President of the Republic of South Africa and Another v Modderklip Boerdery (Pty) Ltd (Agri SA and Others,* Amici Curiae) 2005 (5) SA 3 (CC). The SCA decision is reported as *Modderfontein Squatters, Greater Benoni City Council v Modderklip Boerdery (Pty) Ltd; (Agri SA and Legal Resources Centre,* Amici Curiae*); President of the Republic of South Africa and Others v Modderklip Boerdery (Pty) Ltd (Agri SA and Legal Resources Centre,* Amici Curiae*)* 2004 (6) SA 40 (SCA). See AJ van der Walt 'The state's duty to protect property owners vs the state's duty to provide housing: Thoughts on the *Modderklip* case' (2005) 21 *SAJHR* 144–161.

[182] See the discussion and references in chapter 5.4.3 and 5.4.4.

6.3.7 Communal Land Rights Act 11 of 2004

The Communal Land Rights Act 1 of 2004 was assented to on 14 July 2004. Its date of commencement is yet to be proclaimed. The Act is concerned with tenure security and was therefore promulgated in terms of section 25(6) of the Constitution, as appears from the goals set out in the long title: to provide legal security of tenure by transferring communal land to communities, or by awarding comparable redress.[183]

In essence the Act is intended to improve security of tenure of individuals and communities who hold or use or occupy land communally.[184] Of all those persons and communities 'whose tenure of land is legally insecure as a result of past racially discriminatory laws or practices'[185] it is perhaps especially people who occupy and use rural land communally who have suffered and still suffer most.[186] These land users are affected by weak and insecure tenure that renders them vulnerable to state or private evictions; abuse and unfair treatment by tribal authorities or leaders; lack of access to infrastructure, capital and markets that prevents them from improving the land or their cultivation of it; and general poverty. On the one hand the tribal structures are often the safety net that protects many individuals and families from total destitution,

---

[183] The Act relies strongly on the notion of transition from old order rights to new order rights. Section 1 defines 'old order rights' as:

'a tenure or other right in or to communal land which—
(a) is formal or informal;
(b) is registered or unregistered;
(c) derives from or is recognised by law, including customary law, practice or usage; and
(d) exists immediately prior to a determination by the Minister in terms of section 18, but does not include—
(i) any right or interest of a tenant, labour tenant, sharecropper or employee if such right or interest is purely of a contractual nature; and
(ii) any right or interest based purely on temporary permission granted by the owner or lawful occupier of the land in question, on the basis that such permission may at any time be withdrawn by such owner or lawful occupier'

and 'new order right' as 'a tenure or other right in communal or other land which has been confirmed, converted, conferred or validated by the Minister in terms of section 18'.

[184] Section 1 describes 'community' as 'a group of persons whose rights to land are derived from shared rules determining access to land held in common by such group'. See further W du Plessis, N Olivier & J Pienaar 'A new dispensation for communal land and minerals' (2002) 17 SA Public Law 409–439 at 420–425; G Pienaar 'Security of communal land tenure by registration of individualised title—Is the Communal Land Rights Bill of 2003 the final solution?' (2004) 67 THRHR 244–263.

[185] Section 25(6) of the 1996 Constitution provides that these persons and communities are entitled, to the extent provided by an Act of Parliament, to legally secure tenure or comparable redress. Section 25(9) provides that Parliament shall make the laws referred to in section 25(6). The 2004 Act is the latest of several laws made in this regard, as appears from the sections on other tenure reform laws above.

[186] G Pienaar 'Security of communal land tenure by registration of individualised title—Is the Communal Land Rights Bill of 2003 the final solution?' (2004) 67 THRHR 244–263 at 245 indicates that some 2.4 million households or 13 million people (30% of the total population) fall into this category.

but on the other hand the communal nature of tenure that still dominates rural land holdings often prevents individuals and communities from escaping poverty and improving their economic and social position. It was therefore necessary to devise a tenure reform law that pertains mainly to communal land holding in rural areas and that could combine the virtues of communal land tenure with a land administration system that could offer improved security, fairness, equality and openness.[187]

The Act responds to this challenge with a number of interlocking strategies: (*a*) a so-called land rights enquiry to determine the nature and extent of all human, constitutional, old order and other tenure rights pertaining to certain land, including all competing rights; state interests; the need to promote equal access to land and gender equality; spatial land use planning considerations, and other relevant aspects;[188] (*b*) confirmation of existing 'old order' rights by the minister of land affairs; (*c*) conversion of existing old order rights into ownership or other, comparable 'new order' rights;[189] and (*d*) provision of comparable redress when existing old order rights cannot be rendered secure.[190] The conversion of old order rights into new order rights involves the making of a determination by the minister, who must consider the report of the land rights enquiry, all relevant law (including customary law and law regarding spatial planning, local government and agriculture), the old order rights of all affected parties, the need to provide equitable access to land and the need to promote gender equality.[191] The determination must, where applicable, determine the location and extent of any land to be transferred to a community or person[192] and must specify whether (*a*) the whole of the land should be (or remain) registered in the name of a community; (*b*) the whole of the land should be subdivided into portions that are registered in the name of individuals; (*c*) part of the land should be registered in the name of the community and part subdivided and registered in the name of individuals; and whether (*d*) old order rights should be confirmed, converted into ownership or other new order rights or cancelled.[193]

The four major strategies adopted in the Act are relevant to the constitutional obligation in section 25(6).[194] Firstly, security of tenure is promoted by ascertaining the nature and scope of all existing 'old order' rights in land and by either confirming these rights or converting them into more secure 'new order' rights that can be registered in the name of either an individual or a community. This strategy is aimed at

---

[187]See G Pienaar 'Security of communal land tenure by registration of individualised title—Is the Communal Land Rights Bill of 2003 the final solution?' (2004) 67 *THRHR* 244–263 at 245–251 for a discussion of the problems facing rural users of communal land and the need for reform.
[188]Section 14, read with sections 15–17 of the Act.
[189]Section 18 of the Act.
[190]Section 12 of the Act, read with section 13 and section 18
[191]Section 18(1).
[192]Section 18(2).
[193]Section 18(3).
[194]Section 4(1) repeats the promise of security of tenure or comparable redress that appears in section 25(6) of the Constitution.

individualizing rights and registering them for the sake of greater certainty, security and commercial viability.[195] Secondly, security of tenure is promoted within the communal land holding system by the new statutory requirement in section 19 of the Act that a community whose communal land is, or is to be, registered in its name must make and adopt community rules and have them registered in accordance with the Act.[196] The community rules regulate the administration and use of communal land by the community as landowner within the framework of law governing spatial planning and local government; these rules are binding on the community and its members, must be accessible to the public and are on registration deemed to be a matter of public knowledge.[197] Upon the registration of its rules in terms of section 19(1) a community acquires juristic personality with perpetual succession regardless of changes in its membership and it may, subject to the rules, the Act and any other law, in its own name acquire and hold rights and incur obligations and own, encumber by mortgage, servitude or otherwise and dispose of movable and immovable property and otherwise deal with such property subject to any title or other conditions.[198] Communal land and new order rights are capable of being and must be registered in the name of the community or person entitled to such land or right in terms of the Act and the relevant community rules. When the Minister makes a determination in terms of section 18 the ownership of communal land which is not state land but which is registered in the name of a person, a traditional leader or a communal property association in terms of the Communal Property Associations Act 28 of 1996 or a trust or other legal entity, vests in the community on whose behalf such land is held or in whose interest such registration was effected, subject to limitations and restrictions in relation to and rights or entitlements to such land; and the community succeeds in all respects as the successor in title to such person, traditional leader or traditional leadership, communal property association, trust or other legal entity.[199]

The third significant characteristic is that the Act provides that the holding and administration of communal land shall be subject to constitutional equality provisions, specifically with regard to gender equality. Section 4(2) provides that an old order right held by a married person is, despite any law, practice, usage or registration to the contrary, deemed to be held by all spouses in a marriage in which such person is a

---

[195]G Pienaar 'Security of communal land tenure by registration of individualised title—Is the Communal Land Rights Bill of 2003 the final solution?' (2004) 67 *THRHR* 244–263 provides a detailed analysis and discussion of this function of the original Bill, arguing that the Act would bring a big improvement but still falls short of expectations in two areas: (*a*) the need for a suitable, preferably computerized land information system reflecting the fragmented rights that are administered in the administrative system set up by the Act; and (*b*) a better fit between the role of traditional leaders in the proposed administrative system and their role in terms of the Constitution and the Traditional Leadership and Governance Framework Act 41 of 2003.

[196]Sections 19 and 20 deal with the community rules, the requirements for their registration and amendment.

[197]Section 19(2) and (3).

[198]Section 3.

[199]Section 5.

spouse, jointly in undivided shares irrespective of the matrimonial property regime applicable to such marriage and must, on confirmation or conversion in terms of section 18(3), be registered in the names of all such spouses. Section 4(3) provides that a woman is entitled to the same legally secure tenure, rights in or to land and benefits from land as is a man, and no law, community or other rule, practice or usage may discriminate against any person on the ground of the gender of such person. As in the case of the Communal Property Associations Act 28 of 1996, the rules of a community will have to accommodate constitutional equality and non-discrimination requirements. Section 21 of the Act requires that every community must establish a land administration committee that represents the community, exercising the powers and duties conferred on it by the Act and the rules of the community.[200] The committee is responsible for administration of the community's land, allocation of new order rights to persons, including women, the disabled and the youth, in accordance with the law; the registration of communal land and of new order rights; establishing and maintaining registers and records of all new order rights and transactions affecting them; promoting and safeguarding the interests of the community and its members in their land; promoting co-operation among community members and others in dealing with land; assisting in the resolution of land disputes; liaison with the relevant municipality, Board and any other institution concerning the provision of services and the planning and development of the communal land of the community; and all related matters.[201] If the community has a recognized traditional council it may exercise the functions of the land administration committee, but then the composition of the council has to comply with the democratic and gender-sensitive requirements of section 22 regarding the composition of the committee. In addition, great care is taken to ensure that the Land Rights Boards established in terms of section 25[202] should also reflect the interests of women, the disabled and children in their composition.[203]

The fourth characteristic is that provision is made for comparable redress should it prove impossible to secure the existing tenure of a specific holder of an old order right. Section 12 provides that the Minister may, on application by the holder of an old order right which is insecure as contemplated in section 25(6) of the Constitution and which cannot be made legally secure, determine an award of comparable redress,

---

[200] See section 24.

[201] Section 24.

[202] The Boards are intended to advise the Minister and to advise and assist communities with regard to sustainable land ownership and use, the development of land and the provision of access to land on an equitable basis, liaise with all spheres of government, civil and other institutions, and monitor compliance with the Constitution and the Act: section 28.

[203] Section 26 requires that seven members on each Board should come from the affected communities, of whom at least one each must represent the interests of child-headed households, persons with disabilities, the youth as defined in section 1 of the National Youth Commission Act 19 of 1996, and female-headed households. In addition, at least a third of the Board members must be women. However, when section 2 applies (when the recognized traditional council fulfils the role of the community) just one person is responsible to promote the interests of women, children etcetera.

which may comprise land other than the land to which the applicable old order right relates or a right in such other land; compensation in money or in any other form; or a combination of the above.

Generally speaking the Act embodies an attempt to ensure that those whose communal-style tenure of land is insecure because of past racially discriminatory laws or practices will have access to either secure tenure or comparable redress.[204] At least on the surface it seems reasonably possible that determinations and conversions of insecure land tenure in terms of the Act can result in more secure and equitable land rights. The greatest problems will no doubt occur in situations where the democratic and gender-sensitive land administration foreseen in the Act comes into conflict with established tribal custom that is not democratic and that discriminates against certain members on the basis of gender or family status. It remains to be seen whether the Acts finds application on a large scale and whether it causes conflict.

6.3.8 Constitutional issues

A larger number of—more serious—constitutional issues have been raised in case law with regard to tenure reform laws than any other land reform initiative. One possible explanation for this phenomenon is the fact that tenure reform, much more than restitution or redistribution, involves changes in the law that have direct and clearly perceptible restrictive effects on existing land rights, without compensation. Both restitution and redistribution of land depend largely upon either the use of state land or the acquisition of private land, against payment of either an agreed purchase price or market-related compensation. By contrast, tenure reform mostly involves adjustment of previously weak or vulnerable (black) use and occupation rights, with the inevitable concomitant effect that existing and conflicting or competing (white) land rights are weakened or restricted accordingly, without compensation. This effect is most visible in eviction cases under various land tenure reform laws, where the courts have struggled to come to terms with the fact that anti-eviction measures—intended to strengthen the use and occupation interests of vulnerable land users—inevitably restrict the common law right of landowners to evict unwanted occupiers easily and speedily.

The effect of tenure reform on existing (white) land rights is particularly troublesome when ownership is seen in the traditional way as the strongest and most important of all land rights, which means that an owner is entitled to undisturbed possession unless a contrary right is proven.[205] When ownership is regarded as the paradigm

---

[204]Compare the assessments of W du Plessis, N Olivier & J Pienaar 'A new dispensation for communal land and minerals' (2002) 17 *SA Public Law* 409–439 at 420–425; G Pienaar 'Security of communal land tenure by registration of individualised title—Is the Communal Land Rights Bill of 2003 the final solution?' (2004) 67 *THRHR* 244–263.
[205]See generally AJ van der Walt 'Property rights and hierarchies of power: A critical evaluation of land-reform policy in South Africa' (1999) 64 *Koers* 259–294. Compare further with regard to the
(continued on next page ...)

property right, it appears logical to require that new restrictions should only be imposed on existing ownership rights when they are either justified by the owner's consent or authorized on the basis of strong public interest considerations. In such a situation the statutory imposition of anti-eviction restrictions on a landowner's very strong common law right to evict appears quite drastic, especially in view of the constitutional protection that property enjoys in terms of section 25. This makes it look natural that landowners would object to the anti-eviction restrictions and that the courts would be circumspect and conservative in applying them. If existing rights are purchased or taken over by expropriation against compensation the effects are generally accepted without too much complaint, but when existing rights are affected without any compensation—as in the case of tenure reform laws and especially the anti-eviction provisions—stronger reaction is to be expected.

Reaction against the restrictive effect of the anti-eviction provisions in land tenure reform legislation has adopted two related but distinguishable forms in case law. On the one hand, the most dramatic reaction was to reject the land reform legislation that imposes new restrictions on ownership outright, especially based on the argument that the relevant laws or provisions were unconstitutional for being in conflict with the property guarantee in section 25. A less dramatic reaction appeared in cases where the relevant statutory provisions were not necessarily rejected for being unconstitutional, but where their effect on existing rights was limited through restrictive interpretation.

The most conspicuous example of the dismissive approach that challenges the constitutional validity of tenure reform laws is the decision of the Witwatersrand High Court in *Joubert and Others v Van Rensburg and Others*.[206] A community of landless people occupied residential plots in an informal township that did not comply

---

(... from previous page)
eviction cases and their background in land reform laws AJ van der Walt 'Exclusivity of ownership, security of tenure, and eviction orders: A model to evaluate South African land-reform legislation' 2002 *TSAR* 254–289; AJ van der Walt 'Exclusivity of ownership, security of tenure and eviction orders: A critical evaluation of recent case law' (2002) 18 *SAJHR* 372–420; AJ van der Walt 'Ownership and eviction. Constitutional rights in private law' (2005) 9 *Edinburgh LR* 32–64 (comparing South African and German case law) at 40–49; T Roux 'Continuity and change in a transforming legal order: The impact of section 26(3) of the Constitution on South African law' (2004) 121 *SALJ* 466–492; T Roux 'Pro-poor court, anti-poor outcomes: Explaining the performance of the South African Land Claims Court' (2004) 20 *SAJHR* 511–543. See further R Youngs 'Human rights in the housing sphere: German comparisons' (2004) 15 *The King's College LJ* 145–158 (comparing German case with English case law).

[206] 2001 (1) SA 753 (W). The discussion of this case below is based on passages from AJ van der Walt 'Exclusivity of ownership, security of tenure and eviction orders: A critical evaluation of recent case law' (2002) 18 *SAJHR* 372–420 at 379–385; see footnote 164 above and accompanying text. An application to appeal directly to the Constitutional Court against the order in this case was denied by the Constitutional Court in *Katazile Mkangeli and Others v Joubert and Others* 2001 (2) SA 1191 (CC). The decision *a quo* was overturned by the Supreme Court of Appeal in *Mkangeli and Others v Joubert and Others* 2002 (4) SA 36 (SCA).

with the applicable development laws.[207] Landowners in the vicinity objected to the settlement and approached the court for an ejectment order against the trustees and beneficiaries of the trust and other occupiers of the settlement, based on the lack of compliance with (and consequent contravention of) planning and development laws and the nuisance caused by the settlement. The Witwatersrand High Court granted what amounts to an indirect eviction order based on the duty of the respondent owners and occupiers of the land to comply with the applicable laws and to abate a nuisance.[208]

The interplay between the common law, tenure reform legislation and the Constitution in the foundational logic of the decision is interesting. The eviction order was not based on the superiority of the claimants' (neighbouring landowners) right to possession[209] or on the court's extensive discussion of the constitutional validity of the Extension of Security of Tenure Act 62 of 1997.[210] In the final analysis, the eviction was granted against occupiers who had rights in the land[211] or at least occupied

---

[207]The community previously unlawfully invaded and occupied private property. Private landowners in the vicinity assisted them to acquire a piece of privately owned agricultural land and to set up a trust to purchase and manage the land. Members of the community were allowed to acquire 'rights' to settle on individually demarcated plots on the newly acquired land by making a one-off 'donation' to the trust. Having made these donations and taken possession of the plots allocated to them, the occupiers regarded themselves as owners of these plots. The trust proceeded to 'develop' the land and establish an informal township, and the community moved to the new settlement peacefully, assisted by their benefactors and former neighbours, without complying with the laws that control the establishment of townships. The settlement contravened the Town Planning and Township Ordinance 15 of 1986 (T), but could have been legalised in terms of laws such as the Development Facilitation Act 67 of 1995 or the Communal Property Associations Act 28 of 1996.
[208]Paras [45]–[46] at 799G–802F. The crucial passage is par [45] at 800H–I: 'In regard to ejectment as such it must be remembered that ejectment cannot in this application be granted on the well-known basis of a landowner ejecting an unlawful holder. The respondents are required to bring themselves within lawful limits. If they comply they are not ejected. If they fail to comply it proves that the initial remedies granted by the Court are proved to be [sic] inadequate and ejectment of the excess number of occupiers [beyond the number allowed by planning laws] comes in as a strengthened way of getting matters within legal limits.'
[209]As appears from the facts, such a claim would not have been feasible, because the land was owned by the trust, who allowed the occupiers to occupy the land.
[210]When approached for permission to appeal directly to the Constitutional Court, the latter decided that the initial order was based on private-law issues relating to the validity of the trust, ownership of the land, nuisance and the appropriate remedies for it; and not on the constitutional validity of the Extension of Security of Tenure Act 62 of 1997: *Katazile Mkangeli and Others v Joubert and Others* 2001 (2) SA 1191 (CC) par [12] at 1196H.
[211]When reading the decision it is constantly necessary to remind oneself that the community occupied the land with the permission of the landowners, who were members of the community and who acquired the land for the purpose of settlement by the community, albeit in contravention of planning laws. This consideration is particularly relevant when evaluating passages where the court indirectly compares the occupiers in this case with 'spoliators' and 'impostors' (par [40.1] at 795H–J); or as the 'grabbing' party (par [37.1.5] at 793G) or as occupiers who 'insist[s] on taking— gratis' (par [43.2] at 797G).

the land with the permission of the landowners,[212] and therefore one might have
expected the Extension of Security of Tenure Act 62 of 1997 to apply but, although
the court analysed the Act extensively,[213] it not only refused to grant a controlled
eviction order as intended by the Act, but expressed the opinion[214] that the Act was
unconstitutional because it allowed arbitrary[215] deprivation of (presumably neighbouring landowners') property[216] in conflict with section 25(1) and the deprivation
could not be justified in terms of section 36(1)[217] of the Constitution. In the court's

---

[212]The trial court held that the trustees were the owners of the land and that—bar the statutory
provision that only one residence and one family was allowed to occupy the land lawfully—the
trustees had the right, based on their ownership, to occupy the land: par [12.1] at 773A. The
residents believed that they were owners of the land although in fact they had nothing more than
a contractual agreement, in terms of the trust, with the trustees, who owned the land: par [12.3] at
773E–H.

[213]Paras [26.1]–[44.3] at 799F–785E.

[214]Which apparently did not amount to a finding of unconstitutionality: par [44] at 798E–799F. In
terms of section 172 of the Constitution any court which decides a constitutional matter in its
jurisdiction must declare that any law or conduct that is inconsistent with the Constitution is invalid
to the extent of its inconsistency, something that was apparently considered unnecessary by the
High Court in this case. As pointed out in the Constitutional Court, the constitutional validity of
the Act was not raised as an issue in the papers and was not argued before the court in this matter:
Katazile Mkangeli and Others v Joubert and Others 2001 (2) SA 1191 (CC) par [9] at 195F.

[215]Several arguments were forwarded by the court to support the conclusion that the Act allowed
for arbitrary deprivation, the main thrust apparently being that the law allowed unlawful land
invaders to choose whom to burden with their unlawful occupation of land, holding it on their
own terms: par [39] at 795A–G. The Act is characterised as being in conflict with section 25(1)
because it permits (in the sense of protecting) 'arbitrary' (in the sense of capricious) unlawful
invasion and occupation (by private individuals or groups) of private land: par [39.4] at 795G. This
passage bears no relation and makes no reference to the constitutional discourse on what constitutes
arbitrary state action; see AJ van der Walt *Constitutional property clauses: A comparative analysis* (1999)
333–335; *First National Bank of SA Ltd t/a Wesbank v Commissioner for the South African Revenue
Services and Another; First National Bank of SA Ltd t/a Wesbank v Minister of Finance* 2002 (4) SA 768
(CC) paras [61]–[109] at 797E–815C (see further chapter 4.5).

[216]The court's conclusion that the Act allows deprivation of property seems to rest on two pillars
that are not clearly connected in logic. One line of argument, which takes into account the fact
that the occupiers in this case had the consent of the landowners, is that the Act purports to raise
what is unlawful occupation (in contravention of planning laws) to the level of lawful, *inter alia* by
preventing the court from intervening (and evicting): par [35] at 791J–792F. A second line of argument, which looks irrelevant under the circumstances in view of the fact that the occupiers had the
consent of the landowner, is that occupation, and specifically unlawful occupation, is preferred to
and raised above ownership of land, subjecting the common-law rights of landowners to the whims
of land invaders ('grabbers' in the language of par [37.1.5] at 793G) and to statutory 'indefinite
leases' (paras [36]–[37] at 792F–794H) and similar impositions, without a clear indication of when
the deprivations should be allowed. The provision that eviction was allowed only when it was 'just
and equitable' is described as 'an unguided missile' (par [37.1.2] at 793D, par [44.3] at 799F).

[217]Mostly because the Act was not considered 'law of general application' as meant in section 36(1)
in that it was biased (in favour of occupiers and against landowners: par [42.1] at 797B–C), too broad
(protecting everyone instead of only those in 'situations which really called for protection': par [42.1]

(continued on next page …)

view, the eviction of the occupiers could therefore not be precluded or restricted by the Extension of Security of Tenure Act 62 of 1997.

In view of these remarks and the court's focus on the community's failure to comply with planning and building laws one might expect that the Prevention of Illegal Eviction from and Unlawful Occupation of Land Act 19 of 1998 should have applied, which would again have provided the occupiers with some protection against eviction, but the court held that this Act applied only to situations where the landowner sued for eviction, which was not the case here.[218] The constitutional anti-eviction provision in section 26(3) was not raised or considered at all, probably because the court did not regard its decision as a 'real' eviction order.

The result is that, since the eviction was based on nuisance rather than on the *rei vindicatio*, the protection of land reform laws against possible harm or unfairness resulting from eviction could be bypassed. In addition, the anti-eviction measures in the land reform laws were held to be inapplicable and thus not allowed to protect the occupiers by posing additional limitations or requirements on the granting of the eviction order. Finally, the court did not even consider the possibility that the anti-eviction provision in the Constitution could have any effect on eviction in terms of the common law or that the common law should be developed in terms of constitutional principles—the sacrosanct superiority of the common law and of existing common law rights was taken for granted and regarded as sufficient reason to decide the case in the neighbours' favour. Accordingly, the effective eviction order granted by the court to neighbouring landowners on the basis of nuisance was not allowed to be restricted or controlled in any way by the constitutional anti-eviction principle or by the potentially applicable land-reform statutes. The decision not only failed to subject the common law to constitutional and statutory restrictions but effectively extended its reach by allowing landowners to evict unwanted occupiers not only

---

(... *from previous page*)

at 797B) and too narrow (protecting only occupiers of agricultural land, while the real need for protection was on urban land: par [42.2] at 797D–E). The court argued that the (commonly accepted) approach in terms of which 'every statute other than a private Act is in a certain sense of general application ... will render the constitutional safeguards in ss 25(1) and 36(1) meaningless': par [42.1] at 797A–B. No reference is made to applicable case law or other authorities such as *S v Makwanyane* 1995 (3) SA 391 (CC) [156]; *Dawood and Others v Minister of Home Affairs* 2000 (3) SA 936 (CC) [47]; *President of the Republic of South Africa v Hugo* 1997 (4) SA 1 (CC) [76], [102]–[104]. Compare S Woolman 'Limitation' in M Chaskalson et al (eds) *Constitutional law of South Africa* (2nd service ed 1998) 12–28 ff; J De Waal, I Currie & MG Erasmus *The human rights handbook* (4th ed 2001) 147–154 for a discussion and further references, and see chapters 2.5, 4.4 and 4.5.

[218] Par [25.4.1] at 785B. Flemming AJP nevertheless considered it appropriate to add that the Act 'elevates unlawful occupation above ownership in the sense that even if unlawful occupation is proved, the court can be guided and must be guided by considerations (if any such conduct exists) which are extraneous to the real rights of the owner and the absence of any rights on the part of the occupier' (par [25.4.2] at 785D). The possibility that the Act nevertheless applied and that it meant that an eviction order could not be granted unless the owner launched or supported the application was not considered.

from their own but also from neighbouring land. The court's restrictive reading of the reform laws and extensive application of the common law is echoed in its strongly-worded indications[219] that the court saw itself as fighting a losing battle to uphold the rule of law and the sanctity of existing land rights against a perceived threat of land invasion, lawlessness and land reform.[220] The decision displays no sense of understanding of the role that eviction played in the establishment of apartheid land law or openness to the necessity for and the justification of land reform[221]—on the contrary, it is made very clear that the sanctity of private ownership is considered the highest good, that it is under threat from laws that are perceived to permit and support land invasions and general lawlessness, and that the court sees its duty in protecting ownership against that threat.

The court relied on the constitutional guarantee of ownership against arbitrary deprivation, but the real basis of the decision is the landowner's common law right to undisturbed possession and enjoyment of his or her property, which is argued to include the right to have a nuisance on neighbouring land abated at practically any cost.[222] If the nuisance is caused by (technically) unlawful occupation of the neighbouring land, a court should order the occupiers to leave the land, without considering the socio-economic context of homelessness and without making any effort to balance the need for lawful development against the need for speedy and large-scale provision of housing. Paradoxically, this means that residents whose use of land is unlawful for technical reasons, even though they own the land or occupy it with consent of the owner, are in a worse position than unlawful land invaders: like unlawful land invaders, they can be evicted from the land, but they will not enjoy the protection of the Prevention of Illegal Eviction from and Unlawful Occupation of Land Act 19 of 1998.

The Supreme Court of Appeal overturned this decision,[223] holding that the High Court had no jurisdiction to grant an eviction order in the first place because eviction

---

[219] In places, the strong language of the decision creates the impression of irritability and frustration with what are perceived as the negative effects of the transformation process. See the citations in AJ van der Walt 'Exclusivity of ownership, security of tenure, and eviction orders: A critical evaluation of recent case law' (2002) 18 *SAJHR* 371–419 at 383 footnote 36.

[220] The implication is that the land-reform laws, at least if interpreted in a certain way, would condone and promote lawlessness.

[221] Apart from a general introductory statement to the effect that the court had to strike a balance between opposing rights and interests: par [3.2] at 764C.

[222] Technically, the argument is not new in South African law. There are many similar examples from the apartheid years, where occupiers were also evicted from land (even when they occupied it with the landowner's consent) because they erected and occupied structures that did not comply with planning laws. See AJ van der Walt 'Towards the development of post-apartheid land law: An exploratory survey' (1990) 23 *De Jure* 1–45 at 30–31 with reference to the apartheid-era eviction decisions in *Vena v George Municipality* 1987 (4) SA 29 (C) and *Port Nolloth Municipality v Xhalisa and Others; Luwalala and Others v Municipality of Port Nolloth* 1991 (3) SA 98 (C).

[223] The appeal was heard by the Supreme Court of Appeal because the real basis of the order given by the trial court was the common law and not the land tenure reform legislation or the Constitution

(continued on next page …)

of occupiers who had the consent of the landowner was controlled by the Extension
of Security of Tenure Act 62 of 1997, which granted exclusive jurisdiction with
regard to evictions to the magistrates' courts and the Land Claims Court.[224] Despite
explicit[225] and implicit rejection of the trial court's views on the suitability and constitutional validity of the land tenure reform laws, and although the occupiers were
effectively protected by the Supreme Court of Appeal's decision, neither the Constitutional Court nor the Supreme Court of Appeal entered into a discussion of the
substantive issues concerning the constitutional validity of the Extension of Security
of Tenure Act 62 of 1997, preferring to overturn the initial decision on more or less
technical jurisdiction issues. However, both the SCA and the Constitutional Court
expressed their displeasure with the trial court's anti-reform statements.

Another direct constitutional challenge was mounted against the Extension of
Security of Tenure Act 62 of 1997 in *Nhlabati and Others v Fick*.[226] The case concerned
the right to bury lawful occupiers of agricultural land and their family members on the
farm without consent and against the will of the landowner. In two earlier decisions[227]

(... from previous page)
In an earlier decision concerning direct access on appeal, the Constitutional Court held that the
section of the initial decision that dealt with the constitutionality of the Extension of Security of
Tenure Act 62 of 1997 Act was *obiter*. As pointed out in the Constitutional Court, the constitutional
validity of the Act was not raised as an issue in the papers and was not argued before the court in
this matter: *Katazile Mkangeli and Others v Joubert and Others* 2001 (2) SA 1191 (CC) par [9] at 195F.
The Constitutional Court held that the Witwatersrand High Court's conclusion in this regard was
not the basis of the orders granted in the case, that it had no force and effect, and that there was
no need for the Constitutional Court to make a declaration to that effect or to hear the appeal in
order to say so: par [14] at 197B–C.

[224] *Mkangeli and Others v Joubert and Others* 2002 (4) SA 36 (SCA) par [25] at 47E–F. See further
Magodi and Others v Van Rensburg [2001] 4 All SA 485 (LCC).

[225] The SCA found it necessary to repudiate the remarks concerning the suitability of the Act
explicitly, stating that these remarks were unwarranted and 'should have been avoided': per Brand
JA par [26] at 47G–48B. The Constitutional Court was critical of the trial court's treatment of the
constitutionality issue: *Katazile Mkangeli and Others v Joubert and Others* 2001 (2) SA 1191 (CC) par
[10] at 195G–196A.

[226] 2003 (7) BCLR 806 (LCC); see W du Plessis, N Olivier & J Pienaar 'Expropriation, restitution
and land redistribution: An answer to land problems in South Africa?' (2003) 18 *SA Public Law* 491–
514 at 501–504.

[227] *Serole and Another v Pienaar* 2000 (1) SA 328 (LCC); *Nkosi and Another v Bührmann* 2002 (1) SA
372 (SCA). On the LCC and SCA judgments see T Roux 'Pro-poor court, anti-poor outcomes:
Explaining the performance of the South African Land Claims Court' (2004) 20 *SAJHR* 511–543
at 527–530. The amendment and its history are discussed by the court in *Nhlabati and Others v Fick*
2003 (7) BCLR 806 (LCC) paras [16]–[19] at 811G–812I. On the SCA judgment see AJ van der
Walt 'Property rights v religious rights: *Bührmann v Nkosi*' (2002) 13 *Stell LR* 394–414; W du
Plessis, N Olivier & J Pienaar 'Progress in land reform, illegal occupation of land and judicial
interpretation' (2002) 17 *SA Public Law* 178–209 at 186–187. See further PJ Badenhorst, JM Pienaar
& H Mostert (assisted by M van Rooyen) *Silberberg and Schoeman's The law of property* (4th ed 2003)
503; W du Plessis, N Olivier & J Pienaar 'Land reform: A never-ending process' (2000) 15 *SA Public
Law* 230–254 at 241–243.

it had been decided that the legislature did not intend to include the right to establish a grave in the specific use rights listed in section 6(2) of the Act, and subsequently the Act was amended to include the new section 6(2)(dA), which now includes the right to bury a deceased occupier or member of the occupier's family (who, at the time of that person's death, was residing on the land) in accordance with their religion or cultural belief, if an established practice in respect of the land exists.[228] The occupier enjoys this burial right in balance with the rights of the owner or person in charge of the land and subject to reasonable conditions that may be imposed by the owner or person in charge. In the *Nhlabati* case the owner refused permission for burial of a member of the occupiers' family, arguing that section 6(2)(dA) of the Act was unconstitutional because it violated the protection given to property by section 25 of the Constitution.[229]

The Land Claims Court considered this argument against the background of the Constitutional Court decision in *First National Bank of SA Ltd t/a Wesbank v Commissioner, South African Revenue Service; First National Bank of SA Ltd t/a Wesbank v Minister of Finance*.[230] In view of the analysis of the phrase 'arbitrary conviction' in *FNB* the court first decided[231] that section 6(2)(dA) does not authorise arbitrary appropriation (deprivation) of a grave, because (*a*) the right to appropriate a grave must be balanced with the right of the owner, which means that the right of the owner could in certain circumstances conceivably outweigh the right to a grave;[232] (*b*) an occupier has the right to establish a grave only if there is an established practice of giving permission for burials in the past, which presupposes some kind of pre-existing con-

---

[228]'Established practice' is defined in section 1 of the Act as a practice in terms of which the owner or person in charge of the land or his or her predecessor in title routinely gave permission to people living on the land to bury deceased members of their family on that land in accordance with their religion or cultural belief.

[229]A similar argument was raised and considered but not clearly decided in one of the earlier decisions on burial rights, where it was said that it would amount to an appropriation if an occupier were allowed to take a grave site without permission and against the will of the landowner: *Nkosi and Another v Bührmann* 2002 (1) SA 372 (SCA) par [38] at 384I–J. In *Serole and Another v Pienaar* 2000 (1) SA 328 (LCC) par [16] at 335D it was said that the granting of such a right would amount to granting of a servitude. See the references in *Nhlabati and Others v Fick* 2003 (7) BCLR 806 (LCC) par [27] at 815B–C, par [32] at 817E–F. A second argument, that section 6(2)(dA) was unconstitutional because it intruded upon a functional area of exclusive provincial legislative competence, is not discussed here but was also dismissed: paras [21]–[26] at 813D–815B.

[230]2002 (4) SA 768 (CC). See the discussion of the case in chapter 4.5, 4.6 and 4.7.3 and compare chapter 5.3, 5.8.5 and chapter 7.4. See further on the *FNB* decision T Roux 'Section 25' in S Woolman et al (eds) *Constitutional law of South Africa* (2nd ed 2003 original service Dec 2003) 46-2–46-5, 46-21–46-25.

[231]The *FNB* methodology requires the court to consider the possibility of unconstitutional deprivation first, while raising the issue of unconstitutional expropriation only if there is no such deprivation or if it could be justified under section 36. See the discussion of the *FNB* methodology in chapter 4.5.

[232]*Nhlabati and Others v Fick* 2003 (7) BCLR 806 (LCC) par [31] at 816I.

sensus between the landowner and the occupiers about burials;[233] (c) the establishment of the grave would in most cases constitute a relatively minor intrusion into the landowner's property rights;[234] and (d) the right to bury an occupier or a family member according to section 6(2)(dA) was enacted to fulfil the state's constitutional mandate to provide occupiers legally secure tenure. Considering the importance of the religious or cultural beliefs of many occupiers regarding burial of family members close to their residence, the constitutional mandate would in most cases be sufficient to justify the deprivation of some incidents of ownership.[235]

Again in line with the *FNB* approach, the court next considered the possibility that section 6(2)(dA) might constitute or authorise an unconstitutional expropriation of property. In its earlier *Serole* decision[236] the Land Claims Court stated that granting of a right to establish a grave as of right would amount to the granting of a servitude, which would amount to a *de facto* expropriation without compensation. In *Nhlabati* the court again considered this argument and its implications for the constitutional validity of section 6(2)(dA), without deciding that the section indeed amounted to such an appropriation.[237] The court pointed out that statutory permission for what amounts to an expropriation of a right could either imply that compensation was due or that the absence of compensation was justifiable under section 36 of the Constitution, and concluded that the statutory obligation of a landowner to allow an occupier to appropriate a gravesite on his or her land without compensation is reasonable and justifiable as meant in section 36, having regard to the following circumstances: (a) the right does not constitute a major intrusion on the landowner's property rights; (b) the right is subject to balancing with the landowner's property rights and may sometimes be subject to them; (c) the right exists only where there is an established past practice with regard to grave sites; and (d) the right will enable occupiers to comply with religious or cultural beliefs that forms an important part of their security of tenure, and giving statutory recognition to their security of tenure is in accordance with the constitutional mandate.[238] Accordingly, even if one accepted that section 6(2)(dA) authorised expropriation of grave sites without compensation, in conflict with section 25 of the Constitution,[239] this result would be reasonable and justifiable

---

[233] Par [31] at 817A–B. Note that it is not required that the owner must have allowed the occupier or family involved in a specific dispute to bury their family members in the past—the question is merely whether burials of occupiers took place in the past or not. Moreover, it is the owner of the land in the abstract sense that is involved and not the specific owner at the time of a particular dispute, with the result that a practice would also be established if previous owners allowed burials.
[234] Par [31] at 817B–C.
[235] Par [31] at 817C–D.
[236] *Serole and Another v Pienaar* 2000 (1) SA 328 (LCC) par [16] at 335D. *Serole* was decided by Gildenhuys J, who was again one of the judges in *Nhlabati*.
[237] *Nhlabati and Others v Fick* 2003 (7) BCLR 806 (LCC) paras [32]–[35] at 817D–819E.
[238] Par [35] at 819A–E.
[239] The court made no finding on this point, merely accepting the possibility for argument's sake: par [32] at 817F.

under section 36 of the Constitution. In the final result the constitutional challenge against section 6(2)(dA) was therefore dismissed.

The court's assumption (without deciding the issue) that the establishment of a grave site in terms of section 6(2)(dA) of the Act could constitute an expropriation of a servitude without compensation may well be debatable,[240] but the fact remains that the court decided the constitutional challenge with reference to the social context and the reform-oriented nature of the Act, instead of simply against the background of the presumed inviolability of the common law right of ownership. In this regard *Nhlabati* is one of the most interesting and significant cases to date dealing with the clash between existing common law property rights and land reform legislation that creates conflicting property interests.[241]

Apart from outright constitutional validity challenges, there are also a number of cases in which constitutional issues regarding land tenure reform have been raised more indirectly. The common characteristic in all these cases is that, in instances where either the constitutional or a statutory tenure reform provision was perceived to pose a challenge to or involve a diminution of existing common law property rights, the courts restricted the perceived threat by ignoring, denying or avoiding the application or the implications of section 26(3) of the Constitution[242] or of the reform law or provision involved.[243]

In the first set of cases the question was whether section 26(3) of the Constitution brought about a direct and automatic amendment of the common law, in that it requires additional considerations to be taken into account before an eviction order can be granted. The common law merely requires proof of the applicant's ownership and occupation by someone else,[244] but if the courts have to take into account all relevant circumstances the respondent's social, economic or personal situation might affect the outcome, which would undermine the owner's common law right to a relatively easy and speedy eviction process. The courts have been divided on this issue.

---

[240]See further on this issue chapters 2.5 (limitation issues regarding section 25), 5.2 (definition of expropriation), 5.4 (constructive expropriation) and 5.8 (compensation).

[241]This issue is discussed more fully in chapter 7.4; see also chapter 5.8.5.

[242]The section provides that no person shall be evicted from their home without a court order; that such a court order shall only be granted upon consideration of all relevant considerations; and that no law shall permit arbitrary evictions. See further the discussion in 6.4.3 below and compare chapter 7.3.

[243]The following section is based on and draws from the more detailed discussion in two articles: AJ van der Walt 'Exclusivity of ownership, security of tenure, and eviction orders: A model to evaluate South African land-reform legislation' 2002 *TSAR* 254–289; AJ van der Walt 'Exclusivity of ownership, security of tenure and eviction orders: A critical evaluation of recent case law' (2002) 18 *SAJHR* 372–420. See further especially T Roux 'Continuity and change in a transforming legal order: The impact of section 26(3) of the Constitution on South African law' (2004) 121 *SALJ* 466–492. Further references to literature and the relevant laws and cases are provided in these articles.

[244]*Chetty v Naidoo* 1974 (3) SA 13 (A) at 20A. See AJ van der Walt 'Exclusivity of ownership, security of tenure, and eviction orders: A model to evaluate South African land-reform legislation' 2002 *TSAR* 254–289 at 256–258 for a full discussion of the common law position.

In *Ross v South Peninsula Municipality*[245] the Cape High Court held that section 26(3) amended the common law with regard to eviction by placing and additional burden of proof on the applicant, who must inform the courts of circumstances that would justify the eviction. However, in *Betta Eiendomme (Pty) Ltd v Ekple-Epoh*[246] the Witwatersrand High Court disagreed, holding that 'normal' landlord-tenant situations were not affected by section 26(3) at all.[247] The decision in *Betta Eiendomme* clearly assumes that the common law sets the benchmark, and that the pattern of property holdings as protected in and by the common law is what is normal, to be accepted unless the opposite is proven.[248] The same restrictive approach was followed in *Ellis v Viljoen*,[249]

---

[245] 2000 (1) SA 589 (C); see AJ van der Walt 'Exclusivity of ownership, security of tenure and eviction orders: A critical evaluation of recent case law' (2002) 18 *SAJHR* 372–420 at 394–404. See further T Roux 'Continuity and change in a transforming legal order: The impact of section 26(3) of the Constitution on South African law' (2004) 121 *SALJ* 466–492 at 475–477.

[246] 2000 (4) SA 468 (W). See AJ van der Walt 'Exclusivity of ownership, security of tenure and eviction orders: A critical evaluation of recent case law' (2002) 18 *SAJHR* 372–420 at 397; T Roux 'Continuity and change in a transforming legal order: The impact of section 26(3) of the Constitution on South African law' (2004) 121 *SALJ* 466–492 at 478–482.

[247] The court argued that (*a*) the common law makes it clear that a landowner is entitled to possession of his or her property (par [6.2] at 472E, par [9] at 475B–C); (*b*) the common-law right of ownership 'as recognized before the Constitution has not been affected by the Constitution', and ownership 'still carries within it the right to possession' (par [10.1] at 475D–F); (*c*) neither the text of section 26(3) (par [7.2] at 472I, par [7.3] at 473A, especially par [7.4] at 473D) nor the constitutional obligation to promote the values that underlie the Constitution or the spirit, purport and objects of the Bill of Rights (par [10.1] at 475D–E) requires a restriction of the owner's rights as against an illegal occupier of the land; and (*d*) in the absence of constitutional or legislative interference with the owner's rights, the mere fact that the plaintiff is owner and that the defendant is in possession renders it 'right and proper' that the owner be granted an eviction order 'against someone who has no business interfering with the possession' (par [10.2] at 475F–G). The court arrived at this conclusion by way of a rather restrictive reading of the constitutional provision in section 26(3) (and, by implication, the land-reform statutes in general), arguing that it was aimed at nothing more than protecting lawful owners and occupiers against a repetition of apartheid-style evictions and forced removals: par [7.2] at 472I–J.

[248] Paras [6.2], [10.1], [10.2] at 472E, 475D–G. The clearest statement to this effect appears in par [6.2] at 472E–G: 'I am not ignoring the need to develop the law. There are situations, often novel factual situations, where the law can incline in one direction rather than the other. Policy has really always been part of adjudicating. Any such opportunity or need is clearly distinguishable from the present situation. There is absolute clarity that as from the time when the facts arose which caused "ownership" to vest in applicant, it is applicant only who is entitled to possession except insofar as applicant's own acts burden that right. There is no novelty or uncertain fringe areas. The enquiry must be about what, if anything, in the Constitution conveys with adequate clarity (*a*) that a destruction of such rights or a burden on such rights was created (or authorised); (*b*) how far that detraction goes; and (*c*) if there is no clarity on both these issues, what justification is found in the Constitution not to honour the logical and settled leaning against interference with the existing law when clarity is not given.'

[249] 2001 (5) BCLR 487 (C) 497E–H. See T Roux 'Continuity and change in a transforming legal order: The impact of section 26(3) of the Constitution on South African law' (2004) 121 *SALJ* 466–492 at 482–484.

where the Cape High Court reiterated the view that the common-law right to eviction was a protected property right under section 25 of the Constitution, with the result that an interpretation that deprived private landowners of the common-law right to eviction would amount to an arbitrary deprivation of property in conflict with section 25(1). If one accepts that the Constitution sets the tone and not the common law, that the common law exists only in as far as it does not conflict with the Constitution, the approach set out by the court in *Betta Eiendomme* and *Ellis v Viljoen* is wrong, because then the position would be that the Constitution has amended the common-law right of a landowner to obtain an eviction merely by proving that he or she is the owner and that someone else is in occupation. In view of the constitutional provision, the position would then have to be that a court may no longer grant such an eviction order—if it pertains to residential property—without first considering all the relevant circumstances.

The Supreme Court of Appeal overturned both *Ross* and *Betta Eiendomme* in part, while upholding the restrictive approach to the effect of the Constitution. In *Brisley v Drotsky*[250] the majority of the Court held (contrary to the finding in *Betta Eiendomme*) that section 26(3) of the Constitution was horizontally enforceable[251] and that an eviction order may, in cases of this nature, only be granted once all relevant circumstances have been considered. However, it also decided (contrary to the decision in *Ross*) that section 26(3) did not grant the courts the discretion to deprive a landowner of an eviction order that he or she would otherwise—in the absence of a statutory or other right to occupy—have been entitled to, based on the personal circumstances of the occupier and her family or the availability of alternative accommodation. In the absence of explicit statutory provisions, the personal circumstances of the occupier and the availability of alternative accommodation are therefore not 'relevant circumstances' that section 26(3) forces or allows the courts to take into consideration when deciding whether to grant an eviction order.[252] What other circumstances, apart from the applicant's ownership and the respondent's occupation, could be taken into consideration are not made clear in the decision. In the absence of explicit statutory authority that not only grants the courts an extraordinary discretion to depart from the common law but also specifies the exact factors upon which

---

[250] 2002 (4) SA 1 (SCA) paras [35]–[46] at 19C–22E. For an extensive analysis see T Roux 'Continuity and change in a transforming legal order: The impact of section 26(3) of the Constitution on South African law' (2004) 121 *SALJ* 466–492 at 484–491. As was indicated earlier the courts are still not clear on this issue, or rather on the different issues that overlap around this problem. In *FHP Management (Pty) Ltd v Theron and Another* 2004 (3) SA 392 (C) at 404I–405B the Cape High Court again relied on the common law in a case where the Prevention of Illegal Eviction from and Unlawful Occupation of Land Act 18 of 1998 clearly applies, despite the fact that the Act overrides the common law and requires the courts to consider the position of the occupier and surrounding circumstances before granting an eviction order. In *ABSA Bank Ltd v Murray and Another* 2004 (2) SA 15 (C) paras [10] and [13]–[16] at 21F–G and 22A–H the same Cape Court followed *Ngcobo/Jika* and applied the requirements of the Act.

[251] *Brisley v Drotsky* 2002 (4) SA 1 (SCA) paras [39]–[40] at 20D–G.

[252] Paras [42]–[46] at 21B–22E; Olivier JA dissenting on this point: par [87] at 33C–E.

it should base its exercise of that discretion, the point of departure remains the common law: a landowner is entitled to possession and hence to eviction, and in the absence of a clear legal or statutory right of occupation this right (and the application for an eviction order based on it) cannot be denied by the courts simply with reference to the occupier's personal circumstances or the availability of alternative accommodation. The effect of the constitutional provision in section 26(3) is therefore restricted within the framework of common law ownership.

In deciding eviction cases the courts find it difficult to distinguish between instances where the Prevention of Illegal Eviction from and Unlawful Occupation of Land Act 18 of 1998 applies (clearly overriding the common law), or where the Extension of Security of Tenure Act 62 of 1997 applies (also requiring consideration of contextual matters but not overriding the common law explicitly), or where none of these acts applies and the clash between the common law and the constitutional provision in section 26(3) is more straightforward.[253] The result is that the reformist aims of the legislation are often undermined or frustrated because the common law position is upheld or maintained regardless of the land reform law that applies, the effect of the Constitution and the circumstances of the occupiers.

The more context-sensitive and reform-friendly approach of the Constitutional Court in *Port Elizabeth Municipality v Various Occupiers*[254] countered the restrictive effect of the earlier decisions to a certain extent[255] by saying that the Constitution mandated suitable land reform and therefore formed the interpretive framework within which the anti-eviction provisions must be understood and applied.[256] The Constitutional Court further asserted that the courts not only had the discretion to

---

[253] For the same reason the lower courts do not clearly distinguish between the Supreme Court of Appeal decisions such as *Brisley v Drotsky* 2002 (4) SA 1 (SCA) (dealing with section 26(3) of the Constitution only) and *Ndlovu v Ngcobo; Bekker v Jika* 2003 (1) SA 113 (SCA) (dealing with the Prevention of Illegal Eviction from and Unlawful Occupation of Land Act 18 of 1998, which overrides the common law explicitly); see eg *FHP Management (Pty) Ltd v Theron and Another* 2004 (3) SA 392 (C), which professes to apply both *Brisley* and *Ngcobo/Jika* and ends up simply maintaining the common law, even though it dealt with the 1998 Act. See footnote 258 below.

[254] 2005 (1) SA 217 (CC). *Jaftha v Schoeman and Others; Van Rooyen v Stoltz and Others* 2005 (2) SA 140 (CC) is an interesting anti-eviction decision that deals with the negative duty to refrain from interfering with the right of access to housing under section 26 rather than security of tenure under section 25(6), and the case is therefore discussed in 6.4 below.

[255] It cannot be said that the Constitutional Court's *Port Elizabeth Municipality* decision overrides earlier decisions such as *Brisley*, because the Constitutional Court decision deals specifically with a situation where the Prevention of Illegal Eviction from and Unlawful Occupation of Land Act 18 of 1998 applies. The problem in many of the earlier cases was that this Act does list a (non-exhaustive) set of circumstances that a court should consider when exercising its discretion to grant or refuse an eviction order (eg the interests of women, children, the elderly and other vulnerable persons amongst those to be evicted), but that other anti-eviction laws such as the Extension of Security of Tenure Act 62 of 1997 do not. It could therefore be argued that the *Brisley* approach still holds with regard to evictions that are not carried out in terms of PIE, and particularly evictions in terms of the common law (as was the case in *Brisley*).

[256] Paras [14]–[23] at 225A–229G.

consider other circumstances when deciding an eviction case, but that they were under a constitutional obligation to do so.[257] It remains to be seen whether this decision will have a lasting effect on the way the high courts approach eviction cases in different circumstances, and whether they can succeed in finding the appropriate balance between the property rights of landowners and the housing and security rights of tenants in every individual case, within the conceptual and value framework of the appropriate legislation and case law.[258] In the *Modderklip* decision the Constitutional Court[259] ordered the state to pay compensation to a landowner for the loss that he suffered as a result of the unlawful invasion and occupation of his land and the lack of state provision for efficient enforcement procedures. This decision indicates that the Court was serious when it said that a proper balance had to be struck between the rights of the landowner and the rights of occupiers—prevention of eviction may be a constitutionally sanctioned and morally laudable purpose, but it cannot always take place at the cost of the landowner.

---

[257] Par [23] at 29F: 'The judicial function in these circumstances is not to establish a hierarchical arrangement between the different interests involved, privileging in an abstract and mechanical way the rights of ownership over the right not to be dispossessed of a home, or *vice versa*. Rather, it is to balance out and reconcile the opposed claims in as just a manner as possible, taking account of all the interests involved and the specific factors relevant in each particular case.' The *Port Elizabeth Municipality* case is also discussed in chapter 7.3.4.

[258] In *Davids and Others v Van Straaten and Others* 2005 (4) SA 468 (C) the Cape High Court referred to *Port Elizabeth Municipality v Various Occupiers* 2005 (1) SA 217 (CC) and *Ndlovu v Ngcobo; Bekker v Jika* 2003 (1) SA 113 (SCA) as the relevant case law; and to section 26(3) of the Constitution and the Prevention of Illegal Eviction from and Unlawful Occupation of Land Act 18 of 1998 as the relevant legislation in a case where tenants refused to vacate rental premises from which the landlord tried unsuccessfully to evict them after having cancelled the lease. The Court referred to the Constitutional Court decision in *First National Bank of SA Ltd t/a Wesbank v Commissioner, South African Revenue Service and Another; First National Bank of SA Ltd t/a Wesbank v Minister of Finance* 2002 (4) SA 768 (CC) par [50], where Ackermann J pointed out that '[t]he purpose of s 25 has to be seen both as protecting existing private property rights as well as serving the public interest, mainly in the sphere of land reform but not limited thereto, and also as striking a proportionate balance between these two functions', as well as the decision in *Port Elizabeth Municipality v Various Occupiers* par [19], where Sachs J emphasized the importance of balancing the property rights of landowners with the housing and security rights of tenants: '[t]he Constitution recognises that land rights and the right of access to housing and of not being arbitrarily evicted, are closely intertwined. The stronger the right to land, the greater the prospect of a secure home.' These statements are then used in the judgment as a framework for the decision that eviction was justified in the case, except for the one applicant who was 77 years old and for whom the owners were willing to make a compromise in any event.

[259] The Constitutional Court decision is reported as *President of the Republic of South Africa and Another v Modderklip Boerdery (Pty) Ltd (Agri SA and Others, Amici Curiae)* 2005 (5) SA 3 (CC). The SCA decision is reported as *Modderfontein Squatters, Greater Benoni City Council v Modderklip Boerdery (Pty) Ltd; (Agri SA and Legal Resources Centre, Amici Curiae); President of the Republic of South Africa and Others v Modderklip Boerdery (Pty) Ltd (Agri SA and Legal Resources Centre, Amici Curiae)* 2004 (6) SA 40 (SCA). See AJ van der Walt 'The state's duty to protect property owners vs the state's duty to provide housing: Thoughts on the *Modderklip* case' (2005) 21 *SAJHR* 144–161.

There is some authority in comparative law for constitutional recognition and regulatory (uncompensated) enforcement of anti-eviction legislation, even when it places a dramatic restriction upon the landowner's property rights. One approach is to justify the restrictive working of the anti-eviction laws on the landowner with reference to the lessee's property rights;[260] another is to uphold anti-eviction legislation through balancing of individual entitlements, public interest and social obligations.[261] Both these approaches depend upon the view taken of the constitutional provision that protects tenants against eviction—if the courts think that such a provision vests an independent right in the tenant, even 'normal' eviction proceedings might be subjected to constitutional proportionality or balancing; if not, the risk is that ownership will enjoy hierarchical preference and protection of the constitution might often be hollow for non-owners, as was proved the South African eviction cases discussed earlier. However, in Roman-Germanic (civil-law) systems recognizing a separate and independent property right in favour of a non-owner could be problematic dogmatically unless constitutional property is distinguished clearly from private law ownership.

In *Harrow London Borough Council v Qazi*[262] the House of Lords held that article 8 of the European Convention on Human Rights does not authorize an additional layer of judicial discretion to scrutinize the appropriateness of a landlord's recovery of possession, based on the impact that eviction might have on the home life of the tenant. Proportionality issues, according to the majority, have already been decided on the legislative level and cannot be reopened for every individual case by the judi-

---

[260]The main example is German law; see AJ van der Walt *Constitutional property clauses: A comparative analysis* (1999) 136–139. The *Besitzrecht des Mieters* case (*BVerfGE* 89, 1 (1993)) is especially significant; see AJ van der Walt 'Ownership and eviction: Constitutional rights in private law' (2005) 9 *Edinburgh LR* 32–64 for a discussion in comparison with South African cases. In this case, the German Federal Constitutional Court construed a separate property right in favour of a tenant to protect her against unfair eviction. See further R Youngs 'Human rights in the housing sphere: German comparisons' (2004) 15 *The King's College LJ* 145–158 (comparing German case with English case law).

[261]The general German solution is to establish a balance between the property owner's property rights and the public interest in sufficient provision of housing. This balance is created through social housing legislation that restricts the landowner-landlord's right to evict and to raise rent levels at will. The rent laws have been upheld by the Federal Constitutional Court as successfully finding the right balance between the individual and the social interest. It is usually said that less room exists for interfering with private property through regulatory controls the closer it is to the intimate personal sphere, while more room for regulation exists when the property falls into the commercial sphere, as rental property does. See *BVerfGE* 37, 132 [1974] (*Wohnraumkündigungsschutzgesetz*); *BVerfGE* 38, 248 [1975] (*Zweckentfremdung von Wohnraum*); *BVerfGE* 68, 361 [1985] (*Wohnungskündigungsgesetz*); *BVerfGE* 79, 292 [1989] (*Eigenbedarfskündigung*); *BVerfGE* 89, 1 [1993] (*Besitzrecht des Mieters*); *BVerfGE* 89, 237 [1993] (*Eigenbedarfskündigung*); *BVerfGE* 91, 294 [1994] (*Fortgeltung des Mietepreisbindung*); *BVerfGE* 52, 1 [1979] (*Kleingarten*); *BVerfGE* 87, 114 [1992] (*Kleingarten*) (all Germany); compare *Yee v Escondido* 503 US 519 (1992) (US).

[262][2004] 1 AC 983 (HL). For a discussion see K Gray & SF Gray *Elements of land law* (4th ed 2005) paras 2.70–2.75 at 137–140; 14.16–14.17 at 1495–1497.

ciary. Article 8 does therefore not grant the courts the discretion to scrutinize state housing policy and balance public and private interests. Gray & Gray describe this aspect of the *Qazi* decision as 'a resolute defence of proprietary sovereignty in the face of a much more open-textured form of proprietary morality stemming from a European source'[263] and point out that this decision is difficult to reconcile with the European Court of Human Rights' more recent decision in *Connors v The United Kingdom*,[264] where the European Court was willing to examine the proportionality of the eviction despite the fact that the local authority had already terminated the tenants' licence and was therefore entitled to evict them.

In the South African context the future direction of eviction law, especially but not exclusively in the land reform sphere, will depend largely upon the question whether the courts can find a constitutionally legitimate and socially and politically responsible way of balancing individual property interests against the public interest in secure tenure of housing. The balance that needs to be struck between the property interests of landowners, the housing interests of those who occupy land out of necessity and the public interest will most likely not be found in a confrontational dichotomy or in a hierarchical ordering of pre-existing property rights, constitutional housing rights and the public interest in provision of housing—it is much more likely that the answer is to be found in developing the common law of housing and eviction according to the provisions of section 39(2).

The South African tenure reform laws have so far survived several constitutional challenges, although the most serious constitutional issue with regard to their application is perhaps not their constitutional validity as such but the extent to which the constitutional and statutory reform measures are going to be allowed to amend or change or develop the common law. The effect of the Constitution and of land reform laws on the common law are discussed in chapter 7 in the context of the development of the common law in terms of section 39(2). For present purposes it suffices to say that the constitutional issue, as far as tenure reform is concerned, is whether and how far common law protection of landownership and other common law land rights can be restricted or cut back in order to bolster previously weak and marginalized land rights for the sake of greater security of tenure, without compensation, before it would have to be said that the restriction of existing rights amounted to arbitrary deprivation or uncompensated expropriation of property rights that could not be justified in terms of section 36 of the Constitution.

---

[263] K Gray & SF Gray *Elements of land law* (4th ed 2005) paras 14.16–14.17 at 1497.

[264] (2005) 40 EHRR 189, see K Gray & SF Gray *Elements of land law* (4th ed 2005) paras 2.70–2.73 at 137–139; 14.16–14.17 at 1497. Gray & Gray point out at 1497 that the decision in *Connors* suggests that *Qazi* was decided wrong, but at the same time the European Court has declared further proceedings in *Qazi* inadmissible, which rules out the possibility of it being overturned in Strasbourg. Compare footnote 417 below.

6.4 ACCESS TO LAND AND HOUSING

25. Property

(5) The State must take reasonable legislative and other measures, within its available resources, to foster conditions which enable citizens to gain access to land on an equitable basis.

26. Housing

(1) Everyone has the right to have access to adequate housing.
(2) The State must take reasonable legislative and other measures, within its available resources, to achieve the progressive realization of this right.
(3) . . .

6.4.1 Introduction and overview

Access to land should be distinguished from access to housing, although they are of course linked in that both form an integral part of the larger constitutional purpose of reforming the regime of land rights and land holdings that was established under apartheid.[265] The main link between the two processes is of course that access to housing is more often than not predicated upon access to land, although either of them also has aspects that are not necessarily linked to the other. The main reason for distinguishing between access to land and access to housing in this section is that there are subtle differences between the constitutional provisions that authorize the two processes and, more importantly, that they seem to progress along different legal and administrative routes.

In addition to restitution of dispossessed land rights and tenure reform, the third leg of land reform consists of measures to improve access to land or, as it is also sometimes described, the redistribution of land. Section 25(5) of the Constitution provides that the state must take reasonable legislative and other measures, within its available resources, to foster conditions which enable citizens to gain access to land on an equitable basis. This provision embodies the constitutional mandate for legislative and other measures that promote greater access to land.

Since 1991 various measures and initiatives have been introduced to promote this purpose, mostly by way of legislation that facilitates access to land in some form or executive and administrative initiatives to provide land to those who are unable to gain access through private market channels. The former De Klerk government

---

[265] A similar point was made by Jeannie van Wyk 'The relationship (or not) between rights of access to land and housing: De-linking land from its components' paper presented at the International Property Law Conference, Stellenbosch, 5–6 April 2005. According to Van Wyk the reasons why the two sets of rights should be distinguished include the fact that the two provisions (sections 25(5) and 26 respectively) are different; that the legislation and the governance structures relating to each differ (eg, housing responsibilities occur on all three levels of government, land issues only on the central level); and that housing can conceptually be separated from access to land.

already introduced the Less Formal Township Establishment Act 13 of 1991 as part of their limited pre-democratic land reform programme to facilitate the establishment of urban townships without the normal time-consuming and expensive township establishment procedures.[266] Shortly afterwards and still prior to the 1993 Constitution the Provision of Land and Assistance Act 126 of 1993 was introduced to facilitate the provision and subdivision of land for residential settlement in rural areas.[267] Similarly, the Transformation of Certain Rural Areas Act 94 of 1998 was introduced to undo the remains of certain apartheid tenure regimes in rural areas[268] and the Development Facilitation Act 67 of 1995 was promulgated specifically to promote extraordinary measures to facilitate and speed up the implementation of reconstruction and development projects with regard to both urban and rural land.[269] Other land reform laws that serve restitution or tenure reform goals, such as the Land Reform (Labour Tenants) Act 3 of 1996 and the Communal Property Associations Act 28 of 1996, also serve redistributory purposes in that they facilitate the acquisition of new and possibly stronger and more suitable land rights.[270]

Stated as it is section 25(5) does not create a direct right of access to land; it merely instructs the state to take reasonable legislative and other measures, within its available resources, to foster conditions that would enable citizens to gain access to land on an equitable basis. As such section 25(5) has not yet been used in litigation to gain access to land; and to a large extent its redistributive function has been restricted to the sphere of government policy-making and executive action. Despite the unquestionable value of the policy-making, legislative and executive initiatives that have been taken in honouring the constitutional obligation imposed on the state by section 25(5), none of these statutes or initiatives has raised major constitutional concerns within the framework of section 25(5) of the Constitution to date.

The real action, as far as political and judicial struggles about access to land and housing is concerned, has taken place in the sphere of access to housing in terms of section 26 rather than access to land in terms of section 25 of the Constitution. Section

---

[266]See on this Act PJ Badenhorst, JM Pienaar & H Mostert (assisted by M van Rooyen) *Silberberg and Schoeman's The law of property* (4th ed 2003) 485.

[267]See on this Act PJ Badenhorst, JM Pienaar & H Mostert (assisted by M van Rooyen) *Silberberg and Schoeman's The law of property* (4th ed 2003) 497–499; compare further DL Carey Miller (with A Pope) *Land title in South Africa* (2000) 405–411; AJ van der Walt 'Property rights and hierarchies of power: A critical evaluation of land-reform policy in South Africa' (1999) 64 *Koers* 259–294 at 275.

[268]See on this Act PJ Badenhorst, JM Pienaar & H Mostert (assisted by M van Rooyen) *Silberberg and Schoeman's The law of property* (4th ed 2003) 499; compare further DL Carey Miller (with A Pope) *Land title in South Africa* (2000) 449–455.

[269]See on this Act PJ Badenhorst, JM Pienaar & H Mostert (assisted by M van Rooyen) *Silberberg and Schoeman's The law of property* (4th ed 2003) 533–535; compare further DL Carey Miller (with A Pope) *Land title in South Africa* (2000) 411–448; AJ van der Walt 'Property rights and hierarchies of power: A critical evaluation of land-reform policy in South Africa' (1999) 64 *Koers* 259–294 at 277.

[270]These two acts are discussed in 6.3.1 above.

26(1) provides that everyone has the right to have access to adequate housing; subsection 26(2) adds that the state must take reasonable legislative and other measures, within its available resources, to achieve the progressive realization of this right. As with regard to access to land, a large part of the state's response to its constitutional obligation with regard to access to housing assumed the form of policy frameworks, legislation and executive action, and over the last decade legislation such as the Housing Act 107 of 1997[271] and the Rental Housing Act 50 of 1999,[272] as well as a range of state programmes, incentives and subsidies were introduced to promote access to housing.[273] However, the difference between the promotion of access to land in terms of section 25(5) and of access to housing in terms of section 26(1) and (2) is that the latter has been relied upon in litigation to probe the content and scope of the state's duties and responsibilities with regard to provision of housing, while section 25(5) has not yet been the subject of such litigation with regard to access to land.

Section 26(2) is couched in the same careful language as section 25(5), although there are small differences: both subsections provide that the state 'must take reasonable legislative and other measures, within its available resources', but section 25(5) merely requires the state to 'foster conditions which enable citizens to gain access to land on an equitable basis' while section 26(2) requires that the state 'to achieve the progressive realization of this right'. The formulation of subsection 26(2) is used in other provisions in the Bill of Rights as well and it has been described as a source of 'qualified socio-economic rights',[274] and it is accepted that the social and economic rights in the relevant provisions are, at least to some extent, justiciable.[275] This fact, combined with the sheer extent and urgency of the housing shortage, resulted in a development that is far more active in the fields of litigation and case law than is the case with section 25(5).

---

[271] See on this Act AJ van der Walt 'Property rights and hierarchies of power: A critical evaluation of land-reform policy in South Africa' (1999) 64 *Koers* 259–294 at 278–279.

[272] See on this Act AJ van der Walt 'Exclusivity of ownership, security of tenure, and eviction orders: A model to evaluate South African land-reform legislation' 2002 *TSAR* 254–289 at 269–271. The Act protects tenants against eviction and requires that eviction be preceded by lawful termination of the lease, but the Act does not exclude or override the common law, with the result that eviction at common law is an alternative.

[273] For an overview of early initiatives and schemes see the *White Paper on South African land policy* (1997) at 10; compare AJ van der Walt 'Property rights and hierarchies of power: A critical evaluation of land-reform policy in South Africa' (1999) 64 *Koers* 259–294 at 279.

[274] S Liebenberg 'The interpretation of socio-economic rights' in S Woolman et al (eds) *Constitutional law of South Africa* (2nd ed 2003 original service Dec 2003) at 33–5. This formulation is used with reference to rights that guarantee access to adequate housing (section 26(1)), health care services, sufficient food and water, and social security (section 27(1)).

[275] See S Liebenberg 'The interpretation of socio-economic rights' in S Woolman et al (eds) *Constitutional law of South Africa* (2nd ed 2003 original service Dec 2003) at 33–5, 33–8, referring to the Constitutional Court decision in *Ex parte Chairperson of the Constitutional Assembly: In re Certification of the Constitution of the Republic of South Africa, 1996* 1996 (4) SA 744 (CC) par [78] at 800G–801B.

The case law on access to housing in terms of section 26 falls into two distinct categories, one dealing with the state's duty to provide housing under section 26(1) and (2) and the other concerning the state's duty to protect people from eviction under section 26(3). Since the eviction issue has already been discussed extensively in earlier sections of this chapter,[276] the rest of the section concentrates on the guarantee of access to housing in section 26(1) and (2). With regard to section 26(1) and (2) a negative obligation to refrain from interfering with the right to access to housing is usually distinguished from the notion of a positive obligation to provide access to housing in one form or another.

6.4.2 Access to land in terms of section 25(5)

It was already pointed out above that the state's constitutional obligation to 'take reasonable legislative and other measures, within its available resources, to foster conditions which enable citizens to gain access to land on an equitable basis' has resulted in policy decisions, statutes and executive initiatives, but not in litigation or constitutional challenges. The policy initiatives of the Department of Land Affairs and Agriculture include, as far as redistribution of land is concerned, a proactive land acquisition strategy and a land for housing strategy. In terms of these policies a number of access products have been developed, such as the Land Redistribution for Agricultural Development (which allows beneficiaries to acquire land for agricultural development); the municipal and tribal commonage projects (improving people's access to municipal and tribal land for grazing purposes); Farm Equity Schemes (participants purchase equity in the form of shares in land-based enterprises and receive returns in the form of dividends and capital growth); and settlement schemes (providing people with land for settlement purposes, including grants to assist landless people living under insecure tenure conditions to acquire secure tenure).[277]

Some of the land reform laws introduced since 1994 are specifically aimed at more equitable access to land; others serve restitution or security of tenure and redistribution functions. A complete overview of the relevant legislation falls outside the scope of this chapter, given the fact that this aspect of the land reform process has had little or no direct constitutional implications to date. Two examples will therefore have to suffice for present purposes.[278]

Firstly, chapter II of the Extension of Security of Tenure Act 62 of 1997 provides for long-term security of tenure in either on-site or off-site developments that could

---

[276] See 6.3 above.

[277] On these policies and products see the Department of Land Affairs and Agriculture website at http://land.pwv.gov.za/land_reform/redistribution.htm

[278] For a more extensive overview see DL Carey Miller (with A Pope) *Land title in South Africa* (2000) chapter 8. Important examples of access legislation not discussed here but analysed by Carey Miller are the Provision of Land and Assistance (Provision of Certain Land for Settlement) Act 126 of 1993; the Development Facilitation Act 67 of 1995; and the Transformation of Certain Rural Areas Act 94 of 1998.

benefit lawful occupiers of rural land; state subsidies are made available when land is developed to provide the occupiers with suitable and secure land rights.[279] Secondly, the Land Reform (Labour Tenants) Act 3 of 1996 allows labour tenants to acquire ownership and/or other rights in land in accordance with section 25(5) of the Constitution. Labour tenants who satisfy the requirements in section 1 of the Act may apply for an award of land or land rights and for financial assistance.[280] A claim is lodged with the director-general of land affairs, who informs the landowner and allows him or her to dispute the applicant's status as labour tenant. If the labour tenant proves his or her status the landowner can make proposals for an equitable way of settling the claim; in the absence of such a settlement the Land Claims Court has jurisdiction to make an award.[281] Such an award can involve granting the labour tenant ownership of the land he or she has occupied or other land on the same or on another farm of the owner; an award of other land rights; and an award of ancillary land rights such as water servitudes that are reasonably consistent with the rights enjoyed by the labour tenant.[282] The landowner receives compensation in accordance the Act and with section 25(3) of the Constitution for land and land rights granted to a labour tenant.[283]

6.4.3 Access to housing in terms of section 26: The negative obligation

In as far as section 26(1) and (2) is justiciable, it is accepted that the section creates at least a negative obligation to respect the right to housing. In one of the major cases regarding the so-called qualified socio-economic rights,[284] *Government of the Republic*

---

[279] Section 4. See PJ Badenhorst, JM Pienaar & H Mostert (assisted by M van Rooyen) *Silberberg and Schoeman's The law of property* (4th ed 2003) 501–502; DL Carey Miller (with A Pope) *Land title in South Africa* (2000) 514–516; T Roux 'Chapter 7: The Extension of Security of Tenure Act' in G Budlender, J Latsky & T Roux *Juta's new land law* (1998) 7A–6; W du Plessis, N Olivier & J Pienaar 'Land: Still a contentious issue' (1998) 13 *SA Public Law* 149–169 at 158.

[280] Section 16. See PJ Badenhorst, JM Pienaar & H Mostert (assisted by M van Rooyen) *Silberberg and Schoeman's The law of property* (4th ed 2003) 496; DL Carey Miller (with A Pope) *Land title in South Africa* (2000) 537–544; AJ van der Walt 'Property rights and hierarchies of power: A critical evaluation of land-reform policy in South Africa' (1999) 64 *Koers* 259–294 at 280.

[281] Section 17. The Land Claims Court has exclusive jurisdiction with regard to matters pertaining to the Land Reform (Labour Tenants) Act 31 of 1996; see PJ Badenhorst, JM Pienaar & H Mostert (assisted by M van Rooyen) *Silberberg and Schoeman's The law of property* (4th ed 2003) 494–495; *Dhlamini v Loock* 2001 (3) SA 56 (SCA) (pertaining to eviction of labour tenants).

[282] Section 16. See PJ Badenhorst, JM Pienaar & H Mostert (assisted by M van Rooyen) *Silberberg and Schoeman's The law of property* (4th ed 2003) 496; DL Carey Miller (with A Pope) *Land title in South Africa* (2000) 544.

[283] DL Carey Miller (with A Pope) *Land title in South Africa* (2000) 544–546; see further W du Plessis, N Olivier & J Pienaar 'Land reform: A never-ending process' (2000) 15 *SA Public Law* 230–254 at 240.

[284] The other major Constitutional Court case on this issue, *Minister of Health and Others v Treatment Action Campaign and Others* 2002 (5) SA 721 (CC), dealt with access to health services (specifically the right of access to anti-retroviral medicine for prevention of mother to child transmission of

(continued on next page ...)

of South Africa and Others v Grootboom and Others,[285] this negative duty was described as an implied negative obligation 'placed upon the state and all other entities and persons to desist from preventing or impairing the right of access to adequate housing'. In *Grootboom* the Court based its decision (that the state's housing policy did not meet the requirements in section 26) on the finding that the eviction of the occupiers by the state resulted in a breach of the negative obligation.[286] According to Liebenberg, most commentators agree that the negative obligation to refrain from preventing or impairing the socio-economic rights, as it was recognized in *Grootboom* and worked out in the *Treatment Action Campaign* case, is not subject to the resource-based limitations in section 26(2).[287] It therefore places a direct duty of abstention or restraint upon the state.

(... from previous page)
HIV/AIDS). S Liebenberg 'The interpretation of socio-economic rights' in S Woolman et al (eds) *Constitutional law of South Africa* (2nd ed 2003 original service Dec 2003) 33-5–33-38 discusses the two cases together, and shows how they follow the same conceptual and methodological route by restricting the courts' review power to reasonableness review. See further AJ van der Walt 'A South African reading of Frank Michelman's theory of social justice' (2004) 19 *SA Public Law* 253–307 at 296–298.

[285] 2001 (1) SA 46 (CC) par [34] at 66G–H. For discussion of the *Grootboom* case see S Liebenberg 'The interpretation of socio-economic rights' in S Woolman et al (eds) *Constitutional law of South Africa* (2nd ed 2003 original service Dec 2003) 33-5–33-38; AJ van der Walt 'A South African reading of Frank Michelman's theory of social justice' (2004) 19 *SA Public Law* 253–307 at 294–296; CR Sunstein 'Social and economic rights? Lessons from South Africa' in *Designing democracy: What constitutions do* (2001) 221–237; T Roux T 'Understanding *Grootboom?*—A response to Cass R Sunstein' (2002) 12 *Constitutional Forum* 41–51; D Moseneke 'The fourth Bram Fischer memorial lecture: Transformative adjudication' (2002) 18 *SAJHR* 309–319; M Wesson '*Grootboom* and beyond: Reassessing the socio-economic jurisprudence of the South African Constitutional Court' (2004) 20 *SAJHR* 284–345; J Sloth-Nielsen J 'The child's right to social services, the right to social security, and primary prevention of child abuse: Some conclusions in the aftermath of *Grootboom*' (2001) 17 *SAJHR* 210–231; S Liebenberg 'The right to social assistance: The implications of *Grootboom* for policy reform in South Africa' (2001) 17 *SAJHR* 232–257; P de Vos '*Grootboom*, the right of access to housing and substantive equality as contextual fairness' (2001) 17 *SAJHR* 258–276; M Pieterse 'Coming to terms with judicial enforcement of socio-economic rights' (2004) 20 *SAJHR* 383–417; S Wilson 'Taming the constitution: Rights and reform in the South African education system' (2004) 20 *SAJHR* 418–443; D Bilchitz 'Towards a reasonable approach to the minimum core: Laying the foundations for future socio-economic rights jurisprudence (2003) 19 *SAJHR* 1–26; TJ Bollyky 'R if C > P + B: A paradigm for judicial remedies of socio-economic rights violations' (2002) 18 *SAJHR* 161–200; AJ van der Walt 'Exclusivity of ownership, security of tenure and eviction orders: A critical evaluation of recent case law' (2002) 18 *SAJHR* 372–420. See the discussion of *Grootboom* in 6.4.4 below.
[286] Par [88] at 84I–85A. See further S Liebenberg 'The interpretation of socio-economic rights' in S Woolman et al (eds) *Constitutional law of South Africa* (2nd ed 2003 original service Dec 2003) 33–17.
[287] S Liebenberg 'The interpretation of socio-economic rights' in S Woolman et al (eds) *Constitutional law of South Africa* (2nd ed 2003 original service Dec 2003) 33–18.

In *Jaftha v Schoeman and Others; Van Rooyen v Stoltz and Others*[288] the Constitutional Court again had an opportunity to decide a case upon the basis of this negative obligation. The case originated in a situation where certain very poor, mostly unemployed people who lived in houses they bought with state subsidies under the redistribution and access to housing schemes of the state could not pay relatively small debts they incurred, mostly for daily living expenses, and they were threatened with eviction and sale in execution of their homes.[289] The plaintiffs argued that they have already been provided with housing by the state because they are poor; that the execution proceedings under section 66(1)(a) would result in their losing ownership of and being evicted from their houses; that they would not have a second opportunity to apply for state support in gaining access to housing and would therefore remain homeless afterwards; and that the execution process was unconstitutional because it conflicted with the duty that both the state and private persons had in terms of section 26(1) and (2) of the Constitution not to interfere unjustifiably with their right of access to housing.

The Constitutional Court firstly confirmed that there is indeed a negative content to socio-economic rights and that this negative content at the very least means that 'any measure which permits a person to be deprived of existing access to adequate housing, limits the rights protected in section 26(1).[290] The Court also pointed out

---

[288] 2005 (2) SA 140 (CC). In par [22] at 152D–E the Court pointed out that the question in this case was such that the issues raised by section 25 and by section 26 were different; because of the decision in terms of section 26 it was not necessary to consider a challenge under section 25. In par [31] at 155F–156B the Court pointed out that the other section 26 cases decided by the Court before dealt with the positive obligation and that this was the first case to be decided specifically with reference to the negative obligation, apparently forgetting its decision in *Grootboom* (par [88] at 84I–85A). It is true that *Jaftha* was decided much more directly and extensively on the basis of the negative obligation, while a large part of *Grootboom* was concerned with the possibility of construing a positive obligation as well. In chapter 4.5.5 text accompanying footnotes 144–146 it is argued that *Jaftha* could, on the same reasoning, also have been decided in terms of the *FNB* reading of section 25(1).

[289] The authorizing statute is section 66(1)(a) of the Magistrates' Court Act 32 of 1944; see *Jaftha v Schoeman and Others; Van Rooyen v Stoltz and Others* 2005 (2) SA 140 (CC) par [14] at 150E–G.

[290] *Jaftha v Schoeman and Others; Van Rooyen v Stoltz and Others* 2005 (2) SA 140 (CC) paras [33] at 156G–H, [34] at 156H–157A. The Court thereby reversed the decision of the Cape High Court in *Jaftha v Schoeman and Others; Van Rooyen v Stoltz and Others* 2003 (10) BCLR 1149 (C), where it was said by the High Court in par [39] at 1160D that section 26(1) 'does not give rise to a self-standing and independent right irrespective of the considerations in section 26(2).' The Constitutional Court pointed out in paras [32] at 156C–G, [33] at 156G–H that this finding of the High Court was based on a misreading of the decision in *Minister of Health and Others v Treatment Action Campaign and Others* 2002 (5) SA 721 (CC) par [39] 740H–I, and that it failed to take into account the various statements by the Constitutional Court where the existence of the negative obligation was acknowledged: *Ex Parte Chairperson of the Constitutional Assembly: In re Certification of the Constitution of the Republic of South Africa, 1996* 1996 (4) SA 744 (CC) par [78] at 801A–B; *Government of the Republic of South Africa and Others v Grootboom and Others* 2001 (1) SA 46 (CC) par [34] at 66G–H; *Minister of Health and Others v Treatment Action Campaign and Others* 2002 (5) SA 721 (CC) par [46] at 742G–I.

that section 26 and its emphasis on security of tenure had to be interpreted against the historical background of forced removals and racist evictions during the apartheid era.[291] Against that background, section 26 must be read as a whole, and then it emerges as a provision that is 'aimed at creating a new dispensation in which every person has adequate housing and in which the state may not interfere with such unless it would be justifiable to do so.'[292] In this view, the execution procedure under section 66(1)(a) of the Act clearly limits the negative obligation to respect the plaintiffs' housing rights created by section 26(1), and in the Court's view this limitation is unjustifiable because there will always be instances where it is overbroad, allowing execution in circumstances where the advantage for the creditor are outweighed by the prejudice and hardship caused for the debtor.[293]

In view of the importance of properly regulated debt collection and the interests of creditors the impugned section could not simply be declared unconstitutional and nullified, and therefore the Court preferred judicial overview as a more appropriate remedy. It further elected to implement this remedy by reading words into the section to the effect that creditors who find insufficient movable assets for attachment and sale in execution cannot simply attach and sell immovable property, but have to approach the courts for an order that will authorise sale in execution. In considering such an application the courts have to consider a variety of circumstances such as the size of the debt; its origin and the circumstances under which it arose; the relative balance of the interests of the creditor in recovering the debt versus the interest of the debtor in security of tenure in their home; the availability of alternative ways to recover the debt; and other relevant factors.[294]

The *Jaftha* decision is significant for several reasons. It is obviously important for the extensive and direct manner in which the negative obligation resulting from section 26 was set out, explained and given effect. Because of the decision it is clear that legislation and (state and private) actions that have a negative impact on already existing housing rights of indigent people are regarded as limitations of the negative obligation created by section 26(1) and that such limiting legislation and actions will be unconstitutional unless they are justified under section 36(1). The decision is also important for placing the right of access to housing in section 26, together with the

---

[291] *Jaftha v Schoeman and Others; Van Rooyen v Stoltz and Others* 2005 (2) SA 140 (CC) paras [25]–[26] at 153F–154B.

[292] 2005 (2) SA 140 (CC) par [28] at 154C–155B.

[293] 2005 (2) SA 140 (CC) paras [43], [48], [52] at 158I–159B, 159H–160A, 160I–161A.

[294] 2005 (2) SA 140 (CC) paras [54]–[60] at 161C–163B. The reference to the origin of the debt indicates that debt incurred recklessly and irresponsibly could be treated differently than debt incurred for living expenses, especially when the debtor has attempted and is still willing to make every effort to pay the debt. In considering the limitation issue the Court acknowledged the importance of debt recovery and the interests of creditors, but pointed out that the provision was overbroad in allowing execution and eviction at least in some instances where there is no proportionality between the interests of the creditor (involving a relatively small debt) and the interests of the debtor (who will lose their home and become homeless without any prospect of further state assistance).

prospect of someone losing their home and becoming homeless, securely within a historical context that can and should influence its adjudication: homelessness, insecurity and poverty form part of the legacy of apartheid race-related evictions and forced removals, and therefore the right to housing and to security of tenure should be seen and treated as part of the process of reform and recovery. Thirdly, the decision is significant for the way in which it treats poverty, debt and homelessness as different aspects of one larger socio-economic problem that must be approached holistically, which in turn means that eviction and sale in execution cases have to be adjudicated with due regard for the history and the social and economic background of the affected persons.

6.4.4 Access to housing in terms of section 26: A positive obligation?

Efforts to construe a positive duty to provide access to land and housing have been less successful in the courts, even when these efforts focused on a relatively limited duty to provide a core minimum. The now famous *Grootboom* case[295] involved an application brought by a group of people, including children, who were evicted from private land that they have invaded because of the appalling conditions in the informal settlement where they used to live before. Following the eviction they moved onto a sports field in the area, where they were vulnerable to further eviction and to the elements. They then applied to the Cape High Court for an order against all three levels of government to the effect that the state should provide them with temporary shelter or housing until they could obtain permanent housing. The High Court found no violation of section 26, but gave an order for temporary shelter because of a violation of section 29 with regard to the rights of the children in the group. On appeal the Constitutional Court reversed the High Court order, but held that the state's housing programme nevertheless fell short of the requirements for compliance with section 26(2).[296]

For this finding the Constitutional Court relied on a conjunctive reading of subsections 26(1) and (2), in terms of which subsection (1) delineates the scope of the right and imposes an implied negative duty on the state to respect the right to access to housing.[297] The Court rejected the argument that section 26(1) imposed a minimum core obligation on the state to provide housing, arguing that it would be too difficult for a court to determine in the abstract what the minimum threshold should

---

[295] *Government of the Republic of South Africa and Others v Grootboom and Others* 2001 (1) SA 46 (CC). See footnote 285 above.

[296] See S Liebenberg 'The interpretation of socio-economic rights' in S Woolman et al (eds) *Constitutional law of South Africa* (2nd ed 2003 original service Dec 2003) 33–7 for a short background explanation.

[297] *Government of the Republic of South Africa and Others v Grootboom and Others* 2001 (1) SA 46 (CC) par [34] at 66G–H; compare S Liebenberg 'The interpretation of socio-economic rights' in S Woolman et al (eds) *Constitutional law of South Africa* (2nd ed 2003 original service Dec 2003) 33–17.

be.[298] Instead, the Court opted for another approach altogether, in which the courts would merely asses the reasonableness of state measures to realize the rights set out in progressive realization provisions such as sections 26(2) and 27(2).[299] The Court held that there was a violation of section 26 in that the legislative and other measures taken by the state to realize the right of access to housing were unreasonable because the relevant housing policies made no provision for the urgent needs of people in desperate situations.[300] The housing programmes of the state relied exclusively on formal medium and long term waiting lists, without making any provision for emergencies and crises that require more urgent steps to be taken, and consequently these programmes were not reasonable and had to be amended. No order was given specifically with regard to the applicants in the case. The reasonableness review approach that the Constitutional Court adopted in *Grootboom* has been criticized in the literature, but it was again applied in the *Treatment Action Campaign* case.[301]

In the *Grootboom* case[302] the applicants relied on international law to argue that section 26(1) and (2) should be interpreted with reference to a core minimum that the state was obliged to provide. The core minimum argument proposed by the *amici curiae* and rejected by the Court was based on authority derived from the interpretation that the United Nations Commission developed with reference to the right to adequate housing in article 1 of the 1966 International Covenant on Economic, Social and Cultural Rights, setting out the nature of state parties' obligations

---

[298] Par [33] at 66A–E; compare S Liebenberg 'The interpretation of socio-economic rights' in S Woolman et al (eds) *Constitutional law of South Africa* (2nd ed 2003 original service Dec 2003) 33–24. On minimum core arguments see further S Russell 'Introduction—Minimum state obligations: International dimensions' in D Brand & S Russell (eds) *Exploring the core content of socio-economic rights: South African and international perspectives* (2002) 11–21; P de Vos 'The essential components of the human right to adequate housing—A South African perspective' in D Brand & S Russell (eds) *Exploring the core content of socio-economic rights: South African and international perspectives* (2002) 23–33. The international law sources on core obligations are reviewed and discussed by S Liebenberg 'The interpretation of socio-economic rights' in S Woolman et al (eds) *Constitutional law of South Africa* (2nd ed 2003 original service Dec 2003) 33-6–33-7, 33-10–33-16. See further 6.4.3 below.

[299] Par [95] at 86F–G, compare S Liebenberg 'The interpretation of socio-economic rights' in S Woolman et al (eds) *Constitutional law of South Africa* (2nd ed 2003 original service Dec 2003) 33-33.

[300] Par [95] at 86F–G, par [69] at 79J–80A; compare S Liebenberg 'The interpretation of socio-economic rights' in S Woolman et al (eds) *Constitutional law of South Africa* (2nd ed 2003 original service Dec 2003) 33-34–33-35.

[301] *Minister of Health and Others v Treatment Action Campaign and Others* 2002 (5) SA 721 (CC). See S Liebenberg 'The interpretation of socio-economic rights' in S Woolman et al (eds) *Constitutional law of South Africa* (2nd ed 2003 original service Dec 2003) 33-27–33-32 for a discussion of the criticism.

[302] *Government of the Republic of South Africa and Others v Grootboom and Others* 2001 (1) SA 46 (CC); see text surrounding footnote 285 above. Compare S Liebenberg 'The interpretation of socio-economic rights' in S Woolman et al (eds) *Constitutional law of South Africa* (2nd ed 2003 original service Dec 2003) 33-10–33-16.

under the Covenant.[303] The Commission's argument is largely founded on the notion that the state has a duty to fulfil constitutional rights, which resonates with the state's duty to respect, protect, promote and fulfil the rights in section 7 of the South African Constitution. The Constitutional Court recognized the importance of international law but declined to apply international law on the core minimum standard, arguing that the authority of international law may vary from case to case on a particular point. In this case it was particularly important that South Africa has not ratified the International Covenant on Economic, Social and Cultural Rights (1966), which was therefore not directly binding, despite the significant similarities in phraseology between article 2(1) of the Covenant and section 26(1) and (2) of the Constitution.[304] Although the Covenant was therefore regarded as an important guide in interpreting section 26(1) and (2), the Court was not willing to adopt its interpretation wholesale in the South African context. The result is that efforts to construe a positive 'core' obligation to provide housing on the basis of section 26(1) have so far been unsuccessful.

In another Constitutional Court case, *Minister of Public Works and Others v Kyalami Ridge Environmental Association and Another (Mukhwevo Intervening)*,[305] the right of access to housing and the state's obligations in terms of section 26(2) were approached from a different angle. In this case, the state was already providing emergency accommodation for the victims of a flood and started making plans for their permanent accommodation on state land, but owners of neighbouring properties objected that the state was not specifically authorized to provide permanent housing and that the development did not comply with environmental and planning requirements. The issue was therefore not whether the state was complying with its constitutional obligations, but whether it had exceeded its powers in doing so, particularly when the rights of neighbouring property owners were affected. The point was raised that the flood victims had a constitutional right to be given access to housing and that this right should take precedence over any rights that the neighbours might have under the relevant town planning and environmental legislation.[306] Remarkably, despite the finding that the state was authorized and obliged by section 26 to provide housing for people in a housing crisis, and despite the Court's reference to its earlier decision in *Grootboom*, where it was decided that the state's housing policy, to be reasonable, has

---

[303] Compare S Liebenberg 'The interpretation of socio-economic rights' in S Woolman et al (eds) *Constitutional law of South Africa* (2nd ed 2003 original service Dec 2003) 3-6–33-7, 33-22–33-24.

[304] S Liebenberg 'The interpretation of socio-economic rights' in S Woolman et al (eds) *Constitutional law of South Africa* (2nd ed 2003 original service Dec 2003) 33–11. Significant similarities include the common references to the taking of legislative measures to effect progressive realization of the rights, within the limitations of available resources. Significant differences include the reference to 'right to housing' in the Covenant as opposed to 'right of access to housing' in section 26 and 'appropriate steps' in the Covenant versus 'reasonable steps' in the Constitution.

[305] 2001 (3) SA 1151 (CC). For a discussion see AJ van der Walt 'A South African reading of Frank Michelman's theory of social justice' (2004) 19 *SA Public Law* 253–307 at 288–289.

[306] Par [113] at 1187B–D.

to make special provision for genuine crises and emergencies,[307] the Constitutional Court in *Kyalami* did not simply decide the matter with reference to this overriding constitutional duty but found it necessary to support its decision with the argument that the state, as owner of the land in question, had the same right as any private landowner to develop its property, provided it did so in accordance with the applicable planning and building laws.[308] The Constitutional Court argued that the state acquired its authority to provide housing directly from the Constitution, but that it still had to carry out its obligations in terms of section 26 while at the same time complying with all applicable legislative requirements to ensure that its actions are legal. Since there was nothing to indicate that the state was not planning in due course to satisfy the legality requirements in this case, the objections of the neighbours were overruled.[309] The decision recognized that the state had the authority to take the relevant actions in providing housing in this case, partly because it is owner of the land and partly because it was necessary to carry out its state responsibilities under section 26. The result is that recognition of the state's authority to provide housing in this case was subject to the legality requirement that it had to comply with all relevant environment and planning or development laws.

In a third case on the right of access to housing and the state's obligations under section 26(1) and (2); the *Modderklip* case,[310] the Constitutional Court confirmed the SCA decision in terms of which eviction of a large community of unlawful occupiers from private land had to be postponed until alternative accommodation could be provided for them. The case originated when a community, previously evicted from municipal land that they occupied unlawfully, settled on private land owned by a person who did not simply want to see them evicted and thrown out in the street— he wanted the state to provide alternative accommodation for them first. The landowner had previously obtained an eviction order against the community, but has

---

[307] Par [38] at 1167G–1168C, referring to *Grootboom* paras [40] at 68C–F, [52] at 75D–F, [96] at 86H.

[308] Paras [39] at 1168C–E, [40] at 1168E 1169A, [114] at 1187E–F.

[309] Paras [113], [114] at 1187B–G.

[310] The Constitutional Court decision is reported as *President of the Republic of South Africa and Another v Modderklip Boerdery (Pty) Ltd (Agri SA and Others,* Amici Curiae*)* 2005 (5) SA 3 (CC). The SCA decision is reported as *Modderfontein Squatters, Greater Benoni City Council v Modderklip Boerdery (Pty) Ltd; (Agri SA and Legal Resources Centre,* Amici Curiae*); President of the Republic of South Africa and Others v Modderklip Boerdery (Pty) Ltd (Agri SA and Legal Resources Centre,* Amici Curiae*)* 2004 (6) SA 40 (SCA). In this case, the SCA simultaneously dealt with two related matters; an application for leave to appeal against the judgment in *Modderklip Boerdery (Pty) Ltd v Modder East Squatters* 2001 (4) SA 385 (W) (the 'eviction case') and an appeal against the decision in *Modderklip Boerdery (Edms) Bpk v President van die Republiek van Suid-Afrika* 2003 (6) BCLR 638 (T) (the 'enforcement' case). The discussion in the following paragraphs is based on a case note: AJ van der Walt 'The state's duty to protect property owners vs the state's duty to provide housing: Thoughts on the *Modderklip* case' (2005) 21 *SAJHR* 144–161.

been unsuccessful in having it executed.[311] He consistently maintained that the state has an obligation to remove the one obstacle that prevented him from successfully enforcing the eviction order, namely the provision of alternative accommodation for the community to be evicted. The Supreme Court of Appeal decided that the state indeed has an obligation to protect the landowner's property right under section 25 by assisting him to evict the community, but that it also has an obligation to provide alternative accommodation for the community under section 26.[312] The SCA therefore ordered that the community shall not be removed physically until alternative accommodation has been provided, but that the state shall in the meantime pay the landowner compensation for the loss of use of his property.[313]

Despite an unsubstantiated statement in the High Court and the Supreme Court of Appeal judgments to the effect that section 25(1) operates horizontally,[314] the Supreme Court of Appeal decided that the state had a duty to 'respect, protect, promote and fulfill the rights' in the Bill of Rights as provided in section 7(2) of the Constitution,[315] even when third parties pose a threat to those rights.[316] The Supreme Court of Appeal referred to international law[317] and earlier decisions of the Constitu-

---

[311] See the references to the previous decisions known as the eviction case and the enforcement case in the previous footnote above.

[312] *Modderfontein Squatters, Greater Benoni City Council v Modderklip Boerdery (Pty) Ltd; (Agri SA and Legal Resources Centre,* Amici Curiae*); President of the Republic of South Africa and Others v Modderklip Boerdery (Pty) Ltd (Agri SA and Legal Resources Centre,* Amici Curiae) 2004 (6) SA 40 (SCA) par [41] at 61B–D.

[313] Par [43] at 61I–62E.

[314] The possibility that section 25 may operate horizontally has been mooted but mostly denied in the literature; see chapter 2.4 above and compare further T Roux 'Property' in S Woolman et al (eds) *Constitutional law of South Africa* (2nd ed original service 2003) 46-6–46-8 and sources referred to there. The strongest indication that section 25 does not apply to 'private conduct that is not authorized by law' (Roux at 46–6) is *Phoebus Apollo Aviation CC v Minister of Safety and Security* 2003 (2) SA 34 (CC) par [4] at 35D.

[315] This aspect is mentioned in the SCA decision; see *Modderfontein Squatters, Greater Benoni City Council v Modderklip Boerdery (Pty) Ltd; (Agri SA and Legal Resources Centre,* Amici Curiae*); President of the Republic of South Africa and Others v Modderklip Boerdery (Pty) Ltd (Agri SA and Legal Resources Centre,* Amici Curiae) 2004 (6) SA 40 (SCA) paras [27]–[28] at 55F–56C. See further on the state's duty to protect S Liebenberg 'The interpretation of socio-economic rights' in S Woolman et al (eds) *Constitutional law of South Africa* (2nd ed 2003 original service Dec 2003) 33-10–33-17; AJ van der Walt 'Transformative constitutionalism and the development of South African property law' 2005 *TSAR*, 2006 *TSAR* (forthcoming); see further chapter 7.5.3.

[316] *Modderklip Boerdery (Edms) Bpk v President van die Republiek van Suid-Afrika* 2003 (6) BCLR 638 (T) par [44] at 680I.

[317] *Modderfontein Squatters, Greater Benoni City Council v Modderklip Boerdery (Pty) Ltd; (Agri SA and Legal Resources Centre,* Amici Curiae*); President of the Republic of South Africa and Others v Modderklip Boerdery (Pty) Ltd (Agri SA and Legal Resources Centre,* Amici Curiae) 2004 (6) SA 40 (SCA) at 55I footnote 17.

tional Court[318] and the Supreme Court of Appeal[319] in concluding 'the contrary is not open for argument'.[320] The essence of the original enforcement order and of the main argument in the Court's decision is therefore that the state is obliged in terms of section 7(2) to protect Modderklip's section 25 property right, and that it failed to do so in that it failed to provide the occupiers of the unlawful settlement with housing in accordance with section 26 of the Constitution. In other words, failure to protect one right resulted in failure to protect another right, because the landowner's property right can only be protected properly when suitable housing is provided for the occupiers, who cannot be removed from the land before the state's duty towards them has been honoured first. The basis upon which the state is held responsible for the constitutional infringement in this case is construed entirely with reference to the notion that section 7(2) obliges the state to 'respect, protect, promote and fulfill the rights' in the Bill of Rights, which means that it has certain positive obligations towards the occupiers who are going to be evicted when the enforcement order is carried out and towards the landowner who is being prevented from asserting its rights as long as the state does not carry out its housing duties.[321]

Indirectly this decision implies that the state has a kind of positive duty to provide housing to homeless people, at least in certain circumstances, in order to fulfil its obligations under section 7(2) of the Constitution. The Constitutional Court upheld the SCA's order in essence,[322] although not on the basis that the state's refusal to evict the occupiers and its failure to provide alternative accommodation for the occupiers

---

[318] Particularly *Carmichele v Minister of Safety and Security (CALS intervening)* 2001 (4) SA 938 (CC). See chapter 7.5.3.

[319] *Minister of Safety and Security v Van Duivenboden* 2002 (6) SA 431 (SCA); *Van Eeden v Minister of Safety and Security (Women's Legal Centre Trust as amicus curiae)* 2003 (1) SA 389 (SCA); *Minister of Safety and Security v Hamilton* [2003] 4 All SA 117 (SCA); *Minister of Safety and Security v Carmichele* 2004 (3) SA 305 (SCA). See chapter 7.5.3.

[320] *Modderfontein Squatters, Greater Benoni City Council v Modderklip Boerdery (Pty) Ltd; (Agri SA and Legal Resources Centre,* Amici Curiae*); President of the Republic of South Africa and Others v Modderklip Boerdery (Pty) Ltd (Agri SA and Legal Resources Centre,* Amici Curiae*)* 2004 (6) SA 40 (SCA) par [27] at 55F–56A.

[321] A related and easily confused aspect is the argument that was raised with regard to the state's purported direct constitutional duty in terms of section 165(4)—the duty of the state to assist the courts in ensuring the effectiveness of court orders: *Modderfontein Squatters, Greater Benoni City Council v Modderklip Boerdery (Pty) Ltd; (Agri SA and Legal Resources Centre,* Amici Curiae*); President of the Republic of South Africa and Others v Modderklip Boerdery (Pty) Ltd (Agri SA and Legal Resources Centre,* Amici Curiae*)* 2004 (6) SA 40 (SCA) par [29] at 56D–G. Although this also involves a constitutional state duty, it has to be distinguished from the section 7(2) duties, which are specifically concerned with the protection and promotion of fundamental rights in the Bill of Rights. In any event it was decided that section 165(4) does not force the SAPS to enforce court orders. The question of the sources for an argument based on the state's duty to protect is canvassed in detail in AJ van der Walt 'Transformative constitutionalism and the development of South African property law' 2005 *TSAR*, 2006 *TSAR* (forthcoming). See chapter 7.5.3, where this aspect is discussed.

[322] *President of the Republic of South Africa and Another v Modderklip Boerdery (Pty) Ltd (Agri SA and Others,* Amici Curiae*)* 2005 (5) SA 3 (CC) paras [66], [68] at 27F–G, 28C–G.

breached the landowner's section 25 rights (and the occupiers' section 26 rights), but rather on the alternative argument that it was unreasonable for the state 'to stand by and do nothing in circumstances where it was impossible for [the landowner] to evict the occupiers because of the sheer magnitude of the invasion and the particular circumstances of the occupiers.'[323] In doing so the Constitutional Court used the section 34 right of access to courts (together with suitable and efficient enforcement procedures) as its point of departure rather than the section 25 property rights or section 26 access to housing rights, thereby avoiding the conclusion that the decision acknowledged a positive duty to provide housing under section 26. However, the fact that the Constitutional Court dodged the section 26 argument should not blur the fact that—at least in effect—it relied on the same strategy as the SCA in arriving at its conclusion, namely that the state had certain obligations to protect fundamental rights (including property and access to housing), arising from the Constitution, and that its failure to respond to these obligations was the cause for holding it liable in this case.

6.4.5 Concluding remarks

With regard to access to land and housing the following trends seem to be identifiable. Firstly, most of the actual work on provision of access to land in terms of section 25(5) takes place in the form of government policy making and executive action through various schemes, projects and initiatives, including the provision of subsidies and assistance for those who are unable to access land in the open market and first time purchasers. For the most part, activities of this kind do not have much visible impact on jurisprudence and academic commentary or theory in the sense that they do not show up in litigation and case law and are not discussed in legal academic literature.

Secondly, political and legal pressure for greater access to housing in terms of section 26(1) and (2) does show up in case law resulting from litigation aimed at forcing the state to provide land or housing to specific groups of homeless people. For the most part, this kind of pressure is being exerted on the basis of section 26(1) and (2) and the following general conclusions can so far be made from case law on the matter. (a) It is recognized that the state and everybody else is subject to a negative duty to refrain from preventing or impairing the right of access to housing. (b) This negative obligation is based on section 26(1) but also relates to section 26(3), which prevents people from being evicted unfairly or arbitrarily from their houses. (c) The Constitutional Court tends to read section 26(1) and (2) conjunctively rather than disjunctively when exercising such review powers. (d) The Court has opted for a model of fairly thin reasonableness review of the state's efforts to comply with its constitutional obligations under section 26(2). (e) The Court has so far indicated that a housing programme of the state shall not be reasonable when it relies exclusively on medium and long term waiting lists, without making any provision for emergency

---

[323] Par [48] at 23A–B.

and crisis housing needs that require immediate action. (*f*) The Court has so far rejected the notion of reading a core minimum right to housing into section 26. (*g*) The Court seems to expect the state to comply with general legality requirements in other legislation when fulfilling its duties with regard to provision of housing, even in emergency situations. (*h*) The result of the last few conclusions mentioned above is that efforts to construe a positive duty to provide housing on the basis of section 26 have so far been unsuccessful. (*i*) The latest case law suggests that a new initiative might be developing that might result in stricter control over the state in complying with its constitutional obligation to provide housing, this time via arguments based on the state's duty to protect citizens and their fundamental rights as set out in section 7 of the Constitution or the state's duty to provide suitable and efficient remedies for the enforcement and protection of rights as set out in section 34.

6.5 WATER, MINERAL AND PETROLEUM RESOURCES

24. Environment

Everyone has the right—
  (*a*) to an environment that is not harmful to their health or well-being; and
  (*b*) to have the environment protected, for the benefit of present and future generations, through reasonable legislative and other measures that—
    (i) prevent pollution and ecological degradation;
    (ii) promote conservation; and
    (iii) secure ecologically sustainable development and use of natural resources while promoting justifiable economic and social development.

25. Property

(4) For the purposes of this section—
    (*a*) the public interest includes the nation's commitment to land reform, and to reforms to bring about equitable access to all South Africa's natural resources; and
    (*b*) property is not limited to land.
(8) No provision of this section may impede the state from taking legislative and other measures to achieve land, water and related reform, in order to redress the results of past racial discrimination, provided that any departure from the provisions of this section is in accordance with the provisions of section 36(1).

27. Health care, food, water, and social security

(1) Everyone has the right to have access to—
    (*a*) ...
    (*b*) sufficient food and water; and
    (*c*) ...
(2) The state must take reasonable legislative and other measures, within its available resources, to achieve the progressive realization of each of these rights.

6.5.1 Introduction

Section 25 does not explicitly guarantee access to water, mineral and petroleum or other resources in the same fashion that it does with restitution, tenure security and access to land, but the reform provisions in the Constitution have to be read as a whole, and apart from section 25 there are other provisions in the Bill of Rights that extend the constitutional duty and authority to reform land rights and land holdings to include water and other natural resources. Firstly, section 27(1)(b) of the Constitution guarantees everyone the right of access to sufficient food and water, and section 27(2) provides that the state must take reasonable legislative and other measures, within its available resources, to achieve the progressive realisation of this right. Secondly, section 24 guarantees a right to have the environment protected through reasonable legislative and other measures that would, among other things, secure ecologically sustainable development and use of natural resources while promoting justifiable economic and social development. More particularly, the definition provision in section 25(4) specifies that the notion of the public interest in section 25 'includes the nation's commitment to land reform and to reforms to bring about equitable access to all South Africa's natural resources' and that 'property is not limited to land' and the limitation proviso in section 25(8) includes 'water and related reform' with land reform in stipulating that section 25 may not impede the state from taking legislative and other measures to achieve such reform in order to redress the results of past racial discrimination.[324] None of these provisions creates an general right of access to natural resources, but they do authorise reforms to improve access to natural resources in such a general manner that it could be argued that other natural resources besides water are included in the general authorization for the state to bring about more equitable access to all natural resources. It is therefore clear that, at the very least, section 25 should not be interpreted or applied in such a way that it frustrates or impedes legislative and other measures that are undertaken to achieve reforms with regard to access to water, mineral and petroleum or other similar natural resources.

It would be impossible to discuss all the access rights (apart from land and housing) that are actually or potentially created by sections 24, 25, 26, 27 and 29,[325] and therefore

---

[324]The limitation proviso in section 25(8) is discussed in 6.6 below.

[325]See D Brand & S Russell (eds) *Exploring the core content of socio-economic rights: South African and international perspectives* (2002) for a discussion of a wider range of access rights. A number of recent cases dealt with the efforts of the Department of Environmental Affairs and Tourism to regulate the fishing industry in a way that would simultaneously conserve natural resources, promote economic and sustainable exploitation of fishing resources and establish more equitable access to the fishing industry. See *Minister of Environmental Affairs and Tourism and Others v Pepper Bay Fishing (Pty) Ltd; Minister of Environmental Affairs and Tourism and Others v Smith* 2004 (1) SA 308 (SCA); *Minister of Environmental Affairs and Tourism and Others v Atlantic Fishing Enterprises (Pty) Ltd and Others* 2004 (3) SA 176 (SCA); *Bato Star Fishing (Pty) Ltd v Minister of Environmental Affairs and Others* 2004 (4) SA 490 (CC). On the right to a healthy environment see further M van der Linde & E Basson 'Environment' in S Woolman et al (eds) *Constitutional law of South Africa* (2nd ed 2003 original service) chapter 50.

the following two sections set out the broad outlines of new legislation that controls access to just two major resources, namely water and mineral and petroleum resources, whereafter the most important constitutional issues common to both these areas are considered.

6.5.2 The new water dispensation of 1997–1998

Section 27(1)(b) of the Constitution guarantees everyone the right of access to sufficient water, and section 27(2) provides that the state must take reasonable legislative and other measures, within its available resources, to achieve the progressive realisation of this right. The definition provision in section 25(4) and the limitation proviso in section 25(8) indicate that reforms to improve access to water form part of the state's constitutional obligation to bring about more equitable access to all South Africa's natural resources.

Various legislative measures and other measures have been put in place since 1993 to improve access to water resources. This includes a general drive by the Department of Water Affairs to provide access to water, especially in rural areas,[326] as well as the more specific Free Basic Water strategy aimed at providing every household with a minimum of free water per month.[327] In addition, context-specific provisions in cer-

---

[326] More than 31 million persons (67% of the total population) now have access to free water; more than 29 million of them (54%) are classified as poor: http://www.dwaf.gov.za/FreeBasicWater/ Defaulthome.asp. Special community-based water access efforts are combined with community empowerment and environment conservation efforts in the Working for Water programme which was launched in 1995 in an effort to tackle the problem of invading alien plants and unemployment. It is a multi-departmental initiative led by the departments of Water Affairs and Forestry, Environmental Affairs and Tourism and Agriculture. With 300 projects throughout the country, the programme aims to enhance water security, improve ecological integrity, restore the productive potential of land and promote sustainable use of natural resources and invest in the most marginalized sectors of South African society: http://www.dwaf.gov.za/wfw/. See A Kok & M Langford 'Water' in S Woolman et al (eds) Constitutional law of South Africa (2nd ed 2003 original service) 56B–2–56B7, 56B9–56B–11 on international law with regard to access to water.

[327] As part of the national government's commitment to provide free basic services to the poorest of the poor, the Department of Water Affairs and Forestry issued the Free Basic Water Implementation Strategy Document in May 2001: see http://www.dwaf.gov.za/FreeBasicWater/docs/Implementation%20Strategy%20version%208.3.pdf. The aim of the Free Basic Water strategy is to provide every household with six kiloliters (6000 liters) of free water a month: Implementation Strategy Document (2001) at 5. At present the aim is more modest, namely to provide the poorest households with free water. The Strategy Implementation Document tasks municipalities to identify the relevant households, and section 9(3) of the Document (2001) at 28–29 provides guidelines for identifying poor households. The legislative framework for the strategy consists of the Constitution (section 152 requires local governments to provide services in a sustainable manner); the Local Government: Municipal Systems Act 32 of 2000 (section 74 requires local governments to adopt a tariff policy that complies with all other relevant legislation, and section 75 requires local governments to adopt bylaws to give effect to this tariff policy); and the Water Services Act 108 of 1997 (section 4(3)(c) prohibits discontinuation of basic water services to poor persons who cannot pay for such services and can prove such inability, section 10(1) allows the Minister to prescribe tariffs for the delivery of

(continued on next page ...)

tain land reform statutes ensure that access to water resources forms part of land reform initiatives.[328] However, the major reform initiative with regard to access to water is embodied in two pieces of legislation introduced in 1997–1998, namely the Water Services Act 108 of 1997 and the National Water Act 36 of 1998.

The Water Services Act 108 of 1997 created the legislative framework within which most of the state's activities with regard to access to water resources are authorized and controlled, and it is therefore the most important legislative water access measure that has been promulgated in terms of section 27(1)(b) of the Constitution. The Act is instrumental in implementing the basic right of access to water and in setting up the regulatory framework and the norms and standards for water services providers.[329] In the Preamble the Act recognizes the national government's role as custodian of the nation's water resources, the need for sustainable and coordinated water resource management, and the right of access to water and basic sanitation as set out in section 27(1) of the Constitution.[330] Section 1 of the Act defines 'basic water supply' as 'the prescribed minimum standard of water supply services necessary for the reliable supply of a sufficient quantity and quality of water to households, including informal households, to support life and personal hygiene', and section 3 provides that everyone has a right of access to basic water supply and basic sanitation. Every water services institution must take reasonable measures to realize these rights, every water services authority must take reasonable measures in its water services development plan to realize these rights, and the rights are subject to the limitations in the Act. According to section 4, limitation or discontinuation of water services must be fair and equitable and must provide for reasonable notice of intention to discontinue services; discontinuation may not result in a person being denied access

---

(... from previous page)

water services, and section 10(4) prohibits any service provider from issuing substantially higher tariffs than the national directive). See further A Kok & M Langford 'Water' in S Woolman et al (eds) Constitutional law of South Africa (2nd ed 2003 original service) 56B–1.

[328] The definition of 'rights in land' in section 1 of the Restitution of Land Rights Act 2 of 1994 is wide enough to include water rights; see 6.2 above; see further A Kok & M Langford 'Water' in S Woolman et al (eds) Constitutional law of South Africa (2nd ed 2003 original service) 56B–2. Section 16(1) of the Land Reform (Labour Tenants) Act 3 of 1996 provides for servitudes such as access to water that are reasonably necessary for or consistent with the use rights enjoyed by labour tenants to be included in the rights they can acquire under the Act; see 6.3.3 above.

[329] The long title describes the purpose of the Act as follows: 'To provide for the rights of access to basic water supply and basic sanitation; to provide for the setting of national standards and of norms and standards for tariffs; to provide for water services development plans; to provide a regulatory framework for water services institutions and water services intermediaries; to provide for the establishment and disestablishment of water boards and water services committees and their powers and duties; to provide for the monitoring of water services and intervention by the Minister or by the relevant Province; to provide for financial assistance to water services institutions; to provide for certain general powers of the Minister; to provide for the gathering of information in a national information system and the distribution of that information; to repeal certain laws; and to provide for matters connected therewith.'

[330] These aims are echoed in section 2 as the main objects of the Act.

to basic water services for non-payment where that person proves, to the satisfaction of the relevant water services authority, that he or she is unable to pay for basic services. Chapter II of the Act provides for the setting of national standards regarding the provision of water and tariffs.

The Water Services Act creates the legislative framework within which practical steps are taken to provide households with access to water and is therefore of the greatest practical significance for the provision of water, but for constitutional purposes the new water dispensation that was introduced by the National Water Act 36 of 1998 had much greater impact on the existing water dispensation, and particularly on existing water rights. In the words of the long title, the 1998 Act 'provide[s] for fundamental reform of the law relating to water resources'. Although other initiatives are of course significant in so far as they embody the state's fulfillment of its constitutional obligations with regard to access, the 1998 Act is constitutionally even more important because it scrapped the whole traditional system of water rights and replaced it with a completely new regulatory framework. This obviously had an impact on existing rights, and therefore the effects of the Act have special constitutional significance.

Prior to the 1998 Act water rights were regulated by common law, together with the Water Act 54 of 1956.[331] The main characteristic of the old dispensation was that it was possible to obtain private property rights, particularly ownership, of water. The traditional distinction between private water and public water implied that water from certain sources was held in private ownership, while private use rights were acquired (mostly on the basis of riparian landownership) with regard to public water. While use of private water was also regulated, the distinction between private and public water meant that use rights with regard to private water were strong because they were rooted in the traditional private law notion of ownership and closely connected to private ownership of riparian land. Even in the sphere of public water the connection between use rights and riparian ownership implied that landownership included a strongly privileged position with regard to access to and use of water. The 1998 Act overturned that position completely and radically.

The Act functions on the basis of recognition of the fact that water is a scarce national resource; that this natural resource belongs to all people but is unevenly distributed because the discriminatory laws and practices of the past have prevented equal access to water resources; and that the national government, as public trustee of the nation's water resources, has a responsibility for and authority over water resources to ensure sustainable water resource management, equitable allocation of

---

[331] See further WJ Vos *Principles of South African water law* (2nd ed 1978; previously *Elements of South African water law*). Compare further AJ van der Walt 'Overview of developments since the introduction of the constitutional property clause' (2004) 19 *SA Public Law* 46–89 at 85–86.

water for beneficial use and the redistribution of water.[332] The 1997 *White Paper on a national water policy for South Africa* that preceded the Act already heralded the nature and scope of the reform that was intended: all water resources would, subject to and consistent with the Constitution, be treated as part of the common national resource and, to the extent required to meet the broad objectives of water resource management, would be subject to common regulation and management.[333] There would no longer be ownership of water, but only authorisation to use water.[334] Only water required to meet basic human needs and to maintain environmental sustainability (known as the 'reserve' in the *White Paper* and the Act) would be guaranteed as a right, and all other water uses would be recognised only if they are compatible with and beneficial for the public interest. These uses would be subject to a system of water allocation that promotes optimal use for equitable and sustainable economic and social development.[335] The traditional system of riparian use rights, which was tied to landownership, would effectively be abolished[336] and all users would have to pay the full cost of access to water.[337]

When the National Water Act 36 of 1998 was adopted it embodied the aims and goals set out in the *White Paper* and it made the necessary changes to the water dispensation. The bulk of the Act is concerned with the coordinated management of water as a scarce national resource,[338] but the most interesting provisions for present

---

[332]Preamble to the Act. See further the *White Paper on a national water policy for South Africa*, published by the Department of Water Affairs and Forestry (1997); and compare H Klug 'Water law reform under the new Constitution' (1997) 1(5) *Human Rights & Const LJ SA* 5–10; A Rabie 'Water for the environment' (1998) 61 *THRHR* 111–116. See further A Kok & M Langford 'Water' in S Woolman et al (eds) *Constitutional law of South Africa* (2nd ed 2003 original service) 56B–14.

[333] *White Paper on a national water policy for South Africa* (1997) at 3–4; compare Principles 2 and 3 at 35.

[334]Principle 3 at 35.

[335]Principles 2, 7, 8, 9, 10, 12, 13 and 14 at 35–36. A Rabie 'Water for the environment' (1998) 61 *THRHR* 111–116 at 113, 115 evaluates the 1997 *White Paper*, mainly with regard to its environmental aspects, as radical but satisfactory.

[336]Principles 3 and 4 at 35. See A Rabie 'Water for the environment' (1998) 61 *THRHR* 111–116 at 114.

[337]See the summary at 4; Principle 24 at 36.

[338]Chapter 2 deals with the establishment of a national water resource strategy and catchment management strategies; Chapter 3 with the protection of water resources and prevention of pollution; Chapter 4 with controlled use of water; Chapters 7–9 with water use management through catchment management agencies, water user associations and advisory boards; and Chapter 10 with international water management. Chapter 1 controls government waterworks and Chapter 12 controls the safety of dams. Section 2 describes the purpose of the Act as 'to ensure that the nation's water resources are protected, used, developed, conserved, managed and controlled in ways which take into account amongst other factors—

(*a*) meeting the basic human needs of present and future generations;

(*b*) promoting equitable access to water;

(*c*) redressing the results of past racial and gender discrimination;

(*d*) promoting the efficient, sustainable and beneficial use of water in the public interest;

(continued on next page ...)

purposes are those that regulate the nature and allocation of water rights and especially those that affect existing water rights. The central provisions appear in sections 3 and 4 of the Act, dealing with public power over and private entitlements to the use of water respectively. Section 3 declares the national government, acting through the Minister of Water Affairs and Forestry, the public trustee of the nation's water resources who must ensure that 'water is protected, used, developed, conserved, managed and controlled in a sustainable and equitable manner, for the benefit of all persons and in accordance with its constitutional mandate.'[339] For this purpose, the government is ultimately responsible to ensure that 'water is allocated equitably and used beneficially in the public interest, while promoting environmental values';[340] and it has the power 'to regulate the use, flow and control of all water in the Republic.'[341] Section 4 regulates entitlements to use water, providing that a person may use water 'in or from a water resource for purposes such as reasonable domestic use, domestic gardening, animal watering, fire fighting and recreational use, as set out in Schedule 1' to the Act;[342] that a person 'may continue with an existing lawful water use in accordance with section 34';[343] a person 'may use water in terms of a general authorization or licence under this Act';[344] and—critically—that any entitlement granted to a person by or under the Act replaces any right to use water which that person might otherwise have been able to enjoy or enforce under any other law to take or use water; to obstruct or divert a flow of water; to affect the quality of any water; to receive any particular flow of water; to receive a flow of water of any particular quality; or to construct, operate or maintain any waterwork.[345]

(... from previous page)
  (e) facilitating social and economic development;
  (f) providing for growing demand for water use;
  (g) protecting aquatic and associated ecosystems and their biological diversity;
  (h) reducing and preventing pollution and degradation of water resources;
  (i) meeting international obligations;
  (j) promoting dam safety;
  (k) managing floods and droughts,
and for achieving this purpose, to establish suitable institutions and to ensure that they have appropriate community, racial and gender representation.'
[339] Section 3(1).
[340] Section 3(2).
[341] Section 3(3).
[342] Section 4(1). In section 1 'entitlement' is defined as 'a right to use water in terms of any provision of this Act or in terms of an instrument issued under this Act'.
[343] Section 4(2). The Department of Water Affairs and Forestry published a discussion document on the process of switching all water use rights over from the current system of existing use rights to the new system of use licenses as foreseen in the Act; see *Draft position paper for water allocation reform in South Africa: Towards a framework for water allocation planning* (2005) at http://www.dwaf.gov.za/Documents/Policies/WARdraftJan05.doc.
[344] Section 4(3).
[345] Section 4(4).

Chapter 4, which regulates the use of water, is founded on the principle that the government has overall responsibility for and authority over water resource management, including the equitable allocation and beneficial use of water in the public interest, and hence a person can only be entitled to use water if the use is permissible under the Act. The various types of licensed and unlicensed entitlements to use water are dealt with in Chapter 4.[346] Water use is defined broadly and includes taking and storing of water, activities which reduce stream flow, waste discharges and disposals, controlled activities (which impact detrimentally on a water resource), altering a watercourse, removing water found underground for certain purposes, and recreation.[347] A water use must be licensed unless it is listed in Schedule I or is an existing lawful use or is permissible under a general authorization, or if a responsible authority waives the need for a licence.[348] A person who uses water in terms of a licence must use the water subject to any condition of the relevant authorisation for that use and is subject to any limitation, restriction or prohibition in terms of the Act or any other applicable law.[349]

The most striking change brought about by the Act is that the traditional distinction between public and private water and, together with it, the notion of private ownership of water are abolished and replaced with a uniform system of regulated use rights with regard to public water (which now includes all water).[350] Ownership of water is not recognized in the Act at all, just as private water no longer exists. All water resources are regulated by the Act, leaving no room for the traditional distinction between public and private water and making it clear that all water is regarded and treated as public water. The only references to rights in water occur in the context of various entitlements to use water, and 'entitlement' is defined in section I as a right to use water in terms of the Act. In other words, the only rights in water recognized in the Act are use rights, and they are acquired or allocated and enjoyed subject to the all-encompassing regulatory control of the state.

---

[346]See the Act at http://www.dwaf.gov.za/Documents/Legislature/nw_act/NWA.pdf, explanatory notes accompanying Chapter 4.

[347]Section 21.

[348]Section 22(1).

[349]Section 2(2). Section 26 authorizes the minister to make regulations concerning the use of water. Section 29 sets out the conditions that may be attached to a water use authorization or licence. In issuing a general authorization or licence for water use the responsible authority must take into account all relevant factors, including existing lawful water uses; the need to redress the results of past racial and gender discrimination; efficient and beneficial use of water in the public interest; the socio-economic impact of the water use; the likely effect of the water use to be authorized on the water resource and on other water users; investments already made and to be made by the water user in respect of the water use in question; the strategic importance of the water use to be authorized; and the probable duration of any undertaking for which a water use is to be authorized: section 27.

[350]There is no definition of 'water' in section I, although 'water resource' is defined widely and includes a watercourse, surface water, estuary, or aquifer.

The most significant practical effect of the Act is therefore that the traditional system of water rights is abolished and replaced with a new system, within which all water rights are seen and treated as regulated use entitlements with regard to private water. This change of dispensation obviously affects existing water rights quite dramatically, and the question is how its effect should be explained. An existing lawful water use, with any conditions attached, is recognized but may continue only to the extent that it is not limited, prohibited or terminated by the Act.[351] No licence is required to continue with an existing lawful water use unless the responsible authority requires a person claiming such an entitlement to apply for a licence, although a beneficiary may apply to have her existing use licensed or recognized as a lawful use.[352] However, the responsible authority may require compulsory application for a licence, for instance in areas where the demands for water are approaching or exceed the available supply, where water quality problems are imminent or already exist, or where the water resource quality is under threat.[353] If a licence is required compulsorily the existing use is no longer valid without a licence; if a licence is not granted in such a case the use is no longer permissible; and if a licence is issued it becomes the source of authority for the water use.[354] A person who has applied for a compulsory licence in terms of section 43 in respect of an existing lawful water use and whose application has been refused or who has been granted a licence for a lesser use than the existing lawful water use, resulting in severe prejudice to the economic viability of an undertaking in respect of which the water was beneficially used, may claim compensation for any financial loss suffered in consequence.[355]

The scheme of the Act was obviously to abolish the traditional system of water rights, to replace it with a new regulatory system, to allow for lawful existing uses to continue within certain regulatory parameters, and to put new overarching regulatory standards, requirements and limitations in place in order to achieve the policy goals with regard to control over access to and the use of water. There can be little doubt that the Act embodies a legitimate effort to fulfil the state's constitutional obligations with regard to reform of inequalities in access to water, provision of better access, and imposition of a fair and sustainable water resource management framework. The most important and difficult constitutional issue that remains[356] is whether

---

[351] Part 3 of Chapter 4 deals with existing water uses. See section 34.

[352] See the explanatory note accompanying section 40 of the Act at http://www.dwaf.gov.za/Documents/Legislature/nw_act/NWA.pdf.

[353] Section 43 sets out the procedure for requiring compulsory licenses.

[354] Section 48.

[355] Section 22(6). The procedure for deciding the amount of compensation and making an award is set out in section 22(7)–(10).

[356] AP Burger 'Nuwe Waterwet: Watertribunaal ongrondwetlik?' (1999) 16 *SALJ* 810–814 argued that the water tribunal in section 146(1) of the Act was unconstitutional because the tribunal did not satisfy the independence requirements set out in *De Lange v Smuts NO and Others* 1998 (3) SA 785 (CC) at 814. Subsection 146(5) was substituted by section 3 of the National Water Amendment Act 45 of 1999 in response to some of Burger's criticism regarding the constitution of the tribunal.

the complete abolition of the traditional dispensation—and particularly the scrapping of the category of private water and the apparent impossibility of still holding or acquiring private ownership of water in the new dispensation—is constitutional in view of section 25(1)–(3), and whether it constitutes deprivation or expropriation of existing rights. These issues are discussed in 6.5.4 below.

6.5.3 The new mineral and petroleum resources dispensation of 2002[357]

Section 24 of the Constitution indicates that the state is under a constitutional obligation to take reasonable legislative and other measures to ensure, among other things, sustainable development of natural resources together with justifiable social and economic development. This provision is sufficient in itself to justify reform that would promote access to natural resources such as mining and minerals. It can probably be argued that the references to 'other reforms' in section 25(4) and 25(8) also support reforms intended to improve access to other natural resources such as mineral wealth. The government made it clear that it saw reform of the mining and mineral dispensation as part of its reform brief by introducing the Mineral Development Draft Bill in 2000.[358]

Mineral and mining rights, in various forms and of varying content, are traditionally recognized as valuable and strongly protected private property rights.[359] Their

---

[357]See AJ van der Walt 'Overview of developments since the introduction of the constitutional property clause' (2004) 19 *SA Public Law* 46–89 at 85–86 regarding access laws in general. See further on the new mineral and petroleum dispensation PJ Badenhorst & R Malherbe 'The constitutionality of the Mineral Development Draft Bill 2000' 2001 *TSAR* 462–478, 765–785; PJ Badenhorst 'Beskerming van mineraalregte: 'n *Satyagraha*?' (2001) 64 *THRHR* 643–652; PJ Badenhorst & H Mostert 'Revisiting the transitional arrangements of the Mineral and Petroleum Resources Development Act 28 of 2002 and the constitutional property clause: An analysis in two parts. Part 1: Nature and content of rights acknowledged by the revised transitional provisions' (2003) 14 *Stell LR* 377–400; PJ Badenhorst & H Mostert 'Revisiting the transitional arrangements of the Mineral and Petroleum Resources Development Act 28 of 2002 and the constitutional property clause: An analysis in two parts. Part 2: Constitutionality of the Minerals and Petroleum Resources Development Act's transitional provisions' (2004) 15 *Stell LR* 22–51; PJ Badenhorst & H Mostert (assisted by M Carnelley, RT Stein & M van Rooyen) *Mineral and petroleum law of South Africa: Commentary and statutes* (2004).
[358]GN 4577 in *Government Gazette* 21840 of 18 December 2000. For a discussion see PJ Badenhorst & R Malherbe 'The constitutionality of the Mineral Development Draft Bill 2000' 2001 *TSAR* 462–478, 765–785; PJ Badenhorst 'Beskerming van mineraalregte: 'n *Satyagraha*?' (2001) 64 *THRHR* 643–652.
[359]Arguments to the contrary are misconceived, as is indicated in chapter 3.7.2. In *Ex parte Chairperson of the Constitutional Assembly: In re Certification of the Constitution of the Republic of South Africa, 1996* 1996 (4) SA 744 (CC) par [74] at 799D the Constitutional Court held that it was not necessary to include an explicit guarantee of mineral rights in the property clause to satisfy the certification requirements. In *Lebowa Mineral Trust Beneficiaries Forum v President of the Republic of South Africa* 2002 (1) BCLR 23 (T) at 29G–H the Transvaal High Court decided that this meant that mineral rights were not protected by section 25, but that conclusion is clearly wrong, as is shown in chapter 3.7.2.

creation, recognition and protection were regulated by a host of mining and mineral laws. Mineral and mining rights could be acquired, held, exercised and transferred in accordance with these laws.[360] The intention with the new legislation was to reform the traditional dispensation radically by recognizing the state as guardian of the mineral wealth of the nation; recognizing the state's concomitant power and authority to exercise permanent control over all mineral resources; fulfilling the constitutional obligation to reform property relations and promote the interests of those who have been disadvantaged by past discriminatory laws and practices; and to adjust mineral and mining rights and interests accordingly. In the process, the state would still promote economic growth and development of the nation's mineral resources, and it would still ensure security of titles and interests in minerals and mining, but at the same time access to mineral wealth would be opened up and opportunities would be created for persons and communities from disadvantaged backgrounds to enter into the mining industry or to benefit from it.[361] Clearly, such a radical reform of access to and exploitation of the nation's mineral resources could not be introduced without affecting existing rights, and it should therefore come as no surprise that the attention

---

[360] Even the briefest overview will take the present discussion too far. On the traditional mining and minerals dispensation see BLS Franklin & M Kaplan *The mining and mineral laws of South Africa* (1982); and compare further PJ Badenhorst & R Malherbe 'The constitutionality of the Mineral Development Draft Bill 2000' 2001 *TSAR* 462–478, 765–785; PJ Badenhorst 'Beskerming van mineraalregte: 'n *Satyagraha*?' (2001) 64 *THRHR* 643–652; PJ Badenhorst & H Mostert 'Revisiting the transitional arrangements of the Mineral and Petroleum Resources Development Act 28 of 2002 and the constitutional property clause: An analysis in two parts. Part 1: Nature and content of rights acknowledged by the revised transitional provisions' (2003) 14 *Stell LR* 377–400; PJ Badenhorst & H Mostert 'Revisiting the transitional arrangements of the Mineral and Petroleum Resources Development Act 28 of 2002 and the constitutional property clause: An analysis in two parts. Part 2: Constitutionality of the Minerals and Petroleum Resources Development Act's transitional provisions' (2004) 15 *Stell LR* 22–51; PJ Badenhorst & H Mostert (assisted by M Carnelley, RT Stein & M van Rooyen) *Mineral and petroleum law of South Africa: Commentary and statutes* (2004) chapters 3–11.

[361] See the summary of PJ Badenhorst 'Beskerming van mineraalregte: 'n *Satyagraha*?' (2001) 64 *THRHR* 643–652 at 646. The Act echoes these objectives in section 2. The objects of the Act are to (*a*) recognize the internationally accepted right of the state to exercise sovereignty over all the mineral and petroleum resources within the Republic; (*b*) give effect to the principle of the state's custodianship of the nation's mineral and petroleum resources; (*c*) promote equitable access to the nation's mineral and petroleum resources to all the people of South Africa; (*d*) substantially and meaningfully expand opportunities for historically disadvantaged persons, including women, to enter the mineral and petroleum industries and to benefit from the exploitation of the nation's mineral and petroleum resources; (*e*) promote economic growth and mineral and petroleum resources development in the Republic; (*f*) promote employment and advance the social and economic welfare of all South Africans; (*g*) provide for security of tenure in respect of prospecting, exploration, mining and production operations; (*h*) give effect to section 24 of the Constitution by ensuring that the nation's mineral and petroleum resources are developed in an orderly and ecologically sustainable manner while promoting justifiable social and economic development; and (*i*) ensure that holders of mining and production rights contribute towards the socio-economic development of the areas in which they are operating.

of commentators has been focused on the effects of the new legislation in this regard, even before the 2002 Act was promulgated.[362]

The Mineral and Petroleum Resources Development Act 28 of 2002[363] achieves its reform goals by a process described as conversion of 'old order rights' into 'new order rights', combined with a broader socio-economic development process that revolves around an empowerment Charter that had to be drafted subsequent to the coming into effect of the Act.[364] Various kinds and categories of old order rights are recognized in the Act;[365] among others, actively exercised old order prospecting and

---

[362] PJ Badenhorst has been responsible for the lion's share of comments on the new legislation; see PJ Badenhorst & R Malherbe 'The constitutionality of the Mineral Development Draft Bill 2000' 2001 *TSAR* 462–478, 765–785; PJ Badenhorst 'Beskerming van mineraalregte: 'n *Satyagraha*?' (2001) 64 *THRHR* 643–652; PJ Badenhorst & H Mostert 'Revisiting the transitional arrangements of the Mineral and Petroleum Resources Development Act 28 of 2002 and the constitutional property clause: An analysis in two parts. Part 1: Nature and content of rights acknowledged by the revised transitional provisions' (2003) 14 *Stell LR* 377–400; PJ Badenhorst & H Mostert 'Revisiting the transitional arrangements of the Mineral and Petroleum Resources Development Act 28 of 2002 and the constitutional property clause: An analysis in two parts. Part 2: Constitutionality of the Minerals and Petroleum Resources Development Act's transitional provisions' (2004) 15 *Stell LR* 22–51; PJ Badenhorst & H Mostert (assisted by M Carnelley, RT Stein & M van Rooyen) *Mineral and petroleum law of South Africa: Commentary and statutes* (2004). I concentrated on the latter two-part article and book because they are the most recent and comprehensive, but the earlier articles are also instructive because of Badenhorst's skepticism regarding the validity of the new mineral legislation.

[363] The Act was assented to on 3 October 2002 and commenced on 1 May 2004.

[364] Section 100(1) is entitled 'Transformation of minerals industry' and imposes two sets of socio-economic upliftment and empowerment duties on the responsible minister. Section 100(1) provides that the minister must, within five years from the date on which the Act took effect, and after consultation with the Minister for Housing, develop a housing and living conditions standard for the minerals industry; and develop a code of good practice for the minerals industry in the Republic. Secondly, section 100(2) provides that 'to ensure the attainment of Government's objectives of redressing historical, social and economic inequalities as stated in the Constitution, the minister must within six months from the date on which this Act takes effect develop a broad-based socio-economic empowerment Charter that will set the framework, targets and time-table for effecting the entry of historically disadvantaged South Africans into the mining industry, and allow such South Africans to benefit from the exploitation of mining and mineral resources.' Section 12 of the Act allows the responsible minister to assist 'any historically disadvantaged person to conduct prospecting or mining operations', subject to such conditions as may be suitable.

[365] PJ Badenhorst & H Mostert 'Revisiting the transitional arrangements of the Mineral and Petroleum Resources Development Act 28 of 2002 and the constitutional property clause: An analysis in two parts. Part 1: Nature and content of rights acknowledged by the revised transitional provisions' (2003) 14 *Stell LR* 377–400 list these rights at 381 and discuss them in more detail at 384–393: mineral right; mineral right with a prospecting permit or mining authorisation; consent to prospect, together with a mineral right and with or without a mining authorisation; consent to mine, together with a mineral right and with or without a mining authorisation; prospecting lease, prospecting permit, prospecting licence or prospecting permission referred to in section 44 of the old Minerals Act 50 of 1991, together with a mineral right and with or without a prospecting permit; right to dig or mine or a claim licence referred to in section 47(5) of the old Minerals Act 50 of 1991, together

(continued on next page ...)

mining rights are distinguished from unused old order rights.[366] The Act makes provision for the replacement of most of the old order rights by new order rights, provided that certain procedures are followed as set out in the Act. The central provision underlying the conversion process is that mineral and petroleum resources are part of the common heritage of all South Africans and that the state is custodian of these resources for the benefit of all, with the authority and responsibility to regulate, control and administer the issuing and use of all rights relating to minerals and petroleum resources.[367] It is significant that the Act does not reserve the right to prospect and mine for the state, but it grants control over the issuing and validity of rights to the state so comprehensively that Badenhorst & Mostert describe the effect as implicit reservation or transfer of these rights to the state.[368]

There are various ways in which new order rights could be described as weaker or more insecure than their old order counterparts.[369] The first significant difference is that the new order rights do not automatically vest in the holders of their old order predecessors. In terms of the Act the holders of old order rights have to apply, within a prescribed period, for conversion of their old order rights into new order prospecting

---

(... from previous page)

with a mineral right and with a mining authorisation; permission to prospect or mine in terms of former apartheid laws, together with a mineral right and with a prospecting permit or mining permit; and a temporary permit to continue with prospecting operations or mining operations. See further PJ Badenhorst & H Mostert (assisted by M Carnelley, RT Stein & M van Rooyen) *Mineral and petroleum law of South Africa: Commentary and statutes* (2004) chapters 3–11, 25.

[366] As PJ Badenhorst & H Mostert 'Revisiting the transitional arrangements of the Mineral and Petroleum Resources Development Act 28 of 2002 and the constitutional property clause: An analysis in two parts. Part 1: Nature and content of rights acknowledged by the revised transitional provisions' (2003) 14 *Stell LR* 377–400 at 381 indicate, the distinction hinges on the question whether prospecting or mining was actually being conducted immediately before the Act took effect; see Tables 1, 2 and 3 to Schedule II to the Act for the definitions of 'old order prospecting right', 'old order mining right' and 'unused old order right' respectively.

[367] Section 3.

[368] PJ Badenhorst & H Mostert 'Revisiting the transitional arrangements of the Mineral and Petroleum Resources Development Act 28 of 2002 and the constitutional property clause: An analysis in two parts. Part 1: Nature and content of rights acknowledged by the revised transitional provisions' (2003) 14 *Stell LR* 377–400 at 383; PJ Badenhorst & H Mostert (assisted by M Carnelley, RT Stein & M van Rooyen) *Mineral and petroleum law of South Africa: Commentary and statutes* (2004) at 13-3, 13-5. This view is based on private law logic, according to which the state can only profess to grant rights that previously belonged (in private law) to private rights holders if the rights are first transferred to the state *ex lege*. It is questionable whether this logic is much use in the present context; see the discussion below.

[369] PJ Badenhorst & H Mostert 'Revisiting the transitional arrangements of the Mineral and Petroleum Resources Development Act 28 of 2002 and the constitutional property clause: An analysis in two parts. Part 1: Nature and content of rights acknowledged by the revised transitional provisions' (2003) 14 *Stell LR* 377–400 compare the old order rights and new order rights at 396–399; PJ Badenhorst & H Mostert (assisted by M Carnelley, RT Stein & M van Rooyen) *Mineral and petroleum law of South Africa: Commentary and statutes* (2004) 25-19–25-31. See footnote 376 below and accompanying text.

or mining rights. Unused old order rights, including unseparated mineral rights held
by a landowner, will lapse when the prescribed period expires without an application
for a new order prospecting or mining rights having been lodged or if such application
is unsuccessful.[370] Similarly, holders of actively used old order prospecting and mining
rights have to apply within the prescribed period to have their rights converted into
new order rights and they must comply with the application and registration prescriptions; if they fail the old order rights will lapse.[371] The second major change is that the
new order rights are not permanent like their predecessors (and all real rights in the
traditional private law system). Once granted and registered, a prospecting right or
mining right is a limited real right in the mineral and in the land to which it applies[372]
and the holder acquires the exclusive right to apply for renewal of that right,[373] but at
the same time each of the new order rights is granted or renewed for a limited period
only.[374] A third significant change is that new order prospecting and mining rights may
not be transferred freely like their predecessors—they may be transferred and encumbered, but then only with the written consent of the minister.[375]

The fourth significant distinction between the old and new order rights concerns
their relative or comparative inherent value as measured against their nature and content. Having analysed these rights on a 'before and after' basis, Badenhorst & Mostert
summarize the difference as follows:[376] (a) In situations where the old order right has
been converted or a new order right has been applied for successfully, one limited real
right is exchanged for another limited real right that could either be roughly equal[377]

---

[370]Schedule II to the Act, Item 8.
[371]Schedule II to the Act, Items 6 and 7.
[372]Section 5(1).
[373]Sections 19(1), 25(1).
[374]New order prospecting rights may not be granted for longer than five years and are renewable
once for three years: sections 17(6) and 18(3)–(4). New order mining rights may not be granted for
more than 30 years and may be renewed for not more than 30 years at a time: sections 23(6) and 24(4).
[375]Section 1(1). See further PJ Badenhorst & H Mostert 'Revisiting the transitional arrangements
of the Mineral and Petroleum Resources Development Act 28 of 2002 and the constitutional property clause: An analysis in two parts. Part 1: Nature and content of rights acknowledged by the
revised transitional provisions' (2003) 14 Stell LR 377–400 at 395.
[376]PJ Badenhorst & H Mostert 'Revisiting the transitional arrangements of the Mineral and Petroleum Resources Development Act 28 of 2002 and the constitutional property clause: An analysis
in two parts. Part 1: Nature and content of rights acknowledged by the revised transitional provisions' (2003) 14 Stell LR 377–400 at 396–399; PJ Badenhorst & H Mostert (assisted by M Carnelley,
RT Stein & M van Rooyen) Mineral and petroleum law of South Africa: Commentary and statutes (2004)
chapter 25. Compare the discussion of the constitutionality of these three instances in 6.5.4 below.
[377]Eg in the case of conversion of rights in terms of a mineral lease or prospecting contract and
conversion of rights in terms of statutory mining leases: PJ Badenhorst & H Mostert 'Revisiting the
transitional arrangements of the Mineral and Petroleum Resources Development Act 28 of 2002 and
the constitutional property clause: An analysis in two parts. Part 1: Nature and content of rights
acknowledged by the revised transitional provisions' (2003) 14 Stell LR 377–400 at 397, 398.
Contractual royalties not covered by Item 1, Schedule II to the Act are lost to the state, as Badenhorst
& Mostert indicate, and the duration term of the right could be shorter in the new dispensation.

or arguably lesser[378] in content. (*b*) In instances where applications for new order rights or conversion of old order rights into new order rights are unsuccessful, existing rights will be extinguished and the former holder will lose that right.[379] (*c*) A holder of an old order right who fails to apply for new order rights will also lose those rights when they are terminated after the grace period.[380] The question arises in both these last instances whether there was an expropriation of property rights, whether such expropriation complies with constitutional requirements and whether compensation is payable.[381] The constitutional issues are discussed in the next section below.

6.5.4 Constitutional issues

It is obvious from the discussion above that the new water and mining laws change the existing system of property rights in natural resources quite dramatically, and this inevitably raises constitutional questions.[382] The primary constitutional issue for adjudication relating to the effects of the new laws is whether they constitute deprivation or expropriation of existing property rights and whether such deprivation or expropriation is open to constitutional challenge. The most obvious example that applies to both the water and minerals laws discussed above is that the new laws abolish the old systems of private holdings (private water as well as private mineral and mining

---

[378]Eg in the case of a holder of an unused mineral right that successfully applies for a new order prospecting or mining right, because alienation and encumbrance entitlements are restricted in the new order right, whereas they were not in the old order right under common law: PJ Badenhorst & H Mostert 'Revisiting the transitional arrangements of the Mineral and Petroleum Resources Development Act 28 of 2002 and the constitutional property clause: An analysis in two parts. Part 1: Nature and content of rights acknowledged by the revised transitional provisions' (2003) 14 *Stell LR* 377–400 at 397.

[379]PJ Badenhorst & H Mostert 'Revisiting the transitional arrangements of the Mineral and Petroleum Resources Development Act 28 of 2002 and the constitutional property clause: An analysis in two parts. Part 1: Nature and content of rights acknowledged by the revised transitional provisions' (2003) 14 *Stell LR* 377–400 at 399.

[380]PJ Badenhorst & H Mostert 'Revisiting the transitional arrangements of the Mineral and Petroleum Resources Development Act 28 of 2002 and the constitutional property clause: An analysis in two parts. Part 1: Nature and content of rights acknowledged by the revised transitional provisions' (2003) 14 *Stell LR* 377–400 at 399.

[381]PJ Badenhorst & H Mostert 'Revisiting the transitional arrangements of the Mineral and Petroleum Resources Development Act 28 of 2002 and the constitutional property clause: An analysis in two parts. Part 1: Nature and content of rights acknowledged by the revised transitional provisions' (2003) 14 *Stell LR* 377–400 at 399.

[382]See generally AJ van der Walt 'Overview of developments since the introduction of the constitutional property clause' (2004) 19 *SA Public Law* 46–89 at 85–86, upon which the following analysis is based in part. Apart from that I rely on PJ Badenhorst & H Mostert 'Revisiting the transitional arrangements of the Mineral and Petroleum Resources Development Act 28 of 2002 and the constitutional property clause: An analysis in two parts. Part 2: Constitutionality of the Minerals and Petroleum Resources Development Act's transitional provisions' (2004) 15 *Stell LR* 22–51; PJ Badenhorst & H Mostert (assisted by M Carnelley, RT Stein & M van Rooyen) *Mineral and petroleum law of South Africa: Commentary and statutes* (2004) chapter 25.

rights) and replace them with new systems that attempt, simultaneously, to recognize and uphold existing rights and interests in a new regulatory regime that opens up possibilities of access to the same rights by others. This change of system raises both large and small questions about the constitutional validity of such a scheme—large issues in the sense of whether it is justified and legitimate to replace the whole system of private rights with a new system of licences and permits issued and controlled by the state,[383] and smaller issues with regard to the effects of the new system on existing individual rights.

As far as the large issues are concerned, the question is whether the scheme of abolishing a whole dispensation of existing private rights and replacing it with a state-controlled system of use rights is constitutionally permissible. Does it not boil down to nationalization of water and minerals, without being subjected to the scrutiny that one would expect under section 25 of the Constitution?[384] In this regard it can be argued that the new constitutional dispensation as such allows and authorizes such a transformation of the whole regime of rights, based on a legitimate constitutional goal, namely reform of the previous dispensation that was characterized by inequality and injustices, provided of course that the purpose of the transformation is constitutionally legitimate (eg improvement of more equitable access to these resources) and that the manner of achieving it is constitutionally acceptable. This argument finds support in foreign case law, as is argued below.[385] The *White Paper on a national water policy for South Africa* already anticipated that the new water dispensation foreseen in

---

[383] Interestingly, the old apartheid system of land rights was also a regime of totally state controlled and regulated rights to use land and, as far as black land is concerned, also consisted of use rights under state guardianship.

[384] PJ Badenhorst & H Mostert 'Revisiting the transitional arrangements of the Mineral and Petroleum Resources Development Act 28 of 2002 and the constitutional property clause: An analysis in two parts. Part 2: Constitutionality of the Minerals and Petroleum Resources Development Act's transitional provisions' (2004) 15 *Stell LR* 22–51 at 50–51 argue that the 'destruction of the legal concept of property through the transitional provisions' constitutes 'a steep imposition on property'. In their view, the transitional provisions in the Act amount to over-regulation that could be open to attack for being either an unjustifiable deprivation or a constructive expropriation of property. This argument is arguably misconceived because the authors fail to distinguish between the larger issue discussed here and the smaller issue involving deprivation and expropriation; the latter are restricted to individual property holdings, the former to the property regime as such, and the legitimacy and constitutional validity issues relating to the two are entirely different. Criticism of the systemic reform cannot be based on individual injustices, nor can criticism of individual injustices be based on rejection of the systemic reform. Initial press speculation that mining companies might sue the state for the rights they allegedly lost through the implementation of the new minerals and mining dispensation did not come true; see J Fraser 'Mines will keep right to sue state' *Business Day* 18/10/2004 at http://www.bday.co.za/bday/content/direct/1,3523,1729522–49567233–0,00.html.

[385] Germany: BVerfGE 24, 367 (*Deichordnung*) [1968]; BVerfGE 58, 300 (*Naßauskiesung*) [1981]; BVerfGE 42, 263 (*Contergan*) [1976]. Mauritius: *Societé United Docks and Others v Government of Mauritius* [1985] LRC (Const) 801 (SC, PC); *La Compagnie Sucriere de Bel Ombre Ltee and Others v Government of Mauritius* [1995] 3 LRC 494 PC. See further footnotes 390–392 below.

it would create constitutional questions about the possible expropriation or national-isation of existing water rights. It countered these objections by stating that, while property rights are protected by section 25 of the Constitution, all rights in the Bill of Rights are subject to limitations, that the property clause itself makes provision for corrective action, and that 'not every common law entitlement amounts to a consti-tutionally protected property right',[386] with the result that the changes to and impo-sitions on existing land and water rights brought about by the new water law would amount to regulatory, non-compensable deprivation (or regulation) rather than expropriation of property.[387] In terms of the *White Paper*, all water use rights (including existing rights to public water, private water and underground water) would be placed under centralized state control to improve the distribution and use management, conservation and equality of access to this scarce resource.

Skeptics who were concerned that the constitutionalization of property might provide ammunition with which to attack large-scale systemic reforms tended to focus on often questionable foreign decisions in which it was held that similar or comparable reforms did not affect property or did not constitute expropriation,[388] instead of focusing on more relevant foreign cases indicating that systemic reforms as such could be legitimate. By and large it could be said that concerns in this regard were overstated and misplaced, and that the focus was wrong—the focus should have been on the overall legitimacy of systemic reforms, provided for by the Constitution and authorized in legislation and not just on substantive individual conflicts with the property guarantee. Once the constitutional legitimacy of systemic reform is estab-lished in principle it is much easier to concentrate on smaller issues such as compli-ance with validity and proportionality requirements in individual cases. In other words, it is necessary to distinguish clearly between the larger and the smaller (or the systemic and the individual) aspects when discussing the legitimacy of the changes of dispensation brought about by the water and mineral laws. As far as the larger or systemic issue is concerned the only question is constitutional legitimacy of the scheme, taking into account its effect on the system of private property as such, and not only its effect on individual water or mineral right holders. In principle, a large-scale institutional transformation of a property regime[389] can be constitutionally legit-imate and procedurally valid even when it affects existing rights quite dramatically—there is sufficient comparative material to support this point.

An interesting comparative perspective that supports the constitutional view adopted in the *White Paper* can be gleaned from a number of German cases, where a similar over-arching regulatory regime imposed by legislation replaced the pre-existing

---

[386] *White Paper on a national water policy for South Africa* (1997) at 8 (in section 2.1.7).
[387] Compare Principles 1, 2, 3, 25, 26, 27 at 35–36.
[388] Van der Walt *Constitutional property clauses: A comparative analysis* (1999) 90–91, 484, 271–273.
[389] Such as the possibility to acquire or hold or exercise private property rights in water or nuclear energy sources. I specifically refer to *a* property regime in this limited sense rather than *the* property regime as a whole.

private rights scheme to protect a public interest.[390] In an important early decision,[391] a law practically nationalized all dyke land in the area of Hamburg subsequent to a major flood in the area, the purpose being to place control of the use of dyke land in state hands to improve flood control measures and prevent the recurrence of such a disaster. The Federal Constitutional Court decided that this action was justified by the importance of the purpose, which was clearly in the public interest. A later decision[392] arguably went even further. It concerned private-law claims against a fund which was set up with funds from a delictual settlement between the producers and some victims of a pregnancy drug. The state made a law which transformed the fund into a public-law fund, added public money to the fund, placed it under state control and opened the claims procedure up to potential claimants who were not parties to the original settlement. The transformation of a private-law settlement claim into a statutory claim against a publicly controlled fund was once again justified by the enormous importance of the social interest in ensuring that all victims (and not only those who were parties to the settlement agreement) would receive benefits from the fund, even if the claims of original claimants were reduced in the process. The scheme was upheld even though it replaced the system of private rights with a system of public rights and even though it reduced the money value of the initial claims. The systemic change was justified by the legitimacy of the public purpose for which it was imposed and by judicial acceptance that it was instituted lawfully.

In view of these decisions, which have to be seen against the background of the (much stricter) institutional property guarantee in German law, it is probable that the equally enormous public interest in proper state control over the use and distribution of water (and minerals) will justify the admittedly drastic steps taken to reform South African water (and mineral) law. The legitimacy of the scheme that replaced the old private-property dominated water and mineral dispensations with new, public-property regulatory dispensations has to be evaluated with reference to the overall reformist goals and values in the Constitution and the overall reasonableness of the

---

[390] In the German context this issue is complicated by the so-called institutional property guarantee which is associated with article 14.1 of the German Basic Law, which means that a law which abolishes the institution of property itself (removes the whole or a substantial portion of the world of property from private access) could be unconstitutional. This guarantee does not apply in South African law, but the comparative perspective is nevertheless useful. See AJ van der Walt 'Towards a theory of rights in property: Exploratory observations on the paradigm of post-apartheid property law' (1995) 10 *SA Public Law* 298–345 at 302; DG Kleyn 'The constitutional protection of property: A comparison between the German and the South African approach' (1996) 11 *SA Public Law* 402–445 at 414ff. Although an institutional guarantee is usually associated with a positively framed property guarantee, Kleyn argues that the South African section 25 can still be interpreted in terms of an institutional guarantee, even in the absence of the old section 28(1) of the 1993 Constitution. This is a debatable point, especially since there is no evidence or authority for such a view in comparative law. The most important German decisions are discussed below. Compare article 5 of the Austrian Bill of Rights, and see *VfSlg 9911/1983*.

[391] *BVerfGE* 24, 367 [1968] (*Deichordnung*).

[392] *BVerfGE* 42, 263 [1976] (*Contergan*).

schemes involved, not just with reference to the effect of these changes on individual property holdings. Of course the reasonableness of the new scheme will depend in part on the question whether the new dispensation allows for compensation in cases where the effect of the change was to expropriate individual property holders under the old dispensation, but the mere fact that everyone who had old order rights is affected by the changeover of their rights into new order rights or that some are affected more harshly than others is not sufficient to attack the validity of the scheme, even when the changeover implies some (general and more or less equal) loss of value. Klug[393] suggests that existing water rights were always inherently limited and subject to distribution and use controls, and that the new water law affects the amount and conditions of the actual use rather than take the right away. In this perspective, the new water law is a new regulation (replacing the existing regulation) of the distribution and use of water, and not an expropriation. In view of comparative law, Klug's interpretation looks convincing, given the outline of the water policy and regulatory scheme set out in the Act, albeit perhaps a second-choice explanation that supports the comparative perspective discussed above. Similar considerations apply to the new minerals legislation.

Whether the concomitant systemic changes with regard to existing, individual water or mineral rights amount to individual expropriations (as opposed to the overall validity of the whole scheme) is a different question that has to be answered with regard to the effect of the scheme on a specific individual property owner in a particular case. In this context the fact that the systemic change affects all previous holders of water or mineral rights is not much use, although it can in fact indicate that the change of regime was regulatory rather than expropriatory. If one individual or a small group of persons are expected to bear a disproportionate burden resulting from the change of regime the indication would be stronger that their rights might have been expropriated. These smaller or individual constitutional issues that relate to the effect of the new laws on existing rights are similar to the usual constitutional property questions already discussed earlier in the context of land reform and access to land and housing. With reference to the Mineral and Petroleum Resources Development Act 28 of 2002 Badenhorst & Mostert have raised constitutional concerns of this nature.[394]

---

[393] H Klug 'Water law reform under the new Constitution' (1997) 1(5) *Human Rights & Const LJ SA* 5–10 at 7, after analysis of the nature of existing water rights at 6.

[394] PJ Badenhorst & H Mostert 'Revisiting the transitional arrangements of the Mineral and Petroleum Resources Development Act 28 of 2002 and the constitutional property clause: An analysis in two parts. Part 2: Constitutionality of the Minerals and Petroleum Resources Development Act's transitional provisions' (2004) 15 *Stell LR* 22–51. See further PJ Badenhorst & R Malherbe 'The constitutionality of the Mineral Development Draft Bill 2000' 2001 *TSAR* 462–478, 765–785; PJ Badenhorst 'Beskerming van mineraalregte: 'n *Satyagraha*?' (2001) 64 *THRHR* 643–652; PJ Badenhorst & H Mostert 'Revisiting the transitional arrangements of the Mineral and Petroleum Resources Development Act 28 of 2002 and the constitutional property clause: An analysis in two parts. Part 1: Nature and content of rights acknowledged by the revised transitional provisions' (2003) 14 *Stell LR* 377–400; PJ Badenhorst & H Mostert (assisted by M Carnelley, RT Stein & M van Rooyen) *Mineral and petroleum law of South Africa: Commentary and statutes* (2004) chapter 25.

Their main concern is with the constitutional legitimacy and validity of the 'far-reaching effects the Act's policies of economic empowerment and state custodianship of natural resources may have on existing entitlements with regard to minerals'.[395]

For this purpose, Badenhorst & Mostert identified three 'sets of consequences' brought about by the transitional provisions of the Act, together with three sets of constitutional issues raised by these consequences.[396] In the case of successful conversion of old order rights into new order rights, the main issue is whether the 'degree of imposition on existing rights', caused by new regulatory requirements and restrictions that diminish the nature, scope or lifetime of the rights, amount to deprivation of property or, in extreme cases, to constructive expropriation. In cases where holders of old order rights are unsuccessful in their conversion applications the issue is whether consequent loss of their rights is constitutionally permissible and whether such loss qualifies as expropriation of the rights. In cases where the holders of old order rights fail to apply for conversion they also lose their rights after the grace period and the question again arises whether such loss is constitutionally valid and whether it amounts to expropriation.

Badenhorst & Mostert correctly indicate that the first stage of an inquiry into these issues is to determine whether the old order rights are property. In the Transvaal High Court decision in *Lebowa Mineral Trust Beneficiaries Forum v President of the Republic of South Africa*[397] it was held that mineral rights (in their old order state, prior to the Act) were not protected property under section 25 because the Constitution failed to mention them specifically. As was already argued in chapter 3.7.2, this decision was based on a false reading of the Constitutional Court decision in the *Certification Case*, where it was said that mineral rights were not discrete fundamental human rights and therefore do not need to be specified in the Bill of Rights.[398] As has been pointed out earlier,

---

[395] PJ Badenhorst & H Mostert 'Revisiting the transitional arrangements of the Mineral and Petroleum Resources Development Act 28 of 2002 and the constitutional property clause: An analysis in two parts. Part 2: Constitutionality of the Minerals and Petroleum Resources Development Act's transitional provisions' (2004) 15 *Stell LR* 22–51 at 22.

[396] PJ Badenhorst & H Mostert 'Revisiting the transitional arrangements of the Mineral and Petroleum Resources Development Act 28 of 2002 and the constitutional property clause: An analysis in two parts. Part 2: Constitutionality of the Minerals and Petroleum Resources Development Act's transitional provisions' (2004) 15 *Stell LR* 22–51 at 22. Compare the discussion of the three instances in 6.5.3 above.

[397] 2002 (1) BCLR 23 (T). The decision is discussed in chapter 3.7.2. See further PJ Badenhorst & H Mostert 'Revisiting the transitional arrangements of the Mineral and Petroleum Resources Development Act 28 of 2002 and the constitutional property clause: An analysis in two parts. Part 2: Constitutionality of the Minerals and Petroleum Resources Development Act's transitional provisions' (2004) 15 *Stell LR* 22–51 at 26; PJ Badenhorst, JM Pienaar and H Mostert *Silberberg and Schoeman's The law of property* (4th ed 2002) at 335.

[398] *Ex parte Chairperson of the Constitutional Assembly: In re Certification of the Constitution of the Republic of South Africa, 1996* 1996 (4) SA 744 (CC) par [74] at 799D. In the context of the certification process, the Court held that it was extremely rare for there to be any explicit mention of mineral

(continued on next page ...)

this statement is not authority for the general proposition that mineral rights are not property for purposes of section 25, and it should be accepted that old order mineral rights were and are indeed regarded as property rights for purposes of section 25.[399]

The more serious question is whether the various impacts that the Act has on existing old order mineral rights can pass constitutional muster in view of the requirements for deprivation and expropriation of property in section 25. In testing the effects of the Act on existing old order mineral rights against the constitutional requirements in section 25, Badenhorst & Mostert arrive at the following general results: (*a*) The Act satisfies the requirement of a law of general application, but some of the restrictions imposed by the Act result from the exercise of broad discretionary

---

(... *from previous page*)

rights in a property clause, and that mineral rights as such can therefore not be said to constitute (separate or independent) fundamental human rights that, based on universally recognized practice, deserve to be mentioned and protected explicitly. It cannot be inferred from that statement that mineral rights are not included in the general protection afforded to property of all kinds and categories. In fact, in view of the general formulation of the property clause and the general absence of explicit references to any kind or category of property interests, the converse conclusion seems much more obvious—if property is protected in general, and no mention is made of any specific kind of property, it has to be inferred that any kind of property interest that is not excluded explicitly or by necessary implication is included. This is particularly the case when the relevant category of interests is recognized as property in private law, as old order mineral rights were. See chapter 3.7.2.

[399] PJ Badenhorst & H Mostert 'Revisiting the transitional arrangements of the Mineral and Petroleum Resources Development Act 28 of 2002 and the constitutional property clause: An analysis in two parts. Part 2: Constitutionality of the Minerals and Petroleum Resources Development Act's transitional provisions' (2004) 15 *Stell LR* 22–51 at 26–27 explain that three different kinds of property interests are at stake, and that all three have been recognized as protected property interests already: (*a*) rights to land, including mineral rights under the common law (*Attorney-General v Swissbourgh Mines (Pty) Ltd* 1997 (8) BCLR 1122 (Les CA) regarding registered mining leases; one could also refer to *First National Bank of SA Ltd t/a Wesbank v Commissioner, South African Revenue Service; First National Bank of SA Ltd t/a Wesbank v Minister of Finance* 2002 (4) SA 768 (CC) par [51] at 794E–F, where it was said that ownership of corporeal movables (and land) must 'lie at the heart of our constitutional concept of property, both as regards the nature of the right involved as well as the object of the right'); (*b*) land use rights (*Nkosi v Bührmann* 2002 (1) SA 372 (SCA) par [37] at 385); and (*c*) permissions, licences and concessions granted by the state (for this category Badenhorst & Mostert refer to *Transkei Public Servants Association v Government of the Republic of South Africa* 1995 (5) BCLR 1235 (Tk)). Although one can generally agree with their argument, the authority that Badenhorst & Mostert refer to for the third category is misconstrued. Badenhorst & Mostert at 27 confuse Reich's 'new property' or 'state largesse' with the quite separate category of state-granted licences, permissions and concessions; the latter may in certain instances have market value and be transferable and would therefore not be examples of state largesse at all (outside of Reich's argument). Furthermore, 'new property' or state largesse interests are usually seen as grants for which no rights vest; Reich's point was that there are policy reasons why a right should indeed vest, but by and large this has not been accepted in any legal system—cases where rights in state grants do vest are usually restricted by investment or counter-performance requirements; see chapter 3.7.5 generally and compare AJ van der Walt 'Police-power regulation of intangible property and the constitutional property clause: A comparative analysis of case law' in P Jackson & DC Wilde (eds) *Property law: Current issues and debates* (1999) 208–280.

powers granted to the minister in the Act, and restrictions imposed in this manner could be open to attack.[400] (b) Applicants who lose their old order rights and are unsuccessful in applying for new order rights will have to prove that the loss amounts to an imposition that should be tested against section 25, in which case they can claim compensation if they are able to demonstrate that the imposition amounted to expropriation.[401] (c) Holders who lose their old order rights through non-compliance with application procedures and deadlines could possibly claim compensation on the basis of constructive expropriation, but there is a case to be made that their loss amounts to no more than justifiable deprivation.[402] (d) Holders of old order rights who lose their rights to receive prospecting moneys and royalties should be able to claim compensation for expropriation, especially in cases where these monies become payable to the state.[403] (e) Holders who successfully convert their old order rights into new order rights that are somehow arguably weaker or of lesser content could possibly argue that the deprivation of their rights was not rational or reasonable, especially when they lose the right completely upon termination of the new time limit and non-renewal.[404]

---

[400] PJ Badenhorst & H Mostert 'Revisiting the transitional arrangements of the Mineral and Petroleum Resources Development Act 28 of 2002 and the constitutional property clause: An analysis in two parts. Part 2: Constitutionality of the Minerals and Petroleum Resources Development Act's transitional provisions' (2004) 15 *Stell LR* 22–51 at 29. See further PJ Badenhorst & H Mostert (assisted by M Carnelley, RT Stein & M van Rooyen) *Mineral and petroleum law of South Africa: Commentary and statutes* (2004) 25-22–25-29.

[401] PJ Badenhorst & H Mostert 'Revisiting the transitional arrangements of the Mineral and Petroleum Resources Development Act 28 of 2002 and the constitutional property clause: An analysis in two parts. Part 2: Constitutionality of the Minerals and Petroleum Resources Development Act's transitional provisions' (2004) 15 *Stell LR* 22–51 at 42–43. Item 12(1) to Schedule II to the Act provides for compensation for any person who can prove that his or her property has been expropriated in terms of the Act. Before the expropriation issue can be raised it will be necessary to go through the deprivation test first, because the *FNB* decision implies that the constitutional validity of an expropriation will only come up for decision when it appears that the imposition was either a legitimate and valid deprivation or justifiable in terms of section 36(1): *First National Bank of SA Ltd t/a Wesbank v Commissioner, South African Revenue Service; First National Bank of SA Ltd t/a Wesbank v Minister of Finance* 2002 4 SA 768 (CC) paras [58]–[60]; see chapter 4.5.2.

[402] PJ Badenhorst & H Mostert 'Revisiting the transitional arrangements of the Mineral and Petroleum Resources Development Act 28 of 2002 and the constitutional property clause: An analysis in two parts. Part 2: Constitutionality of the Minerals and Petroleum Resources Development Act's transitional provisions' (2004) 15 *Stell LR* 22–51 at 44–45.

[403] PJ Badenhorst & H Mostert 'Revisiting the transitional arrangements of the Mineral and Petroleum Resources Development Act 28 of 2002 and the constitutional property clause: An analysis in two parts. Part 2: Constitutionality of the Minerals and Petroleum Resources Development Act's transitional provisions' (2004) 15 *Stell LR* 22–51 at 45–46.

[404] PJ Badenhorst & H Mostert 'Revisiting the transitional arrangements of the Mineral and Petroleum Resources Development Act 28 of 2002 and the constitutional property clause: An analysis in two parts. Part 2: Constitutionality of the Minerals and Petroleum Resources Development Act's transitional provisions' (2004) 15 *Stell LR* 22–51 at 47–49.

In the final analysis, every question about the constitutional validity of the effect that the Mineral and Petroleum Resources Development Act 28 of 2002 may have on individual private property in the form of mineral and mining rights will have to be answered on an individual basis, testing the effect of the Act on the rights of a specific rights holder in a specific context.[405] The larger issue concerning the legitimacy of the Act's scheme in effectively removing mineral and mining rights from the sphere of unregulated private property should not confuse the smaller individual issues, which will concern the constitutional validity of a very specific legislative or regulatory deprivation or expropriation of individual property.[406] As was argued above, there are strong arguments and comparative authority to support the idea that the larger issue, namely a large-scale removal of certain property from the sphere of more or less unrestricted or unregulated private property, should not necessarily be problematic if there is constitutional authority and sound policy reasons for doing so. The policy reasons relating to regulation of a vital natural resource, social and economic upliftment and development and promotion of greater equity and more equal access to mineral wealth probably provide a basis for justification of the larger scheme of both the new water and mineral dispensations. In this respect it could therefore be said that the new dispensation brought about by the relevant legislation with regard to water and minerals does not necessarily render these reforms invalid or even constitutionally questionable, even though its effect is that resources that were traditionally available for private property have now either been removed from the sphere of private property altogether or subjected to comprehensive regulatory control that severely restricts the nature and scope (and possibly even the content and duration) of the remaining rights.

As far as the smaller issues relating to the impact of the Act on individual property holdings are concerned, the Act clearly causes a wide range of impositions on private property holdings that can be described as deprivations of property, and each of these deprivations must satisfy the requirements of section 25(1). From the literature it appears that one general problem in this regard might involve the exercise of wide ministerial discretions; judging from constitutional case law the focus with regard to questions relating to ministerial discretion might well fall mainly on arbitrariness arguments. The fact that the Act explicitly recognizes the possibility that its provisions may sometimes result in expropriation of private property and that the Act provides for compensation in such cases indicates that it would be possible to claim compen-

---

[405] PJ Badenhorst & H Mostert 'Revisiting the transitional arrangements of the Mineral and Petroleum Resources Development Act 28 of 2002 and the constitutional property clause: An analysis in two parts. Part 2: Constitutionality of the Minerals and Petroleum Resources Development Act's transitional provisions' (2004) 15 *Stell LR* 22–51 repeatedly recognize this fact

[406] PJ Badenhorst & H Mostert 'Revisiting the transitional arrangements of the Mineral and Petroleum Resources Development Act 28 of 2002 and the constitutional property clause: An analysis in two parts. Part 2: Constitutionality of the Minerals and Petroleum Resources Development Act's transitional provisions' (2004) 15 *Stell LR* 22–51 at 50–51 do confuse these issues; see footnote 384 above and accompanying text.

sation for certain expropriatory effects caused by the transitional arrangements; it also significantly reduces the chances of successfully arguing that those provisions effect arbitrary deprivation. Claimants who wish to avail themselves of this possibility will be faced by the same strategic considerations that affect any expropriation and compensation case in terms of section 25, particularly in so far as the Constitutional Court seems to favour a procedure that requires the deprivation issue to be dealt with first before expropriation is even mentioned. Apart from that, the fact that compensation is provided for could indicate either that all compensation issues under Schedule II of the Act should be treated as constructive expropriation cases, or that they are simply expropriation cases and that the notion of constructive expropriation has no place in the Act except—perhaps—in cases where the imposition amounts to an extraordinarily severe deprivation that affects one individual much more harshly than others, without transferring the property to the state or another beneficiary.

In view of these general remarks it seems possible to conclude that—although the reform legislation with regard to water and minerals does involve serious effects on existing private property holdings—the nature and scope of the constitutional issues that are raised in the process are neither very different from nor more worrying than other, similar concerns resulting from less controversial regulatory legislation with regard to other kinds of property. When compared to land reform legislation, the water and minerals reform laws appear to be neither uniquely interfering nor uniquely troublesome—the problems they cause are comparable and in fact often very similar to the problems caused by land reform laws or by other forms of land use regulation.

6.6 LIMITATION ISSUES

25. Property

(8) No provision of this section may impede the state from taking legislative and other measures to achieve land, water and related reform, in order to redress the results of past racial discrimination, provided that any departure from the provisions of this section is in accordance with the provisions of section 36(1).

36. Limitation of rights

(1) The rights in the Bill of Rights may be limited only in terms of law of general application to the extent that the limitation is reasonable and justifiable in an open and democratic society based on human dignity, equality and freedom, taking into account all relevant factors including—
   (a) the nature of the right;
   (b) the importance of the purpose of the limitation;
   (c) the nature and extent of the limitation;
   (d) the relation between the limitation and its purpose; and
   (e) less restrictive means to achieve the purpose.
(2) Except as provided in subsection (1) or in any other provision of the Constitution, no law may limit any right entrenched in the Bill of Rights.

Limitation issues in general are discussed in chapter 2.5 above. However, a special limitation issue is raised by section 25(8) and it is necessary to refer to this provision in this context.

Section 25(8) provides that no provision of section 25 may impede land and related reforms to redress the results of past imbalances, provided that any departure from the provisions of section 25 is still in accordance with section 36. This raises a number of questions. Analysis of section 25 suggests that the only provisions of section 25 that might possibly impede land reform would be section 25(1), 25(2) and 25(3), and consequently those are the sections from which the state might want to depart in order to promote land reform. However, logically it seems impossible to depart from section 25(1) without also falling foul of section 36(1): any deprivation of property that does not take place in terms of law of general application would be directly in contravention of section 36(1), and any law which permits arbitrary deprivations would be contrary to the demands of section 36(1) as well. Departures from section 25(2) and 25(3) might include expropriations not in terms of a law of general application (which again also contravenes section 36(1)); not for a public purpose or in the public interest (which would also be in contravention of section 36(1)); and without compensation as provided in section 25(2) and 25(3).

It seems, therefore, as if section 25(8) actually raises only one question: would an expropriation, which is aimed at land or related reforms, be acceptable in terms of section 36(1) if the compensation would not be just and equitable in terms of section 25(3)? Moreover, the Constitutional Court's *FNB* decision now raises the question whether expropriation without any compensation might not perhaps fail the initial arbitrary deprivation test and never reach the second stage limitation analysis.[407] This is a difficult question to answer abstractly, but it does seem as if it might in fact be a non-question, because it is highly likely that expropriation without compensation, in circumstances that might satisfy the limitation justification requirements in section 36(1), would also be just and equitable in terms of the contextual considerations in section 25(3).

The real problem is whether expropriation without compensation (or against nominal compensation) is justified in general merely because the expropriation is aimed at land reform. Even in jurisdictions where the property clause does not require compensation explicitly[408] the principle is that expropriation will be unfair in

---

[407] See *First National Bank of SA Ltd t/a Wesbank v Commissioner, South African Revenue Service; First National Bank of SA Ltd t/a Wesbank v Minister of Finance* 2002 4 SA 768 (CC), and compare T Roux 'Section 25' in S Woolman et al (eds) *Constitutional law of South Africa* (2nd ed 2003 original service Dec 2003) 46-2–46-5. Theunis Roux first identified the fact that the *FNB* decision results in all property issues being 'telescoped' or—in his later metaphor—being sucked in by the 'arbitrariness vortex'. See chapter 4.5, 4.6.

[408] Article 5 of the Austrian Bill of Rights; articles 40, 43 of the Irish Constitution. See AJ van der Walt *Constitutional property clauses: A comparative analysis* (1999) 81, 240.

the absence of compensation.[409] On the same basis, if the contextual considerations in subsections 25(1), 25(3) and 36(1) indicate that compensation is required and that a certain measure of compensation is just and equitable, expropriation would probably be unconstitutional if it is not compensated at all or at a lower value than indicated by the normal considerations, simply because it concerns land reform. Of course the considerations in subsections 25(3) and 36(1) may well indicate, in a specific case, that no compensation or a very low measure of compensation would be just and equitable in the particular set of circumstances, but that would have been the case even in the absence of section 25(8).[410] It is, therefore, very hard to determine whether this provision actually means anything. At the moment it looks as if this provision may well be a dead letter, in that it either cannot be applied at all without automatically falling foul of section 36(1), or it does not add anything to the interpretation and application of section 25 that would not have been the case in the absence of this provision anyway.

6.7 CONCLUDING REMARKS

It remains to summarize some of the most important trends emerging from the provisions regarding land reform and access to land, housing and other natural resources in section 25, read together with sections 24, 26 and 27.

The first feature emerging from these provisions and case law dealing with them is that the Constitution either explicitly or implicitly places a range of duties and obligations on the legislature (to make reform laws), the executive and the state administration (to implement these laws as well as various new or amended reform programmes and initiatives), the judiciary (to interpret and apply both existing and new laws and to interpret and develop the common law and customary law) and even on private individuals and institutions (to respect rights) in a certain way to ensure that the rights in the Constitution are respected, protected, promoted and fulfilled. The duties and obligations vary from right to right, and even within different aspects of the same right; from beneficiary to beneficiary and from one context to the next, according to the circumstances of each case; and they also vary according to the person, other private institution or state organ upon which they rest.

As far as the legislature is concerned, its main duty is to make reform laws that would ensure that the rights in sections 24–27 are respected, protected, promoted and fulfilled in line with section 7(2). In this regard it is striking that all the sections

---

[409] In Austria the courts are not quite willing to accept a general compensation duty, but they are forced by the European Convention on Human Rights 1950, which is interpreted as if it required compensation, to fall into line with the rest of the European Union. The same applies to Ireland since it became a member. See AJ van der Walt *Constitutional property clauses: A comparative analysis* (1999) 81, 240.

[410] See the example discussed in chapter 5.8.5 of a case where the circumstances do justify what may amount to expropriation of a servitude without any compensation at all: *Nhlabati and Others v Fick* 2003 (7) BCLR 806 (LCC) paras [32]–[35] at 817D–819E.

involved, from 24 through 27, place more or less explicit obligations on the state to make laws, but section 25 stands out among them for including by far the most extensive and detailed list of law-making duties.[411] It nevertheless appears that case law on the reform laws was so far largely restricted to section 26; even cases in which the laws promulgated in response to section 25(5)–(7) were at stake involved, when the Constitution itself came up at all, section 26(3) rather than or in conjunction with section 25. Conclusions in this regard are therefore somewhat hesitant, but generally speaking the tendency seems to be that the courts employ a reasonableness test when adjudicating the laws made in response to the constitutional duties in sections 24–27. According to this test, as it was set out in the Constitutional Court's *Grootboom* and *Treatment Action Campaign* cases, the laws in question and the policy choices they embody have to be reasonable in the sense that they must establish a programme that is comprehensive and coordinated; must be 'capable of facilitating the realization of the right', balanced and flexible; should not exclude a significant segment of the community; and must include a component that responds to the urgent needs of those in desperate situations.[412] Of course, the reasonableness test was devised in response to the phraseology of sections 26(2) and 27(2), which require 'reasonable legislative and other measures', but this phrase (and therefore the test) could apply to section 25(5) as well, even though that section does not include the limited resources and progressive realization qualifications. Subject to the qualifications, it is possible to say that the legislation that is produced in response to the reform provisions in the Bill of Rights will generally be reviewed with reference to a reasonableness test as it was developed by the Constitutional Court in *Grootboom* and applied in *Treatment Action Campaign*.

A different approach that also has implications for the legislature and the judiciary is followed when the rights of the weak and marginalized are threatened by executive

---

[411] Sections 26(2) and 27(2) are similar qualified progressive realization provisions, requiring the state to take reasonable legislative and other measures, within its available resources, to achieve the progressive realization of the relevant rights (access to housing and water respectively). Section 25(5) contains a similar provision regarding access to land, but instead of the progressive realization qualification it requires the state to foster conditions which enable citizens to gain access on an equitable basis. Section 24(*b*) contains a similar provision with regard to sustainable development of natural resources in general, but does not include the progressive realization or the limited resources qualifications. Sections 25(6) and (7) follow another pattern, simply stating that persons or communities whose tenure of land is insecure or who have been dispossessed of land after a certain date are entitled, to the extent provided for by an act of parliament, to legally secure tenure or comparable redress or to restitution or equitable redress. Section 26(9) requires parliament to make the laws required by section 25(6).

[412] See S Liebenberg 'The interpretation of socio-economic rights' in S Woolman et al (eds) *Constitutional law of South Africa* (2nd ed 2003 original service Dec 2003) 33-32–33-41. The relevant cases are *Government of the Republic of South Africa and Others v Grootboom and Others* 2001 (1) SA 46 (CC); *Minister of Health and Others v Treatment Action Campaign and Others* 2002 (5) SA 721 (CC). See 6.4.3 above.

or administrative action or, in exceptional cases, private action.[413] Judging from a range of cases relating to eviction,[414] debt collection[415] and pound laws,[416] the tendency here is to ensure that administrative and other executive actions that could have a negative impact on persons or groups that have been identified as insecure, vulnerable and marginalized and whose rights are protected in sections 24–27 are subject to judicial overview.[417] This approach implies that laws and legal procedures

---

[413] As appears from the discussion in chapter 2.4 and in 6.4.3 above, this applies to sections 26 and 27 but probably not to section 25. Section 25 probably does not find any horizontal application in the narrow sense (see chapter 2.4), but it is apparently accepted that the so-called negative obligation to respect in section 26(1) does operate horizontally in that private persons are also expected to refrain from interfering with it (see 6.4.3 above).

[414] *Port Elizabeth Municipality v Various Occupiers* 2005 (1) SA 217 (CC). See 6.4.3 above. The case involved eviction under the Prevention of Illegal Eviction from and Unlawful Occupation of Land Act 19 of 1998, which requires the courts to take into account the circumstances before granting an eviction order against unlawful occupiers of land. The Constitutional Court set out the historical, constitutional, political and legislative reform context within which the conflict between the interests of the landowner and of the occupiers must be balanced out.

[415] *Jaftha v Schoeman and Others; Van Rooyen v Stoltz and Others* 2005 (2) SA 140 (CC). See 6.4.3 above. The case concerned sale in execution of a house owned by an indigent person who acquired the house with a state subsidy as part of the access to housing programme, to settle a relatively small debt. The Constitutional Court held that the sale in execution of a person's home to settle debt may only take place under judicial overview, and that all the circumstances must be taken into consideration before allowing it.

[416] *Zondi v Member of the Executive Council for Traditional and Local Government Affairs and Others* 2005 (3) SA 589 (CC). See chapter 7.4. The case was not decided on section 25, although the property clause was raised. The Constitutional Court decided that the pound laws were part of the instruments through which landless black people were oppressed and marginalized by white landowners, and declared certain provisions of the Pound Ordinance unconstitutional, giving the legislature time to rectify the Ordinance as a whole. The offending sections were not allowed to be enforced in the meantime.

[417] Case law of the European Court of Human Rights, dealing with section 8 of the European Convention on Human Rights and Fundamental Freedoms (1950), supports this trend in an interesting way. Section 8(1) of the Convention provides that everyone has the right to respect for (among other things) his private and family life and his home, and section 8(2) that there shall be no interference by a public authority with the exercise of this right except such as is in accordance with the law and is necessary in a democratic society in the interests of national security, public safety or the economic well-being of the country, for the prevention of disorder or crime, for the protection of health or morals, or for the protection of the rights and freedoms of others. In case law on this section the European Court has developed the view that interference will be considered necessary in a democratic society if it answers a pressing social need and is proportionate to the legitimate aim it pursues. In deciding whether a particular interference satisfies this requirement two factors are considered highly relevant (among others): the procedural safeguards available to the affected individual to protect his rights, and the vulnerable position of the individual or group in society. Both considerations correspond with the tendency in South African decisions to ensure that limitations of socially and economically sensitive access rights are subject to judicial overview and that the courts consider all the social and historical circumstances before allowing the limitations. On the European Court's jurisprudence see the explanation in *Connors v The United Kingdom* (2005) 40 EHRR 189 paras [83]–[84]. See further footnote 264 above.

are only constitutionally valid in so far as they either provide for such judicial over-view or when the lack of provision for judicial overview can be overcome by reading in. The tendency in these cases is to require that the courts should consider all the relevant circumstances before granting an order that would have a negative impact on the rights of these persons and groups. Among the considerations to be considered are factors such as the history of apartheid, with its concomitant discrimination against and weakening of persons and groups; the need to change the current unequal distri-bution of property and resources; the history of acquisition and use of land and resources and its effect on poverty and marginalization of persons and groups; and the status of weak and marginalized persons such as the elderly, children, women and so on. This trend ensures that a fairly strong reformist tendency is built into legislation, executive and administrative practice and judicial activity, ensuring that the discrim-inatory and unequal social and economic patterns of the past are not simply entrenched and continued unthinkingly, but that a conscious effort is made by all to change and reform them.

The one area in which the constitutional obligation to reform land law through improved security of tenure and access to land, housing and natural resources still requires considerable attention from the judiciary is the development of the common law and customary law. This topic is discussed in greater detail in chapter 7, but for present purposes it can be said that development of existing law to bring it into line with the constitutional values and objectives has so far largely been restricted to changes (through reading in, reading down, or invalidation, sometimes followed by legislative amendment) to pre-1994 laws, while almost nothing has been achieved as far as development of the unwritten common law and customary law are concerned. The one exception is perhaps the Constitutional Court's decision in *Port Elizabeth Municipality v Various Occupiers*,[418] where the Court at least made a good start on sketching out the paradigm within which the common law with regard to eviction had to be understood and applied; a critical prerequisite for the process of develop-ment.

A final observation involves an interesting general tendency in some tenure reform and access to land laws[419] and the most important access to water and mineral resources laws.[420] These laws promote the reform objects they serve by replacing so-

---

[418] 2005 (1) SA 217 (CC). See 6.4.3 above.

[419] Eg the Communal Property Associations Act 28 of 1996 (see 6.3.4 above) and the Communal Land Rights Act 11 of 2004 (see 6.3.7 above).

[420] The National Water Act 36 of 1998 and the Mineral and Petroleum Resources Development Act 28 of 2002; see 6.5 above. It should be mentioned here that old-order rights in the case of both water and minerals were determined by (privileged, white) ownership of land. In the case of water, ownership of private water and use rights to public water depended on ownership of the land on which the water occurred or of riparian land respectively. In the case of mineral resources mineral rights largely depended on ownership of the land on which the minerals occurred and other exploi-tation rights were mostly accessed through landownership. This fact casts the transformation efforts in a very special light as far as land reform and reform of access to other resources are concerned.

called old order rights by new order rights in two related but different processes. The tenure reform and access to land laws that follow this pattern generally replace weak and insecure old order rights with stronger and secure new order rights, without thereby necessarily abolishing old order rights or the underdeveloped and marginalized system of rights they formed part of. The access to water and mineral resources laws, by contrast, attempt to rectify existing inequalities and lack of access by abolishing the entire existing system of strong, privileged old order rights and replacing it with a whole new system of new order rights that are systemically and qualitatively different from the old order rights. As was pointed out in the discussion of access to water and mineral resources in 6.5 above, this replacement of the whole system of old order rights with a system of qualitatively different new order rights could give rise to constitutional challenges, although there is authority for the general proposition that such a systemic reform could be constitutionally valid if it serves a legitimate constitutional purpose and allows for compensation in individual cases where the reform results in individual loss of rights above and beyond the general systemic changes. Generally speaking the tenure and access to land laws that follow the same pattern but do not abolish an entire system of old order rights should not be open to the same constitutional challenges, although they do have an effect on conflicting old order rights in the sense that these laws generally strengthen land rights that used to be weak and insecure while at the same time inevitably restricting conflicting land rights that used to be much stronger. To date most constitutional challenges against the land reform laws have resulted from this effect, especially in the area of eviction.

Development of Common and Customary Law

7. Rights

(1) This Bill of Rights is a cornerstone of democracy in South Africa. It enshrines the rights of all people in our country and affirms the democratic values of human dignity, equality and freedom

(2) The state must respect, protect, promote, and fulfil the rights in the Bill of Rights.

(3) The rights in the Bill of Rights are subject to the limitations contained in or referred to in section 36, or elsewhere in the Bill.

8. Application

(1) ...

(2) ...

(3) In applying the provisions of the Bill of Rights to natural and juristic persons in terms of subsection (2), a court—

    (*a*) in order to give effect to a right in the Bill, must apply, or where necessary, develop, the common law to the extent that legislation does not give effect to that right; and

    (*b*) may develop rules of the common law to limit the right, provided the limitation is in accordance with section 36(1).

39. Interpretation of Bill of Rights

(1) When interpreting the Bill of Rights, a court, tribunal or forum—
   (a) must promote the values that underlie an open and democratic society based on human dignity, equality and freedom;
   (b) must consider international law; and
   (c) may consider foreign law.
(2) When interpreting any legislation, and when developing the common law or customary law, every court, tribunal or forum must promote the spirit, purport and objects of the Bill of Rights.
(3) The Bill of Rights does not deny the existence of any other rights or freedoms that are recognized or conferred by common law, customary law or legislation, to the extent that they are consistent with the Bill.

7.1 INTRODUCTION[1]

The relationship between the Constitution and pre-1994 sources of law, especially the common law and customary law, is an important and difficult issue. According to section 7(1) of the Constitution, the Bill of Rights 'is a cornerstone of democracy in South Africa' that 'enshrines the rights of all people in our country and affirms the democratic values of human dignity, equality and freedom.' Together with section 2, which provides that the Constitution is the supreme law of the country, this means that all other law, including the common law and customary law, must be consistent with the Constitution. Common law or customary law (or conduct in terms of such law) that is inconsistent with the Constitution is therefore invalid (section 2), but at the same time the Constitution recognizes 'the existence of any other rights or freedoms that are recognized or conferred by common law, customary law or legislation, to the extent that they are consistent' with the Bill of Rights (section 39(3)). Section 8(3) of the Constitution authorizes the courts to develop the common law, either because legislation does not give effect to a right in the Bill of Rights or to limit the right in accordance with section 36(1). Section 39(2) ensures that development of the common law and the customary law will 'promote the spirit, purport and objects of the Bill of Rights.'

One could expect—especially in a reform-oriented context—that rights that enjoy constitutional recognition and protection would be entrenched or developed in legislation, and in some instances special legislation was indeed promulgated to ensure that the constitutional rights would be protected and developed (or limited)

---

[1] This section of chapter 7 is based in part on sections of an article that will be published in two parts as AJ van der Walt 'Transformative constitutionalism and the development of South African property law' 2005 *TSAR*; 2006 *TSAR* (forthcoming).

adequately.[2] However, it is almost impossible to legislate for every conceivable problem in a legal system that is based largely on uncodified common law,[3] and therefore it was obviously necessary to provide judicial maneuvering room for cases that might otherwise fall through the cracks. Section 39(2) is aimed at ensuring that the necessary development of the common law and customary law would—in case of conflict or doubt—favour the constitutional project rather than frustrating it. In this sense, sections 8(3) and 39(2) require development of the common law to ensure that the rights in the Bill of Rights are properly protected (or limited) even when the Constitution itself or supplementary legislation does not provide for such protection (or limitation) in the necessary detail to cover every conceivable individual case.

However, the problem of developing the common law and customary law extends well beyond ensuring that constitutional rights enjoy the protection they deserve even when inadequately provided for in supplementary legislation. A far more complex and intractable problem created by the imposition of the new constitutional order on the largely uncodified systems of common and customary law is to ensure that the supremacy of the Constitution (together with the fundamental rights enshrined in it) is upheld while the integrity of the well-developed and established system of private law is protected, and while the hitherto largely ignored and undervalued system of customary law is afforded due recognition. This problem emerges particularly in instances where proper recognition and protection of constitutional rights involve new or additional limitations or restrictions of existing rights that are protected strongly under the common law, or where 'normal' common law protection of private rights would limit constitutional rights or restrict the application of other constitutional and statutory reform provisions. Section 8(3)(b) authorizes development of the common law to limit constitutional rights in accordance with section 36, but in conflicts between common law and constitutional rights it is always difficult to decide which right or principle should prevail. Generally speaking, two issues arise for adjudication with reference to the relationship between the Constitution and the common or customary law, namely authority (is the restriction of a common law right authorized by a constitutional provision, or does development of the common

---

[2] Eg the Promotion of Equality and Prevention of Unfair Discrimination Act 4 of 2000 (developing the constitutional rights of equality and non-discrimination in section 8 of the Constitution); the Promotion of Administrative Justice Act 3 of 2000 (developing the constitutional right to administrative action in section 33 of the Constitution); and the land reform laws discussed in chapter 6.2, 6.3 and 6.4 (developing the constitutional rights entrenched in section 25(5)–(7) of the Constitution).

[3] South African private law consists of a mixture of largely uncodified common law (of mixed Roman-Dutch and Anglo origin) and ad hoc legislation; see R Zimmermann & DP Visser 'Introduction: South African law as a mixed legal system' in R Zimmermann & DP Visser (eds) *Southern cross: Civil law and common law in South Africa* (1996) 1–30. However, see Ph Thomas 'The South African common law into the twenty-first century' 2005 *TSAR* 292–298 for an interesting qualification: in pluralist, multi-cultural post-constitutional South Africa there is no consensus about what 'our' common law is exactly. Constitutional review affects pre-existing legislation, new legislation and also uncodified common law because all law is subject to the Constitution (section 2) and the Bill of Rights binds the legislature, the executive and the judiciary and 'applies to all law' (section 8(1)).

law justify a limitation of a constitutional right?) and interpretation[4] (should the constitutional (or common law) provision that authorizes the restriction of a common law (or constitutional) right be interpreted narrowly to restrict the scope of the limitation, or should it be interpreted widely to promote the relevant constitutional purpose?). Both issues are discussed in the following sections of this chapter below.

Moreover, the problem extends beyond a simple confrontation between the Constitution and a rule or institution of the common or customary law. Although the South African common law is largely uncodified, it does include a large body of pre-1994 property legislation that controls (for property purposes) areas such as the registration of deeds,[5] sectional title,[6] real security,[7] water[8] and mineral[9] resources and others. Many pre-1994 statutes have been abolished when the apartheid system was dismantled,[10] but many others survived the purge of racially discriminatory laws and are still in force, albeit sometimes in amended, de-racialized form. Over the last 15 years, many new laws have been added, especially in the fields of land reform and reform of access to natural resources.[11] The continued existence of pre-1994 statutes and the introduction of new, post-constitutional legislation combine to create a host of additional problems as far as development of the common law is concerned, ranging from conflicts between pre-1994 statutes and constitutional or new legislative provisions to clashes between new legislative provisions and uncodified common-law principles or institutions. All of these aspects have to be dealt with in view of the constitutional obligation to interpret legislation and develop the common law so as to promote constitutional aims.

Customary law creates its own problems. During the apartheid era customary law was largely ignored and underrated, especially in the context of property law.[12] The

---

[4]See chapter 2.3 on the interpretation of section 25 in general.

[5]Deeds Registries Act 47 of 1937.

[6]Sectional Titles Act 95 of 1986.

[7]Security by Means of Movable Property Act 57 of 1993.

[8]Water Services Act 108 of 1997; National Water Act 36 of 1998; see chapter 6.5.2.

[9]Mineral and Petroleum Resources Development Act 28 of 2002; see chapter 6.5.3.

[10]Especially the primary apartheid laws such as the Land Acts of 1913 and 1936, the Group Areas Act 36 of 1966 and others; see AJ van der Walt 'Towards the development of post-apartheid land law: An exploratory survey' 1990 De Jure 1–45 for details and compare chapter 6.1, 6.2.1, 6.3.1. The majority of apartheid land laws were abolished initially by the Abolition of Racially Based Land Measures Act 108 of 1991.

[11]See footnote 8 above and chapter 6.5.

[12]Tom Bennett is one of the few academics who did pay attention to customary law, including its importance for property regimes and its position in the new constitutional era. See TW Bennett Sourcebook of African customary law (1991) 301–328; TW Bennett 'Redistribution of land and the doctrine of aboriginal title in South Africa' (1993) 9 SAJHR 443–476; TW Bennett Human rights and African customary law under the South African Constitution (1995); TW Bennett 'African land—A history of dispossession' in R Zimmerman & D Visser Southern cross: Civil law and common law in South Africa (1996) 65–94; TW Bennett & CH Powell 'Aboriginal title in South Africa revisited' 1999) 15 SAJHR 449–485.

Constitution now explicitly recognizes customary law[13] in so far as it is consistent with the Constitution[14] and includes customary law in the obligation placed upon courts, tribunals and forums to develop the common law and customary law so as to promote the spirit, purport and objects of the Bill of Rights.[15] Apart from often very difficult decisions regarding the question whether particular rules and institutions of customary law are consistent with constitutional values and principles such as equality,[16] recognition and development of the customary law will also—just like the common law—create conflicts with both pre-1994 and post-1994 legislation and with the common law.[17]

Finally, even seemingly innocuous and apparently technical clashes between different pieces of legislation can (particularly when pre-1994 laws clash with post-1994 laws) require a constitutional solution in the form of interpretation that promotes the spirit, purport and objects of the Bill of Rights.[18]

In all of these cases, the problem is roughly similar: legislation must be interpreted and the common law and customary law have to be developed so as to ensure that constitutional aims and objectives are promoted rather than frustrated. This means that the relevant legislation must be interpreted and the applicable rules and institutions of common or customary law must be applied (and, when necessary, developed) with due recognition of pre-constitutional history and with due respect for constitutional aspirations and goals. Abstractly this may seem like a fairly simple task, but in practice it is the most complex and difficult process that confronts South African lawyers and courts in the constitutional era—the success or failure of this enterprise may well literally determine the future of the new democracy. Some aspects of the problem and considerations that are involved in them are set out and discussed in the following sections of this chapter.

---

[13] See sections 39(3), 211–212.

[14] Sections 2, 39(3).

[15] Section 39(2). Section 8(3), which concerns the application of the Bill of Rights to natural and juristic persons, refers to the development of the common law but does not mention customary law.

[16] See in this regard the decision of the Constitutional Court in *Bhe and Others v Magistrate, Khayelitsha, and Others (Commission for Gender Equality as amicus curiae; Shibi v Sithole and Others; South African Human Rights Commission and Another v President of the Republic of South Africa and Another* 2005 (1) SA 580 (CC). See below text accompanying footnotes 123–128 on this decision concerning the right of inheritance in terms of customary law and the equality principle.

[17] In *Davids and Others v Van Straaten and Others* 2005 (4) SA 468 (C) the respondents in an eviction case claimed that their tenancy of the premises was concluded according to and governed by Muslim law, but the court rejected the argument on the facts.

[18] Section 39(2) specifies that the spirit, purport and objects of the Bill of Rights must be promoted when a court, tribunal or forum interprets any legislation, in addition to instances when it develops the common law or customary law.

7.2 THE HEGEMONY OF COMMON LAW HIERARCHIES

The first consideration that should play a role in developing the common and customary law in line with section 39(2) is the role and influence of the common law during the pre-1994 era. The approach followed in this chapter is informed by a set of interdependent assumptions, namely that the application of the common law played an indirect but significant role in strengthening certain property rights and marginalizing others during the apartheid era; that the hierarchies of recognition and non-recognition, strength and weakness, superiority and inferiority and so on created in the process are still in place even now, fifteen years after the abolition of the primary apartheid laws; that a systemic, fundamental transformation of inequalities in the property regime will require both the strengthening of weak and marginalized rights and the re-evaluation and re-positioning of some existing common law property rights; and that the courts, lawyers and the general public will probably (at least sometimes) resist developments or amendments of the common law that are perceived to weaken the traditional strong position of existing rights at common law.[19] Resistance against constitutionally inspired changes to the common law will not necessarily assume the form of open political or ideological confrontation—in many cases it could take place un- or subconsciously through what has been called the politics of interpretation,[20] for example by opting for a stricter rather than a weaker

---

[19]This line of argument has been developed in the following publications by AJ van der Walt: 'Towards the development of post-apartheid land law: An exploratory survey' 1990 *De Jure* 1–45; 'The future of common law ownership' in AJ van der Walt (ed) *Land reform and the future of land-ownership in South Africa* (1991) 21–35; 'Tradition on trial: A critical analysis of the civil-law tradition in South African property law' (1995) 11 *SAJHR* 169–206; 'Towards a theory of rights in property: Exploratory observations on the conceptual paradigm of post-apartheid property law' (1995) 10 *SA Public Law* 298–345; 'Property rights and hierarchies of power: An evaluation of land reform policy in South Africa' (1999) 64 *Koers* 259–294; 'Modernity, normality, and meaning: The struggle between progress and stability and the politics of interpretation' (2000) 11 *Stell LR* 21–49; 226–243; 'Dancing with codes—Protecting, developing, limiting and deconstructing property rights in the constitutional state' (2001) 118 *SALJ* 258–311; 'Resisting orthodoxy—again: Thoughts on the development of post-apartheid South African law' (2002) 17 *SA Public Law* 258–279; 'Exclusivity of ownership, security of tenure, and eviction orders: A model to evaluate South African land-reform legislation' 2002 *TSAR* 254–289; 'Exclusivity of ownership, security of tenure, and eviction orders: A critical evaluation of recent case law' (2002) 18 *SAJHR* 371–419. See further T Roux 'Continuity and change in a transforming legal order: The impact of section 26(3) of the Constitution on South African law' (2004) 121 *SALJ* 466–492; T Roux 'Pro-poor court, anti-poor outcomes: Explaining the performance of the South African Land Claims Court' (2004) 20 *SAJHR* 511–543; Ph Thomas 'The South African common law into the twenty-first century' 2005 *TSAR* 292–298 at 292.

[20]See Rosemary Coombe '"Same as it ever was": Rethinking the politics of legal interpretation' (1989) 34 *McGill LJ* 603–652; Pierre Schlag 'Rights in the postmodern condition' in A Sarat & TR Kearns (eds) *Legal rights: Historical and philosophical perspectives* (1997) 263–304; Pierre Schlag 'Normativity and the politics of form' (1991) 139 *Univ Penn LR* 801–932; Pierre Schlag '"Le hors de texte, c'est moi": The politics of form and the domestication of deconstruction' (1990) 11

(continued on next page ...)

test when deciding whether a statutory limitation of common law rights was authorized, or by setting higher standards of clarity and explicitness when evaluating the constitutional or statutory authority for or scope of such an interference.[21] In order to overcome such a reform-resistant attitude and the resulting frustration[22] it is necessary to see and evaluate the reform effort in its proper historical perspective, not because that perspective should necessarily justify every reform initiative but because it is impossible to make the necessary judgment call that would justify or condemn a particular initiative without the benefit of the larger picture. After all, lack of contextualized historical consciousness and sensitivity could just as easily result in superficial and facile justification of reforms that should have been struck down as in unjustified, mechanical resistance against all reform. Transformation, or the development of the common law and customary law in line with the new constitutional dispensation, is fundamentally dependent on and influenced by sensitivity for the historical context within which the common law and customary developed and were applied before the introduction of the new Constitution.

The second consideration is the influence of the Constitution. The new constitutional democracy was established in South Africa against the background of a history characterized by inequality and injustice, and the Constitution (together with its supplementary reform legislation) has to be seen and interpreted as an explicit attempt to transform legal and social institutions and power relationships towards greater equality and justice. In that sense, context-sensitive (and therefore transformation-friendly) interpretation, application and (where necessary) development of pre-existing law is a vital part of the larger social and political transformation process embodied in the Constitution. Although the tension between constitutional

---

(... from previous page)

Cardozo LR 1631–1674; Alan Hutchinson 'Part of an essay on power and interpretation (with suggestions on how to make bouillabaisse)' (1985) 60 *NY Univ LR* 850–886; Alan Hutchinson 'Identity crisis: The politics of interpretation' (1992) 26 *New Eng LR* 1173–1219; Alan Hutchinson 'Inessentially speaking (is there politics after postmodernism?)' (1991) 89 *Mich LR* 1549–1636. Duncan Kennedy *A critique of adjudication (fin de siecle)* (1997) 199 explains, in his Sartrean 'bad faith' terminology, un- and subconscious resistance to reform as a strategic aspect of adjudication. See further on the effect of this process in South African law during the post-1994 era AJ van der Walt 'Modernity, normality, and meaning: The struggle between progress and stability and the politics of interpretation' (2000) 11 *Stell LR* 21–49; 226–243; AJ van der Walt 'Dancing with codes—Protecting, developing, limiting and deconstructing property rights in the constitutional state' (2001) 118 *SALJ* 258–311.

[21] See *Brisley v Drotsky* 2002 (4) SA 1 (SCA) and the discussion in chapter 6.3.8. *Brisley* and other related cases are again discussed below.

[22] The Indian courts interpreted the property clause in the then still new Indian Constitution of 1950 in a reactionary rather than a reformist way and struck down reformist legislation, causing conflicts with the reform-oriented government that ultimately resulted in the removal of the property clause from the Indian Bill of Rights: see AJ van der Walt *Constitutional property clauses: A comparative analysis* (1999) 192–206 for an overview of the history and references.

supremacy and the integrity of private law also attracts attention in other legal systems,[23] the historical, social and political context against which this issue features in South Africa is particularly important for proper evaluation of South African reform initiatives. The configuration of a new supreme constitution, judicial power of constitutional review and a strong moral and political impulse towards social and legal transformation inevitably means that all legislative, executive and judicial activity[24] is scrutinized in terms of a set of moral and political judgments regarding the abolition or reform of what is perceived as having been wrong in the past and the promotion and development of what is considered right for the future.[25] In such a constitutionally driven transformative context, reform and development involves more than the 'normal' tension between the stabilizing tendency of existing law and the urge to adapt, renew and develop the law.[26] 'Normal' development of the law,

[23] This problem has enjoyed considerable theoretical attention in German constitutional law and in international law for at least three decades; see AJ van der Walt 'Transformative constitutionalism and the development of South African property law' 2005 TSAR, 2006 TSAR (forthcoming) for references and a discussion of German and international law on this point. Generally speaking, American law does not distinguish between private law and public law as sharply, and the question assumes a different form because of the state action doctrine; see generally LH Tribe American constitutional law (2nd ed 1988) 1688–1720. For various reasons similar or related issues have emerged in Dutch law (see GE van Maanen 'De onrechtmatige rechtmatige overheidsdaad bij de burgerlijke rechter: Zoektocht naar de kwadratuur van de cirkel' in JE Hoitink, GE van Maanen, BPM van Ravels & BJ Schueler Schadevergoeding bij rechtmatige overheidsdaad (2002) 7–89; JM Smits 'Constitutionalisering van het vermogensrecht' in Preadviezen voor de Nederlandse Vereniging voor Rechtsvergelijking (2003) 1–163), English law (see HL MacQueen 'Delict, contract, and the bill of rights: A perspective from the United Kingdom' 2004 (121) SALJ 359–394) and Scots law (see A Boyle, C Himsworth, A Loux & H MacQueen (eds) Human rights and Scots law (2002)); see further D Friedmann & D Barak-Erez (eds) Human rights in private law (2001).

[24] Although this problem affects legislative, administrative and judicial powers, judicial lawmaking features prominently in the literature on this issue because of the critical implications of constitutional review and the countermajoritarian dilemma. Karl Klare 'Legal culture and transformative constitutionalism' (1998) 14 SAJHR 146–188 at 146–188 pays special attention to judicial lawmaking and answers some of the questions raised by majoritarian theory. The best recent South African discussion of the countermajoritarian dilemma is H Botha 'Democracy and rights: Constitutional interpretation in a postrealist world' (2000) 63 THRHR 561–581.

[25] On the dynamic of transformation and its rhetorical codes see AJ van der Walt 'Dancing with codes—Protecting, developing, limiting and deconstructing property rights in the constitutional state' (2001) 118 SALJ 258–311. For an illuminating analysis of the adjudicative issues surrounding transformation see H Botha 'Freedom and constraint in constitutional adjudication' (2004) 20 SAJHR 249–283.

[26] The dynamic described here (existing private law stabilizing the status quo and resisting change) is neither inevitable nor universal, but it seems to be a reasonable explanation of the current South African situation. Klare 'Legal culture and transformative constitutionalism' (1998) 14 SAJHR 146–188 at 146–151 recognizes the tension between democratic lawmaking and transformative adjudication; at 166–172 he identifies the 'disconnect' between the transformative aspirations and potential of the South African Constitution and the pervasive conservatism of South African legal culture as a major source of potential conflict in the project of transformative constitutionalism. See further

(continued on next page ...)

including smaller adaptations that accommodate changes in context or in the needs and requirements of society or of commercial activity, is not seen as a threat to legal stability, but the morally justified and constitutionally authorized privileging of trans-formation entails larger changes that may be perceived as a threat for the stability and integrity of existing law and for legal certainty.[27] Moral and political aspirations towards wide-ranging political, social and legal transformation highlight the tension between constitutional reform and the potentially reactionary tendency of existing law more acutely than 'normal' legal development does.

If one assumes that existing legislation was, with the advent of the new constitu-tional era, overhauled and 'cleansed' of whatever constituted the statutory aspects of the old, unequal and unjust regime, the impression could arise that uncodified private law embodies the stabilizing, change-resistant legacy of the past and that it has to be abolished or changed drastically to promote the transformative process, but that would be an oversimplified perspective on the dynamics of legal change.[28] Although all remnants of discriminatory apartheid law should be identified and abolished, the process of cleansing should be undertaken with care and restraint. Firstly, once the most obvious primary apartheid laws have been abolished it is not necessarily imper-ative to effect all further reforms at once or with great haste—in some cases a certain

---

(... from previous page)
along the same lines AJ van der Walt 'Property theory and the transformation of property law' in Elizabeth Cooke (ed) *Modern studies in property law* (2005) 361–380. For examples that contradict the dynamic of reformist constitution and reactionary private law see AJ van der Walt 'Tentative urgency: Sensitivity for the paradoxes of stability and change in social transformation decisions of the constitutional court' (2001) 16 *SA Public Law* 1–27.

[27] The difference between 'normal' or doctrinal development of private law and transformative development can be compared to the difference between normal scientific development and a paradigm shift as described by T Kuhn *The structure of scientific revolutions* (1962) 52: even 'normal' scientific or doctrinal development (what private law specialists sometimes refer to as interstitial development, ie step-by-step development that fills up gaps on a case-by-case basis, based on HLA Hart *The concept of law* (1961) 37–38) involves some change and therefore resistance. Large-scale transformation, on the other hand, requires fundamental rethinking of the whole paradigm or framework within which all development takes place, and it may therefore imply at least some larger changes as well, even though it does not necessarily mean that everything needs to change or that everything will change radically. However, it may be assumed that resistance against frame-work changes will be stronger than in the case of doctrinal change and, more pertinently, resist-ance against framework change often assumes the form of playing unavoidable changes down by presenting them as (less threatening and less comprehensive) doctrinal changes. For an incisive discussion of approaches to constitutional adjudication and a critique of the interstitial approach see H Botha 'Freedom and constraint in constitutional adjudication' (2004) 20 *SAJHR* 249–283 at 249–283.

[28] See AJ van der Walt 'Tradition on trial: A critical analysis of the civil-law tradition in South African property law' (1995) 11 *SAJHR* 169–206; AJ van der Walt 'Dancing with codes— Protecting, developing, limiting and deconstructing property rights in the constitutional state' (2001) 118 *SALJ* 258–311 for a broad discussion.

reflective slowness may be necessary.[29] Secondly, even when change is clearly necessary and viable it does not mean that everything has to change or that everything must
change radically; change should take place only when and as far as it is necessary.
Finally, in line with the considerations already mentioned, the need for reform does
not justify the abolition of the common law—replacing a well-developed and established uncodified system of common law may prove much more difficult than it
appears, and in the process of all-or-nothing change it is inevitable that many or most
elements of the old system would survive in one form or another anyway, but then
without the built-in restraints and balances of the current system, and ensconced
behind the false impression of being reform-neutral or -positive. In this sense reform
of the common law should not involve complete abolition or a large-scale overhaul
of the whole system of common law rules and institutions, but rather a series of well-
considered, reflective, piecemeal reforms and amendments in response to specific,
clearly identified and well considered needs. The development of the common law
will necessarily have to take place the hard way, requiring difficult value judgments
in every individual case. Where a more general systemic change is required there
seems to be a clear case for statutory reform, rather than leaving it up to the courts.

However, the reflective and piecemeal reform process advocated above should
not be equated with the view that development of the common law must be of an
'interstitial' nature in the sense that changes can or should only take place in the open
spaces between clear and settled principles of the common law.[30] Even the most
settled and established rules and institutions of common law are open to (more or less
radical) change and development, depending upon the constitutional provisions
involved, the historical context and the conflict created by 'normal' or traditional
application of the common law rule.

The problems surrounding development of the common law are illustrated most
strikingly in what may be described as the paradigmatic case for purposes of property
law, namely eviction. Apartheid land law allowed and even fostered evictions and
forced removals that uprooted millions of black South Africans and left them politically, socially and economically marginalised, insecure and vulnerable. The anti-eviction provisions in section 26(3) of the Constitution and in the land reform laws are
meant to stop and, where possible, reverse this process. In addition to laws for restitution of land and positive guarantees of access to housing and land, the 1996 Constitution and some land-reform laws promote greater security of tenure, inter alia by
subjecting evictions to rigorous justification and due-process qualifications and
controls. These laws protect not only occupiers who have a (stronger or weaker) right
to use or occupy land, but even unlawful occupiers of urban and rural land. Clearly,

---

[29] See AJ van der Walt 'Tentative urgency: Sensitivity for the paradoxes of stability and change in
social transformation decisions of the constitutional court' (2001) 16 *SA Public Law* 1–27 for examples of instances where 'tentative urgency' are required. See further in a similar vein K van Marle
'Law's time, particularity and slowness' (2003) 19 *SAJHR* 239–255.
[30] See footnote 27 above.

these reforms affect the common-law right to evict with which landowners traditionally protect their rights against unlawful occupiers. The resulting conflict between
constitutional and statutory anti-eviction provisions and the common law is even
more acute because these reforms strike at the very heart of the common law, namely
the superior position of the private landowner vis-à-vis unlawful occupiers.

Since 1994, some of the anti-eviction provisions and their direct and indirect effect
on the common-law right to evict have been the subject of litigation, making it
possible to identify the contours of a new land-reform oriented jurisprudence in
which the common law regarding eviction is being developed in accordance with the
spirit, purport and objects of the Constitution. In the process the deep tensions
between stability of the common law position and constitutionally mandated change
are revealed. On the one hand it can be argued that the history of apartheid and the
anti-eviction laws clearly justify and require development of the common law that
will restrict the landowner's traditionally almost invulnerable right of eviction; on the
other hand it can be countered that it is not only privately but also politically,
economically and socially important to uphold private landownership against
unlawful land grabbing and land invasions. The tension between these two
approaches illustrates the difficulty of the development issue better than almost any
other aspect of private law;[31] because of its significance the eviction issue has already
featured in several chapters of this book and for the same reason it is again discussed
in the next section below as a paradigm case that illustrates the difficulties of developing the common law.

In the section following the one on eviction, I discuss recent Constitutional Court
and High Court decisions regarding property not necessarily related to eviction. In
that section I argue that, although most cases dealt with legislation, the approach
followed in them and the result of the decisions sometimes amounted to or at least
suggested concomitant developments of or changes to the common law.

Finally, in the last section of the chapter I discuss conceptual and theoretical issues
relating to the development of the common law. This section includes a broad overview of theories regarding the effect of the Constitution on private law and the
courts' reliance on these theories in recent case law, as well as a discussion of other
aspects of the development process.

---

[31] Sanctity of contract is of course equally central to the liberal values that inspire and inform much
of the resistance against development of the common law in so far as it makes inroads into traditional individual freedoms. South African cases such as *Brisley v Drotsky* 2002 (4) SA 1 (SCA) and
Afrox Health Care Bpk v Strydom 2002 (6) SA 21 (SCA) illustrate pretty much the same point in the
field of contract.

7.3 THE PARADIGMATIC CASE: EVICTION[32]

7.3.1 Eviction at common law during the apartheid era

The rules and practices of South African pre-reform-era land law reflect the liberal view that existing land rights (and especially ownership) should be entrenched and protected against unlawful intrusions without first having to assert or prove their historical or socio-political legitimacy. In contrast, sections 25 and 26 of the Constitution, together with the supplementary land-reform programme, indicate the intention to change the still inequitable patterns of land holding in line with the egalitarian, reformist view that the common-law rules and practices of land law entrench unfair existing patterns of social domination and marginalization that need to be amended, inter alia by restricting landowners' traditional entitlement to evict unlawful occupiers.[33] The debate about developing the common law is therefore very much a debate about the integrity and stability of existing rights that were acquired and are held in terms of the common law, as well as a debate about the continuation of traditional perceptions and applications of common law property remedies. South African common law allows a landowner to sue for eviction using the *rei vindicatio*, which is traditionally regarded as the most important real action for the protection of ownership. The requirements for the *rei vindicatio* were set out in *Chetty v Naidoo*:[34] the owner need do no more than allege and prove that he is the owner and that the defendant is holding the property; the *onus* is on the defendant to allege and establish any right to continue to hold against the owner.[35] In a case concerning immovable property, the owner will typically prove that the property is registered in his or her

---

[32] This section is based on and resembles parts of AJ van der Walt 'Exclusivity of ownership, security of tenure, and eviction orders: A model to evaluate South African land-reform legislation' 2002 *TSAR* 254–289 at 254–263; AJ van der Walt 'Exclusivity of ownership, security of tenure, and eviction orders: A critical evaluation of recent case law' (2002) 18 *SAJHR* 371–419. I also made use of R Keightley 'The impact of the Extension of Security of Tenure Act on an owner's right to vindicate immovable property' (1999) 15 *SAJHR* 277–307; Theunis Roux 'Continuity and change in a transforming legal order: The impact of section 26(3) of the Constitution on South African law' (2004) 121 *SALJ* 466–492.

[33] AJ van der Walt 'Exclusivity of ownership, security of tenure, and eviction orders: A model to evaluate South African land-reform legislation' 2002 *TSAR* 254–289 at 254.

[34] 1974 (3) SA 13 (A). See AJ van der Walt 'Exclusivity of ownership, security of tenure, and eviction orders: A model to evaluate South African land-reform legislation' 2002 *TSAR* 254–289 at 256; WE Cooper *Landlord and tenant* (2nd ed 1994) 372–374.

[35] *Chetty v Naidoo* 1974 (3) SA 13 (A) at 20A. This passage was cited and followed in *Pareto Ltd and Others v Mythos Leather Manufacturing (Pty) Ltd* 2000 (3) SA 999 (W) par [5]; *Betta Eiendomme (Pty) Ltd v Ekple-Epoh* 2000 (4) SA 468 (W) par [9]. See further AJ van der Walt 'Exclusivity of ownership, security of tenure, and eviction orders: A model to evaluate South African land-reform legislation' 2002 *TSAR* 254–289 at 256–258; R Keightley 'The impact of the Extension of Security of Tenure Act on an owner's right to vindicate immovable property' (1999) 15 *SAJHR* 277–307 at 283–284.

name and that the defendant occupies it.[36] The onus is then on the occupier to prove that he or she has a valid and enforceable right of occupation against the owner.[37] The position changes when the owner acknowledges (without there being any legal obligation to do so) that the occupier has or had a right of occupation (for example in terms of a lease),[38] in which case the owner has to prove that the right no longer exists or is no longer enforceable.[39]

Although the owner is not allowed at common law to evict without legal process,[40] the protection that this action gives him is very strong. The entitlement to

---

[36]See AJ van der Walt 'Exclusivity of ownership, security of tenure, and eviction orders: A model to evaluate South African land-reform legislation' 2002 *TSAR* 254–289 at 256–258; R Keightley 'The impact of the Extension of Security of Tenure Act on an owner's right to vindicate immovable property' (1999) 15 *SAJHR* 277–307 at 283.

[37]In *Moremi v Moremi and Another* 2000 (1) SA 936 (W) the Witwatersrand High Court held that a statutory lease (created on the basis of an occupation permit in terms of the Conversion of Certain Rights into Leasehold or Ownership Act 81 of 1988) does not create a personal right in favour of the registered lessee only, but that the occupation right forms part of the married couple's joint estate during the marriage, entitling both of them to occupy the premises as the marital home.

[38]The mere assertion that the occupier is in occupation unlawfully or against the will of the owner does not trigger the additional burden of proof: *Chetty v Naidoo* 1974 (3) SA 13 (A) 20C.

[39]The owner can satisfy this additional requirement by proving that, for example, the lease has expired or been terminated. This additional onus will only be placed on the owner in cases where he or she relies on the termination of the right of occupation from the outset or acknowledges the existence of that right, and if the defendant relies on the right as a defence: *Chetty v Naidoo* 1974 (3) SA 13 (A) at 21. See AJ van der Walt 'Exclusivity of ownership, security of tenure, and eviction orders: A model to evaluate South African land-reform legislation' 2002 *TSAR* 254–289 at 256–258; R Keightley 'The impact of the Extension of Security of Tenure Act on an owner's right to vindicate immovable property' (1999) 15 *SAJHR* 277–307 at 284. An owner does not have to prove guilt or unlawfulness on the part of the defendant to obtain an eviction order—once ownership has been established, the plaintiff is entitled to possession unless the defendant proves a right of occupation: see *Hall & Sons Ltd v Kleinsmith* 1963 (4) SA 320 (T); *Krugersdorp Town Council v Fortuin* 1965 (2) SA 335 (T); *Chetty v Naidoo* 1974 (3) SA 13 (A) 20; *Singh v Santam Insurance Ltd* 1997 (1) SA 291 (A).

[40]AJ van der Walt 'Exclusivity of ownership, security of tenure, and eviction orders: A model to evaluate South African land-reform legislation' 2002 *TSAR* 254–289 at 256–258. Rule 6 of the High Court Rules does not allow *ex parte* applications for eviction either; see JM Pienaar 'Recent developments relating to automatic review proceedings in the Land Claims Court' (2001) 34 *De Jure* 162–172 at 169. With regard to eviction of former lessees who are holding over (failing to redeliver the property when the lease terminates), see *London and South African Exploration Co v Moodoosoodam* (1885) 3 HCG 305; *Coakes v Dhanjeesa* (1901) 22 NLR 132 135; compare WE Cooper *Landlord and tenant* (2nd ed 1994) 233. Contractual terms permitting forcible eviction are unlawful and unenforceable: *Blomson v Boshoff* 1905 TS 429; *Nino Bonino v De Lange* 1906 TS 120. The common law does not permit self-help to restore possession, even against allegedly unlawful and illegal occupiers: *Yeko v Qana* 1973 (4) SA 735 (A).

evict is based on the 'normality' assumption[41] that a landowner is entitled to exclusive possession of his or her property—this is what is considered the 'normal state of affairs' that will most likely be upheld in the absence of good reason for not doing so;[42] and any defence has to be raised and proved by the defendant to neutralize this rule.[43] The 'normality' assumption that the owner is entitled to possession unless the occupier could raise and prove a valid defence, usually based on agreement with the owner, formed part of Roman-Dutch law and was deemed unexceptional in early South African law, and it still forms the point of departure in private law. However, it had disastrous results for non-owners under apartheid law because the apartheid

---

[41] AJ van der Walt 'Exclusivity of ownership, security of tenure, and eviction orders: A model to evaluate South African land-reform legislation' 2002 *TSAR* 254–289 at 256–258. The term is used by Rosemary Coombe, who points out that tradition or convention does not present us with a ready-made, neutral and objective source of fixed and stable meaning: in the final analysis, tradition and convention always privileges one view, one perspective, one politics, to the violent exclusion of all others: see R Coombe '"Same as it ever was": Rethinking the politics of legal interpretation' (1989) 34 *McGill LJ* 603–652. 'Normality' reproduces, entrenches and solidifies the inequality, disempowerment and lack of freedom that resulted from the struggles that constituted our culture and our socio-political context: 'Legal meanings are continually mobilized for the maintenance of relations of domination, and legal interpretation plays an integral part in the maintenance of social relations of inequality in our society' (at 651–652). Every instance where we rely on tradition or convention to establish what seems like stable and uncontested meaning is in fact a political choice to affirm or deny, confirm or reject, include or exclude something: 'We have to acknowledge that in legal interpretation we are always affirming the legitimacy of the understandings that are generated by certain varieties of experience and denying the legitimacy of others' (at 631). Thomas Grey 'Property and need: The welfare state and theories of distributive justice' (1976) 28 *Stan LR* 877–902 at 877–879 explains how the basic assumption in favour of retention of the status quo or in favour of reform or redistribution highlights the centrality of property theory in any discussion of social and economic transformation. See further AJ van der Walt 'Modernity, normality and meaning: The struggle between progress and stability and the politics of interpretation' (2000) 11 *Stell LR* 21–49, 226–243 at 231–238.

[42] AJ van der Walt 'Exclusivity of ownership, security of tenure, and eviction orders: A model to evaluate South African land-reform legislation' 2002 *TSAR* 254–289 at 256–258. The lessee's security of tenure is ensured against sale of the property. At common law, the *huur gaat voor koop* rule (lease trumps sale) states that an existing short-term lease of immovable property is not terminated by sale of the property; the purchaser of the property is substituted for the lessor by operation of law and the lessee cannot be evicted by the new owner during the term of the lease, as long as the lessee continues to fulfill his or her obligations under the lease; see *Genna-Wae Properties v Medio-Tronics (Natal)* 1995 (2) SA 926 (A). This rule was again applied in *Davids and Others v Van Straaten and Others* 2005 (4) SA 468 (C). Short-term lessees are also protected by the doctrine of knowledge if the requirements are met. Registered long-term leases of immovable property (10 years or longer and registered in accordance with the Deeds Registries Act 47 of 1937) establish real rights and are protected as such. Unregistered long-term leases are protected (according to the Formalities in Respect of Leases of Land Act 18 of 1969) under the *huur gaat voor koop* rule for the first ten years and under the doctrine of knowledge for the whole term if the requirements are fulfilled. See further *Land- en Landbouontwikkelingsbank van Suid-Afrika v Conradie* 2005 (4) SA 506 (SCA) paras [12]–[13] at 512I–J, 513D–I.

[43] See Joseph William Singer's views about the assignation of 'burdens of persuasion' in property conflicts in American law: Singer *Entitlement: The paradoxes of property* (2000) at 7, 28, 62, 84.

government developed the distinction between owners and non-owners of land to establish and maintain the structural hierarchy that underpins apartheid land law: the strong position of ownership and the (legislatively intensified) weak position of black non-ownership rights of occupation made it easier for the architects of apartheid to effect the evictions and removals required to establish the separation of land holdings along race lines.[44]

Under apartheid land law, the scope of evictions based on the stronger right to possession was extended dramatically. Obviously, the state power of eviction was not unique to apartheid law—most governments have the power to remove people from land when state security, public health or the public interest demands and justifies it. Powers of this nature have vested in the state before and during the apartheid era,[45] and they still do, albeit in a different form.[46] Moreover, the exercise of these powers always has a political edge; law, and particularly this kind of law, is never apolitical. However, during the apartheid era these powers were used for a political purpose that is not justified by widely-shared views of the state's police power or of legitimate state action in the regulation of public and private housing and land use, namely to establish and maintain an unequal and unjust land-use system that was segregated along

---

[44]See AJ van der Walt 'Exclusivity of ownership, security of tenure, and eviction orders: A model to evaluate South African land-reform legislation' 2002 *TSAR* 254–289 at 258; compare AJ van der Walt 'Dancing with codes—Protecting, developing, limiting and deconstructing property rights in the constitutional state' (2001) 118 *SALJ* 258–311 265–279 for a more detailed discussion. Frank Michelman has pointed out to me that this shorthand version of the historical link between Roman-Dutch property law and apartheid land law is neither intellectually intuitive nor historically self-evident to non-South African lawyers. Perhaps the same is true for South African lawyers, although DL Carey Miller & A Pope 'South African land reform' (2000) 44 *JAL* 167–194 at 170–172; Ph Thomas 'The South African common law into the twenty-first century' 2005 *TSAR* 292–298 seem to share my view. The point needs elucidation and further research. For the moment I will restrict myself to the following qualification: by stating that the 'technical' state of Roman-Dutch law was abused to further the purposes of apartheid law I am neither blaming apartheid on Roman-Dutch law nor arguing that it should be abolished. The argument is rather that theoretical assumptions based on the relative strengths and weaknesses of ownership and non-ownership rights in Roman-Dutch made it possible to enact laws that weakened black land rights in such a way that even large-scale forced removals (predicated upon the relative weakness of black land rights) appeared superficially justifiable, especially to those who were willing not to judge the political motivation or the social effects of these laws.

[45]AJ van der Walt 'Exclusivity of ownership, security of tenure, and eviction orders: A model to evaluate South African land-reform legislation' 2002 *TSAR* 254–289 at 259–263. Seemingly 'normal' eviction provisions in statutes such as the Physical Planning Act 88 of 1967, the Health Act 63 of 1977 and the Slums Act 76 of 1979 relate to the health, public safety and public interest functions for which a state organ may sometimes require the right to evict (eg to remove people from a dangerous building or flood plain), but in the apartheid era these laws were applied on a racial basis and so served the agenda of apartheid rather than public health and safety. See AJ van der Walt 'Towards the development of post-apartheid land law: An exploratory survey' (1990) 23 *De Jure* 1–45 at 32.

[46]Apart from health and safety laws, the obvious example is the Prevention of Illegal Eviction from and Unlawful Occupation of Land Act 19 of 1998; see the discussion in chapter 6.3.6.

race lines.[47] The Prevention of Illegal Squatting Act 52 of 1951 not only allowed but actually obliged landowners to evict unlawful squatters from their land, promoting the political agenda of apartheid by introducing a vague and wide-ranging definition of 'unlawful squatting'.[48] It also granted draconian powers of eviction and forced removal to state organs, landowners and the police,[49] and ousted the courts' jurisdic-

[47] Apartheid land law was entrenched in more than a hundred laws, the most important of which, the Prevention of Illegal Squatting Act 52 of 1951 and the Group Areas Act 63 of 1966, criminalized the use and occupation of land on the basis of race: anybody who occupied land designated for a different race group committed a crime. See further the Black Land Act 27 of 1913; Development Trust and Land Act 18 of 1936; Blacks (Urban Areas) Consolidation Act 25 of 1945; Population Registration Act 30 of 1950; Prevention of Illegal Squatting Act 52 of 1951; Reservation of Separate Amenities Act 49 of 1953; Blacks (Prohibition of Interdicts) Act 64 of 1956; Trespass Act 6 of 1959; Regulations for the Administration and Control of Townships in Black Areas 1962; Group Areas Act 36 of 1966; Community Development Act 3 of 1966; Housing Act 4 of 1966; Physical Planning Act 88 of 1967; Regulations for the Administration and Supervision of a Black Urban Residential Area and Related Issues 1968; Black Areas Regulations 1969; Health Act 63 of 1977; Slums Act 76 of 1979; Black Local Authorities Act 102 of 1982; Black Communities Development Act 4 of 1984; National Policy for General Housing Matters Act 102 of 1984; and compare AJ van der Walt 'Towards the development of post-apartheid land law: An exploratory survey' (1990) 23 De Jure 1–45; AJ van der Walt 'Exclusivity of ownership, security of tenure, and eviction orders: A model to evaluate South African land-reform legislation' 2002 TSAR 254–289 at 259–263.

[48] Vena v George Municipality 1987 (4) SA 29 (C) is an example of a situation where the local authority made use of the provision in the Act that rendered occupiers 'unlawful squatters' if the structures they occupied—more often than not self-built shacks—did not comply with building regulations. Of course the informal housing of the people most at risk never complied with these regulations, allowing the local authorities to evict and remove them at will, even when they were occupying land owned by the same authority and even when they have been settled on that land by the same authority in the first place. In the Vena case, the Cape Supreme Court (as it then still was) refused to treat as unlawful squatters people who have been settled on the land by the local authority and who were paying rent to the local authority. The Act was amended soon after to render the lawfulness or title in terms of which the occupier occupied the land irrelevant and to oust the courts' jurisdiction to even consider any aspect of an eviction unless bad faith was proved from the outset. See AJ van der Walt 'Towards the development of post-apartheid land law: An exploratory survey' (1990) 23 De Jure 1–45 at 30; AJ van der Walt 'Exclusivity of ownership, security of tenure, and eviction orders: A model to evaluate South African land-reform legislation' 2002 TSAR 254–289 at 259–263.

[49] Port Nolloth Municipality v Xhalisa and Others; Luwalala and Others v Municipality of Port Nolloth 1991 (3) SA 98 (C) is a case where a municipal authority attempted to evict and remove people who were living in tents in an emergency camp established by the municipal authority on land owned by the municipal authority, simply because the local authority wanted to use the land for something else. The Act allowed the local authority to identify these people as unlawful squatters, forcibly remove them and simply dump them on open ground outside the boundaries of the local authority's jurisdiction (where they would of course be vulnerable to similar treatment by whoever owned that land), but the court refused to allow the eviction (termed a 'civil deportation'). See AJ van der Walt 'Exclusivity of ownership, security of tenure, and eviction orders: A model to evaluate South African land-reform legislation' 2002 TSAR 254–289 at 259–263.

tion to review these actions.[50] During the 1980s, some judges resisted the implementation of increasingly harsh eviction proceedings and forced removals and the ousting of the courts' jurisdiction to review state evictions, but inevitably their efforts merely resulted in further amendments to the legislation and further limitation of the courts' powers.[51]

In this process, the already powerful common-law right to evict was transformed into an even stronger remedy that not only provided strong protection for individual landowners, but also sanctioned the arbitrary exercise of state power to establish and entrench a basically feudal relationship between the state and black occupiers of land. Race-based land laws, backed up by largely uncontrolled state force, denied most black occupiers of land security of tenure and allowed the state to determine, as a matter of political expedience, whether individuals and groups should be removed from land and 'settled' elsewhere as part of the 'huge social experiment' of apartheid.[52] The power to enforce politically motivated, legislatively sanctioned and state-sponsored eviction and (on a larger scale) forced removal thus became a cornerstone of apartheid land law. At least on one level, this represented a significant shift away from the common-law private landowner's traditional power to sue for civil eviction, towards a public-law power to manipulate social relationships for ideological purposes through control over land holdings.

Apartheid land law distinguished itself from 'normal', private land law in the sense that it did not focus on the implicitly political goal of protecting private rights to own, use or exploit land and other natural resources, but on the overtly ideological goal of racial segregation and the establishment of racially segregated patterns of land holding

---

[50]Many apartheid land laws contained an ouster clause, but perhaps the most infamous examples were the regularly amended and extended section 3B(4)(a) of the Prevention of Illegal Squatting Act 52 of 1951 (requiring proof of bad faith before a court could consider or grant any order, judgment or relief founded upon the exercise of the powers under the section); and the Blacks (Prohibition of Interdicts) Act 64 of 1956 (making it possible for the state to prohibit black persons from obtaining an interdict to prevent or terminate state action under certain laws as identified by proclamation in the government gazette). See AJ van der Walt 'Exclusivity of ownership, security of tenure, and eviction orders: A model to evaluate South African land-reform legislation' 2002 TSAR 254–289 at 259–263; and compare further AJ van der Walt 'Towards the development of post-apartheid land law: An exploratory survey' (1990) 23 De Jure 1–45 at 29–32 for more detail and references; compare CH Lewis 'The Prevention of Illegal Squatting Act: The promotion of homelessness' (1989) 5 SAJHR 233–239.

[51]See AJ van der Walt 'Towards the development of post-apartheid land law: An exploratory survey' (1990) 23 De Jure 1–45 at 27–29 (cases relating to the Group Areas Act 36 of 1966), at 29–31 (cases relating to the Prevention of Illegal Squatting Act 52 of 1951); see further AJ van der Walt 'Squatting and the right to shelter' 1992 TSAR 40–55 for a discussion of later case law.

[52]It is now trite in this context to refer to Minister of the Interior v Lockhat 1961 (2) SA 587 (A) 602D, where apartheid was described as 'a colossal social experiment and a long term policy' that must 'inevitably cause disruption and, within the foreseeable future, substantial inequalities', the political wisdom of which had to be left for the supreme legislature as policy-making body to decide upon, and was not for the courts to judge.

and land use.[53] The distinction is illustrated by the fact that the private-law, Roman-Dutch legal organisation of and control over the land rights of white South Africans was by and large left untouched by apartheid law (except in so far as the racial basis of development law privileged white landowners and property developers), while the law relating to black land rights was removed from the sphere of Roman-Dutch private law and largely supplanted or (in the case of customary law in the rural areas) at least supplemented by the (public-law) statutory provisions of the apartheid land laws. I mention this not to suggest that private law rules and practices are neutral or apolitical—all law, particularly all land law, is political. My intention is to emphasise, in the case of apartheid land law, the specific evil of the politics underlying and inspiring the division between the two systems of land law. The land law regime was politicised (in the sense of racialized) in a very specific way by apartheid, and reform of the land law regime inevitably has to proceed from a strongly politicised point of departure to address the legacy of that evil. Quite apart from the fact that all law is obviously closely connected with ideological and political ideals and power structures, the racial-political core of apartheid land law established such a strong duty to transform whatever remains of the apartheid legacy that the political goal of transformation and reform has to assume a direction-giving position in the interpretation and application of current land-reform laws. As far as property law is concerned, the politicized nature of land reform is not a consideration that can be raised against transformation-oriented development of the common law, but much rather an inevitable, fundamental aspect of the reform process as such, because land law is not politically neutral or innocent—both the common law regarding property in land and existing property holdings were fundamentally shaped and affected by the deeply politicized intervention of apartheid laws and policies. As appears from analysis of anti-eviction reform laws and case law, this is an important consideration to keep in mind because it reflexively justifies and in fact necessitates an equally overtly politicized awareness of reform and transformation of the inequalities that remain in existing land holding patterns.

7.3.2 Anti-eviction measures in the land reform era[54]

Tenure reform, one of the three pillars of post-1994 land reform in South Africa,[55] strengthens and secures weak and vulnerable rights and interests in land, in some cases

---

[53]See AJ van der Walt 'Towards the development of post-apartheid land law: An exploratory survey' (1990) 23 *De Jure* 1–45 at 2.

[54]This section is a summary of the results of AJ van der Walt 'Exclusivity of ownership, security of tenure, and eviction orders: A model to evaluate South African land-reform legislation' 2002 *TSAR* 254–289 at 263–289. See the article for more detail about the individual provisions.

[55]AJ van der Walt 'Exclusivity of ownership, security of tenure, and eviction orders: A model to evaluate South African land-reform legislation' 2002 *TSAR* 254–289 at 263–289. The other pillars are restitution (giving back of land rights taken away under apartheid) and redistribution (improving

(continued on next page ...)

regardless of their lawfulness, so that those who have access to land do not lose it unnecessarily, unfairly or arbitrarily.[56] Tenure reform diminishes and removes the threat of further evictions by imposing strict qualification and due-process controls on evictions in so far as they are allowed in the new constitutional framework.[57] The reform laws move away from landownership rights as trumps and towards adjudication of individual eviction cases in a balancing process that takes cognisance of the socio-economic circumstances of the occupiers. It is sometimes argued that this approach injects an arbitrary and unduly politicised element into the process of adjudication[58] but, as was pointed out earlier, the political justification of anti-eviction provisions in land reform laws cannot be properly understood unless the background of apartheid law is taken into account.

Section 26(3) of the Constitution prohibits eviction from and demolition of homes[59] without a court order. This constitutional principle has been copied in a range of reform laws[60] that lay down qualifications for allowing evictions and require-

---

(... from previous page)

access to land). Compare further AJ van der Walt 'Property rights and hierarchies of power: A critical evaluation of land-reform policy in South Africa' (1999) 64 *Koers* 259–294 at 281, and see chapter 6.1, 6.2, 6.3, 6.4. Section 25(6) of the Constitution places an obligation on the state to improve security of tenure by way of appropriate legislation: 'A person or community whose tenure of land is legally insecure as a result of past racially discriminatory laws or practices is entitled, to the

[56] AJ van der Walt 'Exclusivity of ownership, security of tenure, and eviction orders: A model to evaluate South African land-reform legislation' 2002 *TSAR* 254–289 at 263–289.

[57] AJ van der Walt 'Exclusivity of ownership, security of tenure, and eviction orders: A model to evaluate South African land-reform legislation' 2002 *TSAR* 254–289 at 263–289. G Pienaar 'Registration of informal land-use rights in South Africa: Giving teeth to (toothless?) paper tigers?' 2000 *TSAR* 442–468 analyses the possibility of developing a system of registration for informal land-use rights. In terms of the model I use, his proposal implies that the land-use rights are secured with regard to the first consideration, namely to transform them into recognised rights that can trump ownership.

[58] See *Joubert and Others v Van Rensburg and Others* 2001 (1) SA 753 (W) par [41], but see *contra Port Elizabeth Municipality v Peoples Dialogue on Land and Shelter and Others* 2000 (2) SA 1074 (SEC) at 1081H–I. Compare AJ van der Walt 'Exclusivity of ownership, security of tenure, and eviction orders: A model to evaluate South African land-reform legislation' 2002 *TSAR* 254–289 at 263–289.

[59] Note that the provision applies to homes and not to all land, but it is applicable to lawful and unlawful residents: AJ van der Walt 'Exclusivity of ownership, security of tenure, and eviction orders: A model to evaluate South African land-reform legislation' 2002 *TSAR* 254–289 at 263–289.

[60] Eviction provisions appear in the following statutes: the Rental Housing Act 50 of 1999 protects the occupation rights of (lawful) occupiers of (rural and urban) residential property; the Land Reform (Labour Tenants) Act 3 of 1996 protects (lawful) occupiers of agricultural (rural) land; the Extension of Security of Tenure Act 62 of 1997 protects the occupation rights of persons who (lawfully) occupy (rural) land with consent of the landowner; the Interim Protection of Informal Land Rights Act 31 of 1996 protects (lawful) occupiers of (rural and urban) land in terms of informal land rights; the Restitution of Land Rights Act 22 of 1994 protects (lawful and unlawful) occupiers of (urban and rural) land who have instituted a restitution claim; and the Prevention of Illegal Eviction from and Unlawful Occupation of Land Act 19 of 1998 regulates eviction of unlawful occupiers (from urban and rural land).

ments for carrying them out lawfully. The land reform laws that include anti-eviction provisions sometimes overlap and have been adopted piecemeal (and not always coordinated) over a period of time;[61] and some of them serve a wide-ranging, catch-all purpose in ensuring stability and security while others have a more restricted application.[62]

Despite the lack of coordination, and even though individual laws allow for deviations necessitated by the exigencies of the kind of occupation they deal with, the anti-eviction laws display a shared (albeit imperfectly articulated)[63] land-reform policy with regard to the question when eviction should be allowed and how it should be controlled and carried out. Common characteristics make analysis and application of this range of legislation easier.[64] Analysis suggests that land-reform legislation has brought about a more or less ad hoc but nevertheless reasonably standardised set of qualifications, restrictions and controls to ensure that evictions are not undertaken lightly or arbitrarily.[65] The effect of the reform legislation can be summarised as follows:

• Existing rights are neither upheld automatically or by default (as the position was in the common law), nor are they ignored or devalued completely. In some cases existing rights are upheld strongly in the sense that the common law position

---

[61] AJ van der Walt 'Exclusivity of ownership, security of tenure, and eviction orders: A model to evaluate South African land-reform legislation' 2002 TSAR 254–289 at 263–289. Some laws protect lawful and others unlawful occupiers of property, some protect specific categories of occupiers while others have a more general scope, some concentrate on houses and similar structures and others on vacant land, some apply in urban and others in rural areas. See in this respect R Keightley 'The impact of the Extension of Security of Tenure Act on an owner's right to vindicate immovable property' (1999) 15 SAJHR 277–307 at 306 (the applicable legislation has been introduced piecemeal over a period of time, and gives no clear indication of a unifying legislative vision that can assist the courts in interpreting the various lapses, loopholes and gaps creatively with a view to the social and political changes they are supposed to help bring about).

[62] AJ van der Walt 'Exclusivity of ownership, security of tenure, and eviction orders: A model to evaluate South African land-reform legislation' 2002 TSAR 254–289 at 263–289. The picture is complicated by the fact that different courts have jurisdiction over different laws, leaving the applicant with the sometimes unenviable task of deciding where the application should be launched. For a general overview see A Gildenhuys 'Evictions: A quagmire for the unwary' Butterworths Property Law Digest (Sep 1999) 5–11 at 11.

[63] See R Keightley 'The impact of the Extension of Security of Tenure Act on an owner's right to vindicate immovable property' (1999) 15 SAJHR 277–307 at 306; AJ van der Walt 'Exclusivity of ownership, security of tenure, and eviction orders: A model to evaluate South African land-reform legislation' 2002 TSAR 254–289 at 263–289.

[64] AJ van der Walt 'Exclusivity of ownership, security of tenure, and eviction orders: A model to evaluate South African land-reform legislation' 2002 TSAR 254–289 at 263–289 develops an analytic model for the interpretation and application of all the anti-eviction provisions, based on these common characteristics. Details of how the different land reform laws display these characteristics appear in the article.

[65] AJ van der Walt 'Exclusivity of ownership, security of tenure, and eviction orders: A model to evaluate South African land-reform legislation' 2002 TSAR 254–289 at 263–289.

prevails and ownership trumps other interests. In other cases the common law position is amended or reversed, and the security of tenure of occupiers trumps existing ownership rights. In general the nature (content, lawfulness) and duration of occupation and the socio-economic position and vulnerability of the occupiers feature prominently in determining whether the common law position is retained or amended, without being determinative.

- In all cases, strict due-process[66] provisions and requirements are imposed to ensure that evictions are not carried out unlawfully, unfairly or arbitrarily. The constitutional provision in section 26(3) provides the guiding principle in this regard.
- In most cases, special provision is made for urgent and exceptional or temporary evictions.

The overall effect of these statutory amendments is that the landowner's traditionally strong common-law right to obtain an eviction order is qualified substantially with reference to considerations of social, economic and historical fairness and equity, and at the same time eviction orders and proceedings are subjected to strict procedural checks and controls. In principle, this should result in a substantive amendment of the common law, but these statutory amendments and the changes they bring about have not been interpreted uniformly.[67]

7.3.3 Confusion in case law[68]

On the face of it, the constitutional anti-eviction principle in section 26(3) should be the point of departure[69] and all evictions, whether based on the common law or on the land-reform laws, should be subject to it, but the principle of constitutional

---

[66]The term 'due process' is used here together with 'fairness' to indicate that the provisions in question are often of a substantive rather than a merely procedural nature: AJ van der Walt 'Exclusivity of ownership, security of tenure, and eviction orders: A model to evaluate South African land-reform legislation' 2002 TSAR 254–289 at 263–289.

[67]AJ van der Walt 'Exclusivity of ownership, security of tenure, and eviction orders: A model to evaluate South African land-reform legislation' 2002 TSAR 254–289 at 263–289. The case law is discussed and analysed in AJ van der Walt 'Exclusivity of ownership, security of tenure, and eviction orders: A critical evaluation of recent case law' (2002) 18 SAJHR 371–419. See further R Keightley 'The impact of the Extension of Security of Tenure Act on an owner's right to vindicate immovable property' (1999) 15 SAJHR 277–307; T Roux 'Continuity and change in a transforming legal order: The impact of section 26(3) of the Constitution on South African law' (2004) 121 SALJ 466–492.

[68]This section is a summary of the results of AJ van der Walt 'Exclusivity of ownership, security of tenure, and eviction orders: A critical evaluation of recent case law' (2002) 18 SAJHR 371–419. I also made use of R Keightley 'The impact of the Extension of Security of Tenure Act on an owner's right to vindicate immovable property' (1999) 15 SAJHR 277–307; T Roux 'Continuity and change in a transforming legal order: The impact of section 26(3) of the Constitution on South African law' (2004) 121 SALJ 466–492.

[69]See section 8(1) of the Constitution: 'The Bill of Rights [chapter 2 of the Constitution] applies to all law and binds the legislature, the executive, the judiciary, and al organs of state;' AJ van der Walt 'Exclusivity of ownership, security of tenure, and eviction orders: A critical evaluation of recent case law' (2002) 18 SAJHR 371–419.

supremacy does not explain how the anti-eviction principle or provisions should apply or, more particularly, how it should influence the common law, in a given situation. As should perhaps have been expected, the courts have not been consistent in their interpretation and application of the constitutional principle or of the land-reform laws and different approaches to the effect of the anti-eviction provisions have surfaced in case law. Questions about the priority of common law or statutory law often arose in fairly mundane, practical issues such as jurisdiction[70] and burden of proof,[71] and traditional attitudes towards these problems usually favour proceeding in terms of the common law, where the landowner-plaintiff knows exactly what is required when suing for eviction, whereas the land-reform laws usually complicate the landowner-applicant's case considerably.

The most pressing question posed by land reforms relating to evictions is whether a landowner can elect to institute eviction proceedings against obviously unlawful occupiers in terms of common law or whether she is bound to do so in terms of one of the land reform laws. The answer to this question looks deceptively straightforward: section 4(1) of the Prevention of Illegal Eviction from and Unlawful Occupation of Land Act 19 of 1998 distinguishes itself from the majority of land-reform laws[72] by explicitly overriding common law rules,[73] seemingly making it clear that unlawful occupiers (who have no right to occupy) can only be evicted with due regard for the limitations and requirements imposed by the Act.[74] In cases where the occupiers are indeed unlawful invaders, who have settled on the land without permission or any right to do so, the courts have had no difficulty with the provision that the Act

[70] As is explained in footnote 62 above, different courts have jurisdiction with regard to different land-reform laws, and the landowner might find it difficult in some instances to decide in which forum to institute the application.

[71] Land reform laws invariably set higher standards of proof than the common law and require additional information that is often not available to the landowner. Furthermore, the landowner might not want to admit indirectly, by proceeding in a certain forum and in terms of a certain statute, that the occupier enjoys or enjoyed a certain status (eg as residential tenant or labour tenant). See AJ van der Walt 'Exclusivity of ownership, security of tenure, and eviction orders: A critical evaluation of recent case law' (2002) 18 SAJHR 371–419.

[72] Section 13(10) of the Rental Housing Act 50 of 1999 even explicitly allows for common-law eviction to be available in tandem with statutory eviction procedures. Where applicable, the Rent Control Act 80 of 1976 still imposes further restrictions on landlords' right to evict; see Batchelor v Gabie 2002 (2) SA 51 (SCA). See further AJ van der Walt 'Exclusivity of ownership, security of tenure, and eviction orders: A critical evaluation of recent case law' (2002) 18 SAJHR 371–419.

[73] Section 4(1): 'Notwithstanding anything to the contrary contained in any law or the common law, the provisions of this section apply to proceedings by any owner or person in charge of land for the eviction of an unlawful occupier.'

[74] Unlike most other land-reform laws, this Act does not function retroactively, and therefore applies only to evictions instituted since it came into operation on 5 June 1998. See further R Keightley 'The impact of the Extension of Security of Tenure Act on an owner's right to vindicate immovable property' (1999) 15 SAJHR 277–307 at 302–306; AJ van der Walt 'Exclusivity of ownership, security of tenure, and eviction orders: A critical evaluation of recent case law' (2002) 18 SAJHR 371–419.

overrides the common law, and some decisions dealing with such a situation reflect admirable sensitivity for the conflicting claims for protection of existing rights and for promotion of fairness and equity.[75] On the other hand the courts have sometimes been willing to grant common law eviction orders against lawful occupiers, treating them as if they were unlawful land invaders but nevertheless denying them the statutory protection that even unlawful occupiers should have enjoyed.[76] The attitude in some decisions is to interpret the reform laws restrictively and to apply the common law by preference,[77] reasoning that proclaims and upholds existing land rights against a perceived threat of land invasion and lawlessness associated with land reform.[78] Not surprisingly, the worst example of this kind of reactionary logic was overturned by the Supreme Court of Appeal, where it was held that the High Court had no jurisdiction to grant an eviction order in the case.[79] The Supreme Court of Appeal furthermore found it necessary to repudiate the remarks of the trial court concerning the suitability of the Act explicitly, stating that these remarks were unwarranted and 'should have been avoided'.[80]

The worst instances of judicial resistance against the private law effects of anti-eviction provisions were rejected in the literature and overturned on appeal, but cases dealing with these provisions nevertheless abound with examples of other decisions that exemplify an unwillingness to accept the consequences that a reform-friendly, purposive interpretation and application of the anti-eviction provisions would have on private law. The most obvious example of this phenomenon is the series of cases in which the courts had to decide whether the Prevention of Illegal Eviction from and Unlawful Occupation of Land Act 19 of 1998 (PIE) applied to cases of holding over, in other words where a formerly lawful occupier remained in occupation and refused to vacate the property after the source of lawful occupation (such as a lease) was cancelled or had expired.[81] In the initial series of cases it was

---

[75]See e g *Port Elizabeth Municipality v Peoples Dialogue on Land and Shelter and Others* 2000 (2) SA 1074 (SEC); compare further AJ van der Walt 'Exclusivity of ownership, security of tenure, and eviction orders: A critical evaluation of recent case law' (2002) 18 *SAJHR* 371–419 at 377–379.

[76]The worst example is *Joubert and Others v Van Rensburg and Others* 2001 (1) SA 753 (W). Compare further chapter 6.3.8, where the case is discussed extensively.

[77]E g *Joubert and Others v Van Rensburg and Others* 2001 (1) SA 753 (W) par [25.4.2] at 785D. See footnote 76 above.

[78]E g *Joubert and Others v Van Rensburg and Others* 2001 (1) SA 753 (W); see footnote 76 above.

[79]*Mkangeli and Others v Joubert and Others* 2002 (4) SA 36 (SCA) par [24]. See further *Magodi and Others v Van Rensburg* [2001] 4 All SA 485 (LCC). See footnote 76 above.

[80]*Mkangeli and Others v Joubert and Others* 2002 (4) SA 36 (SCA) par [25].

[81]See chapter 6.3.8, where these cases are discussed, and compare AJ van der Walt 'Exclusivity of ownership, security of tenure, and eviction orders: A critical evaluation of recent case law' (2002) 18 *SAJHR* 371–419 at 375–390; T Roux 'Continuity and change in a transforming legal order: The impact of section 26(3) of the Constitution on South African law' (2004) 121 *SALJ* 466–492.

held[82] that PIE did not apply to these instances because it was intended only for situations where land was invaded unlawfully and not for cases where formal housing was initially occupied lawfully in a landlord-tenant situation.[83] In other cases it was decided that the anti-eviction provisions in the Extension of Security of Tenure Act 62 of 1997 did not deprive a landowner of the possibility of evicting occupiers in terms of the common law, despite the fact that the Act prescribed its own, more restrictive eviction requirements and procedures.[84] It was also held in one case that section 26(3) of the Constitution does not apply directly to normal landlord-tenant situations and that the landowner can therefore evict in terms of the common law if she prefers to do so.[85] These decisions clearly assumed that the common law sets the benchmark and that the pattern of property holdings as protected in and by the common law is what is normal, to be applied unless the opposite is proven.[86] The position at common law was taken as given, as clear and fair, and deviations from it are accepted only if and when and in so far as deviation is clearly authorized and required by the Constitution (and other laws). In cases of doubt or (even marginal) uncertainty, the common law default is accepted and any changes are rejected or avoided or minimalized.

In the end this dilemma was placed before the Supreme Court of Appeal, but perhaps unfortunately it reached the SCA in two separate cases, one dealing purely with the direct effect of section 26(3) on the common law and the other concerning the effect of PIE on common law. In *Brisley v Drotsky*[87] the court held that section 26(3) was horizontally enforceable[88] and that an eviction order may indeed only be granted once all relevant circumstances have been considered. However, it also decided that section 26(3) did not grant the courts the discretion to deprive a land-owner of an eviction order that he or she would—in the absence of a statutory or other right to occupy—have been entitled to at common law, based on the personal circumstances of the occupier and her family or the availability of alternative accommodation. In the absence of explicit statutory provisions, the personal circumstances of the occupier and the availability of alternative accommodation are therefore not 'relevant circumstances' that section 26(3) forces or allows the courts to take into

---

[82]With one notable exception: *Bekker and Another v Jika* [2001] 4 All SA 573 (SEC). In *Ross v South Peninsula Municipality* 2000 (1) SA 589 (C) the court decided *obiter* that PIE applied to normal rent situations. See AJ van der Walt 'Exclusivity of ownership, security of tenure, and eviction orders: A critical evaluation of recent case law' (2002) 18 *SAJHR* 371–419 at 385–390.

[83]See chapter 6.3.8. The relevant cases are *ABSA Bank Ltd v Amod* [1999] 2 All SA 423 (W); *Ellis v Viljoen* 2001 (4) SA 795 (C); *Betta Eiendomme (Pty) Ltd v Ekple-Epoh* [2000] 3 All SA 403 (W).

[84]See chapter 6.3.8. The relevant cases are *Skhosana and Others v Roos t/a Roos se Oord and Others* 2000 (4) SA 561 (LCC); *Khuzwayo v Dludla* 2001 (1) SA 714 (LCC).

[85]See chapter 6.3.8. The relevant cases are *Betta Eiendomme (Pty) Ltd v Ekple-Epoh* [2000] 3 All SA 403 (W); *Ross v South Peninsula Municipality* 2000 (1) SA 589 (C).

[86]See chapter 6.3.8. In *Betta Eiendomme (Pty) Ltd v Ekple-Epoh* [2000] 3 All SA 403 (W) this attitude is clear: par [6.2] at 472E–G. See further *Ellis v Viljoen* 2001 (5) BCLR 487 (C) at 497E–H.

[87]2002 (4) SA 1 (SCA) paras [35]–[46] at 19C–22E.

[88]Paras [39]–[40] at 20D–E.

consideration when deciding whether to grant an eviction order.[89] The point of departure is the common law: a landowner is entitled to possession and hence to eviction, and in the absence of a clear legal or statutory right of occupation this entitlement (and the application for an eviction order based on it) cannot be denied with reference to the occupier's personal circumstances or the availability of alternative accommodation. The effect of the constitutional provision in section 26(3) is therefore restricted within the framework of common law ownership. The decision in *Brisley* sets the tone for a restrictive, common law based approach to the transformative effect of section 26(3) of the Constitution, requiring clear and unambiguous statutory authority (in the land reform laws) for any potential or real amendment or limitation of the common law right of a landowner to obtain an eviction order.

In *Ndlovu v Ngcobo; Bekker v Jika*[90] the SCA seemed to adopt exactly the opposite approach, holding that an eviction order cannot be given in the case at hand without considering the personal and socio-economic circumstances of the occupiers. The key to understanding the apparent contradiction between the decisions in *Brisley* and *Ndlovu / Bekker* is the fact that the SCA decided in the latter case that the Prevention of Illegal Eviction from and Unlawful Occupation of Land Act 19 of 1998 (PIE) applied to a tenant who is holding over subsequent to the lawful termination of his lease.[91] In coming to the decision that PIE applied to landlord-tenant situations, Harms JA pointed out that the vulnerability of certain categories of persons—including tenants of urban housing—may well have been a concern when Parliament promulgated PIE, and that interpretation problems caused by lack of clarity in the legislation had to be solved with due consideration for the promotion of the spirit, purport and objects of the Constitution.[92] Once it was decided that PIE applied to the case, the objection raised in *Brisley* fell away and the court was allowed to take into account the circumstances of the occupier, because PIE overrides the common law explicitly on that point, specifying the circumstances that should be considered before an eviction order could be granted.[93]

The result is that the SCA was prepared to develop the common law of eviction according to reform-oriented anti-eviction provisions, provided the considerations in terms of which the common law right to eviction should be restricted are made clear in the relevant legislation—in the absence of a clear statutory discretion to deny the eviction application because of the occupier's personal circumstances (and an indica-

---

[89] Paras [42]–[46] at 21B–22E; Olivier JA dissenting on this point in par [87] at 33C–E.

[90] 2003 (1) SA 113 (SCA). The following paragraphs are based on AJ van der Walt 'Ownership and eviction: Constitutional rights in private law' (2005) 9 *Edinburgh LR* 32–64.

[91] The SCA argued that there was not a sufficiently clear indication of legislative intention to the contrary, and that it could not be discounted that the legislature intended to extend the applicability of PIE to cases of holding over: 2003 (1) SA 113 (SCA) paras [21]–[23] at 125B–H.

[92] Section 39(2) of the Constitution. This passage appears in *Ndlovu v Ngcobo; Bekker v Jika* 2003 (1) SA 113 (SCA) par [16] at 123C–E.

[93] Section 4(1), read with sections 4(6) (occupiers for less than 6 months) and 4(7) (occupiers for longer than 6 months).

tion of the circumstances to be considered in doing so), the court would prefer to stick to the common law and grant an eviction order as soon as the common law requirements have been satisfied. One is left with the impression that the civil courts are uncertain about their role with regard to the development of the common law, especially when confronted by serious limitations on a central institution of private law, namely the entitlement of a landowner to evict unlawful occupiers. Even the seemingly clear constitutional directive in section 26(3) is apparently not enough to convince the courts that a reasonably radical interference with the common law is necessary or legitimate. The Constitutional Court used its opportunity to bring greater clarity in this situation when deciding the important case of *Port Elizabeth Municipality v Various Occupiers*,[94] a case that involved the eviction of unlawful occupiers in terms of PIE.

7.3.4 The *Port Elizabeth Municipality* decision[95]

The Constitutional Court clearly intended its decision in *Port Elizabeth Municipality* to bring some clarity and certainty in an area of the law that was both extremely important and characterized by confusion and uncertainty. The applicability of the decision is limited by the fact that it concerned section 6 of PIE, which applies to evictions by a state organ as opposed to evictions by private landowners, but the decision is nevertheless significant for its approach to the eviction issue in general.

    The first interesting aspect of the decision is the Court's concerted effort to situate adjudication of an eviction case in its proper context, both historically and constitutionally. The decision starts off with a brief overview of the Prevention of Illegal Squatting Act 52 of 1951, which provides the historical context of evictions in the apartheid era,[96] and then proceeds to an overview of the constitutional context within which PIE was promulgated and within which it should be interpreted.[97] The Court emphasizes that politically motivated, legislatively sanctioned and state-sanctioned eviction was a cornerstone of apartheid land law and that section 26(3) of the Constitution and the statutory anti-eviction provisions must be understood as parts of an explicit effort to reverse the history of unjust apartheid evictions. In this approach, PIE has to be understood and applied 'within a defined and carefully calibrated constitutional matrix'[98] of which both sections 25 and 26 form important aspects. Accordingly, the Court argues, much turns on establishing an appropriate constitutional relationship between sections 25 and 26. This relationship should reflect the constitutional recognition that land rights and rights of access to housing (including the right not be evicted arbitrarily) are closely intertwined.[99] In the Court's view, there

---

[94] 2005 (1) SA 217 (CC).
[95] *Port Elizabeth Municipality v Various Occupiers* 2005 (1) SA 217 (CC). See chapter 6.3.8.
[96] Paras [8]–[10] at 222A–224B.
[97] Paras [11]–[23] at 224C–229G.
[98] Par [14] at 225B.
[99] Par [19] at 228B.

are 'three salient features of the way the Constitution approaches the interrelationship between land hunger, homelessness and respect for property rights.'[100] Firstly, the rights of those who have been dispossessed of land are not generally stated in unqualified terms as immediately self-enforcing rights; they usually presuppose the adoption of legislative and other measures by the state. Accordingly, the rights in section 26 are defensive rather than affirmative; they restrict the landowner's right to evict but do not grant independent property rights.[101] The second feature of this interrelated set of provisions is that eviction of people in informal settlements may take place even when it results in the occupiers losing their home.[102] The third feature is that section 26(3) emphasizes the need to seek concrete, case-specific solutions to difficult eviction problems.[103] In the Court's view, 'the Constitution imposes new obligations on the courts concerning rights relating to property not previously recognised by the common law.'[104] The Court's description of this new judicial obligation merits quotation:

> '[The Constitution] counterposes to the normal ownership rights of possession, use and occupation, a new and equally relevant right not arbitrarily to be deprived of a home. The expectations that normally go with title could clash head-on with the genuine despair of people in dire need of accommodation. The judicial function in these circumstances is not to establish a hierarchical arrangement between the different interests involved, privileging in an abstract and mechanical way the rights of ownership over the right not to be dispossessed of a home, or *vice versa*. Rather, it is to balance out and reconcile the opposed claims in as just a manner as possible, taking account of all the interests involved and the specific factors relevant in each particular case.'[105]

Despite the arguably unfortunate reference to people being 'deprived of a home' in the first sentence,[106] this is a highly significant and useful statement of the Court's

---

[100]Par [20] at 228E.

[101]Par [20] at 228E–229A. This contradicts the much-criticized position adopted by the German Federal Constitutional Court in *BVerfGE* 89, 1 [1993] (*Besitzrecht des Mieters*). DP Kommers *The constitutional jurisprudence of the Federal Republic of Germany* (2nd ed 1997) 255 calls it the 'Landlord-Tenant Case'. In this case, the German court adopted the view that the tenant's protected position under anti-eviction provisions in landlord-tenant legislation also qualifies as property (in the limited sense of ownership) for purposes of the property clause in article 14 of the German Basic Law. This decision was heavily criticized for its logic rather than because of the result. For a discussion and further references see AJ van der Walt 'Ownership and eviction: Constitutional rights in private law' (2005) 9 *Edinburgh LR* 32–64.

[102]Par [21] at 229B.

[103]Par [22] at 229C.

[104]Par [23] at 229E.

[105]Par [23] at 229E–G.

[106]Because of the impression it could create that the Court was referring to section 25(1) of the Constitution. Deprivation and expropriation are typically state interferences with private property rights, which means firstly that the actor should be a state organ and secondly that the affected party should have a property right that qualifies for protection under section 25 (as opposed to section 26). It is therefore confusing and serves no purpose to talk of deprivation and expropriation in the

(continued on next page ...)

view of the 'constitutional matrix' within which the development of the common law with regard to eviction should take place. Firstly, the granting of an eviction order is no longer mechanically ensured by proof of the common law requirements—in line with section 26(3), the order can only be granted if eviction is justifiable in view of all the circumstances. Secondly, consideration of the order in view of the circumstances amounts to a balancing exercise in which the rights of the landowner are balanced against the interests of the occupiers. Thirdly, this balancing exercise takes place against the background of the history of eviction in the apartheid era and its lasting and enduring effects on the distribution of land and access to housing today.

Within this matrix, the Court makes it quite clear that eviction does not become impossible, even when it results in someone losing their home. The decision whether to allow the eviction is a highly case-specific one that has to be taken in every individual case, taking into account the historical background, the constitutional context and the circumstances of the parties involved. Because the decision is taken with regard to the facts and the circumstances in every individual case, the strong constitutional sentiment against arbitrary eviction does not mean that eviction will be impossible simply because the occupiers would lose their home, or because they have been in occupation very long, or because the state is evicting them and no provision has been made for alternative accommodation or land. However, the fact that a formal housing programme was in place is an important factor that the court will have to consider, as is the fact that the occupiers have been in occupation for a long time, when no alternative accommodation is available in fact.[107] The Court added that all circumstances have to be considered when deciding whether to allow eviction, even when the court itself had to procure ways of establishing the relevant facts by itself.[108] In addition, it would ordinarily not be just and equitable to grant an eviction order unless proper discussions and, where suitable, mediation had been attempted as alternative ways of settling the matter.[109]

The *Jaftha* decision[110] should be read together with the *Port Elizabeth Municipality* decision[111] in so far as it also involves the effect of section 26(3) of the Constitution on

---

(... from previous page)

context of section 26(3) generally, especially when the landowner is a private person. In the current case the landowner was of course the state and it would have been possible for the occupier to be deprived of property, but what the court has in mind here is probably arbitrary eviction in terms of section 26(3), which would not be a deprivation in terms of section 25(1) unless it was clear that the occupiers had a property right in terms of section 25 and that the state's eviction qualified as a deprivation. See further chapters 4 and 5.

[107] Par [28] at 233G–H.

[108] Par [32] at 235F–236C.

[109] Par [43] at 240E.

[110] *Jaftha v Schoeman and Others; Van Rooyen v Stoltz and Others* 2005 (2) SA 140 (CC). This case is also discussed in chapter 6.4.3 and in 7.4 below.

[111] *Port Elizabeth Municipality v Various Occupiers* 2005 (1) SA 217 (CC). See the discussion above and see further chapter 6.3.8.

common law property and other economic rights. The case dealt with section 66(1)(a) of the Magistrates' Courts Act 32 of 1944, which allows for attachment and sale in execution of private property, including immovable property, to satisfy a debt. In this case the section and the procedure created by it were used to satisfy relatively small debts[112] by attaching and selling in execution the debtor's houses, which were acquired with state subsidies as part of the government's housing programme. In evaluating the effect of the execution procedure in terms of section 66(1)(a) the Court took notice of the backdrop of legislation that made it possible in the apartheid era to summarily evict people from their houses and the intention of section 26(3) of the Constitution 'which speaks directly to the practice of forced removals and summary eviction from land' and which guarantees that this practice will cease, replacing it by a system of strict judicial control over evictions.[113] Against this background, the Court decided, a summary execution procedure that results in eviction of people from their homes without judicial control is untenable, because the procedure is wide enough to allow unscrupulous persons to abuse it by attaching and selling in execution people's homes for insignificant debts. Accordingly, the Court decided that the words 'a court, after consideration of all relevant circumstances, may order execution' should be read into section 66(1)(a) to bring it in line with constitutional requirements.[114]

The effect of these decisions is an indication of the outlines of what may be described as a reform-oriented approach to the development of the common law in the sphere of evictions. Eviction of unlawful occupiers is still possible, but in view of the political and social history of evictions and forced removals it cannot function as it traditionally had—the Constitution and the land reform laws now constitute a new set of parameters within which eviction takes place. Given these parameters it is clear that the position, status, content and protection of landownership have undergone a shift between pre-constitutional common law and post-1994 law. Ownership is still a powerful and well-protected right; it is now even protected in the Constitution itself; but it was also placed within a very specific social, political and constitutional context that affects its adjudication in cases where traditional common law perceptions and enforcement of the landowner's right conflict with the constitutional obligation to protect the land rights of socially, economically and legally marginalised and vulnerable members of society. The new paradigm for adjudication of land rights does not mean that the landowner always loses in such a conflict; it means that he does not automatically win, as he did in common law.

---

[112]R250 and R190 in the two cases respectively; in each case the debt was incurred to buy food. The houses that were attached and sold in execution of the debts must have been worth in excess of R15 000; the amount of state subsidy with which these houses were built and made available to the affected homeowners. See 7.4 below.
[113]Par [28] at 154C–155B.
[114]Par [67] at 165E.

7.4 OTHER DEVELOPMENTS[115]

The Constitutional Court decision in the *Port Elizabeth Municipality* decision[116] is the clearest judicial statement of the courts' attitude towards the development of the common law of property to date, and the effect of the constitutional and statutory anti-eviction provisions is the best example we have so far of common law rules and institutions being developed to promote the spirit, purport and objects of the Bill of Rights. In this section the development of the common law and customary law is discussed with reference to a number of other important constitutional cases outside of the sphere of evictions already discussed earlier. As will appear from the discussion below, most of these cases in fact concerned the interpretation of statutory provisions, but in their effect they acquire at least some importance for the development of the common law.[117]

The *Zondi* case[118] concerned the Pound Ordinance 32 of 1947 (Natal), a piece of apartheid legislation that formed an integral part of the complicated web of common law, customary law and legislation that is often obscured behind references to 'purely private' common law rights. The provisions of the Ordinance gave (mostly white) landowners and pound-keepers the power to seize and impound (mostly black) live-stock found trespassing on (mostly white) land. Pound-keepers were authorised to sell impounded animals to recover the pound fees. Both the impounding and sale of live-

---

[115]Part of this section is based on AJ van der Walt 'Retreating from the *FNB* arbitrariness test already? *Mkontwana v Nelson Mandela Metropolitan Municipality; Bissett v Buffalo City Municipality; Transfer Rights Action Campaign v MEC for Local Government and Housing, Gauteng* (CC)' (2005) 122 *SALJ* 75–89.

[116]*Port Elizabeth Municipality v Various Occupiers* 2005 (1) SA 217 (CC). See the discussion in the previous section above and see further chapter 6.3.8.

[117]In this section I leave three Constitutional Court decisions out of consideration altogether, firstly because they are based on the interpretation of specific (mostly fiscal) legislation and secondly because they are discussed in greater detail elsewhere in the book. The first case is *Harksen v Lane NO* 1998 (1) SA 300 (CC), dealing with the property clause in section 28 of the 1993 interim Constitution; see further chapter 5.2; AJ van der Walt & H Botha 'Coming to grips with the new constitutional order: Critical comments on *Harksen v Lane NO*' (1998) 13 *SA Public Law* 17–41 at 19–26; AJ van der Walt *Constitutional property clauses: A comparative analysis* (1999) 333, 336–339; AJ van der Walt 'Striving for the better interpretation—A critical reflection on the Constitutional Court's *Harksen* and *FNB* decisions on the property clause' (2004) 121 *SALJ* 854–878. The second case is *First National Bank of SA Ltd t/a Wesbank v Commissioner, South African Revenue Service; First National Bank of SA Ltd t/a Wesbank v Minister of Finance* 2002 (4) SA 768 (CC). See the discussion of the case in chapter 4.5 and 4.6; compare chapter 5.4. The third case is *Mkontwana v Nelson Mandela Metropolitan Municipality; Bissett and Others v Buffalo City Municipality; Transfer Rights Action Campaign and Others v Member of the Executive Council for Local Government and Housing, Gauteng and Others* 2005 (1) SA 530 (CC). See chapter 5.2 above and compare AJ van der Walt 'Retreating from the *FNB* arbitrariness test already? *Mkontwana v Nelson Mandela Metropolitan Municipality; Bissett v Buffalo City Municipality; Transfer Rights Action Campaign v MEC for Local Government and Housing, Gauteng* (CC)' (2005) 122 *SALJ* 75–89.

[118]*Zondi v Member of the Executive Council for Traditional and Local Government Affairs and Others* 2005 (3) SA 589 (CC).

stock took place without a court order. The Constitutional Court decided the case against the background of the social, economic and political role that the Ordinance played in the scheme of apartheid land law, particularly in establishing and reinforcing the unequal positions of white landowners and black landless people.[119] The Court held that these provisions violated the constitutional guarantees of equality and access to justice and declared the relevant sections of the Ordinance unconstitutional.[120]

Together with the *Jaftha* decision[121] and the *Port Elizabeth Municipality* decision,[122] the *Zondi* decision contains important guidelines with regard to the development of the common law. Although *Zondi* deals with a statutory provision rather than the common law, and even though it was decided with reference to section 34 rather than section 25, the Court's clearly finds it necessary to penetrate behind the statute and evaluate the effect that it had in establishing the hierarchical privileges that were referred to in *Port Elizabeth Municipality*: the pound ordinances did not establish an extraneous, separate and cleanly divisible piece of legislation that can be distinguished from the common law or from customary law in any intelligible way; nor could the ostensibly a-political regime of white land rights and the hierarchical structure of which it forms the pinnacle be separated from the political ideals of the apartheid land rights system. Instead, proper consideration of the historical, social, economic and political background and context shows that these laws were used to establish and reinforce the superiority of white landownership vis-à-vis black owners of livestock, thereby creating an intricate web of strong common law land rights, weak feudal-like customary law positions with regard to land and movable property, and strong state powers to uphold and enforce this hierarchy of strong and weak, powerful and marginalised, rich and poor.

This methodology of the Court emphasizes two points that are central to the project of developing the common law in view of the Constitution. Firstly, it is always of fundamental importance to consider the reforms and developments required by the Constitution, as well as the common law principles and statutory provisions with which these developments might come into conflict, against their historical background—development of the common law is not a purely prospective, forward-looking project but also a backward-looking and therefore reflective process. The Constitution does not only show the way forward, it also continuously points at and reminds us of the past and those aspects of it that we are trying to come to terms with. Secondly, it is often impossible or unwise to distinguish too sharply between the common law, customary law and legislation in bringing about the developments

---

[119] Paras [38]–[42] at 605A–606F.

[120] The declaration of invalidity was suspended for twelve months to give the provincial legislature an opportunity to amend the ordinance in a suitable way, and various rulings were made to provide for interim justice: paras [126]–[131] at 629C–630F.

[121] *Jaftha v Schoeman and Others; Van Rooyen v Stoltz and Others* 2005 (2) SA 140 (CC). See the discussion in the previous section above and compare chapter 6.3.8.

[122] *Port Elizabeth Municipality v Various Occupiers* 2005 (1) SA 217 (CC). See the discussion in the previous section above and see further chapter 6.3.8.

that are required by the Constitution. In many instances it is an illusion to think that abolition or amendment of the relevant legislation will be sufficient, because apartheid legislation is often deeply ingrained into the common law property positions that survive the purge; and in many ways existing common law rights are not a-political survivals of a regrettable apartheid interlude; they were partly created and reinforced by the apartheid laws, even if they are based on common law institutions that predate apartheid. Even when the apartheid laws have been abolished or suitably amended we still have to consider that they have established and entrenched strong positions of privilege and weak positions of marginality, and developing the common law may sometimes require developments that involve direct changes to those positions.

The most important Constitutional Court decision in which development of customary law was considered is the *Bhe* case.[123] The case concerned the customary law rules of intestate succession, and one of the issues raised was whether the rule of male primogeniture was constitutional in view of the equality provision in section 8 of the Constitution. The Court decided that the rule of male primogeniture, as a centerpiece of the customary law of intestate succession, was inconsistent with current notions of equality and dignity as embodied in the Bill of Rights and that the limitation it imposed on the rights of various persons could not be justified in terms of section 36(1).[124] In arriving at this conclusion, the Court considered various factors that influence current evaluation of this rule of customary law.

Firstly, the central position of the rule of male primogeniture in the customary law of succession has to be seen in the context of its function: in customary law, the law of succession was not primarily concerned with the distribution of the deceased's assets, but with the preservation and perpetuation of the family unit. The successor stepped into the deceased's shoes, inheriting the property of the family unit in a nominal sense only while also becoming responsible for the family obligations of the family head.[125] Secondly, the Court noted that the role of the customary law of succession has been distorted by its embodiment in various apartheid laws and institutions.[126] Thirdly, it is important to consider the social changes that influenced the structure and organization of modern families and communities: many (especially urban) families and communities are no longer structured and organized along traditional lines; and as a result the eldest male child now often inherits the family property without also acquiring the obligations and responsibilities of the head of the family,

---

[123] *Bhe and Others v Magistrate, Khayelitsha, and Others (Commission for Gender Equality as* amicus curiae; *Shibi v Sithole and Others; South African Human Rights Commission and Another v President of the Republic of South Africa and Another* 2005 (1) SA 580 (CC). The rule of male primogeniture was embodied in section 23 of the Black Administration Act 38 of 1927, read with the regulations made under that provision, as well as section 1(4)(b) of the Intestate Succession Act 81 of 1987. See further *Daniels v Campbell NO and Others* 2004 (7) BCLR 735 (CC) (regarding intestate succession in cases of marriages concluded in accordance with Muslim rites).
[124] Par [95] at 622G–623A.
[125] Par [76] at 617D–G.
[126] Paras [82]–[83] at 618H–619B, [89] at 620F.

thereby undermining the social purpose of the traditional rules on inheritance.[127] All these considerations combine to indicate that the limitation of rights brought about by the customary rule of male primogeniture can no longer be justified in terms of section 36(1). The Court considered the legislature to be better placed to bring about the necessary changes that would bring the customary law of succession into line with new constitutional demands, but was nevertheless willing to fashion a case-specific, temporary remedy to ensure that the customary law rule of male primogeniture would not continue to impose unjustifiable limitations on women's and children's rights while the legislature was working on a statutory intervention.[128]

7.5 THEORETICAL AND CONCEPTUAL ISSUES[129]

7.5.1 Introduction

One problem that still requires serious attention is theoretical and conceptual explanation of the development of the common law and customary law. In a nutshell, the theoretical and conceptual issues focus on questions such as the exact definition and explanation of legal reform and transformation and the proper theoretical explanation of the relationship between the Constitution (particularly the rights in the Bill of Rights) and the common and customary law. Why does the Constitution have to have an effect on private law, and exactly how does that effect work in practice? What is the proper role of the judiciary and which developments of or changes to private law should be brought about by the legislature?

When the new South African Constitution explicitly declared itself the supreme law of the land[130] and granted the courts the power of constitutional review[131] it created the adjudicative dilemma of simultaneously upholding the supremacy of the new Constitution and the integrity of a well-developed and established system of private law.[132] The acceptance of a new supreme constitution that entrenches both

---

[127]Par [80] at 618D–E.

[128]Temporary relief was fashioned by making section 1 of the Intestate Succession Act 81 of 1987 applicable to certain intestate deceased estates that would otherwise have been governed by section 23 of the Act. See paras [115]–[116] at 627F–I, [125] at 630D–G, [136] at 634A–E.

[129]This section is based on parts of AJ van der Walt 'Transformative constitutionalism and the development of South African property law' 2005 TSAR; 2006 TSAR (forthcoming).

[130]Section 2: 'This Constitution is the supreme law of the Republic; law or conduct inconsistent with it is invalid, and the duties imposed by it must be performed.' See further sections 7, 8, 38, 39.

[131]Section 172(1): when deciding a constitutional matter within its power, a court must declare a law or conduct that is inconsistent with the Constitution invalid to the extent of its inconsistency, and make any order that is just and equitable, including an order that limits the restrospectivity of the declaration of invalidity and an order to suspend the declaration of invalidity for a period to allow correction.

[132]South African private law consists of a mixture of largely uncodified common law (of mixed Roman-Dutch and Anglo origin) and ad hoc legislation; see R Zimmermann & DP Visser 'Introduction: South African law as a mixed legal system' in R Zimmermann & DP Visser (eds) Southern cross: Civil law and common law in South Africa (1996) 1–30. Constitutional review affects pre-existing

(continued on next page ...)

the judicial power of constitutional review and a strong impulse towards social and legal transformation means that the common law must be developed to promote the spirit, purport and objects of the Bill of Rights, which in turn brings about tension between constitutional pressure towards change and the impulse to uphold existing common law rights for the sake of clarity and legal certainty. Initially, the South African debate about these questions focused mostly on what was referred to as the application issue. The early debate about this point turned on the question of horizontal application.

7.5.2 Horizontal application

The most common application argument assumed that the spirit and values of the new Constitution were basically similar to the 'inherent' values of private law in its 'original' Roman-Dutch form, that these values were untainted by apartheid and that the best way to proceed—once apartheid legislation has been abolished—was to allow private law to develop in its own way and according to its own inherent value system and doctrinal logic. The assumption was that this would eventually produce results substantively similar to those foreseen by the Constitution. To 'colonize' private law by enforcing constitutional values and methods directly, 'from outside', was considered unhelpful and unnecessary and therefore any form of horizontal application beyond indirect and weak 'seepage' of general constitutional values and principles was seen as a grave mistake. There are shades of opinion within the group of academics who argued that private law should be allowed to develop on its own, ranging from the view that there is a completely private sphere where law (including the Bill of Rights) does not penetrate;[133] through the argument that direct horizontal application amounts to unwarranted 'colonization' or 'invasion' of private law;[134] to

---

(... from previous page)

legislation, new legislation and also uncodified common law because all law is subject to the Constitution: section 2; and the Bill of Rights binds the legislature, the executive and the judiciary and 'applies to all law': section 8(1).

[133] See eg JD van der Vyver 'The private sphere in constitutional litigation' (1994) 57 THRHR 360–395. Van der Vyver argues that, according to the text, the 1993 Bill of Rights does not apply to non-state law (internal affairs of non-state institutions), although it 'may have an indirect effect' on those affairs, especially as far as non-discrimination is concerned (section 33(4) of the 1993 Constitution).

[134] D van der Merwe 'Constitutional colonisation of the common law: A problem of institutional integrity' 2000 TSAR 12–32 at 14 describes the 'constitutional way of thinking' as harmful to the integrity of the common law and therefore in the long run harmful to the legal system as a whole, and argues that necessary developments can best be achieved within the institutional framework and methodology of private law itself. See further DW Jordaan 'The Constitution's impact on the law of contract in perspective' (2004) 37 De Jure 58–65. See G Carpenter & C Botha 'Constitutional attack on private law: Are the fears well founded?' (1996) 59 THRHR 126–135 for a critique of the view expounded by Van der Merwe. The strongest critique of the view that common law can and should be shielded from unwarranted 'political' influences via the Constitution is H Botha 'Freedom and constraint in constitutional adjudication' (2004) 20 SAJHR 259–283.

the fairly widespread attitude that private law could be subject to changes inspired by the Constitution, but that those changes should be implemented through legislation while judicial intervention, when it cannot be avoided, should be restricted to small-scale, 'interstitial' or step-by-step development of private law according to its own inherent logic.[135] In all its different shades, this argument was by and large against the horizontal application of the Bill of Rights.

The stronger application argument assumed that the Constitution must have a more direct, fundamental effect on private law and that private law cannot simply be left to gradually 'regain' its inherent virtues according to its own inherent logic. This view was initially expressed in arguments that favoured horizontal application of the fundamental rights in the Constitution, relying on the central argument that the new constitutional order should not countenance the privatization of inequality and discrimination.[136] The mere abolition of apartheid laws would not eradicate apartheid injustices and therefore proactive reform of private law is required; to outlaw and uproot private discrimination and inequality the fundamental rights should be enforceable between private persons and against private institutions, and therefore the

---

[135]See eg A van Aswegen 'Policy considerations in the law of delict' (1993) 56 *THRHR* 171–195 at 171–195; A van Aswegen 'The implications of a bill of rights for the law of contract and delict' (1995) 11 *SAJHR* 50–69; A van Aswegen 'The future of South African contract law' in A van Aswegen (ed) *The future of South African private law* (1994) 44–60; DP Visser 'The future of the law of delict' in A van Aswegen (ed) *The future of South African private Law* (1994) 26–43. G Lubbe 'Taking fundamental rights seriously: The bill of rights and its implications for the development of contract law' (2004) 121 *SALJ* 395–423 at 395–423 is in the same vein but more nuanced and open to some direct constitutional influence in private law.

[136]This was the crux of many early pleas for horizontal application; see eg A Sachs 'Towards a bill of rights in a democratic South Africa' (1990) 6 *SAJHR* 1–24 at 3–4; H Botha 'Privatism, authoritarianism and the constitution: The case of Neethling and Potgieter' (1995) 58 *THRHR* 496–499; LM du Plessis 'Enkele gedagtes oor historiese interpretasie van hoofstuk 3 van die oorgangsgrondwet—*Du Plessis v De Klerk* 1994 6 BCLR 124 (T)' (1995) 58 *THRHR* 504–513; JD van der Vyver 'Constitutional free speech and the law of defamation' (1995) 112 *SALJ* 572–602; G Carpenter & C Botha 'Constitutional attack on private law: Are the fears well founded?' (1996) 59 *THRHR* 126–135 at 126–135; MLM Mbao 'The province of the South African bill of rights determined and redetermined   A comment on the case of *Baloro & Others v University of Bophut hatswana & Others*' (1996) 113 *SALJ* 33–45; S Woolman 'Defamation, application, and the interim constitution: An unqualified and direct analysis of *Holomisa v Argus Newspapers Ltd*' (1996) 113 *SALJ* 428–454; JWG van der Walt 'Justice Kriegler's disconcerting judgment in *Du Plessis v De Klerk*: Much ado about direct horizontal application (read nothing)' 1996 *TSAR* 732–741; JWG van der Walt 'Perspectives on horizontal application: *Du Plessis v De Klerk* revisited' (1997) 12 *SA Public Law* 1–31; S Woolman & D Davis 'The last laugh: *Du Plessis v De Klerk*, classical liberalism, creole liberalism, and the application of fundamental rights under the interim and final constitutions' (1996) 12 *SAJHR* 361–404; H Cheadle & D Davis 'The application of the 1996 constitution in the private sphere' (1997) 13 *SAJHR* 44–66; IM Rautenbach 'The bill of rights applies to private law and binds private persons' 2000 *TSAR* 296–316; JWG van der Walt 'Die toekoms van die onderskeid tussen die publiekreg en die privaatreg in die lig van die horisontale werking van die grondwet' 2000 *TSAR* 416–427, 605–618; S Woolman 'Application' in M Chaskalson et al (eds) *Constitutional law of South Africa* (Revision Service 3 1998).

Constitution has to apply on the horizontal level as well as the purely state-oriented vertical level. Pro-horizontality theorists argued that when the development of the common law had to take place through judicial interpretation and application of the Constitution in private law, the correct method of interpretation and application should be horizontal application of the Bill of Rights, which means that the fundamental rights provisions in the Bill of Rights could when necessary be enforced—in some way or another—in what otherwise was a private law dispute.

Pro-horizontality arguments initially mostly favoured direct horizontal application[137] rather than just indirect horizontal application of fundamental rights or, even more weakly, gradual and indirect 'seepage' of constitutional principles. However, later Johan van der Walt revised his earlier position and argued that indeed[138] 'there is no "extra-legal" private sphere', and that every social practice in fact in some way relies upon and is sanctioned by a legal rule that can—in suitable circumstances—be subjected to constitutional review. Accordingly, as Van der Walt points out, '... the distinction between direct and indirect horizontality is indeed of no real significance for the administration of justice under the Final Constitution.'[139] The only real application issue is, therefore, whether the Constitution applies horizontally, either directly[140] or indirectly,[141] to a private dispute between two private parties, in such a way that the (statutory or common law) private law rules that govern the dispute are open to amendment or influence from the Constitution, even though a state threat against

---

[137] See JWG van der Walt 'Justice Kriegler's disconcerting judgment in *Du Plessis v De Klerk*: Much ado about direct horizontal application (read nothing)' 1996 *TSAR* 732–741; S Woolman 'Defamation, application, and the interim constitution: An unqualified and direct analysis of *Holomisa v Argus Newspapers Ltd*' (1996) 113 *SALJ* 428–454; S Woolman 'Application' in M Chaskalson et al (eds) *Constitutional Law of South Africa* (Revision Service 3 1998); IM Rautenbach 'The bill of rights applies to private law and binds private persons' 2000 *TSAR* 296–316. H Cheadle & D Davis 'The application of the 1996 constitution in the private sphere' (1997) 13 *SAJHR* 44–66 at 57–60 present the clearest argument that some rights apply horizontally and others do not, with the implication that some apply directly horizontally and others do not. C Sprigman & M Osborne 'Du Plessis is *not* dead: South Africa's 1996 constitution and the application of the bill of rights to private disputes' (1999) 15 *SAJHR* 25–51 present the weakest argument to the effect that the 1996 Constitution applies horizontally—in their view, the 1996 Constitution allows indirect horizontal application as foreseen in *Du Plessis v De Klerk* 1996 (3) SA 850 (CC) but does not mandate it.

[138] As Mohamed DP argued in *Du Plessis v De Klerk* 1996 (3) SA 850 (CC) par [79] at 894E–895A.

[139] JWG van der Walt 'Perspectives on horizontal application: *Du Plessis v De Klerk* revisited' (1997) 12 *SA Public Law* 1–31 at 3, 11–12.

[140] Terminology on this point varies to some extent, but I follow the argument as developed by JWG van der Walt and use the term 'direct horizontal application' to refer to instances where a private party can rely directly on a provision in the Constitution to found a cause of action in a private dispute against another private party, without involving or relying upon any other statutory or common law rule.

[141] See footnote 140 above. By extension, this would refer to instances where the cause of action is founded upon a statutory or common law rule, but the interpretation or application of that rule is affected by the Constitution in some way in order to give effect to a specific constitutional provision or to the 'spirit, purport or object' of the Constitution, as it is stated in section 39(2).

either party is not directly in issue. The spectre of privatized injustice and inequality can be addressed adequately through indirect horizontal application understood in this way because every rule and institution of statutory and common law is thereby potentially opened up for constitutional scrutiny and amendment or development.

Pro-horizontality authors accepted that direct horizontal application cases would constitute a small minority, and that the effect of the Constitution on private law would in fact largely take place indirectly via the so-called radiating (or, in a probably weaker version, indirect seepage) effect of constitutional principles and values,[142] but they attach great value to the possibility that private parties with a genuine constitutional complaint against an exercise of private power should not be left without a remedy simply because neither the common law nor legislation provides a suitable remedy. Horizontal application of the Constitution should therefore leave space for the creation of new remedies where these are not provided for adequately by legislation or the common law.[143]

It is probably fair to say that academic commentators now generally accept that the 1996 Constitution enjoys horizontal application in some way; that such horizontal application leaves no room whatever for a 'purely private sphere' unaffected by the Constitution; that the horizontal application of the Constitution implies that any part of the common law can potentially be affected by constitutional provisions, principles and values in one way or another; and that the horizontal application will largely take place indirectly rather than directly, that is, by way of horizontal radiation, seepage or influence upon the common law rather than by way of direct reliance on constitutional provisions to establish a cause of action in purely private disputes. However, commentators leave open the possibility (foreseen by subsections 8(2) and 8(3) of the Constitution) that the horizontal application of the Constitution could vary according to the context of a specific case (particularly the nature of the right involved and any duty imposed by it), and accordingly it is still possible that a specific consti-

---

[142]See JWG van der Walt 'Perspectives on horizontal application: *Du Plessis v De Klerk* revisited' (1997) 12 *SA Public Law* 1–31 at 16–17; JWG van der Walt '*Progressive* indirect horizontal application of the bill of rights: Towards a co-operative relation between common-law and constitutional jurisprudence' (2001) 17 *SAJHR* 341–363 at 343–361; S Woolman 'Application' in M Chaskalson et al (eds) *Constitutional Law of South Africa* (Revision Service 3 1998) at 10-46–10-49.

[143]See JWG van der Walt 'Perspectives on horizontal application: *Du Plessis v De Klerk* revisited' (1997) 12 *SA Public Law* 1–31 at 21–29 (where he argues that open-ended common law institutions such as actions for pure economic loss and abuse of right could be developed to create remedies); Woolman 'Application' in M Chaskalson et al (eds) *Constitutional Law of South Africa* (Revision Service 3 1998) at 10–51. In 'Horizontal application of fundamental rights and the threshold of the law in view of the *Carmichele* saga' (2003) 19 *SAJHR* 517–540 JWG van der Walt identifies the shortcoming in the common law in the procedural rules that determine whether someone would have a fair chance of a hearing and a remedy to protect constitutionally granted or entrenched rights: in view of the common law procedure, lack of a probable cause of action will (as it did in *Carmichele v Minister of Safety and Security* 2003 (2) SA 656 (C)) most likely result in a judgment of absolution from the instance, which means that the issue of finding or developing a suitable remedy never even comes up.

tutional provision could require or prescribe direct rather than indirect horizontal application.[144] Perhaps because it is accepted widely that horizontal application takes place through horizontal radiation or seepage that affects the development of the common law, the distinction between direct and indirect horizontal application seems to have lost most if not all of its urgency in the literature.

The reason for diminishing interest in the horizontal application debate is to be found partly in section 8 of the 1996 Constitution, which makes room for horizontal application much more clearly than was the case with the 1993 Constitution, and partly in case law. Under the 1993 interim Constitution the high courts decided a few cases involving defamation[145] and equality[146] issues in which it was accepted that the Constitution intended to transform South African society, that the inequities and injustices of the past were not restricted to exercises of state power, and that the fundamental rights provisions in the Constitution therefore had to apply horizontally in one way or another to ensure that private law (and the private relations governed by it) was also included in the transformation process. One high court decision that rejected horizontal application of the fundamental rights provisions outright because it would cause 'the whole body of our private law to become unsettled'[147] was subsequently overturned by the Constitutional Court.[148] The decision of the Constitutional Court in *Du Plessis v De Klerk* settled the matter as far as the 1993 Constitution was concerned: resolution of the horizontality issue must ultimately depend upon the specific provisions of the Constitution; general (direct) horizontal application in the sense of direct invocation of constitutional rights in private litigation was not intended; a party in private litigation may nonetheless contend that a statute or executive act relied on by the other party was inconsistent with the Constitution (ie indirect horizontal application); and the fundamental rights provisions do apply to private law, so that government actions or omissions in reliance upon private law may be attacked by a private litigant in a dispute against the state for being inconsistent with the Constitution. Following upon the decision in favour of indirect horizontal application in *Du Plessis v De Klerk*, it could not very likely be argued that there would be no horizontal application under the 1996 Constitution. Since the 1996 Constitution came into power it has therefore been accepted widely that the fundamental rights provisions apply horizontally—the only outstanding issue was: when, and how?

A number of issues feature in what remains of the application debate. The first issue arises from decisions (and academic commentary) in which the effect of the

---

[144]See eg JWG van der Walt 'Perspectives on horizontal application: *Du Plessis v De Klerk* revisited' (1997) 12 *SA Public Law* 1–31 at 11. See further H Cheadle & D Davis 'The application of the 1996 constitution in the private sphere' (1997) 13 *SAJHR* 44–66 at 59.

[145]See eg *Gardener v Whitaker* 1994 (5) BCLR 19 (E); *Holomisa v Argus Newspapers Ltd* 1996 (2) SA 588 (W); *Mandela v Falati* 1995 (1) SA 251 (W).

[146]See eg *Baloro v University of Bophuthatswana* 1995 (8) BCLR 1018 (B); *Motala v University of Natal* 1995 (3) BCLR 374 (D).

[147]*De Klerk v Du Plessis* 1994 (6) BCLR 124 (T).

[148]*Du Plessis v De Klerk* 1996 (3) SA 850 (CC).

Constitution on private law is minimized or even indirectly denied by focusing on internal doctrinal developments in private law that would reach the same result, without reference to the effect of the Constitution. The basic point of departure in these cases is that the development of private law should—and can—take place in terms of the internal dynamics of private law or common law itself, and not under the external force of the Constitution. This approach can have two related and often overlapping results in case law where the development of private law is at stake. One result is to acknowledge that a particular development of the common law is required, but to deny that it takes place under the influence of the Constitution, insisting that the development was inspired by and is accommodated within the 'normal' process of dogmatic development, even in the face of strong evidence that the same court opposed the development in the pre-constitution past. In *National Media Ltd v Bogoshi*[149] the Supreme Court of Appeal insisted that the development of the common law principles with regard to defamation that was at stake in this case occurred and should be explained in terms of the dynamic development of the common law of delict,[150] and not in terms of a development required by the new constitutional values or provisions.

---

[149] 1998 (4) SA 1196 (SCA).

[150] In *Neethling v Du Preez; Neethling v The Weekly Mail* 1994 (1) SA 708 (A) the (then still) Appellate Division of the Supreme Court held that a newspaper could only escape a claim for defamation if it could establish that what was published was true. Furthermore, a rule of strict liability in defamation cases against the media was laid down earlier in *Pakendorf v De Flamingh* 1982 (3) SA 146 (A): see JWG van der Walt '*Progressive* indirect horizontal application of the bill of rights: Towards a co-operative relation between common-law and constitutional jurisprudence' (2001) 17 *SAJHR* 341–363 at 356. In *Bogoshi* the SCA held that the common law was wrongly stated in *Pakendorf* and that the common law principle should be restated correctly: publication of false defamatory allegations of fact would not be regarded as unlawful if, upon consideration of all the circumstances, it was found to have been reasonable to have published the facts in the particular way at the time (at 1212G–H). The *Neethling* case was ignored altogether. Only once the true statement of the common law has been attained in terms of the common law itself does the court deem it necessary to ascertain that the (correctly stated) common law rule is not in conflict with the Constitution. Academic commentators who are against or skeptical of horizontal application might have been expected to regard *Bogoshi* as an excellent decision, but surprisingly some thought that it didn't go far enough in rejecting 'constitutional argument in drag'; see D van der Merwe 'Constitutional colonisation of the common law: A problem of institutional integrity' 2000 *TSAR* 12–32 at 21. Academic commentators in favour of horizontal application and constitutionally inspired development of the common law point out that the avoidance of the true effect of the Constitution in this decision is cynical and misleading; see JWG van der Walt '*Progressive* indirect horizontal application of the bill of rights: Towards a co-operative relation between common-law and constitutional jurisprudence' (2001) 17 *SAJHR* 341–363 at 341–363. See further on this decision H Botha 'Freedom and constraint in constitutional adjudication' (2004) 20 *SAJHR* 249–283 at 253–255: *Bogoshi* treats earlier decisions that undermined press freedom as 'unwarranted deviations from the unfolding logic of the common law' and seeks to cleanse the common law from such errors by overruling (*Pakendorf*) or ignoring (*Neethling*) them; once that has been done the Court declares that the common law balance between press freedom and personal integrity is in line with constitutional demands. In the process, the integral links between apartheid law and restraints on press freedom during the pre-1994 era are ignored or denied.

In many cases this will not make much difference, as the fact that the development takes place is after all the main point, but this attitude does hint at a certain discomfort with the idea that the common law and the Constitution form part of one integral legal system, with the Constitution playing a direction-giving role. This discomfort and the concomitant preference for the common law's own inherent dynamics appeared in a number of earlier SCA decisions until it was decisively rejected by the Constitutional Court. In *Commissioner of Customs and Excise v Container Logistics (Pty) Ltd; Commissioner of Customs and Excise v Rennies Group Ltd t/a Renfreight*[151] the SCA decided that, since the common law grounds for judicial review of administrative action were left intact by the 1993 Constitution, it could set aside such action on common law grounds without considering whether it also fell foul of the constitutional grounds.[152] This decision was set aside by the Constitutional Court with a rather sharply worded remark to the effect that the common law cannot be treated 'as a body of law separate and distinct from the Constitution'—there is just one system of law, of which the common law and the Constitution both form part, with the latter as supreme law shaping and giving force to all law.[153] Although the common law remains relevant to the process, judicial review of the exercise of public power is now a constitutional matter that takes place according to the provisions of the Constitution.[154]

The second result of this attitude is that the courts, even when they acknowledge that development is necessary and that the change is inspired by the Constitution, insist that the development should take place according to the timing, methodology and logic of private law and not according to vague and implicit constitutional values. This could result in necessary developments being minimalized or even frustrated. In *Brisley v Drotsky*[155] and *Afrox Health Care Bpk v Strydom*[156] it was contended that certain contractual clauses[157] should be declared invalid because they were unfair and in conflict with the general principle of good faith. In both cases this argument was rejected, and the result is that general 'provisions such as non-variation and exemption

---

[151] 1999 (3) SA 771 (SCA).

[152] Section 24 of the 1993 Constitution provided for a right to just administrative action. The new provision appears in section 33 of the 1996 Constitution.

[153] *Pharmaceutical Manufacturers Association of SA; In Re: Ex Parte Application of President of the RSA* 2000 (2) SA 674 (CC) par [44] at 696A–B.

[154] Par [51] at 263B.

[155] 2002 (4) SA 1 (SCA).

[156] 2002 (6) SA 21 (SCA). The case is critiqued by H Botha 'Freedom and constraint in constitutional adjudication' (2004) 20 *SAJHR* 249–283 at 249–283, who refers to further discussions of the decision (at 269 footnote 66).

[157] In *Brisley* it was a non-variation clause that required any variation of the initial written document to comply with certain self-imposed formalities; in *Afrox* it was an exemption clause that excluded liability that would otherwise have attached to one of the parties because of the general principles of contract. As G Lubbe 'Taking fundamental rights seriously: The bill of rights and its implications for the development of contract law' (2004) 121 *SALJ* 395–423 at 396 points out, both clauses are 'regarded as permissible manifestations of contractual freedom, even where they occur in standard-form contracts unilaterally drawn up by one of the parties.'

clauses therefore cannot be defeated by direct and explicit recourse to the argument that to enforce them would be unfair and consequently against good faith. Good faith in the sense indicated ... is relevant only to the extent that its precepts are mediated by rules of law.'[158] It was accepted in both cases that public policy—of which open-ended norms such as good faith form part—is now informed by the fundamental values in the Constitution,[159] and that the Constitution might 'spur on the development of new substantive rules of law',[160] but it was nevertheless decided that neither the demands of good faith nor the constitutional values and principles 'were sufficient to outweigh the traditional bias in favour of the strict enforcement of agreements',[161] and consequently the clauses in question were upheld.

Two problems emerge from these decisions. Firstly, the SCA demonstrated a worrying failure to grasp the fundamental difference between central doctrinal values of private law and 'the spirit, purport and object of the Constitution'. On the one hand the SCA relies on a much contested bright-line distinction between (private law) rules and general (*inter alia* constitutional) standards,[162] and on the other hand it elevates private law rules (the right of ownership and strict enforceability of contracts) to the same level as constitutional values and declares the former as deserving of the same protection as any of the 'new' (transformational) values highlighted by the theory of transformative constitutionalism. In doing so, the SCA denied the fundamentally political, transformational nature of the Constitution and of the developments that are necessitated by its adoption at the heart of the post-apartheid legal system. The decision to entrench private law rules such as sanctity of contract on a constitutional foundation[163] sets up a reactionary and potentially destructive barrier in the way of transformation and it blows the tension between stability and transformation up into a constitutional conflict, much in the way that the Indian courts did before the property clause was removed from the Indian constitution.[164] It denies the political history and context of the Constitution's transformative programme and

---

[158] G Lubbe 'Taking fundamental rights seriously: The bill of rights and its implications for the development of contract law' (2004) 121 *SALJ* 395–423 at 398.

[159] In view of the decision in *Carmichele v Minister of Safety and Security (Centre for Applied Legal Studies Intervening)* 2001 (4) SA 938 (CC); see *Brisley v Drotsky* 2002 (4) SA 1 (SCA) par [91] at 34G–H; *Afrox Health Care Bpk v Strydom* 2002 (6) SA 21 (SCA) par [18] at 37D–E.

[160] G Lubbe 'Taking fundamental rights seriously: The bill of rights and its implications for the development of contract law' (2004) 121 *SALJ* 395–423 at 401.

[161] G Lubbe 'Taking fundamental rights seriously: The bill of rights and its implications for the development of contract law' (2004) 121 *SALJ* 395–423 at 401, 414.

[162] This aspect of especially the *Afrox* decision is critiqued extensively by H Botha 'Freedom and constraint in constitutional adjudication' (2004) 20 *SAJHR* 249–283.

[163] See G Lubbe 'Taking fundamental rights seriously: The bill of rights and its implications for the development of contract law' (2004) 121 *SALJ* 395–423 at 415.

[164] See footnote 22 above.

pretends that the development of the law in view of the Constitution is nothing extraordinary—just business as usual.[165]

The second problem is that these decisions failed to develop the common law because, in the absence of extraordinary reasons for doing so, the development in question would have involved an amendment of existing private law rights for which the court—in its own opinion—does not have an explicit statutory discretion, and therefore it simply affirmed the existing private law situation.[166] This argumentative move is illustrated particularly clearly by *Brisley v Drotsky*, which (apart from the contract issue described and analysed by Lubbe) also involved an eviction application which the Court rejected, based on common law logic. This aspect of the *Brisley* case and the Constitutional Court's reaction in the *Port Elizabeth Municipality* case was discussed earlier in this chapter.[167]

The result of the analysis above is that the development of the common law in terms of sections 8 and 39 of the Constitution has not really taken off in any significant sense. Instead, there are signs of uncertainty, hesitation and (in a few cases) even hostility towards the idea that central principles and institutions of the common law might have to be changed (even perhaps dramatically) in order to promote the spirit, purport and objects of the Constitution.

7.5.3 State duty to protect

In more recent cases, the debate about the effect of the Constitution on private law (and therefore about the development of the common law) shifted away from the earlier horizontal application arguments and towards a new set of arguments, based on the state's duty to protect the fundamental rights of citizens against infringements, even if the infringements are caused by the action of other private persons. The most important case in which the duty to protect was referred to as the basis on which the

---

[165]By contrast, the Constitutional Court decided in *Port Elizabeth Municipality v Various Occupiers* 2005 (1) SA 217 (CC) paras [8]–[23] that the historical context within which marginalization and social injustice originated and the constitutional context in which its reform is anticipated have to be taken into account when interpreting and applying laws that amend or reform the common law.

[166]According to T Roux 'Continuity and change in a transforming legal order: The impact of section 26(3) of the constitution on South African law' (2004) 121 *SALJ* 466–492 the eviction part of the *Brisley* decision should be seen as anti-uncertainty rather than anti-constitutional; the SCA was attempting to avoid uncertainty by opting for stability and continuity in the legal position regarding eviction. In view of Henk Botha's analysis of constitutional adjudication (Botha 'Freedom and constraint in constitutional adjudication' (2004) 20 *SAJHR* 249–283, especially at 259) this effort to uphold the rule of law and continuity should not clear the SCA from blame, as it can be described as either denial or bad faith (in Duncan Kennedy's terminology) that avoids 'transformative dialogue about social issues' (see Botha at 259 for references). Botha's criticism of the SCA's position on *stare decisis* in *Afrox* (Botha at 270) is particularly instructive when compared to the approach of Froneman J in *Kate v Member of the Executive Council for the Department of Welfare, Eastern Cape* 2005 (1) SA 141 (SE).

[167]See the discussion of this case and the subsequent decision of the Constitutional Court in *Port Elizabeth Municipality v Various Occupiers* 2005 (1) SA 217 (CC) in 7.3.4 above and in chapter 6.3.8.

common law must be developed in accordance with the Constitution is *Carmichele v Minister of Safety and Security (Centre for Applied Legal Studies Intervening)*.[168] The applicant claimed delictual damages from the respondents on the basis that they owed a legal duty to protect her; that they negligently acted in breach of that duty; and that she consequently suffered damage. The applicant's case was dismissed when the trial court granted an order of absolution from the instance. This order was confirmed by the SCA and the applicant appealed to the Constitutional Court.

The applicant based her application on the argument that the relevant members of the police and the public prosecutors owed her a duty to ensure that she enjoyed her constitutional rights to life, respect for and protection of her dignity, freedom and security, personal privacy and freedom of movement. Counsel argued that the trial court and the SCA erred in not developing the common law, because such development would have resulted in a finding that the respondents owed a legal duty to protect these rights. Neither the trial court nor the SCA had regard to the relevant provisions of the Constitution; they simply held that no such duty existed at common law and therefore granted absolution from the instance.[169]

The Constitutional Court reiterated that the Constitution is the supreme law and that the Bill of Rights applies to all law. The Constitution grants all courts the inherent power to develop the common law, and places an obligation upon the state to respect, protect, promote and fulfil the fundamental rights (section 7(2)). The Constitution also binds the judiciary and provides that the courts must promote the spirit, purport and objects of the Bill of Rights when developing the common law. Accordingly, when the common law deviates from the spirit, purport and object of the Bill of Rights the courts are obliged to develop it 'by removing that deviation.'[170]

The applicant's case was that the common law with regard to wrongfulness should be developed beyond existing precedent. Neither the trial court nor the SCA

---

[168] 2001 (4) SA 938 (CC). For a discussion see JWG van der Walt 'Horizontal application of fundamental rights and the threshold of the law in view of the *Carmichele* saga' (2003) 19 *SAJHR* 517–540 at 517–540. Apart from *Modderfontein Squatters, Greater Benoni City Council v Modderklip Boerdery (Pty) Ltd; (Agri SA and Legal Resources Centre, Amici Curiae); President of the Republic of South Africa and Others v Modderklip Boerdery (Pty) Ltd (Agri SA and Legal Resources Centre, Amici Curiae)* 2004 (6) SA 40 (SCA) other cases in which the duty to protect-construction was referred to are *Minister of Safety and Security v Van Duivenboden* 2002 (6) SA 431 (SCA); *Van Eeden v Minister of Safety and Security (Women's Legal Centre Trust as amicus curiae)* 2003 (1) SA 389 (SCA); *Minister of Safety and Security v Hamilton* 2004 (2) SA 216 (SCA); *Minister of Safety and Security v Carmichele* 2004 (3) SA 305 (SCA).

[169] *Carmichele v Minister of Safety and Security (Centre for Applied Legal Studies Intervening)* 2001 (4) SA 938 (CC) par [32] at 953C–D. See JWG van der Walt 'Horizontal application of fundamental rights and the threshold of the law in view of the *Carmichele* saga' (2003) 19 *SAJHR* 517–540 at 517–540, who argues that the problematic aspect of the common law that had to be developed was the rules of civil procedure that allowed a court to grant absolution from the instance before it can be forced to decide whether a new remedy has to be created or developed in view of the Constitution.

[170] Par [33] at 953E–954A.

embarked upon the required inquiry for such a development.[171] The Constitutional Court adopted a dictum of the European Court of Human Rights in which it was said that the entrenchment of the right to life in the European Convention may, in certain well-defined circumstances, imply a positive obligation on the state to take preventive operational measures to protect an individual whose life is threatened by the criminal acts of another individual.[172] In view of these considerations, and considering the different options for developing the common law that presented themselves in this matter, the Constitutional Court decided that the case for the appellant had sufficient merit to require careful consideration of the complex legal matters raised in it, and that the matter should therefore be referred back to the trial court to continue with the trial.[173] Upon reconsideration the trial court acknowledged that it had erred in not considering the constitutional effect on the case, and decided that there was a gap between the common law (which would not have placed a duty upon the state) and the fundamental rights in the Constitution (which would place a duty to protect upon the state), and that the common law therefore had to be developed in view of section 39(2) of the Constitution to place a duty upon the state. The trial court therefore granted an action for damages to the plaintiff.[174]

One argument in the *Carmichele* case that supports the applicant's claim on the basis of the state's duty to protect is therefore that the Constitution places an obligation upon state organs not to infringe upon the entrenched rights of individuals. In addition, the courts are obliged to develop the common law so as to protect, promote and fulfil those rights; and that implies a further obligation upon the state to take preventive measures—in certain well-defined circumstances—to ensure that other individuals do not infringe upon the entrenched rights of private persons. In the *Modderklip* case[175] similar remarks indicate a shift in South African constitutional theory away from the horizontal application debate and towards the notion of the state's duty to protect private persons against infringements of their fundamental rights by unlawful conduct of other private persons. However, to date little or no academic or judicial attention has been spent on the nature and scope of the duty

[171] Par [40] at 956A–C.
[172] Par [45] at 958B–C, with reference to *Osman v United Kingdom* 29 EHHR 245 par 115 at 305 (also reported as [1998] ECHR 101). In par [48] at 959F the Court also referred to *Z and Others v United Kingdom* application no 29392/95, 10 May 2001 (since reported as [2001] ECHR 329).
[173] Paras [81]—[83] at 970H–971E.
[174] *Carmichele v Minister of Safety and Security* 2003 (2) SA 656 (C). See JWG van der Walt 'Horizontal application of fundamental rights and the threshold of the law in view of the *Carmichele* saga' (2003) 19 *SAJHR* 517–540 at 517–540.
[175] See *Modderfontein Squatters, Greater Benoni City Council v Modderklip Boerdery (Pty) Ltd; (Agri SA and Legal Resources Centre, Amici Curiae); President of the Republic of South Africa and Others v Modderklip Boerdery (Pty) Ltd (Agri SA and Legal Resources Centre, Amici Curiae)* 2004 (6) SA 40 (SCA).

construed in this decision and on how it relates to the idea of developing the common law in accordance with the Constitution.[176]

On the one hand it looks as if the explicit provisions of the Constitution are the origin of the state's duty to protect as it was formulated in *Carmichele* and other cases. Section 7(2) of the Constitution enjoins the state to 'respect, protect, promote, and fulfil the rights in the Bill of Rights', and it seems natural to deduce from that provision that the state has a constitutional duty to promote and protect rights. The Constitutional Court went further in *Carmichele*, adding that the South African Constitution 'is not merely a formal document regulating public power', and that it, like the German Basic Law, 'also embodies ... an objective, normative value system', and that development of the common law in terms of section 39(2) of the Constitution must take place 'within the matrix of this objective normative value system'.[177] This, according to the Constitutional Court, requires development that meets the constitutional objectives of section 39(2) as well as the requirements of developing the common law within its own paradigm.[178] A link is therefore established between the state's duty to protect the fundamental rights in terms of section 7(2) and the obligation to develop the common law according to section 39(2).

In referring to the objective value system inherent in the fundamental rights and the effect of this system of objective normative values the Constitutional Court signalled how far it has moved away from discussing the effect of the Constitution on private law in terms of horizontal application—the focus now seems to be upon the state's duty to protect private individuals and their constitutional rights against infringements by unlawful conduct of other individuals, in view of the explicit provisions of the Constitution or of the objective normative values underlying or embedded in the fundamental rights. However, in discussing this development no mention is made of the horizontal application of the rights in the Constitution. In making this move from horizontal application discourse to duty to protect discourse, the South African courts followed a line of development that resembles a similar development in German constitutional law, but strangely enough German authorities and the well-developed German theory on this point played almost no part in the South African development at all.[179]

---

[176]This section of chapter 7 is partly based on sections of an article in which I explore these issues in more detail and with reference to comparative sources; see AJ van der Walt 'Transformative constitutionalism and the development of South African property law' 2005 *TSAR*; 2006 *TSAR* (forthcoming).

[177]*Carmichele v Minister of Safety and Security (Centre for Applied Legal Studies Intervening)* 2001 (4) SA 938 (CC) par [54] at 961F–H. The same approach was again followed and the link between the value system in the Constitution and development of the common law emphasized in *K v Minister of Safety and Security* 2005 (9) BCLR 835 (CC) paras [14]–[19] at 841B–844F.

[178]*Carmichele* par [55] at 962B.

[179]In the article on which this section of chapter 7 is based I set out and analyse the German debate and the relevant case law and literature extensively; see AJ van der Walt 'Transformative constitutionalism and the development of South African property law' 2005 *TSAR*; 2006 *TSAR* (forthcoming) Part 4.

In the *Carmichele* case,[180] the Constitutional Court referred to case law from the US (against 'positive rights')[181] and from the European Court of Human Rights (in favour of state liability)[182] to substantiate its suggestion that the state (in the form of public bodies such as the police) could be liable to delictual actions from members of the public who claim that the state has failed to protect them against violations of their fundamental rights, even in situations where the actual harm was done by another private person. Apart from the general statement about the objective normative values in the constitution referred to above,[183] no reference was made to German law in *Carmichele*, nor did Ackermann J refer to the German doctrine regarding the state duty to protect in his extensive analysis of German law in *Du Plessis v De Klerk*.[184] German law was not referred to in the subsequent delict cases that followed the *Carmichele* decision either.[185] In subsequent decisions where the facts did not resemble *Carmichele* or the other delictual cases, the courts relied indirectly upon the *Carmichele* decision and the notion of the state's duty to protect rights, but referred only to international law sources.

The *Carmichele* argument on the state's duty to protect the fundamental rights of its citizens was relied on in another SCA decision that was more directly concerned with property. The *Modderklip* case concerned a situation where a landowner was unable to enforce an eviction order against a community of unlawful occupiers on his land because they had nowhere else to go.[186] In *Modderklip* the SCA once again relied on the duty to protect argument, deciding that the state was responsible for the

---

[180] *Carmichele v Minister of Safety and Security (Centre for Applied Legal Studies Intervening)* 2001 (4) SA 938 (CC) paras [45]–[49] at 957F–960B.

[181] *De Shaney v Winnebago County Department of Social Services* 489 US 189 (1988). The case was cited merely to make the point that the state action doctrine precludes state liability in the absence of state action in contravention of a fundamental right, and that the US Supreme Court works from the baseline position that there are no positive rights in the US Constitution; see *Carmichele* par [45] at 957H.

[182] *Osman v United Kingdom* 29 EHHR 245 (also reported as [1998] ECHR 101); *Z and Others v United Kingdom* application no 29392/95, 10 May 2001 unreported (now reported as [2001] ECHR 329). These cases were cited to demonstrate the Court's rejection of the immunity approach that is followed in the UK to safeguard public authorities against delictual claims by members of the public: *Carmichele* par [46] at 958D.

[183] *Carmichele* par [54] at 961F–H.

[184] In *Du Plessis v De Klerk* 1996 (3) SA 850 (CC) Ackermann J dedicated the entire 5 pages of his analysis of German law (paras [92]–[106] at 704F–709E) to a detailed consideration of the reasons why the German courts and scholars rejected (and why South African courts should also reject) direct horizontal application and work with indirect horizontal application only.

[185] Other cases in which the duty to protect-construction was referred to are *Minister of Safety and Security v Van Duivenboden* 2002 (6) SA 431 (SCA); *Van Eeden v Minister of Safety and Security (Women's Legal Centre Trust as amicus curiae)* 2003 (1) SA 389 (SCA); *Minister of Safety and Security v Hamilton* 2004 (2) SA 216 (SCA); *Minister of Safety and Security v Carmichele* 2004 (3) SA 305 (SCA).

[186] *Modderfontein Squatters, Greater Benoni City Council v Modderklip Boerdery (Pty) Ltd; (Agri SA and Legal Resources Centre, Amici Curiae); President of the Republic of South Africa and Others v Modderklip Boerdery (Pty) Ltd (Agri SA and Legal Resources Centre, Amici Curiae)* 2004 (6) SA 40 (SCA).

impasse in enforcing the landowner's property interests: because the state was not honouring its duty to realize and fulfil the occupiers' constitutional right of access to housing they had no alternative accommodation, and until such accommodation was provided the landowner would be unable to enforce his eviction order. The state was therefore instructed to provide alternative housing for the unlawful occupiers, and the owner was awarded compensation against the state for the loss that he suffered as long as the occupiers were present on his land. In making this order the SCA relied on the case law and literature surrounding the General Comments of the UN Committee on Economic, Social and Cultural Rights.[187] This approach to the duty to protect argument is particularly relevant to the South African situation because section 7(2) of the Constitution provides explicitly that '[t]he state must respect, protect, promote, and fulfil the rights in the Bill of Rights.' It is therefore not surprising that the international law cases in which this approach was developed are cited as authority in *Modderklip* for the proposition that the state has a duty to respect, protect and fulfil the section 25 and 26 rights in the South African Constitution. The Constitutional Court upheld the SCA decision but on different grounds, preferring to found the state's duty towards the landowner in this case on section 34 (the right of access to court, including the right to have access to suitable and effective remedies and enforcement procedures). Although the Constitutional Court shifted its focus to section 34 the basic structure of the SCA decision was kept intact and the emphasis was still placed on the state's duty to provide the remedies and enforcement procedures with which a person can protect his or her constitutional rights.[188]

In the *Metrorail* case,[189] the Constitutional Court followed a slightly different line of argument in deciding whether a public company (in which the state is the only shareholder) is accountable to its customers (commuters using the railway service provided by the company) for crimes committed against them by other passengers. The Court argued that the company was a state organ that bore certain obligations in terms of the Legal Succession to the South African Transport Services Act 8 of 1989; that these obligations had to be interpreted in the light of the Bill of Rights because the company was accountable to the broader community in the exercise of its powers; and that the statutory provisions that gave rise to the company's powers and account-

---

[187] Instead of the delictual duty of care cases referred to in *Carmichele*, the *Modderklip* court (SCA) referred to another set of cases relating to the state's duty to protect, fulfil, promote and realize citizens' constitutional rights: *X & Y v The Netherlands* [1985] 8 EHRR 235 (European Court of Human Rights, European Convention on Human Rights); *Union des Jeunes Avocats v Chad* 9th Annual Activity Report 72 (African Commission, African Charter of Human and Peoples' Rights); *The Social and Economic Rights Action Center and the Center for Economic and Social Rights v Nigeria* 15th Annual Activity Report 30 (African Commission, African Charter of Human and Peoples' Rights); *Velásquez Rodríguez v Honduras* 28 ILM 291 (1989) (Inter-American Court of Human Rights). See further on this literature S Liebenberg 'The interpretation of socio-economic rights' in S Woolman et al (eds) *Constitutional law of South Africa* (2nd ed original service 2003) 33-6–33-7.

[188] *President of the Republic of South Africa and Another v Modderklip Boerdery (Pty) Ltd (Agri SA and Others, Amici Curiae)* 2005 (5) SA 3 (CC). See chapters 4.5.5 and 6.4 for a discussion.

[189] *Rail Commuters Action Group and Others v Transnet t/a Metrorail and Others* 2005 (2) SA 359 (CC).

ability had to be interpreted in view of the relevant constitutional provisions and with due regard for the social, economic and political context within which the powers of the company were exercised, to promote the spirit, purport and objects of the Bill of Rights.[190] Accordingly, the company bore a positive obligation, arising from the authorizing statute read with the Constitution, to ensure that reasonable measures were in place to provide for the security of rail commuters.[191] In coming to this decision the Court relied on sections 7, 8 and 39 of the Constitution and not on foreign case law, although the *Osman* decision that was applied in *Carmichele* was again referred to.[192] In the relevant passage, the Court confirmed that the effect of the *Carmichele* decision was to establish that accountability of a public power was one of the considerations that was relevant to the question of whether a legal duty exists for purposes of the law of delict;[193] thereby clarifying the proper relationship between the public law theory of a state duty to protect and the private law doctrine of the duty of care, and (possibly) liability for a claim for delictual damages. The most important aspect of this finding is that the existence of a state duty to protect (accountability) can be an indication of a duty of care and hence of private law liability, so that private law could possibly be developed (in the sense that state liability is extended) to give effect to a transformative, public law or constitutional notion of accountability.

The approach in the *Metrorail* case signifies a move away from the earlier debate about (direct or indirect) horizontal application, while at the same time leaving us in some doubt about the future direction of the debate about the effect of the Constitution on private law. On the one hand, the Court refers to and relies upon the new discourse, opened up in *Carmichele* and similar earlier cases, about the state's duty to protect its citizens' fundamental rights against infringements by other private parties, but without bringing final clarity about the theoretical foundation for this discourse. On the other hand the Court also relies upon the constitutional duty of the courts to develop existing law to promote the spirit, purport and objects of the Constitution according to section 39(2) of the Constitution, without explaining the differences and links between the two processes.

Two further decisions of the Constitutional Court should be mentioned in this regard. In *S v Thebus and Another*[194] the Court stated that development of the

---

[190] Paras [69]–[83] at 397H–402I.

[191] Par [85] at 403E–G. It was unnecessary to decide whether this was a direct constitutional obligation because reliance was placed primarily on the statutory obligations of the company. The Court added that the obligation to ensure the safety of rail commuters could not be placed exclusively on the shoulders of the police, because they were operating under severe capacity restraints; once it was clear that the police could not manage to ensure safety on their own the company had the obligation to take reasonable steps to ensure that rail commuter passengers were safe: paras [91]–[93] at 405G–H, 406D–F.

[192] See paras [71]–[73] at 398E–399F, particularly 399A–B and footnote 77 there.

[193] Par [73] at 399D–F. The Court pointed out that it would not always be necessary or suitable to award delictual damages for a particular breach of a duty to protect citizens' fundamental rights and that other public law remedies (particularly declaratory, mandatory and prohibitory relief) would sometimes be more suitable: par [79] at 401F.

common law under section 39(2) can occur in two instances; firstly when a rule of common law is inconsistent with the Constitution and secondly when a rule of common law is not inconsistent with the Constitution but falls short of its spirit, purport and objects. In the latter case development of the common law would involve adaptation so that the common law 'grows in harmony with the "objective value system" found in the Constitution.' In *K v Minister of Safety and Security*[195] the Court referred to the *Thebus* statement, again confirmed that there is an objective value system inherent in the Constitution and that development of the common law under section 39(2) must take place in accordance with that system, and decided that such development included both more radical changes that occur when obvious inconsistencies with the Constitution are rectified and smaller, incremental development of common law rules. The *Thebus* and *K* decisions indicate that the Court does not rely exclusively on the state duty to protect doctrine for its view of the development of the common law and that the Court's view of development of the common law (although not fully explicated) is linked quite substantially to a notion of the objective system of fundamental values that reside in the Constitution.

7.5.4 Evaluating the shift away from horizontal application

Johan van der Walt[196] wrote with reference to the *Carmichele* case that 'the horizontal application of rights obviously constitutes a critical junction between constitutional and common-law jurisprudence in the resolution of private-law disputes and therefore between the two fields of adjudication that delimit the domains of the Supreme Court of Appeal and the Constitutional Court.' He favours a style of indirect horizontal application that will not allow the civil courts to shy away from development of the common law that goes against the grain of long-standing and perhaps treasured private law principles and institutions, when necessary. The co-operative relation between common law and constitutional jurisprudence that he pleads for can only develop, in his view, if the difference between common law and constitutional law that is upheld in the notion of indirect horizontal application 'remains a creative difference or tension, a difference that in fact accentuates the constitutional challenge to common law. It is to be rejected if the difference that it

---

[194] 2003 (6) SA 505 (CC) par [28].

[195] 2005 (9) BCLR 835 (CC) paras [14]–[19] at 841B–844F. In this case the Court held that the common law rule of vicarious liability had to be developed under section 39(2) to allow state liability in cases where state employees simultaneously acted in pursuance of personal, non-job related purposes (in this case raping a woman whom the policemen offered to assist) and failed to carry out a job-related duty (namely to protect a member of the public). The Court found that the necessary development in this instance was easily accommodated within the common law as it stands, although certain recent decisions did not follow the route of development that was suggested by earlier decisions: paras [48]–[53], [57] at 856G–857I, 858H–859C.

[196] JWG van der Walt '*Progressive* indirect horizontal application of the bill of rights: Towards a co-operative relation between common-law and constitutional jurisprudence' (2001) 17 *SAJHR* 341–363 at 343–361.

invokes between common law and constitutional law is to be conceived in terms of a shield that fends off the constitutional challenge to existing law.'[197] Moreover, Van der Walt argues,[198] this is not a new or strange thing for private law, because the tension characterizes common law institutions themselves—it is the 'tension between a drive towards closure and certainty and a desire to re-open and include what has hitherto been excluded, despite the degree of uncertainty that this re-opening and inclusion re-introduces into the system. This is the age-old tension between clear-cut rules and open-ended principles ...' To this one could perhaps add that the explicit transformation-oriented words of the Constitution, read within its historical and political context, indicate quite clearly that clear-cut rules cannot be allowed to stand in the way of change indicated by open-ended principles that demand the transformation of South African law away from inequality and unfairness and towards greater equality and fairness.

The development of the common law is necessary to ensure that rules and institutions of the common law will not remain unaffected by changes and shifts in emphasis brought about by the new constitutional dispensation. Moreover, such development is authorized by sections 8 and 39 of the Constitution, and the injunction in section 7 to respect, protect, promote and fulfil the rights in the Bill of Rights adds further weight to the process. Consequently, a theory of horizontal application or a theory of state duties to protect fundamental rights is not strictly necessary to enable the South African courts to do whatever is necessary to bring the common law in line with constitutional aims and objectives. However, greater theoretical clarity about the structure and direction of development of the common law is necessary, and attaining such clarity might involve further consideration of the horizontal application and duty to protect constructions. It would probably be unwise to shift the whole burden of developing the common law onto the state duty to protect construction, even though section 7 does provide a useful point of reference for it. On the one hand this construction seems to have been restricted largely to the promotion of socio-economic rights in other jurisdictions, especially in international law, which raises the question whether it is wide enough as a theoretical foundation for everything that needs to be accomplished in terms of development of the common law in the South African context. On the other hand the duty to protect construction suffers from a certain vagueness that leaves much theoretical explanation to be done before the necessary development work can be properly understood and explained. At least in certain areas of private law this does not seem to be the final answer to the development of the common law issue.

It is true that the horizontal application debate has lost much of its initial urgency and fervour, but there is no reason why it should be shelved altogether. An advantage of this construction is that it creates ample room, especially in its German-origin

---

[197] At 355.
[198] At 360. See, much to the same effect, H Botha 'Freedom and constraint in constitutional adjudication' (2004) 20 *SAJHR* 249–283.

radiation language, for useful explanations of the development of the common law through judicial interpretation of common law rules and principles as well as of legislation. Now that the spectre of direct horizontal application seems to have been laid to rest there is room for further development of the notion of indirect horizontal application along the lines suggested by Johan van der Walt, in order to ensure that the influence of the Constitution is felt throughout private law. Apart from the delictual liability cases that were based on the state duty to protect construction, constitutional case law has so far dealt almost exclusively with the interpretation of legislation, which makes it difficult to predict which way the Constitutional Court will move when a case comes up in which it is necessary to develop the common law of property in line with section 39. The existing cases suggest that the Court has not abandoned the wider notion of development altogether for a state duty to protect construction; in fact, if anything the recent cases suggest that the Court is increasingly simply relying on a construction of the duty to develop the common law that is based directly on constitutional provisions such as sections 8 and 39.

APPENDIX 1

Chapters 1 and 2 of the
Constitution of the Republic of South Africa 1996[1]

PREAMBLE

We, the people of South Africa,

Recognise the injustices of our past;

Honour those who suffered for justice and freedom in our land;

Respect those who have worked to build and develop our country; and

Believe that South Africa belongs to all who live in it, united in our diversity.

We therefore, through our freely elected representatives, adopt this Constitution as the supreme law of the Republic so as to

- Heal the divisions of the past and establish a society based on democratic values, social justice and fundamental human rights;
- Lay the foundations for a democratic and open society in which government is based on the will of the people and every citizen is equally protected by law;
- Improve the quality of life of all citizens and free the potential of each person; and
- Build a united and democratic South Africa able to take its rightful place as a sovereign state in the family of nations.

May God protect our people.

CHAPTER 1: FOUNDING PROVISIONS

1. REPUBLIC OF SOUTH AFRICA

The Republic of South Africa is one, sovereign, democratic state founded on the following values:

(1) Human dignity, the achievement of equality and the advancement of human rights and freedoms.

(2) Non-racialism and non-sexism.

(3) Supremacy of the Constitution and the rule of law.

(4) Universal adult suffrage, a national common voters roll, regular elections and a multi-party system of democratic government, to ensure accountability, responsiveness and openness.

2. SUPREMACY OF CONSTITUTION

This Constitution is the supreme law of the Republic; law or conduct inconsistent with it is invalid, and the obligations imposed by it must be fulfilled.

3. CITIZENSHIP

(1) There is a common South African citizenship.

---

[1] The full text of the 1996 Constitution can be found on the Constitutional Court website at http://www.concourt.gov.za/constitution/index.html.

(2) All citizens are—
   (*a*) equally entitled to the rights, privileges and benefits of citizenship; and
   (*b*) equally subject to the duties and responsibilities of citizenship.
(3) National legislation must provide for the acquisition, loss and restoration of citizenship.

4. NATIONAL ANTHEM
The national anthem of the Republic is determined by the President by proclamation.

5. NATIONAL FLAG
The national flag of the Republic is black, gold, green, white, red and blue, as described and sketched in Schedule 1.

6. LANGUAGES
(1) The official languages of the Republic are Sepedi, Sesotho, Setswana, siSwati, Tshivenda, Xitsonga, Afrikaans, English, isiNdebele, isiXhosa and isiZulu.
(2) Recognising the historically diminished use and status of the indigenous languages of our people, the state must take practical and positive measures to elevate the status and advance the use of these languages.
(3) (*a*) The national government and provincial governments may use any particular official languages for the purposes of government, taking into account usage, practicality, expense, regional circumstances and the balance of the needs and preferences of the population as a whole or in the province concerned; but the national government and each provincial government must use at least two official languages.
   (*b*) Municipalities must take into account the language usage and preferences of their residents.
(4) The national government and provincial governments, by legislative and other measures, must regulate and monitor their use of official languages. Without detracting from the provisions of subsection (2), all official languages must enjoy parity of esteem and must be treated equitably.
(5) A Pan South African Language Board established by national legislation must—
   (*a*) promote, and create conditions for, the development and use of
   (*b*) all official languages;
   (*c*) the Khoi, Nama and San languages; and
   (*d*) sign language ; and
   (*e*) promote and ensure respect for
   (*f*) all languages commonly used by communities in South Africa, including German, Greek, Gujarati, Hindi, Portuguese, Tamil, Telegu and Urdu; and
   (*g*) Arabic, Hebrew, Sanskrit and other languages used for religious purposes in South Africa.

CHAPTER 2: BILL OF RIGHTS

7. RIGHTS
(1) This Bill of Rights is a cornerstone of democracy in South Africa. It enshrines the rights of all people in our country and affirms the democratic values of human dignity, equality and freedom.

(2) The state must respect, protect, promote and fulfil the rights in the Bill of Rights.

(3) The rights in the Bill of Rights are subject to the limitations contained or referred to in section 36, or elsewhere in the Bill.

8. APPLICATION

(1) The Bill of Rights applies to all law, and binds the legislature, the executive, the judiciary and all organs of state.

(2) A provision of the Bill of Rights binds a natural or a juristic person if, and to the extent that, it is applicable, taking into account the nature of the right and the nature of any duty imposed by the right.

(3) When applying a provision of the Bill of Rights to a natural or juristic person in terms of subsection (2), a court—

　(a) in order to give effect to a right in the Bill, must apply, or if necessary develop, the common law to the extent that legislation does not give effect to that right; and

　(b) may develop rules of the common law to limit the right, provided that the limitation is in accordance with section 36(1).

(4) A juristic person is entitled to the rights in the Bill of Rights to the extent required by the nature of the rights and the nature of that juristic person.

9. EQUALITY

(1) Everyone is equal before the law and has the right to equal protection and benefit of the law.

(2) Equality includes the full and equal enjoyment of all rights and freedoms. To promote the achievement of equality, legislative and other measures designed to protect or advance persons, or categories of persons, disadvantaged by unfair discrimination may be taken.

(3) The state may not unfairly discriminate directly or indirectly against anyone on one or more grounds, including race, gender, sex, pregnancy, marital status, ethnic or social origin, colour, sexual orientation, age, disability, religion, conscience, belief, culture, language and birth.

(4) No person may unfairly discriminate directly or indirectly against anyone on one or more grounds in terms of subsection (3). National legislation must be enacted to prevent or prohibit unfair discrimination.

(5) Discrimination on one or more of the grounds listed in subsection (3) is unfair unless it is established that the discrimination is fair.

10. HUMAN DIGNITY

Everyone has inherent dignity and the right to have their dignity respected and protected.

11. LIFE

Everyone has the right to life.

12. FREEDOM AND SECURITY OF THE PERSON

(1) Everyone has the right to freedom and security of the person, which includes the right—

　(a) not to be deprived of freedom arbitrarily or without just cause;

　(b) not to be detained without trial;

　(c) to be free from all forms of violence from either public or private sources;

    (*d*) not to be tortured in any way; and

    (*e*) not to be treated or punished in a cruel, inhuman or degrading way.

(2) Everyone has the right to bodily and psychological integrity, which includes the right—

    (*a*) to make decisions concerning reproduction;

    (*b*) to security in and control over their body; and

    (*c*) not to be subjected to medical or scientific experiments without their informed consent.

13. SLAVERY, SERVITUDE AND FORCED LABOUR

No one may be subjected to slavery, servitude or forced labour.

14. PRIVACY

Everyone has the right to privacy, which includes the right not to have—

    (*a*) their person or home searched;

    (*b*) their property searched;

    (*c*) their possessions seized; or

    (*d*) the privacy of their communications infringed.

15. FREEDOM OF RELIGION, BELIEF AND OPINION

(1) Everyone has the right to freedom of conscience, religion, thought, belief and opinion.

(2) Religious observances may be conducted at state or state-aided institutions, provided that—

    (*a*) those observances follow rules made by the appropriate public authorities;

    (*b*) they are conducted on an equitable basis; and

    (*c*) attendance at them is free and voluntary.

(3) (*a*) This section does not prevent legislation recognising—

        (i) marriages concluded under any tradition, or a system of religious, personal or family law; or

        (ii) systems of personal and family law under any tradition, or adhered to by persons professing a particular religion.

    (*b*) Recognition in terms of paragraph (*a*) must be consistent with this section and the other provisions of the Constitution.

16. FREEDOM OF EXPRESSION

(1) Everyone has the right to freedom of expression, which includes—

    (*a*) freedom of the press and other media;

    (*b*) freedom to receive or impart information or ideas;

    (*c*) freedom of artistic creativity; and

    (*d*) academic freedom and freedom of scientific research.

(2) The right in subsection (1) does not extend to—

    (*a*) propaganda for war;

    (*b*) incitement of imminent violence; or

    (*c*) advocacy of hatred that is based on race, ethnicity, gender or religion, and that constitutes incitement to cause harm.

17. ASSEMBLY, DEMONSTRATION, PICKET AND PETITION
Everyone has the right, peacefully and unarmed, to assemble, to demonstrate, to picket and to present petitions.

18. FREEDOM OF ASSOCIATION
Everyone has the right to freedom of association.

19. POLITICAL RIGHTS
(1) Every citizen is free to make political choices, which includes the right—
    (*a*) to form a political party;
    (*b*) to participate in the activities of, or recruit members for, a political party; and
    (*c*) to campaign for a political party or cause.
(2) Every citizen has the right to free, fair and regular elections for any legislative body established in terms of the Constitution.
(3) Every adult citizen has the right—
    (*a*) to vote in elections for any legislative body established in terms of the Constitution, and to do so in secret; and
    (*b*) to stand for public office and, if elected, to hold office.

20. CITIZENSHIP
No citizen may be deprived of citizenship.

21. FREEDOM OF MOVEMENT AND RESIDENCE
(1) Everyone has the right to freedom of movement.
(2) Everyone has the right to leave the Republic.
(3) Every citizen has the right to enter, to remain in and to reside anywhere in, the Republic.
(4) Every citizen has the right to a passport.

22. FREEDOM OF TRADE, OCCUPATION AND PROFESSION
Every citizen has the right to choose their trade, occupation or profession freely. The practice of a trade, occupation or profession may be regulated by law.

23. LABOUR RELATIONS
(1) Everyone has the right to fair labour practices.
(2) Every worker has the right—
    (*a*) to form and join a trade union;
    (*b*) to participate in the activities and programmes of a trade union; and
    (*c*) to strike.
(3) Every employer has the right—
    (*a*) to form and join an employers' organisation; and
    (*b*) to participate in the activities and programmes of an employers' organisation.
(4) Every trade union and every employers' organisation has the right—
    (*a*) to determine its own administration, programmes and activities;
    (*b*) to organise; and
    (*c*) to form and join a federation.

(5) Every trade union, employers' organisation and employer has the right to engage in collective bargaining. National legislation may be enacted to regulate collective bargaining. To the extent that the legislation may limit a right in this Chapter, the limitation must comply with section 36(1).

(6) National legislation may recognise union security arrangements contained in collective agreements. To the extent that the legislation may limit a right in this Chapter, the limitation must comply with section 36(1).

24. ENVIRONMENT

Everyone has the right—

(*a*) to an environment that is not harmful to their health or well-being; and

(*b*) to have the environment protected, for the benefit of present and future generations, through reasonable legislative and other measures that

(*c*) prevent pollution and ecological degradation;

(*d*) promote conservation; and

(*e*) secure ecologically sustainable development and use of natural resources while promoting justifiable economic and social development.

25. PROPERTY

(1) No one may be deprived of property except in terms of law of general application, and no law may permit arbitrary deprivation of property.

(2) Property may be expropriated only in terms of law of general application—

(*a*) for a public purpose or in the public interest; and

(*b*) subject to compensation, the amount of which and the time and manner of payment of which have either been agreed to by those affected or decided or approved by a court.

(3) The amount of the compensation and the time and manner of payment must be just and equitable, reflecting an equitable balance between the public interest and the interests of those affected, having regard to all relevant circumstances, including—

(*a*) the current use of the property;

(*b*) the history of the acquisition and use of the property;

(*c*) the market value of the property;

(*d*) the extent of direct state investment and subsidy in the acquisition and beneficial capital improvement of the property; and

(*e*) the purpose of the expropriation.

(4) For the purposes of this section—

(*a*) the public interest includes the nation's commitment to land reform, and to reforms to bring about equitable access to all South Africa's natural resources; and

(*b*) property is not limited to land.

(5) The state must take reasonable legislative and other measures, within its available resources, to foster conditions which enable citizens to gain access to land on an equitable basis.

(6) A person or community whose tenure of land is legally insecure as a result of past racially discriminatory laws or practices is entitled, to the extent provided by an Act of Parliament, either to tenure which is legally secure or to comparable redress.

(7) A person or community dispossessed of property after 19 June 1913 as a result of past racially discriminatory laws or practices is entitled, to the extent provided by an Act of Parliament, either to restitution of that property or to equitable redress.

(8) No provision of this section may impede the state from taking legislative and other measures to achieve land, water and related reform, in order to redress the results of past racial discrimination, provided that any departure from the provisions of this section is in accordance with the provisions of section 36(1).

(9) Parliament must enact the legislation referred to in subsection (6).

26. Housing

(1) Everyone has the right to have access to adequate housing.

(2) The state must take reasonable legislative and other measures, within its available resources, to achieve the progressive realisation of this right.

(3) No one may be evicted from their home, or have their home demolished, without an order of court made after considering all the relevant circumstances. No legislation may permit arbitrary evictions.

27. Health care, food, water and social security

(1) Everyone has the right to have access to—

(a) health care services, including reproductive health care;

(b) sufficient food and water; and

(c) social security, including, if they are unable to support themselves and their dependants, appropriate social assistance.

(2) The state must take reasonable legislative and other measures, within its available resources, to achieve the progressive realisation of each of these rights.

(3) No one may be refused emergency medical treatment.

28. Children

(1) Every child has the right—

(a) to a name and a nationality from birth;

(b) to family care or parental care, or to appropriate alternative care when removed from the family environment;

(c) to basic nutrition, shelter, basic health care services and social services;

(d) to be protected from maltreatment, neglect, abuse or degradation;

(e) to be protected from exploitative labour practices;

(f) not to be required or permitted to perform work or provide services that—

(i) are inappropriate for a person of that child's age; or

(ii) place at risk the child's well-being, education, physical or mental health or spiritual, moral or social development;

(g) not to be detained except as a measure of last resort, in which case, in addition to the rights a child enjoys under sections 12 and 35, the child may be detained only for the shortest appropriate period of time, and has the right to be—

(i) kept separately from detained persons over the age of 18 years; and

(ii) treated in a manner, and kept in conditions, that take account of the child's age;

(h) to have a legal practitioner assigned to the child by the state, and at state expense, in civil proceedings affecting the child, if substantial injustice would otherwise result; and (*i*) not to be used directly in armed conflict, and to be protected in times of armed conflict.

(2) A child's best interests are of paramount importance in every matter concerning the child.

(3) In this section 'child' means a person under the age of 18 years.

29. EDUCATION

(1) Everyone has the right—

    (*a*) to a basic education, including adult basic education; and

    (*b*) to further education, which the state, through reasonable measures, must make progressively available and accessible.

(2) Everyone has the right to receive education in the official language or languages of their choice in public educational institutions where that education is reasonably practicable. In order to ensure the effective access to, and implementation of, this right, the state must consider all reasonable educational alternatives, including single medium institutions, taking into account—

    (*a*) equity;

    (*b*) practicability; and

    (*c*) the need to redress the results of past racially discriminatory laws and practices.

(3) Everyone has the right to establish and maintain, at their own expense, independent educational institutions that—

    (*a*) do not discriminate on the basis of race;

    (*b*) are registered with the state; and

    (*c*) maintain standards that are not inferior to standards at comparable public educational institutions.

(4) Subsection (3) does not preclude state subsidies for independent educational institutions.

30. LANGUAGE AND CULTURE

Everyone has the right to use the language and to participate in the cultural life of their choice, but no one exercising these rights may do so in a manner inconsistent with any provision of the Bill of Rights.

31. CULTURAL, RELIGIOUS AND LINGUISTIC COMMUNITIES

(1) Persons belonging to a cultural, religious or linguistic community may not be denied the right, with other members of that community—

    (*a*) to enjoy their culture, practise their religion and use their language; and

    (*b*) to form, join and maintain cultural, religious and linguistic associations and other organs of civil society.

(2) The rights in subsection (1) may not be exercised in a manner inconsistent with any provision of the Bill of Rights.

32. ACCESS TO INFORMATION

(1) Everyone has the right of access to—

    (*a*) any information held by the state; and

    (*b*) any information that is held by another person and that is required for the exercise or protection of any rights.

(2) National legislation must be enacted to give effect to this right, and may provide for reasonable measures to alleviate the administrative and financial burden on the state.

33. JUST ADMINISTRATIVE ACTION

(1) Everyone has the right to administrative action that is lawful, reasonable and procedurally fair.

(2) Everyone whose rights have been adversely affected by administrative action has the right to be given written reasons.

(3) National legislation must be enacted to give effect to these rights, and must—

    (*a*) provide for the review of administrative action by a court or, where appropriate, an independent and impartial tribunal;

    (*b*) impose a duty on the state to give effect to the rights in subsections (1) and (2); and

    (*c*) promote an efficient administration.

34. ACCESS TO COURTS

Everyone has the right to have any dispute that can be resolved by the application of law decided in a fair public hearing before a court or, where appropriate, another independent and impartial tribunal or forum.

35. ARRESTED, DETAINED AND ACCUSED PERSONS

(1) Everyone who is arrested for allegedly committing an offence has the right—

    (*a*) to remain silent;

    (*b*) to be informed promptly—

        (i) of the right to remain silent; and

        (ii) of the consequences of not remaining silent;

    (*c*) not to be compelled to make any confession or admission that could be used in evidence against that person;

    (*d*) to be brought before a court as soon as reasonably possible, but not later than 48 hours after the arrest; or the end of the first court day after the expiry of the 48 hours, if the 48 hours expire outside ordinary court hours or on a day which is not an ordinary court day;

    (*e*) at the first court appearance after being arrested, to be charged or to be informed of the reason for the detention to continue, or to be released; and

    (*f*) to be released from detention if the interests of justice permit, subject to reasonable conditions.

(2) Everyone who is detained, including every sentenced prisoner, has the right—

    (*a*) to be informed promptly of the reason for being detained;

    (*b*) to choose, and to consult with, a legal practitioner, and to be informed of this right promptly;

    (*c*) to have a legal practitioner assigned to the detained person by the state and at state expense, if substantial injustice would otherwise result, and to be informed of this right promptly;

    (*d*) to challenge the lawfulness of the detention in person before a court and, if the detention is unlawful, to be released;

    (*e*) to conditions of detention that are consistent with human dignity, including at least exercise and the provision, at state expense, of adequate accommodation, nutrition, reading material and medical treatment; and

    (*f*) to communicate with, and be visited by, that person's—

        (i) spouse or partner;

        (ii) next of kin;

      (iii) chosen religious counsellor; and

      (iv) chosen medical practitioner.

(3) Every accused person has a right to a fair trial, which includes the right—

    (*a*) to be informed of the charge with sufficient detail to answer it;

    (*b*) to have adequate time and facilities to prepare a defence;

    (*c*) to a public trial before an ordinary court;

    (*d*) to have their trial begin and conclude without unreasonable delay;

    (*e*) to be present when being tried;

    (*f*) to choose, and be represented by, a legal practitioner, and to be informed of this right promptly;

    (*g*) to have a legal practitioner assigned to the accused person by the state and at state expense, if substantial injustice would otherwise result, and to be informed of this right promptly;

    (*h*) to be presumed innocent, to remain silent, and not to testify during the proceedings;

    (*i*) to adduce and challenge evidence;

    (*j*) not to be compelled to give self-incriminating evidence;

    (*k*) to be tried in a language that the accused person understands or, if that is not practicable, to have the proceedings interpreted in that language;

    (*l*) not to be convicted for an act or omission that was not an offence under either national or international law at the time it was committed or omitted;

    (*m*) not to be tried for an offence in respect of an act or omission for which that person has previously been either acquitted or convicted;

    (*n*) to the benefit of the least severe of the prescribed punishments if the prescribed punishment for the offence has been changed between the time that the offence was committed and the time of sentencing; and

    (*o*) of appeal to, or review by, a higher court.

(4) Whenever this section requires information to be given to a person, that information must be given in a language that the person understands.

(5) Evidence obtained in a manner that violates any right in the Bill of Rights must be excluded if the admission of that evidence would render the trial unfair or otherwise be detrimental to the administration of justice.

36. LIMITATION OF RIGHTS

(1) The rights in the Bill of Rights may be limited only in terms of law of general application to the extent that the limitation is reasonable and justifiable in an open and democratic society based on human dignity, equality and freedom, taking into account all relevant factors, including—

    (*a*) the nature of the right;

    (*b*) the importance of the purpose of the limitation;

    (*c*) the nature and extent of the limitation;

    (*d*) the relation between the limitation and its purpose; and

    (*e*) less restrictive means to achieve the purpose.

(2) Except as provided in subsection (1) or in any other provision of the Constitution, no law may limit any right entrenched in the Bill of Rights.

37. STATES OF EMERGENCY

(1) A state of emergency may be declared only in terms of an Act of Parliament, and only when—

  (a) the life of the nation is threatened by war, invasion, general insurrection, disorder, natural disaster or other public emergency; and

  (b) the declaration is necessary to restore peace and order.

(2) A declaration of a state of emergency, and any legislation enacted or other action taken in consequence of that declaration, may be effective only—

  (a) prospectively; and

  (b) for no more than 21 days from the date of the declaration, unless the National Assembly resolves to extend the declaration. The Assembly may extend a declaration of a state of emergency for no more than three months at a time. The first extension of the state of emergency must be by a resolution adopted with a supporting vote of a majority of the members of the Assembly. Any subsequent extension must be by a resolution adopted with a supporting vote of at least 60 per cent of the members of the Assembly. A resolution in terms of this paragraph may be adopted only following a public debate in the Assembly.

(3) Any competent court may decide on the validity of—

  (a) a declaration of a state of emergency;

  (b) any extension of a declaration of a state of emergency; or

  (c) any legislation enacted, or other action taken, in consequence of a declaration of a state of emergency.

(4) Any legislation enacted in consequence of a declaration of a state of emergency may derogate from the Bill of Rights only to the extent that—

  (a) the derogation is strictly required by the emergency; and

  (b) the legislation—

    (i) is consistent with the Republic's obligations under international law applicable to states of emergency;

    (ii) conforms to subsection (5); and

    (iii) is published in the national Government Gazette as soon as reasonably possible after being enacted.

(5) No Act of Parliament that authorises a declaration of a state of emergency, and no legislation enacted or other action taken in consequence of a declaration, may permit or authorise—

  (a) indemnifying the state, or any person, in respect of any unlawful act;

  (b) any derogation from this section; or

  (c) any derogation from a section mentioned in column 1 of the Table of Non-Derogable Rights, to the extent indicated opposite that section in column 3 of the Table.

Table of Non-Derogable Rights

1. SECTION NO	2. SECTION TITLE	3. EXTENT TO WHICH THE RIGHT IS PROTECTED
9	Equality	With respect to unfair discrimination solely on the grounds of race, colour, ethnic or social origin, sex religion or language
10	Human dignity	Entirely

1. SECTION NO	2. SECTION TITLE	3. EXTENT TO WHICH THE RIGHT IS PROTECTED
11	Life	Entirely
12	Freedom and security of the person	With respect to subsections (1)(d) and (e) and (2)(c).
13	Slavery, servitude and forced labour	With respect to slavery and servitude
28	Children	With respect to: • subsection (1)(d) and (e); • the rights in subparagraphs (i) and (ii) of subsection (1)(g); and • subsection 1(i) in respect of children of 15 years and younger
35	Arrested, detained and accused persons	With respect to: • subsections (1)(a), (b) and (c) and (2)(d); • the rights in paragraphs (a) to (o) of subsection (3), excluding paragraph (d) • subsection (4); and • subsection (5) with respect to the exclusion of evidence if the admission of that evidence would render the trial unfair.

(6) Whenever anyone is detained without trial in consequence of a derogation of rights resulting from a declaration of a state of emergency, the following conditions must be observed:

(a) An adult family member or friend of the detainee must be contacted as soon as reasonably possible, and informed that the person has been detained.

(b) A notice must be published in the national Government Gazette within five days of the person being detained, stating the detainee's name and place of detention and referring to the emergency measure in terms of which that person has been detained.

(c) The detainee must be allowed to choose, and be visited at any reasonable time by, a medical practitioner.

(d) The detainee must be allowed to choose, and be visited at any reasonable time by, a legal representative.

(e) A court must review the detention as soon as reasonably possible, but no later than 10 days after the date the person was detained, and the court must release the detainee unless it is necessary to continue the detention to restore peace and order.

(f) A detainee who is not released in terms of a review under paragraph (e), or who is not released in terms of a review under this paragraph, may apply to a court for a further review of the detention at any time after 10 days have passed since the previous review, and the court must release the detainee unless it is still necessary to continue the detention to restore peace and order.

(*g*) The detainee must be allowed to appear in person before any court considering the detention, to be represented by a legal practitioner at those hearings, and to make representations against continued detention.

(*h*) The state must present written reasons to the court to justify the continued detention of the detainee, and must give a copy of those reasons to the detainee at least two days before the court reviews the detention.

(7) If a court releases a detainee, that person may not be detained again on the same grounds unless the state first shows a court good cause for re-detaining that person.

(8) Subsections (6) and (7) do not apply to persons who are not South African citizens and who are detained in consequence of an international armed conflict. Instead, the state must comply with the standards binding on the Republic under international humanitarian law in respect of the detention of such persons.

38. Enforcement of rights

Anyone listed in this section has the right to approach a competent court, alleging that a right in the Bill of Rights has been infringed or threatened, and the court may grant appropriate relief, including a declaration of rights. The persons who may approach a court are—

(*a*) anyone acting in their own interest;

(*b*) anyone acting on behalf of another person who cannot act in their own name;

(*c*) anyone acting as a member of, or in the interest of, a group or class of persons;

(*d*) anyone acting in the public interest; and

(*e*) an association acting in the interest of its members.

39. Interpretation of Bill of Rights

(1) When interpreting the Bill of Rights, a court, tribunal or forum—

(*a*) must promote the values that underlie an open and democratic society based on human dignity, equality and freedom;

(*b*) must consider international law; and

(*c*) may consider foreign law.

(2) When interpreting any legislation, and when developing the common law or customary law, every court, tribunal or forum must promote the spirit, purport and objects of the Bill of Rights.

(3) The Bill of Rights does not deny the existence of any other rights or freedoms that are recognised or conferred by common law, customary law or legislation, to the extent that they are consistent with the Bill.

APPENDIX 2

Property Clauses in Selected Foreign Constitutions

1. THE USA[1]

CONSTITUTION OF THE UNITED STATES OF AMERICA 1787

Article [V]

No person shall be held to answer for a capital, or otherwise infamous crime, unless on a presentment or indictment of a Grand Jury, [...] nor be deprived of life, liberty, or property, without due process of law; nor shall private property be taken for public use without just compensation.

Article [XIV], Section 1

[...] No State shall make or enforce any law which shall abridge the privileges or immunities of citizens of the United States; nor shall any State deprive any person of life, liberty, or property, without due process of law; nor deny to any person within its jurisdiction the equal protection of the laws.

2. GERMAN-LANGUAGE CONSTITUTIONS

2.1 FEDERAL REPUBLIC OF GERMANY[2]

Basic Law for the Federal Republic of Germany 1949

Article 14 [Property, inheritance, expropriation]

(1) Property and the right of inheritance shall be guaranteed. Their substance and limits shall be determined by law.

(2) Property entails obligations. Its use should also serve the public interest.

(3) Expropriation shall only be permissible in the public interest. It may only be ordered by or pursuant to a law which determines the nature and extent of compensation. Compensation shall reflect a fair balance between the public interest and the interests of those affected. In case of dispute regarding the amount of compensation recourse may be had to the ordinary courts.

---

[1] The property clause appears in the Fifth Amendment (1791) and Fourteenth Amendment (1868) to the federal Constitution of the US (1787). Source: SE Finer, V Bogdanor & B Rudden *Comparing constitutions* (1996) 102, 117, 120. See further AJ van der Walt *Constitutional property clauses: A comparative analysis* (1999) 398–458; AJ van der Walt 'Compensation for excessive or unfair regulation: A comparative overview of constitutional practice relating to regulatory takings' (1999) 14 *SA Public Law* 273–331 at 280–286, 321.

[2] The property clause appears in article 14 of the German Basic Law (*Grundgesetz* 1949). Source: *Basic Law for the Federal Republic of Germany* (1995) 18 (official translation). See further AJ van der Walt *Constitutional property clauses: A comparative analysis* (1999) 121–163; AJ van der Walt 'Compensation for excessive or unfair regulation: A comparative overview of constitutional practice relating to regulatory takings' (1999) 14 *SA Public Law* 273–331 at 286–290, 321.

2.2 AUSTRIA[3]

Austrian Basic Law of 21 December 1867

Article 5

Property is inviolable. Expropriation against the will of the owner can only occur in cases and in the manner determined by law.

2.3 SWITZERLAND

Federal Constitution of the Swiss Confederation 1874

Article 22*ter*

   1 The right of ownership is guaranteed.

   2 To the extent allowed by their constitutional powers, the Confederation and the Cantons can, by legislation and for reasons of public interest, make provision for expropriation and restrictions on ownership.

   3 In cases of expropriation and restriction of ownership equivalent to expropriation, fair compensation shall be paid.

Federal Constitution of the Swiss Confederation 1999

Article 26

   1 The right to property is guaranteed.

   2 Expropriations and restrictions of ownership equivalent to expropriation shall be fully compensated.

3. THE SPANISH CONSTITUTION[4]

THE SPANISH CONSTITUTION 1978

Article 33

   1 The right to private property and inheritance is recognized.

   2 The social function of these rights shall determine the limits of their content in accordance with the law.

   3 No one may be deprived of this property and rights except for justified cause of public utility or social interest after proper indemnification in accordance with the provisions of law.

---

[3]The property clause in article 5 of the 1867 Austrian Constitution forms part of the old Basic Law of 21 December 1867, which was incorporated into the Constitution of 1929 by reference, see art 149(1). Source: *Austria Documentation: Austrian federal constitutional laws (selection)* (1995) 148, translated by C Kessler. See further AJ van der Walt *Constitutional property clauses: A comparative analysis* (1999) 74–84; AJ van der Walt 'Compensation for excessive or unfair regulation: A comparative overview of constitutional practice relating to regulatory takings' (1999) 14 *SA Public Law* 273–331 at 290–291, 322.

[4]The Spanish property clause appears in article 33 of the 1978 Constitution. Translated from the original Spanish text as published in Boletin del estado 29 December 1978. Source: GH Flanz & EA Hernandez 'Spain' (translated by GH Flanz) in AP Blaustein & GH Flanz (eds) *Constitutions of the countries of the world* (1991) 50. See further AJ van der Walt 'Compensation for excessive or unfair regulation: A comparative overview of constitutional practice relating to regulatory takings' (1999) 14 *SA Public Law* 273–331 at 293–294, 322–323.

4. THE FRENCH CONSTITUTION[5]

DECLARATION OF THE RIGHTS OF MAN AND THE CITIZEN 1789

Hence the National Assembly, in the presence and under the auspices of the Supreme Being, recognizes and declares the following Rights of Man and Citizen.

2 The final end of every political institution is the preservation of the natural and impre-scriptible rights of man. Those rights are liberty, property, security, and resistance to oppression.

17 Property being an inviolable and sacred right, no one may be deprived of it save where public necessity, legally ascertained, clearly requires it; and then on condition of a just and previously determined compensation.

5. THE EUROPEAN CONVENTION[6]

EUROPEAN CONVENTION ON HUMAN RIGHTS AND FUNDAMENTAL FREEDOMS 1950
First Protocol, Article 1

Every natural or legal person is entitled to the peaceful enjoyment of his possessions. No one shall be deprived of his possessions except in the public interest and subject to the conditions provided for by law and by the general principles of international law.

The preceding provision shall not, however, in any way impair the right of a State to enforce such laws as it deems necessary to control the use of property in accordance with the general interest or to secure the payment of taxes or other contributions or penalties.

---

[5]The property provision in article 17 of the Declaration of the Rights of Man and the Citizen forms part of the French Constitution since it was incorporated into the Preamble to the 1946 and the 1958 Constitution. Source: SE Finer, V Bogdanor & B Rudden *Comparing constitutions* (1996) 208–210. See further AJ van der Walt 'Compensation for excessive or unfair regulation: A compar-ative overview of constitutional practice relating to regulatory takings' (1999) 14 *SA Public Law* 273–331 at 295–299, 323.

[6]The European Convention on Human Rights 1950 was signed on 4 November 1950 and came into force on 3 September 1953. The property clause appears in Article 1 of the First Protocol to the European Convention. Article 5 of the First Protocol provides that the Protocol shall be regarded as additional articles to the Convention, and the First Protocol has been ratified by almost all member states who have ratified the Convention. The Convention has not been adopted by the European Union, but was incorporated into Union law by the Maastricht Treaty (article F2). First Protocol to the Convention, Paris, 20 March 1952, Article 1(213 UNTS 221; European TS 5). Source: PM Mtshaulana, J Dugard & N Botha (eds) *Documents on international law: Handbook for law students and constitutional lawyers* (1996) 294–295. See further AJ van der Walt *Constitutional property clauses: A comparative analysis* (1999) 359–376; AJ van der Walt 'Compensation for excessive or unfair regulation: A comparative overview of constitutional practice relating to regulatory takings' (1999) 14 *SA Public Law* 273–331 at 299–302, 323–324. At the time of writing Tom Allen was preparing a manuscript of a book on the property clause in the European Convention and its application in the UK: T Allen *Property and the Human Rights Act 1998* (forthcoming, Hart Publishing, 2005).

6. COMMONWEALTH CONSTITUTIONS

6.1 IRELAND[7]

Constitution of Ireland 1937

40.3.2 The State shall, in particular, by its laws protect as best it may from unjust attack and, in the case of injustice done, vindicate the life, person, good name, and property rights of every citizen.

43.1.1 The State acknowledges that man, in virtue of his rational being, has the natural right, antecedent to positive law, to the private ownership of external goods.

43.1.2 The State accordingly guarantees to pass no law attempting to abolish the right of private ownership or the general right to transfer, bequeath, and inherit property.

43.2.1 The State recognises, however, that the exercise of the rights mentioned in the foregoing provisions of this Article ought, in civil society, to be regulated by the principles of social justice.

43.2. 2 The State, accordingly, may as occasion requires delimit by law the exercise of the said rights with a view to reconciling their exercise with the exigencies of the common good.

6.2 AUSTRALIA

Commonwealth of Australia Constitution 1900

51 The Parliament shall, subject to this Constitution, have power to make laws for the peace, order and good government of the Commonwealth with respect to:—

[...]

(xxxi) The acquisition of property on just terms from any State or person for any purpose in respect of which the Parliament has the power to make laws;

[...]

6.3 MALAYSIA

FEDERAL CONSTITUTION OF MALAYSIA 1957

13 (1) No person shall be deprived of property save in accordance with law.

(2) No law shall provide for the compulsory acquisition or use of property without adequate compensation.

---

[7]The Irish property clause appears in articles 40.3.2 and 43 of the 1937 Constitution. Source: *Bunreacht na hEireann: Constitution of Ireland* (1990) Government Publications 128, 142–144. See further G Hogan & G Whyte (eds) *JM Kelly: The Irish Constitution* (4th ed 2003) chapter 7.7: 'Private property'; AJ van der Walt *Constitutional property clauses: A comparative analysis* (1999) 229–244; AJ van der Walt 'Compensation for excessive or unfair regulation: A comparative overview of constitutional practice relating to regulatory takings' (1999) 14 *SA Public Law* 273–331 at 302–304, 325. See further on the Commonwealth tradition T Allen *The right to property in Commonwealth constitutions* (2000); T Allen 'Commonwealth constitutions and the right not to be deprived of property' (1993) 42 *Int & Comp LQ* 523–552.

Abbreviations

Afr J Int & Comp L	*African Journal of International and Comparative Law*
Am J Comp L	*American Journal of Comparative Law*
Boston Coll Env Affairs LR	*Boston College Environmental Affairs Law Review*
Boston Univ LR	*Boston University Law Review*
Buffalo LR	*Buffalo Law Review*
Cal LR	*California Law Review*
Cambridge LJ	*Cambridge Law Journal*
Can J Law & Jur	*Canadian Journal of Law and Jurisprudence*
Cardozo LR	*Cardozo Law Review*
CILSA	*Comparative and International Law Journal of Southern Africa*
Col LR	*Columbia Law Review*
Cornell LR	*Cornell Law Review*
Crim LR	*Criminal Law Review*
Duke LJ	*Duke Law Journal*
Eur LR	*European Law Review*
Fordham Int LJ	*Fordham International Law Journal*
George Wash LR	*George Washington Law Review*
Harv Civ Rights-Civ Lib LR	*Harvard Civil Rights-Civil Liberties Law Review*
Harv LR	*Harvard Law Review*
Howard LJ	*Howard Law Journal*
Human Rights & Cons LJ SA	*Human Rights and Constitutional Law Journal of Southern Africa*
Human Rights LJ	*Human Rights Law Journal*
Ill Bar J	*Illinois Bar Journal*
Int Lawyer	*International Lawyer*
Int & Comp LQ	*International and Comparative Law Quarterly*
Iowa LR	*Iowa Law Review*
J Crim L	*Journal of Criminal Law*
J Legal Studies	*Journal of Legal Studies*
McGill LJ	*McGill Law Journal*
Maryland LR	*Maryland Law Review*
Mich LR	*Michigan Law Review*
New Eng LR	*New England Law Review*
NY Univ LR	*New York University Law Review*
N Ir LQ	*Northern Ireland Law Quarterly*
Northwestern Univ LR	*Northwestern University Law Review*
Notre Dame LR	*Notre Dame Law Review*
Oregon LR	*Oregon Law Review*
Pepperdine LR	*Pepperdine Law Review*
Solicitors J	*Solicitors Journal*
SAJHR	*South African Journal on Human Rights*
SALJ	*South African Law Journal*
SA Public Law	*South African Public Law*
Southern Cal LR	*Southern California Law Review*
Stanford LR	*Stanford Law Review*
Stell LR	*Stellenbosch Law Review*

Bibliography

A

ACKERMAN B *Private property and the Constitution* (1977)

ALEXANDER GS 'The concept of property in private and constitutional law: The ideology of the scientific turn in legal analysis' (1982) 82 *Col LR* 1545–1599

ALEXANDER GS *Commodity and propriety— Competing visions of property in American legal thought 1776–1970* (1997)

ALEXANDER GS 'Constitutionalising property: Two experiences, two dilemmas' in J McLean (ed) *Property and the constitution* (1999) 88–108

ALEXANDER GS *The global debate over constitutional property* (forthcoming, University of Chicago Press, 2006)

ALLEN T 'Commonwealth constitutions and the right not to be deprived of property' (1993) 42 *Int & Comp LQ* 523–552

ALLEN T 'Commonwealth constitutions and implied social and economic rights' (1994) 6 *Afr J Int & Comp L* 555–570

ALLEN T *The right to property in Commonwealth constitutions* (2000)

ALLEN T *Property and the Human Rights Act 1998* (forthcoming, Hart Publishing, 2005)

ANON 'Manuel injects R6-billion into land restitution' *Mail & Guardian* 23 February 2005

ANTINORI MR 'Does Lochner live in Luxembourg? An analysis of the property rights jurisprudence of the European Court of Justice' (1995) 18 *Fordham Int LJ* 1778–1851

ARENDT H *The human condition* (1958, paperback ed 1989)

B

BADENHORST PJ 'Beskerming van mineraalregte: 'n *Satyagraha*?' (2001) 64 *THRHR* 643–652

BADENHORST PJ & R MALHERBE 'The constitutionality of the Mineral Development Draft Bill 2000' 2001 *TSAR* 462–478, 765–785

BADENHORST PJ & H MOSTERT 'Revisiting the transitional arrangements of the Mineral and Petroleum Resources Development Act 28 of 2002 and the constitutional property clause: An analysis in two parts. Part 1: Nature and content of rights acknowledged by the revised transitional provisions' (2003) 14 *Stell LR* 377–400

BADENHORST PJ & H MOSTERT 'Revisiting the transitional arrangements of the Mineral and Petroleum Resources Development Act 28 of 2002 and the constitutional property clause: An analysis in two parts. Part 2: Constitutionality of the Minerals and Petroleum Resources Development Act's transitional provisions' (2004) 15 *Stell LR* 22–51

BADENHORST PJ & H MOSTERT (ASSISTED BY M CARNELLEY, RT STEIN & M VAN ROOYEN) *Mineral and petroleum law of South Africa: Commentary and statutes* (2004)

BADENHORST PJ, JM PIENAAR & H MOSTERT (ASSISTED BY M VAN ROOYEN) *Silberberg & Schoeman's The law of property* (4th ed 2003)

BARNÉS J 'El Derecho de propiedad en la Constitución Española de 1978' in J Barnés (ed) *Propiedad, expropiación, y responsabilidad: La garantía indemnizatoria en el derecho Europeo y comparado* (1995) 25–66

BARNÉS J (ed) *Propiedad, expropiación, y responsabilidad: La garantía indemnizatoria en el derecho Europeo y comparado* (1995)

BARRY M 'Now something else must happen: *Richtersveld* and the dilemmas of land reform in post-apartheid South Africa' (2004) 20 *SAJHR* 355–382

BELL J *French constitutional law* (1994)

BELL RE 'Confiscation orders under the proceeds of crime legislation' (1998) 49 *N Ir LQ* 38–59

BENNETT TW *Sourcebook of African customary law* (1991)

BENNETT TW 'Redistribution of land and the doctrine of aboriginal title in South Africa' (1993) 9 *SAJHR* 443–476

BENNETT TW *Human rights and African customary law under the South African Constitution* (1995)

BENNETT TW 'African land—A history of dispossession in R Zimmerman & D Visser *Southern cross: Civil law and common law in South Africa* (1996) 65–94

BENNETT TW et al (eds) *Land ownership—Changing concepts* (1985)

BENNETT TW & CH POWELL 'Aboriginal title in South Africa revisited' (1999) 15 *SAJHR* 449–485

BERGER L 'The public use requirement in eminent domain' (1978) 57 *Oregon LR* 203–246

BILCHITZ D 'Towards a reasonable approach to the minimum core: Laying the foundations for future socio-economic rights jurisprudence (2003) 19 *SAJHR* 1–26

BITTLE LF 'Punitive damages and the Eighth Amendment: An analytical framework for determining excessiveness' (1987) 75 *Cal LR* 1433–1471

BLAAUW-WOLF L & J WOLF 'A comparison between German and South African limitation provisions' (1996) 113 *SALJ* 267–296

BOLLYKY TJ 'R if C > P + B: A paradigm for judicial remedies of socio-economic rights violations' (2002) 18 *SAJHR* 161–200

BOTHA H 'Privatism, authoritarianism and the Constitution: The case of Neethling and Potgieter' (1995) 58 *THRHR* 496–499

BOTHA H 'Democracy and rights: Constitutional interpretation in a postrealist world' (2000) 63 *THRHR* 561–581

BOTHA H 'Metaphoric reasoning and transformative constitutionalism' 2002 *TSAR* 612–627, 2003 *TSAR* 1–37

BOTHA H 'Freedom and constraint in constitutional adjudication' (2004) 20 *SAJHR* 249–283

BOTHA H, A VAN DER WALT & J VAN DER WALT (eds) *Rights and democracy in a transformative constitution* (2003)

BOYLE A, C HIMSWORTH, A LOUX & H MACQUEEN (eds) *Human rights and Scots law* (2002)

BOYLE J *Shamans, software and spleens* (1996)

BRAND D & S RUSSELL (eds) *Exploring the core content of socio-economic rights: South African and international perspectives* (2002)

BRINK AP 'Speaking in voices' in *Reinventing a continent: Writing and politics in South Africa 1982–1995* (1996) 12–19

BROWN LN & JS BELL *French administrative law* (4th ed 1993)

BUDLENDER G 'The constitutional protection of property rights: Overview and commentary' in G Budlender, J Latsky & T Roux (eds) *Juta's new land law* (1998) chapter 1

BUDLENDER G, J LATSKY & T ROUX (eds) *Juta's new land law* (1998)

BURGER AP 'Nuwe Waterwet: Watertribunaal ongrondwetlik?' (1999) 16 *SALJ* 810–814

BUTLER DW 'Time-shares conferring ownership' 1985 *Acta Juridica* 315–332

C

CALLIES DL & CG CHIPCHASE '*Palazzolo v. Rhode Island*: Ripeness and "notice" rule clarified and statutory "background principles" narrowed' (2001) 33 *The Urban Lawyer* 907–922

CANDLER LJ 'Tracing and recovering proceeds of crime in fraud cases: A comparison of US and UK legislation' (1997) 31 *Int Lawyer* 3–40

CAREY MILLER DL (with A POPE) *Land title in South Africa* (2000)

CARPENTER G 'Internal modifiers and other qualifications in bills of rights—Some problems of interpretation' (1995) 10 *SA Public Law* 260–282

CARPENTER G & C BOTHA 'Constitutional attack on private law: Are the fears well founded?' (1996) 59 *THRHR* 126–135

CATE FH 'Law in cyberspace' (1996) 39 *Howard LJ* 565–579

CHASKALSON M 'The problem with property: Thoughts on the constitutional protection of property in the United States and the Commonwealth' (1993) 9 *SAJHR* 388–411

CHASKALSON M 'The property clause: Section 28 of the Constitution' (1994) 10 *SAJHR* 131–139

CHASKALSON M 'Stumbling towards section 28: Negotiations over the protection of property rights in the interim Constitution' (1995) 11 *SAJHR* 222–240

CHASKALSON M et al (eds) *Constitutional law of South Africa* (1st ed 1996)

CHASKALSON M & C LEWIS 'Property' in M Chaskalson et al (eds) *Constitutional law of South Africa* (1996) chapter 31

CHEADLE H & D DAVIS 'The application of the 1996 Constitution in the private sphere' (1997) 13 *SAJHR* 44–66

CHEADLE MH, DM DAVIS & NRL HAYSOM *South African constitutional law: The bill of rights* (2002)

CLAASSENS A 'Compensation for expropriation: The political and economic parameters of market value compensation' (1993) 9 *SAJHR* 422–427

COOKE E (ed) *Modern studies in property law* vol I (2002)

COOKE E (ed) *Modern studies in property law* vol II (2005)

COLLY F 'Le Conseil Constitutionnel et le droit de propriété' (1988) 104 *Revue du Droit Public* 135–197

COOMBE R '"Same as it ever was": Rethinking the politics of legal interpretation' (1989) 34 *McGill LJ* 603–652

COOMBE RJ 'The properties of culture and the politics of possessing identity: Native claims in the cultural appropriation controversy' (1993) 6 *Can J Law & Jur* 249–285

COOPER WE *Landlord and tenant* (2nd ed 1994)

COWEN DV *New patterns of landownership. The transformation of the concept of landownership as plena in re potestas* (1984)

COWEN DV 'From sectional to airspace title' 1985 *Acta Juridica* 333–347

COX A 'Law lets down property owner in tenant row' *The Star* 22 October 2004 p 7

CROSS C & R HAINES (eds) *Towards freehold— Options for land and development in South Africa's black rural areas* (1988)

CURRIE DP 'Positive and negative constitutional rights' (1986) 53 *Univ Chicago LR* 864–890

CURRIE DP *The Constitution of the Federal Republic of Germany* (1994)

CURRIE I & J KLAAREN *The Promotion of Administrative Justice Act benchbook* (2001)

D

DAVENPORT TRH 'Some reflections on the history of land tenure in South Africa, seen in the light of attempts by the state to impose political and economic control' 1985 *Acta Juridica* 53–76

DAVIS D, M CHASKALSON & J DE WAAL 'Democracy and constitutionalism: The role of constitutional interpretation' in DH van Wyk, J Dugard, B de Villiers & D Davis (eds) *Rights and constitutionalism: The new South African legal order* (1994) 1–130

DEPARTMENT OF LAND AFFAIRS *White Paper on South African land policy* (1997)

DEPARTMENT OF WATER AFFAIRS AND FORESTRY *White Paper on a national water policy for South Africa* (1997)

DEPARTMENT OF WATER AFFAIRS AND FORESTRY *Draft position paper for water allocation reform in South Africa: Towards a framework for water allocation planning* (2005)

DE KOKER L & JL PRETORIUS 'Conflicting orders in terms of the Proceeds of Crime Act: Some constitutional perspectives' 1998 *TSAR* 39–52, 277–283, 467–483

DE VILLE JR *Constitutional and statutory interpretation* (2000)

DE VOS P '*Grootboom*, the right of access to housing and substantive equality as contextual fairness' (2001) 17 *SAJHR* 258–267

DE VOS P 'The essential components of the human right to adequate housing—A South African perspective' in D Brand & S Russell (eds) *Exploring the core content of socio-economic rights: South African and international perspectives* (2002) 23–33

DE WAAL J, G ERASMUS & I CURRIE *Bill of rights handbook* (4th ed 2001)

DOOLAN B *Constitutional law and constitutional rights in Ireland* (3rd ed 1994)

DU PLESSIS L *Re-interpretation of statutes* (2nd ed 2002)

DU PLESSIS LM 'Enkele gedagtes oor historiese interpretasie van Hoofstuk 3 van die Oorgangsgrondwet – *Du Plessis v De Klerk* 1994 (6) BCLR 124 (T)' (1995) 58 *THRHR* 504–513

DU PLESSIS W & NJJ OLIVIER 'The old and the new property clause' (1997) 1(5) *Human Rights & Const LJ SA* 11–16

DU PLESSIS W, N OLIVIER & J PIENAAR 'The ever-changing land law—1994–1995 reforms' (1995) 10 *SA Public Law* 145–167

DU PLESSIS W, N OLIVIER & J PIENAAR 'Land reform gains momentum during 1996' (1997) 12 *SA Public Law* 251–273

Du Plessis W, N Olivier & J Pienaar 'Land reform continues during 1997' (1997) 12 *SA Public Law* 531–550

Du Plessis W, N Olivier & J Pienaar 'Land: Still a contentious issue' (1998) 13 *SA Public Law* 149–169

Du Plessis W, N Olivier & J Pienaar 'Land issues: An assessment of the failures and successes' (1999) 14 *SA Public Law* 241–270

Du Plessis W, N Olivier & J Pienaar 'Land reform—Trends developing in case law' (1999) 14 *SA Public Law* 528–553

Du Plessis W, N Olivier & J Pienaar 'Land reform: A never-ending process' (2000) 15 *SA Public Law* 230–254

Du Plessis W, N Olivier & J Pienaar 'New measures to expedite land reform' (2000) 15 *SA Public Law* 549–573

Du Plessis W, N Olivier & J Pienaar 'Evictions, restitution, spatial information, the right to housing and minerals: New approaches from the government and the courts' (2001) 16 *SA Public Law* 181–216

Du Plessis W, N Olivier & J Pienaar 'Delays in land reform—South Africa emulating Zimbabwe?' (2001) 16 *SA Public Law* 432–457

Du Plessis W, N Olivier & J Pienaar 'Progress in land reform, illegal occupation of land and judicial interpretation' (2002) 17 *SA Public Law* 178–209

Du Plessis W, N Olivier & J Pienaar 'A new dispensation for communal land and minerals' (2002) 17 *SA Public Law* 409–439

Du Plessis W, N Olivier & J Pienaar '"Your land is safe in South Africa"?' (2003) 18 *SA Public Law* 229–250

Du Plessis W, N Olivier & J Pienaar 'Expropriation, restitution and land redistribution: An answer to land problems in South Africa?' (2003) 18 *SA Public Law* 491–514

Du Plessis W, N Olivier & J Pienaar 'Land matters: New developments 2004 (1)' (2004) 19 *SA Public Law* 212–229

E

Ehrenzeller B, P Mastronardi, RJ Schweizer, & KA Vallender (eds) *Die Schweizerische Bundesverfassung—Kommentar (St Gallen Kommentar)* (2002)

Eisenberg A 'Different constitutional formulations of compensation clauses' (1993) 9 *SAJHR* 412–421

Eisenberg A '"Public purpose" and expropriation: Some comparative insights and the South African bill of rights' (1995) 11 *SAJHR* 207–221

Erasmus HJ, CG van der Merwe & AH van Wyk *Lee and Honoré: Family, things and succession* (2nd ed 1983)

Esbend F 'Surprise ruling on seizure of drunk driving vehicles' *The Herald* 25 May 2005

F

Feenstra R & R Zimmermann (eds) *Das römisch-holländische Recht: Fortschritte des Zivilrechts im 17. und 18. Jahrhundert* (1992)

Finer SE, V Bogdanor & B Rudden *Comparing constitutions* (1996)

Fisher WW 'The development of modern American legal theory and the judicial interpretation of the bill of rights' in MJ Lacey & K Haakonssen (eds) *A culture of rights. The bill of rights in philosophy, politics, and law—1791 and 1991* (1991) 266–365

Forsyth C & I Hare (eds) *The golden metwand and the crooked cord: Essays on public law in honour of Sir William Wade QC* (1998)

Franklin BLS & M Kaplan *The mining and mineral laws of South Africa* (1982)

Fraser J 'Mines will keep right to sue state' *Business Day* 18 October 2004

Friedmann D & D Barak-Erez (eds) *Human rights in private law* (2001)

Frowein JA & W Peukert *Europäische MenschenRechtsKonvention—EMRK Kommentar* (1985)

G

Gibson D *The law of the Charter: general principles* (1986)

Gildenhuys A 'Evictions: A quagmire for the unwary' *Butterworths Property Law Digest* (Sep 1999) 5–11

Gildenhuys A *Onteieningsreg* (2nd ed 2001)

Goldsmith M & MJ Lindeman 'Asset forfeiture and third party rights: The need for further law reform' (1989) 39 *Duke LJ* 1254–1301

GOVENDER K 'The virtues of balancing' (1997) 1(6) *Human Rights & Const LJ SA* 2–3

GRAY K 'Property in thin air' (1991) 50 *Cambridge LJ* 252–307

GRAY K 'Human property rights in land: The propriety of expropriation' (2005) 16 *Stell LR* (forthcoming)

GRAY K & SF GRAY *Elements of land law* (4th ed 2005)

GREY T 'Property and need: The welfare state and theories of distributive justice' (1976) 28 *Stan LR* 877–902

GREY TC 'The disintegration of property' in JR Pennock & JW Chapman (eds) *Property (Nomos XXII)* (1980) 69–85

GUPTA D 'Republic of South Africa's Prevention of Organised Crime Act: A comparative bill of rights analysis' (2002) 37 *Harv Civ Rights–Civ Lib LR* 159–183

H

HADAWAY B 'Executive privateers: A discussion on why the Civil Asset Forfeiture Reform Act will not significantly reform the practice of forfeiture' (2000) 55 *Univ Miami LR* 81–121

HAINES R & CR CROSS 'An historical overview of land policy and tenure in South Africa's black areas' in C Cross & R Haines (eds) *Towards freehold—Options for land and development in South Africa's black rural areas* (1988) 73–92

HARRINGTON MP 'Rethinking *in rem*: The Supreme Court's new (and misguided) approach to civil forfeiture' (1994) 12 *Yale Law & Pol Rev* 281–353

HARRIS DJ, M O'BOYLE & C WARBRICK *Law of the European Convention on Human Rights* (2nd ed 1995)

HART HLA *The concept of law* (1961)

HATHORN M & D HUTCHINSON 'Labour tenants and the law' in C Murray & C O'Regan *No place to rest: Forced removals and the law in South Africa* (1990) 194–213

HINTON M 'Are drug trafficking confiscation orders punitive?' 1992 *Solicitors J* 1264–1265

HOEXTER C (with R Lyster) *The new constitutional and administrative law Vol 2: Administrative law* (2002)

HOFMEYR A 'The role of civil forfeiture in the forthcoming prevention of organised crime legislation: A closer look' 1998 *Responsa Meridiana* 41–61

HOGAN G & G WHYTE (eds) *JM Kelly: The Irish Constitution* (4th ed 2003)

HOGG PW *Constitutional law of Canada* (3rd ed 1992)

HOHFELD WN 'Some fundamental legal conceptions as applied in judicial reasoning' (1913) 23 *Yale LJ* 16–59

HOHFELD WN 'Fundamental legal conceptions as applied in judicial reasoning' (1917) 26 *Yale LJ* 710–770

HOLOUBEK M 'Die Interpretation der Grundrechte in der jüngeren Judikatur des VfGH' in R Machacek, WP Pahr & G Stadler (eds) *70 Jahre Republik: Grund- und Menschenrechte in Österreich. Grundlagen, Entwicklung und Internationale Verbindungen* (1991) 43–83

HUTCHINSON A 'Part of an essay on power and interpretation (with suggestions on how to make bouillabaisse)' (1985) 60 *NY Univ LR* 850–886

HUTCHINSON A 'Inessentially speaking (is there politics after postmodernism?)' (1991) 89 *Mich LR* 1549–1636

HUTCHINSON A 'Identity crisis: The politics of interpretation' (1992) 26 *New Eng LR* 1173–1219

I

IBLER M 'Der Grundrechtsschutz in der spanischen Verfassung am Beispile des Eigentumsschutz' (1999) 54 *Juristen-Zeitung* 287–294

ITZIKOWITZ A 'The prevention and control of money laundering in South Africa' (1999) 62 *THRHR* 88–107

J

JACKSON P & DC WILDE (eds) *Property law: Current issues and debates* (1999)

JANKOWSKI MA 'Tempering the relation-back doctrine: A more reasonable approach to civil forfeiture in drug cases' (1990) 76 *Vir LR* 165–195

JOCHNER MM 'The Supreme Court turns back the clock on civil forfeiture in *Bennis*' (1997) 85 *Ill Bar J* 314–332

JORDAAN DW 'The Constitution's impact on the law of contract in perspective' (2004) 37 De Jure 58–65

K

KASTEN LA 'Extending constitutional protection to civil forfeitures that exceed rough remedial compensation' (1991) 60 George Wash LR 194–244

KEIGHTLEY R 'The impact of the Extension of Security of Tenure Act on an owner's right to vindicate immovable property' (1999) 15 SAJHR 277–307

KENNEDY CH 'Is the Internet a new legal frontier?' (1996) 39 Howard LJ 581–586

KENNEDY D A critique of adjudication (fin de siècle) (1997)

KEYSER-RINGNALDA F 'European integration with regard to the confiscation of the proceeds of crime' (1992) 17 Eur LR 499–515

KLARE K 'Legal culture and transformative constitutionalism' (1998) 14 SAJHR 146–188

KLEYN DG 'The constitutional protection of property rights: A comparison between the German and the South African approach' (1996) 11 SA Public Law 402–445

KLEYN DG & A BORAINE Silberberg & Schoeman: The law of property (3rd ed 1992)

KLUG H 'Water law reform under the new Constitution' (1997) 1(5) Human Rights & Const LJ SA 5–10

KOK A & M LANGFORD 'Water' in S Woolman et al (eds) Constitutional law of South Africa (2nd ed 2003 original service) chapter 56

KOK A 'Why the finding that juristic persons are entitled to the property rights protected by section 25 of the Constitution?' (2004) 67 THRHR 683–686

KUHN T The structure of scientific revolutions (1962)

L

LEVY LW A license to steal: The forfeiture of property (1996)

LEWIS CH 'The modern concept of ownership of land' 1985 Acta Juridica 241–266

LEWIS CH 'The Prevention of Illegal Squatting Act: The promotion of homelessness' (1989) 5 SAJHR 233–239

LEWIS CH 'The right to private property in a new political dispensation in South Africa' (1992) 8 SAJHR 389–430

LIEBENBERG S 'The right to social assistance: The implications of Grootboom for policy reform in South Africa' (2001) 17 SAJHR 232–257

LIEBENBERG S 'The interpretation of socio-economic rights' in S Woolman et al (eds) Constitutional law of South Africa (2nd ed 2003 original service Dec 2003) chapter 33

LUBBE G 'Taking fundamental rights seriously: The bill of rights and its implications for the development of contract law' (2004) 121 SALJ 395–423

M

MACHACEK R, WP PAHR & G STADLER (eds) 70 Jahre Republik: Grund- und Menschenrechte in Österreich. Grundlagen, Entwicklung und Internationale Verbindungen (1991)

MACLEAN J (ed) Property and the constitution (1999)

MACQUEEN HL 'Delict, contract, and the bill of rights: A perspective from the United Kingdom' 2004 (121) SALJ 359–394

MARCHANT BF 'On-line on the Internet: First Amendment and intellectual property uncertainties in the on-line world' (1996) 39 Howard LJ 477–503

MARCUS T 'Land reform—Considering national, class and gender issues' (1990) 6 SAJHR 178–194

MAXEINER JR 'Bane of American forfeiture law—Banished at last?' (1977) 62 Cornell LR 768–902

MBAO MLM 'The province of the South African bill of rights determined and redetermined—A comment on the case of Baloro & Others v University of Bophuthatswana & Others' (1996) 113 SALJ 33–45

MERRILL TW 'The economics of public use' (1986) 72 Cornell LR 61–116

MEYER-LADEWIG J Konvention zum Schutz der Menschenrechte und Grundfreiheiten Handkommentar (2003)

MICHELMAN FI 'Property, utility and fairness: Comments on the ethical foundations of "just compensation" law' (1967) 80 Harv LR 1165–1258

MICHELMAN FI 'Property as a constitutional right' (1981) 38 Wash & Lee LR 1097–1114

MICHELMAN FI 'Possession vs distribution in the constitutional idea of property' (1987) 72 *Iowa LR* 1319 -1350

MICHELMAN FI 'Takings, 1987' (1988) 88 *Col LR* 1600–1629

MICHELMAN FI 'Socio-political functions of constitutional protection for private property holdings (in liberal political thought)' in GE van Maanen & AJ van der Walt (eds) *Property on the threshold of the 21st century* (1996) 433–450

MILLER AR 'Copyright protection for computer programs, databases, and computer-generated works: Is anything new since CONTU?' (1993) 106 *Harv LR* 977–1073

MILTON JRL 'Planning and property' 1985 *Acta Juridica* 267–288

MINDA G *Postmodern legal movements: Law and jurisprudence at century's end* (1995)

MITCHELL A & M HINTON 'Confiscation inquiries—What the Dickens?' (1994) 58 *J Crim L* 201–208

MITCHELL AR, MG HINTON, & SME TAYLOR *Confiscation* (1994)

MOSENEKE D 'The fourth Bram Fischer memorial lecture: Transformative adjudication' (2002) 18 *SAJHR* 309–319

MOSTERT H 'Liberty, social duty and fairness in the context of constitutional property protection and regulation' in H Botha, A van der Walt & J van der Walt (eds) *Rights and democracy in a transformative constitution* (2003) 131–161

MOSTERT H & P FITZPATRICK '"Living in the margins of history on the edge of the country"—Legal foundation and the Richtersveld community's title to land' 2004 *TSAR* 309–323, 498–510

MUNZER SR *A theory of property* (1990)

MURPHY J 'Insulating land reform from constitutional impugnment: An Indian case study' (1992) 8 *SAJHR* 362–388

MURPHY J 'Property rights in the new Constitution: An analytical framework for constitutional review' (1993) 26 *CILSA* 211–233

MURPHY J 'Compensation for nationalization in international law' (1993) 110 *SALJ* 79–99

MURPHY J 'Property rights and judicial restraint: A reply to Chaskalson' (1994) 10 *SAJHR* 386–398

MURPHY J 'Interpreting the property clause in the Constitution Act of 1993' (1995) 10 *SA Public Law* 107–130

MURRAY C & C O'REGAN *No place to rest: Forced removals and the law in South Africa* (1990)

N

NDLANGISA S 'Big guns of business lend a hand to councils: Captains of industry roped in to sort out local government' *The Sunday Times* 31 October 2004 p 4

NEDELSKY J *Private property and the limits of American constitutionalism: the Madisonian framework and its legacy* (1990)

NEDELSKY J 'Should property be constitutionalized? A relational and comparative approach' in GE van Maanen & AJ van der Walt (eds) *Property on the threshold of the 21st century* (1996) 417–432

P

PAPIER HJ 'Art. 14' in T Maunz, G Dürig et al (eds) *Grundgesetz Kommentar* vol II (40th update 2002)

PELLER G 'The metaphysics of American law' (1985) 73 *Cal LR* 1151–1207

PEUKERT W 'Protection of ownership under article 1 of the First Protocol to the European Convention on Human Rights' (1981) 2 *Human Rights LJ* 37–78

PIENAAR GJ 'Eiendomstydsdeling: die aard van die reghebbende se reg' 1986 *TRW* 1–14

PIENAAR GJ 'Ontwikkelings in die Suid-Afrikaanse eiendomsreg in perspektief' 1986 *TSAR* 295–308

PIENAAR G 'Registration of informal land-use rights in South Africa: Giving teeth to (toothless?) paper tigers?' 2000 *TSAR* 442–468

PIENAAR G 'Security of communal land tenure by registration of individualised title—Is the Communal Land Rights Bill of 2003 the final solution?' (2004) 67 *THRHR* 244–263

PIENAAR JM 'Labour tenancy: Recent developments in case law' (1998) 9 *Stell LR* 311–325

PIENAAR JM 'Recent developments relating to automatic review proceedings in the Land Claims Court' (2001) 34 *De Jure* 162–172

PRETORIUS JL & HA STRYDOM 'The constitutionality of civil forfeiture' (1998) 13 *SA Public Law* 385–422

R

RABIE A 'Water for the environment' (1998) 61 *THRHR* 111–116

RABIE MA 'The impact of environmental conservation on land ownership' 1985 *Acta Juridica* 289–313

RADIN MJ 'The liberal conception of property: Cross currents in the jurisprudence of takings' (1988) 88 *Col LR* 1676–1696

RADIN MJ *Contested commodities* (1996)

RAUTENBACH IM *General provisions of the South African bill of rights* (1995)

RAUTENBACH IM 'The Bill of Rights applies to private law and binds private persons' 2000 *TSAR* 296–316

REEVES HS 'Property in cyberspace' (1996) 63 *Univ Chicago LR* 761–799

REICH C 'The new property' (1964) 73 *Yale LJ* 733–787

RONNER AD 'Prometheus unbound: Accepting a mythless concept of civil in rem forfeiture with double jeopardy protection' (1996) 44 *Buffalo LR* 655–776

ROOK D *Property law and human rights* (2001)

ROSE CM 'Property as the keystone right?' (1996) 71 *Notre Dame LR* 329–365

ROSENBERG JA 'Constitutional rights and civil forfeiture actions' (1988) 88 *Col LR* 390–406

ROUX T 'Turning a deaf ear: The right to be heard by the Constitutional Court' (1997) 13 *SAJHR* 216–227

ROUX T 'Chapter 3: The Restitution of Land Rights Act' in G Budlender, J Latsky & T Roux *Juta's new land law* (1998)

ROUX T 'Chapter 7: The Extension of Security of Tenure Act' in G Budlender, J Latsky & T Roux *Juta's new land law* (1998)

ROUX T 'Understanding *Grootboom?*—A response to Cass R Sunstein' (2002) 12 *Constitutional Forum* 41–51

ROUX T 'Property' in MH Cheadle, DM Davis & NRL Haysom *South African constitutional law: The bill of rights* (2002) 429–472

ROUX T 'Section 25' in S Woolman et al (eds) *Constitutional law of South Africa* (2nd ed 2003 original service Dec 2003) chapter 46

ROUX T 'Pro-poor court, anti-poor outcomes: Explaining the performance of the South African Land Claims Court' (2004) 20 *SAJHR* 511–543

ROUX T 'Continuity and change in a transforming legal order: The impact of section 26(3) of the Constitution on South African law' (2004) 121 *SALJ* 466–492

RUBENFELD J 'Usings' (1993) 102 *Yale LJ* 1077–1163

RUBIN GR *Private property, government requisition and the constitution, 1914–1927* (1994)

RUSSELL S 'Introduction—Minimum state obligations: International dimensions' in D Brand & S Russell (eds) *Exploring the core content of socio-economic rights: South African and international perspectives* (2002) 11–21

S

SACHS A *Protecting human rights in a new South Africa* (1990)

SACHS A 'Rights to the land: A fresh look at the property question' in *Protecting human rights in a new South Africa* (1990) 104–138

SACHS A 'Towards a Bill of Rights in a democratic South Africa' (1990) 6 *SAJHR* 1–24

SALLON C & D BEDINGFIELD 'Drugs, money and the law' [1993] *Crim LR* 165–173

SALTZBURG DG 'Real property forfeitures as a weapon in the government's war on drugs: A failure to protect innocent ownership rights' (1992) 72 *Boston Univ LR* 217–242

SARAT A & TR KEARNS (eds) *Legal rights: Historical and philosophical perspectives* (1997)

SAX JL 'Takings and the police power' (1964) 74 *Yale LJ* 36–76

SAX JL 'Takings, private property and public rights' (1971) 81 *Yale LJ* 149–186

SCHLAG P ' "Le hors de texte, c'est moi": The politics of form and the domestication of deconstruction' (1990) 11 *Cardozo LR* 1631–1647

SCHLAG P 'Normativity and the politics of form' (1991) 139 *Univ Penn LR* 801–932

SCHLAG P 'Rights in the postmodern condition' in A Sarat & TR Kearns (eds) *Legal rights: Historical and philosophical perspectives* (1997) 263–304

SCHMIDT-BLEIBTREU B 'Art. 14' in B Schmidt-Bleibtreu & F Klein *Kommentar zum Grundgesetz* (9th ed 1999) 369–413

SCHOOMBEE JT 'Group areas legislation—The political control of ownership and occupation of land' 1985 *Acta Juridica* 77–118

SCHWELB E 'The protection of the right of property of nationals under the First Protocol to the European Convention on Human Rights' (1964) 13 *Am J Comp L* 518–541

SILBERBERG H *The law of property* (1975; 4th ed 2003 by PJ Badenhorst, JM Pienaar & H Mostert)

SIMON WH 'The invention and reinvention of welfare rights' (1985) 44 *Maryland LR* 1–37

SIMON WH 'Rights and redistribution in the welfare system' (1986) 38 *Stanford LR* 1431–1516

SINGER JW *Property law: Rules, policies, and practices* (1993)

SINGER JW 'No right to exclude: Public accommodations and private property' (1996) 90 *Northwestern Univ LR* 1283–1497

SINGER JW 'Property and social relations: From title to entitlement' in GE van Maanen & AJ van der Walt (eds) *Property on the threshold of the 21st century* (1996) 69–90

SINGER JW 'Property and equality: Public accommodations and the constitution in South Africa and the United States' (1997) 12 *SA Public Law* 53–86

SINGER JW *Entitlement: The paradoxes of property* (2000)

SINGER JW & JM BEERMAN 'The social origins of property' (1993) 6 *Can J of Law & Jur* 217–248

SKWEYIYA Z 'Towards a solution to the land question in post-apartheid South Africa: Problems and models' (1990) 6 *SAJHR* 195–214

SLOTH-NIELSEN J 'The child's right to social services, the right to social security, and primary prevention of child abuse: Some conclusions in the aftermath of *Grootboom*' (2001) 17 *SAJHR* 210–231

SMITH L '*In rem* forfeiture proceedings and extraterritorial jurisdiction' (1996) 45 *Int & Comp LQ* 902–909

SMITS JM 'Constitutionalisering van het vermogensrecht' in *Preadviezen voor de Nederlandse Vereniging voor Rechtsvergelijking* (2003) 1–163

SNIJDERS HJ & EB RANK BERENSCHOT *Goederenrecht* (1994)

SONNEKUS JC 'Borgstelling, verjaring en verwarring' 2003 *TSAR* 350–376

SOUTHWOOD MD *The compulsory acquisition of rights* (2000)

SPRIGMAN C & M OSBORNE 'Du Plessis is *not* dead: South Africa's 1996 Constitution and the application of the Bill of Rights to private disputes' (1999) 15 *SAJHR* 25–51

STRAFER GR 'Civil forfeitures: Protecting the innocent owner' (1985) 37 *Univ Florida LR* 841–861

SUNSTEIN CR 'Social and economic rights? Lessons from South Africa' in *Designing Democracy: What Constitutions Do* (2001) 221–237

T

TAGGART M 'Expropriation, public purpose and the Constitution' in C Forsyth & I Hare (eds) *The golden metwand and the crooked cord: Essays on public law in honour of Sir William Wade QC* (1998) 91–112

TAYLOR WW 'The problem of proportionality in RICO forfeitures' (1990) 65 *Notre Dame LR* 885–895

THOMAS DA 'The Criminal Justice Act 1993: (1) Confiscation orders and drug trafficking' [1994] *Crim LR* 93–100

THOMAS PH 'The South African common law into the twenty-first century' 2005 *TSAR* 292–298

TRIBE LH *American constitutional law* (2nd ed 1988)

TRIBE LH & MC DORF *On reading the Constitution* (1991)

U

UNDERKUFFLER LS 'On property: An essay' (1990) 100 *Yale LJ* 127–148

UNDERKUFFLER-FREUND LS 'Takings and the nature of property' (1996) 9 *Can J Law & Jur* 161–205

UNDERKUFFLER LS *The idea of property: Its meaning and power* (2003)

V

VALENDER KA 'Art. 26' in B Ehrenzeller, P Mastronardi, RJ Schweizer, & KA Vallender (eds) *Die Schweizerische Bundesverfassung—Kommentar (St Gallen Kommentar)* (2002) 328–352

VAN ASWEGEN A 'Policy considerations in the law of delict' (1993) 56 *THRHR* 171–195

VAN ASWEGEN A 'The future of South African contract law' in A van Aswegen (ed) *The future of South African private law* (1994) 44–60

VAN ASWEGEN A (ed) *The future of South African private law* (1994)

VAN ASWEGEN A 'The implications of a bill of rights for the law of contract and delict' (1995) 11 *SAJHR* 50–69

VAN DER LINDE M & E BASSON 'Environment' in S Woolman et al (eds) *Constitutional law of South Africa* (2nd ed 2003 original service) chapter 50

VAN DER MERWE CG *The law of things* in WA Joubert (ed) *The law of South Africa* vol 27 (published separately as *The law of things* 1987)

VAN DER MERWE CG *Sakereg* (2nd ed 1989)

VAN DER MERWE D 'Land tenure in South Africa: A brief history and some reform proposals' 1989 *TSAR* 663–692

VAN DER MERWE D 'Land tenure in South Africa: Changing the face of property law' (1990) 1 *Stell LR* 321–335

VAN DER MERWE D 'Constitutional colonisation of the common law: A problem of institutional integrity' 2000 *TSAR* 12–32

VAN DER POST DJ 'Land law and registration in some of the black rural areas of Southern Africa' 1985 *Acta Juridica* 213–266

VAN DER VYVER JD 'The private sphere in constitutional litigation' (1994) 57 *THRHR* 360–395

VAN DER VYVER JD 'Constitutional free speech and the law of defamation' (1995) 112 *SALJ* 572–602

VAN DER VYVER JD 'Property in international human rights law' in GE van Maanen & AJ van der Walt (eds) *Property law on the threshold of the 21st century* (1996) 451–486

VAN DER WALT AJ 'Bartolus se omskrywing van *dominium* en die interpretasies daarvan sedert die vyftiende eeu' (1986) 49 *THRHR* 305–321

VAN DER WALT AJ 'The effect of environmental conservation measures on the concept of landownership' (1987) 104 *SALJ* 469–479

VAN DER WALT AJ 'Developments that may change the institution of private ownership so as to meet the needs of a non-racial society in South Africa' (1990) *Stell LR* 26–48

VAN DER WALT AJ 'Towards the development of post-apartheid land law: An exploratory survey' (1990) 23 *De Jure* 1–45

VAN DER WALT AJ (ed) *Land reform and the future of landownership in South Africa* (1991)

VAN DER WALT AJ 'Introduction' in AJ van der Walt (ed) *Land reform and the future of landownership in South Africa* (1991) 1–7

VAN DER WALT AJ 'Der Eigentumsbegriff' in R Feenstra & R Zimmermann (eds) *Das römisch-holländische Recht: Fortschritte des Zivilrechts im 17. und 18. Jahrhundert* (1992) 485–520

VAN DER WALT AJ 'The fragmentation of land rights' (1992) 8 *SAJHR* 431–450

VAN DER WALT AJ 'Squatting and the right to shelter' 1992 *TSAR* 40–55

VAN DER WALT AJ 'Ownership and personal freedom: Subjectivism in Bernhard Windscheid's theory of ownership' (1993) 56 *THRHR* 569–589

VAN DER WALT AJ 'Notes on the interpretation of the property clause in the new constitution' (1994) 57 *THRHR* 181–203

VAN DER WALT AJ 'Property rights, land rights, and environmental rights' in DH van Wyk, J Dugard, B de Villiers & D Davis (eds) *Rights and constitutionalism: The new South African legal order* (1994) 455–501

VAN DER WALT AJ 'Marginal notes on powerful(l) legends: Critical perspectives on property theory' (1995) 58 *THRHR* 396–420

VAN DER WALT AJ 'Unity and pluralism in property theory: A review of property theories and debates in recent literature: Part I' 1995 *TSAR* 15–29

VAN DER WALT AJ 'Subject and society in property theory: A review of property theories and debates in recent literature: Part II' 1995 *TSAR* 322–345

VAN DER WALT AJ 'Rights and reforms in property theory: A review of property theories and debates in recent literature: Part III' 1995 *TSAR* 493–526

VAN DER WALT AJ 'Towards a theory of rights in property: Exploratory observations on the paradigm of post-apartheid property law' (1995) 10 *SA Public Law* 298–345

VAN DER WALT AJ 'Tradition on trial: A critical analysis of the civil-law tradition in South African property law' (1995) 11 *SAJHR* 169–206

VAN DER WALT AJ 'The limits of constitutional property' (1997) 12 *SA Public Law* 275–330

VAN DER WALT AJ 'Compensation for excessive or unfair regulation: A comparative overview of constitutional practice relating to regulatory takings' (1999) 14 *SA Public Law* 273–331

VAN DER WALT AJ 'The constitutional property clause: Striking a balance between guarantee and limitation' in J MacLean (ed) *Property and the constitution* (1999) 109–146

VAN DER WALT AJ 'Police-power regulation of intangible property and the constitutional property clause: A comparative analysis of case law' in P Jackson & DC Wilde (eds) *Property law: Current issues and debates* (1999) 208–280

VAN DER WALT AJ 'Property rights and hierarchies of power: A critical evaluation of land-reform policy in South Africa' (1999) 64 *Koers* 259–294

VAN DER WALT AJ *Constitutional property clauses: A comparative analysis* (1999)

VAN DER WALT AJ 'Civil forfeiture of instrumentalities and proceeds of crime and the constitutional property clause' (2000) 16 *SAJHR* 1–45

VAN DER WALT AJ 'Protecting social participation rights within the property paradigm: A critical reappraisal' in E Cooke (ed) *Modern studies in property law* vol I (2002) 27–41

VAN DER WALT AJ 'Moving towards recognition of constructive expropriation?' (2002) 65 *THRHR* 459–473

VAN DER WALT AJ 'Sosiale geregtigheid, prosedurele billikheid, en eiendom: Alternatiewe perspektiewe op grondwetlike waarborge' (2002) 13 *Stell LR* 59–82, 206–229

VAN DER WALT AJ 'Negating Grotius—The constitutional validity of statutory security rights in favour of the state' (2002) 18 *SAJHR* 86–113

VAN DER WALT AJ 'Property rights v religious rights: *Bührmann v Nkosi*' (2002) 13 *Stell LR* 394–414

VAN DER WALT AJ 'Exclusivity of ownership, security of tenure, and eviction orders: A model to evaluate South African land-reform legislation' 2002 *TSAR* 254–289

VAN DER WALT AJ 'Exclusivity of ownership, security of tenure, and eviction orders: A critical evaluation of recent case law' (2002) 18 *SAJHR* 371–419

VAN DER WALT AJ 'Overview of developments since the introduction of the constitutional property clause' (2004) 19 *SA Public Law* 46–89

VAN DER WALT AJ 'A South African reading of Frank Michelman's theory of social justice' (2004) 19 *SA Public Law* 253–307

VAN DER WALT AJ 'The property clause in the new Federal Constitution of the Swiss Confederation 1999' (2004) 15 *Stell LR* 326–332

VAN DER WALT AJ 'Striving for the better interpretation—A critical reflection on the Constitutional Court's *Harksen* and *FNB* decisions on the property clause' (2004) 121 *SALJ* 854–878

VAN DER WALT AJ 'Ownership and eviction: Constitutional rights in private law' (2005) 9 *Edinburgh LR* 32–64

VAN DER WALT AJ 'Retreating from the *FNB* arbitrariness test already? *Mkontwana v Nelson Mandela Metropolitan Municipality; Bissett v Buffalo City Municipality; Transfer Rights Action Campaign v MEC for Local Government and Housing, Gauteng* (CC)' (2005) 122 *SALJ* 75–89

VAN DER WALT AJ 'Property theory and the transformation of property law' in Elizabeth Cooke (ed) *Modern studies in property law* vol II (2005) 361–380

VAN DER WALT AJ 'The state's duty to protect property owners vs the state's duty to provide housing: Thoughts on the *Modderklip* case' (2005) 21 *SAJHR* 144–161

VAN DER WALT AJ 'Transformative constitutionalism and the development of South African property law' 2005 *TSAR*; 2006 *TSAR* (forthcoming)

VAN DER WALT AJ & H BOTHA 'Coming to grips with the new constitutional order: Critical comments on *Harksen v Lane NO*' (1998) 13 *SA Public Law* 17

VAN DER WALT AJ & GJ PIENAAR *Introduction to the law of property* (4th ed 2002)

VAN DER WALT JWG 'Justice Kriegler's disconcerting judgment in *Du Plessis v De Klerk*: Much ado about direct horizontal application (read nothing)' 1996 *TSAR* 732–741

VAN DER WALT JWG 'Perspectives on horizontal application: *Du Plessis v De Klerk* revisited' (1997) 12 *SA Public Law* 1–31

VAN DER WALT JWG 'Die toekoms van die onderskeid tussen die publiekreg en die privaatreg in die lig van die horisontale werking van die grondwet' 2000 *TSAR* 416–427, 605–618

VAN DER WALT JWG '*Progressive* indirect horizontal application of the Bill of Rights: Towards a co-operative relation between common-law and constitutional jurisprudence' (2001) 17 *SAJHR* 341–363

VAN DER WALT JWG 'Horizontal application of fundamental rights and the threshold of the law in view of the *Carmichele* saga' (2003) 19 *SAJHR* 517–540

VANDEVELDE KJ 'Developing property concepts' (1980) 29 *Buffalo LR* 333–340

VAN MAANEN GE 'De onrechtmatige rechtmatige overheidsdaad bij de burgerlijke rechter: Zoektocht naar de kwadratuur van de cirkel' in JE Hoitink, GE van Maanen, BPM van Ravels & BJ Schueler *Schadevergoeding bij rechtmatige overheidsdaad* (2002) 7–89

VAN MAANEN GE & AJ VAN DER WALT (eds) *Property on the threshold of the 21st century* (1996)

VAN MARLE K 'Law's time, particularity and slowness' (2003) 19 *SAJHR* 239–255

VAN ONSELEN C 'Sunday Essay' *Sunday Times* 18 May 1997 p 25

VAN ONSELEN C *The seed is mine: The life of Kas Maine, A South-African sharecropper 1894–1985* (1996)

VAN WYK DH, J DUGARD, B DE VILLIERS & D DAVIS (eds) *Rights and constitutionalism: The new South African legal order* (1994)

VAN WYK J 'The relationship (or not) between rights of access to land and housing: Delinking land from its components' paper presented at the International Property Law Conference, Stellenbosch, 5–6 April 2005

VISSER C 'Rent control' 1985 *Acta Juridica* 349–368

VISSER D 'The future of the law of delict' in A van Aswegen (ed) *The future of South African private Law* (1994) 26–43

VOS WJ *Principles of South African water law* (2nd ed 1978; previously *Elements of South African water law*)

W

WENDT R 'Eigentum, Erbrecht und Enteignung' in M Sachs (ed) *Grundgesetz Kommentar* (3rd ed 2002) 607–666

WILSON S 'Taming the constitution: Rights and reform in the South African education system' (2004) 20 *SAJHR* 418–443

WOOLMAN S 'Defamation, application, and the Interim Constitution: An unqualified and direct analysis of *Holomisa v Argus Newspapers Ltd*' (1996) 113 *SALJ* 428–454

WOOLMAN S 'Out of order? Out of balance? The limitation clause of the final Constitution' (1997) 13 *SAJHR* 102–134

WOOLMAN S 'Application' in M Chaskalson et al (eds) *Constitutional law of South Africa* (Revision Service 3 1998) chapter 10

WOOLMAN S 'Limitation' in M Chaskalson et al (eds) *Constitutional law of South Africa* (1st ed 1996, 5th rev service 1999) chapter 12

WOOLMAN S et al (eds) *Constitutional law of South Africa* (2nd ed 2003)

WOOLMAN S & D DAVIS 'The last laugh: *Du Plessis v De Klerk*, classical liberalism, creole liberalism, and the application of fundamental rights under the Interim and Final Constitutions' (1996) 12 *SAJHR* 361–404

Y

YOUNGS R 'Human rights in the housing sphere: German comparisons' (2004) 15 *The King's College LJ* 145–158

Z

ZIFF B & PRATIMA V RAO (eds) *Borrowed power: Essays on cultural appropriation* (1997)

ZIMMERMANN R & DP VISSER 'Introduction: South African law as a mixed legal system' in R Zimmermann & DP Visser (eds) *Southern cross: Civil law and common law in South Africa* (1996) 1–30

ZIMMERMANN R & DP VISSER (eds) *Southern cross: Civil law and common law in South Africa* (1996)

Index of Legislation

Constitutions

Legislation

Index of Cases

Guyana

India

Inter-American Court of Human Rights

Ireland

Zimbabwe

Subject Index

495